Volvo
240 Series
Owners
Workshop
Manual

Colin Brown

Models covered
All Volvo 240, 244 and 245 models including special
editions; 1986 cc, 2127 cc & 2316 cc; sohc

Does not fully cover B230K 'Heron head' engine
Does not cover Diesel, Turbo or ohv engine variants

(270-7S1)

ABCDE
FGHIJ
KLM

Haynes Publishing Group
Sparkford Nr Yeovil
Somerset BA22 7JJ England

Haynes Publications, Inc
861 Lawrence Drive
Newbury Park
California 91320 USA

Acknowledgements

Thanks are due to the Champion Sparking Plug Company Limited who supplied the illustrations showing spark plug conditions, to Holt Lloyd Limited who supplied the illustrations showing bodywork repair, and to Duckhams Oils who provided lubrication data. Certain other illustrations are the copyright of AB Volvo and are used with their permission. Thanks are also due to Sykes-Pickavant, who provided some of the workshop tools, to John Tallis Motors Limited, Bathwick Hill, Bath, and to the Yeovil Motor Company Limited for their kind assistance. Special thanks go to all those people at Sparkford who helped in the production of this manual.

© **Haynes Publishing Group 1991**

A book in the **Haynes Owners Workshop Manual Series**

Printed by J. H. Haynes & Co. Ltd, Sparkford, Nr Yeovil, Somerset BA22 7JJ, England

ISBN 1 85010 402 6

British Library Cataloguing in Publication Data
Brown, Colin. *1942-*
   Volvo 240 series owners workshop manual.
   1. Automobiles - Maintenance & repair.
   I. Title   II. Series
   629.28'722
   ISBN 1-85010-402-6

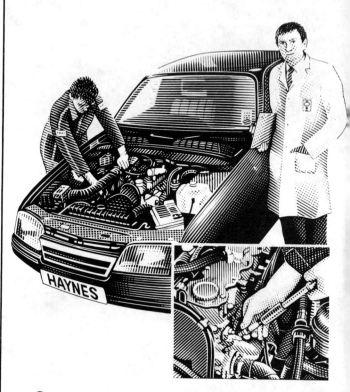

Contents

Early Volvo 245DL Estate

1979 model Volvo 244DL Saloon

About this manual

Its aim

The aim of this manual is to help you get the best value from your vehicle. It can do so in several ways. It can help you decide what work must be done (even should you choose to get it done by a garage), provide information on routine maintenance and servicing, and give a logical course of action and diagnosis when random faults occur. However, it is hoped that you will use the manual by tackling the work yourself. On simpler jobs it may even be quicker than booking the car into a garage and going there twice, to leave and collect it. Perhaps most important, a lot of money can be saved by avoiding the costs a garage must charge to cover its labour and overheads.

The manual has drawings and descriptions to show the function of the various components so that their layout can be understood. Then the tasks are described and photographed in a step-by-step sequence so that even a novice can do the work.

Its arrangement

The manual is divided into twelve Chapters, each covering a logical sub-division of the vehicle. The Chapters are each divided into Sections, numbered with single figures, eg 5; and the Sections into paragraphs (or sub-sections), with decimal numbers following on from the Section they are in, eg 5.1, 5.2, 5.3 etc.

It is freely illustrated, especially in those parts where there is a detailed sequence of operations to be carried out. There are two forms of illustration: figures and photographs. The figures are numbered in sequence with decimal numbers, according to their position in the Chapter – eg Fig. 6.4 is the fourth drawing/illustration in Chapter 6. Photographs carry the same number (either individually or in related groups) as the Section or sub-section to which they relate.

There is an alphabetical index at the back of the manual as well as a contents list at the front. Each Chapter is also preceded by its own individual contents list.

References to the 'left' or 'right' of the vehicle are in the sense of a person in the driver's seat facing forwards.

Unless otherwise stated, nuts and bolts are removed by turning anti-clockwise, and tightened by turning clockwise.

Vehicle manufacturers continually make changes to specifications and recommendations, and these, when notified, are incorporated into our manuals at the earliest opportunity.

Whilst every care is taken to ensure that the information in this manual is correct, no liability can be accepted by the authors or publishers for loss, damage or injury caused by any errors in, or omissions from, the information given.

Project vehicles

The vehicles used in the preparation of this Manual, and which appear in many of the photographic sequences include a 1977 Volvo 244DL Saloon, a 1978 Volvo 245GLE Estate and a 1988 Volvo 240GL Estate.

Introduction to the Volvo 240 series

The Volvo 240 series of Saloons and Estate cars represents all that has become synonymous with the word Volvo – safety, reliability and rugged longevity. Volvo do not change things for the sake of change, but for improvement to an already high standard of build. The result, evident in the latest range of vehicles, is a tribute to Scandinavian thoroughness and pride of product.

Despite being well equipped with the more modern vehicle innovations, the Volvo 240 retains a certain simplicity and ease of maintenance which the home mechanic will find to his or her liking.

All engine options are derived from the basic B21 unit, with carburettor or fuel injection options. Transmission options comprise: four-speed manual with overdrive, five-speed manual, three-speed automatic and three-speed automatic with lock-up fourth (overdrive).

Retaining the engine in-line, rear-wheel-drive configuration, with all-round disc braking, rigid safety cage and proven suspension, Volvo have produced one of the safest, most reliable vehicles around today, beloved of load carriers everywhere.

1981 model Volvo 245GL Estate

1988 model Volvo 240GL Saloon

General dimensions, weights and capacities

Dimensions
Length:
    1975 to 1976 .... 192.8 in (4897 mm)
    1977 to 1980 .... 192.1 in (4879 mm)
    1981 on .... 188.6 in (4790 mm)
Overall height:
    Saloon .... 56.2 in (1427 mm)
    Estate .... 57.5 in (1461 mm)
Overall width .... 67.3 in (1709 mm)
Wheelbase:
    Manual steering .... 103.9 in (2639 mm)
    Power steering 1979 on .... 104.3 in (2649 mm)
Front track:
    1975 to 1976 .... 55.9 in (1420 mm)
    1977 on with 5^1/$_2$" wide wheels .... 56.3 in (1430 mm)
Rear track:
    1975 to 1976 .... 53.15 in (1350 mm)
    1977 on with 5^1/$_2$" wide wheels .... 53.5 in (1359 mm)
Turning circle (between kerbs) .... 32 ft 6 in (10 m)

Weights
Kerb weight (approximately, unladen with full fuel tank and
dependent on version) .... 2701 to 3153 lb (1225 to 1430 kg)
Maximum trailer weight up to 1983 .... 2002 lb (908 kg)
1984 on .... 3300 lb (1500 kg)
Maximum roof rack load .... 220 lb (100 kg)

Capacities
Engine oil (drain, filter change and refill) .... 6.8 pints (3.85 litres)
Manual transmission:
    M40 and M45 .... 1.3 pints (0.75 litre)
    M41 .... 2.8 pints (1.6 litres)
    M46 .... 4.0 pints (2.3 litres)
    M47 .... 2.3 pints (1.3 litres)
Automatic transmission:
    BW35 .... 11 pints (6.4 litres)
    BW55 pre-1979 .... 11.5 pints (6.5 litres)
    1979 on (with deeper sump) .... 12 pints (6.9 litres)
    AW70 and 71 .... 13 pints (7.5 litres)
Rear axle:
    type 1030 .... 2.3 pints (1.3 litres)
    type 1031 .... 2.8 pints (1.6 litres)
Cooling system:
    Manual transmission .... 16.7 pints (9.5 litres)
    Automatic transmission .... 16.4 pints (9.3 litres)
Fuel tank .... 13.2 gals (60 litres)

Dimensions, weights and capacities

Jacking, towing and wheel changing

Jacking

Use the jack supplied with the vehicle only for wheel changing during roadside emergencies. Chock the wheel diagonally opposite the wheel being removed.

When raising the vehicle for repair or maintenance, use a hydraulic trolley jack, supplemented with axle stands once the vehicle is raised. Place the jack under the side jacking points, as indicated, raise the vehicle, then position an axle stand under one of the main chassis members before lowering the vehicle slowly onto the axle stand. Never work underneath the vehicle while it is supported only with a trolley jack, or the vehicle jack. If both front wheels or both rear wheels are required to be clear of the ground, then it is permissible to use a trolley jack positioned under the final drive unit for the rear wheels, and under the front chassis crossmember between the front wheels.

It is always preferable, and certainly recommended, that the vehicle is placed over an inspection pit or raised on a lift if these are available, or drive the vehicle onto ramps.

Towing

Towing eyes are welded to the front and rear of the vehicle (photos). The rear eye should only be used for the emergency towing of another vehicle. For trailer towing, a properly fitted towing bracket should be used. Before the vehicle is towed, the following precautions should be observed. Unlock the steering wheel by turning the ignition key to position one. With the engine inoperative, greater pressure will be required to operate the brake pedal, as there will be no servo assistance. Observe the current law regarding towing of vehicles. Drive as smoothly as possible, keeping the tow rope taut at all times to avoid jerking. Additionally, on automatic vehicles, set the selector lever to neutral, and check that the transmission fluid level is normal. The maximum towing speed for automatics is 10 mph (20 km/h), and the maximum towing distance is 20 miles (30 km). If these conditions cannot be met, or if transmission failure has occurred, then a specialist towing firm must be used, who will tow the vehicle with the rear wheels clear of the ground.

Front towing eye – arrowed (panel in bumper removed)

Rear towing eye

Wheel changing

To change a roadwheel, first park on firm, level ground if possible. Apply the handbrake and engage reverse gear (or 'P' on automatic). The spare tyre, jack and tool kit are stowed in the luggage compartment (photos). Prise off the 'Volvo' emblem from the centre of the wheel hub (if fitted) (photo), then pull off the wheel trim. Slacken the wheel nuts. Position the jack under the vehicle jacking point nearest to the wheel to be changed and chock the wheel diagonally opposite. Raise the jack until the top attachment point can be engaged in the vehicle jacking point (photo) and its foot is almost touching the ground. Raise the jack further so that it is just beginning to take the weight of the vehicle, then check that the top attachment is still in engagement with the vehicle jacking lug (photo). Raise the vehicle until the wheel is clear of the ground. Remove the wheel nuts and remove the wheel.

Fit the spare wheel and secure it with the wheel nuts. Tighten the nuts until they are snug, final tightening being carried out when the vehicle weight is on the ground. Lower the jack slowly until the wheel takes the weight of the vehicle, then remove the jack from the jacking point. Tighten the wheel bolts in diagonal sequence, to the specified torque (see Chapter 10), especially where alloy wheels are concerned. Refit the wheel trim and emblem panel. Have the wheel balanced at the earliest opportunity.

Note: *later models have a location peg on the wheel hub and a hole drilled in the wheel flange in order that the wheel is refitted in correct relationship, thus maintaining wheel balance. However, where the spare wheel has been fitted, or a new tyre, the wheel should still be checked for balance to eliminate vibration.*

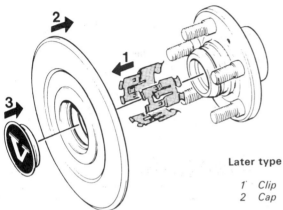

Later type roadwheel hub cap

1 Clip   3 Emblem
2 Cap

Removing the cover from the jack stowage on an early Estate car

Cover removed showing the jack

Spare wheel stowage – 1988 Estate ...

... and the jack

Removing the 'Volvo' emblem from later type wheel trim

Engaging the vehicle jack in a jacking point

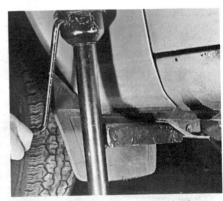

Raising the vehicle on the jack

Buying spare parts and vehicle identification numbers

Buying spare parts

Spare parts are available from many sources, for example: Volvo garages, other garages, accessory shops and motor factors. Our advice regarding spare parts is as follows.

Officially appointed Volvo garages – This is the best source for all parts, and may be the only place some parts which are specific to your vehicle may be obtained (eg, cylinder head, gearbox internal components, badges and internal trim etc). It is also the only place you should buy parts if your vehicle is under warranty – non-Volvo parts may invalidate the warranty. To ensure the correct part is obtained, it is necessary to give the storeman your vehicle chassis, engine or gearbox number, and if possible to take the 'old' part with you for added identification. Remember that some parts are available on a factory exchange basis, which is cheaper than just buying a new part. It obviously makes sense to go to your Volvo dealer, as they are best equipped to advise and supply you.

Other garages and accessory shops – These are often very good places to buy materials and parts needed for regular maintenance (eg, spark plugs, bulbs, drivebelts, oils and greases etc.) They also sell general accessories, usually have convenient opening hours, charge lower prices, and can often be found not far from home.

Motor factors – Good factors will stock all the more important parts which wear out relatively quickly and have a high turnover rate (eg, clutch components, pistons, valves, exhaust systems, brake components, etc. Motor factors will often supply new or reconditioned parts on an exchange basis – this can save a considerable amount of money.

Vehicle identification numbers

The accompanying diagrams show the location of the various identification plates stamped or rivetted to the vehicle. These plates give very useful information regarding the identification of the vehicle and major components (photos).

Additionally, a service plate mounted on the right-hand door pillar behind the front door (early models), or on a plate in front of the radiator (later models) gives further component manufacturer information, and a tyre inflation pressure plate is fixed on the inside of the fuel filler lid.

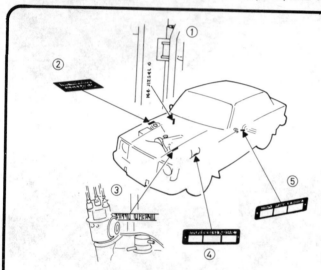

Vehicle identification plates (early models)

1 Type and model year designation and chassis number
2 Vehicle type designations, code number for colour and upholstery – plate inside front wing
3 Type designation, serial number and part number of engine
4 Type designation, serial number and part number of transmission unit
5 Final drive reduction ratio, part number and serial number of rear axle.

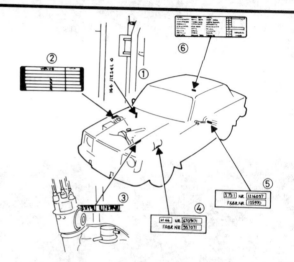

Vehicle identification plates (later models)

1 Type and model year designation
2 Type designation, maximum permitted load and colour code
3 Type designation and part number of engine
4 Type designation, serial number and part number of transmission unit
5 Final drive reduction ratio, part number and serial number of rear axle
6 Service plate – below the rear window on right-hand side (Saloon) or in large storage compartment (Estate)

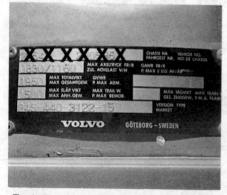

Typical vehicle type designation plate

Engine serial number

Rear axle identification plate

General repair procedures

Whenever servicing, repair or overhaul work is carried out on the car or its components, it is necessary to observe the following procedures and instructions. This will assist in carrying out the operation efficiently and to a professional standard of workmanship.

Joint mating faces and gaskets

Where a gasket is used between the mating faces of two components, ensure that it is renewed on reassembly, and fit it dry unless otherwise stated in the repair procedure. Make sure that the mating faces are clean and dry with all traces of old gasket removed. When cleaning a joint face, use a tool which is not likely to score or damage the face, and remove any burrs or nicks with an oilstone or fine file.

Make sure that tapped holes are cleaned with a pipe cleaner, and keep them free of jointing compound if this is being used unless specifically instructed otherwise.

Ensure that all orifices, channels or pipes are clear and blow through them, preferably using compressed air.

Oil seals

Whenever an oil seal is removed from its working location, either individually or as part of an assembly, it should be renewed.

The very fine sealing lip of the seal is easily damaged and will not seal if the surface it contacts is not completely clean and free from scratches, nicks or grooves. If the original sealing surface of the component cannot be restored, the component should be renewed.

Protect the lips of the seal from any surface which may damage them in the course of fitting. Use tape or a conical sleeve where possible. Lubricate the seal lips with oil before fitting and, on dual lipped seals, fill the space between the lips with grease.

Unless otherwise stated, oil seals must be fitted with their sealing lips toward the lubricant to be sealed.

Use a tubular drift or block of wood of the appropriate size to install the seal and, if the seal housing is shouldered, drive the seal down to the shoulder. If the seal housing is unshouldered, the seal should be fitted with its face flush with the housing top face.

Screw threads and fastenings

Always ensure that a blind tapped hole is completely free from oil, grease, water or other fluid before installing the bolt or stud. Failure to do this could cause the housing to crack due to the hydraulic action of the bolt or stud as it is screwed in.

When tightening a castellated nut to accept a split pin, tighten the nut to the specified torque, where applicable, and then tighten further to the next split pin hole. Never slacken the nut to align a split pin hole unless stated in the repair procedure.

When checking or retightening a nut or bolt to a specified torque setting, slacken the nut or bolt by a quarter of a turn, and then retighten to the specified setting.

Locknuts, locktabs and washers

Any fastening which will rotate against a component or housing in the course of tightening should always have a washer between it and the relevant component or housing.

Spring or split washers should always be renewed when they are used to lock a critical component such as a big-end bearing retaining nut or bolt.

Locktabs which are folded over to retain a nut or bolt should always be renewed.

Self-locking nuts can be reused in non-critical areas, providing resistance can be felt when the locking portion passes over the bolt or stud thread.

Split pins must always be replaced with new ones of the correct size for the hole.

Special tools

Some repair procedures in this manual entail the use of special tools such as a press, two or three-legged pullers, spring compressors etc. Wherever possible, suitable readily available alternatives to the manufacturer's special tools are described, and are shown in use. In some instances, where no alternative is possible, it has been necessary to resort to the use of a manufacturer's tool and this has been done for reasons of safety as well as the efficient completion of the repair operation. Unless you are highly skilled and have a thorough understanding of the procedure described, never attempt to bypass the use of any special tool when the procedure described specifies its use. Not only is there a very great risk of personal injury, but expensive damage could be caused to the components involved.

Tools and working facilities

Introduction

A selection of good tools is a fundamental requirement for anyone contemplating the maintenance and repair of a motor vehicle. For the owner who does not possess any, their purchase will prove a considerable expense, offsetting some of the savings made by doing-it-yourself. However, provided that the tools purchased meet the relevant national safety standards and are of good quality, they will last for many years and prove an extremely worthwhile investment.

To help the average owner to decide which tools are needed to carry out the various tasks detailed in this manual, we have compiled three lists of tools under the following headings: *Maintenance and minor repair, Repair and overhaul,* and *Special.* The newcomer to practical mechanics should start off with the *Maintenance and minor repair* tool kit and confine himself to the simpler jobs around the vehicle. Then, as his confidence and experience grow, he can undertake more difficult tasks, buying extra tools as, and when, they are needed. In this way, a *Maintenance and minor repair* tool kit can be built-up into a *Repair and overhaul* tool kit over a considerable period of time without any major cash outlays. The experienced do-it-yourselfer will have a tool kit good enough for most repair and overhaul procedures and will add tools from the *Special* category when he feels the expense is justified by the amount of use to which these tools will be put.

It is obviously not possible to cover the subject of tools fully here. For those who wish to learn more about tools and their use there is a book entitled *How to Choose and Use Car Tools* available from the publishers of this manual.

Maintenance and minor repair tool kit

The tools given in this list should be considered as a minimum requirement if routine maintenance, servicing and minor repair operations are to be undertaken. We recommend the purchase of combination spanners (ring one end, open-ended the other); although more expensive than open-ended ones, they do give the advantages of both types of spanner.

Combination spanners - 10, 11, 12, 13, 14 & 17 mm*
Adjustable spanner - 9 inch
Spark plug spanner (with rubber insert)
Spark plug gap adjustment tool
Set of feeler gauges
Brake bleed nipple spanner
Screwdriver - 4 in long x $^1/4$ in dia (flat blade)
Screwdriver - 4 in long x $^1/4$ in dia (cross blade)
Combination pliers - 6 inch
Hacksaw (junior)
Tyre pump
Tyre pressure gauge
Oil can
Fine emery cloth (1 sheet)
Wire brush (small)
Funnel (medium size)

(UNF (Imperial) fastenings may be found on components such as the propeller shaft, air conditioning compressor and power steering gear.

Repair and overhaul tool kit

These tools are virtually essential for anyone undertaking any major repairs to a motor vehicle, and are additional to those given in the *Maintenance and minor repair* list. Included in this list is a comprehensive set of sockets. Although these are expensive they will be found invaluable as they are so versatile - particularly if various drives are included in the set. We recommend the ½ in square-drive type, as this can be used with most proprietary torque wrenches. If you cannot afford a socket set, even bought piecemeal, then inexpensive tubular box spanners are a useful alternative.

The tools in this list will occasionally need to be supplemented by tools from the *Special* list.

Sockets (or box spanners) to cover range in previous list
Reversible ratchet drive (for use with sockets)
Extension piece, 10 inch (for use with sockets)
Universal joint (for use with sockets)
Torque wrench (for use with sockets)
'Mole' wrench - 8 inch
Ball pein hammer
Soft-faced hammer, plastic or rubber
Screwdriver - 6 in long x $^5/16$ in dia (flat blade)
Screwdriver - 2 in long x $^5/16$ in square (flat blade)
Screwdriver - 1$^1/2$ in long x $^1/4$ in dia (cross blade)
Screwdriver - 3 in long x $^1/8$ in dia (electricians)
Pliers - electricians side cutters
Pliers - needle nosed
Pliers - circlip (internal and external)
Cold chisel - $^1/2$ inch
Scriber
Scraper
Centre punch
Pin punch
Hacksaw
Valve grinding tool
Steel rule/straight-edge
Allen keys (inc. splined/Torx type if necessary)
Selection of files
Wire brush (large)
Axle-stands
Jack (strong trolley or hydraulic type)

Special tools

The tools in this list are those which are not used regularly, are expensive to buy, or which need to be used in accordance with their manufacturers' instructions. Unless relatively difficult mechanical jobs are undertaken frequently, it will not be economic to buy many of these tools. Where this is the case, you could consider clubbing together with friends (or joining a motorists' club) to make a joint purchase, or borrowing the tools against a deposit from a local garage or tool hire specialist.

The following list contains only those tools and instruments freely available to the public, and not those special tools produced by the vehicle manufacturer specifically for its dealer network. You will find occasional references to these manufacturers' special tools in the text of this manual. Generally, an alternative method of doing the job without the vehicle manufacturers' special tool is given. However, sometimes, there is no alternative to using them. Where this is the case and the relevant tool cannot be bought or borrowed, you will have to entrust the work to a franchised garage.

> Valve spring compressor
> Piston ring compressor
> Balljoint separator
> Universal hub/bearing puller
> Impact screwdriver
> Micrometer and/or vernier gauge
> Dial gauge
> Stroboscopic timing light
> Dwell angle meter (contact breaker ignition only)/tachometer
> Universal electrical multi-meter
> Cylinder compression gauge
> Lifting tackle
> Trolley jack
> Light with extension lead

Buying tools

For practically all tools, a tool factor is the best source since he will have a very comprehensive range compared with the average garage or accessory shop. Having said that, accessory shops often offer excellent quality tools at discount prices, so it pays to shop around.

There are plenty of good tools around at reasonable prices, but always aim to purchase items which meet the relevant national safety standards. If in doubt, ask the proprietor or manager of the shop for advice before making a purchase.

Care and maintenance of tools

Having purchased a reasonable tool kit, it is necessary to keep the tools in a clean serviceable condition. After use, always wipe off any dirt, grease and metal particles using a clean, dry cloth, before putting the tools away. Never leave them lying around after they have been used. A simple tool rack on the garage or workshop wall, for items such as screwdrivers and pliers is a good idea. Store all normal wrenches and sockets in a metal box. Any measuring instruments, gauges, meters, etc, must be carefully stored where they cannot be damaged or become rusty.

Take a little care when tools are used. Hammer heads inevitably become marked and screwdrivers lose the keen edge on their blades from time to time. A little timely attention with emery cloth or a file will soon restore items like this to a good serviceable finish.

Working facilities

Not to be forgotten when discussing tools, is the workshop itself. If anything more than routine maintenance is to be carried out, some form of suitable working area becomes essential.

It is appreciated that many an owner mechanic is forced by circumstances to remove an engine or similar item, without the benefit of a garage or workshop. Having done this, any repairs should always be done under the cover of a roof.

Wherever possible, any dismantling should be done on a clean, flat workbench or table at a suitable working height.

Any workbench needs a vice: one with a jaw opening of 4 in (100 mm) is suitable for most jobs. As mentioned previously, some clean dry storage space is also required for tools, as well as for lubricants, cleaning fluids, touch-up paints and so on, which become necessary.

Another item which may be required, and which has a much more general usage, is an electric drill with a chuck capacity of at least 5/16 in (8 mm). This, together with a good range of twist drills, is virtually essential for fitting accessories such as mirrors and reversing lights.

Last, but not least, always keep a supply of old newspapers and clean, lint-free rags available, and try to keep any working area as clean as possible.

Spanner jaw gap comparison table

Jaw gap (in)	Spanner size
0.250	1/4 in AF
0.276	7 mm
0.313	5/16 in AF
0.315	8 mm
0.344	11/32 in AF; 1/8 in Whitworth
0.354	9 mm
0.375	3/8 in AF
0.394	10 mm
0.433	11 mm
0.438	7/16 in AF
0.445	3/16 in Whitworth; 1/4 in BSF
0.472	12 mm
0.500	1/2 in AF
0.512	13 mm
0.525	1/4 in Whitworth; 5/16 in BSF
0.551	14 mm
0.563	9/16 in AF
0.591	15 mm
0.600	5/16 in Whitworth; 3/8 in BSF
0.625	5/8 in AF
0.630	16 mm
0.669	17 mm
0.686	11/16 in AF
0.709	18 mm
0.710	3/8 in Whitworth; 7/16 in BSF
0.748	19 mm
0.750	3/4 in AF
0.813	13/16 in AF
0.820	7/16 in Whitworth; 1/2 in BSF
0.866	22 mm
0.875	7/8 in AF
0.920	1/2 in Whitworth; 9/16 in BSF
0.938	15/16 in AF
0.945	24 mm
1.000	1 in AF
1.010	9/16 in Whitworth; 5/8 in BSF
1.024	26 mm
1.063	11/16 in AF; 27 mm
1.100	5/8 in Whitworth; 11/16 in BSF
1.125	11/8 in AF
1.181	30 mm
1.200	11/16 in Whitworth; 3/4 in BSF
1.250	11/4 in AF
1.260	32 mm
1.300	3/4 in Whitworth; 7/8 in BSF
1.313	15/16 in AF
1.390	13/16 in Whitworth; 15/16 in BSF
1.417	36 mm
1.438	17/16 in AF
1.480	7/8 in Whitworth; 1 in BSF
1.500	11/2 in AF
1.575	40 mm; 15/16 in Whitworth
1.614	41 mm
1.625	15/8 in AF
1.670	1 in Whitworth; 11/8 in BSF
1.688	111/16 in AF
1.811	46 mm
1.813	113/16 in AF
1.860	11/8 in Whitworth; 11/4 in BSF
1.875	17/8 in AF
1.969	50 mm
2.000	2 in AF
2.050	11/4 in Whitworth; 13/8 in BSF
2.165	55 mm
2.362	60 mm

Safety first!

Professional motor mechanics are trained in safe working procedures. However enthusiastic you may be about getting on with the job in hand, do take the time to ensure that your safety is not put at risk. A moment's lack of attention can result in an accident, as can failure to observe certain elementary precautions.

There will always be new ways of having accidents, and the following points do not pretend to be a comprehensive list of all dangers; they are intended rather to make you aware of the risks and to encourage a safety-conscious approach to all work you carry out on your vehicle.

Essential DOs and DON'Ts

DON'T rely on a single jack when working underneath the vehicle. Always use reliable additional means of support, such as axle stands, securely placed under a part of the vehicle that you know will not give way.

DON'T attempt to loosen or tighten high-torque nuts (e.g. wheel hub nuts) while the vehicle is on a jack; it may be pulled off.

DON'T start the engine without first ascertaining that the transmission is in neutral (or 'Park' where applicable) and the parking brake applied.

DON'T suddenly remove the filler cap from a hot cooling system – cover it with a cloth and release the pressure gradually first, or you may get scalded by escaping coolant.

DON'T attempt to drain oil until you are sure it has cooled sufficiently to avoid scalding you.

DON'T grasp any part of the engine, exhaust or catalytic converter without first ascertaining that it is sufficiently cool to avoid burning you.

DON'T allow brake fluid or antifreeze to contact vehicle paintwork.

DON'T syphon toxic liquids such as fuel, brake fluid or antifreeze by mouth, or allow them to remain on your skin.

DON'T inhale dust – it may be injurious to health (see *Asbestos* below).

DON'T allow any spilt oil or grease to remain on the floor – wipe it up straight away, before someone slips on it.

DON'T use ill-fitting spanners or other tools which may slip and cause injury.

DON'T attempt to lift a heavy component which may be beyond your capability – get assistance.

DON'T rush to finish a job, or take unverified short cuts.

DON'T allow children or animals in or around an unattended vehicle.

DO wear eye protection when using power tools such as drill, sander, bench grinder etc, and when working under the vehicle.

DO use a barrier cream on your hands prior to undertaking dirty jobs – it will protect your skin from infection as well as making the dirt easier to remove afterwards; but make sure your hands aren't left slippery. Note that long-term contact with used engine oil can be a health hazard.

DO keep loose clothing (cuffs, tie etc) and long hair well out of the way of moving mechanical parts.

DO remove rings, wristwatch etc, before working on the vehicle – especially the electrical system.

DO ensure that any lifting tackle used has a safe working load rating adequate for the job.

DO keep your work area tidy – it is only too easy to fall over articles left lying around.

DO get someone to check periodically that all is well, when working alone on the vehicle.

DO carry out work in a logical sequence and check that everything is correctly assembled and tightened afterwards.

DO remember that your vehicle's safety affects that of yourself and others. If in doubt on any point, get specialist advice.

IF, in spite of following these precautions, you are unfortunate enough to injure yourself, seek medical attention as soon as possible.

Asbestos

Certain friction, insulating, sealing, and other products – such as brake linings, brake bands, clutch linings, torque converters, gaskets, etc – contain asbestos. *Extreme care must be taken to avoid inhalation of dust from such products since it is hazardous to health.* If in doubt, assume that they *do* contain asbestos.

Fire

Remember at all times that petrol (gasoline) is highly flammable. Never smoke, or have any kind of naked flame around, when working on the vehicle. But the risk does not end there – a spark caused by an electrical short-circuit, by two metal surfaces contacting each other, by careless use of tools, or even by static electricity built up in your body under certain conditions, can ignite petrol vapour, which in a confined space is highly explosive.

Always disconnect the battery earth (ground) terminal before working on any part of the fuel or electrical system, and never risk spilling fuel on to a hot engine or exhaust.

It is recommended that a fire extinguisher of a type suitable for fuel and electrical fires is kept handy in the garage or workplace at all times. Never try to extinguish a fuel or electrical fire with water.

Note: *Any reference to a 'torch' appearing in this manual should always be taken to mean a hand-held battery-operated electric lamp or flashlight. It does NOT mean a welding/gas torch or blowlamp.*

Fumes

Certain fumes are highly toxic and can quickly cause unconsciousness and even death if inhaled to any extent. Petrol (gasoline) vapour comes into this category, as do the vapours from certain solvents such as trichloroethylene. Any draining or pouring of such volatile fluids should be done in a well ventilated area.

When using cleaning fluids and solvents, read the instructions carefully. Never use materials from unmarked containers – they may give off poisonous vapours.

Never run the engine of a motor vehicle in an enclosed space such as a garage. Exhaust fumes contain carbon monoxide which is extremely poisonous; if you need to run the engine, always do so in the open air or at least have the rear of the vehicle outside the workplace.

If you are fortunate enough to have the use of an inspection pit, never drain or pour petrol, and never run the engine, while the vehicle is standing over it; the fumes, being heavier than air, will concentrate in the pit with possibly lethal results.

The battery

Never cause a spark, or allow a naked light, near the vehicle's battery. It will normally be giving off a certain amount of hydrogen gas, which is highly explosive.

Always disconnect the battery earth (ground) terminal before working on the fuel or electrical systems.

If possible, loosen the filler plugs or cover when charging the battery from an external source. Do not charge at an excessive rate or the battery may burst.

Take care when topping up and when carrying the battery. The acid electrolyte, even when diluted, is very corrosive and should not be allowed to contact the eyes or skin.

If you ever need to prepare electrolyte yourself, always add the acid slowly to the water, and never the other way round. Protect against splashes by wearing rubber gloves and goggles.

When jump starting a car using a booster battery, for negative earth (ground) vehicles, connect the jump leads in the following sequence: First connect one jump lead between the positive (+) terminals of the two batteries. Then connect the other jump lead first to the negative (–) terminal of the booster battery, and then to a good earthing (ground) point on the vehicle to be started, at least 18 in (45 cm) from the battery if possible. Ensure that hands and jump leads are clear of any moving parts, and that the two vehicles do not touch. Disconnect the leads in the reverse order.

Mains electricity and electrical equipment

When using an electric power tool, inspection light etc, always ensure that the appliance is correctly connected to its plug and that, where necessary, it is properly earthed (grounded). Do not use such appliances in damp conditions and, again, beware of creating a spark or applying excessive heat in the vicinity of fuel or fuel vapour. Also ensure that the appliances meet the relevant national safety standards.

Ignition HT voltage

A severe electric shock can result from touching certain parts of the ignition system, such as the HT leads, when the engine is running or being cranked, particularly if components are damp or the insulation is defective. Where an electronic ignition system is fitted, the HT voltage is much higher and could prove fatal.

Routine maintenance

The maintenance schedule which follows is that recommended by the manufacturer, and is the minimum required. Where the vehicle is operated under adverse conditions which includes frequent stop-start driving, use as a taxi, frequent and prolonged motorway driving and driving on unmade roads, the intervals should be reduced – consult your dealer.

Every 250 miles (400 km), weekly, or before a long journey

Check tyre pressures and condition of the tyre treads (Chapter 10, Section 27)
Check engine oil level (Chapter 1, Section 3)
Check coolant level (Chapter 2, Section 2)
Check brake fluid (and where applicable, clutch fluid) level (Chapter 9, Section 2 and Chapter 5, Section 2)
Top up the washer reservoirs (Chapter 12, Section 26), adding a screen wash such as Turtle Wax High Tech Screen Wash
Inspect engine and underside of vehicle for leaks
Check the function of main-line electrical services – lights, horn, wipers (Chapter 12) etc.

Every 6000 miles (10 000 km) or six months, whichever comes first

Brake servo – check (Chapter 9, Section 21)
Selector linkage (automatics) – check and adjust (Chapter 6, Section 44)
Tyres – inspect thoroughly (Chapter 10, Section 27)
Gearbox or automatic transmission – check oil level and top-up as necessary (Chapter 6, Section 2 or 41)
Rear axle – check oil level and top up as necessary (Chapter 8, Section 2)
Engine oil and oil filter – renew (Chapter 1, Sections 3 and 4)
Hydraulic clutch – check for leaks and rectify as necessary (Chapter 5)
Brake system – check for leaks and rectify as necessary (Chapter 9)
Power steering system – check oil level and top up as necessary (Chapter 10, Section 14)
Coolant – check for leaks and rectify as necessary (Chapter 2)
Battery electrolyte level – check and top up as necessary (Chapter 12, Section 3)
Carburettor dashpot fluid – check and top up (Chapter 3)
Warm start valve (B200K and B230K) – check operation (Chapter 3, Section 28)
Spark plugs – renew (except long-life plugs) (Chapter 4, Section 3)
Contact breaker points (mechanical ignition) – renew (Chapter 4, Section 6)
Ignition timing (mechanical) – check and adjust (Chapter 4, Sections 13 and 14)
Choke – check and adjust (Chapter 3)
Idle speed and CO content – check and adjust (Chapter 3)
Kickdown cable (automatics) – check and adjust (Chapter 6, Section 45)

Every 12 000 miles (20 000 km) or twelve months, whichever comes first

Handbrake – check and adjust (Chapter 9, Section 12)
Headlamp/windscreen wash systems – check (Chapter 12, Section 26)
Doors, bonnet, boot and tailgate hinges – lubricate (Chapter 11)
Front wheel bearings – check and adjust (Chapter 10, Section 3)
Steering – check: have alignment checked and adjusted as necessary (Chapter 10, Section 5)

Front suspension – check (Chapter 10)
Brake pads – check for wear (Chapter 9, Sections 5 and 11)
Brake hoses and pipelines – check for leaks and damage (Chapter 9, Section 24)
Rear suspension – check (Chapter 8)
Clutch (mechanical) – check and adjust (Chapter 5, Section 3)
Propeller shaft – check bearings and for damage (Chapter 7, Section 2)
Exhaust system – check (Chapter 3, Section 17)
Fuel lines – check for damage and leaks (Chapter 3)
Engine – check for leaks and cleanliness
Underseal/paintwork – check (Chapter 11)
Coolant – check concentration of anti-freeze (Chapter 2, Section 2)
Accessory drivebelts (alternator, power steering pump etc) – check and adjust (Chapter 2, Section 14)
Exhaust manifold – check for leaks and check-tighten bolts (Chapter 3, Section 19)
Distributor (mechanical) – lubricate felt pad (Chapter 4, Section 11)
Battery – check charge (Chapter 12, Section 4)
Spark plugs (long-life) – renew (Chapter 4, Section 3)

Every 24 000 miles (40 00 km) or two years, whichever comes first

Automatic transmission – renew ATF (Chapter 6, Section 42)
In-line fuel filter – renew (Chapter 3, Section 64)
Crankcase ventilation system – check and clean (Chapter 3, Section 21)
Valve clearances – check and adjust (Chapter 1, Section 5)
Engine compression – check (Chapter 1, Section 14)
Air filter – renew (Chapter 3, Section 6)
Coolant – renew (Chapter 2, Sections 4, 5 and 6)
Brake/clutch fluid – renew by bleeding (Chapter 9, Section 25 and Chapter 5, Section 4)
Rear brake band (BW35 only) – check and adjust (Chapter 6, Section 47)

Every 36 000 miles (60 000 km) or three years, whichever comes first

Camshaft drivebelt – renew (Chapter 1, Section 6)

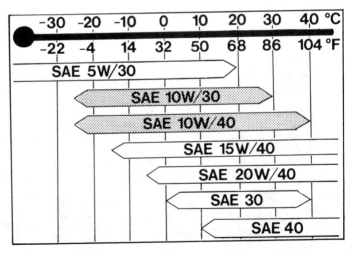

Engine oil viscosity/ambient temperature range chart

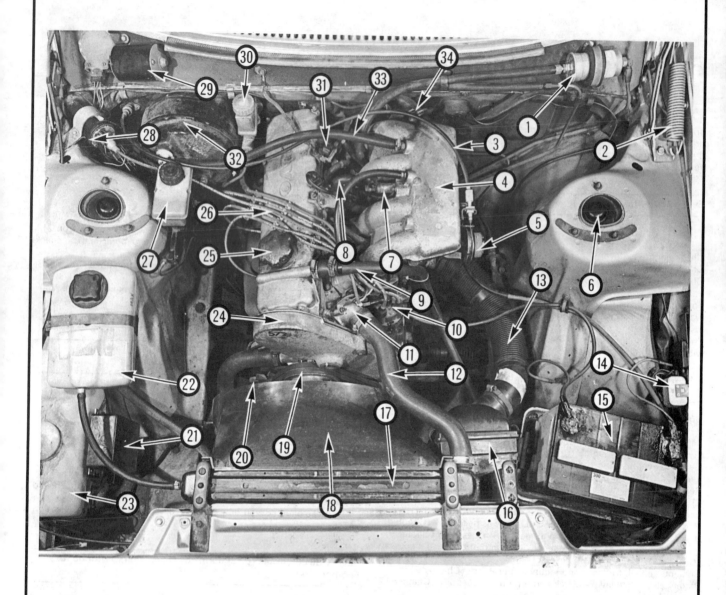

Under-bonnet view of a Volvo 245GLE Estate

1 In-line fuel filter
2 Bonnet hinge spring
3 Accelerator cable
4 Inlet manifold
5 Throttle pulley
6 Suspension tower
7 Cold start injector
8 Auxiliary air valve
9 Crankcase ventilation hose

10 Distributor
11 Thermostat housing
12 Top radiator hose
13 Air inlet ducting
14 Headlight main beam step relay
15 Battery
16 Air filter housing
17 Radiator

18 Cooling fan shroud
19 Cooling fan pulley
20 Alternator
21 Ignition control unit
22 Coolant expansion tank
23 Windscreen/headlight wash reservoir
24 Camshaft drivebelt cover
25 Engine oil filler cap

26 Spark plug HT leads
27 Brake fluid reservoir
28 Ignition coil
29 Windscreen wiper motor
30 Clutch fluid reservoir
31 Ignition timing sender
32 Brake vacuum servo
33 Vacuum hose
34 Engine oil dipstick

Under-bonnet view of a Volvo 240GL Estate

1 Engine oil dipstick
2 Throttle pulley
3 Automatic transmission dipstick
4 Carburettor
5 Windscreen wiper motor
6 Bonnet hinge spring
7 Suspension tower
8 Carburettor air intake ducting
9 Fuel pump
10 Inlet manifold
11 Thermostat housing
12 Power steering fluid reservoir cap
13 Headlight main beam step relay
14 Battery
15 Air filter housing
16 Crankcase ventilation hose
17 Top radiator hose
18 Cooling fan shroud
19 Camshaft drivebelt cover
20 Alternator
21 Radiator
22 Windscreen/headlight wash reservoir
23 Coolant expansion tank
24 Accelerator cable
25 Engine oil filler cap
26 Brake fluid reservoir
27 Spark plug HT leads
28 Kickdown cable (automatic transmission)
29 Ignition timing sender
30 Ignition coil
31 Brake vacuum servo
32 Idle solenoid valve
33 Distributor
34 Vacuum hose (brake servo)

Front underside view of a Volvo 245GLE Estate

1 Exhaust pipe	7 Front towing eye	14 Engine oil drain plug
2 Front brake caliper	8 Cooling fan	15 Sump reinforcing plate
3 Control arm	9 Crankshaft pulley	16 Automatic transmission
4 Balljoint	10 Power steering pump pulley	17 Gearbox support member
5 Steering (track) rod	11 Air filter (carburettor)	18 Propeller shaft
6 Carburettor hot air intake ducting	12 Front axle crossmember	19 Hot air collector plate (air intake system)
	13 Engine oil sump	

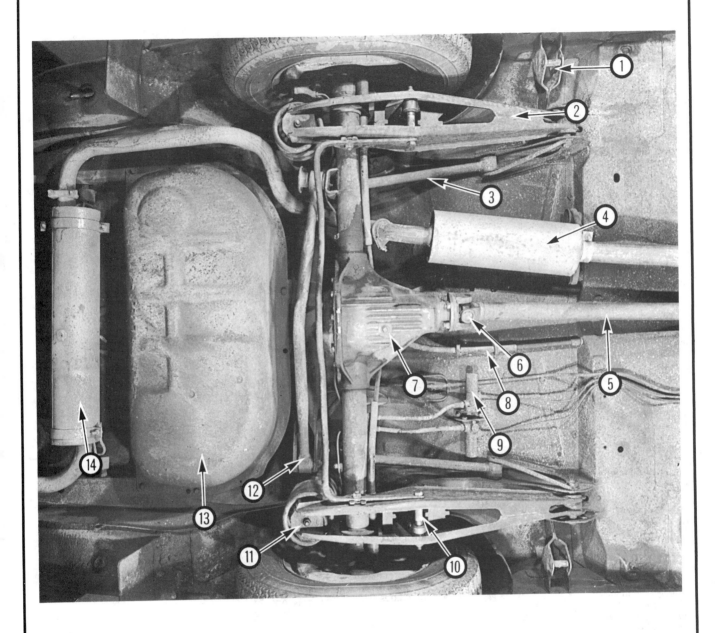

Rear underside view of a Volvo 245GLE Estate

1 Rear jacking point	5 Propeller shaft	8 Handbrake cable	11 Suspension spring lower
2 Trailing arm	6 Propeller shaft universal	9 Brake valve	mounting
3 Reaction rod	joint	10 Shock absorber lower	12 Anti-roll bar
4 Front silencer	7 Rear axle drain plug	mounting	13 Fuel tank
			14 Rear silencer

Conversion factors

Length (distance)

Inches (in)	X	25.4	= Millimetres (mm)	X 0.0394	= Inches (in)
Feet (ft)	X	0.305	= Metres (m)	X 3.281	= Feet (ft)
Miles	X	1.609	= Kilometres (km)	X 0.621	= Miles

Volume (capacity)

Cubic inches (cu in; in³)	X	16.387	= Cubic centimetres (cc; cm³)	X 0.061	= Cubic inches (cu in; in³)
Imperial pints (Imp pt)	X	0.568	= Litres (l)	X 1.76	= Imperial pints (Imp pt)
Imperial quarts (Imp qt)	X	1.137	= Litres (l)	X 0.88	= Imperial quarts (Imp qt)
Imperial quarts (Imp qt)	X	1.201	= US quarts (US qt)	X 0.833	= Imperial quarts (Imp qt)
US quarts (US qt)	X	0.946	= Litres (l)	X 1.057	= US quarts (US qt)
Imperial gallons (Imp gal)	X	4.546	= Litres (l)	X 0.22	= Imperial gallons (Imp gal)
Imperial gallons (Imp gal)	X	1.201	= US gallons (US gal)	X 0.833	= Imperial gallons (Imp gal)
US gallons (US gal)	X	3.785	= Litres (l)	X 0.264	= US gallons (US gal)

Mass (weight)

Ounces (oz)	X	28.35	= Grams (g)	X 0.035	= Ounces (oz)
Pounds (lb)	X	0.454	= Kilograms (kg)	X 2.205	= Pounds (lb)

Force

Ounces-force (ozf; oz)	X	0.278	= Newtons (N)	X 3.6	= Ounces-force (ozf; oz)
Pounds-force (lbf; lb)	X	4.448	= Newtons (N)	X 0.225	= Pounds-force (lbf; lb)
Newtons (N)	X	0.1	= Kilograms-force (kgf; kg)	X 9.81	= Newtons (N)

Pressure

Pounds-force per square inch (psi; lbf/in²; lb/in²)	X	0.070	= Kilograms-force per square centimetre (kgf/cm²; kg/cm²)	X 14.223	= Pounds-force per square inch (psi; lbf/in²; lb/in²)
Pounds-force per square inch (psi; lbf/in²; lb/in²)	X	0.068	= Atmospheres (atm)	X 14.696	= Pounds-force per square inch (psi; lbf/in²; lb/in²)
Pounds-force per square inch (psi; lbf/in²; lb/in²)	X	0.069	= Bars	X 14.5	= Pounds-force per square inch (psi; lbf/in²; lb/in²)
Pounds-force per square inch (psi; lbf/in²; lb/in²)	X	6.895	= Kilopascals (kPa)	X 0.145	= Pounds-force per square inch (psi; lbf/in²; lb/in²)
Kilopascals (kPa)	X	0.01	= Kilograms-force per square centimetre (kgf/cm²; kg/cm²)	X 98.1	= Kilopascals (kPa)
Millibar (mbar)	X	100	= Pascals (Pa)	X 0.01	= Millibar (mbar)
Millibar (mbar)	X	0.0145	= Pounds-force per square inch (psi; lbf/in²; lb/in²)	X 68.947	= Millibar (mbar)
Millibar (mbar)	X	0.75	= Millimetres of mercury (mmHg)	X 1.333	= Millibar (mbar)
Millibar (mbar)	X	0.401	= Inches of water (inH₂O)	X 2.491	= Millibar (mbar)
Millimetres of mercury (mmHg)	X	0.535	= Inches of water (inH₂O)	X 1.868	= Millimetres of mercury (mmHg)
Inches of water (inH₂O)	X	0.036	= Pounds-force per square inch (psi; lbf/in²; lb/in²)	X 27.68	= Inches of water (inH₂O)

Torque (moment of force)

Pounds-force inches (lbf in; lb in)	X	1.152	= Kilograms-force centimetre (kgf cm; kg cm)	X 0.868	= Pounds-force inches (lbf in; lb in)
Pounds-force inches (lbf in; lb in)	X	0.113	= Newton metres (Nm)	X 8.85	= Pounds-force inches (lbf in; lb in)
Pounds-force inches (lbf in; lb in)	X	0.083	= Pounds-force feet (lbf ft; lb ft)	X 12	= Pounds-force inches (lbf in; lb in)
Pounds-force feet (lbf ft; lb ft)	X	0.138	= Kilograms-force metres (kgf m; kg m)	X 7.233	= Pounds-force feet (lbf ft; lb ft)
Pounds-force feet (lbf ft; lb ft)	X	1.356	= Newton metres (Nm)	X 0.738	= Pounds-force feet (lbf ft; lb ft)
Newton metres (Nm)	X	0.102	= Kilograms-force metres (kgf m; kg m)	X 9.804	= Newton metres (Nm)

Power

Horsepower (hp)	X	745.7	= Watts (W)	X 0.0013	= Horsepower (hp)

Velocity (speed)

Miles per hour (miles/hr; mph)	X	1.609	= Kilometres per hour (km/hr; kph)	X 0.621	= Miles per hour (miles/hr; mph)

Fuel consumption*

Miles per gallon, Imperial (mpg)	X	0.354	= Kilometres per litre (km/l)	X 2.825	= Miles per gallon, Imperial (mpg)
Miles per gallon, US (mpg)	X	0.425	= Kilometres per litre (km/l)	X 2.352	= Miles per gallon, US (mpg)

Temperature

Degrees Fahrenheit = ($°C \times 1.8$) + 32

Degrees Celsius (Degrees Centigrade; °C) = ($°F - 32$) $\times$ 0.56

*It is common practice to convert from miles per gallon (mpg) to litres/100 kilometres (l/100km),
where mpg (Imperial) x l/100 km = 282 and mpg (US) x l/100 km = 235

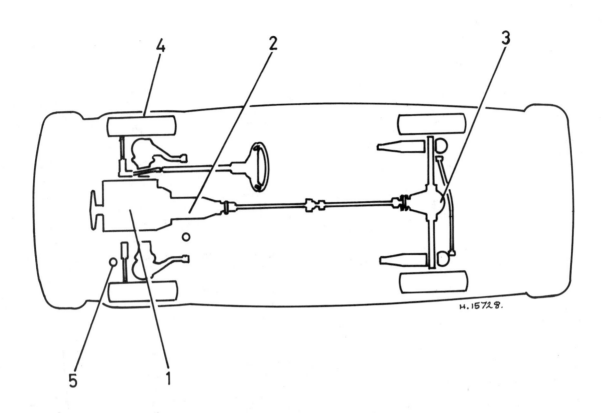

H.15728.

Recommended lubricants and fluids

Component or system	Lubricant type/specification	Duckhams recommendation
1 Engine	Multigrade engine oil, viscosity SAE 10W/30 to API SE (up to 1983) or API SF (from 1984)	Duckhams QXR, Hypergrade, or 10W/40 Motor Oil
2A Manual gearbox (with or without overdrive) M40 and M41	Hypoid gear oil, viscosity SAE 80W/90 or 80/90, to API-GL-4	Duckhams Hypoid 80
M45*, M46* and M47*	ATF type F or G, or Volvo Thermo-oil part number 1 161 243-9 (from 1982 only for M46)	Duckhams Q-Matic
2B Automatic transmission BW35 and BW55 AW70 and AW71	ATF type F or G Dexron IID type ATF	Duckhams Q-Matic Duckhams D-Matic
3 Rear axle Without limited slip differential With limited slip differential	Hypoid gear oil, viscosity SAE 90, to API-GL-5 Hypoid gear oil, viscosity SAE 90, to API-GL-56, with Volvo additive part number 1 161 129-0	Duckhams Hypoid 90S Duckhams Hypoid 90DL
4 Front wheel bearings	General purpose lithium based grease	Duckhams LB 10
5 Power steering reservoir	ATF type A, F or G	Duckhams Q-Matic
Hydraulic system	Hydraulic fluid to DOT 4	Duckhams Universal Brake and Clutch Fluid

*Do not mix oil types

Fault diagnosis

Introduction

The vehicle owner who does his or her own maintenance according to the recommended schedules should not have to use this section of the manual very often. Modern component reliability is such that, provided those items subject to wear or deterioration are inspected or renewed at the specified intervals, sudden failure is comparatively rare. Faults do not usually just happen as a result of sudden failure, but develop over a period of time. Major mechanical failures in particular are usually preceded by characteristic symptoms over hundreds or even thousands of miles. Those components which do occasionally fail without warning are often small and easily carried in the vehicle.

With any fault finding, the first step is to decide where to begin investigations. Sometimes this is obvious, but on other occasions a little detective work will be necessary. The owner who makes half a dozen haphazard adjustments or replacements may be successful in curing a fault (or its symptoms), but he will be none the wiser if the fault recurs and he may well have spent more time and money than was necessary. A calm and logical approach will be found to be more satisfactory in the long run. Always take into account any warning signs or abnormalities that may have been noticed in the period preceding the fault – power loss, high or low gauge readings, unusual noises or smells, etc – and remember that failure of components such as fuses or spark plugs may only be pointers to some underlying fault.

The pages which follow here are intended to help in cases of failure to start or breakdown on the road. There is also a Fault Diagnosis Section at the end of each Chapter which should be consulted if the preliminary checks prove unfruitful. Whatever the fault, certain basic principles apply. These are as follows:

Verify the fault. This is simply a matter of being sure that you know what the symptoms are before starting work. This is particularly important if you are investigating a fault for someone else who may not have described it very accurately.

Don't overlook the obvious. For example, if the vehicle won't start, is there petrol in the tank? (Don't take anyone else's word on this particular point, and don't trust the fuel gauge either!) If an electrical fault is indicated, look for loose or broken wires before digging out the test gear.

Cure the disease, not the symptom. Substituting a flat battery with a fully charged one will get you off the hard shoulder, but if the underlying cause is not attended to, the new battery will go the same way. Similarly, changing oil-fouled spark plugs for a new set will get you moving again, but remember that the reason for the fouling (if it wasn't simply an incorrect grade of plug) will have to be established and corrected.

Don't take anything for granted. Particularly, don't forget that a 'new' component may itself be defective (especially if it's been rattling round in the boot for months), and don't leave components out of a fault diagnosis sequence just because they are new or recently fitted. When you do finally diagnose a difficult fault, you'll probably realise that all the evidence was there from the start.

Electrical faults

Electrical faults can be more puzzling than straightforward mechanical failures, but they are no less susceptible to logical analysis if the basic principles of operation are understood. Vehicle electrical wiring exists in extremely unfavourable conditions – heat, vibration and chemical attack – and the first things to look for are loose or corroded connections and broken or chafed wires, especially where the wires pass through holes in the bodywork or are subject to vibration.

Carrying a few spares can save you a long walk!

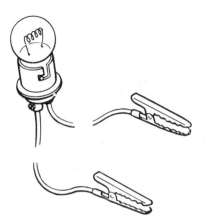

A simple test lamp is useful for tracing minor electrical faults

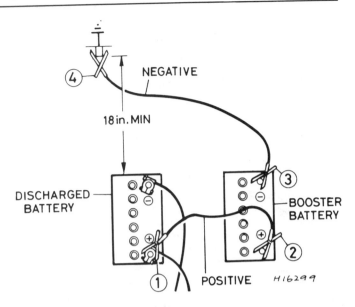

Jump start lead connections for negative earth vehicles – connect leads in order shown

All metal-bodied vehicles in current production have one pole of the battery 'earthed', ie connected to the vehicle bodywork, and in nearly all modern vehicles it is the negative (–) terminal. The various electrical components – motors, bulb holders etc – are also connected to earth, either by means of a lead or directly by their mountings. Electric current flows through the component and then back to the battery via the bodywork. If the component mounting is loose or corroded, or if a good path back to the battery is not available, the circuit will be incomplete and malfunction will result. The engine and/or gearbox are also earthed by means of flexible metal straps to the body or subframe; if these straps are loose or missing, starter motor, generator and ignition trouble may result.

Assuming the earth return to be satisfactory, electrical faults will be due either to component malfunction or to defects in the current supply. Individual components are dealt with in Chapter 12. If supply wires are broken or cracked internally this results in an open-circuit, and the easiest way to check for this is to bypass the suspect wire temporarily with a length of wire having a crocodile clip or suitable connector at each end. Alternatively, a 12V test lamp can be used to verify the presence of supply voltage at various points along the wire and the break can be thus isolated.

If a bare portion of a live wire touches the bodywork or other earthed metal part, the electricity will take the low-resistance path thus formed back to the battery: this is known as a short-circuit. Hopefully a short-circuit will blow a fuse, but otherwise it may cause burning of the insulation (and possibly further short-circuits) or even a fire. This is why it is inadvisable to bypass persistently blowing fuses with silver foil or wire.

Spares and tool kit

Most vehicles are supplied only with sufficient tools for wheel changing; the *Maintenance and minor repair* tool kit detailed in *Tools and working facilities*, with the addition of a hammer, is probably sufficient for those repairs that most motorists would consider attempting at the roadside. In addition a few items which can be fitted without too much trouble in the event of a breakdown should be carried. Experience and available space will modify the list below, but the following may save having to call on professional assistance:

Spark plugs, clean and correctly gapped
HT lead and plug cap – long enough to reach the plug furthest from the distributor
Distributor rotor, condenser and contact breaker points (as applicable)
Drivebelt(s) – emergency type may suffice
Spare fuses
Set of principal light bulbs
Tin of radiator sealer and hose bandage
Exhaust bandage
Roll of insulating tape
Length of soft iron wire
Length of electrical flex
Torch or inspection lamp (can double as test lamp)

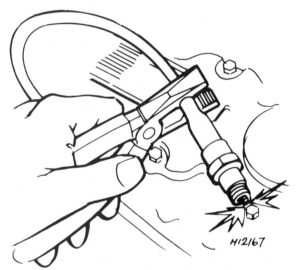

Crank engine and check for spark. Note use of insulated tool. Also, refer to Chapter 4 before carrying out this test on vehicles with electronic ignition. Use a spare plug – removing one from the engine could create a fire hazard.

Battery jump leads
Tow-rope
Ignition water dispersant aerosol
Litre of engine oil
Sealed can of hydraulic fluid
Worm drive clips

If spare fuel is carried, a can designed for the purpose should be used to minimise risks of leakage and collision damage. A first aid kit and a warning triangle, whilst not at present compulsory in the UK, are obviously sensible items to carry in addition to the above.

When touring abroad it may be advisable to carry additional spares which, even if you cannot fit them yourself, could save having to wait while parts are obtained. The items below may be worth considering:

Clutch and throttle cables
Cylinder head gasket
Alternator brushes
Tyre valve core

One of the motoring organisations will be able to advise on availability of fuel etc in foreign countries.

Engine will not start

Engine fails to turn when starter operated
Flat battery (recharge, use jump leads, or push start)
Battery terminals loose or corroded
Battery earth to body defective
Engine earth strap loose or broken
Starter motor (or solenoid) wiring loose or broken
Automatic transmission selector in wrong position, or inhibitor switch faulty
Ignition/starter switch faulty
Major mechanical failure (seizure)
Starter or solenoid internal fault (see Chapter 12)

Starter motor turns engine slowly
Partially discharged battery (recharge, use jump leads, or push start)
Battery terminals loose or corroded
Battery earth to body defective
Engine earth strap loose
Starter motor (or solenoid) wiring loose
Starter motor internal fault (see Chapter 12)

Starter motor spins without turning engine
Flywheel gear teeth damaged or worn
Starter motor mounting bolts loose

Engine turns normally but fails to start
Damp or dirty HT leads and distributor cap (crank engine and check for spark) – try moisture dispersant such as Holts Wet Start
Dirty or incorrectly gapped distributor points (if applicable)
No fuel in tank (check for delivery at carburettor)
Excessive choke (hot engine) or insufficient choke (cold engine)
Fouled or incorrectly gapped spark plugs (remove, clean and regap)
Other ignition system fault (see Chapter 4)
Other fuel system fault (see Chapter 3)
Poor compression (see Chapter 1)
Major mechanical failure (eg camshaft drive)

Engine fires but will not run
Insufficient choke (cold engine)
Air leaks at carburettor or inlet manifold
Fuel starvation (see Chapter 3)
Ballast resistor defective, or other ignition fault (see Chapter 4)

Engine cuts out and will not restart

Engine cuts out suddenly – ignition fault
Loose or disconnected LT wires
Wet HT leads or distributor cap (after traversing water splash)
Coil or condenser failure (check for spark)
Other ignition fault (see Chapter 4)

Engine misfires before cutting out – fuel fault
Fuel tank empty
Fuel pump defective or filter blocked (check for delivery)
Fuel tank filler vent blocked (suction will be evident on releasing cap)
Carburettor needle valve sticking
Carburettor jets blocked (fuel contaminated)
Other fuel system fault (see Chapter 3)

Engine cuts out – other causes
Serious overheating
Major mechanical failure (eg camshaft drive)

Engine overheats

Ignition (no-charge) warning light illuminated
Slack or broken drivebelt – retension or renew (Chapter 2)

Ignition warning light not illuminated
Coolant loss due to internal or external leakage (see Chapter 2)
Thermostat defective
Low oil level
Brakes binding
Radiator clogged externally or internally
Engine waterways clogged
Ignition timing incorrect or automatic advance malfunctioning
Mixture too weak

Note: *Do not add cold water to an overheated engine or damage may result*

Low engine oil pressure

Gauge reads low or warning light illuminated with engine running
Oil level low or incorrect grade
Defective gauge or sender unit
Wire to sender unit earthed
Engine overheating
Oil filter clogged or bypass valve defective
Oil pressure relief valve defective
Oil pick-up strainer clogged
Oil pump worn or mountings loose
Worn main or big-end bearings

Note: *Low oil pressure in a high-mileage engine at tickover is not necessarily a cause for concern. Sudden pressure loss at speed is far more significant. In any event, check the gauge or warning light sender before condemning the engine.*

Engine noises

Pre-ignition (pinking) on acceleration
Incorrect grade of fuel
Ignition timing incorrect
Distributor faulty or worn
Worn or maladjusted carburettor
Excessive carbon build-up in engine

Whistling or wheezing noises
Leaking vacuum hose
Leaking carburettor or manifold gasket
Blowing head gasket

Tapping or rattling
Incorrect valve clearances
Worn valve gear
Worn timing belt
Broken piston ring (ticking noise)

Knocking or thumping
Unintentional mechanical contact (eg fan blades)
Worn drivebelt
Peripheral component fault (generator, water pump etc)
Worn big-end bearings (regular heavy knocking, perhaps less under load)
Worn main bearings (rumbling and knocking, perhaps worsening under load)
Piston slap (most noticeable when cold)

Chapter 1 Engine

Contents

Specifications

B21 engine

General

Type	4-cylinder, in-line, ohc
Application:	
B21A	Carburettor models
B21E	Fuel injection models
Bore	3.622 in (92.0 mm)
Stroke	3.150 in (80 mm)
Cubic capacity	129.7 cu in (2127 cc)
Compression ratio:	
B21A up to 1978	8.5:1
B21A 1979 to 1983	9.3:1
B21A 1984	10.0:1
B21E	9.3:1
Output:	
B21A up to 1975	97 bhp (71 kW) at 5000 rpm
B21A 1976 to 1978	100 bhp (74 kW) at 5250 rpm
B21A 1979 to 1983	107 bhp (79 kW) at 5500 rpm
B21A 1984	102 bhp (75 kW) at 5250 rpm
B21E	123 bhp (90 kW) at 5500 rpm
Torque:	
B21A	125 lbf ft (170 Nm) at 2500 to 3000 rpm
B21E 1975 to 1980	125 lbf ft (170 Nm) at 3500 rpm
B21E 1981 to 1983	119 lbf ft (162 Nm) at 3500 rpm
Compression pressures (all types warm engine, using starter)	128 lbf/in² (883 kPa)
Maximum deviation between cylinders	28 lbf/in² (193 kPa)
Firing order	1-3-4-2 (No 1 cylinder at front of engine)

Cylinder head

Height	5.756 in (146.1 mm)
Minimum after machining	5.736 in (145.6 mm)
Maximum warp (for use without machining):	
Across diagonals	0.020 in (0.50 mm)
Across width	0.010 in (0.250 mm)

Renew cylinder head if warp is greater than 0.039 in (1.0 mm) longitudinally or 0.020 in (0.5 mm) crosswise

Cylinder bores
Standard sizes:
  C .... 3.6220 to 3.6224 in (92.0 to 92.01 mm)
  D .... 3.6224 to 3.6228 in (92.01 to 92.02 mm)
  E .... 3.6228 to 3.6232 in (92.02 to 92.03 mm)
  G .... 3.6236 to 3.6240 in (92.04 to 92.05 mm)
1st oversize .... 3.6417 in (92.5 mm)
2nd oversize .... 3.6614 in (93.0 mm)
Wear limit .... 0.004 in (0.10 mm)

Pistons
Height .... 2.79 in (71.0 mm)
Weight .... 19.42 ± 0.21 oz (555 ± 6.0 g)
Maximum variation in same engine .... 0.42 oz (12.0 g)
Piston clearance in bore .... 0.0004 to 0.0015 in (0.01 to 0.04 mm)

Piston rings
Width:
  Upper compression ring (version 1) .... 0.0779 to 0.0784 in (1.978 to 1.990 mm)
  Upper compression ring (version 2) .... 0.0680 to 0.0685 in (1.728 to 1.740 mm)
  Lower compression ring .... 0.0779 to 0.0784 in (1.978 to 1.990 mm)
  Oil scraper ring (version 1) .... 0.1866 in (4.74 mm)
  Oil scraper ring (version 2) .... 0.1567 to 0.1572 in (3.978 to 3.990 mm)
Axial clearance in groove:
  Upper and lower compression ring .... 0.0015 to 0.0028 in (0.040 to 0.072 mm)
  Oil scraper ring .... 0.0012 to 0.0024 in (0.030 to 0.062 mm)
End gap:
  Upper compression ring .... 0.0138 to 0.0256 in (0.35 to 0.65 mm)
  Lower compression ring .... 0.0138 to 0.0217 in (0.35 to 0.55 mm)
  Oil scraper ring .... 0.0098 to 0.0236 in (0.25 to 0.60 mm)

Gudgeon pins
Gudgeon pins (general):
  Arrangement .... Fully floating with circlips at both ends
  Fit in con-rod .... Sliding fit
  Fit in piston .... Push fit
Gudgeon pin diameter:
  Standard .... 0.945 in (24.00 mm)
  Oversize .... 0.947 in (24.05 mm)

Valves
Inlet valves:
  Seat angle in cylinder head .... 45°
  Valve seat angle .... 44° 30'
  Seat width in cylinder head .... 0.063 in (1.6 mm)
  Valve head diameter .... 1.732 in (44 mm)
  Stem diameter .... 0.3132 to 0.3138 in (7.955 to 7.970 mm)
Exhaust valves:
  Seat angle in cylinder head .... 45°
  Valve seat angle .... 44.5°
  Seat width in cylinder head .... 0.080 in (2 mm)
  Valve head diameter .... 1.378 in (35 mm)
  Stem diameter .... 0.3130 to 0.3136 in (7.945 to 7.960 mm)
Valve clearances – inlet and exhaust:
  Checking value:
    Cold .... 0.012 to 0.016 in (0.30 to 0.40 mm)
    Hot .... 0.014 to 0.018 in (0.35 to 0.45 mm)
  Setting value:
    Cold .... 0.014 to 0.016 in (0.35 to 0.40 mm)
    Hot .... 0.016 to 0.018 in (0.40 to 0.45 mm)

Valve guides
Length .... 2.047 in (52 mm)
Inner diameter .... 0.3150 to 0.3159 in (8.000 to 8.022 mm)
Height above cylinder head face:
  Inlet .... 0.606 to 0.614 in (15.4 to 15.6 mm)
  Exhaust .... 0.705 to 0.713 in (17.9 to 18.1 mm)
Valve stem-to-guide clearance:
  Inlet, new .... 0.0012 to 0.0024 in (0.030 to 0.060 mm)
  Exhaust, new .... 0.0024 to 0.0035 in (0.060 to 0.090 mm)
  Wear limit, both .... 0.0059 in (0.15 mm)

Valve springs
Free length .... 1.77 in (45 mm)
With load of 62 to 70 lb (28 to 32 kg) .... 1.50 in (38 mm)
With load of 156 to 174 lb (72 to 80 kg) .... 1.06 in (27 mm)

Valve tappets

Diameter	1.4557 to 1.4565 in (36.975 to 36.995 mm)
Adjuster shim thickness	0.13 to 0.18 in (3.3 to 4.5 mm) in steps of 0.002 in (0.05 mm)

Camshaft

Marking max lift height:	
B21A 1975	A/0.39 in (9.8 mm)
B21A 1976 to 1983	L/0.41 in (10.5 mm)
B21A 1984	L/0.39 in (9.8 mm)
B21E	D/0.44 in (11.2 mm)
Number of bearings	5
Journal diameter	1.1791 to 1.1799 in (29.950 to 29.970 mm)
Radial clearance	0.0012 to 0.0028 in (0.030 to 0.071 mm)
Endfloat	0.004 to 0.016 in (0.1 to 0.4 mm)
Valve clearance for camshaft setting (cold engine)	0.028 in (0.7 mm)
Inlet valve should then open at:	
B21A 1975	5° BTDC
B21A 1976 to 1987	13° BTDC
B21A 1984	10° BTDC
B21E	15° BTDC
Diameter of camshaft bearings	1.1811 to 1.819 in (30.000 to 30.021 mm)

Timing gears

Number of teeth:	
Crankshaft gear	19
Intermediate gear	38
Camshaft gear	38
Drivebelt	123

Intermediate shaft

Number of bearings	3
Diameter bearing journal:	
Front	1.8494 to 1.8504 in (46.975 to 47.000 mm)
Intermediate	1.6939 to 1.6949 in (43.025 to 43.050 mm)
Rear	1.6900 to 1.6909 in (42.925 to 42.950 mm)
Radial clearance	0.0008 to 0.0030 in (0.020 to 0.075 mm)
Endfloat	0.008 to 0.018 in (0.20 to 0.46 mm)
Diameter of bearing in block:	
Front	1.8512 to 1.8524 in (47.020 to 47.050 mm)
Intermediate	1.6957 to 1.6968 in (43.070 to 43.100 mm)
Rear	1.6917 to 1.6929 in (42.970 to 43.000 mm)

Crankshaft

Endfloat (maximum)	0.0098 in (0.25 mm)
Big-end bearing clearance	0.0009 to 0.0028 in (0.024 to 0.070 mm)
Main bearings clearance	0.0011 to 0.0033 in (0.028 to 0.083 mm)
Main bearing journals:	
Diameter:	
Standard	2.4981 to 2.4986 in (63.451 to 63.464 mm)
Undersize 1	2.4882 to 2.4886 in (63.197 to 63.210 mm)
Undersize 2	2.4781 to 2.4786 in (62.943 to 62.956 mm)
Width on crankshaft for flange bearing shell:	
Standard	1.5339 to 1.5354 in (38.960 to 39.000 mm)
Oversize 1	1.5378 to 1.5394 in (39.061 to 39.101 mm)
Oversize 2	1.5418 to 1.5434 in (39.163 to 39.203 mm)
Maximum ovality	0.0027 in (0.07 mm)
Maximum taper	0.0019 in (0.05 mm)
Big-end bearing journals:	
Bearing seat width	1.179 to 1.183 in (29.95 to 30.05 mm)
Diameter:	
Standard	2.1255 to 2.1260 in (53.987 to 54.000 mm)
Undersize 1	2.1155 to 2.1160 in (53.733 to 53.746 mm)
Undersize 2	2.1055 to 2.1060 in (53.479 to 53.492 mm)
Maximum ovality	0.0019 in (0.05 mm)
Maximum taper	0.0019 in (0.05 mm)

Connecting rods

Endfloat on crankshaft	0.006 to 0.0014 in (0.15 to 0.35 mm)
Length between centres	5.71 ± 0.0039 in (145 ± 1 mm)
Permissible weight difference between con-rods on same engine	0.035 oz (10 grammes)

Flywheel

Permissible axial throw (max)	0.002 in (0.05 mm) at diameter of 5.9 in (150 mm)

Lubrication system

Oil type/specification	Multigrade engine oil, viscosity SAE 10W/30 to API SE (up to 1983) or API SF (from 1984) (Duckhams QXR, Hypergrade, or 10W/40 Motor Oil)

Oil capacity:

With oil filter	6.8 Imp pints (3.85 litres)
Without oil filter	5.9 Imp pints (3.35 litres)
Oil pressure at 2000 rpm (engine warm)	37 to 85 psi (2.5 to 6.0 kg/cm²)
Oil filter – type	Full flow, Champion C102 (all models)

Oil pump:

Type	Gear type pump
Number of teeth on each gear	9
Endfloat	0.0008 to 0.0047 in (0.02 to 0.12 mm)
Radial clearance	0.0008 to 0.0035 in (0.02 to 0.09 mm)
Backlash	0.0059 to 0.0138 in (0.15 to 0.35 mm)

Relief valve spring length:

Free length	1.54 in (39.2 mm)
With load of 11 ± 0.8 lb (5 ± 0.4 kg)	1.03 in (26.25 mm)
With load of 15 ± 1.8 lb (7 ± 0.8 kg)	0.83 in (21 mm)

B23 engine (where different to B21)
General

Bore	3.780 in (96.0 mm)
Cubic capacity	141.2 cu in (2316 cc)

Compression ratio:

B23A 1981 to 1984	10.3:1
B23E 1979 to 1984	10.0:1

Output:

B23A 1981 to 1984	112 bhp (82 kW) at 5000 rpm
B23E 1979 to 1980	140 bhp (103 kW) at 5750 rpm
B23E 1981 to 1983	136 bhp (100 kW) at 5500 rpm
B23B 1984	131 bhp (96 kW) at 5400 rpm

Torque:

B23A 1981 to 1984	136 lbf ft (185 Nm) at 2500 rpm
B23E 1979 to 1980	141 lbf ft (191 Nm) at 4500 rpm
B23E 1981 to 1983	140 lbf ft (190 Nm) at 4500 rpm
B23E 1984	140 lbf ft (190 Nm) at 3600 rpm

Cylinder bores
Standard sizes:

C	3.7795 to 3.7799 in (96.0 to 96.01 mm)
D	3.7799 to 3.7803 in (96.01 to 96.02 mm)
E	3.7803 to 3.7807 in (96.02 to 96.03 mm)
G	3.7811 to 3.7815 in (96.04 to 96.05 mm)
1st oversize	3.7913 in (96.3 mm)
2nd oversize	3.7992 in (96.5 mm)
Wear limit	0.004 in (0.10 mm)

Pistons
Height:

B23A	3.0079 in (76.4 mm)
B23E:	
Type 1	3.1653 in (80.4 mm)
Type 2	3.0079 in (76.4)

Weight:

B23A	19.95 ± 0.25 oz (570 ± 7 g)
B23E	
Type 1	19.42 ± 0.21 oz (555 ± 6 g)
Type 2	19.95 ± 0.25 oz (570 ± 7g)
Maximum variation in same engine	0.42 oz (12.0 g)
Piston clearance in bore (as B21 except for B23E Type 1)	0.0019 to 0.0027 in (0.05 to 0.07 mm)

Camshaft
Marking/max lift height:

B23A 1975	A/0.39 in (9.8 mm)
B23A 1976 on	A/0.41 in (10.5 mm)
B23E 1979 to 1980	H/0.472 in (12.0 mm)
B23E 1981 to 1983	K/0.471 in (11.95 mm)
B23E 1984	A/0.41 in (10.5 mm)

Inlet valve opening timing (cold) at 0.028 in (0.7 mm) clearance:

B23A 1975	5° BTDC
B23A 1976 on	13° BTDC
B23E 1979 to 1980	21° BTDC
B23E 1981 to 1983	15° BTDC
B23E 1984	13° BTDC

B200 engine (where different to B21)
General

Bore	3.5 in (88.9 mm)

Displacement	1986 cc (121 cu in)
Compression ratio	10:1
Output (DIN):	
B200K	101 bhp (74 kW) at 5400 rpm
B200E	117 bhp (86 kW) at 6000 rpm
Torque (DIN):	
B200K	118 lbf ft (160 Nm) at 2400 rpm
B200E	117 lbf ft (158 Nm) at 3800 rpm

Cylinder head

Material	Light alloy
Height	5.756 in (146.1 mm)
Minimum height after refacing	5.736 in (145.6 mm)

Cylinder block

Material	Cast-iron
Bore grade:	
C	3.5000 to 3.5004 in (88.90 to 88.91 mm)
D	3.5004 to 3.5008 in (88.91 to 88.92 mm)
E	3.5008 to 3.5012 in (88.92 to 88.93 mm)
G	3.5016 to 3.5020 in (88.94 to 88.95 mm)
Wear limit	0.004 in (0.1 mm)

Pistons

Height	2.752 in (69.9 mm)
Weight difference between pistons	0.56 oz (16.0 g) max
Clearance in bore:	
1985 models	0.0001 to 0.0010 in (0.003 to 0.027 mm)
1986 on models	0.0004 to 0.0011 in (0.010 to 0.030 mm)

Piston rings

Height:	
Top compression	0.0681 to 0.0685 in (1.728 to 1.740 mm)
Second compression	0.0681 to 0.0685 in (1.728 to 1.740 mm)
Oil scraper	0.1368 to 0.1374 in (3.475 to 3.490 mm)
Piston ring-to-groove clearance:	
Top compression	0.0024 to 0.0036 in (0.060 to 0.092 mm)
Second compression	0.0012 to 0.0025 in (0.030 to 0.062 mm)
Oil scraper	0.0008 to 0.0022 in (0.020 to 0.055 mm)
Piston ring end gap:	
Top compression	0.012 to 0.020 in (0.30 to 0.50 mm)
Second compression	0.012 to 0.022 in (0.30 to 0.55 mm)
Oil scraper	0.010 to 0.020 in (0.25 to 0.50 mm)

Gudgeon pins

Diameter:	
Standard	0.9055 in (23.00 mm)
Oversize	0.9075 in (23.05 mm)
Length	2.36 in (60.0 mm)

Valve springs

Free length – B200K and B200E	1.77 in (45.0 mm)

Camshaft

B200K:	
Marking	L
Maximum lift height	0.386 in (9.8 mm)
Inlet valve opens	5° BTDC
B200E:	
Marking	A
Maximum lift height	0.41 in (10.5 mm)
Inlet valve opens	13° BTDC
Endfloat	0.008 to 0.020 in (0.2 to 0.5 mm)

Crankshaft

Endfloat	0.0032 to 0.0106 in (0.080 to 0.270 mm)
Main bearing running clearance	0.0009 to 0.0028 in (0.024 to 0.072 mm)
Big-end bearing running clearance	0.0009 to 0.0026 in (0.023 to 0.067 mm)
Diameter (standard)	2.1654 in (55.0 mm) nominal
Undersize:	
1	2.1555 in (54.75 mm) nominal
Maximum ovality	0.0002 in (0.004 mm)
Maximum taper	0.0002 in (0.004 mm)
Big-end crankpins:	
Diameter (standard)	1.9291 in (49.0 mm) nominal

Undersize:
  1 .... 1.9193 in (48.75 mm) nominal
  2 .... 1.9094 in (48.50 mm) nominal
  Maximum ovality .... 0.0001 in (0.004 mm)
  Maximum taper .... 0.0002 in (0.004 mm)

Connecting rods
Endfloat on crankshaft .... 0.010 to 0.018 in (0.25 to 0.45 mm)
Length between centres .... 5.98 (152.0 mm)
Maximum weight difference between connecting rods .... 0.7 oz (20.0 g)

Flywheel
Run-out (axial throw) maximum .... 0.0008 in (0.02 mm) at diameter of 3.9 in (100 mm)

B230 engine (where different to B200)
General
Bore .... 3.780 in (96.0 mm)
Displacement .... 2316 cc (141.2 cu in)
Compression ratio:
  B230A 10.3:1
  B230E 10.3:1
  B230K 10.5:1
Output (DIN):
  B230A .... 110 bhp (81 kW) at 5000 rpm
  B230E .... 133 bhp (98 kW) at 5400 rpm
  B230K .... 116 bhp (85 kW) at 5100 rpm
Torque (DIN):
  B230A .... 138 lbf ft (187 Nm) at 2500 rpm
  B230E .... 144 lbf ft (195 Nm) at 3600 rpm
  B230K .... 142 lbf ft (192 Nm) at 3000 rpm

Cylinder block
Bore grades .... As for R23

Pistons
Height .... 2.5472 in (64.7 mm)
Clearance in bore .... 0.004 to 0.0012 in (0.010 to 0.030 mm)

Piston rings
Piston ring-to-groove clearance:
  Top compression .... 0.0024 to 0.0036 in (0.060 to 0.092 mm)
  Second compression .... 0.0016 to 0.0028 in (0.040 to 0.072 mm)
  Oil scraper .... 0.0012 to 0.0025 in (0.030 to 0.065 mm)
Piston ring end gap:
  Top compression .... 0.012 to 0.022 in (0.30 to 0.55 mm)
  Second compression .... 0.012 to 0.022 in (0.30 to 0.55 mm)
  Oil scraper .... 0.012 to 0.024 in (0.30 to 0.60 mm)

Gudgeon pins
Length .... 2.56 in (65.0 mm)

Camshaft
B230A:
  Marking .... A
  Maximum lift height .... 0.413 in (10.5 mm)
  Inlet valve opens .... 13° BTDC
B230K:
  Marking .... T
  Maximum lift height .... 0.390 in (9.9 mm)
  Inlet valve opens .... 7° BTDC
B230E:
  Marking V
  Maximum lift height .... 0.448 in (11.37 mm)
  Inlet valve opens .... 11° BTDC

Torque wrench settings – all engines

Cylinder head bolts (see also Section 9)	lbf ft	Nm
Early types (with recessed head):		
Stage 1	43	60
Stage 2	80	110
Stage 3	Run engine till warm, cool 30 minutes	
Stage 4	Loosen bolt 1 by 30°, then retighten to Stage 2	
Stage 5	Repeat, in sequence, on bolts 2 to 10	
Later type (with hexagon head):		
Stage 1	15	20
Stage 2	43	60
Stage 3	Angle-tighten by 90°	

Note: *Discard bolts after 5 uses, or if bolts are stretched*

Main bearing cap bolts	80	110
Big-end bearing nuts or bolts (B21/B23 engines):		
Used	46	63
New	51	70
Big-end bearing nuts or bolts (B200/B230 engines)**:		
Stage 1	15	20
Stage 2	Angle-tighten by 90°	Angle-tighten by 90°
Flywheel (use new bolts)	51	70
Camshaft sprocket bolt	37	50
Intermediate shaft sprocket bolt	37	50
Camshaft bearing cap nuts	15	20
Crankshaft pulley/sprocket centre bolt (B21/B23 engines)	122	165
Crankshaft sprocket centre bolt (B200/B230 engines):		
Stage 1	44	60
Stage 2	Angle-tighten by 60°	Angle-tighten by 60°
Camshaft belt tensioner bolt	37	50
Oil sump bolts	8	11

Oiled threads unless otherwise stated in text
** *Renew bolts if length exceeds 2.185 in (55.5 mm)*

1 General description

The engine is a four-cylinder, in-line, overhead cam, water-cooled unit. All versions are derived from the B21, the larger engines having increased bore/stroke.

The overhead camshaft acts directly on the valve 'buckets' (tappets), and is driven by a toothed belt from a sprocket on the crankshaft. This belt also drives the intermediate shaft which in turn drives the distributor, fuel pump (carburettor engines) and oil pump. The alternator, air conditioning and power steering are all driven by V-belt from the crankshaft pulley, as is the water pump.

The cylinder head is of cast aluminium, and of crossflow design. The valve guides and seats are pressed in place.

The crankshaft runs in five main bearings of the white-metal-lined shell type, the same type of bearing also being used on the connecting rod 'big-end' bearings. The cylinder block is of cast iron with the cylinders bored directly into it.

Later versions, introduced in 1985, were called the B200 and B230, and although these engines are improved and uprated, the basic servicing/overhaul procedures are the same. Do, however, make sure you use the correct Specifications for the engine being worked on.

The B230K 'Heron head' engine was introduced in 1987. This engine has a new design of cylinder head, which is flat, the pistons being dished to form a combustion chamber in their crowns. This has resulted in better fuel consumption without reduction in performance, and an increase in compression ratio with a lowering of the required fuel octane rating. No further specific details were available on this engine at the time of writing.

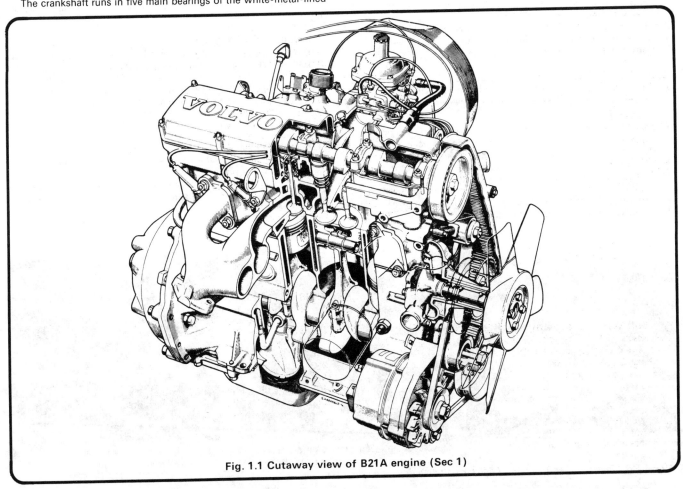

Fig. 1.1 Cutaway view of B21A engine (Sec 1)

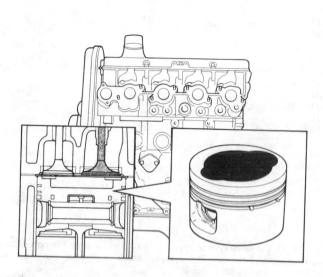

Fig. 1.2 View of B230K 'Heron head' (Sec 1)

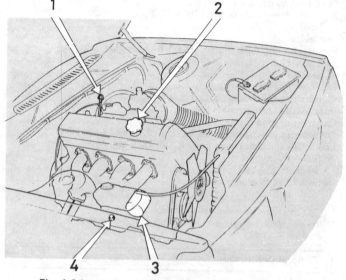

Fig. 1.3 Location of oil change components (Sec 3)

1 Oil dipstick   *3 Oil filter*
2 Oil filler cap   *4 Sump drain plug*

2 Routine maintenance

1 At the intervals specified in the *Routine maintenance* Section at the beginning of this Manual, carry out the following operations.
2 Weekly, or before a long journey, check the engine oil level (Section 3).
3 Periodically check all round the engine for signs of leakage.
4 Renew the engine oil and oil filter (Sections 3 and 4).
5 Check and adjust the valve clearances (Section 5).
6 Renew the camshaft drivebelt (Section 6).
7 Carry out a compression check (Section 14).

3 Engine oil – level checking, draining and refilling

Level checking
1 The vehicle should be parked on level ground, and a period of at least one minute should elapse from the engine last being run.
2 Open the bonnet and remove the engine oil level dipstick (photo).
3 Wipe the dipstick clean on a piece of non-fluffy rag, then re-insert it in the dipstick tube, ensuring it is pushed fully down.
4 Withdraw the dipstick, and inspect the end of it to establish the oil level (photo). The level should be maintained between the 'MAX' and 'MIN' marks (the cross-hatched section).

5 The difference between the 'MAX' and 'MIN' marks is approximately 2 pints (1.0 litres).
6 If the oil needs replenishing, remove the cap from the oil filler on the valve cover, and pour in a quantity of the specified oil to raise the level to that indicated (photo). Allow time for the oil to drain down, or a false reading may be obtained, with subsequent over-filling. Mop up any spillage.
7 On completion, refit the dipstick and oil filler cap, and close the bonnet.

Draining and refilling
8 Again the vehicle should be parked on level ground. The oil will drain more readily and carry away more contaminants if the engine has been recently run, but beware of scalding if the oil is really hot.
9 Place a suitable receptacle under the oil drain plug, then remove the plug and allow the oil to drain from the sump (photo).
10 Clean the drain plug and its seating area on the sump. Fit a new sealing washer before refitting the plug to the sump when all the oil has drained out, and tighten it securely.
11 Refer to Section 4 for oil filter changing.
12 Fill the engine with the specified quantity and quality of oil as described in earlier paragraphs.
13 On completion, run the engine until it reaches normal operating temperature and check for leaks from the drain plug (and filter if it has been renewed). Stop the engine and re-check the oil level.
14 Dispose of the old oil safely: remember it is toxic and inflammable.

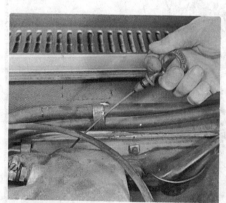

3.2 Removing the engine oil dipstick

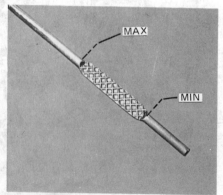

3.4 'MAX' and 'MIN' marks on dipstick

3.6 Filling the engine with oil

4 Oil filter – renewal

1 The oil filter should be renewed at the same time as the oil is renewed.

2 After draining the oil as described in Section 3 (if the filter alone is being changed, there is no need to drain the oil, only the oil in the filter will be lost), and proceed as follows.

3 Unscrew the filter from the side of the engine block (photo). It may only be hand-tight, but if it is too tight, use a strap or chain wrench on it. Be prepared for spillage.

4 Mop up any spillage, and clean all round the filter base on the engine block. Make sure that the sealing ring has come away with the old filter.

5 Grease the seal on the new filter, and screw the new filter into the filter base, using only moderate hand pressure.

6 After filling the engine with oil as described in Section 3, run the engine and check for leaks from the filter base. If it does leak, tighten the filter a little more, but do not over-tighten.

5 Valve clearances – checking and adjusting

1 Disconnect or remove such items as HT leads, vacuum and breather hoses, and for more ease of access, the accelerator cable, in order to remove the camshaft cover. Also remove the ignition timing sender socket and where applicable, the auxiliary air valve.

2 Remove the nuts and lift off the camshaft cover. Note the earth lead under the nuts. Recover the gasket.

3 Using a ring spanner on the crankshaft pulley nut, bring the engine to TDC, number one cylinder on the compression stroke. Remove the spark plugs to make turning the engine easier. Number one cylinder is at TDC on compression when the notch on the crankshaft pulley is in line with the zero mark on the timing scale, and both cam lobes of that cylinder are both pointing obliquely upwards. The cylinders are numbered one to four from the front of the engine. (See also Section 6, paragraph 4).

4 With the engine in this position, measure and record the clearance between the base of the front cam lobe and the upper face of the tappet shim beneath it. Do this by inserting various thicknesses of feeler blade until a firm sliding fit is obtained.

5 Repeat the measurement on the second cam and again record the clearance (photo).

6 Turn the crankshaft through 180° until the cam lobes on number three cylinder are facing upwards. Repeat the measurement on these valves.

7 Turn the engine a further 180° and repeat the operation on number four cylinder, then a further 180° and measure number two.

8 Refer to the Specifications and check the recorded clearances against those specified. If the clearances are within tolerances, commence reassembly. If not, adjust the clearances as follows.

9 A special tool for removing the shims is used by Volvo, which does make the task very much easier, but one can get by using a wedge-shaped tool which will fit between the camshaft and the rim of the tappet, so that the tappet can be depressed against the valve spring, but still leave the shim free to be removed (photos).

10 Turn the tappet so that the notch in the rim is facing the side of the engine.

11 Depress the tappet by whatever method is chosen, and hold the tappet down while the shim in the top of the tappet is prised up so that it can be gripped with long-nosed pliers and removed (photo). The tappet can be released. Measure and record the shim thickness, using a micrometer.

12 Now calculate the correct thickness of shim, as shown in the following example:

Specified clearance (A) = 0.016 in (0.40 mm)
Measured clearance (B) = 0.011 in (0.28 mm)
Original shim thickness (C) = 0.156 in (3.95 mm)
Shim thickness required = C – A + B = 0.151 in (3.83 mm)

3.9 Engine oil drain plug in sump

4.3 Engine oil filter

5.5 Measuring a valve clearance

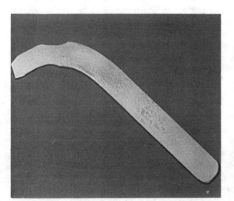
5.9A Wedge-shaped piece of scrap metal for depressing the tappets

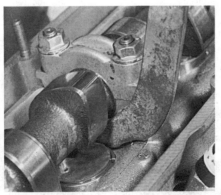
5.9B Tool being used to depress a tappet

5.11 Removing a shim

5.13 Shim thickness marking

5.16 Ensure half-moon shaped seal is in place

5.17A Fitting the valve cover gasket

5.17B Earth strap between valve cover and bulkhead

5.17C Ignition sender

5.17D Spark plug HT leads and bracket

In this example, the shim thickness to be fitted would have to be 0.15 in (3.85 mm) or 0.150 in (3.80 mm), giving clearances of 0.015 in (0.38 mm) and 0.017 in (0.43 mm).
Note: *The shims are supplied in metric sizes, and it would be advisable to use the metric scale when calculating shim thickness.*
13 Lubricate the new shim before depressing the tappet and fitting the shim back into the recess in the tappet. The side with the shim thickness marked on it should face downwards, into the tappet (photo). Release the tappet and check that the shim is seating correctly.
14 Repeat the procedure on the other tappet if necessary, and on the other valves in sequence, as described for measurement in paragraphs 3 to 7. Do not turn the crankshaft with shims missing from the tappets, as the cam lobes may jam in them.
15 When all the shim thicknesses have been calculated and adjusted, turn the engine through several complete turns (using the starter motor or the crankshaft bolt), and then check all valve clearances once more.
16 Before refitting the camshaft cover, check that the half-moon shaped rubber seal in the rear of the cylinder head is in good condition (B21/B23 engines only), and renew it if signs of oil leakage are apparent (photo).
17 Fit the camshaft cover, using a new gasket, remembering the components held under the retaining nuts (earth lead, ignition sender, HT lead bracket) (photos).
18 Reconnect the HT leads, vacuum hoses, etc, and run the engine, checking that there are no leaks from the camshaft cover.

6 Camshaft drivebelt – removal, refitting and tensioning

1 The procedure given here describes the procedure with the engine *in situ*.
2 Remove the cooling fan shroud, and for greater ease of access, the cooling fan (see Chapter 2). On B200/B230 engines, the fan and pulley must be removed for access anyway. Remove the accessory drivebelts (Chapter 2, Section 14).

3 Remove the camshaft drivebelt cover. On some engines this is in two halves, the lower half can be removed later.
4 Using a ring spanner on the crankshaft pulley bolt, turn the engine to TDC, number one cylinder on compression stroke. This is indicated when the mark on the camshaft sprocket is in line with the mark on the camshaft cover or sprocket guide plate (photo).
5 Similarly, the marks on the crankshaft sprocket and front oil seal housing should be in alignment (the pulley mark cannot be used, because the timing marks are on the cover which has been removed), as should the marks on the intermediate shaft sprocket, which determines ignition timing.
6 The crankshaft pulley now has to be removed. On B21/B23 engines, the pulley is secured by the ring of six bolts, which are not too difficult to remove without moving the engine from its TDC position, but on B200 and B230 engines, the pulley is held by the centre bolt, which is much tighter (photo).
7 On B200/B230 engines, to prevent the engine turning while the bolt is undone, remove the starter motor and have an assistant jam the starter ring gear on the flywheel with a lever.
8 On all types of engine, check the alignment of the marks after the pulley has been removed.
9 On engines with a split belt cover, remove the lower half.
10 Loosen the camshaft drivebelt tensioner pulley nut (photo), then pull the belt tight by hand to compress the tensioner spring, and tighten the pulley nut. The belt will now be released from tension and can be slipped off the sprockets.
Note: *If the belt is to be used again, mark the direction of rotation on it so that it can be refitted the same way.*
11 Once the belt is removed, **do not** turn the camshaft or crankshaft, or the valves/pistons may strike each other, causing damage.
12 Inspect the drivebelt for contamination with oil or grease, cracking or fraying. Renew it if its condition is in doubt.
13 Check the tensioner roller by spinning it. If it feels rough, or has excessive play, it should be renewed (Section 8).
14 Before refitting the belt, check all the alignment marks once more.
15 Slip the belt back over the sprockets and tensioner roller, remembering its direction of rotation if the old belt is being re-used.

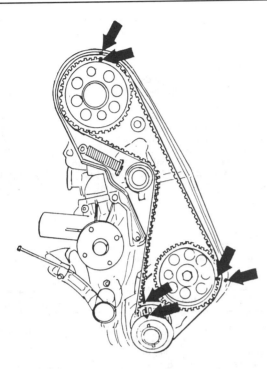

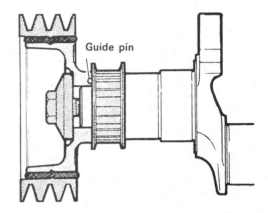

Fig. 1.5 Crankshaft pulley and sprocket arrangement on
B200/B230 engines (Sec 6)

Fig. 1.4 Timing gear sprocket alignment marks (arrowed),
No 1 cylinder at TDC on compression stroke (Sec 6)

The two lines on the outside of the belt must be opposite the
crankshaft sprocket mark.

16 Give a final check of the alignment marks before releasing the
tensioner nut. Allow the tensioner to take up its natural position, then
tighten the nut.

17 Refit the lower belt cover where applicable, then fit the crankshaft
pulley. On B200/B230 engines, this will again involve preventing the
engine from turning. Note the alignment pin or dowel, used on both
types of engine.

18 On all types of engine, turn the crankshaft through two full
revolutions, coming to rest with the TDC marks again lined up. Check
that all marks are in alignment. If not the procedure will have to be
repeated.

19 Refit the drivebelt cover, accessory drivebelts, pulleys, fan etc.

20 Run the engine until it reaches normal operating temperature, then
stop the engine.

21 Remove the camshaft drivebelt tensioner bolt plug from the cover
(photo), and loosen the tensioner bolt, and then re-tighten it and refit
the plug.

22 Check the ignition timing (Chapter 4, Section 14).

23 If a new belt has been fitted, repeat paragraph 21 after
approximately 600 miles (1000 km).

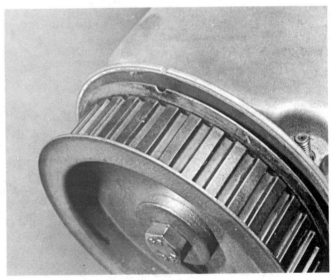

6.4 Camshaft sprocket and cover marks

6.6 Removing the crankshaft pulley
(B21/B23)

6.10 Loosen the tensioner nut

6.21 Tensioner nut access plug

7 Camshaft – removal and refitting

Note: *If a new camshaft is to be fitted because of wear to the existing camshaft, the lubrication system must be flushed with **two** consecutive oil and oil filter changes **before** removing the old camshaft. Drain the oil and renew the filter, then run the engine for 10 minutes. Fresh oil and a new filter **must** by provided for the new camshaft. Non-compliance with this instruction may cause rapid wear of the new camshaft.*

1   Remove the camshaft drivebelt as described in Section 6, but the belt can remain on the lower sprockets.

2   Prevent the camshaft from turning by inserting a suitable tool through the holes in the sprocket, or by using a strap wrench, while the sprocket retaining bolt is loosened (photo). **Do not** allow the camshaft to turn, or the valves may strike the pistons.

3   Remove the sprocket bolts, guide plate, sprocket and rear guide plate, noting their relative positions (photos).

4   Remove the camshaft cover, noting the earth lead, HT lead bracket and ignition timing sender secured under the nuts. Recover the gasket.

5   Check that the camshaft bearing caps are marked so that they can be replaced in the same position, before progressively slackening the cap nuts. Ensure the camshaft (which is under pressure from the valve springs) does not stick and jump up when suddenly released. Remove the bearing caps (photos).

6   Lift out the camshaft complete with front oil seal. The lobe edges may be sharp, so be careful (photo).

7   To measure camshaft endfloat, remove all the tappets and shims, keeping them in strict order of removal for refitting, then refit the camshaft and rear bearing cap.

8   Measure the endfloat between the bearing cap and the camshaft flange (photo).

9   Excessive endfloat, if not caused by wear in the camshaft itself, can be corrected by renewing the rear bearing cap.

10   Refit the tappets and shims in their original positions.

11   Before refitting the camshaft, liberally oil all components. Use clean engine oil, or the special camshaft lubricant which may be supplied with a new camshaft.

12   Fit the camshaft into place on the bearings, with number one cylinder lobes facing obliquely upwards and the camshaft sprocket guide pin also pointing upwards.

13   Apply sealant to the mating surfaces of the front and rear bearing caps (photo).

14   Fit the caps in their respective positions, then fit and tighten the bearing cap nuts progressively a little at a time until the caps bottom. Tighten the nuts to the specified torque.

15   Lubricate a new oil seal and fit it in place on the front of the camshaft, tapping it home with a piece of tubing (photo).

16   Refit the camshaft sprocket and associated components, which is a reversal of removal, and tighten the sprocket bolt to the specified torque.

17   Refit and tension the camshaft drivebelt (Section 6).

18   If any new parts have been fitted, check and adjust the valve clearances as described in Section 5.

19   If a new camshaft has been fitted, it should be run in at moderate engine speeds for about 5 minutes, or as directed by the manufacturers.

8 Camshaft drivebelt tensioner – removal and refitting

1   Remove the camshaft drivebelt cover and line up the sprocket timing marks as described in Section 6.

2   Loosen the tensioner roller nut.

3   Compress the spring using large water pump pliers, or by the method described in Section 6, then insert a pin through the hole in the spring shaft to prevent it expanding when removed (photo).

4   Remove the roller nut and ease the spring and roller off their spigots.

5   Refit in reverse order, removing the pin on completion (photo).

7.2 Restrain the camshaft and loosen the sprocket retaining bolt

7.3A Removing the bolt, washer and front guide plate ...

7.3B ... and the sprocket

7.5A Camshaft bearing cap markings (arrowed)

7.5B Removing a camshaft bearing cap nut

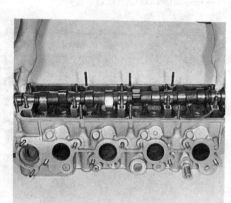

7.6 Lifting off the camshaft

7.8 Measuring camshaft endfloat

7.13 Apply sealant to the shaded areas shown on the bearing cap

7.15 Fitting a new oil seal

8.3 Insert a pin through the hole in the spring shaft (arrowed)

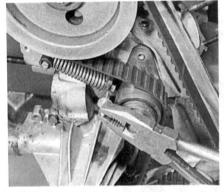

8.5 Removing the restraining pin

9 Cylinder head bolts – removal, inspection and refitting

Note: *The cooling system must be drained before removing the cylinder head bolts.*

1 There are two types of bolt, as shown in Fig. 1.6. The two types should not be mixed on the same cylinder head.

2 Early types are socket-headed with separate washers, later types are hexagon-headed with a machined collar.

3 The bolts should be removed by unscrewing them a half a turn at a time, in the reverse order of tightening (Fig. 1.7), until all tension is relieved and they can be removed by hand.

4 The above procedure is important to minimise risk of the cylinder head being warped.

5 The bolts should be thoroughly degreased and inspected for necking (stretching) and renewed if this condition is evident.

6 Later type bolts should only be used a maximum of five times. Where doubt exists as to this, they should be renewed.

7 Before refitting, the bolts having been degreased as previously mentioned, the threads should be lubricated with clean engine oil. Also clean the thread holes in the cylinder block.

8 Fit the cylinder head bolts, screwing them down as far as possible by hand, ensuring they are not cross-threaded.

9 Tighten the bolts a little at a time, in the sequence shown in Fig. 1.7, to the specified torque.

10 Early type bolts should be check-tightened in the following manner:

> (a) *Run the engine till it reaches normal operating temperature, switch off and allow the engine to cool for 30 minutes.*
> (b) *Loosen bolt number 1 (in the tightening sequence) by approximately 30°.*
> (c) *Re-tighten to the specified maximum torque.*
> (d) *Repeat, in sequence, on the remaining bolts.*

11 It is emphasised that correct tightening of the cylinder head bolts is essential if the cylinder head is not to become warped.

12 Where angle-tightening of the bolts is called for, a simple template cut from card can be used as a guide.

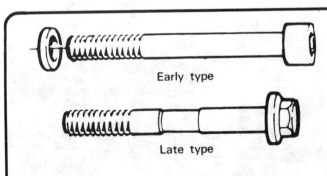

Early type

Late type

Fig. 1.6 Two types of cylinder head bolt (Sec 9)

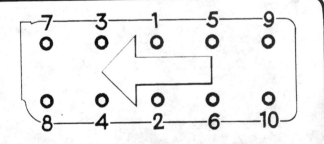

Fig. 1.7 Numerical tightening sequence of cylinder head bolts (Sec 12)

10　Cylinder head – removal and refitting

1　The procedure given here is for removing the cylinder head with the engine *in situ*.
2　Disconnect the battery negative terminal.
3　Drain the cooling system (See Chapter 2).
4　Disconnect the spark plug leads, vacuum hoses and crankcase ventilation hoses.
5　On fuel injection engines, remove the auxiliary air valve, and disconnect the injectors and cold start injector.
6　Disconnect the radiator top hose from the thermostat housing.
7　Remove the camshaft drivebelt as described in Section 6, and on B200/B230 engines, remove the camshaft sprocket and spacer washer, and remove the camshaft tensioner stud.
8　Remove the carburettor or disconnect all services to it and remove it with the inlet manifold (see Chapter 3).
9　On fuel injection models, disconnect the accelerator cable (see Chapter 3).
10　Where fitted, disconnect the Pulsair system hoses (Chapter 3).
11　Refer to Chapter 3 and remove the inlet and exhaust manifolds.
12　Check round the cylinder head, and disconnect any remaining electrical leads (temperature sensor, ignition timing sender, etc).
13　Remove the camshaft cover and recover the gasket.
14　Remove the cylinder head bolts as described in Section 9.
15　Lift off the cylinder head. On B200/B230 engines, it will be necessary to bend the drivebelt cover forwards a little. If the cylinder head is stuck, do not attempt to lever it from the block, but break the seal by gently tapping with a soft-faced mallet.
16　Set the head down on a bench, supported on a couple of wooden blocks.
17　Remove the old cylinder head gasket, and remove all traces of it from the cylinder block and head.
18　Commence refitting by positioning a new cylinder head gasket over the locating dowels in the cylinder block. Check that all the water and oil ways line up, which will indicate that the gasket is the right way up. The gasket is assembled dry (photo).

19　Check that the O-ring seal is positioned in the water pump recess (photo).
20　Gently lower the cylinder head onto the cylinder block, making sure it sits down over the locating dowels (photo). Also make sure that the camshaft is in the 'No 1 firing' position, otherwise the valves may contact the piston.
21　Refit the cylinder head bolts as described in Section 9.
22　The remaining procedure is a reversal of removal, finally checking the valve clearances before starting the engine.
23　Re-tighten early type cylinder head bolts as described in Section 9, paragraph 10.

11　Cylinder head – dismantling

1　Remove the cylinder head as described in Section 10.
2　Remove the spark plugs or injectors if still fitted.
3　Remove the half-moon shaped rubber seal (when fitted) at the rear of the cylinder head.
4　Remove the thermostat housing (photo) and thermostat and the coolant temperature sensor.
5　Remove the camshaft as described in Section 7.
6　Lift out the tappets and shims. Keep them in strict order of removal, as they must be refitted in the same position (photo).
7　Remove the rubber seals from the top of the valve stems.
8　Use a valve spring compressor (or similar home-made tools as depicted) to compress a valve spring (photo).
9　Extract the valve stem collets. This is more easily done using a pencil magnet (photo). Carefully release the spring compressor.
10　Lift off the valve spring upper seat and valve spring (photo).
11　Remove the valve. Note that only the inlet valves have oil seals, which should be removed along with the spring lower seats (photo).
12　Remove the remaining valve assemblies, keeping all components in order for refitting.
13　Remove temperature sensors, the thermal timer etc (as applicable), noting their locations for refitting (photo).

10.18 A new cylinder head gasket in position

10.19 O-ring seal fitted to water pump

10.20 Cylinder head in position

11.4 Thermostat housing and lifting eye

11.6 Lifting out a tappet

11.8 Compressing a valve spring to remove the collets, using home-made tools

11.9 Extracting the collets with a pencil magnet

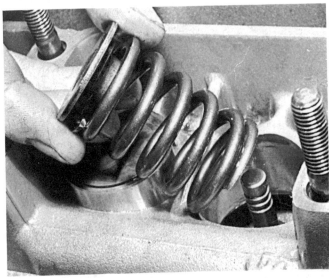

11.10 Lifting out the valve spring

11.11 Removing an inlet valve stem oil seal

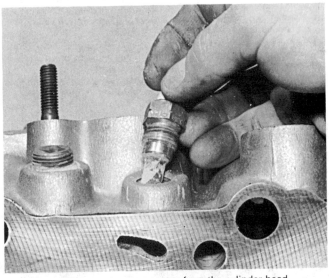

11.13 Removing a temperature sensor from the cylinder head

12 Cylinder head – overhaul

1   With the cylinder head removed and dismantled as described in Sections 10 and 11, remove all traces of carbon from around the valve ports and guides.
2   This should be done using a wooden scraper or flexible wire brush, as the aluminium head is soft and easily scored. (Paint stripper is good for removing stubborn deposits and traces of cylinder head gasket, but satisfy yourself that it will not attack the cylinder head itself).
3   On completion, wash the head in clean paraffin and blow dry, cleaning out all the coolant channels and valve guides.
4   Using a straight edge placed diagonally across the cylinder head face from corner to corner, try to insert a feeler blade between the straight edge and the head to ascertain any warping. Repeat across the other diagonal, and in three places across the width of the head. Tolerances are given in the Specifications. If the head is outside these tolerances, have it skimmed by a specialist. Note the minimum head height, also given in the Specifications.
5   Take each valve in turn and remove any carbon build-up on the stems or valve face. Inspect the valve face for signs of burning or pitting.

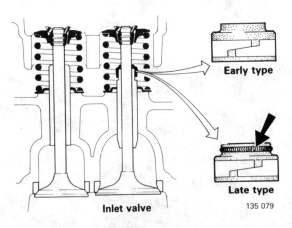

Fig. 1.8 Early and late type valve guide seals (Sec 12)

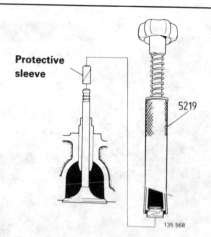

Protective sleeve

5219

135 568

Fig. 1.9 Special tool for fitting valve stem oil seals (Sec 12)

6   Similarly, inspect the valve seats in the cylinder head. Light scoring or pitting of valves and seats can be removed by valve grinding, but anything more serious will necessitate the seats or valves being refaced which is a job for a specialist.

7   Place each valve into its guide in turn, and check for wear in the valve stems or guides. This is best done using a dial test indicator, with the valve held 0.04 to 0.08 in (1.0 to 2.0 mm) from the seat. Try to rock the stem in the guide to show any wear. Limits are given in the Specifications.

8   If the wear limits are exceeded, try again using a new valve, and if there is still no improvement, the valve guides must be worn and will need renewing. Again this is a job for a specialist.

9   The valves can now be ground in to their seats, either to mate new valves to their seats, or improve the seating of existing valves.

10 Place the cylinder head upside down on a couple of wooden blocks, high enough for the valves to be inserted fully into the guides.

11 Smear a trace of grinding paste onto the seat face, and fit a valve grinding tool to the valve. Using a semi-rotary action, grind the valve head to its seat, lifting it occasionally to re-distribute the paste. When a dull matt, even, surface is produced on both the valve seat and valve face, clean off the paste and repeat the operation using a finer grade of paste. When a smooth, unbroken ring of light grey matt finish is produced on both the valve seat and valve, the operating is complete (photos).

12 Remove all traces of grinding paste from the valve, valve seat and valve guide by washing in paraffin and blowing dry. It is most important that no trace of grinding paste is left.

13 Measure the valve spring free length, and if possible the compressed length, against the tolerances given in the Specifications. Weak springs should be renewed. Renew the springs in any case if they have seen much service.

14 Inlet valve stem oil seals should be renewed as a matter of course. Note that there are two types of seal – only the later type should be used.

13 Cylinder head – reassembly

1   Before reassembly begins, give all components a coating of clean engine oil.

2   Fit each valve assembly in turn in the following sequence.

3   Insert the valve stem into the valve guide (photo) and fit the spring lower seat, dished side upwards.

4   On the inlet valves, fit a valve stem oil seal (photo), pushing it down over the stem with a piece of suitable-sized tubing. There is a special tool for this purpose. The seal is easily damaged on the edges of the collet rings, so use the protective sleeve supplied over the end of the stem.

5   Fit the valve spring and spring upper seat.

6   Compress the spring and fit the two collets, ensuring they are located properly in the grooves in the stem. A dab of grease will help in locating them.

7   Release the spring compressor carefully, then give each valve stem a sharp tap with a soft mallet to seat the collets (photo).

8   Fit the rubber seals to the valve stem ends (photo).

9   Oil the tappets and insert them into their respective bores. Fit the

12.11A Applying grinding paste to a valve

12.11B Grinding-in a valve

13.3 Inserting a valve into a valve guide

13.4 Fitting a new inlet valve stem seal

13.7 Valve collets seated properly

13.8 Fit the rubber seal to the valve tips

13.9 Fitting a shim to a tappet

shims into the tappets, and record the thickness of each shim for later reference (photo).

10 Fit the camshaft and front oil seal as described in Section 7. Do not forget to fit the half-moon shaped seal in the rear of the cylinder head.

11 Fit the camshaft sprocket and guide plates as described in Section 7. On B200 and B230 engines, the sprocket will have to be removed when the cylinder head is refitted to the engine.

12 Check and adjust the valve clearances as described in Section 5, using a strap wrench to turn the camshaft.

13 Refit the thermostat and housing, coolant temperature sensor and thermal timer if applicable, using new gaskets, sealing washers or sealant as appropriate.

14 Compression checking

1 A compression tester is required for the compression test. These are not too expensive and worthwhile obtaining. The type which screws into the spark plug hole, as opposed to those with a rubber bung which is just pressed into the hole, is best.

2 As a safety precaution to prevent damage to the ignition circuit, disconnect the negative terminal (terminal 1) on the coil.

3 The purpose of a compression test is to detect wear in the cylinder bores or piston rings, or in the valve gear or head gasket.

4 The engine should be at normal operating temperature, the battery fully charged and all spark plugs removed.

5 Have an assistant ready to crank the engine on the starter motor, fit the compression tester to number one cylinder spark plug hole, and crank the engine with the accelerator pedal fully depressed (throttle wide open). Record the highest pressure reading obtained. (Some testers have a needle which will stay at the highest pressure until reset, which is very useful).

6 Repeat the test on the remaining three cylinders.

7 The result should be compared with the specified pressures given in the Specifications.

8 If the pressure in any one of the cylinders is low, squirt some clean engine oil into that cylinder through the spark plug hole and allow the oil to run round and into the piston rings. Repeat the test on that cylinder.

9 If there is temporary increase in the pressure, it indicates wear in the cylinder bore or piston rings.

10 If there is no improvement, it suggests leaking or burnt valves, or a blown cylinder head gasket.

11 A low reading from two adjacent cylinders is probably due to a blown head gasket between these cylinders.

12 On completion of testing, refit the spark plugs and LT lead on the coil.

15 Oil pressure checking

1 A pressure gauge, and an adaptor to fit the oil pressure transmitter threads and connect to the oil pressure gauge hose will be required.

2 Remove the oil pressure transmitter from the cylinder block (it is situated down by the oil filter).

3 Fit the adaptor and connect the oil pressure gauge and hose to it.

4 The oil pressure should be checked with the engine filled to the correct level with the specified oil, and with a new oil filter having been fitted. The engine should be at normal operating temperature and running at 2000 rpm.

5 If the specified oil pressure is not obtained, re-check the oil level and inspect the engine for leaks.

6 If the oil level is correct and there is no leakage, suspect the pressure relief valve in the oil pump of malfunction, or a worn oil pump.

7 If these are in order, there is probably wear in the crankshaft bearings.

16 Oil sump – removing and refitting

Note: *On pre-1980 engines, a shallower sump was used, and the front axle crossmember and steering shaft do not have to be removed/released.*

1 The following procedure described the removal of the sump with the engine *in situ*.

2 Drain the engine oil, then refit the drain plug and tighten it.

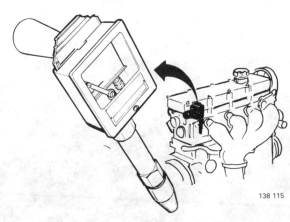

Fig. 1.10 Typical compression tester (Sec 14)

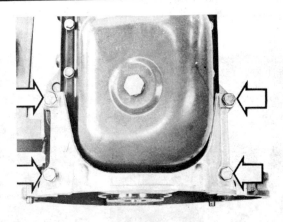

Fig. 1.11 Oil sump reinforcing bracket bolts (arrowed) (Sec 16)

Fig. 1.12 Removing the sump, engine *in situ* (Sec 16)

3 Remove the engine splash guard from the underside of the engine.
4 Remove the nuts from the engine mountings on the front axle crossmember.
5 Remove the lower pinch-bolt from the lower steering shaft joint (see Chapter 10), and loosen the upper pinch-bolt, then slide the joint up and off the steering pinion shaft.
6 Attach lifting gear to the engine front lifting eye and raise the engine slightly.
7 Remove the left-hand engine mounting.
8 Remove the bolts securing the front axle crossmember and lower the crossmember.
9 Remove the oil sump reinforcing bracket (photo).
10 Remove the bolts securing the sump to the engine block.
11 Pull the sump down, and rotate it to clear obstructions to remove it from the engine.

12 Clean the inside of the sump out in petrol and dry it thoroughly.
13 Remove all traces of old gasket from the mating surfaces of the sump and cylinder block.
14 Small irregularities in the sump mating face, caused by over-tightening of the retaining bolts, may be chamfered down, but if this is severe and causing leakage, renew the sump.
15 Fitting a new sump is a reversal of removal, using a new gasket (the lug faces the starter motor bracket), and tightening the retaining bolts to the specified torque (photo). (Stick the gasket to the sump or block with grease.)
16 Make sure the drain plug is tight, then refill the engine with oil.

17 Oil pump – removal and refitting

Note: *There are two versions, the procedure for both types being similar, the difference being in the oil pick-up strainer. On later versions, the pick-up is longer to account for the deeper sump. Specifications for both types of pump is the same.*
1 Remove the sump as described in Section 16.
2 Remove the retaining bolts and lift out the pump (photo). Note the drain hose retaining bracket under one of the retaining bolts on 1981-on models.
3 When refitting the pump which is a reversal of the removal procedure, use new seals on the delivery tube (photo) and ensure that the oil pump driveshaft engages with the dogs on the drive pinion from the intermediate shaft.
4 Guide the delivery tube carefully into the oil gallery in the cylinder block to avoid damage to the seal. Coat the seals with clean engine oil to ease their fitting (photo).
5 On 1981-on models, make sure the clamp for the oil trap drain hose is in position under the retaining bolt, and that it clamps the hose securely.
6 Ensure the lower end of the hose is tucked in behind the pump. Do not cut the hose, as its length is critical.

16.9 Removing the reinforcing bracket

16.15 Fitting the sump. Note the new gasket

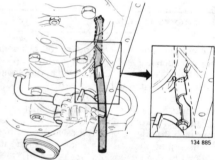

Fig. 1.13 Correct positioning of oil drain tube (Sec 17)

17.2 Removing the oil pump

17.3 Fitting the delivery tube to the pump. New seal (arrowed) is in position in the pump

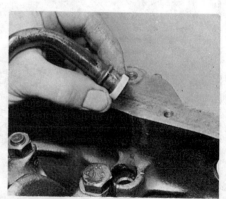

17.4 Guiding the delivery tube into place in the cylinder block

18 Oil pump – overhaul

1 Apart from the strainer assembly, the two versions of oil pump are the same.
2 Pull the delivery pipe from its socket in the pump.
3 On early versions, the strainer assembly has to be removed from the pump to gain access to the bolts securing the two halves of the pump.
4 On both types, remove the bolts and separate the two halves of the pump, being careful not to lose the spring of the relief valve (photos).
5 Remove the spring and plunger (or ball on early versions) from the relief valve assembly.
6 Lift out the pump gears. The drive gear engages with the shaft of the pinion gear, which will have remained in the engine, in mesh with the intermediate shaft (photos).

7 Clean all components, especially the filter screen, in clean petrol, and then dry them using non-fluffy rag, or preferably by blow drying (a hair dryer can be very useful here).
8 Reassemble the gears to the pump housing, and measure the backlash, side clearance and endfloat (photos). Refer to the Specifications for tolerances.
9 Inspect the relief valve ball or plunger for scoring or pitting, and renew as necessary, Similarly, any chipping of gears or excessive wear in the gear teeth will mean renewal. It is probable that only a complete pump is available.
10 Remove the gears from the housing, and coat all components in clean engine oil before reassembly, which is a reversal of dismantling (photo).
11 Refit the assembled pump as described in Section 17.

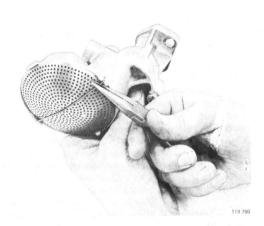

Fig. 1.14 Removing the strainer on an early type pump (Sec 18)

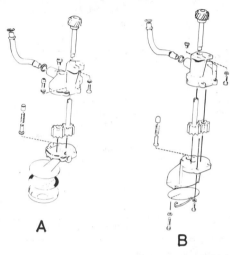

Fig. 1.15 Exploded view of oil pump assembly (Sec 18)

A Later type   B Early type

18.4A Removing the pump securing bolts

18.4B Separating the two halves of the pump

18.6A Remove the idler gear ...

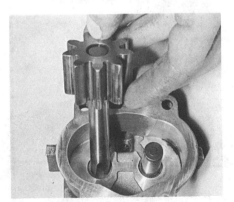

18.6B ... and drivegear

18.8A Measuring side clearance in the gears

18.8B Measuring gear endfloat

18.10 Fitting the relief valve plunger

19.2 Pilot bearing retaining circlip

19.3 Removing the pilot bearing

19 Crankshaft pilot bearing – renewal

Note: *The pilot bearing is only fitted to manual transmission models. Automatic transmission versions use a guide sleeve.*
1   Remove the clutch as described in Chapter 5.
2   Prise out the bearing retaining circlip (photo).
3   Remove the bearing using a slide hammer or similar tool (photo).
4   Fit the new bearing, driving it home as far as it will go using a socket or piece of tubing, which will act upon the bearing outer race and not on the inner race, which would cause damage to the bearing. Secure with a new circlip.
5   Refit the clutch, again as described in Chapter 5.

20 Flywheel/driveplate – removal and refitting

Flywheel (manual transmission)
1   Remove the gearbox (Chapter 6)
2   Remove the clutch (Chapter 5).

3   Make alignment marks across the flywheel and end of the crankshaft, so that it is refitted in the same relative position. Note the location of the dowel pins, if fitted (Fig. 1.16) – these are not found on all models.
4   Prevent the flywheel from turning by jamming the teeth of the ring gear against a screwdriver, and remove the retaining bolts (photo). Do not drop the flywheel – an extra pair of hands at this point would be useful, as the flywheel is quite heavy. Lift the flywheel off the crankshaft.
5   New bolts must be used for reassembly.
6   Refit the flywheel, using the new bolts, and put a dab of thread-locking compound on their threads, and tighten them to the specified torque, preventing the flywheel from turning as before (photos).
7   Refit the clutch and gearbox.

Driveplate (automatic transmission)
8   Remove the transmission and proceed as from paragraph 3 above, ignoring reference to the clutch and dowel pins. Note the two large washers either side of the driveplate (Fig. 1.17).

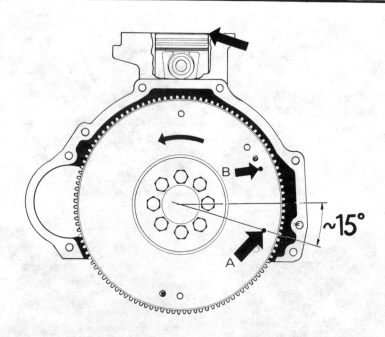

Fig. 1.16 Location of the flywheel in relation to the crankshaft. Do not confuse pin A with pin B (Sec 20)

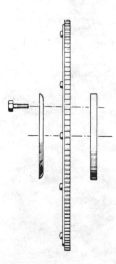

Fig. 1.17 Driveplate and washers on automatic transmission (Sec 20)

20.4 Removing the retaining bolts

20.6A Applying thread-locking fluid

20.6B Preventing the flywheel from turning while the bolts are tightened

21 Flywheel/driveplate – examination and renovation

1   Inspect the flywheel or driveplate for cracks or other damage, paying particular attention to the flywheel in the area where the clutch friction plate contacts it.
2   If the driveplate shows signs of damage or wear, it must be renewed complete.
3   Small cracks or scoring in the flywheel can be removed by having the flywheel re-surfaced by a specialist. Anything more drastic will necessitate renewal.
4   Inspect the flywheel (or driveplate) ring gear, and renew as necessary (see Section 22).
5   Flywheel run-out can be checked during reassembly, when the flywheel is attached to the crankshaft.

22 Flywheel ring gear – renewal

Note: *If the ring gear on the driveplate of automatic transmission models is worn, the complete driveplate must be renewed. The ring gear cannot be renewed separately.*
1   Remove the flywheel as described in Section 2.
2   Drill through the old ring gear at a point between two teeth, being careful not to drill into the flywheel itself.
3   Using a cold chisel at the point of drilling, split the ring gear and lever it off. It is advisable to wear some kind of eye protection during this operation.
4   Clean the seat on the flywheel were the ring gear fits.
5   Heat the new ring gear to 230°C (446°F) in an oven or oil bath, or

using the flame from a welding torch. If using a welding torch, scraps of 40/60 solder placed on the ring gear will indicate when the correct temperature has been reached as the solder will melt at 220 to 230°C (428 to 446°F). Do not overheat the ring, or its temper will be lost.
6   Using tongs, fit the ring gear to the flywheel, inner chamfer toward the flywheel. Tap the gear home with a soft drift, and allow it to cool.
7   Once cool, check the fit of the ring gear on the flywheel, before refitting the assembly as described in Section 20.

23 Crankshaft rear oil seal – renewal

1   Remove the flywheel or driveplate as described in Section 20.
2   Before removing the oil seal, check and note whether the seal is flush with the end of the carrier housing, or recessed into it.
3   Carefully prise out the oil seal using a small screwdriver, being careful not to scratch the surfaces on which the seal bears.
4   Clean the crankshaft and carrier housing, and inspect the crankshaft for wear where the seal bears upon it. There will be a ridge if it is worn (photo).
5   Lubricate the new oil seal, crankshaft and carrier housing seal bearing surfaces with clean engine oil, then fit the new seal, lips facing inwards, and use a piece of tubing of suitable size to tap the seal into the housing. Do not twist the seal, but keep it square on to the crankshaft.
6   If there was any wear evident on the crankshaft, tap the seal in so that it is slightly more recessed than the old seal. The seal may be recessed by up to 0.24 in (6.0 mm) within the carrier, before machining of the crankshaft is necessary.
7   Refit the flywheel or driveplate.

Fig. 1.18 Fitting the flywheel ring gear. Inset shows chamfer (Sec 22)

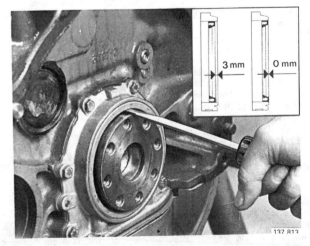
Fig. 1.19 Levering out the oil seal – note insertion depth (Sec 23)

23.4 Wear ridge left by old seal

25.5 Removing a connecting rod bearing cap

24 Oil seals (front) – renewal

1   The front oil seal on the camshaft is dealt with in Section 7 (there is no rear seal on the camshaft).
2   Remove the intermediate shaft sprocket or crankshaft sprocket (Section 40) for access to whichever seal is defective.
3   Prise out the old seal, being careful not to scratch the surfaces on which the seal bears.
4   Clean the areas on the shaft and housings where the seal bears, and inspect them for scoring or wear which could cause premature failure of the new seal.
5   If these faults are evident, then renewal of the shaft in question may be the only solution to the oil leakage. It may be possible to remove light scoring by machining.
6   Lubricate the new seal and the housings in which it fits with clean engine oil, and then fit the seal, lips inwards, tapping it home using a piece of tubing of suitable size.
7   Refit the remaining disturbed components.

25 Pistons and connecting rods – removal and refitting

1   Remove the cylinder head (Section 10), the sump and oil pump (Sections 16 and 17).
2   Feel around the inside top surface of the cylinder bores for a wear ridge which, in some cases, it is recommended be removed with a ridge reamer or scraper, as the ridge can cause damage to the piston rings as they are removed. However, a ridge big enough to cause this amount of damage would almost certainly indicate that new pistons/rings and a cylinder rebore are required anyway.
3   Turn the crankshaft to bring two of the connecting rod bearing caps into a position where the caps can be removed.
4   Check that there are identification marks stamped on the caps and connecting rods. If not, mark then with centre-punch dots so that they can be refitted to their original positions.
5   Remove the cap nuts, and pull off the cap and bearing shell (photo). It may need tapping with a soft-faced mallet to free it. Keep the shell with its cap.
6   Push the connecting rod and piston up and out of the cylinder bore. Recover the remaining bearing shell if it is loose, and refit the cap and shell to its connecting rod.
7   Repeat the operation on the remaining pistons and connecting rods, turning the crankshaft as necessary.
8   Examine the cylinder bores (Section 32) and the pistons and connecting rods (Section 26). Also inspect the crankshaft bearing journals (Section 28). If after examination the cylinder bores or crankshaft need further attention, necessitating removal of the engine, the cylinder head will have to be temporarily refitted in order to remove the engine.

25.13A Using a piston ring compressor

25.13B Slot on piston crown must face forwards when piston is fitted in cylinder

9 All components having been inspected and any rectification work carried out, reassembly can commence.

10 Before the pistons are refitted, the cylinder bores should be honed to remove the shiny glaze formed on them in use. Use coarse emery cloth or a proprietary 'glaze buster' hone. The idea is to achieve a coarse, cross-hatched effect on the cylinder bores, which will help the pistons to bed-in more quickly. Block off the bottom of the bores with rag to prevent filings contaminating the crankshaft, and clean both the bores and crankshaft thoroughly on completion.

11 Smear the pistons and cylinder bores with clean engine oil.

12 Check that the bearing shells are in position in the connecting rod and bearing cap, and that the piston ring gaps are evenly spaced around the piston (they should not all line up).

13 Fit a piston ring compressor to the piston, and then fit the piston and connecting rod assembly into its original bore. The arrow or slot on the piston crown should face forwards (photos).

14 Tap the piston down into the bore with the handle of a hammer, ensuring the compressed piston rings enter the bore without fouling. Do not force them in.

15 Oil the crankpin journals and pull the connecting rod down onto the crankshaft. Fit the connecting rod cap and tighten the nuts to the specified torque (photo).

16 Repeat on the remaining cylinders, turning the crankshaft as necessary.

17 On completion, check that the crankshaft is reasonably free to turn. Some tightness is to be expected, especially if new bearings or pistons/rings have been fitted, but excessive tightness or harshness should be investigated.

18 Refit the cylinder head, oil pump and sump.

26 Pistons and connecting rods – examination and renovation

1 Before dismantling the piston assemblies, check that each piston and connecting rod have identification marks and orientation marks, so that they are reassembled in exactly the same positions.

2 Remove a circlip from the piston and push out the gudgeon pin, which should be a sliding fit in the piston. Remove the piston from the connecting rod (photos).

3 Examine the piston for cracks, scoring and burning. If new standard size pistons are required, note that they come in four grades to match the grading of the cylinders. The grading letter is stamped on the piston crown and on the cylinder block adjacent to each cylinder.

4 Measure the diameter of each piston at 90° to the gudgeon pin, and about 0.28 in (7.0 mm) above the lower edge of the skirt. Subtract this measurement from the bore diameter (see Section 32) to obtain the running clearance. Tolerances are given in the Specifications.

5 If new rings are to be fitted to the existing pistons, remove the old rings by expanding them over the top of the piston. Several old feeler blades, inserted around the ring, will prevent the lower rings dropping into empty grooves. The oil control ring is in three sections.

6 Before fitting new piston rings, their end gaps must be checked by inserting them into the cylinder bore and pushing them down with a piston until they are about 0.6 in (15.0 mm) above the bottom of the bore, and square on to it (photo). Gap sizes are given in the Specifications. If the gap is too small, the ends of the rings can be filed down to size, but this should not normally be necessary.

7 Clean out the piston ring grooves using an old piece of piston ring as a scraper. Be careful not to scratch the soft aluminium surfaces of the grooves, and wear gloves, as the edges of piston rings can be sharp (photo).

8 Check the clearance of the new rings in the grooves. If the clearance is beyond that given in the Specifications, the pistons should be renewed.

9 Check the fit of the gudgeon pin in both the piston and connecting rod. It should be a tight sliding fit. If any perceptible play exists, consult your Volvo dealer.

10 Fit the rings to the pistons, starting with the lower ring, which is the oil control ring. Note the piston ring profiles, and observe the 'TOP' marking on the second compression ring. Unless the top ring is stepped, it can be fitted either way up. (See Section 32, paragraph 5.) The rings are easily broken, so do not expand them too far (photos).

11 Lubricate the gudgeon pin and fit the connecting rod to the piston, ensuring the piston and rod are the right way round (see Fig. 1.22) before inserting the gudgeon pin and securing it with the circlip.

25.15 Tightening the conrod cap bolts to the specified torque

Fig. 1.20 Measuring piston ring clearance in groove using a feeler gauge (Sec 26)

Fig. 1.21 Piston ring profiles (Sec 26)

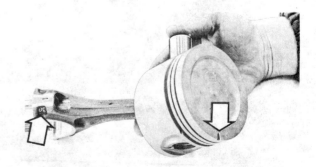

Fig. 1.22 Slot on piston head must point forwards, and numbers on connecting rod must face right-hand side of engine – oil filter side (Sec 26)

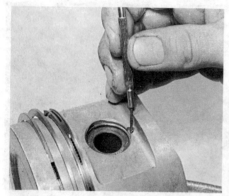

26.2A Removing a piston circlip

26.2B Push or pull out the gudgeon pin

26.6 Measuring piston ring end gap

26.7 Cleaning a piston ring groove

26.10A Fitting the piston rings

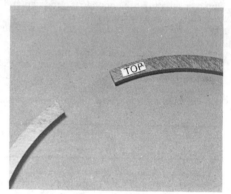

26.10B Take note of the markings on the rings

27 Crankshaft and main bearings – removal

The engine must be removed for this operation.
1   With the pistons and connecting rods removed as described in Section 25, turn the cylinder block upside down.
2   Remove the front and rear oil seal housings if not already done (photo). On early models remove the crankshaft front spacer sleeve, retrieve the Woodruff key and note which way round the sleeve is fitted.
3   If there is a possibility that the existing main bearing shells could be used again, the crankshaft endfloat should be measured to see if it is within limits (see Section 29).

4   Check that there are identification marks on the main bearing caps, and if not make punch marks on them (one to five from the front of the engine).
5   Remove the main bearing cap bolts, lift off the caps (tap them gently with a soft-faced mallet if they are stuck) and keep each bearing shell with its cap.
6   Lift out the crankshaft (photo).
7   On B21/B23 engines, endfloat is taken up by the flanged main bearing shells fitted to No 5 bearing, but on B200/B230 engines, two thrustwashers are inserted on each side of the centre main bearing. Retrieve these two washers.
8   Remove the upper halves of the main bearing shells from their seats in the crankcase. Keep them in order if they are to be re-used (photo).

27.2 Removing the rear oil seal housing

27.6 Lifting out the crankshaft

27.8 Bearing shell upper halves

28 Crankshaft and main bearings – examination and renovation

1   Examine the crankpins and main journal surfaces for signs of wear, scratches or scoring. Using a micrometer, measure the journals in several places to determine any out-of-round or taper. Tolerances are given in the Specifications. If the tolerances are exceeded, the crankshaft should be re-ground and undersize bearing shells fitted, or renewed completely.

2   Inspect the bearing shells for wear, scoring or pitting. There should be no sign of the copper underlay showing through the white metal lining. As refitting used shells is false economy, they should be renewed anyway, having come thus far.

3   On engines with separate thrustwashers, these should be renewed if the crankshaft endfloat was excessive.

4   One accurate method of determining wear in the bearings is by use of Plastigage. The crankshaft should be located in position in the crankcase on its bearings, and a filament of Plastigage placed across the bearing shell in the bearing cap or on the journal itself. The cap is then fitted and tightened to the specified torque. The cap is then removed and the Plastigage filament, which will have been flattened to a width corresponding to the bearing clearance, measured against the scale supplied with the Plastigage kit. This clearance is then compared with the tolerance given in the Specifications, indicating whether or not the wear is excessive (photos).

5   The crankshaft can be roughly tested for cracking by suspending it on a cord and striking it with a metal object, when it should give a clear, bell-like note if it is intact, while if it is cracked the result will be a dull note. Have it professionally tested if suspect.

6   Take the opportunity of renewing the crankshaft pilot bearing while it is accessible – see Section 19.

29 Crankshaft and main bearings – refitting

1   Clean the bearing shell locations in the cylinder block thoroughly using a non-fluffy rag.

2   Fit the bearing shells to their locations, ensuring the locating lugs in the shell fit into the recess in the cylinder block. If the same bearings are being re-used, ensure they are refitted to the same locations.

3   All the bearing shells are the same, except for No 5 which has thrust flanges on the side – B21 and B23 engines only (photo).

4   On B200/B230 engines, smear some grease onto the thrust-washers and fit them to either side of the centre main bearing in the crankcase. The slotted sides face outwards.

5   Squirt oil onto the shells in the crankcase (photo).

6   Clean the crankshaft bearing journals, and then gently lower the crankshaft into position on the bearings in the crankcase, making sure that the shells and thrustwashers are not disturbed.

7   Inject oil into the crankshaft oilways.

8   Fit the bearing shells to the main bearing caps as described for fitting to the cylinder block, then give them a coat of oil.

9   Fit the main bearing caps to their correct position, ensuring they are the right way round and that they fit right down onto the crankshaft and bearings.

10 Fit the bolts to the main bearing caps, tightening them finger-tight.

11 Try turning the crankshaft, which should rotate smoothly, without harshness. Any binding or excessive stiffness should be investigated, the most likely cause being dirt in, or under, the bearing shells.

12 Tighten the main bearing cap bolts to the specified torque, and then repeat the turning test mentioned above. Some stiffness is to be expected in a new assembly (photo).

13 Check the crankshaft endfloat. This is best done using a dial test indicator set up on the end of the crankshaft when it is levered fully one way, and then levered in the opposite direction. On those engines which have integral thrust flange on No 5 bearing, the endfloat can also be measured by inserting feeler blades between the thrust flange and the web.

14 Fit the rear oil seal carrier, using a new gasket, and trim the protruding ends of the gasket level with the crankcase sump mating surface (photos).

15 Fit a new rear oil seal as described in Section 23.

16 On early models, fit the spacer sleeve to the crankshaft (bevelled edge forwards) (photo). Do not forget the Woodruff key.

17 Fit the front oil seal housing (provided the intermediate shaft is

28.4A Plastigage filament placed on a shell

28.4B Measuring the width of the crushed filament

29.3 Rear main bearing shell has thrust flanges

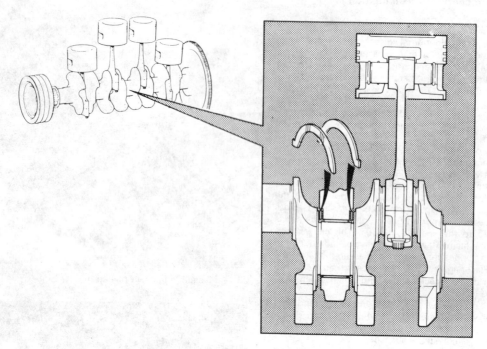

Fig. 1.23 Thrustwashers which control endfloat (B200/B230) (Sec 29)

installed), and trim off the gasket ends using a sharp blade. The camshaft drivebelt backplate can also be fitted at this stage, but if not, leave out the bolts from the oil seal housing which also secure the cover (photos).

18 Fit the front oil seals (Section 24).
19 Fit the crankshaft and intermediate shaft sprockets and associated components.

29.5 Oiling a main bearing shell

29.12 Tightening the main bearing cap bolts

29.14A Fitting the rear oil seal housing ...

29.14B ... and trimming the gasket

29.16 Fitting the crankshaft spacer sleeve. Woodruff key is already in position

29.17A Fitting the front oil seal housing ...

29.17B ... and drivebelt backplate

30.5A Removing the oil pump pinion cover on early 'A' engine

30.5B Removing the oil trap on later models

30.5C Pinion cover on early fuel injection model

30.6 Removing the intermediate shaft

30 Intermediate shaft – removal and refitting

1   If the engine has not been stripped for overhaul, carry out the following operations.
2   Remove the front oil seal housing (Section 40).
3   Remove the distributor (Chapter 4).
4   Remove the fuel pump (Chapter 3) – not fuel injection models.
5   Remove the oil pump pinion gear. This is accessible after removing the cover on the side of the cylinder block on early models. On 1981-on models, remove the oil trap of the crankcase ventilation system, and on fuel injection models, the cover incorporates a bracket for the fuel/air control unit (photos).
6   Withdraw the shaft from the cylinder block, being careful not to damage the bearings (photo).
7   Give the shaft a coat of clean engine oil before refitting, which is a reversal of removal.

31 Intermediate shaft – examination and renovation

1   Inspect the bearing journals on the shaft for wear. Measure the journals and compare the results with the tolerances given in the Specifications. Check the gear teeth for cracks and chipping. Renew the shaft if it is worn or damaged.
2   If the intermediate shaft bearings in the cylinder block are worn or damaged, then they will have to be renewed by your Volvo dealer or specialist.

32 Cylinder block and bores – examination and renovation

1   The cylinder bores should be examined for taper, ovality and deep scoring. Feel the top of the bores for a ridge where the piston rings end

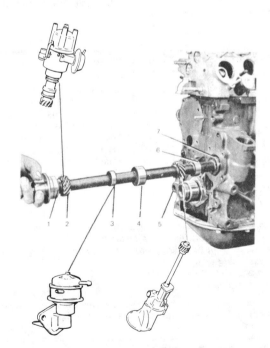

Fig. 1.24 Removing the intermediate shaft (Sec 30)

1   Front bearing
2   Distributor gear
3   Fuel pump cam
4   Centre bearing
5   Oil pump drivegear
6   Manufacturing support
7   Rear bearing

their travel. If this ridge is excessive, indicating wear, the engine will probably have been suffering from excessive oil consumption accompanied by blue smoke from the exhaust.

2   To determine cylinder wear, measure the bore diameter in several positions around the circumference using a dial gauge placed just below the wear ridge, and again at the bottom of the bore, which is not subject to wear. If the difference is more than 0.004 in (0.1 mm), then the cylinders should be rebored and oversize pistons fitted.

3   Oil control rings can be obtained and fitted to the existing pistons to overcome slight wear in the cylinders, but their benefit is short-lived.

4   If new pistons and/or rings are to be fitted to old bores, de-glaze the cylinders as described in Section 25.

5   If there is a wear ridge at the top of the cylinders and new piston rings are being fitted, then either the top piston ring must be stepped so that it will not strike the ridge, ('ridge dodger' pattern), or the ridge must be removed using a ridge reamer.

6   Thoroughly inspect the crankcase for cracks and damage. Make sure all oilways and passages are unblocked, even if the block has been sent to a specialist for rebore (perhaps even more so in this case). Also clean out all water ways, removing corrosion and other deposits.

Fig. 1.25 Engine mounting bolts on front axle – arrowed (Sec 33)

33 Engine mountings – removing and refitting

1   The procedure given here is for removal of the mountings with the engine *in situ*. When removing the engine, it is only necessary to remove the bolts securing the mountings to the front axle crossmember to release them.

2   There are two front mountings, bolted to the front axle crossmember. The rear of the engine is supported through the transmission unit by the transmission support mounting.

3   Attach lifting gear to the engine, and take the weight off the mounting to be removed. Do not be tempted to jack the engine from under the oil sump.

4   Remove the bolts securing the mounting to the axle crossmember.

5   Remove the nut securing the mounting to the engine bracket and lift out the mounting. Alternatively, the engine-to-mounting bolts could be removed (photo).

6   For greater ease of access, the power steering pump hoses can be moved aside, and the oil filter (right-hand side) and inlet manifold support tube (left-hand side) removed.

7   Refitting is a reversal of removal.

33.5 Removing the front engine-to-mounting bolts

34 Major operations possible with the engine *in situ*

1   The components listed below may be removed and refitted with the engine *in situ*, although this may not necessarily be the best course of action. For instance, if the connecting rod bearings or piston rings need attention, it is likely that there are other areas which also need attention, and as the sump and cylinder head would have to be removed, which is a lot of work, consideration should be given to removing the engine for complete overhaul.

Camshaft drivebelt
Camshaft
Cylinder head and valve gear
Crankshaft and intermediate shaft front oil seals
Crankshaft rear oil seal (gearbox, clutch and flywheel removed)
Flywheel (gearbox and clutch removed)
Crankshaft pilot bearing (gearbox and clutch removed)
Oil sump and oil pump
Pistons and connecting rods
Engine mountings

2   The engine must be removed for removal/overhaul of the crankshaft and main bearings, and intermediate shaft.

35 Engine removal – general

1   The engine can be removed and refitted with the transmission unit attached, although with the weight involved, it is better to remove the engine on its own, especially where automatic transmission is fitted. The weight of the engine alone is approximately 350 lb (159 kg).

2   Although not strictly necessary, we removed the front grille, cover

35.2A Cover plate ...

35.2B ... and stay

35.3 Front axle crossmember retaining bolts

36.29 Lifting out the engine

plate and support stay to give better access (photos).

3 It is also better to remove the bolts from the front axle crossmember and lower it after the weight of the engine has been taken on the sling and the engine mountings removed. This gives a lot more room to manoeuvre the engine, especially if it is being removed with the transmission unit attached (photo).

4 Make sure the lifting gear is suitable for the task, and securely attached to the engine lifting eyes on the cylinder head.

5 At least two people will be required to lift the engine out, and three would be a definite advantage.

36 Engine – removal (without transmission)

1 Disconnect the battery and remove it from the vehicle (Chapter 12). Also remove the bonnet (Chapter 11).

2 Drain the cooling system and remove the radiator (Chapter 2).

3 Disconnect the air inlet trunking to the carburettor/air flow control unit and remove the air filter and housing (Chapter 3).

4 Remove the coil-to-distributor HT lead (Chapter 4).

5 Disconnect the accelerator cable and choke cable, and kickdown cable where fitted (Chapters 3 and 6).

6 Disconnect the brake servo vacuum hose (Chapter 9).

7 Disconnect the fuel supply line, and where fitted the return line (Chapter 3).

8 Disconnect the various crankcase ventilation hoses, and where fitted the Pulsair system hoses (Chapter 3). Mark them for refitting to avoid confusion.

9 Disconnect the ignition system electrical connections from around the engine.

10 Disconnect the starter motor (Chapter 12).

11 Disconnect the engine earth strap, between the valve cover and engine bulkhead.

12 Where fitted, disconnect the air conditioner clutch electrical lead.

13 Remove the power steering pump without disconnecting the hoses, and tie it to one side out of the way.

14 Disconnect the heater hoses at the rear of the engine where they pass through the engine bulkhead.

15 Remove the starter motor (Chapter 12).

16 Disconnect the exhaust downpipe at the exhaust manifold flange. Also release the bracket on the clutch bellhousing (Chapter 3).

17 Raise and support the vehicle on secure axle stands. Remove the engine splash guard (Chapter 11).

18 Drain the engine oil (Section 3).

19 Remove the lower engine-to-transmission bolts accessible from below. Also remove the flywheel/driveplate lower cover.

20 On automatic transmission models, unbolt the torque converter from the driveplate. Turn the crankshaft as necessary to gain access to the bolts through the starter motor hole, or from underneath the engine.

21 When applicable remove the air conditioning compressor drivebelt, then remove the bolts from the compressor securing bracket, and lift the pump to one side. **Do not** disconnect the hoses (see Chapter 10, Section 50).

22 Support the transmission unit on a jack.

23 Attach lifting gear to the engine, using the lifting eyes on the cylinder head, and just take the weight of the engine.

24 Remove the remaining engine-to-transmission bolts from the top of the engine.

25 Remove the bolts from the engine mountings on the front axle crossmember.

26 When lifting the engine, it will be easier if the axle crossmember bolts are removed and the crossmember lowered out of the way (this is especially so when removing the engine with the gearbox attached, see Section 35).

27 Have a final check round the engine bay and ensure that nothing has been missed and left connected.

28 Raise the engine slightly and draw it forwards, pulling it clear of the input shaft of the transmission unit. Do not allow the weight of the engine to be taken by the input shaft.

29 Continue lifting the engine, keeping it clear of all obstructions, and tilted down towards the rear (photo). Have an assistant watch to see that nothing is fouled or trapped.

30 Once clear of the engine bay, swing the engine out and set it down on the bench or blocks of wood on the floor, preventing it from toppling over, and remove the lifting gear.

37 Engine – removal (with transmission)

1 Proceed as in Section 36, paragraphs 1 to 18, but as there is no need to remove the starter motor, instead just disconnect the leads to it.

Manual transmission models

2 Disconnect the clutch cable at the operating fork (cable-operated clutch) or on hydraulic clutches, remove the circlip or bolts securing the slave cylinder to the bellhousing and move the cylinder to one side without disconnecting the hose.

3 Remove the gear lever (Chapter 6).

Automatic transmission models

Note: *Because of the weight involved, it is not recommended that the engine and automatic transmission unit be removed together. However, if suitable lifting gear is available, proceed as follows.*

4 Disconnect the selector linkage.

Manual and automatic transmission models

5 Disconnect the reversing light switch, and where fitted the overdrive connections, and ignition timing sender (photo).

6 Unbolt the propeller shaft from the gearbox/transmission unit (Chapter 7). Also disconnect the speedometer cable, when applicable.

7 Support the transmission unit on a jack, and remove the bolt from the transmission support bearing.

8 Remove the transmission support crossmember (Chapter 6).

9 Attach lifting gear to the engine using the lifting eyes on the cylinder head.

10 Remove the bolts securing the engine mountings to the front axle crossmember.

11 Take the weight of the engine on the lifting gear. Check that no connections have been overlooked.

12 Remove the engine mountings, then if wished remove the bolts securing the front axle crossmember to the chassis and lower the crossmember (see Section 35).

13 Carefully lower the jack from under the transmission unit, at the same time starting to lift the engine out. Have an assistant watch to see that nothing is fouled or trapped.
14 Keep the engine tilted towards the rear, and guide it up and out of the engine bay.
15 Set the engine down on supporting blocks, preventing it from toppling.

38 Engine – separation from transmission

1   Remove the starter motor.
2   Remove the bellhousing-to-engine nuts and bolts. Also remove the flywheel/driveplate bottom cover plate.
3   On manual transmission models, with the aid of an assistant, withdraw the gearbox and bellhousing assembly from the engine (photo). Do not allow the weight of the unit to fall on the input shaft once it is clear of the locating dowels.
4   On automatic transmission models, remove the bolts securing the torque converter to the driveplate, turning the engine to gain access to the bolt heads either through the starter motor hole or from underneath. Make an alignment mark across the torque converter and driveplate for reassembly.
5   With the aid of an assistant, withdraw the transmission unit from the engine. Make sure that the torque converter stays in the bellhousing.

39 Engine – dismantling (general)

1   The essential preliminary to dismantling an engine is cleaning. The ideal way to do this is to brush the engine all over with paraffin or a similar commercial solvent. Allow it to stand for a while and then hose it down. Where the dirt is thick and deeply embedded, work the solvent into it with a wire brush. If the engine is very dirty, a second application may be necessary here and there. Finally, wipe down the outside of the engine with a rag. If it is not possible to use a pressure hose to remove the dirt and solvent, cleaning will be much more laborious, but however laborious it is, it will pay in the long run. After all, the engine has got to be cleaned at the end of the dismantling process, so it might just as well be as clean as possible at the start.
2   Clean each part as the engine is stripped. Try to ensure that everything taken off – down to the smallest washer – goes back exactly where it came from and exactly the same way round. This means laying the various bits and pieces out in a tidy manner. Nuts, bolts and washers may often be replaced finger tight from where they were removed.
3   Most parts can easily be cleaned by washing them in paraffin and wiping down with a cloth, but do not immerse parts with oilways in paraffin. They are best wiped down with a petrol or paraffin dampened cloth, and the oilways cleaned out with nylon pipe cleaners.
4   Re-use of old gaskets is false economy. Oil and water leaks will always result even if nothing worse. Always use genuine Volvo gaskets obtainable from Volvo garages.
5   Do not throw the old gaskets away as the engine is stripped down. These may be used for checking the pattern of new ones, or as templates for making gaskets for which replacements are difficult to obtain. Hang up the old gaskets as they are removed.
6   Generally speaking, when stripping an engine it is best to work from the top down, at least once you have removed the gearbox. Support it with wood blocks so that it stands firmly on its sump or the base of the crankcase to start with. When the stage of removing the crankshaft and connecting rods is reached, turn it on its side or upside down, and carry out all subsequent work with it in this position.

40 Engine – dismantling for overhaul

1   With the engine removed, remove the ancillary components as follows, with reference to the relevant Sections or Chapters as necessary:

   (a) Alternator and mounting brackets (Chapter 12)
   (b) Exhaust manifold and Pulsair pipework where fitted (Chapter 3)

37.5 Disconnect the ignition setting sender

38.3 Separating the transmission from the engine – support the transmission as it is withdrawn

   (c) Cooling fan and water pump (Chapter 2)
   (d) Distributor (Chapter 4)
   (e) Inlet manifold with carburettor or injection components (Chapter 3)
   (f) Spark plugs (Chapter 4)
   (g) Clutch pressure and driven plates (Chapter 5)
   (h) Ignition sensor(s) (mainly Bendix Rex system) (Chapter 4)
   (i) Auxiliary air valve, fuel injection (Chapter 3)
   (j) Crankshaft pulley (see Section 6)

2   Remove the coolant transfer pipe (photo).
3   Remove the fuel pump (photo) or the fuel injection components from the side of the engine (Chapter 3).
4   Remove the bolt from the dipstick tube bracket and remove the tube and bracket (photo).
5   Remove the oil pump drive pinion (Section 30, paragraph 5).
6   Remove the cylinder head (Section 10).
7   Jam the starter ring gear and remove the crankshaft sprocket centre bolt. This bolt is very tight. Also remove the intermediate shaft sprocket bolt, restraining the sprocket with a strap wrench or with a bar through one of the holes.
8   Remove the sprockets. On early models, also remove the spacer from the crankshaft (photos). Remove the intermediate shaft (Section 30).

40.2 Disconnecting the coolant transfer pipe

40.3 Removing the fuel pump

40.4 Removing the oil dipstick tube

40.8A Removing the crankshaft sprocket and guide plate

40.8B Removing the intermediate shaft sprocket

40.9 Remove the bolts from the rear cover

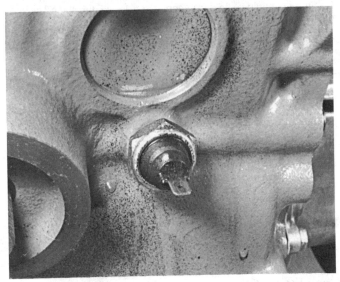

40.13 Oil pressure switch

9   Remove the camshaft drivebelt rear cover, and the front oil seal housing (photo).
10   Remove the flywheel or driveplate (Section 26).
11   Remove the oil sump, oil pump, and oil filter (Sections 16, 17 and 4).
12   Remove the pistons and connecting rods (Section 25). Also remove the crankshaft (Section 27).
13   Work around the engine and remove the engine mounting brackets, and any pressure/temperature transmitters if they are still in place (photo).

41 Engine – reassembly after overhaul

Note: *The reassembly procedure is basically a reversal of dismantling, and the order in which it is undertaken largely a matter of choice. The following sequence is intended as a guide only.*
1   Refit the oil pressure switch to the cylinder block.
2   Refit the crankshaft, pistons and connecting rods (Sections 29 and 25). Also refit the intermediate shaft.
3   Refit the oil pump and oil sump (Sections 16 and 17).
4   Refit the flywheel or driveplate (Section 20).
5   If not already done, fit the crankshaft and intermediate shaft sprockets and associated components.
6   Fit the crankshaft pulley (Section 6).
7   Refit the water pump (Chapter 2).
8   Refit the cylinder head (Section 10).
9   Refit the oil pump drive pinion, making sure it engages with the intermediate shaft splines and the teeth on the oil pump driveshaft.
10   Fit the cover or the crankcase ventilation oil trap, using a new O-ring seal.
11   Refit the oil dipstick tube and insert the dipstick.
12   Refit the coolant transfer pipe to the side of the cylinder block.
13   Refit the remaining components listed in Section 40, paragraph 1. If preferred, leave delicate items such as the alternator and fit once the engine is installed.

42 Engines – reconnection to transmission

Manual transmission models
1   Make sure the clutch is correctly centred, and that the release components are fitted to the bellhousing.
2   Put a smear of molybdenum grease on the input shaft splines and the release arm pivot point, and where the arm contacts the release bearing.

3   Offer the transmission to the engine, making sure the input shaft enters the clutch components and engages with the pilot bearing in the crankshaft. At no stage allow the weight of the gearbox to hang on the input shaft. Turn the crankshaft or input shaft as necessary to allow the splines to line up.
4   Make sure the locating dowels on the engine enter the bellhousing, then fit and tighten the bellhousing-to-engine retaining bolts.

Automatic transmission models
5   Ensure the torque converter is fully engaged with the transmission unit. Put a smear of molybdenum grease on the converter locating spigot.
6   Offer the transmission unit to the engine, engaging the locating dowels, then fit and tighten the retaining bolts.
7   Fit the torque converter-to-driveplate bolts, observing the alignment marks made previously, and tighten them in criss-cross fashion to the specified torque (Chapter 6).

All models
8   Refit the starter motor, and where applicable, the flywheel/driveplate bottom cover.

43 Engine – refitting

1   Refitting the engine is basically a reversal of the removal procedure given in Sections 36 and 37, with the following additional points.

Without transmission
2   Ensure that the clutch is correctly centered, or the torque converter is fully engaged on the transmission. Carry out the greasing operation given in Section 42.
3   Lower the engine into the engine bay, ensuring that it does not foul any components or pipework.
4   On manual transmission models, guide the input shaft into the clutch, turning the crankshaft or rocking the engine to line up the splines. Do not allow the engine to drop too low and put pressure on the input shaft. The engine and transmission must be at the same angle for the shaft to enter.
5   Once the bellhousing is fully engaged on the locating dowels, fit and tighten the bellhousing-to-engine bolts, and on automatic transmission models, fit and tighten the converter-to-driveplate bolts.
6   Fit the starter motor and bottom cover.

With transmission
7   After fitting the engine/transmission unit, on manual models, fit the gear lever and if necessary adjust the reverse select detent (see Chapter 6). Connect up the reversing light switch, and where fitted the overdrive solenoid.
8   On automatic models, reconnect the selector lever linkage, and adjust it as described in Chapter 6. Also reconnect and adjust the kickdown cable.

With or without transmission
9   Refill the engine with the specified engine oil (Section 3).
10 Refill the cooling system (Chapter 2).
11 Refer to Section 44 before starting the engine.

44 Initial start-up after overhaul

1   Have a final check round the engine and transmission unit to ensure that all connections have been made, no bolts are left undone, and that all tools and rags etc have been removed.
2   Check that the alternator (and where fitted the power steering and air conditioning pump) drivebelts are tensioned correctly.
3   Check that the engine oil and coolant levels are correct, and that there is fuel in the tank.
4   Check that the battery electrolyte level is topped up, and that the battery is fully charged.
5   Start the engine. It may take several turns of the engine on the starter motor to get fuel pumped through the empty system.
6   Keep a close eye on the engine oil pressure warning light, checking that it goes out when the engine starts. (There may be a delay of a few seconds while the new oil filter fills with oil.)
7   Keep the engine running at fast idle speed, and check all round the engine and transmission unit for signs of leakage. As the engine becomes hot, there will be smells or burning, and smoke may come from exhaust components, but do not worry unless this should become excessive, in which case stop the engine and investigate.
8   Check the ignition timing (Chapter 4). Check the idle and CO content adjustment, and the adjustment of the accelerator, choke and kickdown cables as necessary (Chapter 3).
9   Stop the engine, allow it to cool and re-check the engine oil and coolant levels, restoring them as required.
10 Where applicable, check-tighten the cylinder head bolts (Section 9).

45 Fault diagnosis – engine

Symptom	Reason(s)
Engine fails to start	Discharged battery
	Loose battery connection
	Loose or broken ignition leads
	Moisture on spark plugs, distributor cap, or HT leads
	Incorrect spark plug gaps
	Cracked distributor cap or rotor
	Other ignition system fault
	Dirt or water in fuel
	Empty fuel tank
	Faulty fuel pump
	Other fuel system fault
	Faulty starter motor
	Low cylinder compressions
Engine idles erratically	Intake manifold air leak
	Leaking head gasket
	Incorrect valve clearances
	Worn camshaft lobes
	Faulty fuel pump
	Loose crankcase ventilation hoses
	Idle adjustment incorrect
	Uneven cylinder compression

45 Fault diagnosis – engine

Symptom	Reason(s)
Engine misfires	Spark plugs worn or incorrectly gapped Dirt or water in fuel Idle adjustment incorrect Burnt out valve Leaking cylinder head gasket Distributor cap cracked Incorrect valve clearances Uneven cylinder compressions Worn carburettor Other fuel or ignition system fault
Engine stalls	Idle adjustment incorrect Intake manifold air leak Ignition timing incorrect
Excessive oil consumption	Worn pistons, cylinder bores or piston rings Valve guides and valve stem seals worn Oil leaks
Engine backfires	Idle adjustment incorrect Ignition timing incorrect Incorrect valve clearances Intake manifold air leak Sticking valve
Engine noises	See *Fault diagnosis* at beginning of Manual

Chapter 2 Cooling system

Contents

Specifications

General (all engines)

System type .... Water-based coolant, pump-assisted circulation, pressurised and thermostatically controlled.

Coolant .... Water and ethylene glycol based antifreeze – Volvo type A up to 1981, type C 1981 on (Duckhams Universal Antifreeze and Summer Coolant)

Capacity:
  Manual transmission .... 16.7 pints (9.5 litres) approx
  Automatic transmission .... 16.4 pints (9.3 litres) approx
Expansion tank relief valve:
  Opens at .... 9.4 to 12.3 lbf/in² (65 to 85 kPa)
  Vents inward at .... 1 lbf/in² (7 kPa)
Thermostat:

	T1	T2	T3
Identity mark	82	87	92
Starts to open at	82°C (180°F)	87°C (189°F)	92°C (198°F)

Drivebelt deflection .... 0.20 to 0.40 in (5.0 to 10.0 mm)

Torque wrench setting

	lbf ft	Nm
Fixed fan retaining bolts	6.6	9

1 General description

The cooling system is of the sealed type, with closed radiator and an expansion tank. There is no radiator filler cap, the cap in the expansion tank being used for this purpose. The heating system is fed by pipe from the cylinder block, the return being connected to the pump inlet.

During operation, with the coolant below the operating temperature of the thermostat, the radiator and expansion tank remain closed from the cylinder block and heater, coolant only circulating through these components. As the coolant temperature reaches the operating temperature of the thermostat, the thermostat will begin to open and allow coolant to flow through the radiator, thus being cooled in the process before being returned to the cylinder block.

As the coolant temperature rises, the coolant will expand, this excess of volume being 'taken up' by the expansion tank. Conversely, on cooling, the expansion tank provides a reservoir of coolant which will automatically be drawn back into the radiator. Provided that the specified level of coolant is kept in the expansion tank, no air can enter the system, and frequent topping-up of the system is eliminated.

Circulation of the coolant is by centrifugal pump, which is mounted on the front face of the cylinder block, and driven by belt from the crankshaft pulley.

Three types of cooling fan for forced cooling of the coolant are fitted, according to model and year of manufacture, these being a fixed fan, fan with viscous coupling or a thermally-controlled fan with viscous coupling.

The cooling system is pressurized to increase the boiling point of the coolant. The expansion tank cap incorporates a pressure relief valve which allows steam to vent should the maximum pressure be exceeded. Another valve in the cap allows air back in as the system cools, so preventing the formation of vacuum.

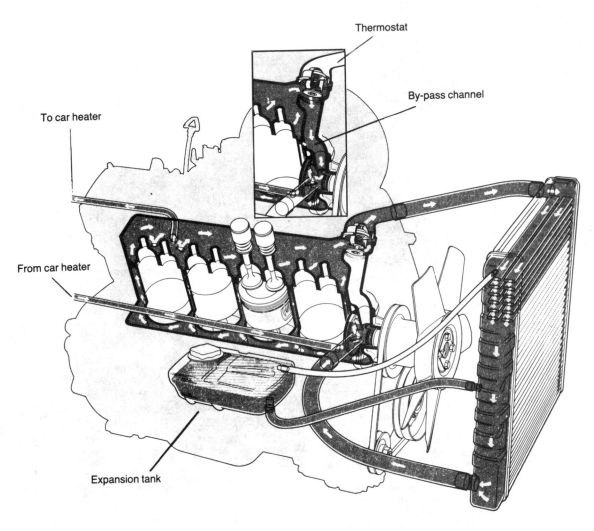

Fig. 2.1 General view of the cooling system (Sec 1)

2 Routine maintenance

1   Weekly, or before a long journey, check the level of coolant in the expansion tank, when the engine is cold.

2   The level should be maintained between the MIN and MAX marks on the side of the tank (photo).

3   If topping-up is necessary, wait for the system to cool down if it is hot. **There is a risk of scalding if the cap is removed whilst the system is hot.** Place a thick rag over the expansion tank cap and slacken it to release any pressure. When pressure has been released, carry on unscrewing the cap and remove it.

4   Top up to the 'MAX' mark with the specified coolant – see Section 3 (photo). In an emergency plain water is better than nothing, but remember that it is diluting the proper coolant. Do not add cold water to an overheated engine whilst it is still hot.

5   Refit the expansion tank cap securely when the level is correct. Check for leaks if there is a frequent need for topping-up – losses from this type of system are normally minimal.

6   Every 6000 miles or six months, check the antifreeze concentration using a proprietary tester of the hydrometer or floating ball type.

7   Every 12 000 miles or 12 months, inspect the condition of the alternator/water pump, power steering, and if fitted the air conditioning pump, drivebelts for signs of cracking or fraying, and for correct tension. Renew or adjust as described in Section 14.

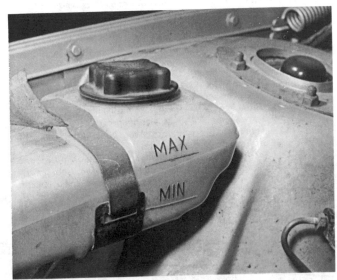

2.2 Expansion tank 'MAX' and 'MIN' marks

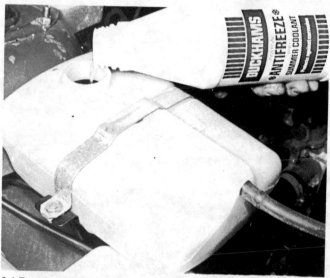

2.4 Topping-up the cooling system through the expansion tank

Fig. 2.2 Cooling system drain points and expansion tank cap – arrowed (Sec 4)

3 Antifreeze mixture

1   It is essential that an antifreeze mixture is maintained in the cooling system all year round as protection not only against frost in winter, but also for anti-corrosion purposes the year through.
2   The mixture should be made up of 50% clean water and 50% antifreeze.
3   Two types of antifreeze have been used by Volvo and are: type A (red), used on pre-1981 models, and type C (blue), used on post-1981 models.
4   When dealing with a system which has previously been filled with type A antifreeze, use type A for topping-up. Alternatively, up to 25% (ie approximately 4 pints/2.3 litres) of type C mixture may be used. If a greater made-up volume than this is required, or doubt exists as to the percentages, the system should be drained and filled with the type C antifreeze. The same applies to the use of non-Volvo antifreeze (eg Duckhams Universal Antifreeze and Summer Coolant).
5   The 50-50 ratio of water to antifreeze will give adequate protection against freezing for normal winter conditions in the UK.

4 Cooling system – draining

Note: *The system is best drained when the coolant is warm but not hot, after a recent run, but care should be taken when removing the expansion tank cap, as the sudden drop in pressure can cause the coolant to boil violently. Cover the cap with a cloth when removing.*
1   Turn the heater control to the maximum heat position.
2   Disconnect the battery negative lead.
3   Remove the cap from the expansion tank. **Caution:** *Danger of scalding if the coolant is hot.*
4   If available, push a piece of tubing on to the drain cock on the right-hand side of the engine block to prevent spillage, open the drain cock and catch the coolant in a suitable container.
5   Similarly, disconnect the radiator lower hose and drain the remaining coolant from the system (photo).
Note: *If the coolant is not due for change (see Section on routine maintenance), and is in good clean condition, it may be used again.*
6   On completion, close the drain cock, remove the tubing if used, and re-connect the lower radiator hose.
7   Dispose of the old coolant safely if it is not to be re-used. It is poisonous.

5 Cooling system – flushing

1   If coolant renewal has been neglected or the percentage of antifreeze allowed to become diluted, rust, scale and sediment may

4.5 Lower radiator hose (arrowed)

begin to block the coolant passageways.
2   To restore cooling efficiency, the system should be flushed as follows.
3   Drain the system as described in Section 4.
4   Remove the thermostat as described in Section 9, then temporarily refit the thermostat housing cover.
5   Disconnect the radiator lower hose at the radiator end, and insert a garden hose into the end of the radiator hose, jamming it in place with some rag.
Note: *Before continuing, allow the engine to become quite cool. The introduction of cold water into a hot engine can cause cracking of the block or head.*
6   Turn on the garden hose and flush through the system until fresh clean water flows from the radiator bottom outlet.
7   If contamination is particularly bad, reverse flush using the same procedure, but through the top hose. After reverse-flushing, carry out a normal flush before continuing. If the water still does not run clear, the radiator may be flushed with a good proprietary cleaning agent, such as Holts Radflush or Holts Speedflush.
8   Refit the thermostat using a new seal, and re-connect the radiator hoses, not forgetting to close the cylinder block drain cock.
9   Refill the system as described in Section 6.
Note: *Proprietary flushing compounds are available, but should only be used in extreme cases, following the manufacturer's instructions closely.*

6 Cooling system – filling

1   Before refilling the cooling system, check that all hoses are in good condition and their securing clips tight.
2   Check that the cylinder block drain cock is closed.
3   To guard against corrosion and the effects of cold weather in winter, always fill the system with a water/antifreeze mixture. Never use only water, even in summer.
4   Set the heater control to the maximum heat position.
5   Remove the expansion tank cap, and slowly fill the system with the coolant mixture, to the 'MAX' level marked on the side of the expansion tank.
6   Refit the expansion tank cap, run the engine till it reaches normal operating temperature, and check all components and hose connections for leakage.
7   Allow the engine to cool, and re-check the level of coolant in the expansion tank, topping-up as necessary.
Note: *The system is self-bleeding, and no special bleeding procedure is required.*

7 Fan shroud – removal and refitting

1   Remove the two screws from the top edge of the shroud (photo).
2   Lift the shroud to disengage the locating lug at the bottom edge.
3   The shroud can be manoeuvred rearwards for access to the radiator, or up and out of the engine compartment, as required.
4   Refit in the reverse order.

8 Radiator – removal and refitting

1   Disconnect the battery, then drain the cooling system as described in Section 4.
2   Remove the fan shroud as described in Section 7.

3   Disconnect the top and bottom radiator hose, and the hose(s) to the expansion tank (photos).
4   On vehicles with automatic transmission, disconnect the oil cooler pipelines and blank off the pipe ends. Be careful to keep dirt out.
5   Remove the two retaining brackets at the top of the radiator (photos).
6   Lift out the radiator, being careful not to bump it against the fan or adjacent bodywork (photo).
7   Inspect the radiator for signs of leakage, which will show as stained or corroded areas. Brush away any debris.
8   If the radiator is suspected of leaking, a garage or radiator specialist will pressure-test it and advise on repairs, but it would probably be better to renew it. In an emergency minor leaks from the radiator may be cured by using a radiator sealant such as Holts Radweld, with the radiator and associated plumbing *in situ*.
9   Flushing the radiator can be more thoroughly carried out with it removed from the vehicle, as can cleaning of the matrix.
10 Refitting is a reversal of removal, but ensure that the radiator fits into the lower locating pads (photo), and is flush with the front panel. The gap between the front panel and the radiator can be sealed, if desired, using plastic foam strip available from your Volvo dealer. This will give a more positive flow of air through the radiator.

9 Thermostat – removal, testing and refitting

1   Disconnect the battery and drain sufficient coolant to bring the level below the thermostat housing.
2   Disconnect the radiator top hose at the thermostat housing end (photo).
3   Remove the two nuts from the thermostat housing and remove the top cover, noting the lifting bracket.
4   Lift out the thermostat.
5   Clean both mating surfaces of the housing and cover thoroughly.
6   The thermostat can be tested by immersing it in a pan of cool water and bringing it to the boil, when it should open within 2 minutes, and close upon removal from the water and cooling. Precise opening

7.1 Fan shroud retaining screw (arrowed)

8.3A Disconnect the top radiator hose ...

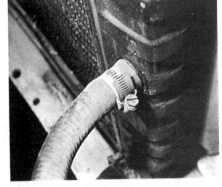
8.3B ... and the upper ...

8.3C ... and lower expansion tank hoses

8.5A Radiator retaining bracket ...

8.5B ... being removed

8.6 Lifting out the radiator

8.10 Radiator lower locating pad.

9.2 Thermostat housing hose clip (arrowed)

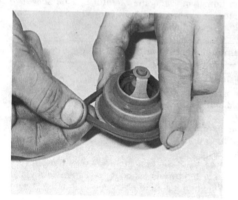

9.9A Fitting a new seal to the thermostat

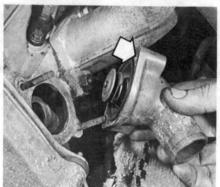

9.9B Refitting the thermostat housing. Note the new seal (arrowed)

10.7 Lower radiator hose clip (A) and heater return pipe securing bolt (B)

temperatures are given in the Specifications.

7   If the thermostat is to be renewed, ensure the new one is of the correct temperature range for your vehicle (see Specifications).

8   It is not recommended that the vehicle be run for long periods without the thermostat fitted.

9   Refitting is a reversal of removal, but use a new seal around the thermostat (photos).

10 The thermostat is installed with the spring towards the engine.

10 Water pump – removal and refitting

Note: *Defective water pumps are indicated by water/steam leaks from the shaft seal and noisy or rough operation, accompanied by excessive play in the shaft (checked with the drivebelt tension released). No repairs are possible to the pump, and an exchange unit should be fitted.*

1   Disconnect the battery.

2   Drain the cooling system as described in Section 4.

3   Remove the fan shroud.

4   Remove the alternator/power steering/air conditioning drivebelts as applicable, with reference to Section 14.

5   Refer to Section 13 and remove the cooling fan.

6   Refer to Chapter 1 and remove the timing belt cover.

7   Disconnect the radiator lower hose from the pump (photo).

8   Remove the bolt securing the heater return pipe first, then remove the remaining bolts and nuts and lift off the water pump.

Note: *On vehicles equipped with the Pulsair system the bolt securing the return pipe from the heater can be difficult to remove. Undo the nut at the rear of the bolt, then loosen the remaining pump securing bolts, move the pump out slightly and the bolt may then be removed. On both types, the hexagonal headed bolts should be replaced with an Allen type bolt, to aid future removal.*

9   Clean the mating surfaces of the pump and cylinder block.

10 Refitting is a reverse of removal, but use a new gasket between the

pump and cylinder block, and fit new seals to the pump-to-cylinder head outlet and the heater return pipe (photos).

11 Fit the retaining bolts finger-tight, then lever the pump upwards, maintaining this upward pressure while the bolts are finally tightened (photo). This is to get a good seal on the pump-to-cylinder head connection.

12 Refit the other disturbed components, then refill the cooling system (Section 6). Run the engine and check for leaks.

11 Temperature gauge sender – removal and refitting

1   The temperature gauge sender is situated on the left-hand side of the cylinder head just under the inlet manifold (photo).

2   To remove the sender, disconnect the battery and drain the coolant to below the level of the sender.

3   Disconnect the electrical lead, then unscrew the sender from the head.

4   Refit in the reverse order, using a new sealing washer if applicable and applying a little sealant to the threads of the sender.

12 Cooling fan – general description

1   Three types of cooling fan may be fitted according to model year and engine type. They are:

(a) Fixed fan
(b) Viscous coupling fan (of which there are two types)
(c) Thermo-viscous coupling fan

2   All the fans are driven by belt from the crankshaft pulley.

3   The fixed fan rotates at the same speed as the coolant pump.

4   The viscous coupling fan speed is dependent on engine speed – at low engine speeds, fan rotation is relatively slow, increasing up to a

10.10A Pump-to-cylinder block gasket

10.10B Pump-to-cylinder head outlet seal

10.11 Lever the pump upwards before tightening the bolts

11.1 Temperature gauge sender

point with engine speed, beyond which it will **not** increase. This reduces noise and drag at high speed.
5   The thermally-controlled viscous coupling is similar to the viscous coupling, but with added temperature control.
6   A bi-metal spring, located in the centre of the coupling, senses radiator temperature (by the air passing through the radiator and over the coupling), and controls oil flow within the coupling via a valve. At low temperatures, the valve is closed, and the fan 'slips' more than at high temperatures, when the valve is fully open, allowing high fan speed.
7   Neither of the viscous couplings are repairable by the home mechanic, and if they become defective they should be renewed.

13 Fan and pulley – removal and refitting

1   On all types, disconnect the battery and remove or push back the fan shroud.
2   Remove the water pump/alternator drivebelt (see Section 14) if the pulley is to be removed.

Fixed fan
3   Remove the four retaining bolts from the fan hub (photo).
4   Lift off the plate, large washer, fan and boss, and if wished the pulley, noting their positions (photos).
5   Refitting is a reversal of this procedure.

Viscous coupling fan (type 1)
6   Remove the centre bolt and bush and pull off the fan and coupling.
7   The fan can be removed from the coupling by undoing the four securing nuts and bolts.
8   The hub assembly is similarly bolted to the water pump flange.
9   Refit in the reverse order.

Viscous coupling fan (type 2)
10 The procedure is similar to that described above, but the coupling cannot be removed from the fan.

Thermally-controlled viscous coupling
11 Remove the four nuts securing the coupling to the water pump flange, and lift off the fan and coupling.
12 The fan is secured to the coupling by studs and nuts.
13 Refit in the reverse order.

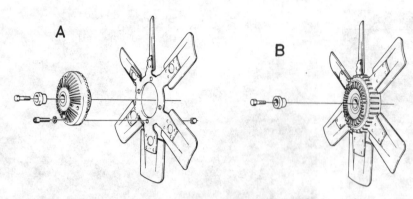

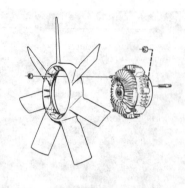

Fig. 2.3 Viscous coupling fan – type 1 (A) type 2 (B) (Sec 13)

Fig. 2.4 Thermally-controlled viscous coupling (Sec 13)

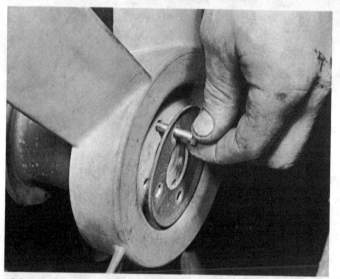

13.3 Removing the fan retaining bolts

13.4A Lift off the fan ...

13.4B ... boss ...

13.4C ... and pulley

14 Drivebelts – removal, refitting and tensioning

1 The water pump, alternator, and where fitted, the power steering pump and air conditioning compressor, are all driven (directly or indirectly) by belt from the crankshaft pulley.

2 Some models have twin belts driving the alternator and water pump, and a variety of arrangements may be found driving the other equipment.

3 All drivebelts should be inspected at the specified intervals (see Section 2), for fraying, splitting, cracking or oil contamination. The tension should also be checked and adjusted as described in the following paragraphs.

4 To remove a belt, first loosen the tensioning mechanism or strap nut or bolt, then the component-to-mounting bracket bolts – not the bracket-to-engine block bolts (photos).

5 Push the component inwards to release tension in the belt, and slip the belt off the pulleys. Obviously, to reach the inner belts, the outer ones must be removed first.

6 Fit the new belt(s) over the pulleys. Nip up the nuts and bolts so that the component can just be moved. On early models, lever outwards against the component (photo) to tension the belt so that the specified deflection is obtained, then tighten the tensioning strap nut and bolt, then the mounting bolts. Be careful when levering not to damage the component – use a wooden or plastic lever.

7 On later models, a positive tensioner is employed, and correct tension is achieved by screwing the tensioner bolt in or out, after loosening the mounting bolts, and tightening them on completion.

8 On air conditioning pumps where the pump is fixed in its mountings and cannot be moved in or out, the belt tension is adjusted by increasing or decreasing the number of shims fitted between the two halves of the crankshaft pulley. To remove the outer half of the pulley, undo the bolts in the hub.

9 Where twin belts are used to drive a component, they should be renewed as a pair.

10 A drivebelt is correctly tensioned when, using moderate thumb pressure midway along the belt's longest run, it can be deflected between the limits given in the Specifications.

Fig. 2.5 Drivebelt arrangement without power steering (Sec 14)

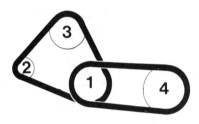

Fig. 2.6 Drivebelt arrangement with power steering (Sec 14)

1 Crankshaft pulley	3 Fan
2 Alternator	4 Power steering pump

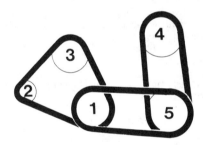

Fig. 2.7 Drivebelt arrangement with power steering and air conditioning (Sec 14)

1 Crankshaft pulley	3 Fan
2 Alternator	4 Power steering pump
	5 Air conditioning compressor

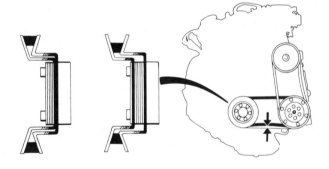

Fig. 2.8 Crankshaft pulley adjustment shims (Sec 14)

14.4A Later 'positive' tensioning mechanism on the alternator ...

14.4B ... and power steering pump

14.4C An alternator mounting bolt (arrowed) ...

14.4D ... and power steering pump bolt (arrowed)

14.6 Levering the alternator outwards with a piece of wood

15 Fault diagnosis – cooling system

Symptom	Reason(s)
Overheating	Insufficient coolant in system Broken or incorrectly tensioned drivebelt (too loose) Radiator blocked either internally or externally Blockage in other part of system Kinked or collapsed hose causing restriction Thermostat inoperative or missing Fuel system fault (weak mixture) Ignition timing incorrectly set or automatic advance faulty Cylinder head gasket blown Exhaust system partially blocked Engine oil level too low Brakes binding Idle speed compensation device malfunction (vehicles with air conditioning only)
Engine running too cool	Thermostat faulty, missing, or incorrect heat range
Loss of coolant	Loose hose clips Hoses perished, cracked or split Radiator leaking Defective cap on expansion tank Blown cylinder head gasket Cracked cylinder head or cylinder block Leak from heater (indicated by wet carpets)
Oil and/or combustion gases in coolant	Cylinder head gasket blown Cylinder head or block cracked

Note: *A blown cylinder head gasket is indicated by excessive water and steam issuing from the exhaust (not to be confused with the normal condensation and vapour, especially on cold mornings), accompanied by rapid and persistent loss of coolant. Check the flatness of the cylinder head and cylinder block mating faces (see Chapter 1).*

Chapter 3 Fuel and exhaust systems

Contents

Specifications

General

System type:
  'A' engines .... Sidedraught, constant depression carburettor
  'K' engines .... Fixed jet, downdraught carburettor
  'E' engines .... Continuous Injection (CI) fuel injection system
Fuel tank capacity:
  Total .... 13.2 Imp gal (60.0 litres)
  Expansion chamber .... 1.1 Imp gal (5.0 litres)
  Reserve (red section of gauge) .... 1.76 Imp gal (8.0 litres)
Fuel octane rating:
  B21A, 1975 to 1978 .... 91 to 93 RON (UK 3-star)
  B21E .... 91 to 93 RON (UK 3-star)
  B230K .... 95 RON (UK 4-star, or premium unleaded)
  All other models .... 97 or 98 RON (UK 4-star)

Air cleaner

Application:
  Models 1974 to 1978 (B21A engine) .... Champion W199 (round type)
  All other models (except 240, 244, 245 – 2127 cc engine) .... Champion U531 (panel type)

Idle and CO content adjustment

Note: *Pulsair system disconnected and plugged where applicable.*

	Idle speed (rpm)	CO content (%) Setting	Checking
B21A 1975 to 1977	850	2.5	1.5 to 4.0
B21A:			
1978	900	2.5	2.0 to 3.5
1979 to 1983	900	2.0	1.5 to 3.0
1984	900	1.5	1.0 to 2.5
B23A 1981 to 1984	900	2.0	1.5 to 3.0
B21E 1975 to 1980	900	2.0	1.0 to 3.0*
B21E 1981 to 1984	900	1.0	0.5 to 2.0
B23E 1979 to 1980	950	2.0	1.5 to 2.5
B23E 1981 to 1984	900	1.0	0.5 to 2.0
B200K	900	1.5	1.0 to 2.5
B200E	900	1.0	0.5 to 2.0
B230A	900	2.0	1.5 to 3.0
B230K (manual)	800	1.0	0.5 to 1.5
B230K (automatic)	900	1.0	0.5 to 1.5
B230E	900	1.0	0.5 to 2.0

4.0, 1975 to 1977

Carburettor engines
Fuel pump

Type	Mechanical diaphragm, operated from intermediate shaft
Pump pressure	2.2 to 4.0 lbf/in² (15.0 to 27.0 kPa) at 1000 rpm

SU HIF 6

Application	B21A engine
Metering needle designation	BDJ
Damping fluid	ATF (Duckhams Q-Matic)
Damping piston endfloat	0.043 to 0.067 in (1.1 to 1.7 mm)
Float needle valve diameter	1.75 mm
Fast idle speed	1250 to 1350 rpm

Solex (Zenith) 175 CD

Application	B21A engine
Metering needle designation:	
1975	B2BB (early) B1ED (late)
1976 on	B1EE
Damping fluid	ATF (Duckhams Q-Matic)
Damping piston endfloat	0.039 to 0.071 in (1.0 to 1.8 mm)
Float needle valve diameter	2.0 mm
Float height	See text
Temperature compensator designation	60L
Temperature compensator opening commences	68°F (20°C)
Fast idle speed	1250 to 1350 rpm

Pierburg (DVG) 175 CDUS

Application	B21A, B23A and B230A engines
Metering needle designation:	
B21A	PN
B23A and B230A	DC
Damping fluid	ATF (Duckhams Q-Matic)
Damping piston endfloat	0.020 to 0.060 in (0.5 to 1.5 mm)
Float needle valve diameter	2.5 mm
Float height	0.28 to 0.36 in (7.0 to 9.0 mm)
Fast idle speed	1250 to 1350 rpm

Solex Cisac (B200K)

Main jet (primary)	145
Main jet (secondary)	140
Air correction jet (primary)	160
Air correction jet (secondary)	135
Idle fuel jet	35
Part load enrichment jet	60
Idling solenoid jet	43
Float level	1.33 in (33.8 mm)
Choke flap gap	0.122 in (3.1 mm)
Fast idle cam gap	0.075 in (1.90 mm)

Solex Cisac (B230K) – where different to above

Main jet (primary)	142
Main jet (secondary)	125
Air correction jet (primary)	130
Air correction jet (secondary)	160
Idling solenoid jet	46

Fuel injection engines

Type .... Continuous injection (CI)

Injectors
B21E up to 1978	007 (or use 015)
B21E, B23E, B200E and B230E 1979 on	015
Opening pressure:	
007	43.5 to 52 lbf/in² (300 to 360 kPa)
015 (up to August 1982)	46.4 to 55 lbf/in² (320 to 380 kPa)
015 (September 1982 on)	50.7 to 59.4 lbf/in² (350 to 410 kPa)

Auxiliary air valve
Resistance	40 to 60 ohms
Fully open at	−22°F (−30°C)
Fully closed at	158°F (70°C)

Control pressure regulator
Resistance	20 to 30 ohms
Airflow sensor plate rest position (maximum control pressure, engine warm and fuel pump running)	0 to 0.012 in (0 to 0.3 mm) below venturi waist

Main fuel pump
Capacity (at 72 lbf in) (500 kPa), 12 volt supply and at 68°F (20°C):	
Up to 1979	1.4 pints (0.8 litre) per 30 seconds
1980 on	1.76 pints (1.0 litre) per 30 seconds

Tank pump
Consumption (12 volt supply):	
B21B, B23B and early B200B/B230B	1 to 2 A
Later models	3 to 4 A

Pressures
Line pressure	62 to 77 lbf/in² (450 to 530 kPa)
Rest pressure (after 20 minutes)	22 lbf/in² (150 kPa) minimum
Control pressure (warm engine)	50 to 54 lbf/in² (345 to 375 kPa)
Control pressure (cold engine)	See graph (in text)

1 General description

All models have a rear-mounted fuel tank, fuel being drawn from the tank by a mechanical pump in the case of carburettor engines, and by an electric pump where fuel injection systems are fitted. The latter also has a lift pump in the fuel tank, integral with the fuel sender, from 1977 on.

The carburettor fitted depends on model year and engine, but basically all 'A' engines have a constant-depression type carburettor of SU, Zenith or Pierburg make. Later versions (B200K and B230K) have a fixed-jet Solex Cisac carburettor.

The fuel injection system fitted to all 'E' engines is of the continuous injection type.

All models have an automatic hot air intake system, the degree of automatic control being more sophisticated the later the model.

Later versions of the constant-depression carburettors may have additional control devices such as an idling bypass system and a warm start valve.

All engines have some form of crankcase ventilation system, again, the later the model, the more complex the system.

The exhaust system is made of aluminised steel, suspended from the vehicle on rubber mountings. Later models have a 'long-life' system fitted.

Note: *Before attempting to make any adjustments to the carburettor or fuel injection system; ensure that all controls are adjusted correctly (ie accelerator cable, choke control, kickdown cable etc.).*

Warning: *When working on any part of the fuel system, disconnect the battery negative terminal, and take all necessary precautions against fire and other hazards. Read the Safety first! Section at the beginning of this Manual.*

2 Routine maintenance

1 At the intervals specified in the *Routine maintenance* Section at the beginning of this Manual, carry out the following operations, appropriate to the model in question.

2 Check the oil level in the carburettor dashpot ('A' engines only) and top up as necessary (see relevant Section according to carburettor fitted).

3 Check the warm start valve for correct operation (Section 28).

4 Check and adjust the choke control, kickdown cable (automatic transmission models) and idle speed and CO content (refer to relevant Section according to carburettor or CI system fitted).

5 Inspect the exhaust system, and check-tighten the exhaust manifold retaining nuts (Section 17).

6 Renew the air filter (Section 6).

7 Clean out the crankcase ventilation system, and check the EGR system and Pulsair system for correct operation (Sections 21 to 23).

8   On fuel injection systems, renew the in-line filter in the engine compartment (Section 64).

3   Tamperproof plugs – general

1   Certain adjustment screws on the carburettor are now sealed by a tamperproof plug, usually of aluminium or plastic.
2   These plugs are fitted to discourage, and to detect, unauthorised adjustment of the carburettor by non-qualified operators.
3   In some EEC countries (though not yet in Britain), it is an offence against anti-pollution laws to drive a vehicle with missing plugs or plugs which have been removed and refitted.
4   Therefore, before removing a plug for adjustment, ensure you will not be breaking local or national anti-pollution laws by so doing. If necessary obtain and fit new plugs on completion of the adjustment(s).

4   Idle speed and CO adjustment – general

1   In the majority of cases, especially on more recent models, the idle speed and CO adjustment requires the use of an accurate tachometer (revolution counter) and a CO meter (exhaust gas analyser) as the two adjustments are usually tied in with one another.
2   If these two pieces of equipment are not available, then the adjustment should be carried out by your Volvo dealer or other specialist.
3   The equipment should be connected to the vehicle in accordance with the equipment manufacturer's instructions, and adjustment made as described in the appropriate Section, using the Specifications at the beginning of this Chapter.
4   Before attempting any adjustment to the carburettor or fuel injection system, ensure the ignition system, valve clearances and crankcase ventilation system are all in good condition and set correctly. The accelerator cable and choke cable should also be checked and adjusted correctly.
5   See also Section 3 on tamperproof plugs fitted to the carburettor.

5   Unleaded fuel – general

1   Unleaded fuel is becoming more widely available, and should theoretically become commonplace as time progresses.
2   In general, the use of unleaded fuel in engines not specifically designed to be run on it, will cause rapid wear of the valve seats.
3   Although it is understood that all post-1987 Volvo models covered by this Manual are able to run on unleaded fuel, you should consult your Volvo dealer before so doing, as alteration to ignition settings may be required.
4   Your Volvo dealer should also be consulted if it is intended to use unleaded fuel on models produced before 1987.

6   Air filter – renewal

1   The air filter should be renewed at the intervals given in the *Routine maintenance* Section at the beginning of this Manual. More frequent renewal may be necessary in dusty conditions.
2   There are two types of air filter; one fitted directly to the carburettor (early models) and one remotely-sited ('E' engines and later carburettor engines).

Early types

3   Remove the three bolts securing the filter housing to the carburettor, and pull back the housing (photo).
4   Separate the two halves of the housing and lift out the filter. Wipe clean inside the housing, being careful not to get dirt into the carburettor.
5   Refit in the reverse order to removal.

Later types

6   Undo the clips securing the cover to the main housing. Two types may be encountered (photo).

6.3 Removing the air filter housing bolts on early models

6.6 Later type air filter housing securing clips

6.7A Removing an air filter

6.7B Removing another type of air filter – note 'TOP' marking

7.7A Hot air intake ducting around the engine bay

7.7B Hot air intake ducting under the headlight

7   Pull the cover off the housing and remove the filter (photos). Wipe clean inside the housing, being careful not to get dirt into the inlet tract.
8   Refit in the reverse order, making sure the lugs which secure the bottom edge of the filter are located properly.
Note: *The word 'UP' (or TOP) stamped on the filter should face towards the incoming air.*

7   Air inlet and pre-heating ducting (B21 and B23) – removal and refitting

1   Both the early and later type of air inlet ducting contains an automatic intake air pre-heating device, controlled by a thermostat. (Some early fuel injection models do not have pre-heating.)
2   The hot air for the system is drawn from a collector plate fitted around the exhaust downpipe just below the exhaust manifold.

Early types
3   Removal and refitting are straightforward, with reference to Fig. 3.1.
4   The thermostat operation can be checked by observing the end of the control flap spindle at different engine temperatures (ie hot and cold). It can also be checked on the bench using a hair dryer.
5   If the unit appears to be defective, the complete assembly should be renewed.

Later types
6   A later system is shown in Fig. 3.4.
7   The hot air intake ducting connection to the air filter housing passes around the lower part of the engine bay, and under the headlight unit (photos).
8   To remove the filter housing and thermostat assembly, first remove the filter as described in Section 6.
9   Remove the fixing clamp from the top of the housing.
10 Disconnect the hot air duct from the bottom of the filter housing.
11 Lift the housing up and out of the engine bay.
12 The thermostat and control flap assembly are held in the housing by plastic clips, which should be depressed to remove the assembly (photos).
13 The operation of the thermostat can be checked by blowing hot air from a heat gun or hair dryer over it, and watching to see if the flap moves.
14 If it fails to operate, fit a new thermostat.
15 When fitting the thermostat and flap assembly to the housing, ensure the flap spindle locates in the pivot point before snapping in the spring clips (photo).
16 The remaining procedure is a reversal of removal.
Note: *If a new filter housing is being fitted to models with the Pulsair system, drill out the Pulsair pipe connection in the top of the housing using a 0.57 in (14.5 mm) drill, and on 1981 on models, plug the hole in the top of the housing.*

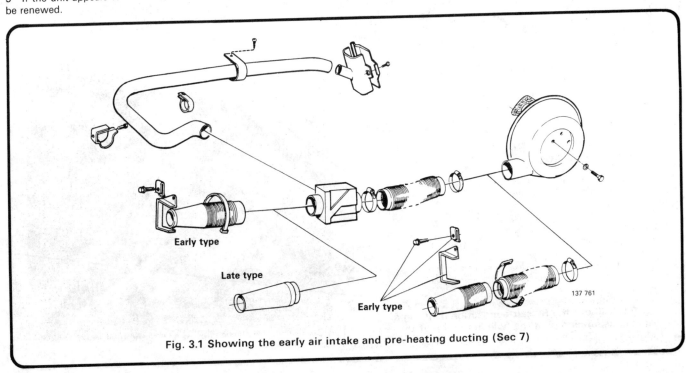

Early type

Late type

Early type

137 761

Fig. 3.1 Showing the early air intake and pre-heating ducting (Sec 7)

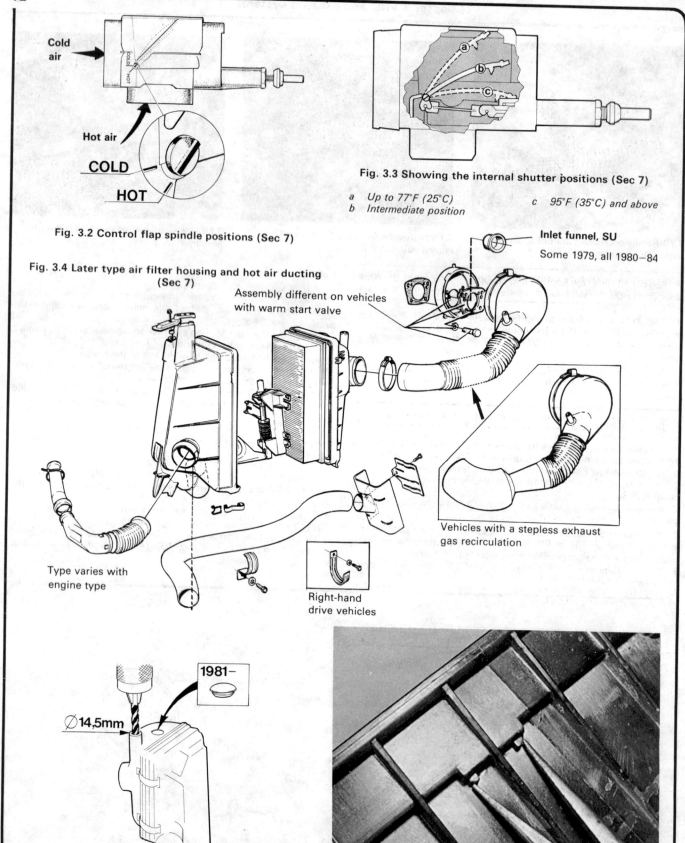

Cold air

Hot air

COLD

HOT

Fig. 3.2 Control flap spindle positions (Sec 7)

Fig. 3.3 Showing the internal shutter positions (Sec 7)

a   Up to 77°F (25°C)   c   95°F (35°C) and above
b   Intermediate position

Fig. 3.4 Later type air filter housing and hot air ducting
(Sec 7)

Assembly different on vehicles
with warm start valve

Inlet funnel, SU

Some 1979, all 1980–84

Vehicles with a stepless exhaust
gas recirculation

Type varies with
engine type

Right-hand
drive vehicles

1981–

Ø14,5mm

134 833

Fig. 3.5 Drill out the Pulsair connection if fitting a
new housing, and plug the hole in the top of the
housing (Sec 7)

7.12A Depressing the plastic clips to release the thermostat and
control flap assembly

7.12B Thermostat and control flap assembly removed

7.15 Ensure the flap spindle is located correctly (arrowed)

9.1 Mechanical fuel pump mounted on the cylinder block

8 Hydro-temperature controlled air inlet (B200 and B230) – general description

1 The system is similar to that described in Section 7, but the thermostat is controlled by a sensor mounted in the air inlet duct just in front of the carburettor, and connected to the thermostat by capillary tube.
2 Care should be exercised when removing the air inlet ducting not to damage the capillary tube.

9 Fuel pump (carburettor engines) – removal and refitting

1 The fuel pump on carburettor engines is a mechanical, diaphragm type pump, mounted on the left-hand side of the cylinder block, and driven by a cam off the intermediate shaft (photo).
2 Three types of pump may be encountered, as shown in Figs. 3.7 and 3.8.
3 If the pump becomes defective and the filter is clean (Section 10), the complete pump should be renewed as follows.
4 Disconnect the battery negative lead. Disconnect the inlet and outlet fuel lines from the pump, being prepared for some spillage. Block off the ends of the pipes to prevent dirt entry.
5 Remove the nuts securing the pump to the studs on the cylinder block, and lift off the pump. Recover the gasket and any spacers.
6 Refitting is a reversal of removal, using a new gasket between the pump and the cylinder block.

10 Fuel pump filter (carburettor engines) – renewal

1 Renewable filters are fitted to Pierburg, Sofabex and SEV fuel pumps.
2 To remove the filter, first disconnect the battery. Refer to Figs. 3.7 and 3.8, and remove the screw(s) securing the top cover on the pump.
3 Lift out the filter.
4 Fit a new filter in reverse order, using a new sealing ring under the cover.

11 Fuel pump (carburettor engines) – testing

1 The correct way is to fit a pressure gauge using a T-piece in the fuel line between the pump and the carburettor, then start the engine and check that the pressure is as given in the Specifications.
2 If no gauge is available, disconnect the fuel line from the pump to the carburettor at the carburettor end, and direct the end of the hose into a suitable container.
3 Disable the ignition system by disconnecting the positive LT leads from the ignition coil (terminal '15' or '+'). It is important that no sparks are produced during the test, and that fuel is not spilled onto a hot exhaust. Take appropriate fire precautions.
4 Have an assistant crank the engine on the starter. Fuel should be ejected into the container in regular bursts. If not, the pump is

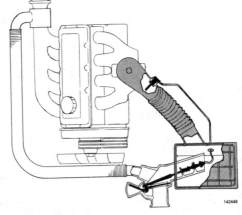

Fig. 3.6 Hydro-temperature controlled system in later models (Sec 8)

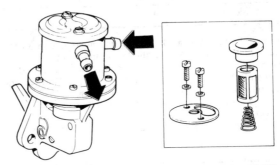

Fig. 3.7 Sofabex SEV type fuel pump (Secs 9 and 10)

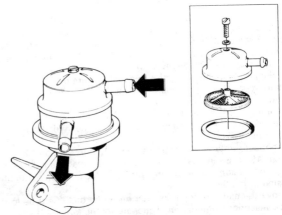

Fig. 3.8 Pierburg type fuel pump (Secs 9 and 10)

defective, or something is amiss on the tank side of the pump.

5 Remake the original fuel and electrical connections. Dispose of the fuel in the container safely.

12 Fuel tank sender unit – removal and refitting

1 The fuel tank sender unit, which transmits the fuel level in the tank to the fuel gauge, is screwed into the top of the fuel tank beneath the boot/luggage area floor.

2 The sender unit differs between carburettor and fuel injection engines.

3 On most fuel injection engines, there is an integral fuel pump incorporated in the unit (see Section 68).

4 Both types incorporate a filter on the bottom of the outlet (suction) pipe, which may need to be cleaned periodically (see Section 13).

5 Removal and refitting procedures for both types are similar, and are as follows.

Note: *A special tool is required to remove the sender from the top of the tank. This tool could easily be made up from scrap metal (see Fig. 3.9).*

6 Disconnect the battery negative terminal. Ensure adequate ventilation and take appropriate fire precautions.

7 Remove the fuel tank filler cap to release any residual pressure in the system.

8 Remove the floor panels from the boot/luggage area to uncover the panel in the floor over the sender unit.

9 Disconnect the leads to the sender unit. There is an earth lead fitted under a separate screw.

10 Remove the screws from the panel and pull the panel up out of the way.

11 Disconnect the fuel lines from the sender unit.

12 Using the tool, unscrew the sender unit from the top of the tank. (A couple of large screwdrivers or tyre levers may be used at a pinch.)

13 Lift out the sender unit, complete with filter, and on fuel injection engines, the internal pump.

14 Refitting is a reversal of removal, using a new seal lubricated with glycerine under the sender unit, and renewing the sealing mastic around the floor panel if it has become hardened with age.

13 Fuel tank filter – renewal

1 Remove the fuel tank sender unit as described in Section 12.

2 Pull the filter from the end of the fuel outlet (suction) pipe.

3 There are two types of filter, depending on age and model. Note how the end of the early type pipe is angled to prevent blockage.

4 Fit a new filter, pushing it fully on to the pipe.

5 Refit the sender as described in Section 12.

Note: *On some early tanks with a drain plug, the filter may be accessible from below after draining the tank and removing the access plug.*

14 Fuel tank – removal and refitting

Note: *Several different fuel tanks have been fitted to different models, especially on fuel injection engines. Only later-type fuel tanks are available as spares, and if it is intended to replace an older type tank with a new one, the advice of your Volvo dealer should be sought, as several modifications may be involved.*

1 Disconnect the battery negative terminal. Ensure there is adequate ventilation, and take appropriate fire precautions throughout the operation.

2 Where fitted, undo the drain plug and drain the fuel into a suitable container. Where there is no drain plug, the fuel will have to be siphoned out.

3 Disconnect the tank sender unit as described in Section 12.

4 On pre-1977 'E'-engined models, disconnect the external fuel and electrical connections to the external pump and accumulator, mounted on the side of the tank.

5 Remove the clips securing the filler neck and breather tube to the tank, and disconnect the rubber sections from the tank.

6 Either support the tank with a jack, or have an assistant help support the tank while the tank securing bolts are removed.

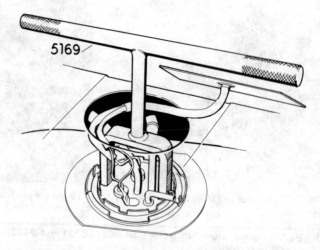

Fig. 3.9 Showing the special tool for removing the sender unit (Sec 12)

Fig. 3.10 Sealing arrangement of the sender unit (Sec 12)

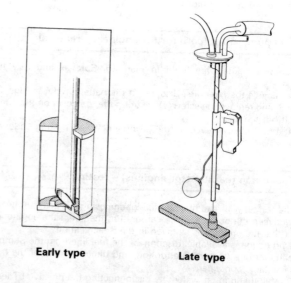

Early type   **Late type**

Fig. 3.11 Early and late type fuel tank filters (Sec 13)

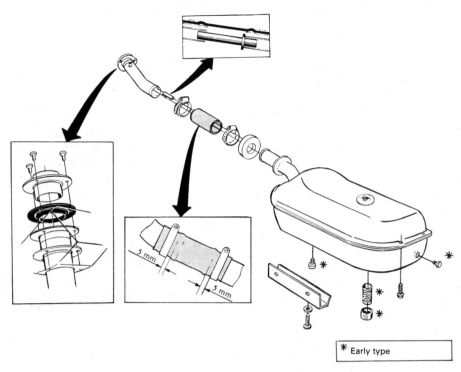

* Early type

Fig. 3.12 Fuel tank assembly up to 1978 (Sec 14)

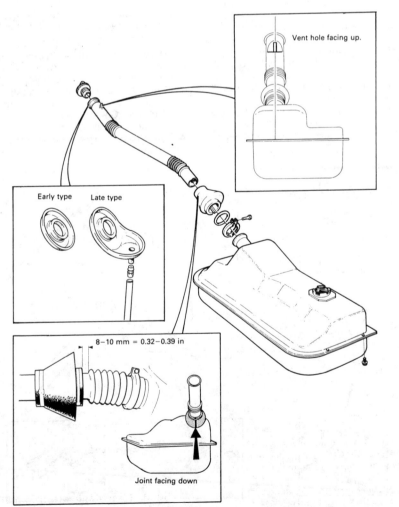

Fig. 3.13 Fuel tank assembly fitted to later models (Sec 14)

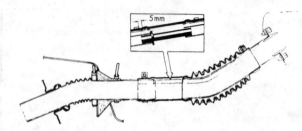

Fig. 3.14 Later type fuel filler hose arrangement (Sec 14)

7   The tank may well remain in position, being held by the mastic sealant around its edge. Cut through the sealant to release the tank, then lower the tank to the ground.
8   Repair of a leaking tank must only be undertaken by professionals. Even when the tank is empty, it may still contain explosive vapours. **Do not** attempt to weld or solder the tank. 'Cold' repair compounds are available, and these are suitable for DIY use.
9   Refitting is a reversal of removal, using new seals where they are fitted between connections, and renew the sealant between the tank and boot floor. If a new tank is being fitted, give it a coat of anti-corrosion paint before fitting.

15 Fuel hoses and pipeline connections – general

1   Older type fuel lines were made of metal, but increasingly a plastic material is being used.
2   Periodically inspect the fuel lines for leakage and security of clamps and clips.
3   When undoing or tightening connections, use two spanners to avoid twisting the hose.
4   To renew a nipple in a plastic hose, proceed as follows.
5   Cut the hose at right-angles some 3/4 in (20.0 mm) in from the old union.
6   Make a horizontal cut in the end of the hose about 1 3/4 in (45.0 mm) long.
7   Using a heat gun or hair dryer, gently warm the end of the hose, then grip it in a pair of pliers and push in the new nipple.
8   Fold back the cut ends of the hose, and secure in position with a pipe clip.

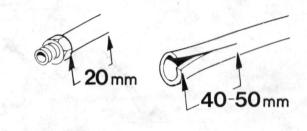

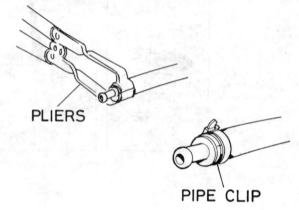

Fig. 3.15 Fitting a new nipple to plastic hose (Sec 15)

16 Exhaust system – general description

1   The exhaust system is a 'two-box' system in three sections, made of aluminised steel. As from 1987, all models have a long-life system which is more resistant to corrosion.
2   The downpipe is joined to the exhaust manifold by a flanged joint.
3   Most other joints are a push fit, one pipe inside the other, secured by U-clamps. On some models there is a bell-mouthed joint with an 'olive' (tapered sealing ring) forward of the front silencer.
4   The system is suspended from the underside of the vehicle by rubber mounting bushes or rubber rings.

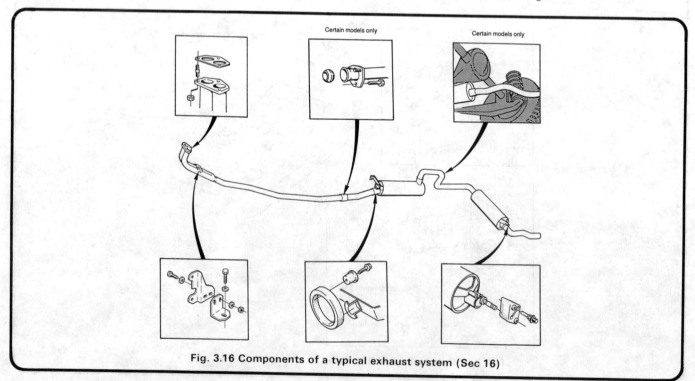

Fig. 3.16 Components of a typical exhaust system (Sec 16)

17 Exhaust system – inspection and repair

1 The exhaust system should be inspected periodically for corrosion, causing holes and splits, especially around the welded joints of the silencers. Inspect pipe joints for leakage and the security of mountings.
2 Examine the exhaust system with the engine running (make sure the transmission is in neutral and the handbrake is on). Any exhaust gas leakage can readily be felt. Small holes can be found more easily if the tailpipe is partly obstructed with a wad of cloth.
3 Allow the system to cool before checking the rubber mountings by pulling them by hand and checking for cracking and perishing of the mountings.
4 Perished mountings should be renewed.
5 Holts Flexiwrap and Holts Gun Gum exhaust repair systems can be used for effective repairs to exhaust pipes and silencer boxes, including ends and bends. Holts Flexiwrap is an MOT approved permanent exhaust repair. In some instances a badly corroded and holed exhaust will need to be replaced either in part or whole.
6 Renewal is really a job for the exhaust specialist who can do the job in a fraction of the time it will take at home.

18 Exhaust system – removal and refitting

1 Disconnect the downpipe-to-exhaust manifold joint (photo).
2 Raise and support the vehicle. Disconnect the bracket on the clutch bellhousing (photo).
3 Remove the U-clamp from the rear section of the exhaust system, and free the rear section from its mountings by removing the bolts from the rubber support bushes and unhooking the rubber rings (photos).
4 Work the rear section free from the centre section, and lift it out from over the rear axle. (If a section is to be renewed and the sliding joint is seized, saw through the old section.)
5 Once the rear section is removed, it is a relatively simple matter to disconnect and remove the centre section and the downpipe.
6 Refitting is a reversal of removal, using new clamps and suspension rubber rings where necessary, anti-seize compound on all fastenings and a proprietary exhaust assembly/sealing compound on all joints. Use a new gasket between the downpipe-to-exhaust manifold flange, and if necessary a new olive in the bell-mouthed joint.
7 When refitting the rear silencer, ensure it is inclined forwards, as shown in Fig. 3.17. It is marked 'IN' on the end which must be connected to the exhaust pipe.
8 Do not fully tighten the mounting and clamp bolts until satisfied that the system is hanging correctly without straining the mountings. No part of the system must be closer than 3/4 in (20 mm) to the body. Carry out final tightening from the downpipe-to-manifold joint rearwards.
9 Run the engine and check for leaks. Stop the engine and allow the system to cool, then re-check the tightness of the mounting and clamp bolts.

19 Exhaust manifold – removal and refitting

1 Disconnect the exhaust downpipe from the exhaust manifold. It may be necessary to release the exhaust support bracket on the clutch bellhousing.
2 Where fitted, disconnect the Pulsair manifold and the EGR pipe.
3 Remove the nuts securing the manifold to the cylinder head studs, and lift the manifold off (photo). Note the location of the engine lifting eye.
4 Refit in the reverse order, using new gaskets, and tighten the nuts progressively working from the centre outwards (photo).
Note: *The word OUT (or UT) should face outwards when fitting the gaskets.*

20 Inlet manifold – removal and refitting

1 Disconnect the battery negative terminal.
2 Remove the carburettor, or disconnect all services to it and leave it in place on the manifold. On fuel injection engines, disconnect the air inlet trunking.
3 Disconnect any breather or vacuum hoses connected to the manifold, making notes or identifying marks if necessary.
4 On 'E' engines, disconnect the cold start injector (photo).
5 Disconnect the accelerator cable, if not already done.
6 Drain the coolant system to below the level of the cylinder head (Chapter 2).
7 Disconnect any coolant pipes from the inlet manifold. Also disconnect the EGR pipe, when so equipped.
8 Undo the nuts securing the manifold to the cylinder head, and lift it off the studs.
9 Refit in reverse order, using new gaskets and tightening the nuts progressively, working from the centre outwards (photo).

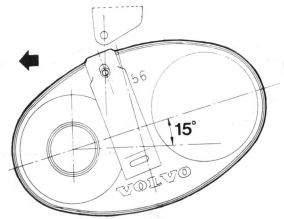

Fig. 3.17 Rear silencer mounting position – arrow points to front of car (Sec 17)

18.1 Downpipe-to-exhaust manifold joint disconnected

18.2 Exhaust pipe bracket on the clutch bellhousing

18.3A Typical U-clamp and rubber suspension rings

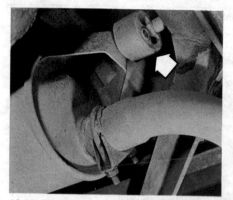

18.3B Rubber support bush (arrowed)

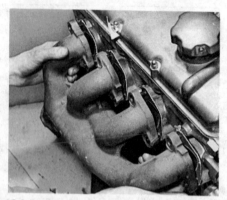

19.3 Removing the exhaust manifold

19.4 Exhaust manifold refitted – note the engine lifting eye

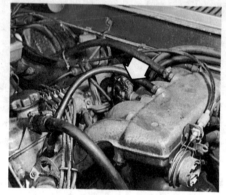

20.4 Cold start injector (arrowed) on 'E' engines

20.9 Refitting the inlet manifold (carburettor engine shown)

21 Crankcase ventilation system – general description

1 A closed crankcase ventilation system, is fitted to all engines.
2 The crankcase gases are now allowed to vent directly to atmosphere, as in an 'open' type system, but are drawn from the crankcase or valve cover using the vacuum at the inlet manifold, and re-directed into the inlet manifold for combustion, thereby reducing pollution of the atmosphere by unburnt oil fumes and blow-by gas.

3 A flame trap and oil separator are fitted in the hose between the crankcase and the inlet manifold.
4 A calibrated nipple at the hose connection to the inlet manifold regulates the flow of gases into the inlet manifold, preventing the gas/air ratio becoming too high and upsetting the fuel/air mixture ratio, and also ensures the vacuum in the crankcase does not become excessive.
5 There are no moving parts in the system, and servicing is limited to periodically cleaning out the hoses and oil separator.

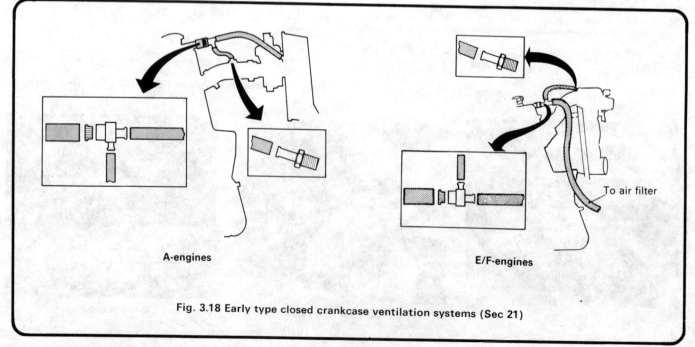

A-engines

E/F-engines

To air filter

Fig. 3.18 Early type closed crankcase ventilation systems (Sec 21)

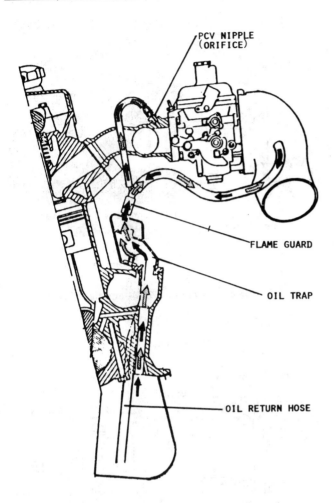

Fig. 3.19 Sectional view of crankcase ventilation system on 'A' engines (Sec 21)

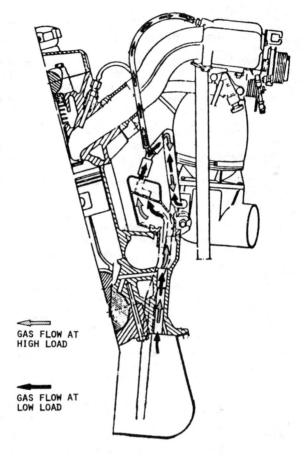

Fig. 3.20 Sectional view of crankcase ventilation system on 'E' engines (Sec 21)

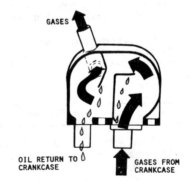

Fig. 3.21 Sectional view of later type oil trap (Sec 21)

22 EGR system – general description

1   An exhaust gas recirculation (EGR) system is fitted to 1987 B230K engines. Under certain conditions, a small quantity of exhaust gas is fed back into the inlet manifold. This lowers the level of harmful oxides of nitrogen (NOx) in the exhaust gas.
2   The system consists of an exhaust gas recirculation valve, a vacuum amplifier and a thermostatic control valve.
3   The thermostatic valve senses the temperature of the engine coolant, and opens at a temperature of 131°F (55°C), bringing the system into use.
4   The vacuum amplifier controls the connection between the inlet manifold and the EGR valve, controlling the opening of the valve according to engine load (vacuum).
5   The vacuum amplifier senses engine load by being connected to the depression at the throttle butterfly and to the air filter housing, giving it two reference points.
6   In this way the EGR valve is continually controlled, allowing the optimum amount of exhaust gas into the inlet manifold for recombustion under all engine conditions.
7   The vacuum amplifier and the EGR valve are adjusted as a matched pair during assembly, and if either becomes defective, then both the amplifier and EGR valve should be renewed.
8   Faults in the EGR system may cause rough idle, backfiring and poor performance. Consult a Volvo dealer or other specialist if faults are suspected.
9   No further information was available at the time of writing.

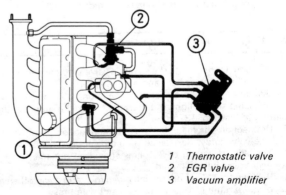

1   Thermostatic valve
2   EGR valve
3   Vacuum amplifier

Fig. 3.22 Schematic view of EGR system (Sec 22)

23 Pulsair system – general description

1 The Pulsair system is fitted to all B230K engines from 1987 onwards.

2 The purpose of the system is to create a cleaner exhaust gas by injecting air into the exhaust manifold, which results in some of the hydrocarbons and carbon monoxide gases being burned.

3 The pipework which is fitted to the exhaust manifold is connected to the air filter housing via two non-return valves.

4 The system utilises the 'pulses' created in the exhaust system to draw clean air from the air inlet, and inject it into the exhaust manifold.

5 When the pressure in the exhaust system rises, the non-return valves close, preventing the exhaust gases entering the air filter housing.

6 Servicing of the system consists of periodically cleaning the hoses, and checking the non-return valves by disconnecting the hoses and blowing through the valves.

7 When blown through from the air inlet side, the valves should open, and when blown through from the exhaust side, the valves should close. Valves which are suspect should be renewed.

Note: *Whenever adjustments are being carried out to the carburettor, the Pulsair system should be disconnected at the air filter housing, and the hose plugged.*

8 No further information was available at the time of writing.

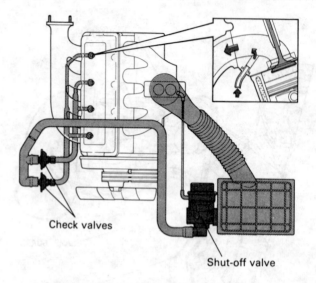

Fig. 3.23 Pulsair system on B230K engines (Sec 23)

24 Idling bypass system – general description

1 The idling bypass system is fitted to 1978 on models with 'A' engines.

2 It consists of a solenoid valve, screwed into the inlet manifold, and connected electrically to the ignition switch.

3 The inlet manifold and carburettor have channels bored in them, through which a quantity of the fuel/air mixture can flow, bypassing the throttle valve.

4 When the ignition is switched on, the solenoid valve operates and opens the bypass channel, and closes when the ignition is switched off, giving greater control of the idling system and preventing running-on.

5 Idle speed on carburettors with a bypass system should be set by using the adjuster screw in the bypass channel, and not by the throttle valve adjuster screw.

6 Where the idle speed cannot be set satisfactorily using the bypass adjustment screw, the basic setting of the carburettor main jet, needle and throttle valve should be checked and adjusted as described in the relevant Section.

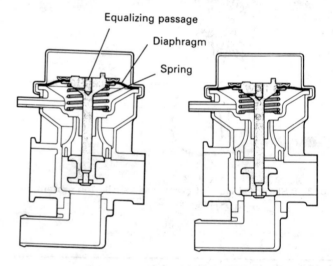

Fig. 3.24 Showing the operation of the shut-off valve

25 Idle speed – vehicles with air conditioning

1 On some vehicles fitted with air conditioning a solenoid valve, which opens when the air conditioning is switched off, is fitted on the carburettor or inlet manifold.

2 The solenoid valve controls a bypass channel around the throttle valve, similar to the idle bypass system, but there is no adjusting screw.

3 The solenoid valve allows more fuel/air mixture to the engine when the air conditioner is in use, preventing a drop in idle speed.

26 Idling bypass valves – testing

1 Disconnect the lead to the solenoid valve, and connect up a 12 volt test lamp between the lead and a good earth.

2 Switch on the ignition (and air conditioning if appropriate), when the test lamp should light. If it does not, check the supply to the valve, starting at fuse No. 13.

3 Connect an ohmmeter between the connection on top of the valve and the valve body. Resistance should be approximately 30 ohms.

4 Similarly, a reading of 30 ohms should be obtained between the connector and inlet manifold.

5 Remove the valve from the inlet manifold, and clean off any carbon deposits from the valve seat, using a stiff wire brush.

Note: *Carbon deposits are caused by:*

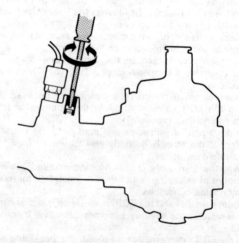

Fig. 3.25 Idling bypass solenoid valve and adjuster screw (Sec 24)

(a) Blocked or defective crankcase ventilation system
(b) Dirty or incorrectly fitted air cleaner or air intake system
(c) Poor quality fuel

6 These defects should be rectified before refitting the valve.
7 Smear the threads of the solenoid valve with grease or anti-seize compound before refitting.

27 Warm start valve – general description

1 The warm start valve is fitted to certain models from mid-1980 on.
2 On early Solex and Pierburg carburettors, it is mounted on the engine bulkhead, and on SU and later versions of the above, it is mounted on the inner wheel arch. From 1984 it is mounted directly on to the carburettor.
3 The valve is connected to the carburettor float chamber by tubing (via connections on the air inlet ducting) and is electrically-operated via the ignition switch.
4 The valve provides for better warm starting, by evacuating the fuel vapour which forms in the float chamber to atmosphere when the ignition is switched off. The valve closes as soon as the ignition is switched on.
5 A kit is available from your dealer for fitting the warm start valve to 1979 vehicles.
6 Malfunction of the warm start valve can cause difficult warm starting, high fuel consumption, high CO level at idle and rough running.

28 Warm start valve – testing

1 With the ignition switched off it should be possible to blow through the valve from the carburettor side to the vent tube side.
2 With the ignition switched on, the valve should close and it should not be possible to blow through it.
3 If the valve fails to operate, check the electrical supply to it, and its earth before renewing the valve.
Note: *The length and type of tubing connected between the carburettor and the remotely-mounted warm start valve is critical, and should not be renewed by unspecified tubing or engine performance may be affected.*

29 SU HIF 6 carburettor – general description

1 The variable choke SU carburettor is a relatively simple instrument. It differs from most other carburettors in that instead of having a number of various fixed jets for different conditions, only one variable jet is fitted to deal with all possible conditions.
2 Air passing rapidly through the carburettor draws petrol from the jet so forming the fuel/air mixture. The amount of petrol drawn from the jet depends on the position of the tapered carburettor needle, which moves up and down the jet orifice according to the engine load and

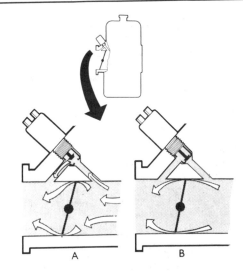

Fig. 3.26 Idle speed increase solenoid valve on vehicles with air conditioning (Sec 25)

A Air conditioner on   B Air conditioner off

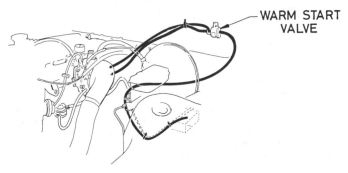

Fig. 3.27 Warm start valve layout (Sec 27)

Solex and Pierburg carburettors: Upper 17.3 in (440.0 mm). Lower 18.5 in (470.0 mm)
SU carburettors: Upper 20.9 in (530.0 mm). Lower 17.3 in (440.0 in)

throttle opening, this effectively altering the size of jet so that exactly the right amount of fuel is metered for the prevailing road conditions.
3 The position of the tapered needle in the jet is determined by engine vacuum. The shank of the needle is held at its top end in a piston which slides up and down the dashpot in response to the degree of manifold vacuum.
4 With the throttle fully open, the full effect of inlet manifold vacuum is felt by the piston which has an air bleed into the choke tube on the outside of the throttle. This causes the piston to rise fully, bringing the needle with it. With the accelerator partially closed, only slight inlet manifold vacuum is felt by the piston (although, of course, on the engine side of the throttle the vacuum is greater), and the piston only rises a little, blocking most of the jet orifice with the metering needle.
5 To prevent the piston fluttering and giving a richer mixture when the accelerator is suddenly depressed, an oil damper and light spring are fitted inside the dashpot.

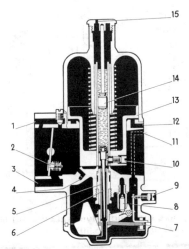

Fig. 3.28 Sectional view of the SU HIF 6 carburettor (Sec 29)

1 Solenoid valve (idle bypass) channel	5 Fuel jet	10 Retaining screw
2 Overrun valve (certain models only)	6 Metering needle	11 Float chamber vent
3 Idle channel (1978 on)	7 Bi-metal spring	12 Suction piston vent
4 Choke channel	8 Needle valve (float chamber)	13 Suction piston
	9 CO adjustment screw	14 Damper piston
		15 Vent hole

6   The only portion of the piston assembly to come into contact with the piston chamber or dashpot is the actual central piston rod. All the other parts of the piston assembly, including the lower choke portion, have sufficient clearance to prevent any direct metal to metal contact which is essential if the carburettor is to function correctly.
7   From 1978, a bypass idling system is used (see Section 24.)

30 SU HIF 6 carburettor – idle speed adjustment

Note: *See Sections 3 and 4 before commencing.*
1   Disconnect the accelerator control rod ball end, and check that the throttle valve operates smoothly without binding, and that the spindle is not loose. If it is, then the carburettor should be overhauled.
2   Remove the air cleaner or inlet duct, and check that with the throttle valve fully open, it is at 90° to the vertical. Adjust by bending the stop lug on the throttle spindle.
3   On 1978 to 1981 models, if the throttle valve adjustment has been disturbed, set it as follows. Undo the locknut on the throttle valve adjusting screw, and unscrew the adjuster until the throttle valve is fully closed. Screw the adjuster in to obtain the initial opening shown in Fig. 3.30. On completion, tighten the adjuster locknut and seal it with paint. There should be no need to repeat this adjustment.
4   Refit the air cleaner or inlet duct and reconnect the accelerator control rod.
5   Check that the choke control is pushed fully in, and that the lever cam is clear of the fast idle adjusting screw.
6   Check that the oil level in the damper chamber is correct, topping-up as necessary.
7   Connect up a tachometer.
8   Start the engine and allow it to reach normal operating temperature.
9   Set the engine idle speed as follows. On models without an idling by-pass system (see Section 24) adjust the throttle adjusting screw in or out to obtain the specified idling speed (Fig. 3.72). On models with an idling bypass system, adjust the idling bypass system adjusting screw to obtain the specified idling speed (Fig. 3.25).
10 If the correct idle speed cannot be obtained on the bypass adjusting screw, check the throttle valve setting as follows.
Note: *This method should also be used where running-on has been a problem.*
11 Screw the idle bypass adjusting screw in until it bottoms, then out again by four complete turns.
12 Set the engine idle speed to 1100 to 1200 rpm using the throttle adjusting screw.
13 Reduce the engine idle speed to that specified by screwing in the idle bypass adjusting screw.
14 On completion, tighten all adjuster screw locknuts and remove the tachometer. Seal the throttle adjusting screw locknut with paint if it was disturbed.

31 SU HIF 6 carburettor – CO adjustment

Note: *This adjusting screw is sealed with a plug (see Section 3). See also Section 4 on CO adjustment.*
1   Start the engine and allow it to reach normal operating temperature.
2   Connect the CO meter in accordance with the meter manufacturer's instructions.
3   Increase engine speed to approximately 1500 rpm for about 30 seconds to allow cold fuel to enter the carburettor.
4   Reduce engine speed to idle, and gently tap the damper chamber on the carburettor to ensure the piston is not sticking.
5   Check the CO content and adjust the screw (see Fig. 3.33) as necessary to obtain the specified reading. Screw in to increase and out to decrease CO content.
6   Check and adjust the idle speed as described in Section 30, then recheck the CO content.
7   When both idle speed and CO content are correct, stop the engine and disconnect the test gear.

32 SU HIF 6 carburettor – fast idle adjustment

Note: *Adjust the idle speed (Section 30) before attempting fast idle adjustment.*
1   Pull out the choke control lever approximately 1.0 in (25.0 mm) so that the index mark on the choke lever cam is opposite the fast idle adjustment screw.
2   Connect a tachometer. Start the engine and check that the fast idle is as specified. If not, loosen the locknut on the adjuster screw and turn the screw until the specified speed is reached. On completion, tighten the locknut.
3   Push the choke control fully in, and check that there is a gap between the choke lever cam and the head of the adjuster screw.

33 SU HIF 6 carburettor – removal and refitting

1   Disconnect the battery negative lead. Remove the air cleaner, or air cleaner duct, as described in Sections 6 or 7.
2   Disconnect the fuel inlet pipeline and blank off the open end.
3   Disconnect the distributor vacuum pipe at the carburettor.
4   Disconnect the choke cable from the carburettor.
5   Snap back the locking tab on the accelerator ball end, and pull the ball end from the throttle control lever.
6   Remove the carburettor retaining nuts and lift off the carburettor. Cover the inlet manifold opening with rag to keep dirt and dampness out.

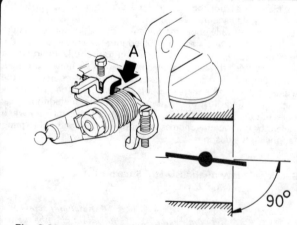

Fig. 3.29 Checking the throttle valve full-open position – SU HIF 6 carburettor (Sec 30)

Adjustment point A arrowed

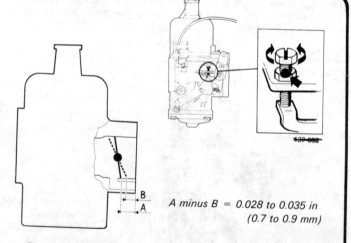

Fig. 3.30 Throttle valve basic setting diagram – SU HIF 6 carburettor (Sec 30)

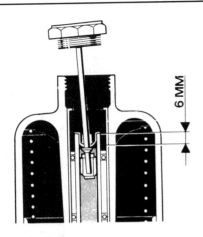

Fig. 3.31 Damper fluid level. This also applies to Solex and some Pierburg carburettors (Sec 30)

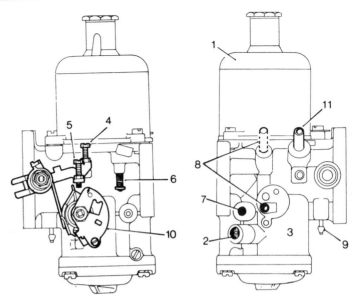

Fig. 3.32 SU HIF 6 carburettor adjustment points and other features (Sec 30)

1   Piston/suction chamber
2   Jet adjusting screw
3   Float chamber
4   Throttle adjusting screw
5   Fast idle adjusting screw
6   Piston lifting pin
7   Fuel inlet

8   Vent tube (alternative positions)
9   Auto ignition connection
10 Cold start enrichment lever (cam lever)
11 Crankcase ventilation tube

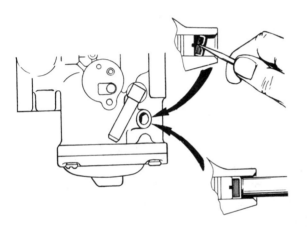

Fig. 3.33 CO adjustment screw and sealing plug (Sec 31)

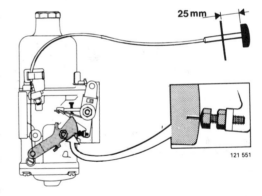

Fig 3.34 SU HIF 6 carburettor fast idle adjustment (Sec 32)

7   Refitting is a reversal of removal, using a new gasket under the carburettor, making sure all traces of old gasket are removed.
8   After refitting, adjust the idle speed, CO content and fast idle as described in Sections 30, 31 and 32.
9   After fitting the accelerator control rod, adjust the rod to give the clearance shown in Fig. 3.35.

34 SU HIF 6 carburettor – dismantling and reassembly

Note: *Check the cost and availability of spares before commencing carburettor overhaul. A new or reconditioned carburettor may be a more satisfactory solution if the old one is generally worn. If it is decided to overhaul, obtain a carburettor repair kit which will contain gaskets, O-rings and similar items, which should be renewed as a matter of course.*
1   Remove the carburettor as described in Section 33, then give the outside a good clean in solvent or petrol to remove any grime. Place the carburettor on a bench which has been lined with clean newspaper.
2   Undo the cap at the top of the carburettor and withdraw it complete with the small damper piston. Empty the oil from the dashpot.
3   Mark the position of the float chamber cover relative to the body and remove it by unscrewing the four screws holding it down. Empty out any fuel still in the fuel chamber.

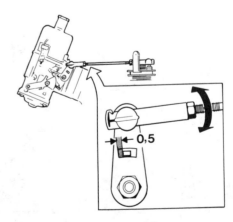

Fig. 3.35 Accelerator link rod adjustment – SU HIF 6 carburettor. Dimension in mm (Sec 33)

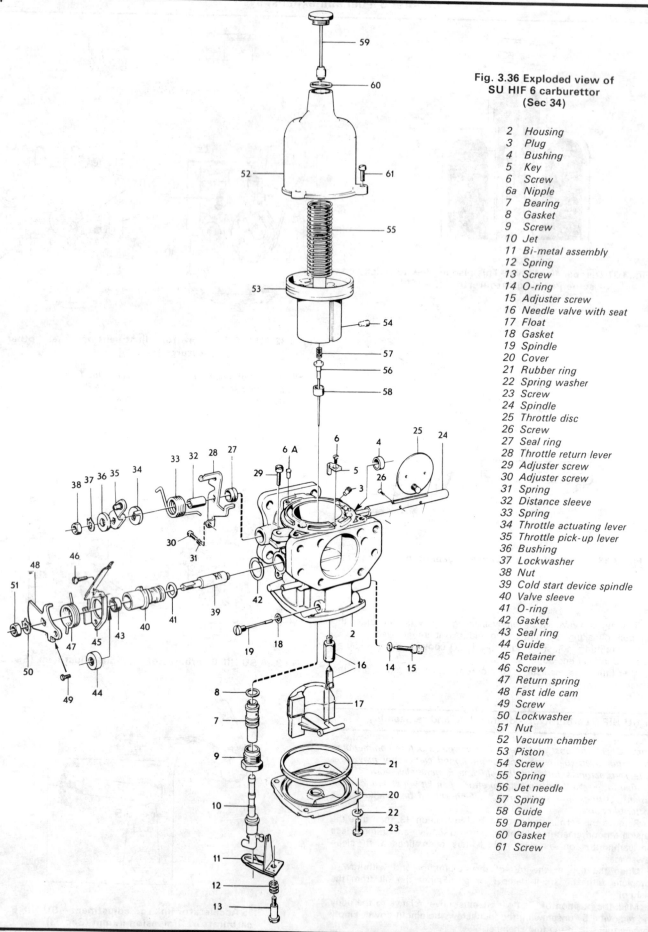

Fig. 3.36 Exploded view of
SU HIF 6 carburettor
(Sec 34)

2 Housing
3 Plug
4 Bushing
5 Key
6 Screw
6a Nipple
7 Bearing
8 Gasket
9 Screw
10 Jet
11 Bi-metal assembly
12 Spring
13 Screw
14 O-ring
15 Adjuster screw
16 Needle valve with seat
17 Float
18 Gasket
19 Spindle
20 Cover
21 Rubber ring
22 Spring washer
23 Screw
24 Spindle
25 Throttle disc
26 Screw
27 Seal ring
28 Throttle return lever
29 Adjuster screw
30 Adjuster screw
31 Spring
32 Distance sleeve
33 Spring
34 Throttle actuating lever
35 Throttle pick-up lever
36 Bushing
37 Lockwasher
38 Nut
39 Cold start device spindle
40 Valve sleeve
41 O-ring
42 Gasket
43 Seal ring
44 Guide
45 Retainer
46 Screw
47 Return spring
48 Fast idle cam
49 Screw
50 Lockwasher
51 Nut
52 Vacuum chamber
53 Piston
54 Screw
55 Spring
56 Jet needle
57 Spring
58 Guide
59 Damper
60 Gasket
61 Screw

4 The float is held to the body by a spindle having a screw head on it (shown in Fig. 3.36). Unscrew and remove the spindle with its sealing washer, remove the float, unscrew the needle valve socket and remove it and the needle. It is normal to renew the needle valve and socket when overhauling the carburettor. Renew the float and spindle too if they are worn.

5 Dismantle the various control linkages, being sure that it is understood how the linkages work before they are taken off. It is an easy matter to sort this out before taking them apart, but much more difficult when they are in bits.

6 Unscrew the nut holding the fast idle cam – having first straightened its tab washer, take off the cam and its spring which is contained in a small housing behind it. Undo the two screws holding down this housing, and pull on the spindle which held the fast idle cam and the whole cold start assembly will come out of the body. It is shown in Fig. 3.36.

7 Undo the screws holding the throttle disc into its shaft, being careful not to put too much pressure on the shaft in the process (support it with the other hand). Remove the disc and withdraw the throttle shaft.

8 Mark the flanges and remove the top part of the body (suction chamber) and the piston. Be careful of the needle on the end of the piston – a good idea is to stand the piston on a narrow-necked jar with the needle hanging inside it.

9 Unscrew the jet adjusting screw and remove the bi-metal assembly holding the jet.

10 The carburettor is now sufficiently dismantled for inspection to be carried out. One or two adjusting screws and the like have been left in the body, but it is recommended that these are only removed when actually ensuring that the various channels are clear. Generally speaking, the SU carburettor is very reliable, but even so it may develop faults, which are not readily apparent unless a careful inspection is carried out, yet may nevertheless affect engine performance. So it is well worthwhile giving the carburettor a good look over when it has been dismantled.

11 Inspect the carburettor needle for ridging. If this is apparent it will probably be found that there is corresponding wear on the inside of the jet. If the needle is ridged, it must be renewed. Do not attempt to rub it down with abrasive paper as carburettor needles are made to very fine tolerances.

12 When refitting the needle locate it in the piston as shown in Fig. 3.38.

13 Inspect the jet for wear. Wear inside the jet will accompany wear on the needle. If any wear is apparent on the jet, renew it. It may be unhooked from the bi-metal spring and this may be used again (see Fig. 3.39).

14 Inspect the piston and the carburettor body (suction chamber) carefully for signs that these have not been in contact. When the carburettor is operating, the main piston should not come into contact with the carburettor body. The whole assembly is supported by the rod of the piston which slides in the centre guide tube, this rod being attached to the cap in the top of the carburettor body. It is possible for wear in the centre guide to allow the piston to touch the wall of the body. Check for this by assembling the small piston in the carburettor body and sliding the large one down, rotating it about the centre guide tube at the same time. If contact occurs and the cause is worn parts, renew them. In no circumstances try to correct piston sticking by altering the tension of the return spring, though very slight contact with the body may be cured – as a temporary measure – by polishing the offending portion of the body wall with metal polish or extremely fine wet and dry paper.

15 The fit of the piston in the suction chamber can be checked by plugging the air hole in the body and assembling the piston in the chamber without its return spring, fitting the damper piston without filling the dashpot with oil. If the assembly is now turned upside down, the piston should sink to the bottom in 5 – 7 seconds. If the time is appreciably less than this, the piston and suction chamber should both be replaced since they are matched to each other.

16 Check for wear on the throttle shaft and bushes through which it passes. Apart from the nuisance of a sticking throttle, excessive wear here can cause air leaks in the induction system adversely affecting engine performance. Worn bushes can be extracted and new bushes fitted if necessary. For inspection and overhaul of the choke assembly, see Section 36.

17 Reassembly is a straightforward reversal of the dismantling process. During reassembly the float level must be checked and

Fig. 3.37 Jet and float assembly on SU HIF 6 carburettor (Sec 34)

1 Fixing screw for bi-metal assembly
2 Spring
3 Bi-metal assembly
4 Float valve retainer
5 Drilling to cold start valve

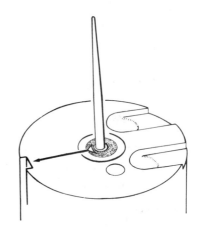

Fig. 3.38 Correct relationship of carburettor needle and retainer to piston (Sec 34)

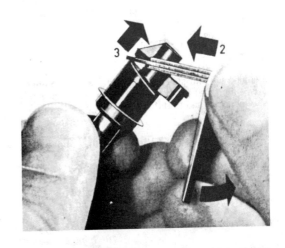

Fig. 3.39 Removing the bi-metal strip from the jet (Sec 34)

adjusted if necessary as described in Section 35. When assembling the jet, screw up the adjusting screw so that the upper edge of the jet comes level with the bridge, then turn it 2½ turns clockwise. This gives the initial position for jet adjustment. Fig. 3.37 shows the jet assembled on the bi-metallic strip in the main body, and also indicates the correct positioning of the float valve retainer on the tab on the float arm.

18 When the carburettor is assembled, the dashpot should be filled with automatic transmission fluid to within 0.25 in (6 mm) of the top of the cylinder before re-inserting the damper piston.

35 SU HIF 6 carburettor – float level setting

1 With the carburettor upside down and the float chamber cover removed, the float should be the specified distance below the carburettor body (see Fig. 3.40).
2 Adjustment is by bending the steel tag on the float arm. Do not bend the float arm itself.
Note: *Some types have a plastic tag and not a steel one, in which case no adjustment is possible, nor should it be necessary.*

36 SU HIF 6 carburettor – choke assembly

1 The choke (cold start) assembly can be seen in Figs. 3.41 and 3.42.
2 As the spindle, which also carries the fast idle cam, turns, a V-shaped slot in the spindle progressively opens a channel between the float chamber and throttle chamber. At the same time, a small air bleed channel is opened so that air is mixed with the extra fuel supplied.
3 The fast idle cam operates the throttle by acting on the adjusting screw on a lever on the throttle spindle.
4 The whole assembly can be removed from the carburettor (see Section 34, paragraph 6) for cleaning and overhaul. If the spindle or housing show signs of wear, they should be renewed. When refitting the assembly, the notch in the gasket should face upwards, and the O-ring seal should be oiled before fitting.

37 Solex (Zenith) 175 CD carburettor – general description

1 Originally known as a Stromberg, this carburettor is similar in many respects to the SU HIF 6 carburettor, being a constant depression, sidedraught type carburettor.
2 The main difference is in the suction chamber, where the piston is fixed to a rubber diaphragm, and not sealed directly against the sides of the chamber.
3 As the depression felt in the upper part of the chamber alters with engine speed and load, the piston moves up and down in response, moving the fuel metering needle which is fixed to the piston, in and out of the fuel jet.
4 The carburettor is fitted with a temperature compensator, which allows more air into the idle circuit in relation to temperature. As the compensator warms up, more air is admitted. This reduces variations in idle speed relative to temperature.
5 There is also a warm start valve, which offsets the effects of fuel vapour from the float chamber during high under-bonnet temperatures, which can lead to difficulty in starting (see Section 27).

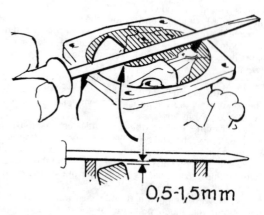

Fig. 3.40 Setting float level on SU HIF 6 carburettor (Sec 35)

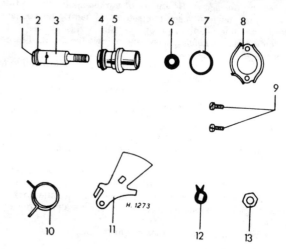

Fig. 3.41 SU HIF 6 carburettor – choke assembly (Sec 36)

1 Circlip	8 Spring retainer
2 Washer	9 Fixing screws
3 Spindle	10 Return spring
4 Rubber ring	11 Fast idle cam
5 Housing	12 Tab washer
6 Rubber seal for spindle	13 Nut
7 Gasket	

Fig. 3.42 Operation of the assembled choke (Sec 36)

A Disengaged	10 Spring retainer
B Engaged	11 Screw
1 Carburettor housing	12 Packing
2 Channel from float chamber	13 V-slot
3 Stop tab for lever	14 Valve housing
4 Channel for additional air	15 Rubber ring
5 Tab washer	16 Spindle
6 Cam for fast idle	17 Washer
7 Nut	18 Circlip
8 Sealing	19 Channel to carburettor
9 Return spring	throttle chamber

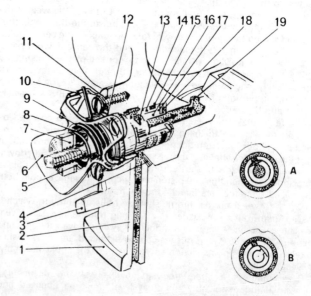

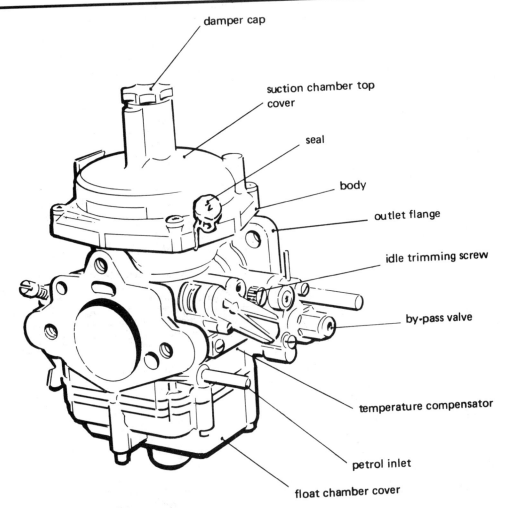

damper cap

suction chamber top cover

seal

body

outlet flange

idle trimming screw

by-pass valve

temperature compensator

petrol inlet

float chamber cover

Fig. 3.43 View of Solex (Zenith) 175 CD carburettor (Sec 37)

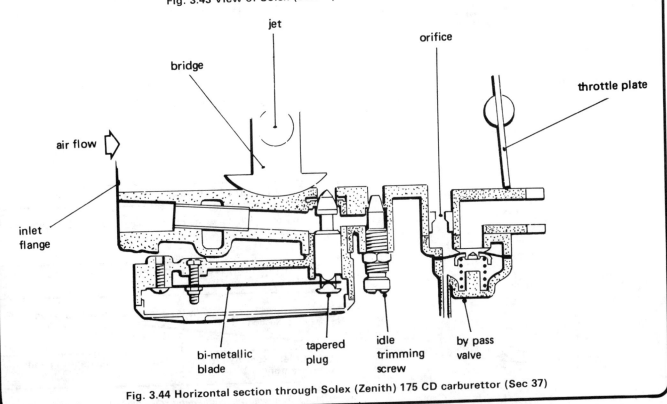

jet

bridge

orifice

throttle plate

air flow

inlet flange

bi-metallic blade

tapered plug

idle trimming screw

by pass valve

Fig. 3.44 Horizontal section through Solex (Zenith) 175 CD carburettor (Sec 37)

38 Solex (Zenith) 175 CD carburettor – idle speed and CO adjustment

Note: *Adjustment of the CO content requires the use of a special tool. If this tool is not available, the adjustment should be left to your dealer. See also Sections 3 and 4.*

Idle speed adjustment

1   The procedure is basically the same as described for the SU HIF 6 carburettor in Section 30, which should be followed, noting the following points:

(a) *Idle speed is adjusted on the throttle valve adjusting screw on models before 1977, and on later models on the idle bypass adjustment screw (Fig. 3.45).*

(b) *If the specified idle speed cannot be set on the idle bypass screw, then the throttle valve should be set and adjusted, which again is similar to the procedure for the SU carburettor.*

CO content – fine adjustment

2   The preliminary operations are as described for the SU carburettor, and the volume screw (Fig. 3.46) is used to adjust the CO content. However, only small adjustments can be made on this screw, and basic setting, or a larger adjustment, requires the use of a special tool.

CO content – basic setting

Note: *On models up to 1977, the main jet is adjusted. This requires the use of press tools, and should be done by a Volvo dealer or other specialist. On 1977-on models, the air valve metering needle is adjusted. The special tool required is readily available from most motor factors and accessory shops. One such tool is Sykes-Pickavant carburettor adjuster no 660480.*

1977-on models

3   Screw the volume control screw fully in.

4   Remove the damper piston from the suction chamber.

5   Fit the special tool, making sure the lugs on the tool engage with the air valve, or the diaphragm may be damaged when the tool is turned (Fig. 3.43).

6   Connect a CO meter in accordance with the meter manufacturer's instructions, but do not start the engine yet.

7   Adjust the CO content in the desired direction by screwing the tool in or out so moving the needle up or down. Moving the needle up increases CO content, and *vice versa*.

Note: *The full range is four turns, and if the correct CO content cannot be achieved in this manner, the needle must be reset to its basic position as described in Section 41.*

8   Remove the tool, top up the dashpot and refit the damper piston.

9   Run the engine as described in Section 31, paragraphs 1, 3 and 4.

10 Read the CO meter and try the effect of the volume control screw. If the CO content can still not be brought within limits, stop the engine and repeat the basic setting procedure from paragraph 3.

11 Re-adjust the idle speed as necessary to keep it within the specified limits during CO content adjustment.

12 When both idle speed and CO content are correct, stop the engine and disconnect the test gear.

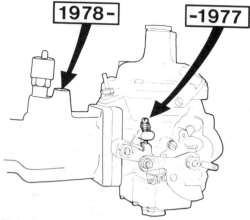

Fig. 3.45 Showing idle speed adjustment points on Solex (Zenith) carburettor (Sec 38)

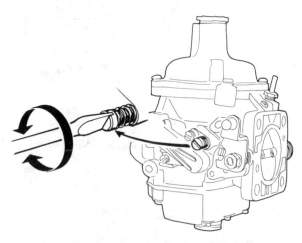

Fig. 3.46 Volume control screw on Solex (Zenith) carburettor (Sec 38)

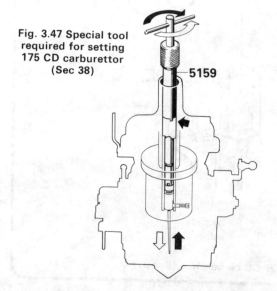

Fig. 3.47 Special tool required for setting 175 CD carburettor (Sec 38)

5159

39 Solex (Zenith) 175 CD carburettor – fast idle adjustment

1   The procedure is as described in the SU HIF 6 carburettor in Section 32.

40 Solex (Zenith) 175 CD carburettor – removal and refitting

1   The procedure is basically the same as for the SU HIF 6 carburettor. Refer to Section 33.

41 Solex (Zenith) 175 CD carburettor – dismantling and reassembly

Note: *The removal, refitting and adjustment of the metering needle in* the air valve and the main fuel jet require the use of special tools. If these tools are not available, do not disturb the needle or jet. If either of these components need renewing or adjustment and the tools are not available, the work will have to be done by your Volvo dealer. Refer also to the note at the beginning of Section 34. The diaphragm can be renewed without removing the carburettor.

1　Remove the carburettor as described in Section 40. Clean it externally and take it to a clean workbench.

2　Remove the damper piston from the suction chamber. Inspect the damper piston for scoring and wear (with the chamber filled to the correct level, there should be a fair amount of resistance felt when the damper is pushed down into the bore of the chamber). Also check the axial clearance as shown in Fig. 3.49.

3　Mark the alignment of the suction chamber cover to the carburettor body, then remove the four screws and lift off the cover.

4　Retrieve the spring, then lift out the diaphragm and air valve, being careful not to bend or damage the needle.

5　Inspect the diaphragm for perishing or splits, renewing it as a matter of course unless it is in perfect condition. It is secured to the air valve by four screws and a collar. Note the locating lug formed in the diaphragm edge which fits in the carburettor body, and ensure the new diaphragm is fitted to the air valve in the same position as the old one. If cleaning the old diaphragm, only use paraffin, not petrol or similar solvents.

6　Inspect the needle for wear, ridging, bending and ovality. The raised washer at the base of the needle should be flush with the face of the air valve. On pre-1977 models, the needle can be adjusted to bring the washer flush by undoing the grub screw in the side of the air valve and moving the needle by hand. On later models the special tool used for mixture adjustment is required.

7　If adjustment is needed on these later models, refer to Section 38, which gives the adjustment procedure for CO content, but adjust the needle so that the raised washer is flush with the air valve, which is the basic setting. The needle is then adjusted up or down to adjust the CO content as described in Section 38 when the carburettor is reassembled. Note that the metering needle designation mark is stamped on the shank of the needle.

8　The needle can be removed by removing the grub screw on pre-1977 mdels, and by also using the special tool on later models.

9　Remove the throttle valve spindle linkages, noting the position of the return springs. Only later springs are available as spares, and if a new spring is fitted to the throttle lever, then the collar on the washer should be filed down to accept the new spring.

10　Check the throttle valve spindle for wear, which can cause air leaks into the carburettor. If the spindle is worn, remove the screws from the throttle valve (the screwed ends are peened over and may need cutting off), remove the throttle valve and tap out the spindle. When refitting, use new spindle seals and centralise the throttle valve before peening over the retaining screws.

Note: The bushes in the carburettor body are made of steel and are unlikely to wear before the spindle. If the bushes are worn, the carburettor must be renewed.

11　Make a mark across the float chamber and carburettor body, then remove the screws securing the chamber to the body. Remove the float chamber and recover the gasket.

12　Tip out any fuel remaining in the float chamber and dispose of it safely. Clean out any sediment. If the plug in the float chamber on early models is removed for any reason, a new plug must be fitted. (In fact the plug will have to be removed for subsequent CO adjustment.)

13　Pull out the float pivot pin and remove the float. Shake the float to see if there is any fuel inside of it, indicating a leak, in which case renew the float.

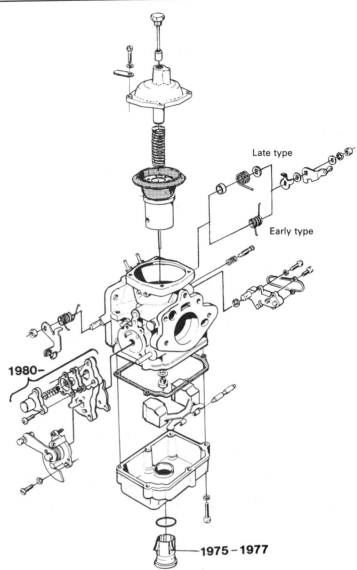

Fig. 3.48 Exploded view of Solex (Zenith) 175 CD carburettor (Sec 41)

Fig. 3.49 Damper piston axial clearance (Sec 41)

A = 0.04 to 0.07 in (1.0 to 1.8 mm)

Fig. 3.50 Locating lug (arrowed) in diaphragm edge (Sec 41)

14 Remove the float needle valve, and check that the filter mesh is clean and the needle is free to move. Clean or renew as necessary.

15 Remove the temperature compensation valve from the side of the carburettor. The valve should move under light pressure and return to its original position when released.

16 Centralise the valve after loosening screw 'B' in Fig. 3.53, tightening the screw on completion. The temperature at which the valve opens is adjusted on screw 'C', and should be as given in the Specifications.

17 Remove the choke valve and inspect the valve plates for scoring. Light marks can be removed using fine grinding paste, but make sure all paste is removed, using petrol, on completion.

18 On 1980-on models, remove the cold start vacuum valve, and inspect the diaphragm for splits. It would be as well to renew it any way, as they do stretch with age.

19 Inspect the main jet, and if it shows signs of ovality it should be renewed. This is a specialist job, requiring press tools. Have it done by a Volvo dealer or carburettor specialist.

20 Refit the float needle valve, using a new washer under it, then fit the float back to its hinge assembly.

21 Invert the carburettor, and check the float height is as specified in Fig. 3.56 with the float resting on the needle valve.

22 Adjust the float height by bending the tang which contacts the needle valve. Do not bend the float arm.

23 Assemble and refit the remaining components, which is a reversal of removal, using new gaskets and seals where fitted.

24 Check the basic setting of the throttle valve on 1978 and later models as follows. Bend the throttle lever stop so that the throttle valve is fully closed, then bend the stop to obtain the specified throttle valve opening dimension as shown in Fig. 3.30 for the SU HIF 6 carburettor.

25 Refit the carburettor as described in Section 40, then check and adjust idle speed and CO content as described in Section 38, and the fast idle speed as described in Section 39.

42 Pierburg (DVG) 175 CDUS carburettor – general description

1 The Pierburg (DVG) carburettor is similar in principle and construction to the Solex (Zenith) 175 CD carburettor.

2 The main different is in the temperature compensation of the main jet, which is achieved by using a floating jet which is spring-loaded against a bi-metallic washer. As temperature increases, the bi-metallic washer expands and moves the jet up against the spring pressure, thus weakening the mixture.

3 A manual choke (cold start device) is fitted, and from 1980 an additional vacuum valve is fitted, which gives increased control of the mixture when the choke is in operation.

4 On 1981-on B23 models, a modified damper reservoir and piston are fitted, which automatically keeps the damper fluid at the correct level, provided the reservoir is kept topped up.

43 Pierburg (DVG) 175 CDUS carburettor – idle speed and CO adjustment

Refer to Sections 3 and 4.

Idle speed

1 Disconnect the accelerator control rod from the carburettor, and check that the throttle valve and spindle operate smoothly. Reconnect the control rod.

2 Check the operation of the choke lever, ensuring that it does not contact the throttle lever stop when the control is pushed fully in, and that it opens fully when the control is pulled fully out. Push the control fully in for this adjustment.

3 Ensure the damper/reservoir fluid level is correct (Fig. 3.31 or 3.59).

4 Where fitted, disconnect the Pulsair system hose at the air cleaner, and plug the end of the hose.

5 Start the engine and allow it to reach normal operating temperature.

6 Adjust the idle speed to that specified, using the idle bypass adjustment screw.

7 If the correct idle speed cannot be achieved using the idle bypass

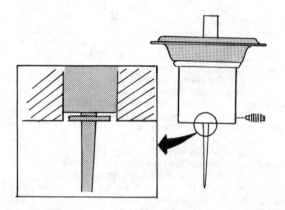

Fig. 3.51 Correct location of needle in air valve (Sec 41)

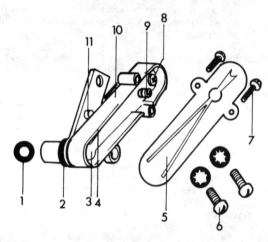

Fig. 3.52 Temperature compensation valve on Solex (Zenith) 175 CD carburettor (Sec 41)

1	Rubber seal	7 Screw for cover
2	Rubber seal	8 Cross-slotted screw
3	Valve	9 Adjustment nut
4	Bi-metal spring	10 Housing
5	Cover	11 Identity label
6	Screw for temperature compensator	

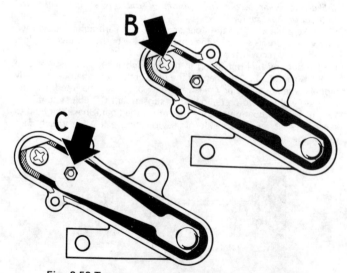

Fig. 3.53 Temperature valve adjustment (Sec 41)

B Centralising screw   C Temperature adjuster

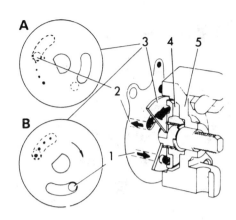

Fig. 3.54 Choke valve assembly Solex (Zenith) 175 CD
carburettor (Sec 41)

A   Choke 'off'   3   Pierced disc
B   Choke 'on'   4   Channel disc
1   Passage from float chamber   5   Housing
2   Passage to throttle chamber

Fig. 3.56 Float level on Solex (Zenith) 175 CD carburettor
(Sec 41)

A = 0.350 to 0.510 in (9.0 to 13.0 mm)
B = 0.590 to 0.670 in (15.0 to 17.0 mm)

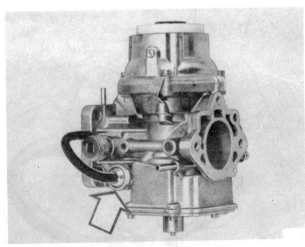

Fig. 3.57 Cold start vacuum valve Pierburg carburettor
(Sec 42)

Fig. 3.55 Cold start vacuum valve fitted to 1980-on
models (Sec 41)

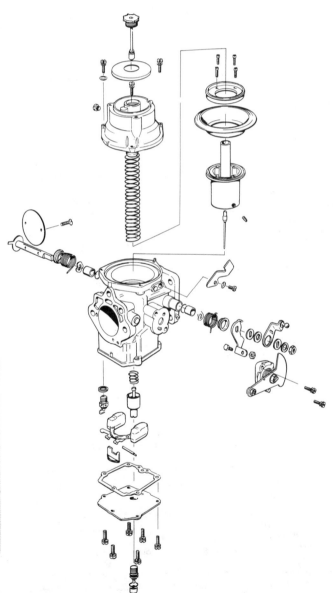

Fig. 3.58 Exploded view of Pierburg (DVG) 175 CDUS
carburettor (Sec 42)

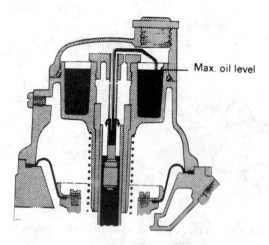

Fig. 3.59 Sectional view of modified damper reservoir (Sec 42)

Fig. 3.60 Adjusting idle speed on Pierburg (DVG) carburettor (Sec 43)

screw, check the basic setting of the throttle valve as described in Section 47.

CO content

8   CO content is adjusted on the sealed screw on the underside of the carburettor. The sealing plug can be prised out and a new one fitted on completion, but see Section 3.

9   Prepare the engine as described in paragraphs 1 to 5, and connect up a CO meter in accordance with the meter manufacturer's instructions.

10 Adjust the CO content to the specified value. Turning the screw to raise the jet reduces CO content, and turning it to lower the jet increases CO content.

11 With the engine still running, reconnect the Pulsair hose (having removed the plug). The CO content should drop when the hose is connected, showing that the system is working, and the CO content should not be re-adjusted.

12 Check and adjust idle speed as described earlier, re-check CO content from paragraph 9. When both adjustments are correct, stop the engine and remove the test equipment. Fit a new tamperproof plug if necessary.

44 Pierburg (DVG) 175 CDUS carburettor – fast idle adjustment

1   Adjustment of the fast idle is as described in Section 39 for the Solex (Zenith) 175 CD carburettor.

45 Pierburg (DVG) 175 CDUS carburettor – removal and refitting

1   Removal and refitting is basically as described for the earlier type carburettors, noting the following points:

(a) An insulation flange is fitted between the carburettor and the inlet manifold on some 1979-80 models without the warm start valve.

(b) The warm start valve is fitted to 1980-on models (see Section 27).

(c) There are two types of float chamber cover, the later types identified by the cast strengthening webs. If an early type air filter duct (without a recess in its rear edge) is being fitted with a later type float chamber cover, two gaskets should be used between the carburettor and air filter duct.

(d) The gasket between the carburettor and manifold should be fitted with the 'humps' at the top and bottom.

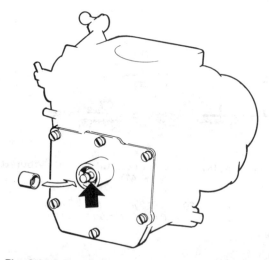

Fig. 3.61 CO (mixture) screw on Pierburg (DVG) carburettor (Sec 43)

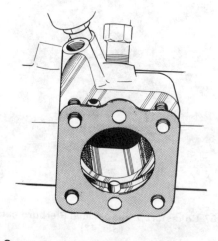

Fig. 3.62 Correctly fitted carburettor flange gasket (Sec 45)

46 Pierburg (DVG) 175 CDUS carburettor – dismantling and reassembly

Refer to the notes at the beginning of Section 34.

1   Remove the carburettor as described in Section 45, then clean down the outside in solvent to remove all grime.

2   Remove the damper piston from the top of the carburettor. On B23 models, this means removing the top cover from the reservoir first and disconnecting the oil suction tube. Do not lose the retaining spring.

3   Remove the screws from the suction chamber cover, lift off the cover and retrieve the spring.

4   Lift out the diaphragm, air valve and fuel metering needle, being careful not to damage or bend the needle.

5   Check the throttle valve and spindle for smooth operation.

6   If the spindle is loose in the bushes, renew the spindle and seals, which is a similar procedure to that described for earlier carburettors, with reference to Fig. 3.63. Note the assembly marks on the throttle valve, which should face towards the inlet side of the carburettor.

7   Check the throttle valve basic setting by bending the tang on the throttle lever so that the valve is fully closed.

8   Now bend the tang to give the specified opening (see Fig. 3.30, the dimensions are the same).

9   Remove the float chamber cover.

10 Pull out the float lever spindle and remove the float, unhooking the spring as you do so.

11 Shake the float to see if there is any fuel inside, indicating a leak, and renew if necessary.

12 Check the float valve for free movement. If it is sticky, remove it from the carburettor and clean it in solvent, or renew the valve. Use a new sealing washer under the valve when refitting.

13 Refit the float assembly and spindle, and ensure the spring is fitted between the float and the float valve.

14 Check the float level setting by tilting the carburettor on its side, ten degrees or so from the vertical, so that the float is hanging down under its own weight (Fig. 3.65).

15 The plastic bracket should be depressed and the ball of the float valve should not be pressed into the valve during the measurement. Adjust if necessary by bending the metal tongue which bears on the valve.

16 Check the main jet for wear (ovality) and renew as necessary.

17 The jet and bi-metallic washers are renewed as a complete assembly, and pull out of the carburettor bridge. Do not lose the return spring, and fit it into the bridge before refitting the jet assembly.

18 Basic setting of the jet is done after the float chamber cover is refitted by screwing in the jet adjusting screw until the jet is the specified depth below the face of the bridge (Fig. 3.66).

19 Check that the outer part of the damper cylinder is a tight fit in the suction chamber cover.

20 Also check that the lower edge of the inner part of the damper cylinder is flush with the underside of the air valve piston face. This can be adjusted by gently tapping the cylinder with a soft drift and hammer.

21 Check the diaphragm for splits and perishing, and renew as necessary. It is secured to the air valve by screws and a collar. (Renew the diaphragm as a matter of course at time of overhaul.)

22 Take note of the relationship of the lug on the diaphragm rim, which locates in the rim of the carburettor body, and fit the new diaphragm to the air valve in the same position.

23 Check the metering needle for wear, ridging, bending and ovality, and renew as necessary.

24 The needle is secured in the air valve by a grub screw. When refitting, the flat side of the needle retainer faces the grub screw, and the collar of the needle should be level with the air valve face. The needle designation is stamped on the needle shank.

25 Fit the needle, air valve and diaphragm assembly back to the carburettor, ensuring the locating lug fits into the recess in the carburettor rim. Make sure the needle fits into the jet, and do not force the air valve down.

26 Fit the spring and suction chamber cover, noting the cast alignment marks on the cover and carburettor.

27 After tightening the securing screws, check that the air valve falls freely under its own weight and strikes the bridge with an audible metallic click.

28 If it does not, check the alignment of the needle and jet.

29 On 1980-on models with a vacuum valve, check the condition of the hose between the carburettor flange and the valve. It should be renewed if it shows signs of deterioration.

30 Disconnect the hose from the carburettor flange, and suck through it to check if the valve is functioning. The valve must pass air when suction is applied. If it does not, renew it by unscrewing it from the carburettor and refitting a new valve.

31 Check the choke linkage and cold start valve assembly, which is as described for earlier carburettor types.

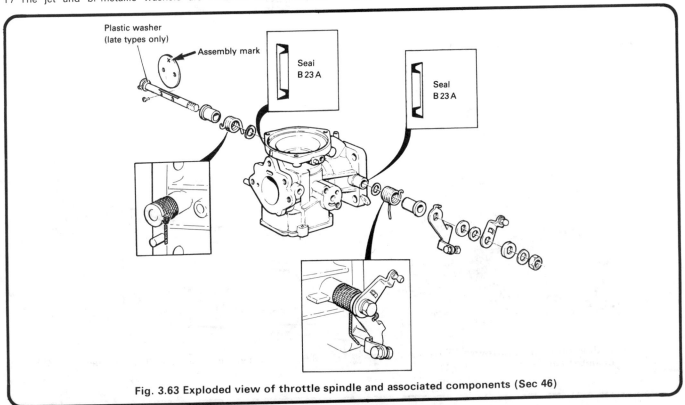

Fig. 3.63 Exploded view of throttle spindle and associated components (Sec 46)

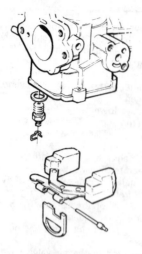

Fig. 3.64 Float assembly (Sec 46)

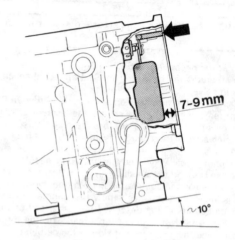

Fig. 3.65 Checking float level on Pierburg (DVG) carburettor (Sec 46)

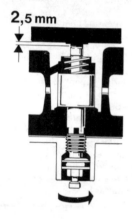

Fig. 3.66 Basic setting of jet (Sec 46)

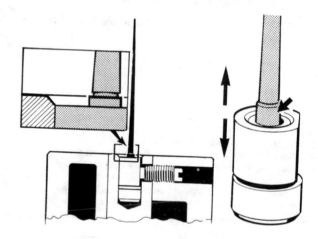

Fig. 3.67 Location of needle in air valve (Sec 46)

Fig. 3.68 Alignment marks (arrowed) between suction chamber and carburettor body (Sec 46)

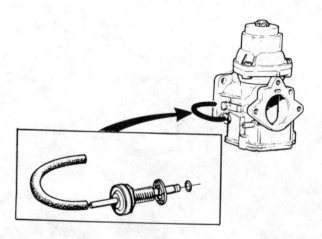

Fig. 3.69 Vacuum valve fitted to 1980-on models (Sec 46)

32 Check the axial play of the damper piston, also as described for earlier carburettors (Fig. 3.49). The dimension required for this carburettor is 0.02 to 0.06 in (0.5 to 1.5 mm).

33 The remaining reassembly procedure is a reversal of dismantling, using new gaskets and seals where these are fitted.

34 On B21 types, fill the damper cylinder with the specified fluid to within $1/4$ in (6.0 mm) of the top of the cylinder.

35 On B23 types, refit the damper, then push in the fluid suction tube, which should face forwards. Do not forget the retaining spring. Fit the reservoir cover and fill the reservoir with the specified fluid.

36 Refit the carburettor as described in Section 45.

37 Check and adjust the accelerator cable (Section 59), and check and adjust the idle speed, CO content and fast idle speed as described in Sections 43 and 44.

47 Pierburg (DVG) 175 CDUS carburettor – throttle valve basic setting

1 The idle speed/CO content cannot be set correctly as described in Section 43, or the engine tends to run-on after being switched off, the basic setting of the throttle valve should be checked and adjusted as follows.

2 Run the engine until it reaches normal operating temperature.

3 Screw in the idle bypass valve adjustment screw gently until it bottoms.

4 Now turn the screw out by four complete turns.

5 Adjust engine speed to 1100 to 1200 rpm by bending the lug on the throttle lever.

6 Re-adjust engine idle speed to the specified value, using the idle bypass screw.

7 Check and adjust CO content as necessary.

48 Solex Cisac (B200K) carburettor – general description

1 Fitted to B200K engines, the Solex Cisac carburettor is a fixed-jet, twin-barrel, downdraught type.

2 An idling solenoid valve is fitted to the carburettor to shut off fuel supply when the ignition is turned off, preventing engine run-on.

3 The primary and secondary throttle valves are preset in the factory, and should not be adjusted in service.

4 The carburettor also incorporates a part-load enrichment valve, an accelerator pump, and a vacuum-operated choke control valve (although the choke operation is still manual).

5 The idling channels in the carburettor are heated by an electric thermistor plate in the base of the carburettor.

49 Solex Cisac (B200K) carburettor – idle and CO adjustment

Refer to Sections 3 and 4.

1 Remove the air inlet duct from the top of the carburettor.

2 Check that the throttle valves operate smoothly, and that the secondary valve does not start to move until the primary valve is $2/3$ open.

3 Check and adjust the accelerator cable as described in Section 59.

4 Check and adjust the operation of the choke as described in Section 50.

5 Check and adjust the fast idle cam as described in Section 51.

6 Refit the air cleaner duct, and ensure that all crankcase ventilation hoses are connected correctly. Disconnect and plug the Pulsair hoses, when applicable.

7 Connect a tachometer and CO meter to the engine, in accordance with the meter manufacturer's instructions.

8 Start the engine and allow it to reach normal operating temperature.

9 Adjust the idle speed to the specified value with the idling (volume) control screw.

10 Check the CO content. If adjustment is required, prise out the plug from the CO adjustment screw (see also Section 3).

11 Adjust the CO content to that specified by screwing in to decrease

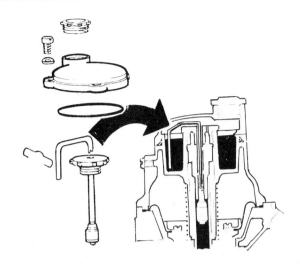

Fig. 3.70 Damper reservoir and oil suction tube assembly (Sec 46)

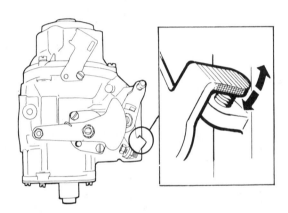

Fig. 3.71 Adjusting throttle valve basic setting on Pierburg (DVG) carburettor (Sec 47)

CO, and out to increase. Re-adjust the idle speed if necessary, and repeat until both idle speed and CO content are as specified.

12 On completion, stop the engine, fit a new tamperproof plug to the screw and remove the test equipment. Unplug and re-connect the Pulsair hoses, when applicable.

Note: *If no CO meter is available, a reasonable setting can be achieved by turning the adjuster screw in until the idle speed becomes erratic, then screwing the adjuster out until the idle becomes smooth. It may now be necessary to adjust the idle speed, and this setting should be regarded as a temporary measure until the CO content can be adjusted by your dealer. This should be done at the earliest opportunity.*

50 Solex Cisac (B200K) carburettor – choke adjustment

1 Remove the air inlet duct from the top of the carburettor. Check that, with the choke pushed fully in, there is no slackness in the operating cable.

2 Tighten the cable by loosening the cable clamp bolt in the choke lever, pulling the cable tight and then tightening the clamp bolt. The cable must not be so tight as to pull the choke lever off its stop – just take up any slack.

3 Check for smooth operation of the choke linkage, and that the secondary throttle valve is disengaged when the choke control is pulled fully out. (The bottom of the choke lever on the carburettor strikes against a latch, which disengages the throttle valve.)

4 Check the operation of the choke vacuum valve by pulling out the

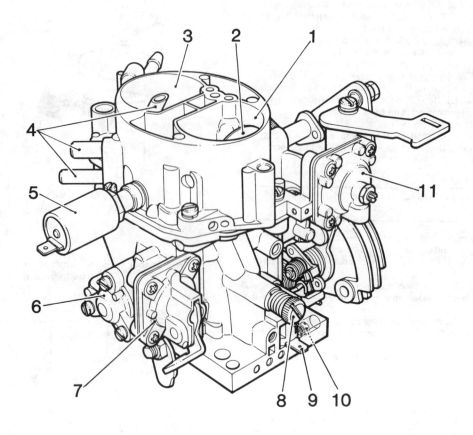

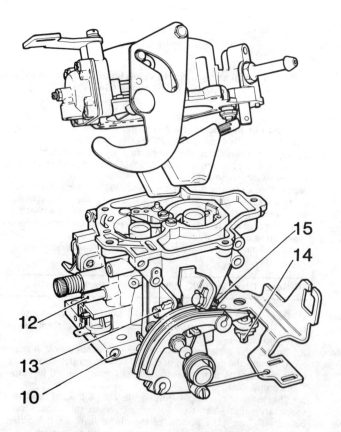

Fig. 3.72 Exploded view of Solex Cisac carburettor (Sec 48)

1   Primary barrel
2   Choke (cold start) flap
3   Secondary choke
4   Float chamber vents
5   Fuel cut-off solenoid
6   Part load enrichment device
7   Accelerator pump
8   Idle speed screw
9   Thermistor heater for idling channels
10 CO (mixture) screw
11 Choke control vacuum unit
12 Vacuum take-off (distributor advance)
13 Primary throttle valve adjustment screw
14 Secondary throttle valve adjustment screw
15 Fast idle adjustment screw

Note: 13 and 14 should not be adjusted in service

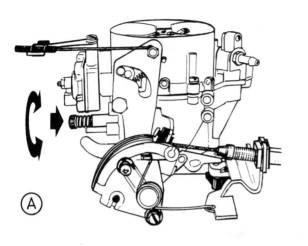 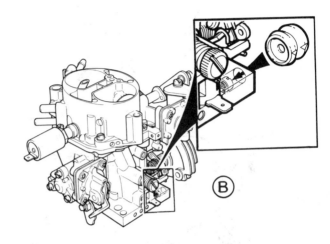

Fig. 3.73 Idle speed adjustment screw (A) and CO adjustment screw (B) – Solex Cisac carburettor (Sec 49)

choke control to fully close the choke flap.

5   Push the vacuum unit pullrod right in until it bottoms. Make sure the rod is not at an angle, or the reading will be false.

6   The gap between the carburettor wall and the top edge of the choke flap should be as shown in Fig. 3.74. It can be checked by using a suitable size of drill.

7   Adjust the gap by loosening the locknut on the adjuster and turning the screw in or out to obtain the specified gap. Tighten the locknut on completion.

8   Check the fast idle adjustment (Section 51), then refit the air inlet duct.

51 Solex Cisac (B200K) carburettor – fast idle adjustment

1   With the choke control pushed fully in, the gap between the fast idle adjustment screw and the choke lever cam should be as specified in Fig. 3.75.

2   Adjust the gap by loosening the locknut and turning the screw in or out. Tighten the locknut on completion.

52 Solex Cisac (B200K) carburettor idling cut-off solenoid valve – testing

1   The valve can be tested for correct operation by switching the ignition on and off. A clicking sound should be heard from the valve with each operation of the switch.

2   Indications of a faulty valve are:

   (a) If the valve does not open, the engine will stall at idle.
   (b) If the valve fails to close, the engine may run-on after the ignition is switched off.

3   Removing and refitting of the valve are covered in Section 54.

53 Solex Cisac (B200K) carburettor – removal and refitting

1   Disconnect the battery negative terminal.

2   Remove the air inlet duct from the carburettor.

3   Disconnect the fuel and ventilation hoses.

4   Disconnect the throttle and choke control cables.

5   Disconnect the idling solenoid and idling channel heater leads.

6   Remove the four securing nuts, and lift the carburettor from the manifold.

7   Refit in reverse order, using a new gasket on either side of the insulation flange, and ensure the crankcase ventilation and warm start hoses are connected correctly, or performance will be affected.

8   Check and adjust the accelerator and choke control cables as described in Sections 50 and 59.

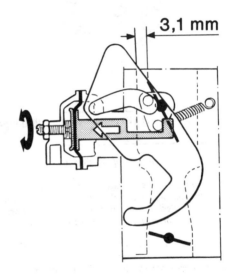

Fig. 3.74 Choke vacuum control adjustment diagram for Solex Cisac carburettor (Sec 50)

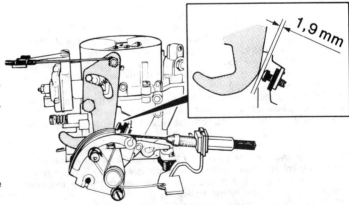

Fig. 3.75 Fast idle adjustment on Solex Cisac carburettor (Sec 51)

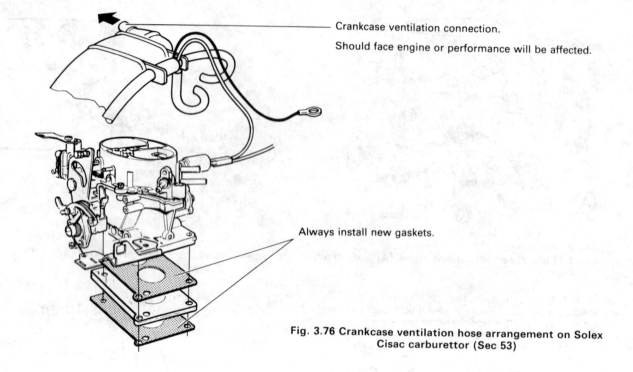

Crankcase ventilation connection.

Should face engine or performance will be affected.

Always install new gaskets.

Fig. 3.76 Crankcase ventilation hose arrangement on Solex
Cisac carburettor (Sec 53)

54 Solex Cisac carburettor (B200K) – dismantling and reassembly

Refer to the note at the beginning of Section 34.

Note: *Both the primary and secondary throttle valves are preset in the factory, and should not be adjusted in service. Do not remove the throttle valves or spindles. If wear is suspected in this area (which should only be evident after very high mileage), consult your Volvo dealer.*

1   Remove the carburettor as described in Section 53, and wash down the exterior surfaces in solvent.
2   Remove the screws from the top cover and lift off the cover and float assembly.
3   Extract the float hinge pin and remove the float.
4   Shake the float to see if there is any fuel inside, indicating a leak, and renew as necessary.
5   Remove the idling solenoid valve from the side of the carburettor. It should only be screwed in finger-tight.
6   Check that the fuel inlet valve (float valve) is free to move and not sticking. Renew the valve, or remove it and clean it in clean petrol. Use a new washer under the valve when refitting.
7   Note that there is a filter screen in the inlet pipe union. Remove the union and take out the filter. Clean the filter in petrol. Partial blockage of this filter will cause poor performance at full throttle.
8   Remove the cover from the choke pull-down vacuum unit (do not lose the spring), and inspect the diaphragm for splits. Renew as necessary before refitting the unit.
9   If the choke lever is removed for any reason, do not lose the ball and spring fitted beneath it, and refit them before fitting the lever.
10 If the choke flap is removed, the screws should be refitted using thread-locking fluid.
11 Tip out any fuel remaining in the float chamber and dispose of it safely. Remove the jets (one at a time to avoid mixing), and blow through them and their channels using compressed air. Do not probe the jets with wire. Use a bristle from a nylon brush to clear stubborn blockages, or soak the jets in a cleaning solvent.
12 If the idle (volume) screw and CO content adjusting screws are removed, on refitting them they should be adjusted as follows. Screw both screws in until they bottom, then screw the idle screw out 5 full turns, and screw the CO content screw out 8 full turns. This is a basic setting, both screws being re-adjusted when the carburettor is refitted.

13 Remove the covers from the accelerator pump and part-load enrichment valve, retrieving their springs, and inspect the diaphragms for splitting. Renew as necessary.
14 Clean the mating faces of the cover and carburettor body, making sure no traces of gasket are left sticking to them.
15 Check that all linkages are working smoothly, and apply a little engine oil to the pivot points.
16 Assemble the float to the top cover, fit a new cover gasket, and check the float level by inverting the cover and measuring the distance between the face of the gasket and the high point of the float, which should be as shown in Fig. 3.78.
17 Adjust by bending the lug which contacts the float valve needle.
18 Fit the top cover and float assembly to the carburettor body and tighten the securing screws.
19 Fit the idle solenoid valve, srewing it in finger-tight only.
20 Refit the carburettor as described in Section 53, then check and adjust the choke and throttle cables, idle speed CO content, and the fast idle speed, with reference to the relevant Sections.

55 Solex Cisac (B200K) carburettor idling channel heater – testing

1   This is a thermistor type heating element which keeps the idling channels warm to prevent icing.
2   To check the operation of the device, an ammeter will be required. Switch on the ignition, connect the ammeter between the connector plug and the thermistor (Fig. 3.79).
3   At 68°F (20°C) the ammeter should read 1 amp. As the thermistor warms up, the reading should drop. If there is no initial reading, withdraw the thermistor retaining roll pin and cap, and thoroughly clean all contact surfaces. If there is still no reading, use a test lamp or voltmeter to verify the presence of supply voltage at the connector.

56 Solex Cisac (B230K) carburettor – general description

1   The Solex Cisac carburettor fitted to B230K engines is a slightly modified version of that fitted to B200K engines.
2   The choke control valve is vacuum-operated, opening in two

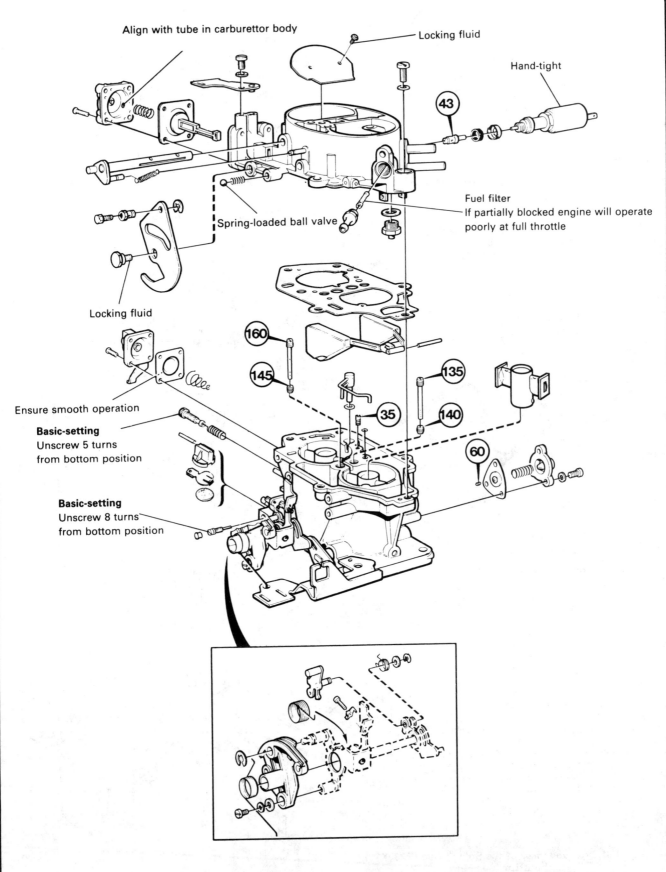

Align with tube in carburettor body

Locking fluid

Hand-tight

43

Fuel filter
If partially blocked engine will operate
poorly at full throttle

Spring-loaded ball valve

Locking fluid

Ensure smooth operation

Basic-setting
Unscrew 5 turns
from bottom position

Basic-setting
Unscrew 8 turns
from bottom position

160

145

135

35

140

60

Fig. 3.77 Exploded view of Solex Cisac (B200K) carburettor (Sec 54)

Circled numbers indicate jet sizes

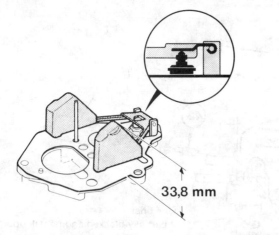

33,8 mm

Fig. 3.78 Float level setting for Solex Cisac
carburettor (Sec 54)

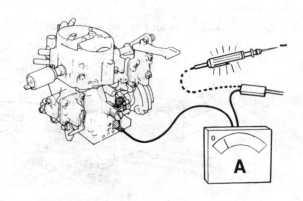

Fig. 3.79 Idle channel heater test circuit (Sec 55)

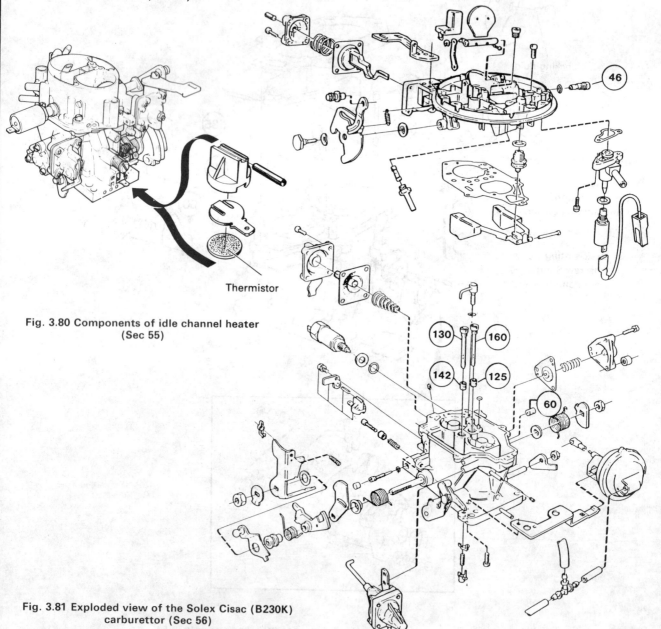

Thermistor

Fig. 3.80 Components of idle channel heater
(Sec 55)

Fig. 3.81 Exploded view of the Solex Cisac (B230K)
carburettor (Sec 56)

Jet sizes shown (circled)

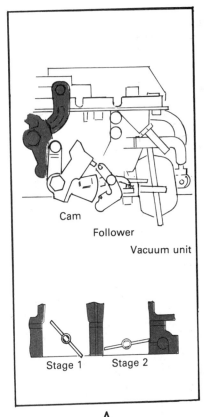

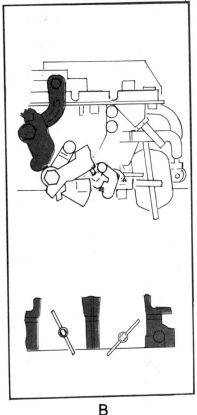

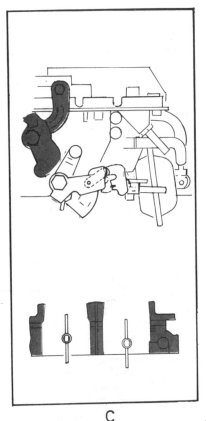

A   B   C

Fig. 3.82 Vacuum-operated second stage throttle – Solex Cisac (B230K) carburettor (Sec 56)

A   Closed   *B   Partly open*   *C   Fully open*

stages in response to the vacuum in the inlet manifold.
3   The throttle is modified to reduce spring force. The idle speed adjustment screw acts directly on the throttle linkage.
4   An electro-magnetic hot start valve, wired through the ignition switch, operates as follows:

  (a) *When the ignition is switched off, the valve opens the float chamber vent to atmosphere.*
  (b) *When the ignition is switched on, the valve closes the float chamber vent.*
  (c) *When the starter motor is energised, the valve opens the float chamber vent.*

5   A fuel cut-off valve reduces fuel consumption by cutting the idle circuit fuel supply when decelerating from engine speeds above 1350 rpm. A micro-switch, mounted on the throttle control pulley, operates the cut-off solenoid valve control unit, interrupting fuel supply during these conditions. The solenoid re-opens when engine speed drops below 1350 rpm, or the accelerator pedal is depressed. The solenoid valve also acts as a fuel cut-off valve when the ignition is switched off, preventing run-on.
6   The accelerator jet is only fitted to stage one, since stage two is isolated during moderate acceleration.
7   The second stage throttle valve is operated by vacuum, engine speed and load determining its opening.
8   No specific adjustment or overhaul data were available at the time of writing.

57 Accelerator pedal – removal and refitting

Note: *Refer to Section 60 for cruise control components.*
1   Remove the cover box from the top of the pedal.
2   Disconnect the accelerator pedal from the top of the pedal by extracting the split pin and removing the pin.
3   Remove the bolts from the pivot point brackets and lift the pedal away.
4   Refit in reverse order, and check and adjust the accelerator cable as described in Section 59.

58 Accelerator cable – removal and refitting

1   Disconnect the link rod between the throttle lever and the throttle pulley (not on Solex Cisac types).
2   Loosen the cable adjuster until the cable eye end can be removed from the pulley.
3   Pull out the locking clip and release the cable adjuster from the bracket. On some types, the adjuster locknuts will have to be completely undone (photo).
4   Disconnect the cable attachment point at the top of the accelerator

58.3 Disconnecting the accelerator cable adjuster

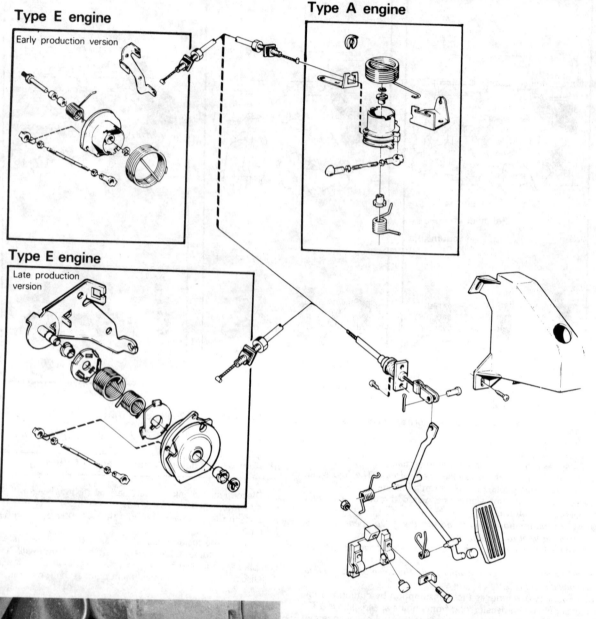

Type E engine

Early production version

Type A engine

Type E engine

Late production version

Fig. 3.83 Accelerator pedal and throttle control components
(Secs 57 and 58)

58.5 Accelerator cable housing on engine bulkhead being removed

pedal. This is secured by a split pin and clevis pin. It will be necessary to remove the pedal cover box for access.

5   Remove the two screws from the cable housing where the cable passes through the engine bulkhead (photo).

6   Withdraw the cable from the interior into the engine bay.

7   Fitting a new cable is a reversal of removal, adjusting the cable and link rod as described in Section 59 on completion.

59 Accelerator cable and link rod – adjustment

Note: *See also Chapter 6 for automatic transmission kickdown cable, and Section 65 for fuel injection system, if applicable.*

SU HIF 6 carburettor

1   Disconnect the carburettor-to-throttle pulley link rod.

2 Check that the throttle valve and linkage moves freely without binding.

3 Check the pulley return spring is in the correct position for manual or automatic transmission (Fig. 3.84).

4 Loosen the accelerator cable adjuster, and check that when turned against the spring and then released, the pulley springs back against the stop.

5 Now tighten the cable adjuster until the accelerator cable is tight, but the pulley still contacts the stop when released.

6 Check that the pulley contacts the opposite stop when the accelerator pedal is fully depressed.

7 Reconnect the link rod, and adjust its length by undoing the locknuts on the balljoint ends, and turning the rod so that the clearance shown in Fig. 3.85 on the throttle lever is obtained.

8 Tighten the locknuts on completion.

Solex (Zenith) 175 CD carburettor

9 The procedure is the same, but the throttle lever arrangement is different (Fig. 3.85).

Pierburg (DVG) 175 CDUS carburettor

10 The procedure is as described for the SU HIF 6 carburettor but again the throttle lever arrangement is different (Fig. 3.86).

Solex Cisac carburettor

11 The procedure is similar, but there is no throttle pulley or link rod.

12 Adjust the cable so that the throttle quadrant contacts both the closed and open stops, with the cable just taut when the pedal is released.

---

60 Choke cable – removal, refitting and adjustment

No specific procedures exist for choke cable removal and refitting. The following paragraphs are intended as a general guide.

1 Disconnect the battery negative lead.

2 If necessary remove the air cleaner or air inlet duct for access.

3 Disconnect the choke cable inner and outer from the fastenings on the carburettor.

4 Inside the car, free the choke control from the facia, removing trim as necessary for access. Disconnect the warning light switch wires (when applicable).

5 Pull the choke cable into the car, and remove it with the control.

6 Refit by reversing the removal operations, adjusting the cable as follows.

7 Adjust the relative positions of the cable inner and outer at the carburettor end, so that with the control pushed home and the choke operating lever fully off, there is barely perceptible slack in the cable inner. Tighten the cable fastenings in this position.

8 Have an assistant operate the choke control, and check that the operating lever moves over its full range.

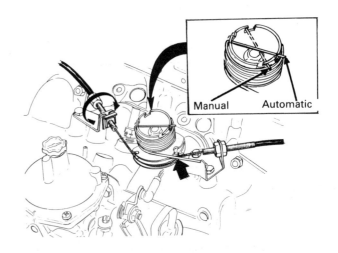

Fig. 3.84 Location of pulley return spring on manual and automatic versions (Sec 59)

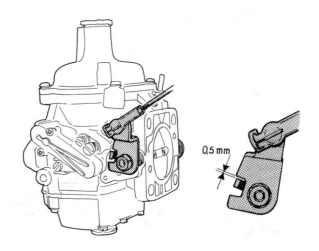

Fig. 3.85 Throttle lever clearance – Solex/Zenith 175 CD shown (Sec 59)

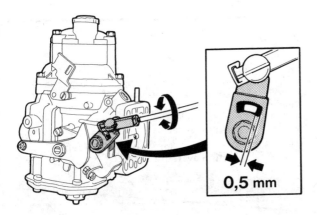

Fig. 3.86 Throttle lever clearance – Pierburg (DVG) carburettor (Sec 59)

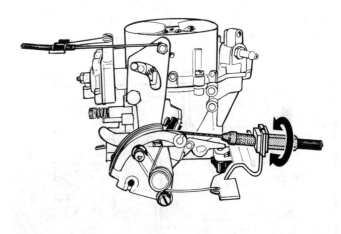

Fig. 3.87 Adjusting the accelerator cable on the Solex Cisac carburettor (Sec 59)

61 Fault diagnosis – carburettor engines

Note: *High fuel consumption and poor performance are not necessarily due to carburettor faults. Make sure that the ignition system is properly adjusted, that the brakes are not binding and that the engine is in good mechanical condition before tampering with the carburettor.*

Symptom	Reason(s)
Smell of petrol when engine is stopped	Leaking pipes or unions Leaking fuel tank
Smell of petrol when engine is idling	Leaking fuel lines or unions between pump and carburettor Overflow of fuel from float chamber due to wrong level setting, ineffective needle valve or punctured float
Excessive fuel consumption for reasons not covered by leaks or float chamber faults	Worn needle and/or jet Sticking needle or piston Brakes binding Inappropriate driving habits or adverse conditions
Difficult starting, uneven running, lack of power, cutting out	Blockages in carburettor Float chamber fuel level too low or needle valve sticking Fuel pump not delivering sufficient fuel Split or cracked diaphragm in suction chamber (when applicable) Intake manifold gaskets leaking or manifold fractured
Difficulty in starting not associated with faults already given	Over-rich mixture entering cylinders as a result of too much use of choke control or depressing the accelerator pedal when starting
Engine does not respond properly to throttle pedal	Sticking piston or needle Damper piston not working properly Fluid level in dashpot low
Engine idling speed drops markedly after a long period of idling (in warm weather especially)	Defective temperature compensator (when applicable) Hot start valve sticking in run position
Engine does not take up proper idling speed when throttle released	Sticking controls Defective bypass valve

62 Fuel injection system – general description

The fuel injection system used in the 240 series is a continuous injection (CI) system, mechanically operated, with one injector per cylinder, in which the injectors spray fuel continuously while the engine is running.

The fuel supply is regulated by continually measuring the air volume entering the engine and matching the fuel to it.

The components and their functions are as follows:

Air flow sensor – Measures the volume of air entering the engine, and is integral with the fuel distributor. Sensor plate movement is determined by incoming air working against fuel control pressure. Thus a change in fuel pressure will affect the movement of the plate.

Fuel distributor – Controls and distributes the fuel to the injectors. A pressure regulator controls both line and rest pressures. In 1978, a new distributor was introduced, which blocks off the fuel return line when the engine is switched off. The fuel distributor incorporates a plunger, which is in contact with the airflow sensor arm, and rises and falls with it according to airflow. This movement is used to regulate the fuel supply. The fuel distributor and airflow sensor together are sometimes known as the control unit.

Tank pump – Introduced in 1977, although it may be found fitted to earlier models. The pump supplies fuel to the main fuel pump, preventing cavitation, and incorporates a non-return valve.

Main fuel pump – Provides the main fuel pressure to the system. It incorporates a non-return valve to maintain pressure (rest pressure) in the system when the engine is not running.

Fuel accumulator – damps out fuel pump pulses, and also helps retain rest pressure.

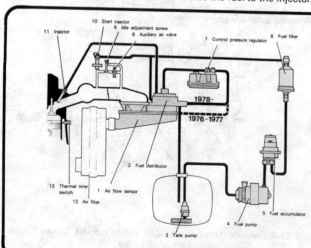

Fig. 3.88 Schematic diagram of the CI fuel injection system (Sec 62)

10 Start injector
9 Idle adjustment screw
8 Auxiliary air valve
11 Injector
7 Control pressure regulator
6 Fuel filter
1978-
1976-1977
2 Fuel distributor
12 Thermal time switch
1 Air flow sensor
13 Air filter
3 Tank pump
4 Fuel pump
5 Fuel accumulator

Fuel filter – Installed in-line between the pump and the control unit. Its paper element traps foreign deposits in the fuel.

Control pressure regulator – Regulates fuel/air mixture during cold start conditions and during engine warm-up period. The regulator lowers fuel pressure during the above engine conditions, creating a richer mixture by allowing greater deflection of the airflow sensor plate.

Auxiliary air valve – Provides additional air for fast idle during cold start and warm-up.

Idle adjustment screw – Controls idle speed by increasing or decreasing airflow in a bypass around the throttle valve.

Cold start injector – Supplies extra fuel during cold start conditions. It is controlled by a thermal time switch, screwed into the cylinder head.

Injectors – Atomise the injected fuel.

63 CI system – idle speed and CO adjustment

Refer to Sections 3 and 4.

Idle speed

1   Run the engine until it has reached normal operating temperature. Connect a tachometer (rev counter) in accordance with the meter manufacturer's instructions.

2   Adjust the idle speed to that specified by turning the idle screw in or out as necessary (photo).

63.2 Idle speed adjustment screw (arrowed)

3   If the specified idle cannot be achieved on the idle screw, check the airflow sensor plate, as described in Section 70.

CO content

Note: *An Allen key is used to adjust the CO content and this Allen key*

must not be left in position on the adjuster screw between adjustments, or damage to the airflow sensor plate may result.

4   The engine should be at normal operating temperature, and a CO meter connected in accordance with the meter manufacturer's instructions. Disconnect and plug the Pulsair hoses, when so equipped. Rev the engine briefly.

5   Check and record the CO level and compare it with that specified.

6   If adjustment is required, remove the plug covering the adjustment screw (see also Section 3) and turn the screw clockwise to increase the CO content and anti-clockwise to reduce CO content (photo). Remove the Allen key and rev the engine before taking another CO reading.

7   Re-adjust the idle speed if necessary. Carry on until both idle speed and CO content are correct.

8   On completion, fit a new plug to the adjuster screw orifice and remove all test equipment.

64 Fuel filter – renewal

1   The in-line fuel filter is mounted on the engine bulkhead (photo). It may be on the left- or right-hand side depending on model year.

2   The filter should be renewed at the intervals given in the *Routine maintenance* Section at the beginning of this Manual.

3   To renew the filter, first disconnect the battery negative terminal. Take appropriate fire precautions, and ensure adequate ventilation.

4   Clean around the filter unions. Disconnect the pipelines to the filter, being prepared for fuel spray and spillage, and use two spanners, one to hold the filter and one to undo the pipeline union.

5   Pull the filter from its housing. The filter is of the disposable cartridge type, dispose of the old cartridge carefully.

6   Fitting a new filter cartridge is a reversal of the removal procedure. Observe the arrows on the filter cartridge showing the direction of fuel flow.

7   Run the engine and check that there are no leaks from the filter unions.

65 CI system accelerator cable and linkage – adjustment

Note: *See also Chapter 6 for automatic transmission kickdown cable.*

1   Disconnect the throttle lever-to-pulley link rod by snapping back the tab and pulling the ball end from the socket on the throttle lever (photo).

2   Check that the throttle pulley moves freely and contacts both steps.

3   Tighten or loosen the accelerator cable adjuster if necessary until the cable is taut without pulling the pulley from the closed stop. Have an assistant depress the accelerator pedal fully, and check that the full-open stop makes contact.

4   Adjust the link rod length to fit between the pulley and throttle lever without disturbing the setting of either.

65.1 Accelerator control linkage
1   Accelerator cable adjuster
2   Throttle pulley
3   Closed stop
4   Full-open stop
5   Link rod
6   Throttle lever stop and adjuster screw

63.6 CO adjustment screw (air intake trunking removed for clarity)

64.1 In-line fuel filter in the engine bay

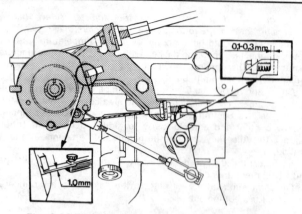

Fig. 3.89 Throttle pulley adjustment (Sec 65)

5   Refit the link rod. Refer to Fig. 3.89. Insert a feeler blade 0.04 in (1 mm) thick between the closed stop and the stop lug. Measure the clearance between the throttle lever stop and the adjuster screw: it should be 0.004 to 0.012 in (0.1 to 0.3 mm). Turn the adjuster screw if necessary until the clearance is correct, then remove the feeler blade.

66 CI System components – removal and refitting

1   Disconnect the battery negative terminal. Take appropriate fire precautions, and ensure good ventilation throughout procedures involving fuel spillage. Remember that fuel lines may still be pressurized when disconnecting components.

Injectors

2   Remove the injector retaining bolt (photo).
3   Pull the injector and fuel hose from the cylinder head (photo).
4   Use two spanners to undo the injector-to-fuel hose union (photo).
5   The injector can be removed from the holder casting, and the seals, which become hard and brittle with age, should be renewed before refitting, which is a reversal of removal (photo). Note that new injectors are filled with a preservative wax before storage. This wax must be flushed out of the injector before it is fitted. Take advice from the seller of the injectors.

Air/fuel control unit

Note: *The fuel distributor, which is secured to the top of the control unit can be removed separately if so desired by disconnecting the unions and removing the three screws securing the distributor to the control unit, but take care that the distributor plunger does not fall out during the operation. It is also necessary to take stringent precautions against the entry of dirt.*
6   Remove the fuel filler cap to release residual pressure.
7   Disconnect the air intake ducting from the airflow sensor, and on pre-1978 models, disconnect the electrical plug from the sensor.
8   Clean round all the fuel hose connections before disconnecting them, having marked each one so that they are replaced in their correct positions.
9   Remove the nuts from the attachment brackets, and lift the unit from the engine bay (photo).
10 Refit in the reverse order, using new sealing washers on all banjo unions (photo).
11 After refitting, check that the airflow sensor plate moves freely over its full range before fitting the intake ducting.
12 The basic setting of the control unit should now be adjusted as follows.
13 On models up to 1977, withdraw the connector on the airflow sensor.
14 On 1978-on models, a test relay, made up as described in Section 69, must be connected as shown in Fig. 3.94.
15 Disconnect the ignition control unit.
16 Disconnect one injector hose at the distributor end.
17 Switch on the ignition.
18 Turn the CO adjustment screw (see Section 63) clockwise until fuel just starts to flow from the disconnected union.
19 Now back off the CO screw (anti-clockwise) by half a turn.
20 Switch off the ignition.

21 Re-connect the injector hose, and remake all electrical connections.
22 Check and adjust idle speed and CO content as described in Section 63.

Cold start injector

23 Unplug the electrical connector (photo).
24 Disconnect the fuel hose union (photo).
25 Remove the Allen bolts securing the injector to the manifold, noting the earth lead (photo).
26 Pull out the cold start injector (photo).
27 Use new sealing washers on refitting, which is a reversal of removal (photo).

Auxiliary air valve

28 Unplug the electrical connector (photo).
29 Disconnect the air hoses from the top and bottom of the valve (photo).
30 Remove the two Allen bolts securing the air valve to the manifold, and remove the valve (photo).
31 Refit in the reverse order to removal.
Note: *Different valves are fitted to different models. They can be identified by the number stamped on the lower face of the valve.*

Control pressure regulator

32 Unplug the electrical connector (photo).
33 Disconnect the fuel hose unions. They are different sizes, and so cannot be confused when refitting. The hoses can be disconnected at the regulator or air/fuel control unit end.
34 Unbolt and remove the unit from the engine (photos).
35 Refit in reverse order, using new sealing washers on the banjo unions.
Note: *If it is proved by testing that the control pressure regulator is defective, it should be renewed, as no repairs to it are possible. After refitting, check and adjust the control pressure, idle speed and CO content as described in Section 63.*

Thermal timer

36 The thermal timer is screwed into the cylinder block or head, into the coolant channels, so first remove the coolant expansion tank cap to release any pressure in the system. For the same reason, ensure the engine is cool before removing the timer, to avoid risk of scalding.
37 Disconnect the electrical lead from the timer.
38 Unscrew the timer and plug the hole to minimise coolant loss.
39 Refit in reverse order, using sealant on the threads of the timer, and top up the coolant system on completion.

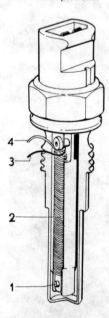

Fig. 3.90 Thermal timer (Sec 66)

1   Contacts   3   Lead to starter motor
2   Bi-metallic spring   4   Lead to cold start injector

66.2 Injector retaining bolt (arrowed)

66.3 Pulling the injector from the cylinder

66.4 Using two spanners to undo the union

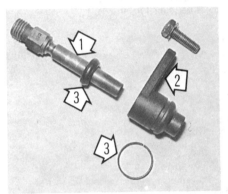

66.5 Injector dismantled
1 Nozzle   3 Seals
2 Holder

66.9 Air/fuel control unit removed from the engine
1 Fuel distributor   3 CO adjustment screw
2 Sensor plate

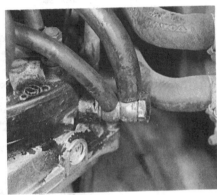

66.10 Banjo union on fuel distributor

66.23 Pulling off the electrical connector

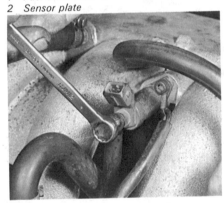

66.24 Removing the fuel hose union

66.25 Note the earth lead (arrowed) under the retaining bolt

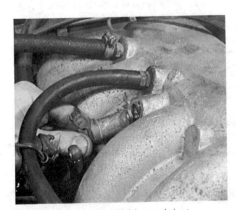

66.26 Pulling out the cold start injector

66.27 Components of the cold start injector (seals arrowed)

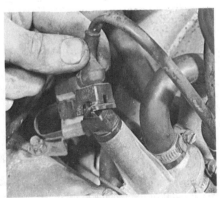

66.28 Pulling the connector from the air valve

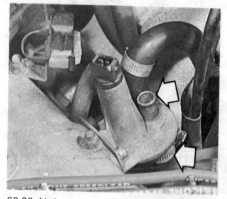
66.29 Air hose connections (arrowed)

66.30 Air valve removed

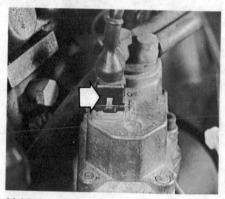
66.32 Electrical connector on control pressure regulator (arrowed)

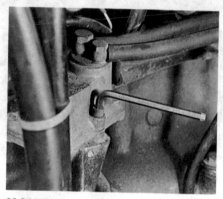
66.34A Remove the retaining bolts ...

66.34B ... and remove the unit

Relays

40 On 1975 models, the main fuel pump relay and tank pump relay are the same, and are interchangeable.
41 They are mounted under the left-hand side facia panel, towards the centre of the vehicle.
42 On 1976–77 models, the relays are different and are not interchangeable. The tank pump relay can be identified by it having a yellow lead (among others) connected to it. Both are mounted under the left-hand facia.
43 From 1978 on, one electronic relay replaces the two fitted earlier, and is mounted under the facia on the left-hand side. It should be noted that this relay carries out the function of stopping the fuel pump running if the engine stops with the ignition still switched on. The electrical contact on the airflow sensor, which previously carried out this function, is no longer fitted.

67 Fuel pump and accumulator (CI system) – removal and refitting

Note: *There are two systems. On early (pre-1977) models, the pump is mounted externally on the side of the fuel tank and there may or may not be an internal tank pump. On post-1977 models, there is an internal tank pump, integral with the fuel gauge sender unit, and also an external pump mounted underneath the vehicle just in front of the left-hand rear wheel arch.*

Early types

1 Raise and support the vehicle. Clean round all the hose connections so that dirt will not get into the pump.
2 Disconnect the battery negative terminal.
3 Pinch the fuel inlet hose with a clamp.
4 Disconnect the fuel inlet and outlet hoses.
5 Remove the retaining nuts, the fuel pump and accumulator, and the guard plate.

6 Disconnect the electrical plug and the fuel accumulator hoses.
7 Separate the bracket, rubber mountings, accumulator and fuel pump.
8 Refitting is the reverse of removal. Always fit a new fuel hose between the fuel accumulator and the fuel pump at every removal.

Later types

9 Remove the bolts securing the mounting plate to the vehicle underbody, and tilt the plate, with the pump and accumulator, down (photos).
10 The remaining procedure is as described for the earlier version in paragraphs 1 to 8.

68 Fuel tank pump and filter – removal and refitting

1 The fuel tank pump is integral with the fuel tank level sender unit, and its removal and refitting is described in Sections 12 and 13.
2 With the sender unit removed as described in Section 12, undo the two nuts securing the electrical connections to the pump.
3 Remove the clamp screw and pull the pump from the sender unit.
4 Remove the filter from the bottom of the pump. It is a push fit.
5 Refit in reverse order, ensuring that the filter does not hamper the action of the float on the sender unit.

69 CI system – test equipment

1 The test procedures in Section 70 require the use of some special equipment, which while not difficult to obtain, may be expensive. If the tools are not available, your Volvo dealer will have to carry out the work.

Test relay

2 This relay should be available from your Volvo dealer, and should

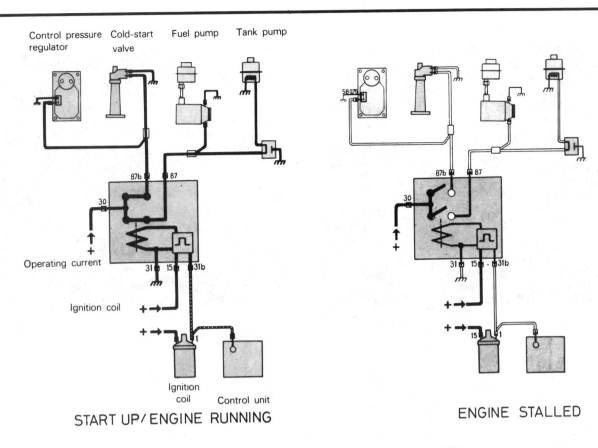

Fig. 3.91 Operation of electronic pump relay (Sec 66)

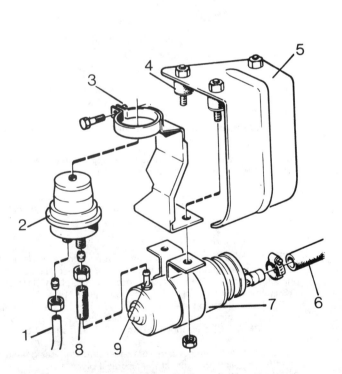

Fig. 3.92 Fuel pump and accumulator – early version (Sec 67)

1   Outlet hose
2   Accumulator
3   Bracket
4   Rubber mounting
5   Guard plate
6   Inlet hose
7   Fuel pump
8   Pump to accumulator hose
9   Non-return valve

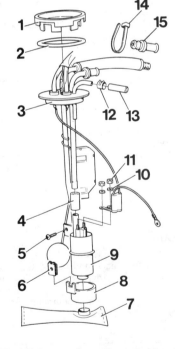

Fig. 3.93 Tank pump and sender unit (Sec 68)

1   Cap
2   O-ring seal
3   Sender unit
4   Hose
5   Screw
6   Spring clip
7   Filter
8   Bracket
9   Tank pump
10 Washer
11 Nut
12 Clip
13 Hose
14 Clip and 15 Nipple (modification to 1975 vehicles only)

67.9A Fuel pump mounting plate retaining bolts (arrowed)

67.9B Mounting plate tilted down to reveal accumulator (1), fuel pump (2) and non-return valve (3)

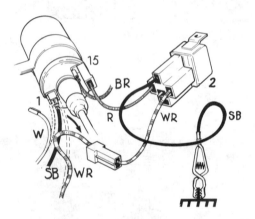

Fig. 3.94 Wiring diagram for test relay (Sec 69)

1 Coil (distributor side)	SB Black
2 Relay	WR White/red
15 Coil (battery side)	BR Brown
W White	R Red

be wired up as shown in Fig. 3.94. It is essential on 1978-on models, in order to run the fuel pump for test purposes (see also Section 70, paragraph 5).

Pressure gauge

3   Essential for testing fuel line pressures. It should be calibrated from 0 to 100 lbf/in² (0 to 7 bar), and connected to a three-way cock. Sufficient unions and adaptors for connecting the gauge are also required.
4   A multi-meter or voltmeter and ohmmeter are useful for checking supply to a unit, and for continuity within it.

70 CI system components – test procedures

1   Refer to Section 69 for details of test equipment.
2   Stringent precautions should be taken against fume intoxication and fire hazard, especially where fuel is being sprayed from injectors.
3   All other relevant engine systems (eg ignition system) should be in good order, and the battery must be in a state of full charge for the tests to be accurate.
4   Before starting any test procedures, disconnect the electrical plugs on the control pressure regulator and auxiliary air valve, and only

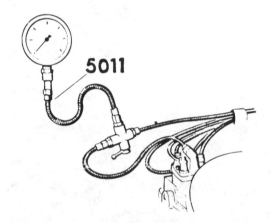

Fig. 3.95 Pressure gauge and three-way cock (Sec 69)

connect them when the test requires it. These units heat up when connected with the fuel pump running, which could result in false readings.
5   As a safety precaution, the plug to the ignition control unit should be disconnected. This is also necessary on some models to enable the fuel pump to be started.

Cold start injector

6   The engine should be cold (at ambient temperature). Remove the injector from the cylinder head, leaving the fuel hose and electrical lead connected, and position the injector nozzle into a clean glass jar.
7   Switch on the ignition and crank the engine.
8   Check the injection time using a stopwatch. Injection time will vary according to engine temperature from 7.5 seconds at –4°F (–20°C), to zero at 95°F (35°C) and above. At 68°F (20°C), it should be about 2 seconds.
9   If the injector continues to spray fuel after the designated time period has elapsed, disconnect the electrical plug.
10   If the injector then stops, suspect the thermal timer of malfunction.
11   If injection continues, the start injector is at fault and should be renewed.
12   If no fuel injection occurs during the test, disconnect the plug from the injector, connect a voltmeter across the plug terminals, and repeat the test.
13   If voltage is present for the specified period during cranking, the injector is faulty. No voltage suggests a fault in the thermal timer or supply wiring.

14 After correct operation of the injector is established, carry out an injector leak test as follows.

15 On 1975–77 models, disconnect the plug from the airflow sensor. On 1978-on models, connect up the test relay as described in Section 69.

16 Switch on the ignition – the fuel pump should start running (this can be checked by feeling the fuel filter which should vibrate slightly)

17 Check that the leak rate from the injector is no more than one drop per minute. If it is greater than this, renew the injector.

Air/fuel control unit

18 Remove the air intake trunking from the control unit.

19 Check the centralisation of the sensor plate by passing a thin feeler blade or a slip of paper around its periphery. The plate should not touch the venturi sides at any point. Adjust the plate by loosening the central nut and moving the plate as necessary. Tighten the nut on completion.

20 Check that there is no side-play in the plate and arm. If there is, the arm pivot should be reconditioned (see Section 72).

21 Ensure that the plate operates over its full range without restriction.

22 Switch on the gnition and run the fuel pump, either by connecting the test relay (Section 69) or by disconnecting the airflow sensor plug (early models only).

23 Lift the sensor plate, for a short while only, and check that the injectors make a buzzing sound, indicating that they are working, and that they stop when the plate is returned to its rest position.

Note: *The control pressure in the system offers some resistance to lifting of the plate, which should not be confused with jamming.*

24 Switch off the ignition.

25 If the airflow sensor jams at any stage during the test, it should be reconditioned.

26 If the injectors continue to buzz when the plate is in the rest position, the fuel distributor has jammed, and should be cleaned or renewed.

27 If the injectors do not work when the plate is lifted, the line pressure is incorrect (perhaps because the fuel pump is not working).

28 Check the line and control pressures as described later in the test procedures, then measure the resting height of the airflow sensor plate.

29 The fuel pump must be running and control pressure must be at its maximum value, so the control pressure regulator must have been energised for at least five minutes.

30 Check the rest height of the plate, which should be level with the venturi waistline, or at most 0.012 in (0.3 mm) below it.

31 Adjust the height by expanding or compressing the spring on the underside of the plate.

32 Switch off the ignition.

33 It is emphasised that the correct rest height of the sensor plate is dependent on the control pressure being correct, and if this is not the case, it is pointless attempting to adjust the plate height.

34 Remove all test equipment and restore disturbed electrical connections.

Auxiliary air valve

35 The valve should be tested when the engine is cold.

36 Disconnect the electrical lead and the air hoses to the valve.

37 Shine a torch through the valve to establish that it is partly open.

38 If it is not, and cannot be opened when tapped (to simulate engine vibration), it should be renewed.

39 Connect the electrical plug to the valve and run the fuel pump (paragraph 22). The valve should close completely after about 5 minutes at ambient temperature. Again gentle tapping to simulate engine vibration will help it to close. (It is necessary to run the fuel pump, because the electrical supply to the valve is via the fuel pump relay.)

40 If the valve fails to close, check that there is voltage at the plug connections, and if so the valve should be renewed.

Line and control pressures

41 Switch off the ignition.

42 Connect a pressure gauge with a three-way cock (see Section 69) between the control pressure regulator and the fuel distributor.

43 Switch on the ignition and run the fuel pump (paragraph 22). Turn the three-way cock so that the line from the fuel distributor is open to the pressure gauge, and the control pressure regulator is isolated.

44 Read off the pressure on the gauge, which should be as specified. This is the line pressure.

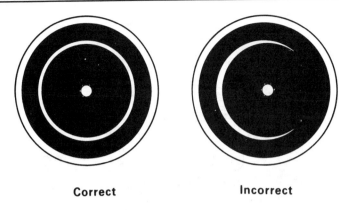

Correct   **Incorrect**

Fig. 3.96 Adjustment of airflow sensor plate (Sec 70)

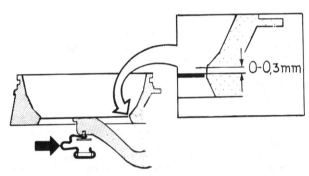

Fig. 3.97 Rest height adjustment of airflow sensor plate (Sec 70)

45 If it is too low, the cause may be leakage on the pressure side of the pump, a defective accumulator, a defective tank pump or clogged tank or main filter.

46 If the pressure is too high, the cause may be a blocked fuel return line, or it may be that the line pressure regulator is defective.

47 Once the line pressure is set correctly, the control pressure can be checked as follows.

48 Turn the three-way cock to the central position, so that pressure from both lines is open to the gauge. The control pressure regulator should be cold (at ambient temperature).

49 The control pressure varies with regulator temperature, and should be as shown in the graph (Fig. 3.99).

50 Too high a pressure is due to a blocked fuel return line. If the pressure is too low, the test should be repeated with a new pressure regulator.

51 With the cold pressure correct, connect the plug to the control pressure regulator and allow the pump and regulator to run for at least 5 minutes to warm up.

52 Check the warm pressure, which should be as given in the Specifications.

53 Again, too high a pressure is due to a blocked fuel return line.

54 Too low a pressure may be because the control regulator is not heating up – check for voltage at the plug.

55 If voltage is present but the regulator has not warmed up, it should be renewed.

56 With the line and control pressures correct, the rest pressure can be checked.

57 Leave the three-way cock in position 2 (as when reading control pressure).

58 Switch on the ignition, and allow the pump to run for about 5 minutes to stabilise control pressure. (Obviously the control pressure regulator must be connected.)

59 Switch off the ignition, and wait for the pressure to stabilise.

60 The rest pressure should stabilise at or above the minimum given in the Specifications. Low rest pressure is a cause of hot-start difficulty.

61 If pressure drops too low, check for leakage in the fuel line from the control pressure regulator. On 1975–77 models, it may be that the control pressure regulator allows too much fuel to flow through. Test

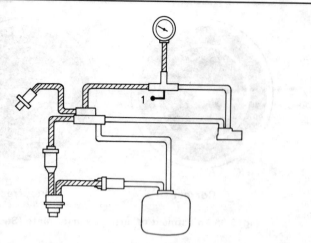

Fig. 3.98 Measuring line pressure (1) and control pressure (2) (Sec 70)

with a new regulator. On 1978-on models, check the needle valve in the line pressure regulator, and clean or renew as necessary.

62 Other causes are a defective fuel pump non-return valve or external leakage.

63 On completion, remove the test equipment and restore original electrical connections.

Injectors and fuel distributor

64 Remove the injectors from their recesses in the cylinder head and place each one on a piece of clean rag.

65 Switch on the ignition and run the fuel pump (paragraph 22).

66 Inspect the injector nozzles. It is normal for the nozzles to become moist, but they should not drip.

67 Switch off the ignition.

68 If the injectors have leaked, there is an internal fault in the fuel distributor, and it should be renewed.

69 Check the injectors at rest pressure by slowly lifting the airflow sensor plate to open the metering slots (ignition still off).

70 The injectors may become moist, but should not drip fuel within 15 seconds. If one or more injectors leak, have them cleaned and tested, or renewed.

71 Check injector delivery rate by placing each injector into identical-sized glass jars or tubes.

72 Run the fuel pump (paragraph 22). Lift the airflow sensor plate by half its full travel, and wait until the jars are nearly full before releasing the sensor plate.

73 Each injector should start delivering fuel at the same time, and the amount of fuel delivered from each injector should be equal, within 20%.

74 If the deviation is greater than 20%, swap injectors and hoses at the fuel distributor and repeat the test.

75 If the deviation follows the injector, the injector or hose is at fault. If the previously good injector appears to malfunction, the fuel distributor is faulty and should be renewed.

76 The spray pattern of the injectors can be checked by holding the injector in a glass jar. Examples of good and bad spray patterns are shown in Fig. 3.101.

77 Any further testing of the injectors should be done by your Volvo dealer who has the necessary test equipment.

Tank pump

78 A defective tank pump can cause the following symptoms:

(a) Increased noise level at the main pump
(b) Poor engine performance generally, and low top speed
(c) Juddering and engine cut-out

79 Initial response to these problems is to check the line fuse in the luggage compartment on 1975 to 78 models, or fuse number 5 in the fusebox on later models.

80 If the fuse is intact, check the current drawn by the pump (see Specifications).

81 If both these are in order, check the fuel tank for blockage (Section 68).

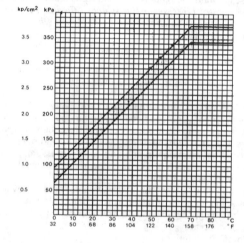

Fig. 3.99 Control graph (cold engine) pressure (Sec 70)

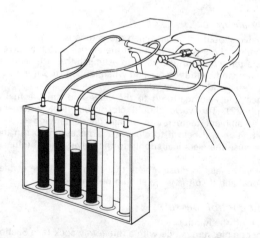

Fig. 3.100 Checking injector delivery using measuring tubes (Sec 70)

82 If the fuel tank filter is clean, or the current draw is not as specified, renew the tank pump.

Main fuel supply

83 To check the operation of the fuel pump, disconnect the ignition system control unit.

84 On 1975 to 77 models, disconnect the plug on the airflow sensor.

85 On 1978-on models, connect up the test relay as described in Section 69.

86 Switch on the ignition – the pump should start running. This can be checked by feeling the in-line fuel filter in the engine bay, which will vibrate slightly when the pump is running.

87 If the pump does not run, check the fuses, leads and relay(s). Relays can only be checked by substitution.

88 Pump output pressure is checked during the pressure checking procedures (paragraphs 41 to 63). Delivery may be checked if wished by disconnecting the fuel filter and running the delivery pipe into a measuring vessel; minimum delivery capacity is given in the Specifications. If delivery is low but pressures are correct, this can only be due to a blockage.

71 Line pressure – adjusting

1 Line pressure (and through it, the control and rest pressures, which are dependent upon line pressure) is adjusted by adding or removing shims from under the spring and valve of the pressure regulator in the fuel distributor. The procedure is included in Section 72.

2 Unless the necessary seals, shims and pressure gauges are available, it is not recommended that adjustment be undertaken by the home mechanic.

3 Adjusting the line pressure by this method should only be considered after all other tests have established that there is no other fault in the system, and scrupulous cleanliness should be observed at all times.

4 On models up to 1977, for every 0.004 in (0.1 mm) increase in shim thickness, line pressure will be increased by 0.9 lbf/in^2 (6 kPa). On later models the corresponding increase is 2.2 lbf/in^2 (15 kPa). Shims are available in various thicknesses.

72 CI system air/fuel control unit – overhaul

Note: *Scrupulous cleanliness is essential during the overhaul procedure, and great care should be taken not to damage or scratch the control plungers. Renew all seals and gaskets, where fitted, on reassembly.*

1 Remove the control unit as described in Section 66. Remove the Allen screws and separate the upper and lower halves of the unit.

2 Remove the three plain-headed screws securing the fuel distributor to the control unit and lift off the distributor. Be extremely careful not to drop the control plunger, and recover the O-ring seal.

3 Remove the control plunger from the distributor and clean it in petrol, using a soft brush. Do not use any abrasive materials on it. Also clean the fuel distribution slots.

4 Unscrew the pressure regulator plug, and withdraw the pressure regulator plunger and associated components, keeping them in order. Remember they are under spring pressure when removing them.

5 If any plungers are scored or otherwise damaged, or if the control plunger sticks in the distributor, the complete fuel distributor must be renewed. Do not attempt to dismantle it any further.

6 Remove the stopper plate assembly. Remove the two circlips from the end of the airflow sensor pivot shaft. Remove the plugs, spring and balls, noting which side the spring is situated.

7 Loosen the sensor plate lever securing screws, and then tap out the pivot shaft. Lift out the lever, plate and arm.

8 Examine all parts for wear or damage and renew as necessary.

9 Reassemble the airflow sensor plate and arm, lightly greasing the shaft and balls. Centre the lever before tightening the retaining screws, ensuring the CO adjustment screw is opposite the drilled hole in the housing.

10 Refit the stopper plate assembly.

11 Centralise the sensor plate as described in Section 70, paragraph 19, then check the plate for full and free movement throughout its full range of travel.

12 Adjust the rest height position of the plate as described in Section

70, paragraph 30. Set the plate flush with the waistline, because it will move downwards when control pressure is applied.

13 Reassemble the pressure regulator and fit it back to the control unit (see also Section 71).

14 Refit the fuel distributor, making sure the control plunger does not fall out during the operation. Tighten the screws evenly.

15 Refit the upper half of the airflow control unit to the lower half, using a new gasket. On completion check that the airflow sensor plate and lever move freely.

16 Refit the air/fuel control unit as described in Section 66.

17 Carry out pressure tests as described in Section 70.

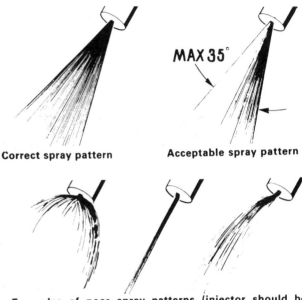

Correct spray pattern   **Acceptable spray pattern**

Examples of poor spray patterns (injector should be replaced)

Fig. 3.101 Injector spray patterns (Sec 70)

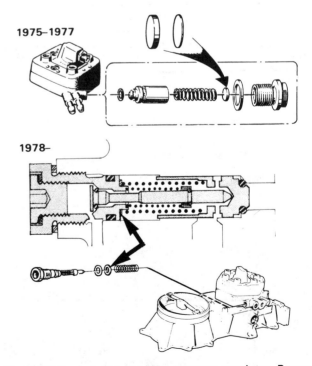

1975–1977

1978–

Fig. 3.102 Exploded view of the pressure regulator. Pressure adjustment shims arrowed (Sec 71)

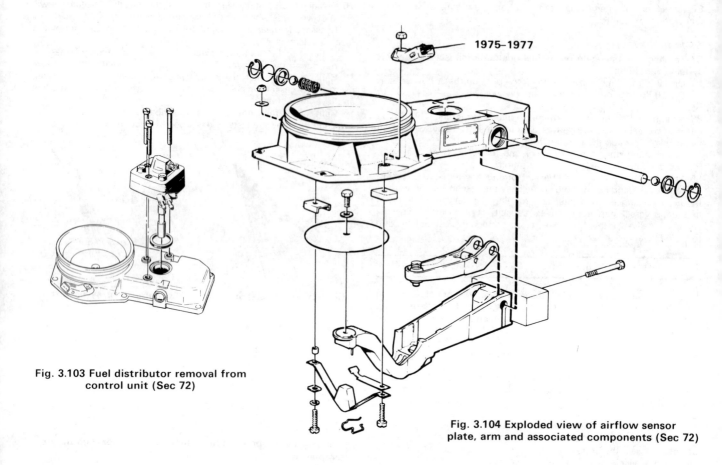

Fig. 3.103 Fuel distributor removal from
control unit (Sec 72)

1975–1977

Fig. 3.104 Exploded view of airflow sensor
plate, arm and associated components (Sec 72)

73 Fault diagnosis – fuel injection system

Note: *High fuel consumption and poor performance are not necessarily due to fuel system faults. Make sure that the ignition system is properly adjusted, that the brakes are not binding and that the engine is in good mechanical condition before tampering with the injection system.*

Symptom	Reason(s)
Smell of petrol when engine is stopped	Leaking fuel pipes or unions Leaking fuel tank
Smell of petrol when engine is idling	Leaking fuel lines or unions in fuel distribution system
Difficult starting with cold engine	Leak in the intake system Airflow sensor plate maladjusted Fuel distributor or airflow sensor sticking or binding Line pressure too low Control pressure too high Auxiliary air valve not opening Cold start injector faulty Thermal time switch faulty Blocked fuel lines or filters
Difficult starting with warm engine	Leak in the intake system Airflow sensor plate maladjusted Fuel distributor or airflow sensor sticking or binding Line pressure too low Cold start injector leaking Air/fuel control unit leaking Control pressure incorrect Rest pressure incorrect Injectors leaking

Symptom	Reason(s)
Uneven running	Control pressure incorrect Cold start injector leaking Air/fuel control unit leaking Auxiliary air valve not closing Injectors leaking Defective injector O-ring seal Air leak in intake system
Poor performance, lack of power	Cold start injector leaking Control pressure too high Fuel starvation, blocked fuel lines, filters, injectors or fuel distributor Intake system leaking Tank pump defective
Excessive fuel consumption not accounted for by external leaks	Control pressure too low Cold start injector leaking Faulty injectors Brakes binding Inappropriate driving style or adverse conditions

Chapter 4 Ignition system

Contents

Specifications

System type

Early 'A' engines .... Mechanical with contact breaker
Early 'E' engines .... Electronic, breakerless (TSZ-2)
B200E, B200K and B230E TZ-28H
B230K .... Bendix Rex

Firing order .... 1–3–4–2 (No 1 at front of engine)

HT leads
Application:
    All models up to 1976 .... Champion CLS 1 boxed set
    All models 1977 to 1984 .... Champion CLS 12 boxed set
    All models .1984-on .... Champion CLS 13 boxed set

Spark plugs
B21A .... Champion N9YCC or N9YC
B23A .... Champion N9YCC or N9YC
B21E .... Champion N7YCC or N7YC
B23E .... Champion N7YCC or N7YC
B200K and B230A .... Champion N9YCC or N9YC
B200E, B230E and B230K .... Champion N7YCC or N7YC
Electrode gap:
    N9YCC and N7YCC .... 0.032 to 0.035 in (0.8 to 0.9 mm)
    N9YC and N7YC .... 0.028 to 0.032 in (0.7 to 0.8 mm)

Ballast resistor
Resistance:
    Early 1979 models with contact breaker .... 0.9 ± 0.1 ohms
    Later models with contact breaker .... 1.3 ± 0.1 ohms
    TSZ-2 system .... 0.9 ± 0.1 ohms

Ignition timing (°BTDC, vacuum hose disconnected and plugged)

Engine type	Static, or at 700 to 800 rpm	at 2500 rpm
B21A:		
1975	12	24 to 28
1986 to 1978	15	32 to 36
1979 to 1983	12	28 to 32
1984 on	7	17 to 23
B21E 1975 to 1983	8	28 to 33
B23A:		
1982	5	19 to 24
1983 on	7	17 to 22
B23E:		
1979 to 1983	5	25 to 30
1984	10	24 to 29
B200K	7	17 to 23
B200E	10	24 to 28
B230A	7	17 to 23
B230A (with M45 WR gearbox)	5	15 to 23
B230E	10	24 to 28
B230K	12	–

Ignition coil

'A' engines up to 1978
Primary resistance .... 2.7 to 3.0 ohms
Secondary resistance .... 8.0 to 11.0 K ohms

'A' engines 1979 on and 'E' engines with TSZ-2
Primary resistance .... 1.9 ohms
Secondary resistance .... 9.5 ± 1.5 K ohms

TZ-28H and Bendix coils
Primary resistance .... 0.6 to 0.9 ohms
Secondary resistance .... 6.5 to 8.5 K ohms

Distributor

Contact breaker type – 'A' engines
Direction of rotation .... Clockwise
Contact breaker gap (minimum) .... 0.016 in (0.40 mm)
Dwell angle .... 62 ± 3°

TSZ-2 type – 'E' engines
Direction of rotation .... Clockwise
Resistance of impulse sender .... 0.95 to 1.25 K ohms
Air gap (minimum) .... 0.010 in (0.25 mm)

TZ-28 type .... No data available

Rotor arm (all types)
Resistance (approximately) .... 4.0 to 6.0 K ohms

Torque wrench settings

	lbf ft	Nm
Spark plugs (unoiled)	15 to 22	20 to 30

1 General description

The ignition system is designed to deliver the spark to each cylinder at the right time in order to ignite the fuel/air mixture. It must do this under all engine conditions of speed and load.

There are several different types of ignition system in use in different models. Early 'A' engines use a conventional mechanical system with contact breaker points which interrupt the Low Tension (LT) side of the circuit. Through the action of the coil, the LT is changed to High Tension (HT) current, which is then distributed to each cylinder in turn by the distributor. In each cylinder the spark plug causes the HT current to jump a gap set between the spark plug electrodes, which results in the spark which ignites the fuel/air mixture. It can be seen that the spark must be delivered at the right time to each cylinder (just before top dead centre (BTDC) on the compression stroke when both inlet and exhaust valves are closed) in order to obtain the best power output from the engine. The optimum ignition timing varies with engine speed (centrifugal advance) and load (vacuum advance).

Early 'E' engines use a basic form of electronic ignition (TSZ-2), or breakerless ignition, which as its name implies has no contact breaker points, the interruption of the LT circuit being achieved by an impulse sender in the distributor and an electronic control unit, which then sends the current to the coil where the HT current is produced. Centrifugal and vacuum advance are still determined mechanically.

B200 and B230 engines (excluding B230K) are equipped with an updated electronic ignition system designated TZ-28H.

B230K engines are equipped with the 'Bendix Rex' system which is an entirely new concept in electronic ignition systems, more fully described in Sections 16 to 19. With this system, ignition advance is determined and applied electronically.

Warning – high-voltage ignition systems
When working on any ignition system, take care to avoid electric shock produced from the HT side of the system. When the engine is running, do not touch any part of the system. When tracing faults use well-insulated tools. The voltages produced by electronic systems could prove fatal.

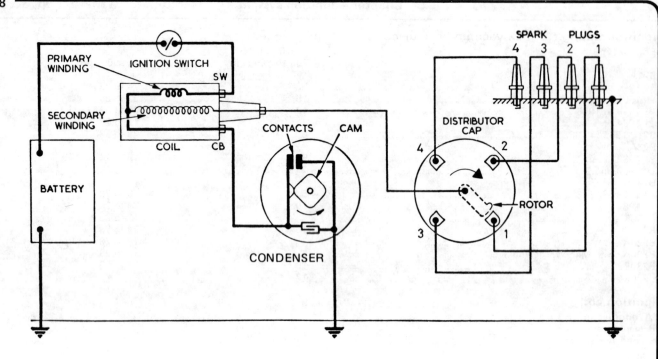

Fig. 4.1 Schematic diagram of the contact breaker type circuit (Sec 1)

(LT circuit in heavy line)

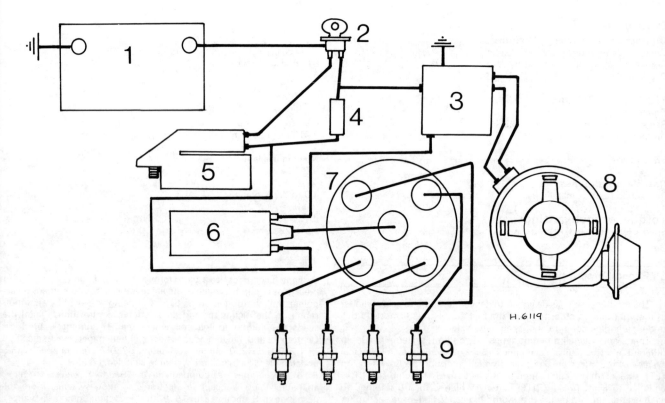

H.6119

Fig. 4.2 TSZ-2 breakerless ignition system (Sec 1)

1	Battery	4	Ballast resistance	7	Distributor cap
2	Ignition switch	5	Starter motor	8	Impulse sender
3	Control unit	6	Ignition coil	9	Spark plugs

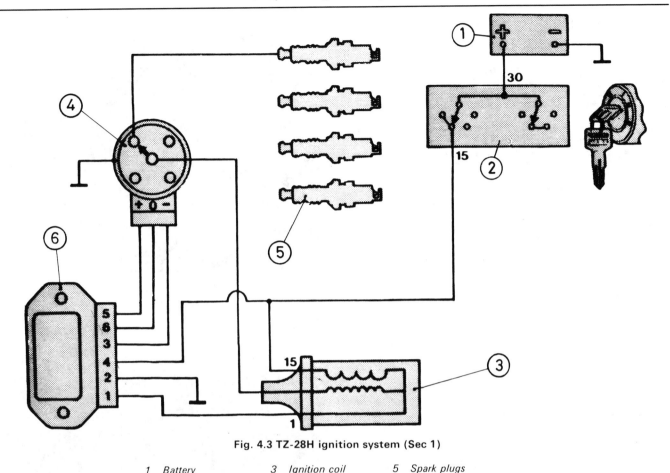

Fig. 4.3 TZ-28H ignition system (Sec 1)

1	Battery	3	Ignition coil	5	Spark plugs
2	Ignition switch	4	Distributor	6	Electronic control unit

2 Routine maintenance

1 At the intervals specified in the *Routine maintenance* Section at the beginning of this Manual, carry out the following operations.
2 Renew the spark plugs (Section 3).
3 Inspect the distributor cap, HT leads and rotor arm (Section 4).
4 Check and adjust the contact breaker gap, and renew the points if necessary, on mechanical systems (Section 6).
5 Inspect all ignition system components for security of terminals, corrosion of terminals and general cleanliness.
6 Check and adjust ignition timing (Sections 13 and 14).
7 Keep all components clean and dry. The application of water-repellent spray at regular intervals can be beneficial, especially in wet weather.
8 Lubricate the felt pad at the top of the distributor shaft on contact breaker distribution with a few drops of oil (photo). Be careful not to get oil onto the contact breaker points.

3 Spark plugs – removal, inspection and renewal

1 The correct functioning of the spark plugs is vital for the correct running and efficiency of the engine. It is essential that the plugs fitted are appropriate for the engine, and the suitable type is specified at the beginning of this chapter. If this type is used and the engine is in good condition, the spark plugs should not need attention between scheduled replacement intervals. Spark plug cleaning is rarely necessary and should not be attempted unless specialised equipment is available as damage can easily be caused to the firing ends.
2 Allow the engine to cool before removing the spark plugs.
3 Disconnect the battery negative lead.
4 Remove any air cleaner ducting or other components in order to give easy access to all four plugs.
5 Number the spark plug leads before removal using sticky tape or

tie-on labels so that they can be refitted correctly. (Later models have the leads already marked.)
6 Pull the leads off the spark plugs, grasping the connector and not the lead.

2.8 Lubricating the distributor shaft felt pad

7   Clean out the spark plug recesses in the cylinder head using a brush, or by blowing them out with air (bicycle pump or similar).

8   Remove the spark plugs using a spark plug socket or box spanner (photo).

9   Inspect the spark plugs. Much can be learned about engine and fuel system condition from the state of the plugs.

10   Spark plugs should be renewed at the intervals given in the *Routine maintenance* Section at the beginning of this Manual.

11   The electrode may be set by bending it carefully using a spark plug adjusting tool. Do not try to bend the centre electrode or the ceramic core may be damaged.

12   Check the spark plug leads, giving them a wipe down and checking the connections for security, renewing any which appear faulty.

13   Fit new plugs, starting them off by hand, and be absolutely certain that they are not cross threaded before tightening them to the specified torque using a torque wrench. In the absence of a torque wrench, tighten the new plugs approximately one quarter of a turn beyond where the base of the plug contacts the cylinder head.

14   Refit the spark plug leads, ensuring each one is fitted to the correct plug, and push each connector firmly down onto the plug. Make sure the other ends of the leads are still making good contact with the distributor.

15   Reconnect the battery and start the engine. If it is difficult to start or runs erratically, then the leads are probably mixed up.

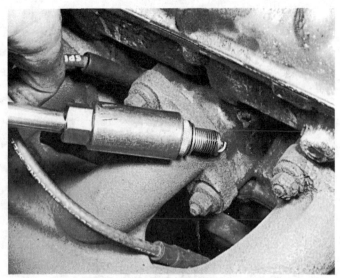
3.8   Removing a spark plug

4   Distributor cap, HT leads and rotor arm – removal, inspection and refitting

1   Disconnect the battery negative lead.

2   Undo the clips or screws which hold the distributor cap in place. The clips may need levering off with a screwdriver (photo).

3   Pull off the rotor arm and inspect the tip. It can be cleaned with emery cloth or a fine file. Check the plastic body and renew the rotor if it is cracked, or if the resistance, checked between the tip and the centre of the rotor, is much more or less than that specified.

4   Mark each HT lead so that you can replace them in the same position, then pull the leads from the distributor cap, the coil and the spark plugs. Pull on the rubber end caps, grasping them firmly, and not on the leads themselves, which can lead to damage of the connectors.

5   Inspect the leads, making sure they are not cracked. Check the connectors for corrosion, and that they are a good tight fit on the spark plugs and distributor cap. Do not forget the connection to the coil. Renew any leads which are defective, although this is best done as a set. Note that some models use copper-cored leads with resistive connectors, whilst others use resistive leads.

6   Inspect the inside of the distributor cap for thin crack-like lines running between the terminals. These lines indicate current leakage (known as tracking). If there is evidence of tracking, renew the cap. Check the carbon contact in the centre of the cap, ensuring it is free to move in and out. Clean the terminal posts if they have a hard deposit built up on them. Clean the inside of the cap and give it a light spray with water-repellent fluid (photo).

7   Refitting of all components is a reversal of removal, making sure that all connections are pushed fully home and in the correct location.

4.2 Location of the distributor – one cap clip arrowed

5   Engine speed limiter – general

1   All B200 and B230 engines are equipped with an engine speed limiter.

2   This most commonly takes the form of a spring-loaded contact in the distributor rotor arm.

3   At 6200 rpm, the weight overcomes the force of the spring and allows the two contacts to touch, shorting out the ignition.

4.6 Showing the inside of the distributor cap
1   *Spring-loaded terminal*   2   *Outer terminal posts*

Are your plugs trying to tell you something?

Normal.
Grey-brown deposits, lightly coated core nose. Plugs ideally suited to engine, and engine in good condition.

Heavy Deposits.
A build up of crusty deposits, light-grey sandy colour in appearance.
Fault: Often caused by worn valve guides, excessive use of upper cylinder lubricant, or idling for long periods.

Lead Glazing.
Plug insulator firing tip appears yellow or green/yellow and shiny in appearance.
Fault: Often caused by incorrect carburation, excessive idling followed by sharp acceleration. Also check ignition timing.

Carbon fouling.
Dry, black, sooty deposits.
Fault: over-rich fuel mixture.
Check: carburettor mixture settings, float level, choke operation, air filter.

Oil fouling.
Wet, oily deposits. Fault: worn bores/piston rings or valve guides; sometimes occurs (temporarily) during running-in period.

Overheating.
Electrodes have glazed appearance, core nose very white – few deposits. Fault: plug overheating. Check: plug value, ignition timing, fuel octane rating (too low) and fuel mixture (too weak).

Electrode damage.
Electrodes burned away; core nose has burned, glazed appearance. Fault: pre-ignition. Check: for correct heat range and as for 'overheating'.

Split core nose.
(May appear initially as a crack). Fault: detonation or wrong gap-setting technique. Check: ignition timing, cooling system, fuel mixture (too weak).

WHY DOUBLE COPPER IS BETTER FOR YOUR ENGINE.

Unique Trapezoidal Copper Cored Earth Electrode — 50% Larger Spark Area — Copper Cored Centre Electrode

Champion Double Copper plugs are the first in the world to have copper core in both centre <u>and</u> earth electrode. This innovative design means that they run cooler by up to 100°C – giving greater efficiency and longer life. These double copper cores transfer heat away from the tip of the plug faster and more efficiently. Therefore, Double Copper runs at cooler temperatures than conventional plugs giving improved acceleration response and high speed performance with no fear of pre-ignition.

Champion Double Copper plugs also feature a unique trapezoidal earth electrode giving a 50% increase in spark area. This, together with the double copper cores, offers greatly reduced electrode wear, so the spark stays stronger for longer.

 FASTER COLD STARTING

 FOR UNLEADED OR LEADED FUEL

 ELECTRODES UP TO 100°C COOLER

 BETTER ACCELERATION RESPONSE

 LOWER EMISSIONS

 50% BIGGER SPARK AREA

 THE LONGER LIFE PLUG

Plug Tips/Hot and Cold.
Spark plugs must operate within well-defined temperature limits to avoid cold fouling at one extreme and overheating at the other.
Champion and the car manufacturers work out the best plugs for an engine to give optimum performance under all conditions, from freezing cold starts to sustained high speed motorway cruising.
Plugs are often referred to as hot or cold. With Champion, the higher the number on its body, the hotter the plug, and the lower the number the cooler the plug. For the correct plug for your car refer to the specifications at the beginning of this chapter.

Plug Cleaning
Modern plug design and materials mean that Champion no longer recommends periodic plug cleaning. Certainly don't clean your plugs with a wire brush as this can cause metal conductive paths across the nose of the insulator so impairing its performance and resulting in loss of acceleration and reduced m.p.g.
However, if plugs are removed, always carefully clean the area where the plug seats in the cylinder head as grit and dirt can sometimes cause gas leakage.
Also wipe any traces of oil or grease from plug leads as this may lead to arcing.

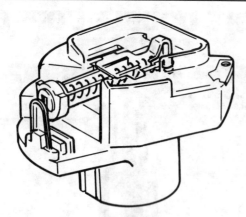

Fig. 4.4 Engine speed limiter – spring-loaded contact type (Sec 5)

6 Contact breaker points – inspection, renewal and adjusting

1   Disconnect the battery negative terminal.
2   Unclip and remove the distributor cap.
3   Remove the rotor arm and plastic cover.
4   Turn the crankshaft until the heel of the contact breaker is resting on the highest point of one of the lobes of the cam. (The crankshaft can be turned using a spanner on the pulley bolt, or on manual gearbox models by engaging top gear, jacking up one rear quarter and turning a rear wheel. Either way it will be easier if the spark plugs are removed.)
5   Inspect the contacts. If they are pitted, burnt or have a hard grey deposit on them, they should be renewed. **Note:** *Contacts can be resurfaced using a fine file or emery cloth, but if they are badly worn they should be renewed. One cause of badly burned and pitted points is a defective condenser, and it may be considered worthwhile to renew the condenser whenever the points are renewed. If the points are in good condition, proceed to paragraph 12 to check the gap.*
6   Disconnect the LT lead to the points.
7   Remove the screw securing the points to the baseplate (photo) and lift them off the post.
8   Before fitting new points, clean the contact faces with methylated spirit to remove any preservative which may be on them. Also put a smear of petroleum jelly on the distributor cam.
9   Fit the new points over the post, then screw in the securing screw, but do not fully tighten it yet.
10   Reconnect the LT lead.
11   Turn the crankshaft until the heel of the contact is resting on the highest point of one of the cam lobes.
12   Using clean feeler blades, measure the gap between the contacts, which should be as specified (photo). Feeler blades of the specified thickness should be a firm sliding fit (neither loose nor tight) between the contacts.

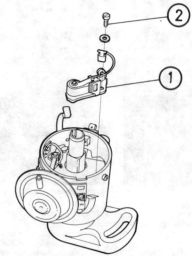

Fig. 4.5 Contact breaker points assembly (Sec 6)

1   Contact breaker   2   Securing screw

13   Adjust the gap by inserting a screwdriver blade in the slot in the moveable contact and between the two dimples by the slot, and lever the contact in or out as required (photo).
14   Once the gap is set, tighten the securing screw.
15   Turn the engine through one complete revolution, and re-check the gap, adjusting as necessary.
16   Refit the plastic cover and rotor arm.
17   Refit the distributor cap and secure it in place with the clips.
18   Reconnect the battery.
Note: *The procedure given here must be regarded as an initial setting only and the points gap should be adjusted by checking the dwell angle. The dwell angle is the number of degrees of distributor cam rotation during which the contact breaker points are closed; ie the period from when the points close after being opened by one cam lobe, until they are opened again by the next cam lobe. The advantages of setting the points by this method are that any wear of the distributor shaft or cam lobes is taken into account and the inaccuracies associated with using feeler gauges are eliminated. In general a dwell meter should be used in accordance with the meter manufacturer's instructions.*
19   Check the ignition timing (Sections 13 and 14) and adjust as necessary.

7 Condenser – removal and refitting

1   Disconnect the battery negative terminal.
2   Remove the distributor cap, rotor arm and plastic cover.
3   Disconnect the LT cable from the condenser.

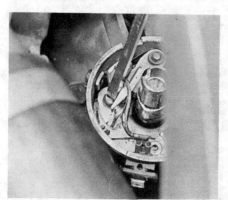

6.7 Undoing the contact breaker points securing screw

6.12 Measuring the contact breaker gap

6.13 Lever the points here to adjust the gap

4   Remove the screw securing the condenser to the distributor body.
5   Refitting the condenser is a reversal of removal.
Note: *The condenser is an often-overlooked component of the ignition system. Apart from helping to produce a good spark, it also protects the contact points from excess erosion due to sparking across them. If the points are showing signs of this pitting and burning, it is a good indication that the condenser needs renewing.*

8   Coil – testing, removal and refitting

For Bendix-Rex system, see Section 19.
1   Different coils are fitted to mechanical and electronic ignition systems, and are not interchangeable even though they may look the same.
2   Inspect the coil for obvious signs of malfunction – cracks, terminal corrosion, loose terminals etc. Some coils are fitted with oil: if the oil is leaking out, the coil must be renewed.
3   Disconnect the LT and HT leads (photo), noting their locations for refitting.
4   Use a multi-meter or ohmmeter to check the coil resistance. Primary resistance is checked between the two LT terminals, and HT resistance between an LT and the HT terminal. Values are given in the Specifications.
5   If the values differ greatly from that specified, the coil should be renewed.
6   Remove the coil by disconnecting the leads and loosening the bracket bolt sufficiently to slide the coil from the bracket.
7   Refitting is a reversal of removal.

9   Ballast resistor – testing, removal and refitting

1   Certain models, notably all 'A' engines from 1979 on, and 'E' engines with TSZ-2 electronic ignition, are fitted with a ballast resistor, which is wired in series with the ignition coil.
2   When the starter is energised, the ballast resistor is bypassed and full battery power is applied to terminal 15 of the coil, through terminal 16 on the starter motor solenoid. This gives a good spark for starting the engine.
3   As soon as the engine has started, voltage reaches the coil through the ballast resistor, reducing the flow of current through the coil.
4   If the engine fires when the starter motor is operated but will not run, it is likely that the ballast resistor is defective or disconnected.
5   To test the ballast resistor, first disconnect the wires to the ballast resistor.
6   Using a multi-meter or ohmmeter, test the resistance through the ballast resistor, which should be as given in the Specifications. Renew it if not.
7   Remove the ballast resistor by removing its securing bolt (if fitted).
8   Fit and connect a new resistor.
9   Do not be tempted to bypass a defective ballast resistor, as the excessive flow of current will damage the coil and other ignition system components.

10 Distributor – removal and refitting

For Bendix-Rex systems see Section 19.
1   Disconnect the battery negative terminal if wished.
2   Unclip the distributor cap and lift off the cap, laying it to one side (photo).
3   Where fitted, disconnect the vacuum hose and the LT terminal (photos). On some types, the LT connector is a push fit and on others the screw must be undone.
4   Turn the crankshaft (see Section 6, paragraph 4) until the rotor arm faces towards the scribed mark on the rim of the distributor body. It may be necessary to remove the rotor arm, take off the plastic cover and refit the rotor arm temporarily in order to see the mark (photo). Be careful that the distributor cap clips do not foul the arms of the rotor.
5   Make alignment marks between the base of the distributor and the engine. Remove the distributor lock bolt and lift out the distributor.
6   When refitting the distributor, which is a reversal of the removal procedure, turn the rotor arm 60° clockwise away from the alignment mark on the rim, then insert the distributor. As the gears mesh, the rotor

8.3 Showing the coil with (A) LT and HT terminals and (B) bracket bolt

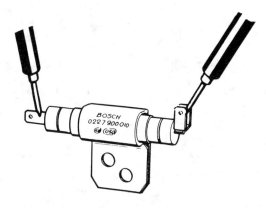

Fig. 4.6 Testing the resistance of a ballast resistor (Sec 9)

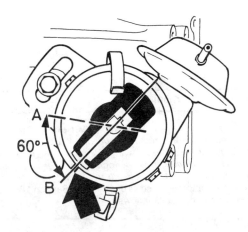

Fig. 4.7 Rotor arm position when refitting the distributor (Sec 10)

A   Position before fitting   *B   Position after fitting*

10.2 Distributor with cap removed

10.3A Disconnecting the vacuum hose ...

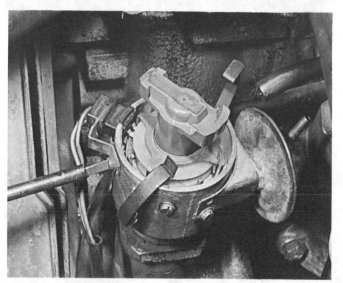

10.3B ... and LT terminal

10.4 Rotor lined up with the mark on the distributor rim (arrowed)

will turn back to line up with the mark. If it does not, take it out and try again.

7   Check the ignition timing (Sections 13 and 14) and adjust if necessary.

11 Distributor – overhaul

Note: *If the side play in the distributor shaft exceeds the specified tolerance, consideration should be given to obtaining a service exchange unit, as wear here would indicate a generally worn distributor which would be uneconomic to repair. In any case individual components may be difficult to obtain.*

1   With the distributor removed as described in Section 10 and placed in a padded vice, proceed as follows.

Contact breaker type

2   Remove the contact breaker assembly as described in Section 6.

3   Remove the condenser and LT terminal as described in Section 7.

4   Remove the circlip securing the vacuum unit pullrod to the baseplate, and unhook the pullrod.

5   Remove the vacuum unit securing screw and lift away the vacuum unit.

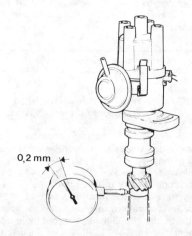

0,2 mm

Fig. 4.8 Measuring play in the distributor rotor shaft (Sec 11)

0.2 mm = maximum allowable play

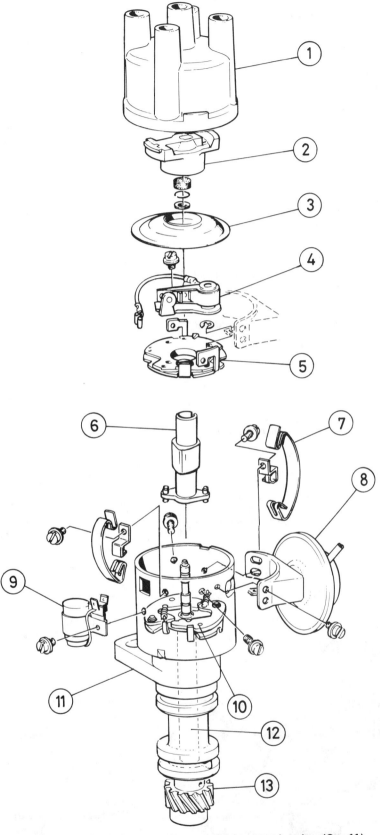

Fig. 4.9 Exploded view of distributor with contact breaker (Sec 11)

1 Distributor cap
2 Rotor arm
3 Plastic cover
4 Contact breaker assembly
5 Baseplate
6 Cam lobe
7 Distributor cap clips
8 Vacuum unit
9 Condenser
10 Centrifugal weights
    assembly
11 Distributor body
12 Distributor drive shaft
13 Skew gear

6   Remove the screws which secure the cap clips and the baseplate, then remove the clips and baseplate.

7   The mechanical advance and retard mechanism can now be seen. The springs do weaken with time, and would benefit from being renewed. Unhook them carefully from their posts, noting that they are not identical, so refit them in their correct positions.

8   Grease the weights assembly and ensure they are free to move on their pivots.

9   Apply vacuum to the vacuum unit and check that the pullrod moves in.

10 If it does not, the diaphragm is probably at fault, and a new vacuum unit should be obtained and fitted.

11 Reassembly is a reversal of removal, noting the following points:

   (a) Apply a few drops of engine oil to the felt wick at the top of the rotor shaft.
   (b) Place a smear of grease or petroleum jelly on the cam lobes where the fibre heel of the contact breaker runs.
   (c) Refit the distributor as described in Section 10.

Breakerless type (TSZ-2)

12 Remove the circlip and washer from above the rotor (photos).

13 Lever the rotor gently off the shaft using two screwdrivers placed under opposite sides of the rotor, being careful not to lose the locating pin.

14 Remove the second circlip from above the impulse sender (photo).

15 Remove the screw securing the vacuum unit to the distributor (photo).

16 Remove the block connector from the side of the distributor (photo), and the cap clips. These screws also secure the impulse sender.

17 Lift out the impulse sender, at the same time removing the vacuum unit, which is hooked onto the post on the underside of the stator (photos).

18 Overhaul of the centrifugal weights is as described for the mechanical distributor, and the same comments about wear in the shaft also apply (photo).

19 Refitting is a reversal of removal, noting the following points:

   (a) Tap the locating pin which locks the rotor in till it is flush with the rotor (photo).
   (b) Measure the air gap between the rotor and stator arms using a feeler gauge, carefully bending the rotor arms if necessary to obtain the correct clearance (photo), which is given in the Specifications.

Note: The impulse sender can be tested in-situ by disconnecting the cable which goes to the coil and checking the resistance across the two terminals, which should be as given in the Specifications. If it is not, renew the sender.

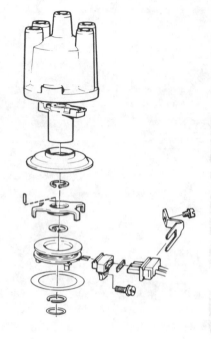

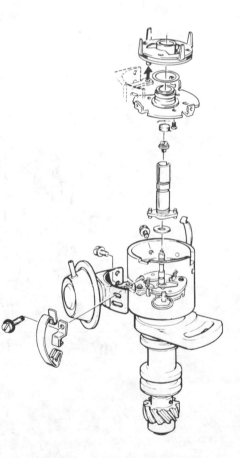

Fig. 4.10 Exploded view of TSZ-2 distributor (Sec 11)

11.12A Removing the circlip ...

B200 and B230 (TZ-28H) type

20 Overhaul procedures for this type of distributor are similar to that described for earlier breakerless types. If the trigger wheel (rotor) is bent, it must be renewed.

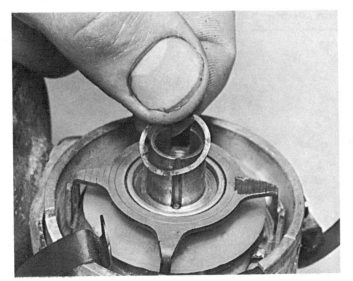
11.12B ... and washer

11.14 Circlip above the impulse sender (arrowed)

11.15 Securing screw for vacuum unit

11.16 Removing the block connector

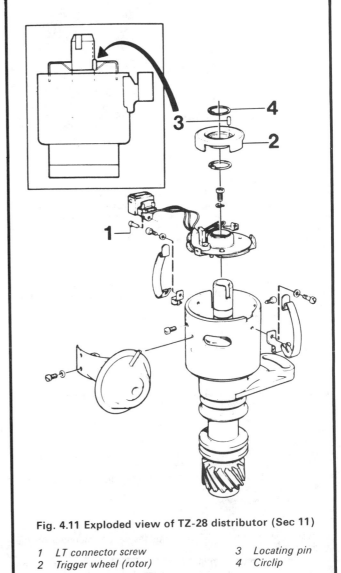
Fig. 4.11 Exploded view of TZ-28 distributor (Sec 11)

1   LT connector screw   3   Locating pin
2   Trigger wheel (rotor)   4   Circlip

11.17A Lifting out the impulse sender

11.17B Showing the screws which secure the two halves of the impulse sender together (A) and the vacuum pullrod spigot (B)

11.18 Centrifugal weights assembly

11.19A Tapping in the pin which locks the rotor

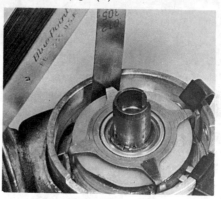

11.19B Measuring the air gap

B230K (Bendix) type

21 The distributor's only function is to distribute current to the spark plugs. Therefore there are no internal components like impulse senders or advance and retard mechanisms, these functions being performed electronically. Overhaul is therefore limited to the rotor arm and shaft. It is unlikely that the shaft will need attention, except in very high mileage vehicles.

12 Control units (electronic ignition) – testing, removal and refitting

1 Testing of control units is best left to your Volvo dealer, who has the necessary equipment and is best able to diagnose faults accurately. Where test information is available, it will be given in the following text.
2 In general, control units are solid state, transistorized units with no user-serviceable parts inside, and if diagnosis reveals malfunction, the only option is to renew the control unit.

TSZ-2

3 Disconnect the battery negative lead if wished.
4 The control unit is situated in the engine bay, mounted on the windscreen washer reservoir bracket (photo).
5 To remove the unit, disconnect the plug on its underside, remove the securing screws and remove the unit.
6 Refit in the reverse order.

TZ-28H

7 Proceed as for the TSZ-2 unit, but the unit is mounted on the left-hand inner wing.
8 The control unit earth connection can be checked by disconnecting the plug, and using a multi-meter. checking between terminal 2 on the plug and an earthing point. Resistance should be zero. If the test meter shows infinity, then there is a break in the earth connection.

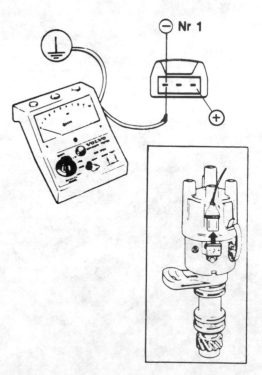

Fig. 4.12 Checking the control unit through the distributor cable (Sec 12)

12.4 Control unit (TSZ-2)
1   Multi-plug
2   Securing screws

9   Check the ignition coil primary resistance between terminal 1 and 4 on the connector. Resistance should be between 0.6 and 0.9 ohms. If it is outside these limits, the coil or wiring is defective.
10 Reconnect the plug at the control unit, and disconnect the plug at the distributor. Measure the resistance between the distributor connector and a good earth (see Fig. 4.12). Resistance should be zero. If the test meter shows infinity, then either there is a break in the wire from number three terminal on the control unit, or the control unit is faulty.
11 Connect the battery and switch on the ignition. The voltage at the distributor positive connection (also shown in Fig. 4.12) should be 11.5 volts. If less than this value, either there is a break in the wire from terminal 5 on the control unit, or the control unit is defective.
12 To check the distributor impulse sender, move the rubber dust cover on the control unit to one side, reconnect the distributor and turn on the ignition. Measure the voltage at terminal 6 on the control unit. Turn the crankshaft with a spanner. Every time a rotor vane passes the pick-up, the voltmeter should read 1.8 to 8.0 volts. In between, the voltage should drop to 0.7 volts. If the voltage is correct in both cases, then the control unit is defective, and if there is some other voltage displayed, the impulse sender in the distributor is defective. **Caution:** *HT voltages will be generated during this test. Take precautions against electric shock.*

Bendix Rex
13 See Section 19.

13 Ignition timing – static

Contact breaker system
1   Turn the engine until No 1 piston is approaching TDC on the compression stroke, and the timing mark on the crankshaft pulley is opposite the appropriate mark (as given in Specifications at the beginning of this Chapter) on the timing scale (photo).
2   Release the clamp bolt on the distributor mounting, and with the distributor cap removed, turn the distributor housing until the contact breaker points are just opening. This can be checked by connecting a test lamp between the distributor low tension terminal and a good earth and switching on the ignition. When the points have just opened, the test lamp will light up.
3   Tighten the clamp bolt and remove the test lamp, switch off the ignition and refit the distributor cap.
4   It is recommended that the timing is now checked with a stroboscope as described in the following Section.

Breakerless systems (except Bendix Rex)
5   Static timing as described above is not possible. Provided the

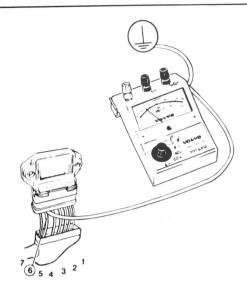

Fig. 4.13 Checking impulse sender (Sec 12)

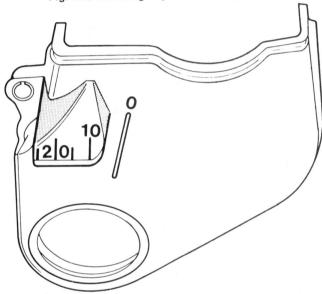

Fig. 4.14 Later type timing marks (Sec 13)

13.1 Timing marks on the timing belt case on early models

distributor has been correctly fitted (Section 10), the timing will be close enough for the engine to be run and dynamic timing to be performed.

Bendix Rex
6   See Section 17.

14 Ignition timing – dynamic

1   It is necessary to use this method where a breakerless type distributor is fitted. The method is recommended for all types of ignition. (For Bendix Rex systems, see also Section 17.)
2   Clean the timing mark on the crankshaft pulley and the timing scale on the cover. Mark the appropriate setting with quick-drying white paint (or chalk).
3   Run the engine to normal operating temperature.
4   Disconnect the vacuum pipe from the distributor and plug it.
5   Connect a stroboscope in accordance with the manufacturer's instructions, usually between No 1 spark plug and No 1 HT lead.
6   Make sure the engine idling speed is correctly set.
7   Start the engine and point the stroboscope at the white marks. They will appear stationary, and if the ignition timing is correctly set they will be in alignment. If they are not directly opposite each other, release the clamp bolt on the distributor mounting and turn the distributor one way or the other until the marks line up. Tighten the clamp bolt.
8   If the engine is now revved up, the pulley mark will move away from the fixed mark, indicating that the centrifugal advance mechanism is operating. If the vacuum pipe is reconnected, the movement of the timing mark in relation to the fixed point will be greater when the engine speed is increased. This indicates that the vacuum advance is operating. Special test equipment is needed for accurate checking of centrifugal and vacuum advance.

15 Ignition timing sender

1   Most models are equipped with a connector (on the valve cover) which carries ignition timing information (photo).
2   The connector is only of use to Volvo dealers or other specialists having the necessary test equipment.

16 Bendix Rex ignition system – general description

1   The Bendix Rex electronic ignition system is fitted to B230K engines.

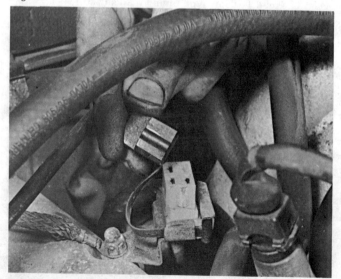

15.1 Ignition timing sender connection on the valve cover

2   It is an advanced micro-processor controlled system, which varies the ignition point in response to several electronic sensors which transmit engine speed, load, temperature and knock (if present) to a centralised control unit, which then sends current via an amplifier/coil unit and the distributor, to the spark plugs.
3   The control unit also operates a carburettor-mounted solenoid valve, which cuts off fuel supply during deceleration, giving a cleaner exhaust, and reduced fuel consumption.
4   Mounted adjacent to the accelerator cable pulley is an idling switch, which establishes a fixed ignition point during idling, and informs the control unit when the accelerator is closed, the control unit then cutting off fuel supply if appropriate.
5   Between these sensors and the control unit, the ignition is advanced and retarded for every load condition of the engine, and fuel supply switched on and off as necessary.

17 Bendix Rex ignition system – ignition timing

1   Static timing is set in production and cannot be adjusted. It is determined by the position of the flywheel.
2   Dynamic timing can be checked using the strobe method described in Section 14, but as all advance and retard functions are carried out electronically, its only value is in fault diagnosis.

18 Bendix Rex ignition system – testing

1   The system is best tested by your Volvo dealer who has the necessary test equipment. No test values were available at the time of writing. If the various sensors are suspected of malfunction, they can be removed and substituted with a serviceable item as described in the following Section.

19 Bendix Rex ignition components – removal and refitting

Control unit
1   The control unit is mounted inside the vehicle under the dashboard.
2   Disconnect the multi-plug, remove the mounting screws and withdraw the unit.

Amplifier/coil unit
3   The unit is mounted in the engine bay, on the left-hand inner wing.
4   Disconnect the multi-plugs on the unit, remove the mounting screws and withdraw the unit.

Distributor
5   The distributor's only function is to 'distribute' HT current to the spark plugs. Therefore there are no contact breakers, senders or advance and retard mechanisms inside. No removal and refitting information was available at the time of writing.

Fuel cut-off solenoid valve
6   The fuel cut-off solenoid is screwed into the carburettor body.
7   To remove it, disconnect the electrical lead and unscrew the solenoid.
8   Use a new sealing washer under the valve on refitting.

Pressure sensor
9   The pressure sensor is connected to the inlet manifold by vacuum tube and to the control unit by cable, and is mounted on the left-hand suspension tower.
10   Disconnect the vacuum tube and electrical cable, remove the mounting screws and remove the unit.

Speed position transducer
11   The speed position transducer is bolted to the rear end of the engine just above the flywheel.
12   To remove it, disconnect the cable and remove the mounting bolts.
Note: *The transducer senses the passage of holes drilled in the flywheel for this purpose, from which it can detect crank angle, engine speed and top dead centre.*

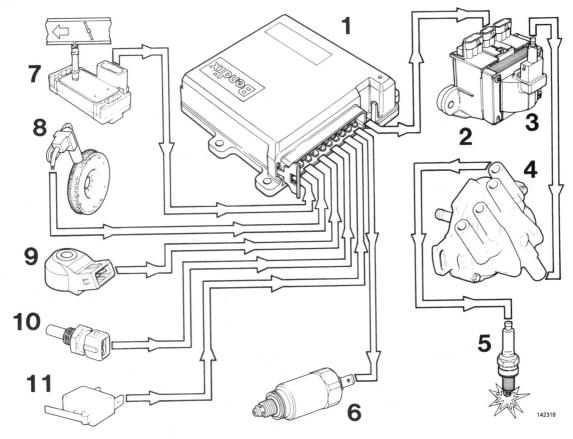

Fig. 4.15 Bendix Rex ignition system components (Sec 19)

1	Control unit	4	Distributor	7	Pressure sensor
2	Power amplifier	5	Spark plug	8	Speed position transducer
3	Coil	6	Solenoid valve	9	Knock sensor

10 Temperature sensor
11 Idling switch

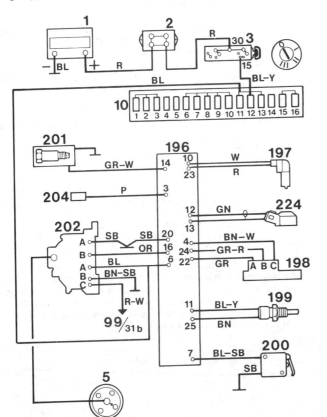

Fig. 4.16 Wiring diagram – Bendix Rex ignition system (Sec 19)

1 Battery
2 Junction box
3 Ignition switch
5 Distributor
10 Fusebox
99 Fuel pump relay
196 Control unit
197 Speed-position transducer
198 Pressure sensor
199 Temperature sensor
200 Idling switch
201 Fuel cut-off solenoid valve
202 Power stage – ignition coil
204 Diagnostic test socket
224 Knock sensor

For colour code, refer to wiring diagrams in Chapter 12

Knock sensor

13 The knock sensor is screwed into the cylinder block between the second and third cylinders, on the left-hand side of the engine.
14 Disconnect the lead and unscrew the sensor. Use a new sealing washer on refitting.

Temperature transmitter

15 The temperature transmitter is screwed into the cylinder head.
16 Partially drain the cooling system. Disconnect the electrical lead and unscrew the transmitter. Use a new sealing washer on refitting.

Idling switch

17 The idling switch is mounted adjacent to the accelerator cable pulley.
18 Disconnect the lead, remove the mounting screws and remove the switch.
Note: *On refitting the switch adjust it within the limits of its mounting holes so that the contacts are closed at idle, but open as soon as any accelerator movement takes place.*

All components

19 Unless otherwise stated, refitting is a reversal of removal.

20 Fault diagnosis – ignition system (contact breaker type)

Failures of the ignition system will either be due to faults in the HT or LT circuits. Initial check should be made by observing the security of spark plug terminals, LT terminals, coil and battery connections. More detailed investigation and the explanation and remedial action in respect of symptoms of ignition malfunction are described in the following sub-Sections. Also see Section 9 for models with a ballast resistor.

Engine fails to start

1 If the engine fails to start and the car was running normally when it was last used, first check there is fuel in the fuel tank. If the engine turns over normally on the starter motor and the battery is evidently well charged, then the fault may be in either the high or low tension circuits. First check the HT circuit. **Note:** *If the battery is known to be fully charged, the ignition light comes on, and the starter motor fails to turn the engine check the tightness of the leads on the battery terminals and also the security of the earth leads to their connections on the body. It is quite common for the leads to have worked loose, even if they look and feel secure. If one of the battery terminal posts gets very hot when trying to work the starter motor this is a sure indication of a faulty connection to that terminal.*
2 One of the commonest reasons for bad starting is wet or damp spark plug leads and distributor. Remove the distributor cap. If condensation is visible internally, dry the cap with a rag and also wipe over the leads. Damp starting problems can be cured by the use of Holts Wet Start. To prevent the problem recurring Holts Damp Start can be used to provide a sealing coat so excluding any further moisture from the ignition system. Holts Cold Start will help to start a car when only a very poor spark occurs. Replace the cap.
3 If the engine still fails to start, check that current is reaching the plugs, by disconnecting each plug lead in turn at the spark plug end, and hold the end of the cable about 3/16 in (5 mm) away from the cylinder block. Spin the engine on the starter motor.
4 Sparking between the end of the cable and the block should be fairly strong with a regular blue spark. (Hold the lead with rubber to avoid electric shocks). If current is reaching the plugs, then remove them and clean and regap them. The engine should now start.
5 If there is no spark at the plug leaks take off the HT lead from the centre of the distributor cap and hold it to the block as before. Spin the engine on the starter once more. A rapid succession of blue sparks between the end of the lead and the block indicates that the coil is in

order and that the distributor cap is cracked, the rotor arm faulty, or the carbon brush in the top of the distributor cap is not making good contact with the spring on the rotor arm. Possibly the points are in bad condition. Clean and reset them as described in this Chapter.
6 If there are no sparks from the end of the lead from the coil, check the connections at the coil end of the lead. If it is in order start checking the low tension circuit.
7 Use a 12V voltmeter or a 12V bulb and two lengths of wire. With the ignition switch on and the points open test between the low tension wire to the coil (it is marked 15 or +) and earth. No reading indicates a break in the supply from the ignition switch. Check the connections at the switch to see if any are loose. Refit them and the engine should run. A reading shows a faulty coil or condenser, or broken lead between the coil and the distributor.
8 Take the condenser wire off the points assembly and with the points open, test between the moving point and earth. If there now is a reading, then the fault is in the condenser. Fit a new one and the fault is cleared.
9 With no reading from the moving point to earth, take a reading between earth and the (1 or –) terminal of the coil. A reading here shows a broken wire, which will need to be renewed between the coil and distributor. No reading confirms that the coil has failed and must be renewed, after which the engine will run once more. Remember to refit the condenser wire to the points assembly. For these tests it is sufficient to separate the points with a piece of dry paper while testing with the points open.

Engine misfires

10 If the engine misfires regularly, run it at a fast idling speed. Pull off each of the plug caps in turn and listen to the note of the engine. Hold the plug cap in a dry cloth or with a rubber glove as additional protection against a shock from the HT supply.
11 No difference in engine running will be noticed when the lead from the defective circuit is removed. Removing the lead from one of the good cylinders will accentuate the misfire.
12 Remove the plug lead from the end of the defective plug and hold it about 3/16 in (5.0 mm) away from the block. Restart the engine. If the sparking is fairly strong and regular, the fault must lie in the spark plug.
13 The plug may be loose, the insulation may be cracked, or the points may have burnt away giving too wide a gap for the spark to jump. Worse still, one of the points may have broken off. Either renew the plug, or clean it, reset the gap, and then test it.
14 If there is no spark at the end of the plug lead, or if it is weak and intermittent, check the ignition lead from the distributor to the plug. If the insulation is cracked or perished, renew the lead. Check the connections at the distributor cap.
15 If there is still no spark, examine the distributor cap carefully for tracking. This can be recognised by a very thin black line running between two or more electrodes, or between an electrode and some other part of the distributor. These lines are paths which now conduct electricity across the cap thus letting it run to earth. The only answer is a new distributor cap.
16 Apart from the ignition timing being incorrect, other causes of misfiring have already been dealt with under the section dealing with the failure of the engine to start. To recap – these are that:

a) *The coil may be faulty giving an intermittent misfire.*
b) *There may be a damaged wire or loose connection in the low tension circuit.*
c) *The condenser may be short circuiting.*
d) *There may be a mechanical fault in the distributor (broken driving spindle or contact breaker spring).*

17 If the ignition timing is too far retarded or the automatic advance mechanisms are not working, it should be noted that the engine will tend to overheat, and there will be a quite noticeable drop in power. If the engine is overheating and the power is down, and the ignition timing is correct, then the carburettor should be checked, as it is likely that this is where the fault lies.

21 Fault diagnosis – ignition system (breakerless type)

Symptom	Reason(s)
Engine fails to start	Discharged battery or loose connections Fault in system component Disconnected system leads Incorrect air gap
Engine starts and runs but misfires	Faulty spark plug Cracked distributor cap Worn advance mechanism Incorrect timing Poor earth connections Incorrect air gap or faulty pick-up unit
Engine overheats	Incorrect timing Advance weights seized (retarded) Perforated vacuum pipe
Engine 'pinks'	Timing too advanced Advance weights seized (advanced) Broken weight spring

Chapter 5 Clutch

Contents

Specifications

General

Clutch type	Single dry plate with diaphragm spring
Actuation	Hydraulic or cable, according to model
Diameter	8.5 in (215.9 mm)

Adjustment

Hydraulic type	Automatic in use
Cable type (free play at release arm)	0.04 to 0.12 in (1.0 to 3.0 mm)
Clutch pedal travel	6.3 in (160.0 mm)

Pressure plate

Warpage (maximum)	0.008 in (0.2 mm)

Hydraulic fluid type/specification ....

Hydraulic fluid to DOT 4 (Duckhams Universal Brake and Clutch Fluid)

1 General description

1 The clutch is a single dry plate, diaphragm spring type, cable- or hydraulically operated, according to model, via a release arm and bearing.
2 The main components of the clutch are the pressure plate (also called the cover), which incorporates the diaphragm spring, the driven plate (or friction plate or disc) and the release arm and bearing.
3 The pressure plate is bolted to the flywheel, the driven plate is sandwiched between them, but free to move axially on the splines of the gearbox input shaft.
4 With the engine running and the clutch pedal released, the diaphragm spring forces the driven plate against the flywheel, thus transmitting drive from engine to gearbox.

5 When the clutch pedal is depressed, the release arm causes the release bearing to press upon the diaphragm spring, which relieves the pressure on the driven plate and interrupts the drive.
6 Hydraulically-operated clutches need no adjustment during service, but cable-operated clutches must be adjusted periodically to compensate for wear in the friction linings on the driven plate.
7 On early models, the clutch hydraulic system had its own reservoir, then in approximately 1984–5 model year, the system shared the brake fluid reservoir. Later models have returned to having a separate reservoir.
Warning: *Asbestos hazard. As with the brakes, the clutch friction linings may contain asbestos. Any dust in or around the pressure plate, friction plate and bellhousing should be assumed to contain asbestos and treated accordingly.*

2 Routine maintenance

1 At the intervals given in the *Routine maintenance* Section at the beginning of this Manual, carry out the following operations.
2 Check the level of hydraulic fluid in the reservoir when applicable (photo). The level should be maintained about the 'MIN' mark. Inspect the system pipelines and slave cylinder for leaks. The need for frequent topping-up of the reservoir would indicate such a leak, and this should be investigated. When the reservoir is shared with the braking system, both systems will have to be inspected.
3 When renewing the brake fluid, renew the fluid in the clutch hydraulic system (Section 4).
4 Check the clutch adjustment on models with cable actuation (Section 3).

3 Clutch cable – removal, refitting and adjustment

1 Raise and support the vehicle. Slacken the adjuster locknut and screw the adjuster in to release all tension in the cable.
2 Unhook the return spring from the release arm, then release the cable end from the arm.
3 Gain access to the clutch pedal, then remove the split pin from the clevis pin, remove the clevis pin and disconnect the cable end.
4 Pull the cable through the engine bulkhead, into the engine bay.
5 Refit in the reverse order, routing the cable to the right-hand side of the steering shaft.
6 Make sure the rubber buffer in the release arm is installed correctly.
7 Screw in the adjuster to give the specified free play in the release arm (see Specifications), tightening the adjuster locknut on completion.

4 Clutch hydraulic system – bleeding

1 Fill the reservoir with the specified hydraulic fluid.
2 Raise and support the vehicle. Slacken the bleed screw on the slave cylinder, and then fit a length of plastic tubing over the bleed screw. The tube must be a tight fit on the screw.
3 Place the other end of the tube in a jar containing clean hydraulic fluid, sufficient to keep the end of the tube submerged.
4 Have an assistant depress the clutch pedal. Tighten the bleed screw when the pedal is fully depressed. Now release the pedal, slacken the bleed screw and depress the pedal again. Continue this process until air-free fluid emerges from the end of the tube. Keep the reservoir level topped up, or air will enter the system through the reservoir and the bleeding procedure will have to recommence.
5 On completion, tighten the bleed screw and remove the plastic tubing.
6 The use of one-man bleeding equipment is described in Chapter 9.

5 Clutch – removal and refitting

1 Remove the engine or gearbox as desired (photo).
2 Make alignment marks across the flywheel and pressure plate.
3 Remove the pressure plate-to-flywheel bolts progressively and in diagonal pattern, to reduce the possibility of warping the pressure plate.
4 Once the spring pressure is released, remove the bolts completely and lift off the pressure and driven plates. Take a note of which way round the driven plate faces.
5 Inspect the components as described in Section 7.
6 Before commencing to refit the clutch components, clean any oil or grease off the friction surfaces of the pressure plate or flywheel. Make sure your hands are clean, to avoid contamination of the driven plate.

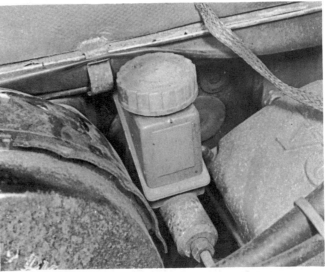
2.2 Clutch hydraulic fluid reservoir on the master cylinder

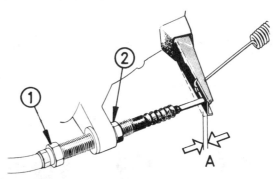
Fig. 5.1 Release arm free play adjustment (Sec 3)

1 Adjuster   A = 0.04 to 0.12 in (1.0 to 3.0 mm)
2 Locknut

Fig. 5.2 Correct fitting of the rubber buffer in the release arm (Sec 3)

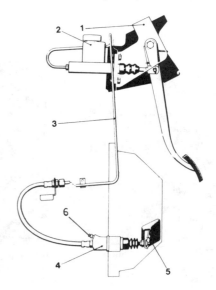

Fig. 5.3 Clutch hydraulic system (Sec 4)

1 Pedal bracket   4 Slave cylinder
2 Master cylinder   5 Release arm
3 Hydraulic pipeline 6 Bleed screw

7 Inspect the pilot bearing in the crankshaft and renew it if necessary as described in Chapter 1, Section 19.

8 When refitting the clutch assembly, it is vital that the driven plate is centralised in the pressure plate in order that the gearbox input shaft can be inserted. 'Universal' alignment tools are available, or one can be made from the likes of a broom handle. The important point is that it should be a snug fit in the pilot bearing and the splines of the driven plate.

9 Offer the driven plate up to the flywheel (photo). Make sure the plate is the right way round. Generally they are marked flywheel side (photo) (Schwungrad).

10 Place the pressure plate in position, observing the alignment marks if applicable, and insert the retaining bolts finger-tight, then insert the alignment tool (photo).

11 Check that the driven plate is centralised with the pressure plate, then tighten the pressure plate bolts, again progressively and in diagonal pattern.

12 Remove the alignment tool and visually check the alignment of pilot bearing, driven plate and pressure plate. If they are not central, difficulty will be encountered when refitting the gearbox.

13 Refit the gearbox, or engine as applicable.

Note: *On later models, the flywheel dowel pins have been repositioned. As the pressure plate fits over these dowel pins, early clutch assemblies cannot be fitted to later engines (1984 on approximately). Later clutch assemblies are drilled to fit both pin positions.*

6 Clutch release arm and bearing – removal and refitting

1 Whenever the engine or gearbox is removed, take the opportunity to inspect the release arm and bearing. Check the bearing for smoothness of operation, cracking or blueing due to overheating. Renew as necessary.

2 Remove the engine or gearbox. Remove the bellhousing dust cover from the release arm.

3 Disconnect the release arm from the ball-stud pivot. On some models this may be held by a spring clip.

4 Slide the release bearing and arm off the guide sleeve and separate them (photos).

5 Clean the guide sleeve and splines of the gearbox shaft, and grease them with a heat-resistant grease or anti-seize compound.

6 Fill the groove in the release bearing with the same grease, then refit the bearing to the arm, and also grease the bearing-to-arm pivot point.

7 Refitting is a reversal of removal, but make sure the spring on the ball-stud pivot (when applicable) is located correctly. Also be careful not to get grease onto the clutch friction surfaces.

7 Clutch components – inspection

1 Clean the clutch driven plate, cover and flywheel in a solvent to remove all grease and oil. Take precautions against dust inhalation, which may contain asbestos.

2 Inspect the friction surfaces of the flywheel and pressure plate for scoring or cracks (photo). Score marks of less than 0.040 in (1.0 mm) are acceptable, anything deeper will mean a new component. Flywheels can be machined by specialist firms, but see Chapter 1.

3 Inspect the pressure plate for warping by laying a straight edge across it and using feeler gauges to detect warp. Limits are given in the Specifications.

4 Inspect the 'fingers' of the diaphragm spring for wear, especially where it contacts the release bearing. Signs of blueing indicate overheating.

5 Inspect the driven plate linings for wear. If the lining is worn down to, or almost down to, the rivet heads, the plate must be renewed. If the linings are oil contaminated or show a hard black glaze, the plate should be renewed and the cause of the oil contamination rectified.

6 In practice, it is usual to renew the driven plate and pressure plate together, and also to fit a new release bearing if it is showing any signs of wear, in order to delay early repetition of the clutch removal process.

5.1 Showing clutch with gearbox removed (five of the pressure plate-to-flywheel bolts arrowed)

5.9A Fitting the driven plate and pressure plate

5.9B 'Flywheel side' marking on driven plate

5.10 Clutch centering tool in position

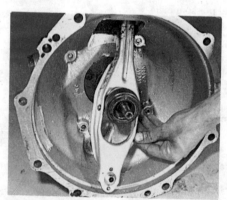

6.4A Release arm and bearing on a cable-operated clutch ...

6.4B ... and on a hydraulic type

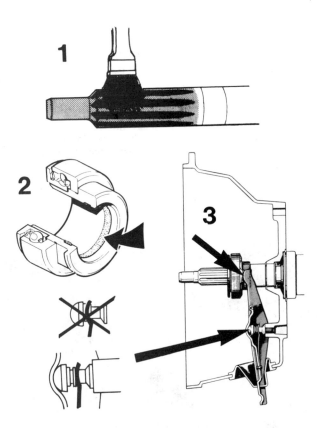

Fig. 5.4 Clutch release component lubrication. Inset shows correct fitting of spring clip on bell-stud pivot (Sec 6)

1   Input shaft splines   3   Arm pivot points
2   Groove in bearing

8 Clutch pedal – removal and refitting

1   Remove the soundproofing panels from under the dash.
2   Release the pedal return spring.
3   Slacken the adjuster and unhook the clutch cable, or disconnect the master cylinder pushrod clevis pin, as applicable.
4   Remove the nut from the pedal pivot bolt, then tap out the pivot bolt and retrieve the pedal and return spring.
5   Clean the assembly and inspect the pivot bushes for wear, renewing them as necessary.
6   Use molybdenum disulphide grease to lubricate the pivot points and pivot bolt, and the cable or pushrod attachment points.
7   Refit in the reverse order, and on cable-operated clutches, adjust the release arm free travel on completion (Section 3).

9 Clutch master cylinder – removal, overhaul and refitting

1   Connect up the end of a suitable length of tubing to the bleed screw of the slave cylinder and place the other end in a jar. Undo the bleed screw one turn and pump the clutch pedal up and down until the clutch fluid reservoir is empty of fluid. Remove the tube and tighten the bleed screw.
2   Disconnect the fluid outlet pipe from the master cylinder. Also disconnect the pipe which connects the master cylinder to the fluid reservoir, on models where the reservoir is shared with the braking system. Protect the paintwork against fluid spillage; wash off spilt fluid immediately.
3   Remove the panel under the dashboard, and then disconnect the pushrod from the clutch pedal by removing the clevis pin.
4   Unscrew and remove the bolts from the master cylinder mounting flange and remove the master cylinder.

7.2 Flywheel friction surface, showing light scoring and a small crack

5   Clean away all external dirt before taking the master cylinder to a totally clean working area.
6   Pull off the dust-excluding cover and withdraw the pushrod.
7   Extract the circlip now visible at the end of the master cylinder and remove the washer, piston, seals and return spring.
8   Examine the surfaces of the piston and the cylinder bore for rust, scoring or bright wear areas. If such conditions are evident, renew the master cylinder complete.
9   If these components are unmarked and in good condition, discard the rubber seals and wash each part in clean hydraulic fluid or methylated spirit. **Do not use any other fluid.**
10 Obtain a repair kit which will contain all the necessary seals and other renewable items.
11 Dip the new seals in clean hyraulic fluid and position them on the piston using the fingers only.
12 Insert the spring, piston and seals and washer carefully into the master cylinder and secure with the circlip.
13 Insert the pushrod and refit the dust cover.
14 Refitting the master cylinder is a reversal of the removal procedure.
15 Check that there is a clearance of 0.04 in (1 mm) between the pushrod and the piston. If not, adjust the clearance by turning the

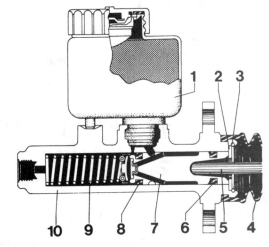

Fig. 5.5 Sectional view of the clutch master cylinder (Sec 9)

1   Fluid reservoir   6   Piston seal
2   Washer   7   Piston
3   Circlip   8   Piston seal
4   Dust cover   9   Spring
5   Pushrod   10 Cylinder body

adjusting nuts on each side of the pushrod yoke that connects to the pedal.
16 Refit the pedal mounting cover panel under the dashboard.
17 Fill up the master cylinder reservoir with hydraulic fluid and bleed the system as described in Section 4.

10 Clutch slave cylinder – removal, overhaul and refitting

1 Disconnect the flexible hose from the rigid hydraulic pipe by unscrewing the union nut from the latter.
2 Disconnect the hose from its securing bracket, and plug the open end of the fluid line to avoid loss of fluid.
3 On early models, extract the circlip and withdraw the slave cylinder from the clutch housing. On later models, unbolt and remove the slave cylinder.
4 Clean away all external dirt from the slave cylinder and remove the rubber dust cover and pushrod.

5 Extract the circlip (which is now visible at the end of the cylinder) and withdraw the piston assembly and spring.
6 Inspect the surfaces of the piston and cylinder bores for rust, scoring or bright wear areas. If these are evident, the complete slave cylinder must be renewed.
7 If the components are in good condition, wash them in clean hydraulic fluid or methylated spirit. **Do not use any other fluid.**
8 Obtain a repair kit which will contain a new seal and other renewable items.
9 Dip the new piston seal in clean hydraulic fluid and manupulate into position on the piston using the fingers.
10 Refit the spring and piston assembly into the cylinder and secure with the circlip. Refit the pushrod and dust cover (photos).
11 On early models check that the domed nut is located on the pushrod as shown in Fig. 5.6, and if necessary loosen the locknut, re-position the domed nut then tighten the locknut.
12 Refitting is a reverse of the removal procedure. The system must be topped up with the specified hydraulic fluid and then bled, as described in Section 4.

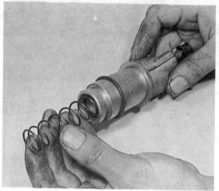
10.10A Insert the spring ...

10.10B ... followed by the piston. Make sure it is the right way round

10.10C Fitting the dust cover and pushrod

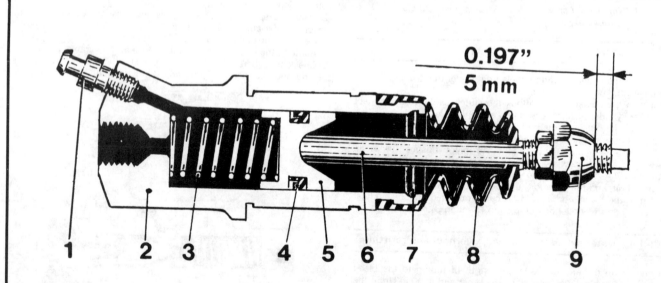
Fig. 5.6 Sectional view of an early type slave cylinder (Sec 10)

1 Bleed screw
2 Cylinder body
3 Spring
4 Seal
5 Piston
6 Pushrod
7 Stop ring
8 Dust cover
9 Domed nut (early models only)

11 Fault diagnosis – clutch

Symptom	Reason(s)
Judder when taking up drive	Clutch friction surfaces worn Oil contamination on friction surfaces Worn splines on gearbox shaft or driven plate Pressure plate worn or defective Engine or gearbox mountings worn
Clutch drag (failure to release)	Air in hydraulic system Driven plate sticking on splines Release arm free play excessive Gearbox shaft seized in crankshaft bearing Driven plate rusted to flywheel (after long periods of disuse)
Clutch slip (increase in engine speed without increase in vehicle speed)	Friction surfaces worn or oil contaminated Pressure plate defective Release arm free play insufficient

Noise when depressing clutch pedal:
    Engine stopped
 	
    Engine running
	Pedal pivot dry (needs lubrication)
	Clutch cable or release arm pivot dry
	Release bearing dry or worn
	Pressure plate spring diaphragm fingers worn or damaged

Chapter 6 Transmission

Contents

Specifications

Part A: Manual gearbox
General

Type .... 4 or 5 forward speeds and reverse. Overdrive on some models
Identification:
   M40 .... 4-speed, early models (to 1976)
   M41 .... 4-speed with overdrive, early models
   M45 .... 4-speed, later models (to 1984)
   M46 .... 4-speed with overdrive, later models
   M47 .... 5-speed (1984 on)

Ratios (typical)

	M40/41	M45/46	M47
1st	3.41 : 1	3.71 : 1	4.03 : 1
2nd	1.99 : 1	2.16 : 1	2.16 : 1
3rd	1.36 : 1	1.37 : 1	1.37 : 1
4th	1.0 : 1	1.0 : 1	1.0 : 1
5th	–	–	0.83 : 1
Reverse	3.25 : 1	3.68 : 1	3.68 : 1

Lubrication

Lubricant type/specification:

M40, M41 .... Hypoid gear oil, viscosity SAE 80W/90 or 80/90, to API-GL-4 (Duckhams Hypoid 80)

M45*, M46* and M47* .... ATF type F or G, or Volvo Thermo-oil part number 1 161 243-9 (from 1982 only for M46) (Duckhams Q-Matic)

*Do not mix oil types

Lubricant capacity (drain and refill, approx):

M40, M45 .... 1.3 pints (0.75 litre)
M41 .... 2.8 pints (1.6 litres)
M46 .... 4.1 pints (2.3 litres)
M47 .... 2.3 pints (1.3 litres)

Clearances and endfloats

M45/46

Reverse gear to gear selector .... 0.004 to 0.04 in (0.1 to 1.0 mm)

Endfloat:
Input shaft .... 0.0004 to 0.008 in (0.1 to 0.20 mm)
Layshaft (cast iron casing) .... 0.001 to 0.004 in (0.025 to 0.10 mm)
Layshaft (aluminium casing) .... 0.0012 in (0.03 mm) endfloat to 0.0020 in (0.05 mm) preload*
Mainshaft .... 0.0004 to 0.008 in (0.01 to 0.20 mm)

*No preload is allowed if a vibration damper is fitted – see Section 24.

M47 (where different to above)

Reverse gear to gear selector .... 0.004 to 0.10 in (0.1 to 2.5 mm)

Endfloat:
Layshaft .... 0.0004 to 0.004 in (0.01 to 0.10 mm)
5th gear synchroniser hub .... 0.0004 to 0.008 in (0.01 to 0.20 mm)

Torque wrench settings

	lbf ft	Nm
Output flange nut (M40)	70 to 77	95 to 105
Bellhousing bolts (M45/6/7)	26 to 37	35 to 50
Gearbox top cover bolts (M45/6/7)	11 to 18	15 to 25
Output flange nut (M45/47):		
M16	52 to 66	70 to 90
M20	66 to 81	90 to 110
Rear cover bolts	26 to 37	35 to 50
Layshaft bolt (M47)	26 to 33	35 to 45
5th gear synchro nut (later type M47)	89	120
Drain plug	20 to 30	27 to 40
Bearing retainer plate bolts (M47)	11 to 18	15 to 25

Part B: Overdrive

Reduction ratio .... 0.8 : 1
Lubricant type/capacity .... See Part A Specifications

Torque wrench settings

	lbf ft	Nm
Solenoid valve	37	50
Oil sump bolts	7	10
Output flange nut	130	175
Pressure filter plug	16	22
Overdrive-to-intermediate flange nuts	9	12
Overdrive main-to-rear casing nuts	9	12

Part C: Automatic transmission

Type .... Borg Warner 35 (3-speed), Borg Warner 55 (3-speed), or Aisan Warner 70 or 71 (3-speed plus overdrive 4th)

Borg Warner 35

Fluid type/specification .... ATF type F or G (Duckhams Q-Matic)
Fluid capacity (from dry) .... 11.3 pints (6.4 litres) approx
Converter size .... 9.5 in (240 mm)
Converter ratio .... 1 : 1 to 2 : 1
Reduction ratio:
1st speed .... 2.39 : 1
2nd speed .... 1.45 : 1
3rd speed .... 1 : 1
Reverse .... 2.09 : 1

Borg Warner 55

Fluid type/specification .... ATF type F or G (Duckhams Q-Matic)
Fluid capacity (from dry)*:
Pre-1979 .... 11.4 pints (6.5 litres) approx
1979 on (with deep oil sump) .... 12.1 pints (6.9 litres) approx

*Includes approximately 4.4 pints (2.5 litres) in torque converter

Torque converter size	9.5 in (240 mm)
Torque converter ratio	1 : 1 to 2 : 1
Reduction ratios:	
1st speed	2.45 : 1
2nd speed	1.45 : 1
3rd speed	1 : 1
Reverse	2.21 : 1

Aisan Warner 70 and 71

Fluid type/specification	Dexron 11D type ATF (Duckhams D-Matic)
Fluid capacity (from dry)*	13.2 pints (7.5 litres) approx
*Includes approximately 4.4 pints (2.5 litres) in torque converter	
Converter size	9.8 in (248 mm)
Converter ratio	2 : 1 to 1 : 1
Reduction ratios:	
1st speed	2.45 : 1
2nd speed	1.45 : 1
3rd speed	1 : 1
4th speed (overdrive)	0.69 : 1
Reverse	2.21 : 1

Torque wrench settings

	lbf ft	Nm
Converter housing to transmission case	8 to 13	11 to 18
Converter to driveplate	25 to 30	35 to 41
Oil sump bolts	8 to 13	11 to 18
Oil drain plug	9 to 12	12 to 17
Brake band adjuster locknut	30 to 40	41 to 45
Starter inhibitor switch contact	6 to 8	8 to 11
Kickdown cable connection at transmission case	8 to 9	11 to 12
Oil cooler connection nipple	12 to 15	17 to 21
Oil cooler connection nut	10 to 12	14 to 17
Speedometer gear locknut	4 to 7	6 to 10
BW55		
Converter housing to engine	26 to 37	35 to 50
Driveplate to converter:		
M12 bolts	41 to 66	55 to 90
M10 bolts	30 to 37	41 to 50
Converter housing cover:		
M6 bolts	4 to 6	6 to 9
M8 bolts	13 to 19	18 to 25
Sump (oil pan):		
Yellow gasket	4 to 7	6 to 10
Blue gasket	6 to 9	8 to 12
Output flange	30 to 37	41 to 50
Oil cooler pipe union	15 to 22	20 to 30
Oil filler pipe nut	48 to 52	65 to 70
Drain plug	9 to 13	12 to 17
*AW70/71**		
Driveplate to torque converter	30 to 36	41 to 49
Sump (oil pan)	3 to 3.5	4 to 5
Drain plug	13 to 17	18 to 23

*Other torque wrench settings as given for type BW55

PART A: MANUAL GEARBOX

1 General description

There are five different designations of manual gearbox in use on the 240 series. All are derived from the same basic unit, and are as follows:

M40 – 4-speed
M41 – 4-speed with overdrive
M45 – modified 4-speed
M46 – modified 4-speed with overdrive
M47 – 5-speed

The M40/41 types were fitted to early models, and were replaced with the modified M45/46 in 1976. The M45/46 was again modified in 1979, a simpler version being introduced. The 5-speed M47 was introduced in 1984, and is basically the M45 with a 5th gear housed in a separate unit on the rear of the gearbox. Some modifications to the 5th gear components took place in 1986.

All units have synchromesh on all forward gears, gear changing being by floor-mounted remote gear lever via mechanical linkage.

The overdrive unit is electro-hydraulic, controlled by a switch in the gear lever, and operates on top gear only. On later models, the overdrive is automatically disengaged when changing down to 3rd gear. The overdrive is covered in detail in Part B of this Chapter.

2 Routine maintenance and oil seal renewal

1 Every 6000 miles or six months, or if prompted by unusual noises or evidence of leakage, check the gearbox oil level as follows.
2 Drive the vehicle over a pit, or raise and support it so that it is still level.
3 Clean the area round the filler/level plug on the side of the gearbox. Unscrew and remove the plug (photo).
4 Oil should be up to the level of the bottom of the plug hole. Insert a clean piece of stiff wire if necessary to check.
5 Top up if necessary with the specified oil. Do not overfill: allow any surplus to drip out of the plug hole.
6 Refit and tighten the filler/level plug, using a new sealing washer if necessary. (Early models use taper seating plugs without washers. Apply a dab of sealant on the plug threads if leakage is a problem.)

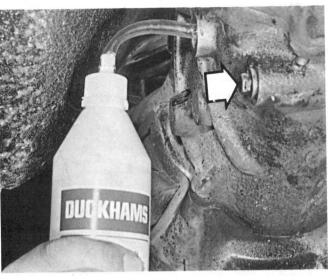

2.3 Filling the gearbox with oil – note also drain plug (arrowed)

7 Frequent need for topping-up can only be due to leakage, which should be found and rectified.
8 Oil changing is no longer specified as a routine operation, although a drain plug is provided for the owner who wishes to do so. It would be beneficial to clean the overdrive oil filter screen, on models so equipped, at the same time (Section 29).
9 In the event of leakage, the drive flange oil seal can be renewed without removing the gearbox. Proceed as follows.
10 Raise and support the vehicle.
11 Unbolt the propeller shaft from the drive flange and move it aside.
12 Counterhold the flange and undo its central nut.
13 Draw off the flange, using a puller if necessary. Do not try to hammer it off. Be prepared for oil spillage.
14 Prise out the old oil seal and clean up its seat. Inspect the seal rubbing surface on the flange: clean it, or renew the flange if necessary.
15 Lubricate the new seal and fit it, lips inwards, using a piece of tube to tap it home. On the M47 gearbox, the seal should be recessed by 2.5 mm (0.1 in).
16 On the gearboxes with overdrive, apply locking compound to the output shaft splines. Be careful not to contaminate the seal.
17 Refit the flange and secure it with the nut, tightened to the specified torque.
18 Refit the propeller shaft.
19 Top up the gearbox oil.
20 Lower the vehicle. Check for leaks after the next run.

---

3 Gear lever – removal, overhaul and refitting

Note: *This procedure applies specifically to 1979 and later models fitted with the M45, M46 and M47 transmissions. No information is available for earlier models, but the procedure is believed to be similar.*
1 Unclip the gear lever gaiter from the console and slide the gaiter up the gear lever.
2 Drive out the roll pin at the lower end of the gear lever, using a reaction bar to prevent straining the linkage.
3 On models with overdrive, remove the facia trim side panel and disconnect the overdrive wiring. Use a length of cord tied to the cable to assist in re-routing when refitting (see Fig. 6.4).
4 On models with overdrive, prise out the top of the gear lever knob and disconnect the overdrive switch.
5 Remove the gear lever.
6 Grip the gear lever in a soft-jawed vice, then use a soft mallet to tap off the knob (photo).
7 Remove the screw (steel pullrod only) and withdraw the reverse detent knob (photo).
8 Remove the pullrod, spring and interlock sleeve (photo).
9 Remove the screw and separate the sleeve from the pullrod. Note

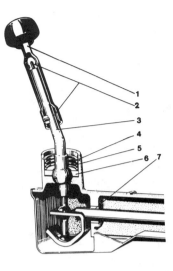

Fig. 6.1 Cutaway view of the early type gear lever (Sec 3)

1 Gear lever – upper part
2 Rubber bushes
3 Gear lever – lower part
4 Circlip
5 Spring
6 Washer
7 Selector rod

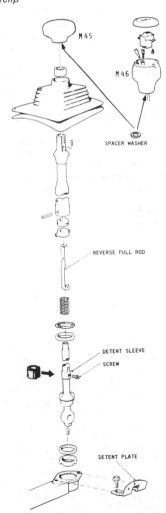

Fig. 6.2 Components of later type gear lever (Sec 3)

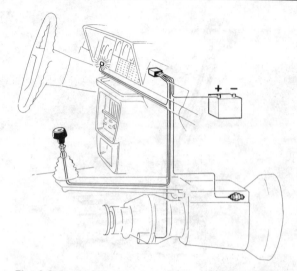

Fig. 6.3 Overdrive wiring runs – later models (Sec 3)

that the sleeve has been modified (Fig. 6.5), and the later type should always be fitted, together with a 0.08 in (2.0 mm) thick, 0.63 in (16.0 mm) diameter washer beneath the gear lever knob, to ensure that the sleeve clears the detent bracket.

10 Bend the end of the steel pullrod as shown in Fig. 6.6 to prevent it rattling.

11 Soak the plastic pullrod in water for one hour before fitting.

12 Fit the spring and interlock sleeve to the pullrod, apply locking fluid to the screw then tighten it.

13 Grease the steel pullrod and fit the reverse detent knob to the rod and secure it with the screw.

14 Fit the pullrod to the lever, then grip the lever in a soft-jawed vice and tap the knob into position.

15 Fit the lever to the stub on the gearbox, and secure by tapping in the pin.

16 Engage 1st gear and use a feeler gauge to check that the clearance between the reverse detent plate and the detent screw is between 0.02 and 0.06 in (0.5 and 1.5 mm). Engage 2nd gear and check that the clearance is the same. If necessary, loosen the bolts and adjust the reverse detent plate as necessary.

17 Re-connect the overdrive cable if fitted, connecting the switch at the top of the gear lever and pushing the switch back into the knob.

18 Refit the gear lever gaiter.

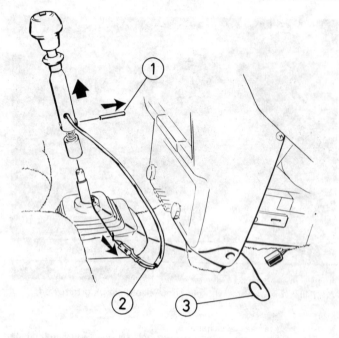

Fig. 6.4 Re-routing overdrive wiring – use a length of cord as shown (Sec 3)

1   Pin   2   Overdrive cable
                            3   Cord

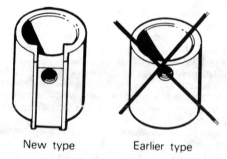

New type   Earlier type

Fig. 6.5 Different types of pullrod interlock sleeve (Sec 3)

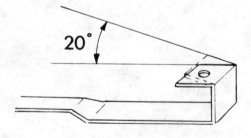

Fig. 6.6 Pullrod bending diagram (Sec 3)

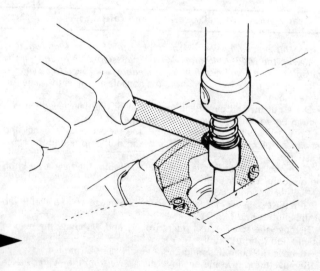

Fig. 6.7 Checking reverse detent clearance with a feeler blade (Sec 3)

3.6 Removing the gear lever knob

3.7 Withdrawing the reverse detent knob (plastic pullrod type). It need not be removed completely once the rod is released

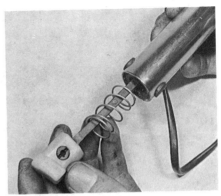
3.8 Removing the pullrod (plastic type), spring and interlock sleeve

4 Gear lever – disconnecting for gearbox removal

Note: *On models with overdrive, disconnect the overdrive cable as described in Section 3*

M40/41 type
1 Remove the gear lever gaiter.
2 Using circlip pliers, remove the circlip from the gear lever ball end housing.
3 Lift out the spring and washer.
4 Lift out the gear lever.

M45, 46 and 47 type
5 Remove the grub screw (4 mm Allen key) from the selector rod fork end underneath the vehicle, push out the pin and disconnect the fork.
6 Remove the gear lever gaiter.
7 Remove the bolts from the reverse detent bracket and lift out the bracket.
8 Remove the circlip and lift out the gear lever.
Note: *On some models, the reversing light switch is mounted on the gear lever carrier, and must be removed prior to lowering the gearbox.*

All types
9 Re-connection of the gear lever is a reversal of the above procedures on all types.
10 On completion, adjust the reverse detent bracket if necessary as described in Section 3.

5 Reversing light switch – removal and refitting

M40/41 type
1 The reversing light switch is mounted on the top left-hand rear gearbox casing.
2 Raise and support the vehicle. Disconnect the battery and the electrical cables to the switch.
3 Unscrew the switch from the gearbox casing.
4 Refit in the reverse order, using a new sealing washer under the switch.

M45/46 type (up to 1980)
5 Gain access to the rear of the centre console and disconnect the reversing light connector.
6 Remove the gear lever gaiter.
7 Bend a piece of stiff wire into a hook, and insert it down between the left-hand side soundproofing and tunnel. (This is to pull the cable back through when refitting).
8 Raise and support the vehicle. Remove the bolts from the right-hand side of the gearbox crossmember.
9 Feed the reversing light cable down through the side of the tunnel and soundproofing to the underside of the vehicle. Free the cable from the gear lever carrier.
10 Unscrew and remove the reversing light switch from the gearbox housing, using a cranked open-ended 22 mm spanner.
11 Fit a new switch, using a new sealing washer under the switch.

Fig. 6.8 Gearlever grub screw on M45/46/47 gearbox (Sec 4)

Fig. 6.9 Reverse detent bracket bolts (arrowed) (Sec 4)

12 Hook the cable through the wire (see paragraph 7), and pull the cable through to the inside of the vehicle. Secure the cable to the gear lever carrier.
13 Refit the gearbox crossmember bolts. Lower the vehicle.
14 Connect the cable, check the operation of the reversing light, then refit the console side panel and gear lever gaiter.

M45/46 (1980 on) and M47 types
15 Raise and support the vehicle. Position a jack under the gearbox and just take the weight.
16 Remove the gearbox crossmember bolts.
17 Unhook the rubber hooks supporting the exhaust silencer.
18 Lower the gearbox sufficiently to allow room to unscrew the

6.2 Gearbox support crossmember securing
bolts

6.3A Gearbox centre support block bolt
(later models)

6.3B Support block-to-gearbox bolts (later
models)

reversing light switch, working from under the vehicle or inside the
engine bay.
19 Disconnect the electrical leads, and unscrew the switch from the
gearbox housing.
20 Fitting a new switch is a reversal of this procedure, using a new
sealing washer under the switch.

6 Gearbox support crossmember – removal and refitting

1 The gearbox support crossmember is bolted to the floorpan either
side of the transmission tunnel, underneath the gearbox.
2 To remove it, raise and support the vehicle and take the weight of
the gearbox on a jack. Remove the bolts at either end of the
crossmember (photo).
3 Remove the bolt(s) from the centre support block (photos) (this
has been modified several times, and varies between models).
4 Lift the crossmember over the exhaust and remove it from the
vehicle.
5 Refit in the reverse order.

7 Gearbox (all types) – removal and refitting

Note: *The M40/41 gearbox can be removed from the bellhousing,
leaving the bellhousing attached to the engine. On all other types the
gearbox and bellhousing are removed together. The procedure given
here for the M40/41 is for removal, leaving the bellhousing in position.
If the bellhousing is to be removed with the gearbox, the procedure is
similar to that described for M45/46 gearboxes.*

Removal – M40/41 type
1 On models with overdrive, see Section 33, paragraph 1.
2 Disconnect the battery (Chapter 12). Remove the gearlever
(Section 4).
3 Raise and support the vehicle. Drain the gearbox (Section 2).
4 Position a trolley jack under the gearbox and take its weight.
5 Remove the gearbox support crossmember (Section 6).
6 Remove the engine rear mounting.
7 Disconnect the exhaust bracket (Chapter 3).
8 Disconnect the propeller shaft from the output flange and hang it
out of the way (Chapter 7).
9 Disconnect the speedometer cable.
10 Place a piece of wood between the rear of the engine and the
bulkhead. Lower the gearbox on the jack until the upper gearbox bolts
can be reached. A socket with a long extension, and a universal joint,
will be needed.
11 Disconnect any electrical cables still attached to the gearbox (this
can vary between models).
12 Remove the right upper and lower left gearbox retaining bolts.
These must be replaced with guide pins, which could be made up from
old bolts with the heads cut off and screwdriver slots cut in to the
shank.
13 Remove the remaining two bolts, then slide the gearbox rearwards

off the guide pins, and lower the gearbox to the ground. Do not allow
the weight of the gearbox to hang on the input shaft.

Removal – M45/46 and 47 types
Note: *On these gearboxes, the clutch bellhousing and gearbox are
removed together. The procedure is similar to that given for M40/41
gearboxes with the following additional points.*
14 Disconnect the clutch cable/slave cylinder (Chapter 5).
15 Disconnect the front exhaust silencer mounting rubber support
rings (Chapter 3).
16 Remove the starter motor (Chapter 12).
17 Remove the engine-to-bell housing bolts, and lower the gearbox
to the ground.

Refitting – all types
18 Refit by reversing the removal operations, noting the following
points.

> (a) *Apply a smear of molybdenum-based grease to the input
>   shaft splines*
> (b) *Make sure that the clutch driven plate is properly centred, and
>   that the clutch release components have been fitted in the
>   bellhousing*
> (c) *Adjust the clutch cable (when applicable)*
> (d) *Refill or top up the gearbox oil*

8 Gearbox overhaul – general

1 Before overhauling a gearbox, consideration should be given to the
comparative cost of a reconditioned exchange unit, which in terms of
time is often a better course of action. Additionally, for overhaul a
range of pullers is required, and the use of a large vice is almost
essential. If these are not available, an exchange unit becomes even
more attractive.
2 Before starting the overhaul, give the gearbox a thorough wash in
solvent to remove all the grime. Any grit which finds its way inside the
gearbox will accelerate wear after rebuild when the gearbox is in use.
3 During dismantling, as components are removed, keep them in
order, and do not mix them up. This will not only help in reassembly,
but adjacent parts 'bed in' together, and any wear will show up more
readily and enable corrective action to be taken.

9 Gearbox (all types) – inspection

1 With the gearbox dismantled, give all components a good clean in
a solvent and then dry them off using non-fluffy rag, or preferably air
dry using an old hair dryer, or one of the new heat guns is very useful.
2 Inspect all components for wear, cracks, chipping etc, and the
bearings for harshness of operation or blueing due to overheating. It
would be better to renew them as a matter of course, having come this
far.
3 The thrust washers would also benefit from being renewed.

9.5 Fitting a circlip to lock gears/hubs to shaft

10.1A Fitting a sliding key to a synchroniser unit ...

10.1B ... and a spring

4   All oil seals should be renewed, not forgetting the one in the clutch bellhousing.

5   Some retaining circlips are available in various thicknesses, and the thickest compatible circlip should be used at reassembly (photo).

6   Inspect the selector forks for cracks and wear, especially on their engaging lugs. Later types have renewable brass inserts.

7   Inspect the selector shafts for wear and parallelism. Renew the detent balls and springs if necessary.

8   Before reassembly, coat all components in the specified gearbox oil.

10 Synchroniser units – dismantling and reassembly

1   The synchroniser assemblies consist of the inner hub and outer sleeve together with the three keys, which are tensioned by the springs (photos).

2   Each assembly then has a synchroniser ring (or cone), which fits into the sleeve over the keys.

Note: *When assembled correctly, the two key tensioning springs (one on either side of the unit) much be hooked into the same key, one running clockwise, the other anti-clockwise. The free end of the spring must curve away from the hub (Fig. 6.10).*

3   On M45, 46 and 47 types, on 3rd/4th synchroniser, the cut-out portions of the hub should align with the ground teeth on the sleeve. If there is a machined groove in the sleeve, the groove should face the flat side of the hub (Fig. 6.11).

4   The synchroniser units should be inspected for wear as for the other components, and any worn parts renewed. As this is the most likely cause of gearbox overhaul anyway, it is probably better to renew the complete synchroniser assemblies. It may not be possible to obtain individual components in any case.

11 Gearbox (M40/41) – dismantling into major assemblies

1   On M41 types, remove the overdrive unit as described in Section 33.

2   On M41 types, remove the circlip securing the overdrive oil pump eccentric to the shaft and remove the eccentric. It is keyed to the shaft, so do not lose the key.

3   The procedure from now on is the same for both M40 and M41 types, except where differences are pointed out.

4   Remove the top cover and lift off the cover and gasket.

5   Remove the springs and the balls which will be found under them.

6   Remove the protective cover from the end of the selector rods (photo).

7   Remove the screws securing the selector forks and dogs to the selector rods.

8   Push the centre selector rod rearwards into 1st gear position, then drive out the roll pin by a fraction of an inch, making sure it does not contact 1st gear.

9   Now push the selector rod forwards, so that the pin will clear 1st gear, and drive it out completely.

10 Remove the selector rods (photo), being careful to hold the forks

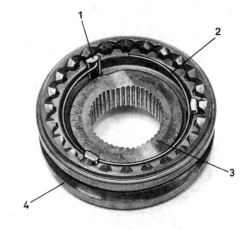

Fig. 6.10 Synchromesh unit (Sec 10)

1   *Sliding key*   3   *Hub*
2   *Spring*   4   *Sleeve*

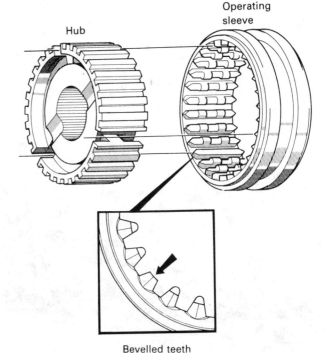

Fig. 6.11 Relationship of synchro hub to sleeve (Sec 10)

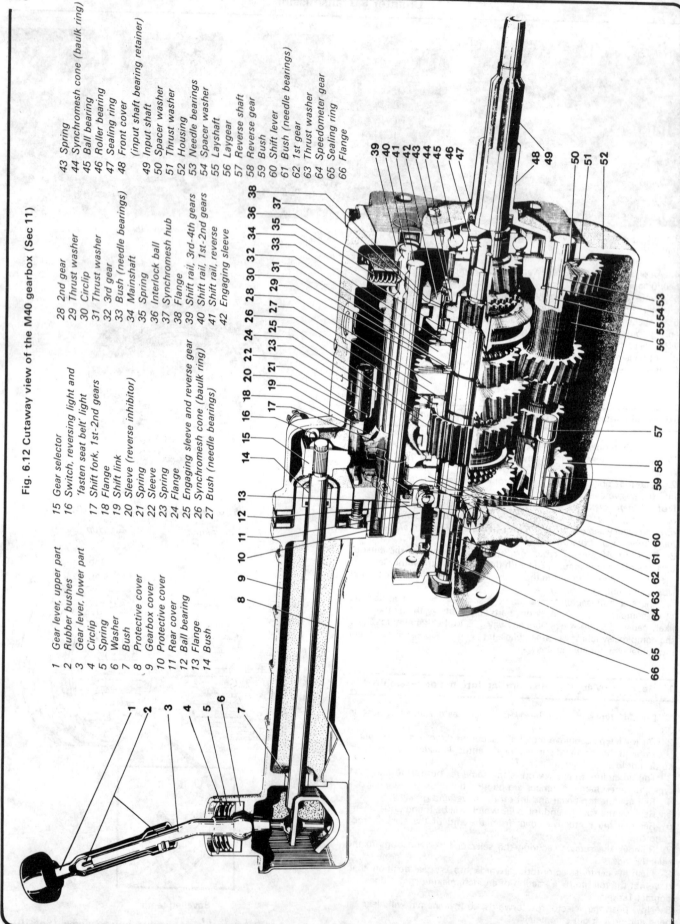

Fig. 6.12 Cutaway view of the M40 gearbox (Sec 11)

1 Gear lever, upper part
2 Rubber bushes
3 Gear lever, lower part
4 Circlip
5 Spring
6 Washer
7 Bush
8 Protective cover
9 Gearbox cover
10 Protective cover
11 Rear cover
12 Ball bearing
13 Flange
14 Bush

15 Gear selector
16 Switch, reversing light and 'fasten seat belt' light
17 Shift fork, 1st-2nd gears
18 Flange
19 Shift link
20 Sleeve (reverse inhibitor)
21 Spring
22 Sleeve
23 Spring
24 Flange
25 Engaging sleeve and reverse gear
26 Synchromesh cone (baulk ring)
27 Bush (needle bearings)

28 2nd gear
29 Thrust washer
30 Circlip
31 Thrust washer
32 3rd gear
33 Bush (needle bearings)
34 Mainshaft
35 Spring
36 Interlock ball
37 Synchromesh hub
38 Flange
39 Shift rail, 3rd-4th gears
40 Shift rail, 1st-2nd gears
41 Shift rail, reverse
42 Engaging sleeve

43 Spring
44 Synchromesh cone (baulk ring)
45 Ball bearing
46 Roller bearing
47 Sealing ring
48 Front cover (input shaft bearing retainer)
49 Input shaft
50 Spacer washer
51 Thrust washer
52 Housing
53 Needle bearings
54 Spacer washer
55 Layshaft
56 Laygear
57 Reverse shaft
58 Reverse gear
59 Bush
60 Shift lever
61 Bush (needle bearings)
62 1st gear
63 Thrust washer
64 Speedometer gear
65 Sealing ring
66 Flange

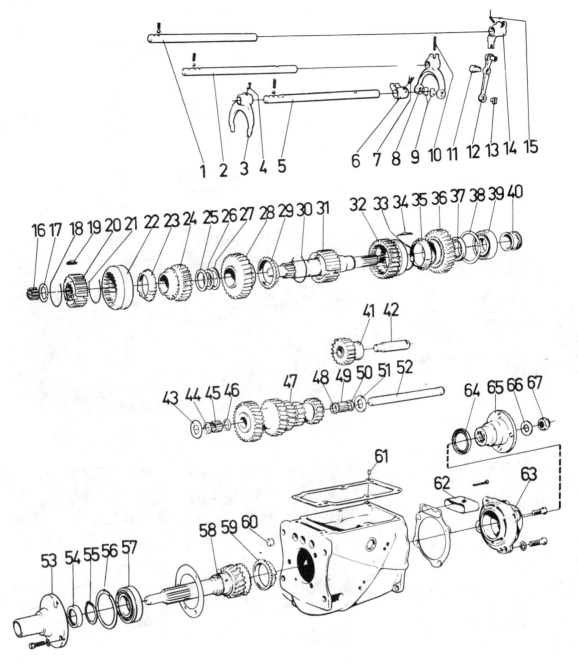

Fig. 6.13 Exploded view of the M40 gearbox (Sec 11)

1 Reverse selector rod	18 Spring	35 Synchromesh cone	52 Layshaft
2 1st-2nd selector rod	19 Flange	36 1st gear	53 Front cover
3 Selector fork	20 Synchromesh hub	37 Thrust washer	54 Sealing ring
4 Screw	21 Spring	38 Circlip	55 Circlip
5 3rd-4th selector rod	22 Engaging sleeve, 3rd-4th	39 Ball bearing	56 Circlip
6 Dog	23 Synchromesh cone	40 Speedometer pinion	57 Ball bearing
7 Screw	24 3rd gear	41 Reverse gear	58 Input shaft
8 Selector fork	25 Thrust washer	42 Shaft	59 Synchromesh cone
9 Flange pins	26 Circlip	43 Thrust washer	60 Cap plug
10 Tensioning pin	27 Thrust washer	44 Spacer washer	61 Guide pin
11 Bearing pin	28 2nd gear	45 Roller bearing	62 Protective cover
12 Lever	29 Synchromesh cone	46 Spacer washer	63 Bearing housing
13 Flange pin	30 Spring	47 Intermediate gear	64 Sealing ring
14 Selector dog	31 Mainshaft	48 Spacer washer	65 Flange
16 Roller bearing	32 Engaging sleeve, 1st-2nd	49 Nacelle roller bearing	66 Washer
17 Circlip	33 Spring	50 Spacer washer	67 Nut
	34 Flange	51 Thrust washer	

square to the rods as they are withdrawn, or they will foul up. Lift out the forks and dogs.

11 Engage two gears at once to lock the gearbox, then undo the flange nut (it will be tight) and use a puller to remove the flange. (On models with overdrive, this will not be necessary as the flange has already been removed.)

12 Remove the bolts from the mainshaft bearing housing at the rear of the gearbox (photo).

13 Similarly, remove the screws from the input shaft housing (photo), followed by the housing itself.

14 Turn the bearing housings so that both ends of the layshaft are exposed, and drive out the layshaft. The layshaft must be driven out rearwards.

Note: *The layshaft runs in needle roller bearings which are not caged, and as the shaft is driven out, the bearings will drop into the bottom of the casing, along with the layshaft gears. These should be retrieved*

when the main and input shafts are removed. Volvo produce a special tool to prevent this happening, but if this is not available, do not worry at this stage. Methods of refitting will be discussed later.

15 Pull the mainshaft out rearwards (photo), complete with rear bearing housing on non-overdrive models.

16 Drive out the input shaft forwards (photo). Note the roller bearings on which the mainshaft runs (photo).

17 Retrieve the laygear and needle roller bearings (photos).

18 Drive out or extract the reverse gear shaft and lift out reverse gear.

19 Remove the reverse selector assembly if wished.

12 Mainshaft (M40/41) – dismantling

1 Remove the circlip from the 3rd/4th synchroniser hub (photos).

11.6 Removing the protective cover from the end of the selector rods

11.10 Pulling out a selector rod

11.12 Removing the bolts from the mainshaft bearing housing

11.13 Removing the input shaft housing

11.15 Mainshaft assembly being removed

11.16A Pulling out the input shaft

11.16B Needle bearings in the input shaft which support the mainshaft

11.17A Removing the laygear

11.17B Layshaft, laygear and needle roller bearings

12.1A Mainshaft assembly

12.1B Removing the circlip from the synchroniser hub

12.2A Slide off the hub, sleeve ...

12.2B ... and ring

12.2C Removing 3rd gear

12.5A Second gear circlip ...

12.5B ... being removed

12.6 ... followed by 2nd gear

12.11A Removing the circlip from the bearing housing ...

12.11B ... and lifting out the bearing

12.12A Removing the speedometer drive gear ...

12.12B ... noting the spring position

2 Slide off the hub, sleeve and synchroniser ring, followed by 3rd gear (photos).

3 It may be necessary, if the hub is tight, to pull off the whole assembly, along with 3rd gear using a puller.

4 With 3rd gear removed, slide off the thrust washer behind 3rd gear.

5 Remove the circlip and thrust washer from in front of 2nd gear (photos).

6 Slide off 2nd gear and synchroniser ring (photo).

7 Now remove 1st/2nd gear engaging sleeve and 1st gear synchroniser ring. The hub is part of the mainshaft, so the springs and sliding keys will have to be removed separately.

8 Using 1st gear as a support, drive or pull the mainshaft from the bearing housing.

9 Remove 1st gear and thrust washer from the mainshaft.

10 Prise out the oil seal from the bearing housing.

11 Remove the circlip from the bearing housing (photo), and lift out the bearing (photo).

12 Remove the speedometer drivegear from the housing (photo), taking note of the spring position (photo). (This does not apply to models with overdrive.)

13 Mainshaft (M40/41) – reassembly

1 Using a suitable mandrel, press the ball-bearing into the bearing housing.

2 Select a circlip which fits snugly in the groove and fit it in place.

3 On M40 types, fit the speedometer gear into the housing.

4 Fit a new seal into the front of the housing, again using a suitable mandrel to press it home.

5 Assembly 1st/2nd gear synchroniser assembly onto the mainshaft, referring to Section 10.

M40 type

6 On M40 types, fit the 1st/2nd gear synchroniser ring, 1st gear and thrust washer onto the shaft.

7 Fit the shaft into the bearing housing, ensuring the speedometer gear is in position, and press it fully home.

M41 type

8 On M41 types, place the bearing housing onto a support tube, the diameter of which will take the shaft. Place the tube in a vice, and fit the thrust washer, 1st gear and synchroniser ring to the housing.

9 Now drop the shaft down into the housing, pressing it fully home.

10 Select and fit a circlip behind the cover.

11 Fit the key and oil pump eccentric, and lock them in place with a circlip.

Both types

12 On both types fit the synchroniser ring, 2nd gear and thrust washer onto the shaft, then select and fit a circlip.

13 Fit the 3rd gear thrust washer, 3rd gear and synchroniser ring.

14 Assemble 3rd/4th gear synchroniser (see Section 10) and fit to the shaft, ensuring the machined groove faces rearwards.

15 Select and fit a circlip to the end of the shaft.

14 Gearbox (M40/41) – reassembly

1 Fit the reverse selector assembly if it has been removed.

2 Fit the reverse gear and shaft. The end of the shaft with the machined groove should protrude out of the casing by the specified amount (see Fig. 6.15).

3 Fit the input shaft ball-bearing (if removed), pressing it onto the shaft as far as it will go using a piece of tubing.

4 Select and fit the input shaft bearing-to-shaft circlip – see Section 9. Also fit the bearing outer circlip.

5 The layshaft needle roller bearings now have to be fitted. This can be done by using a length of plastic or copper tubing of diameter equal to, or just smaller than, the layshaft, and of equal length to the laygear assembly (photo).

6 Fit the layshaft to the laygear assembly, then fit the needle roller bearings (there are 21 of them in each bearing), not forgetting the washers at each end (photos). Use plenty of grease which will help to keep the bearings in place. Now push the length of tubing through the

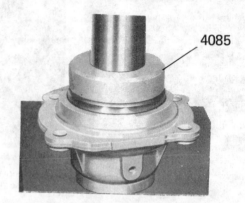

Fig. 6.14 Fitting the mainshaft bearing into its housing using mandrel 4080 (Sec 13)

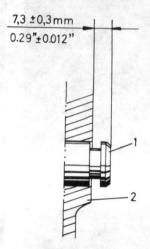

7,3 ±0,3mm
0.29"±0.012"

Fig. 6.15 Fitting the reverse pinion shaft (M40) (Sec 14)

1 Reverse shaft   2 Gearbox casing

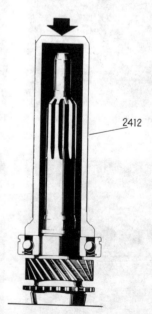

Fig 6.16 Fitting the ball-bearing on the input shaft (Sec 14)

laygear, pushing out the layshaft as you do so. The tubing is left inside the laygear while further reassembly continues, and then the process is reversed when the layshaft is finally fitted, pushing out the tube (photos).

7 Stick the layshaft thrust washers in place inside the casing, using grease to keep them in place.

8 Fit the gasket to the mainshaft bearing housing, again using a smear of grease to keep it in place.

9 Place the laygear assembly into the gearbox casing (large gears towards the input shaft end).

10 Fit the roller bearings into the input shaft bearing, using plenty of grease to keep them in place. (There are 14 of them).

11 Check that the layshaft washers are still in position.

12 Fit the synchroniser ring to the input shaft, and then carefully push the shaft into its housing (photo).

13 Carefully pass the mainshaft through the other end of the casing, and engage it with the input shaft. Make sure that none of the bearings become dislodged, and press the bearing and housing in as far as they will go.

14 Now carefully invert the gearbox so that the laygear comes to rest on the mainshaft and loosely in line with the layshaft holes.

15 Align the laygear with the holes, check that the thrust washers are still in position, then carefully push the layshaft through the holes and the laygear, pushing out the plastic tubing as you do so.

16 If the needle bearings should come out, dismantle the gearbox and start again.

17 Press a new oil seal into the input shaft housing, and fit a new gasket, making sure that the hole in the gasket lines up with the hole in the casing (photo). (This is an oil passageway for lubrication of the bearing.)

14.5 Using a piece of tubing to retain the bearings

14.6A Fit a washer ...

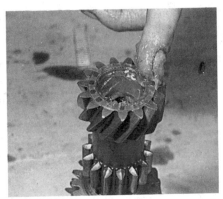
14.6B ... using plenty of grease ...

14.6C ... to retain the bearings ...

14.6D ... and outer washer ...

14.6E ... before inserting the tubing

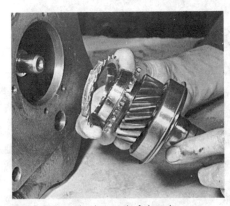
14.12 Fitting the input shaft into its housing

14.17 The hole in the casing which should not be covered by the gasket

14.19 Fitting the mainshaft bearing housing bolts

18 Fit the input shaft housing, using new O-ring seals under the screw heads.

19 On M40 types, fit the mainshaft bearing housing bolts and tighten them fully (photo). On M41 types, check that the oil pump eccentric is fitted, as previously described, and fit the overdrive unit as described in Section 33.

20 Position the selector forks in place.

21 Insert the centre (1st/2nd) selector rod, and tap in a new roll pin to secure the fork to the rod (photos).

22 Insert 3rd/4th gear selector rod, angling the selector dog towards the centre shaft. Fit and tighten the dog and fork securing screws. The use of thread-locking compound is recommended.

23 Fit the reverse selector rod and secure its dog.

24 Place the detent balls into their holes, and place the springs over them.

25 Fit the gearbox cover using a new gasket, and tighten down the bolts.

26 Check the operation of the selectors, and that the shafts turn freely.

27 Fit the protective cover over the ends of the selector shafts.

28 On M40 types, fit the output flange and nut. Counterhold the flange and tighten the nut to the specified torque.

29 Fill the gearbox with the recommended oil and refit as described in Section 7.

15 Gearbox (M45/46) pre-1979 – dismantling into major assemblies

1 Remove the gear lever carrier (photo).

2 Remove the sleeve and knock out the pin securing the selector rod (photo).

M45 type

3 On M45 types, counterhold the output flange and undo the output flange nut – this will be tight.

4 Remove the flange, using a puller if it is tight (photo).

M46 type

5 On M46 types, if the overdrive has been removed with the gearbox, remove the overdrive unit as described in Section 33.

6 Remove the circlip, then remove the oil pump eccentric which is keyed to the shaft – don't lose the key.

7 Remove the overdrive intermediate flange. Recover the bearing shims.

Both types

8 Remove the bolts securing the clutch bellhousing to the gearbox and separate the two. The bolts (or Allen screws) are reached from inside the bellhousing. Recover the input shaft bearing shim.

9 Remove the bolt from the locking plate and remove the speedometer drive pinion – M45 only (photo).

10 Remove the gearbox top cover (photos).

11 Lift out the three springs (photo) and retrieve the three balls which are under them.

12 Remove the rear cover (photo) and slide off the speedometer drivegear (M45 only). Recover the bearing shims.

13 Use a pin punch to remove the roll pins from the selector forks and dogs (photo). The selector rods will have to be moved to-and-fro, in order to remove the roll pins without them causing damage to the gears.

14 Remove the selector rods, forks and forward gear selectors. Identify them for subsequent refitting.

15 Remove the circlip securing the mainshaft bearing to the shaft, and then use two levers to ease the bearing from the housing (photos). Recover the thrust washer.

16 Prise out the layshaft bearing outer races, which will allow the layshaft to be lowered (photo).

17 Pull out the input shaft together with its ball-bearing (photo).

18 Remove 4th gear synchroniser ring from the end of the mainshaft and lift out the mainshaft (photo), keeping the synchroniser ring with it.

19 Lift out the layshaft (photo).

20 Use a soft drift to tap out the reverse gear shaft rearwards, then lift out the shaft and gear.

21 Unhook the reverse gear selector fork from the selector rod by turning the rod.

22 Remove the reverse gear selector rod.

14.21A Inserting the centre selector rod

14.21B Fit a new roll pin ...

14.21C ... and drive it home

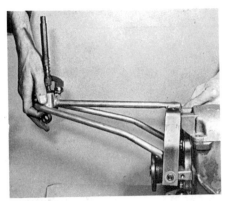

15.1 Removing the gear lever carrier

15.2 Sleeve and pin (arrowed) which secure the rod

15.4 Pulling off the output flange

15.9 Removing the speedometer drive pinion

15.10A Lift off the top cover

15.10B Inside the cover is the selector mechanism

15.11 Remove the three springs that hold down the balls

15.12 Removing the rear cover

15.13 The roll pins that secure the forks and selectors (arrowed)

15.15A Easing out the mainshaft bearing with levers ...

15.15B ... before lifting it out

15.16 Layshaft taper roller bearing with outer races removed

15.17 Pulling out the input shaft, complete with bearing and circlips

15.18 Lift out the mainshaft ...

15.19 ... followed by the layshaft

16 Layshaft (M45/46) pre-1979 – dismantling and reassembly

1   The layshaft and gears are a single unit, and all that can be done is the removal of the taper roller bearings from each end (photo).
2   Pull the bearings off, using a puller if they are tight.
3   Inspect the bearings and layshafts gears with reference to Section 9. If the laygear show signs of excess wear or damage, the whole unit should be renewed.
4   Fit new bearings, pressing them fully on to the shaft.

17 Input shaft (M45/46) pre-1979 – dismantling and reassembly

1   The input shaft runs in the ball-bearing which fits into the casing, and its inner end contains the taper roller bearing which locates with the mainshaft.
2   Remove the circlips from the bearing, if not already carried out, then pull the bearing from the shaft.
3   Remove the taper roller bearing from inside the housing at the other end of the shaft.
4   Inspect the shaft and bearings with reference to Section 9.
5   Grease a new taper roller bearing and push it into position in the shaft.
6   Press on a new ball-bearing and fit the retaining circlip to lock it to the shaft. Do not fit the external circlip yet.

18 Mainshaft (M45/46) pre-1979 – dismantling

1   Remove 1st gear and synchroniser ring from the mainshaft (photo).

Fig. 6.17 Input shaft, showing the roller bearing in position (Sec 17)

2   Remove the circlip for 1st/2nd synchroniser hub, and press off the hub and 2nd gear.
3   Repeat the operation for 3rd/4th hub and gear (photo).
4   With all the components removed, inspect them as described in Sections 9 and 10.

19 Mainshaft (M45/46) pre-1979 – reassembly

1   Assemble both synchroniser hubs as described in Section 10.
2   Press 3rd gear and its synchroniser ring, and 3rd/4th gear synchroniser hub onto the shaft. The flat side of the hub should face inboard (towards 3rd gear).
3   Ensure the synchroniser ring slots fully over the keys.
4   Fit the circlip to retain 3rd/4th synchroniser hub.

16.1 Layshaft assembly with taper bearings (arrowed)

18.1 Removing 1st gear and synchroniser ring

18.3 Components of the mainshaft (hubs and sleeves assembled). 1st/2nd synchro hub has not been removed

5 Press 2nd gear and synchroniser ring, and 1st/2nd synchroniser hub, onto the other end of the shaft, and lock in place with a circlip.
6 Fit the synchroniser ring and 1st gear.

20 Gear selector mechanism (M45/46) pre-1979 – dismantling and reassembly

1 Unhook the return spring and remove the selector plate from the top cover, held by three bolts. (On later types it may be held by circlips).
2 Remove the roll pin from the selector rod and remove the rod and selector dog.
3 Prise out the seal in the cover and renew it, pressing in a new seal, spring side facing inwards.
4 After inspection and renewal of any worn parts, reassemble the selector mechanism which is a reversal of dismantling.

21 Rear cover (output flange) oil seal (M45) pre-1979 – renewal

Note: *This operation can be carried out* in situ *after removal of the propeller shaft and drive flange. See Section 2.*
1 Prise out the oil seal from the rear cover.
2 Grease the lips of the new oil seal, then use a socket of suitable diameter to tap the seal back into the cover.
3 The spring side of the seal should face inwards, and the seal pressed in until the seal's inner lips are flush with the casting on the inner face of the cover.

22 Clutch bellhousing seal (M45/46) pre-1979 – renewal

1 The seat fits into the release bearing sleeve, the procedure being the same as described for the rear cover oil seal, pressing the seal in as far as it will go.

23 Gearbox (M45/46) pre-1979 – reassembly

1 Fit the reverse gear selector rod, lever and selector dog. Do not fit the roll pin at this stage.
2 Fit the reverse gear and shaft (photo).
3 The shaft end should be flush with the housing ± 0.002 in (0.05 mm) (photo).
4 Adjust the clearance between the selector lever and reverse gear to 0.004 to 0.04 in (0.1 to 1.0 mm) by tapping the pivot in or out of the housing. Fit the roll pin to the selector dog and rod.
5 Place the layshaft in the bottom of the casing.
6 Place the mainshaft into the casing with the rear end protruding, then fit the thrust washer onto the mainshaft.
7 Fit the mainshaft bearing and fit the external circlip round the bearing.
8 Push the mainshaft and bearing into the housing. **Warning:** *Ensure that no gear teeth become jammed together during this operation, and keep the bearing square on to the housing.* When correctly fitted, the bearing external circlip should be hard against the casing.
9 Place 4th gear synchroniser ring onto the front end of the mainshaft.
10 Push the input shaft and bearing into engagement with the end of the mainshaft, pushing the input shaft in as far as it will go.
11 Lift up the layshaft and position each end bearing in the holes in the casing.
12 Now pull out the input shaft sufficiently to fit the external circlip round the bearing, then push the shaft and bearing back in until the circlip is hard against the casing.
13 Tap in the layshaft outer races (photo).
14 Using a depth gauge, measure the distance between the front face of the input shaft bearing and the surface of the gearbox casing (photo).
15 Also measure the distance between the face of the bellhousing and the bearing seat in the bellhousing. Add to this measurement 0.010 in

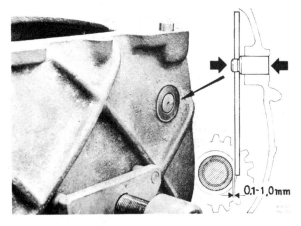

Fig. 6.18 Adjusting the clearance between the selector lever and reverse gear (Sec 23)

Fig. 6.19 Fitting the mainshaft bearing (Sec 23)

Fig. 6.20 Input shaft with external circlip (arrowed) fitted (Sec 23)

(0.25 mm) to allow for the thickness of the gasket.
16 From this combined measurement, subtract the measurement taken in paragraph 14.
17 Subtract the specified endfloat from the result obtained in paragraph 16 to give the required thickness of the input shaft bearing shim. For example:

Depth of bearing seat plus gasket thickness = 5.32 mm
Protrusion of bearing above gearbox casing = 4.65 mm
Difference = 0.67 mm
Specified endfloat = 0.01 to 0.20 mm
Difference minus endfloat = 0.47 to 0.66 mm

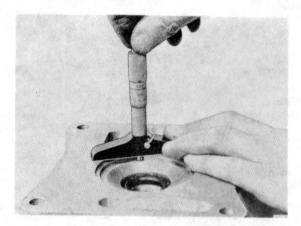

Fig. 6.21 Measuring the distance between the front face of the input shaft bearing and surface of the gearbox casing (Sec 23)

23.2 Reverse gear and shaft

Shims are available in various thicknesses. In the above example, a shim of 0.50 or 0.60 mm would be used.

18 Smear the bellhousing gasket and the selected shim with grease, fit them in position, and fit the bellhousing to the gearbox. Tighten the retaining bolts to the specified torque.

19 Fit the selector forks into the synchroniser hubs.

20 Slide the selector rods into position through the forks, at the same time fitting the dogs. Tap in the roll pins until they are flush (photos).

21 Determine the thickness of shims for the layshaft and mainshaft by a similar method as described for the input shaft. Permissible tolerances are given in the Specifications. Do not forget to include the gasket thickness of 0.0098 in (0.25 mm). **Note:** *On M46 types, the mainshaft measurement is taken from the face of the intermediate flange surface to the bearing seat surface. On all types, layshaft bearing shim thickness is determined by subtracting the specified endfloat from the depth of the bearing outer race below the casing (including gasket).*

22 Fit the speedometer drive to the mainshaft – M45 only (photo).

23 Stick the rear cover gasket and the selected mainshaft shim in place on the rear cover with grease.

24 Similarly, stick the layshaft shim in place on the layshaft outer race.

25 Fit the rear cover, and tighten the bolts to the specified torque.

26 Fit the output flange. Hold the flange and tighten the nut to the specified torque (photo).

27 On M46 types, carry out paragraphs 23 to 25, but obviously using the intermediate flange in place of the rear cover.

28 Fit the top cover gasket in place.

29 Fit the balls into their holes and position the springs over them.

30 Position the selector rods in the same plane, move the selector rod in the cover to the central position, and fit the top cover.

31 Tighten the top cover bolts.

23.3 Checking the protrusion of the reverse gear shaft

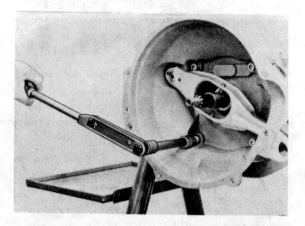

Fig. 6.22 Fitting the clutch bellhousing (Sec 23)

23.13 Layshaft outer race being fitted

23.14 Measuring the protrusion of the input shaft bearing

23.20A Fit the selector rods, dogs and forks ...

23.20B ... and lock each one with a roll pin (arrowed)

23.22 Speedometer gear fitted to the mainshaft

23.26 Fitting the output flange

23.32 Reversing light switch

32 Fit the reversing light switch (photo). **Note:** *If the switch was previously fitted to the gear lever carrier, it should be moved and fitted to the cover.*
33 Check the operation of all gears, and the gearbox for smooth operation.
34 On M46 types, refit the overdrive as described in Section 33.
35 Fit a new rubber ring to the selector rod joint, then fit the selector rod and knock in the securing pin and fit the sleeve.
36 Fit the gear lever carrier (photo).
37 Fill the gearbox with the specified oil and refit as described in Section 7.

23.36 Fitting the gear lever carrier

24 Gearbox (M45/46) 1979 on – dismantling and reassembly

1 The procedure is basically the same as described for the pre-1979 gearbox, noting the following differences.
2 Only one selector rod is used in place of the three on earlier types.
3 The selector plate is held in place by guides and the top cover, and the spring keeps the plate tensioned to the right.
4 Movement of the selector plate via the selector rod and gear lever is controlled within the guides and slots.
5 A leaf spring in the underside of the cover keeps reverse selector in position, and the three lugs locate over the guides (see Fig. 6.26).
6 Although the procedures for dismantling the modified gearbox into major assemblies are similar to those for earlier types, this is not true of many of the components, which are not interchangeable with earlier gearboxes. These include:

(a) *The input shaft which has 22 splines, which means a different clutch driven plate*
(b) *3rd and 4th gears and synchroniser have been modified*
(c) *The shift forks are made of steel, with renewable brass friction pads*
(d) *On later gearboxes, a vibration damper is fitted to the 1st gear end of the mainshaft to reduce noise levels. This vibration damper can be fitted to gearboxes as a modification, but note that if a damper is fitted, then a modified 1st/2nd synchroniser ring should also be fitted. Refer to Sections 25 and 26 on the M47 gearbox for details*

Note 1: *If a vibration damper is fitted, the layshaft must **not** be preloaded (see paragraphs 17 to 24), as this may cause stiffness of gear changing. The original shims can be re-used.*
Note 2: *Where a vibration damper is fitted, a clutch driven plate without pre-damping springs should also be used.*
Note 3: *Later gearboxes may have been modified in respect of the 1st, 2nd and 3rd gears, which run on needle roller bearings and not the bushes as previously fitted. The bushes can be replaced by the needle*

roller bearings on the earlier gearboxes, but to improve gearbox performance, shims should be fitted under the brass ring on the synchroniser. These shims should also be fitted to gearboxes which have needle roller bearings already fitted, but no shims. The procedure for fitting the shims is as follows.
7 Assemble the mainshaft with a brass ring behind 1st/2nd synchroniser ring.
8 Fit the needle roller bearing and 1st gear.
9 Remove the thrust washer from behind 1st gear (this thrust washer is not used where a vibration damper is fitted, use the washer provided with the vibration damper).
10 Support the mainshaft in a vice resting on 2nd gear. Do not tighten the vice, as the shaft must be free to move.
11 Push down on the shaft to seat 1st gear locking circlip correctly.
12 Fit the thrust washer (non-vibration damper) or other washer (vibration damper).
13 Measure the clearance between the washer and 1st gear (Fig. 6.28).
14 The clearance should be as near as possible to 0.004 in (0.10 mm).
15 Dismantle the mainshaft and fit suitable shims behind the brass ring on 1st/2nd synchroniser ring to give the correct clearance.
16 Reassemble the mainshaft.

Layshaft bearing shim calculation

17 This procedure applies to M45/46 gearboxes with an aluminium casing, regardless of whether or not a vibration damper and needle roller bearings are fitted.
18 After renewal of the layshaft, layshaft bearings, or the gearbox casing, the required shim thickness must be determined as follows.
19 Place the layshaft in the casing. Fit the front bearing race and drive it in from the outside of the casing, using a piece of tube. Leave the race protruding by a small amount (1 mm/0.04 in approx) – it will adopt its correct position in the next step.
20 Fit the bellhousing and its gasket. Secure it with the four bolts, tightened to the specified torque.
21 Invert the gearbox so that it stands on the bellhousing. Fit the layshaft rear bearing outer race and drive it into position. Rotate the layshaft while driving in the race; it is correctly fitted when a slight resistance to turning is felt.
22 Use a depth gauge, or a straight-edge and feeler blades, to measure accurately the distance from the rear end face of the casing (with gasket fitted) to the rear bearing outer race (photo). Select shims from the thicknesses available to make up a total thickness equal to the distance measured, or close enough to it to fall within the specified tolerance. For example:

Distance measured = 1.52 mm
Allowed tolerance = 0.03 mm endfloat to 0.05 mm preload
Acceptable shim thickness = (1.52 − 0.03) to (1.52 + 0.05)
= 1.49 to 1.57 mm

24.22 Measuring the depth of the layshaft bearing race

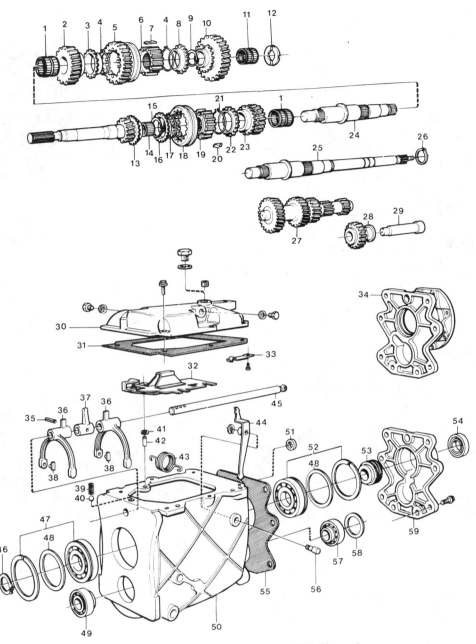

Fig. 6.23 Exploded view of later type M45/46 gearbox
(Sec 24)

1 Needle roller bearing	16 Synchro baulk ring	32 Selector plate	47 Input shaft bearing and
2 2nd gear	17 Synchro spring	33 Leaf spring	circlip
3 Synchro baulk ring	18 3rd/4th synchro sleeve	34 Intermediate flange (M46)	48 Shims
4 Synchro springs	19 Synchro-hub	35 Roll pin	49 Layshaft front bearing
5 1st/2nd synchro sleeve	20 Key	36 Selector forks	50 Gearcase
(with reverse gear)	21 Synchro spring	37 Selector dog	51 Oil seal
6 Synchro hub	22 Synchro baulk ring	38 Fork tips	52 Mainshaft bearing and
7 Key	23 3rd gear	39 Detent spring	circlip
8 Synchro baulk ring	24 Mainshaft (M45)	40 Detent ball	53 Speedometer worm
9 Circlip	25 Mainshaft (M46)	41 Washer	54 Oil seal (M45)
10 1st gear	26 Circlip	42 Pin	55 Gasket
11 Needle roller bearing	27 Layshaft/laygear	43 Spring	56 Pivot pin
12 Thrust washer	28 Reverse idler gear	44 Reverse selector lever	57 Layshaft rear bearing
13 Input shaft	29 Idler gear shaft	45 Selector shaft	58 Shim
14 Input shaft roller bearing	30 Top cover	46 Circlip	59 End casing (M45)
15 Circlip	31 Gasket		

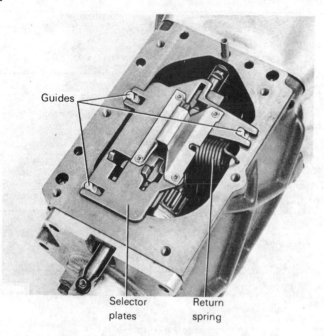

Fig. 6.24 Selector plate on later M45/46 gearboxes (Sec 24)

Fig. 6.25 View inside the later M45/46 gearbox (Sec 24)

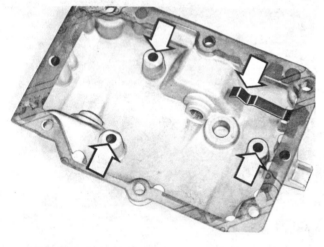

Fig. 6.26 Underside of later M45/46 gearbox cover (Sec 24)

Fig. 6.27 Modified mainshaft assembly (Sec 24)

1 Brass ring   3 Needle roller bearing
2 1st/2nd synchroniser ring   4 1st gear

Fig. 6.28 Measuring the clearance between 1st gear and washer (Sec 24)

163

23 Shims are available in the following thicknesses:

> 0.05 mm
> 0.10 mm
> 0.15 mm
> 0.35 mm
> 0.50 mm
> 0.70 mm
> 1.00 mm

Therefore in the above example, shim packs of 1.50 or 1.55 mm could be made up, both of which fall within tolerance.

24 Note that when a vibration damper is fitted, preload is not permitted. In that case, the acceptable shim thickness in the above example would be 1.49 to 1.52 mm, giving endfloat between 0.03 mm and zero.

25 Remove the bellhousing and gasket, the layshaft and its races, and proceed with gearbox reassembly.

25 Gearbox (M47) – dismantling

Note: *From 1986, the 5th gear and synchroniser are fitted to the layshaft and not the mainshaft. Removal and refitting is virtually the same as described below and in Section 26. No specific procedures had been established at the time of writing.*

1 An exploded view of the M47 (5-speed) gearbox appears in Fig. 6.29.

2 With the exception of the 5th gear assembly, which is contained within a housing bolted to the rear of the gearbox, the M47 is virtually

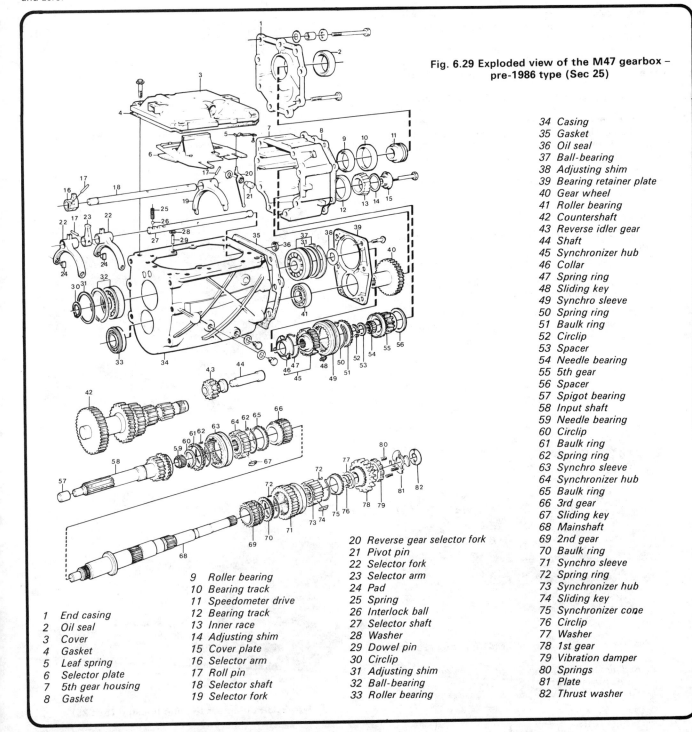

Fig. 6.29 Exploded view of the M47 gearbox – pre-1986 type (Sec 25)

34 Casing
35 Gasket
36 Oil seal
37 Ball-bearing
38 Adjusting shim
39 Bearing retainer plate
40 Gear wheel
41 Roller bearing
42 Countershaft
43 Reverse idler gear
44 Shaft
45 Synchronizer hub
46 Collar
47 Spring ring
48 Sliding key
49 Synchro sleeve
50 Spring ring
51 Baulk ring
52 Circlip
53 Spacer
54 Needle bearing
55 5th gear
56 Spacer
57 Spigot bearing
58 Input shaft
59 Needle bearing
60 Circlip
61 Baulk ring
62 Spring ring
63 Synchro sleeve
64 Synchronizer hub
65 Baulk ring
66 3rd gear
67 Sliding key
68 Mainshaft
69 2nd gear
70 Baulk ring
71 Synchro sleeve
72 Spring ring
73 Synchronizer hub
74 Sliding key
75 Synchronizer cone
76 Circlip
77 Washer
78 1st gear
79 Vibration damper
80 Springs
81 Plate
82 Thrust washer

1 End casing
2 Oil seal
3 Cover
4 Gasket
5 Leaf spring
6 Selector plate
7 5th gear housing
8 Gasket

9 Roller bearing
10 Bearing track
11 Speedometer drive
12 Bearing track
13 Inner race
14 Adjusting shim
15 Cover plate
16 Selector arm
17 Roll pin
18 Selector shaft
19 Selector fork

20 Reverse gear selector fork
21 Pivot pin
22 Selector fork
23 Selector arm
24 Pad
25 Spring
26 Interlock ball
27 Selector shaft
28 Washer
29 Dowel pin
30 Circlip
31 Adjusting shim
32 Ball-bearing
33 Roller bearing

the same as the M45 (1979 on), and has been subject to the same modifications.

3   Before dismantling the gearbox, the 5th gear assembly must be removed as follows.

4   Remove the top cover.

5   Remove the gear selector plate and lift off the washers, spring and ball.

6   Remove the gearchange lever support bracket and remote control rod.

7   Lock two gears at once by moving the selector rods, and then remove the nut from the output flange.

8   Remove the output flange, using a puller if it is tight.

9   Remove the speedometer drivegear (when fitted).

10 Remove the bolts, and then remove the end cover plate and gasket.

11 Remove the bolt from the end of the layshaft, and take off the washer and shim.

12 Refit the bolt by about six threads, and use it and a puller engaged with the square cut-outs in the housing, to pull off the end housing.

13 Remove the housing gasket and the selector rod oil seal.

14 Pull the speedometer drivegear (when fitted), washer, roller bearing and washer from the mainshaft.

15 Using a puller, remove 5th gear from the layshaft.

16 Remove the layshaft end-bolt.

17 Remove 5th gear, needle bearing, bush and synchroniser ring from the mainshaft.

18 Drive out the roll pin from 5th gear selector fork, remove the synchroniser hub circlip, and slide the assembly (including the fork), from the mainshaft and selector shafts.

19 If the hub is left on the shaft, remove it with a puller and take off the shim, retaining it for later.

20 Remove the bearing retainer plate from the rear face of the gearbox, and place the shim to one side.

21 The remaining procedure is basically the same as for the later M45 gearbox, but note the following modifications:

(a) 1st, 2nd and 3rd gears run on needle roller bearing in place of bushes

(b) A vibration damper is fitted to the 1st gear end of the mainshaft

(c) Where a vibration damper is fitted, a brass ring is also fitted to the rear of the 1st/2nd synchroniser hub

22 The damper can be dismantled by levering off the washer and separating the brake plate from the damper cone. Do not lose the springs (photos).

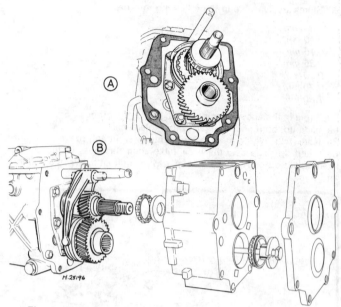

Fig. 6.30 5th speed gear arrangement on M47 gearbox
(Sec 25)

A   Pre-1986   B   1986 on

Fig. 6.31 Gear selector plate, washers, spring and ball
(Sec 25)

Fig. 6.32 Selector components – M47 gearbox (Sec 25)

1   Roll pins   4   5th selector fork
2   Main selector shaft   5   1st/2nd selector fork
3   5th selector shaft   6   3rd/4th selector fork

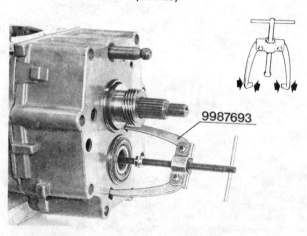

Fig. 6.33 Pulling off the end housing (Sec 25)

Fig. 6.34 Removing the speedometer drive assembly from the mainshaft (Sec 25)

Fig. 6.35 Pulling off the 5th gear from the layshaft (Sec 25)

Fig. 6.36 5th gear components (Sec 25)

1   Needle roller bearing   2   Spacer

Fig. 6.37 1st gear and vibration damper (Sec 25)

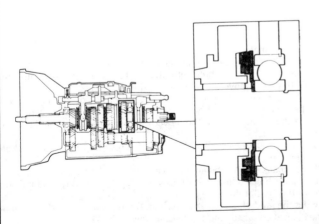

Fig. 6.38 Sectional view of the 1st gear vibration damper (Sec 25)

25.22A Prise off the vibration damper washer ...

25.22B ... and remove the springs

Fig. 6.39 1st gear vibration damper assembly on mainshaft
(Sec 26)

1 Brass ring   3 1st gear
2 Synchroniser ring   4 Vibration damper

26 Gearbox (M47) – reassembly

1   The reassembly of the M47 gearbox follows the same basic
procedure as for the later type of M45 (1979 on), bearing in mind the
following differences.

Mainshaft reassembly
2   Ensure the brass ring is fitted to 1st/2nd gear synchroniser hub on
the mainshaft.
3   Fit the synchroniser ring, needle bearing and 1st gear, then fit the
circlip.
4   Press the vibration damper onto the end of the shaft, washer facing
the end of the shaft.
5   After fitting, it should be very difficult to turn the vibration damper
washer.
6   If the mainshaft bearing or the bearing retainer plate has been
renewed, the shim thickness must be recalculated as follows.
7   Measure the distance between the bearing race and rear face of the
casing.
8   Measure the distance between the face of the bearing retainer plate
and the bearing seat.
9   Subtract the measurement taken in paragraph 7 from that taken in
paragraph 8.
10 From this value, subtract the maximum and minimum endfloat
tolerances (0.0004 to 0.008 in (0.01 to 0.20 mm)). The thickness of
shim to be fitted lies between these two values.
11 Fit the shim in the bearing seat in the retainer plate.
12 Fit the bearing retainer plate to the rear face of the gearbox.
13 Check the turning force required to turn the mainshaft with 1st gear
selected, which should be 7 to 22 lbf in (0.8 to 2.5 Nm) (a piece of
string wound round the mainshaft and pulled by a spring balance will
give an approximate value, if the spring balance reading is multiplied
by the radius of the shaft).

Reassembly of 5th gear components
14 If a new synchro unit is to be fitted, the hub will have to be pressed
onto the shaft and the clearance between the hub face and the circlip
measured. If the clearance is greater than 0.008 in (0.20 mm) then it
must be reduced by inserting a shim behind the hub. Shims are
available in four thicknesses.
15 If the original synchro is to be refitted, use the original shim.
16 Fit the synchro-hub circlip.
17 Locate the three synchro sliding keys in the synchro-hub. Engage
the 5th speed selector fork in the groove of the synchro sleeves so that
the chamfered teeth are towards the sliding keys.
18 Fit the sleeve and fork simultaneously, at the same time holding the
synchro springs engaged in the sliding keys. The ends of the springs
should engage in the same key but run in opposite directions.

Fig. 6.40 5th gear synchroniser hub circlip (arrowed)
(Sec 26)

19 Secure the selector fork to the shaft with a roll pin.
20 Grease the needle bearings and insert them with the spacer, in 5th
speed mainshaft gear.
21 Fit the synchroniser ring and fit both 5th speed gears to their shafts.
Screw in the layshaft bolt with washer to draw the gear onto the
layshaft, then remove the bolt and washer.
22 Fit the washer, roller bearing (taper towards end of shaft) the thrust
washer ring and speedometer gear (if applicable) to the mainshaft.
23 Fit the bearing tracks (if renewed) and selector shaft seal into 5th
gear housing.
24 Grease a new gasket and fit it with 5th gear housing to the end of
the gearbox.
25 Fabricate some tubular distance pieces and fit them to the rear
cover plate bolts. Screw in the bolts to 35 lbf ft (50 Nm) to hold the 5th
gear housing tightly.
26 Fit the layshaft rear bearing (without shim), the cover washer, with
the splines engaged, and tighten the bolt.
27 Check the layshaft endfloat, preferably using a dial gauge. The
endfloat must be as given in the Specifications. Select shims from the
five thicknesses available to give the specified endfloat. Fit the shim,
washer and new self-locking bolt. Tighten the bolt to the specified
torque.
28 Remove the bolts and temporary spacers, fit the seals and (if

Fig. 6.41 Checking 5th gear synchroniser hub-to-circlip clearance (Sec 26)

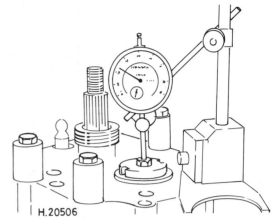

H.20506

Fig. 6.42 Measuring layshaft endfloat (Sec 26)

applicable) the speedometer driven gear to the rear cover.
29 Grease a new gasket and locate the rear cover. Fit the gearchange rod and support bracket, screw in the bolts and tighten to the specified torque.
30 Lock up two gears at once by moving the selector rods within the top cover aperture. Fit the drive flange and tighten a new nut to

specified torque. Return the gears to neutral.
31 Fit the washers, selector plate, interlock ball and the spring.
32 Grease a new gasket and fit the top cover to the gearbox. Tighten the bolts to specified torque.
33 Fill the gearbox with the specified oil and refit as described in Section 7.

27 Fault diagnosis – manual gearbox

Symptom	Reason(s)
Weak or ineffective synchromesh	Synchronising components worn, split or damaged
Jumps out of gear	Incorrectly assembled synchro units Synchro units badly worn Selector fork rod groove badly worn Incorrect assembly of selector components
Excessive noise	Incorrect grade of oil in gearbox or oil level too low Bearings worn or damaged Gear teeth excessively worn or damaged Shimming of layshaft and/or mainshaft incorrect (M45/46/47 gearbox) Layshaft thrust washers worn (M40)
Excessive difficulty in engaging gear	Clutch pedal adjustment incorrect Gear lever adjustment incorrect (M45/46/47) Selector components worn or damaged

Note: *It is not necessarily a good idea to dismantle the gearbox in an attempt to rectify a minor fault. A gearbox which is noisy, or on which the synchro can be beaten by a quick change, may carry on for a long time in this state. Piecemeal renewal of components can actually increase noise by presenting different wear surfaces to each other.*

PART B: OVERDRIVE UNIT

28 General description

The overdrive is essentially an extra gearbox, driven by the output shaft of the main gearbox and producing on its own output shaft a step-up ratio of 0.797:1. The 'gear change' is controlled hydraulically, the hydraulic control valve being operated by a solenoid. The electrical connections to the solenoid are taken through a switch on the cover of the main gearbox which ensures that overdrive can only be brought into operation when the car is in top gear. The activating switch for the whole system is mounted in the top of the gear lever knob.

A cutaway illustration of the overdrive and an exploded view are shown in Fig. 6.43 and 6.44.

The heart of the overdrive is the epicyclic gear system, whose components are shown in Fig. 6.43. These parts are assembled on the elongated mainshaft which extends from the main gearbox. Two of

these parts, the planet carrier and the unidirectional clutch, are splined to the mainshaft and always revolve, therefore, at mainshaft speed. The unidirectional clutch sits inside the output shaft and ensures that if nothing else is driving the output shaft, it will be driven by the gearbox mainshaft. In this manner the 1 : 1 ratio is obtained. When this occurs, the planet carrier and the annulus on the output shaft are revolving at the same speed, so the planet gears within the planet carrier are not being driven forwards or backwards and remain stationary on their splines. This means that the sun wheel must also be revolving at the same speed as the planet carrier and the annulus. The sun wheel is splined to the sliding clutch member and this too is revolving at the mainshaft speed. In practice the sliding clutch member is held against the tapered extension of the mainshaft when the 1 : 1 ratio is required and the whole gear system is locked together (Fig. 6.45).

To obtain the step-up ratio, the sliding clutch member is drawn away from the output shaft annulus and comes up against the outer casing of the gearbox which holds it stationary. It is still splined to the sun wheel, so this, too, is prevented from turning.

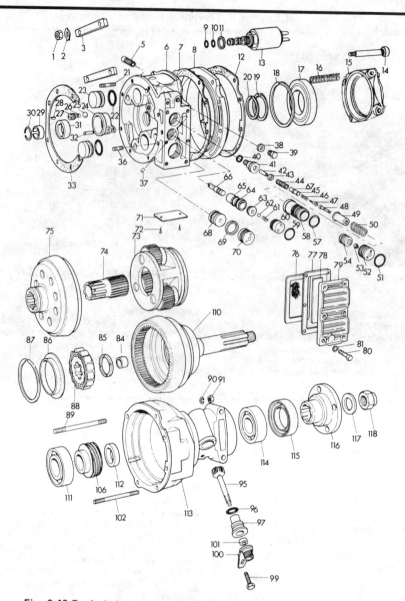

Fig. 6.43 Exploded view of the overdrive unit shown on its side (Sec 28)

1	Nut	28	Key	58	Cylinder
2	Lockwasher	29	Resilient ring	59	O-ring
3	Bridge piece	30	Circlip	60	Plug
5	Breather	31	Eccentric	61	Spring
6	Front casing	32	Piston pin	62	Ball
7	Gasket	33	Gasket	63	Non-return body
8	Brake ring	36	Stud	64	O-ring
9	O-ring	37	Orifice nozzle	65	Pump body
10	O-ring	38	Seal	66	Pump plunger
11	Seal	39	Plug	67	Washer
12	Gasket	40	O-ring	68	Pressure filter
13	Solenoid	41	End piece	69	Seal
14	Bolt	42	Piston	70	Plug
15	Thrust bearing retainer	43	Washer	71	Data plate
16	Spring	44	Spring	72	Screw
17	Thrust bearing	45	Retainer	73	Planet gear and carrier
18	Circlip	46	Spring	74	Sunwheel
19	Circlip	47	Screw	75	Clutch sliding member
20	Circlip	48	Screw	76	Screen filter
21	Stud	49	Holder	77	Gasket
22	Piston seal	50	Spring	78	Magnet
23	Piston	51	O-ring	79	Baseplate
24	Connecting rod	52	Plug	80	Bolt
25	Non-return ball	53	Nut	81	Resilient washer
26	Non-return valve spring	54	Piston	84	Bush
27	Plug			85	Thrust washer

86	Oil thrower
87	Circlip
88	One-way clutch
89	Stud
90	Resilient washer
91	Nut
95	Speedometer pinion*
96	O-ring*
97	Bush*
99	Bolt*
100	Retainer*
101	Oil seal*
102	Stud
106	Speedometer driving gear*
110	Output shaft
111	Ball bearing
112	Spacer
113	Rear casing
114	Ball bearing
115	Oil seal
116	Flange
117	Washer
118	Nut

*Not applicable to models with electronic speedometer

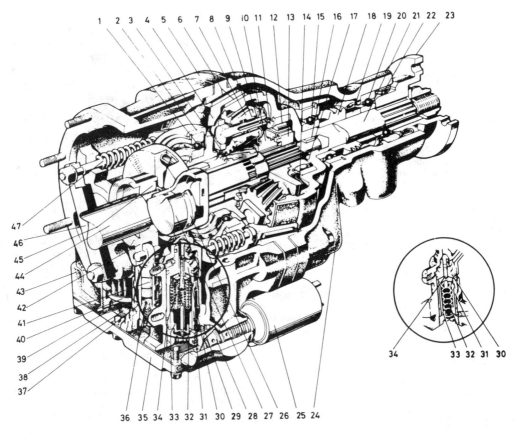

Fig. 6.44 Cutaway view of the overdrive unit. Inset shows later type pressure relief valve (Sec 28)

1	Thrust bearing	14	Oil trap
2	Thrust bearing retainer	15	Ball bearing
3	Sunwheel	16	Bush
4	Clutch sliding member	17	Thrust washer
5	Brake ring	18	Speedometer driving gear *
6	Clutch member linings	19	Spacer
7	Planet gear	20	Ball bearing
8	Needle bearing	21	Output shaft
9	Shaft	22	Oil seal
10	Planet carrier	23	Coupling flange
11	Oil thrower	24	Rear casing
12	One-way clutch rollers	25	Solenoid
13	One-way clutch	26	Piston seal

27	Piston	40	Pressure filter
28	Operating valve	41	Pump plunger
29	Orifice nozzle	42	Connecting rod
30	Cylinder top	43	Front casing
31	Cylinder	44	Input shaft (gearbox
32	Spring		mainshaft)
33	Large piston	45	Eccentric
34	Small piston	46	Bridge piece
35	Baseplate	47	Spring
36	Check valve for oil pump		
37	Pump cylinder	*Not applicable to models with	
38	Magnet	electronic speedometer	
39	Screen filter		

The planet carrier continues to revolve at mainshaft speed, but because the sun wheel is stationary the planet wheels turn around their spindles in the planet carrier. This means that the outer teeth of the planet wheel (which mesh with the annulus) are moving relative to the planet carrier, and this makes the annulus move faster than the planet carrier.

The sliding member is bolted to bridge pieces. Behind these bridge pieces are hydraulically operated pistons which are able to push the bridge pieces away from the case against the action of the clutch return springs when the hydraulic pressure is great enough. This means that changing gear is simply a matter of raising the oil pressure applied to the pistons. The oil pressure is generated in the first instance by a piston pump which is driven by a cam on the mainshaft extension. A solenoid valve controls the application of oil pressure to the pistons.

The overdrive hydraulic system incorporated a pressure relief valve, a pick-up strainer and a pressure filter.

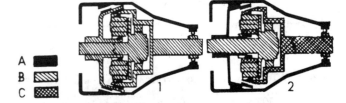

Fig. 6.45 Operating principle of overdrive (Sec 28)

1	Direct drive	B	Parts rotating at speed of
2	Overdrive		input shaft
A	Non-rotating parts	C	Parts rotating faster than
			input shaft

29 Oil filter screen – removal, cleaning and refitting

Caution: *If the vehicle has recently been running, the oil in the overdrive unit may be hot enough to scald.*

1   The oil filter screen should be cleaned whenever the oil in the

gearbox is renewed.

2   Raise and support the vehicle. Place a suitable container beneath the overdrive unit sump. Unbolt and remove the sump (photo) and drain the oil from the overdrive. Remove the filter screen.

3   Inspect the filter screen and magnet in the sump closely, before cleaning, for metal particles or other debris indicating internal wear or damage, in which case overhaul may be necessary.

4   Clean the filter screen, magnet and sump plate in a solvent, then allow to dry.

5   Remove all traces of gasket from the mating surfaces.

6   Fit a new gasket to the sump, and place the magnet and filter screen in position on the sump plate.

7   Position the sump plate, with the magnet and screen, in place on the overdrive unit, then fit and tighten the bolts to the specified torque.

8   Top up the main gearbox oil level, as described in Section 2.

30 Oil pressure filter – removal and refitting

1   The oil pressure filter can be removed after the oil sump and filter screen have been removed as described in Section 29.

2   Looking up at the overdrive unit with the sump removed, you will see three plugs: two large, on the outside, and one smaller plug in the centre. The right-hand plug looking forward, covers the pressure filter. **Note:** *The centre plug covers the non-return valve, and the left-hand plug the pressure relief valve.*

3   Tap the pressure filter plug with a plastic mallet, which will make it easier to remove, then undo the plug using a peg spanner inserted in the holes provided.

4   Remove the plug, then the seal and oil filter.

5   Clean the filter in solvent, renewing it if necessary.

6   Fit the filter, and use a new oil seal on the plug before refitting the plug and tightening it to the specified torque. **Note:** *In order to torque-load the plug effectively, make up a tool as shown in Fig. 6.47 and use a spring balance to apply the torque.*

7   Refit the oil sump as described in Section 29.

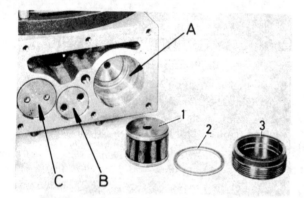

Fig. 6.46 Showing the three plugs under the sump (Sec 30)

A   Filter   1   Pressure filter
B   Non-return valve   2   Seal
C   Pressure relief valve   3   Plug

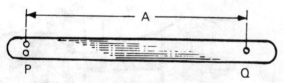

Fig. 6.47 Tool for applying correct torque to plugs (Sec 30)

A = 12 in (305 mm)
P Pegs for holes in plugs
Q Balance hole

Balance reading of 16 lbs (7.26 kg) =
16 lbf ft (2.2 kg m) of torque

31 Solenoid valve – removal, testing and refitting

1   The solenoid valve is mounted on the left-hand side of the overdrive unit.

2   Raise and support the vehicle. Disconnect the battery negative terminal.

3   Disconnect the electrical leads to the solenoid valve.

4   Thoroughly clean the area around the valve to remove all road grime. The ingress of dirt into the overdrive unit can be disastrous.

5   Using a slim 1 in AF spanner, unscrew the solenoid valve from the

29.2 Removing the sump to expose the filter screen (overdrive unit removed)

overdrive unit (photo).

6   To check the operation of the valve, block off the holes between the O-ring seals using the fingers, then blow down on the plunger. The plunger should not pass any air.

7   Now connect a 12 volt supply to the solenoid terminals and repeat the operation, this time with the holes unblocked. Again the plunger should not pass any air.

8   Renew the solenoid if the above conditions cannot be met.

9   Refit the solenoid in the reverse order, using new 'O'-ring seals and tighten the solenoid to the specified torque. (A 'crow's foot' spanner, or a variation of the spring balance technique shown in Fig. 6.47, will be needed to determine the torque.)

10 Check the gearbox oil level and top up if necessary.

32 Output shaft oil seal – renewal

Refer to Section 2.

33 Overdrive unit – removal and refitting

1   Before removing the overdrive unit, residual torque in the internal mechanism must be released by driving the vehicle with overdrive engaged, and then disengaging the overdrive while the clutch is depressed.

2   Raise and support the vehicle. Disconnect the propeller shaft as described in Chapter 7.

3   Disconnect the battery negative terminal, then disconnect the electrical leads at the solenoid.

4   Disconnect the speedometer cable, if fitted to the overdrive.

5   Support the gearbox on a jack, then remove the bolts from the gearbox crossmember.

6   Lower the gearbox and overdrive unit on the jack sufficiently to reach the uppermost bolts securing the overdrive to the intermediate flange.

7   Remove all the overdrive-to-intermediate flange nuts or bolts.

8   Pull the overdrive unit rearwards to separate it from the intermediate flange and lift it clear of the mainshaft and out from under the vehicle. **Note:** *If the overdrive unit will not separate from the intermediate flange, gentle use of a plastic mallet may loosen it, or a slide hammer could be bolted to the output flange. If none of these measures work, do not force the unit from the flange, but dismantle the unit in sequence, working from the rear, until it can be moved.*

9   Refitting is a reversal of removal, using a new gasket between the overdrive and the intermediate flange, and tightening the flange nuts or bolts to the specified torque.

10 Top up the gearbox oil, road test the vehicle, then check the oil level again.

34 Speedometer drive oil seal and bearing – renewal

1   Raise and support the vehicle. Disconnect the speedometer drive cable by removing the locking plate and unscrewing the knurled end of the cable, then pulling it from the housing.
2   Using a spanner on the machined flats of the bearing housing, unscrew the housing and lift out the bearing, housing and drive pinion.
3   The drive pinion and bearing can now be removed from the housing.
4   Prise the O-ring from the housing and clean the housing in solvent.
5   Coat all new parts in clean gearbox oil, then fit the O-ring to the housing.
6   Push a new seal into the housing, followed by the bearing and drive pinion.
7   Refit the housing to the overdrive and reconnect the speedometer cable in the reverse order of removal.
8   Check and top up the gearbox oil level.

35 Overdrive – dismantling

1   With the overdrive removed from the gearbox, clean it externally and clamp it in a soft-jawed vice.
2   Disconnect the earth lead from the solenoid. Unscrew and remove the solenoid, using a 1 in AF open-ended spanner with thin jaws.
3   Slacken the six nuts which secure the main and rear casings (photo). Remove four of the nuts, leaving two (opposite and on long studs) which should be slackened alternately a little at a time until the spring pressure separating the casings is relieved. Note the location of the solenoid earth lead under one of the nuts. Recover the special washers.
4   Remove the bridge piece nuts and the bridge pieces themselves (photo). The nuts will be under spring pressure at first.
5   Separate the main and rear casings.
6   Remove the planet gears and carrier, the sun wheel with cone clutch and springs, and the brake ring (photos).
7   Clamp the main casing in the vice. Unbolt and remove the filter screen and the oil sump.
8   Remove the two pistons, using long-nosed pliers if necessary (photo).
9   Using a peg spanner or (at a pinch) a pair of circlip pliers, unscrew the pressure filter (large) plug. Remove the washer and filter (photo).
10   Similarly remove the non-return valve (small) plug. Remove the spring, ball and valve seat (photos). The sleeve and pump plunger can then be removed if wished.
11   Finally unscrew the relief valve plug. Remove the piston, springs and plunger, being careful not to lose any shims. The valve sleeve may be extracted if necessary (photos).
12   Further dismantling depends on the work to be undertaken. The thrust bearing can be removed from its cage after removing the two circlips and separating the cage from the sun wheel and cone clutch (photo).
13   The unidirectional clutch can be removed from the rear casing after removing the circlip and the oil thrower. Recover the thrust washer.
14   To remove the output shaft bearings, the flange must be removed and the shaft pressed out of the rear casing. The front bearing can then be pulled off the shaft and the rear bearing driven out of the casing. There is a spacer between the two bearings, as well as the speedometer driving gear on early models.

36 Overdrive unit – overhaul

1   As with the gearbox, renewal of a well-worn unit may be more satisfactory than overhaul. Check the price and availability of spare parts, and the price of new or reconditioned unit before proceeding.
2   Flush oilways and control orifices with solvent and blow them dry.
3   Examine hydraulic system components such as pistons, valves and valve seats for wear and damage. Renew as necessary.
4   Wash the bearings and the one-way clutch in solvent. Check for roughness and visible damage.
5   Clean out the groove in front of the annulus (ring gear). Dirt will collect here as a result of centrifugal force.
6   Examine the gears for wear and damage. Do not try to dismantle

31.5 Removing the solenoid (overdrive unit removed)

35.3 Undoing an overdrive casing nut

35.4 Removing a bridge piece

35.6A Removing the planet gear set ...

35.6B ... and the sun wheels, cone clutch and springs

35.8 Removing a piston

35.9 Removing the pressure filter

35.10A Unscrewing the non-return valve plug

35.10B Remove the non-return valve spring ...

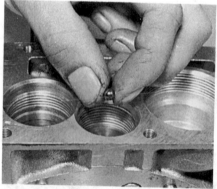

35.10C ... the ball ...

35.10D ... and the valve seat

35.11A Removing the relief valve piston ...

35.11B ... the small spring ...

35.11C ... the large spring ...

35.11D ... and the plunger with shims

35.11E Removing the relief valve sleeve

35.12 The thrust bearing in its cage

37.7 Refitting the oil pump sleeve and plunger

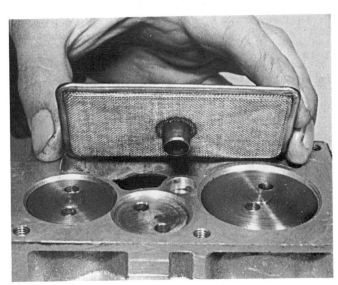

37.11 Fitting the oil filter screen

37.13 Fitting a casing gasket

37.16 Fitting a casing stud nylon washer

the planet gear set.
7   Check the brake ring for cracks, and the clutch linings for burning or abrasion.
8   Check the condition of the clutch springs. They should by 55.5 ± 1.5 mm (2.185 ± 0.059 in) long.
9   Check the solenoid using a 12 volt battery and an ammeter. Current consumption should be approximately 2A and the solenoid plunger should move in and out without sticking. (see Section 31).
10 Renew the oil filter screen and the pressure filter unless they are in perfect condition.
11 All parts must be perfectly clean, and reassembly must take place under clean conditions, to avoid subsequent trouble with the hydraulic system.
12 If the pressure relief valve components are renewed, it will be necessary to have a Volvo dealer or other specialist perform hydraulic pressure tests to determine the correct quantity of shims required.

37 Overdrive – reassembly

1   Press the output shaft bearings into the rear casing and onto the shaft. Do not forget the spacer (or the speedometer driving gear, when applicable). Press the output shaft into the casing and fit a new flange oil seal.
2   Refit the thrust washer, the one-way clutch inner race and the roller cage. Fit the oil thrower and circlip, then check the operation of the one-way clutch.
3   Refit the output flange, using locking compound on the splines. Do not contaminate the oil seal. Counterhold the flange and tighten the nut to the specified torque.

4   Refit the planet gear set to the output shaft, lining up the splines.
5   Fit the thrust bearing to its cage. Assemble the cage, sun wheel and cone clutch. Make sure the clutch linings are clean and dry, then lubricate them with ATF.
6   Refit the relief valve components and secure them with the plug, using a new O-ring.
7   Refit the oil pump sleeve and plunger, lubricating them with ATF (photo). The groove and bevel on the sleeve must align with the pressure filter recess, and the chamfer on the plunger ring must face forwards.
8   Refit the non-return valve seat and ball. Fit the spring into the plug and refit the plug, using a new O-ring.
9   Fit the pressure filter, washer and plug.
10 Tighten all the plugs with a peg spanner.
11 Fit the oil filter screen, a new cover gasket and the sump (photo). Tighten the cover bolts.
12 Lubricate the two pistons and insert them into their bores. Make sure they are the right way round.
13 Refit the brake ring to the rear casing, using a new gasket. Fit another new gasket on the main casing side of the brake ring (photo).
14 Refit the sun wheel/cone clutch assembly. Fit the clutch springs over the bearing cage studs.
15 Fit the main and rear casings together, being careful not to displace the gasket. Fit the piston bridge pieces and the nuts, tightening the nuts against spring pressure.
16 Fit the main-to-rear casing nuts, using new nylon washers (photo). Remember the solenoid earth tag. Tighten the nuts progressively to the specified torque, then recheck the tightness of the bridge piece nuts.
17 Refit and tighten the solenoid.

38 Fault diagnosis – overdrive unit

Symptom	Reason(s)
Failure to engage	Low oil level
	Electrical fault (check gear lever switch, inhibitor switch on gearbox top cover, or solenoid valve connections first)
	Sticking solenoid valve
	Overdrive clutch*
	Blocked filter screen or pressure filter, or other blockage
	Non-return valve inoperative
	Pressure relief valve inoperative

*This can sometimes be freed by driving the vehicle at 40 to 45 mph (70 to 80 km/h) in 4th gear with overdrive engaged. Depress the clutch, rev the engine to 5000 rpm, then quickly release the clutch.

Failure to disengage*	Electrical fault
	Pressure relief valve inoperative
	One-way clutch sticking
	Solenoid valve sticking
	Oil blockage in system

*Do not reverse the vehicle with overdrive engaged, or damage may result.

Overdrive slips when engaged	Worn friction linings
	Solenoid valve faulty
	Blocked filter screen or pressure filter
	Non-return valve faulty
	Pressure relief valve faulty
Noisy operation*	General wear
Noise in normal drive, disappearing when overdrive engaged	Cone clutch (thrust) bearing worn
Noise in both normal and overdrive, which disappears during overdrive engagement	Front and rear shaft bearings worn
Noise which reduces in frequency when overdrive engaged	Gearbox output shaft bearing worn

*If the engine is switched off while the overdrive is still engaged, noise from the overdrive may be evident the next time the overdrive is engaged. This is normal and should not be confused with other symptomatic noises.

PART C: AUTOMATIC TRANSMISSION

39 General description

Three types of automatic transmission may be fitted, depending on model. They are as follows:

Borg Warner 35 – a three-speed unit fitted to early B21A and B21E engined models.
Borg Warner 55 – a three-speed unit derived from the BW35 and fitted to later B21A, B21E, B23A and B23E models.
Aisan Warner 70 and 71 – a three-speed unit with a lock-up fourth speed overdrive, again derived from the BW55 and built in conjunction with the Japanese firm Aisan. Fitted to later B23A and B23E models, and to the B200E, B200K, B230A, B230E and B230K models.

All the transmissions are fully automatic, gearchanging being dependent on engine speed and load. A kickdown facility provides instant downshift (road speed permitting) when the accelerator pedal is fully depressed for overtaking etc. Manual control of all speeds is available through the floor-mounted speed select lever, and mechanical linkage to the transmission unit.

Drive from the engine is transmitted via the torque converter, a three-element hydro-kinetic unit which provides a fluid coupling and a variable torque multiplication ratio. The planetary gearbox is hydraulically controlled through a valve assembly, which automatically selects the correct gear for engine speed and load.

A fluid cooler, which is part of the cooling system radiator, is used to cool the transmission fluid, the fluid cooler and transmission unit being connected by a flow and return pipeline.

A parking lock is incorporated in the transmission unit, which is a pawl type lock.

40 Routine maintenance

Note: *Because of the complex nature of automatic transmission units and the need for scrupulously clean working conditions and specialised equipment, maintenance and overhaul should be confined to those operations described in the following Sections.*

1 At the intervals laid down in the *Routine maintenance* Section at the beginning of this Manual, carry out the following operations.
2 Check the fluid level in the transmission unit (Section 41).
3 Renew the fluid in the transmission unit (Section 42).
4 Check and adjust the kickdown cable (Section 45).
5 Adjust the rear brakeband (BW35 only) (Section 47).

41 Fluid level – checking and topping-up

1 Warm up the transmission fluid by driving the vehicle for at least 10 miles. Park on level ground and allow the engine to idle.
2 Move the gear selector through all positions (apply the footbrake) and finish in position P. Wait two minutes.
3 Still with the engine idling, withdraw the transmission dipstick. Wipe it with a clean lint-free cloth, re-insert it fully, withdraw it again and read the level. Use the 'hot' markings on the dipstick. (The 'cold' markings are for reference when refilling with fresh fluid; an accurate level check can only be made with the fluid hot.)
4 If topping-up is necessary, this is done via the dipstick tube. Only use fresh transmission fluid of the specified type, and take great care not to introduce dirt into the transmission. Do not overfill: the distance from 'MIN' to 'MAX' on the dipstick represents half a litre (not quite a pint) of fluid.
5 Refit the dipstick, making sure it is fully home, and stop the engine.
6 Check for leaks if frequent topping-up is required.

42 Fluid – draining and refilling

Warning: *ATF can become extremely hot during use, and care should be exercised when draining to avoid scalding.*

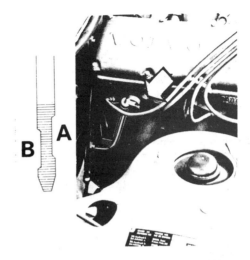

Fig. 6.48 Early type dipstick (Sec 41)

A Hot   *B Cold*

Fig. 6.49 Later type dipstick (Sec 41)

A Cold   *B Hot*

Transmission units with a drain plug

1 Remove the drain plug from the sump at the bottom of the transmission unit (photo), and drain the fluid into a suitable container for disposal.
2 Refit the drain plug on completion, and fill the unit with fresh fluid as described in Section 41.

Transmission units without a drain plug

3 Disconnect the fluid dipstick tube at its lower end, and drain the fluid as above. Reconnect the dipstick on completion and refill the unit as described in Section 41.

42.1 Automatic transmission drain plug

All units

4   It is recommended that the transmission sump be removed at the time of fluid change so that the magnet and pick-up filter can be cleaned. Observe scrupulous cleanliness when doing this, and use a new sump gasket on reassembly. If clean working conditions are not available, have the job done by a Volvo dealer or other specialist.

5   Where cases of fluid contamination are encountered, the fluid cooler should also be flushed as described in Section 43, and in severe cases your Volvo dealer should be consulted.

43 Fluid cooler – flushing

1   The transmission fluid is cooled by passing it through a cooler incorporated in the right-hand side of the radiator. On some models an auxiliary cooler is also mounted in front of the radiator. After removing the transmission or draining the fluid for any reason, it is worthwhile cleaning the old fluid from the cooler.

2   To clean the standard cooler first overfill the transmission by approximately 0.5 Imp pt (0.3 litre).

3   Disconnect the fluid return pipe from the rear of the transmission (photo) and position a container beneath it.

4   With P selected and the handbrake applied, have an assistant start the engine and let it idle.

5   Switch off the engine when clean fluid comes out, then reconnect the return pipe and top up the fluid level as described in Section 41.

6   To clean the auxiliary cooler disconnect the pipes at the standard cooler then use a pump to force new fluid through the cooler until it emerges from the return pipe.

7   Re-connect the pipes, then top up the fluid level as described in Section 41.

44 Selector lever linkage – adjustment (all types)

1   First check that all bushes in the linkage are in good condition and renew any which are worn.

2   Engage 'D' and move the lever towards the stop in the gate. Measure the clearance between the lever and stop. This clearance should be equal to, or greater than, the same measurement between the lever and stop with the lever in '2'.

3   The clearance can be adjusted from under the vehicle by disconnecting the linkage fork (which may be at either end, depending on model) and turning the fork in or out for coarse adjustment, or using the knurled adjuster sleeve for fine adjustment. Visible thread on the link rod must not exceed 1.38 in (35 mm) on completion of adjustment.

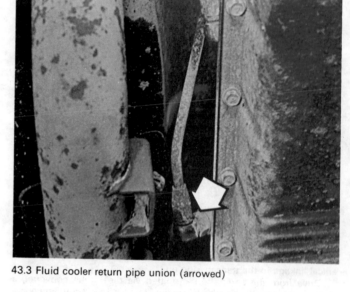

43.3 Fluid cooler return pipe union (arrowed)

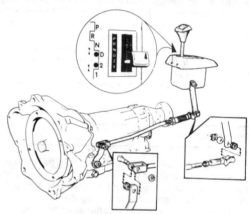

Fig. 6.50 Selector lever adjustment (Sec 44)

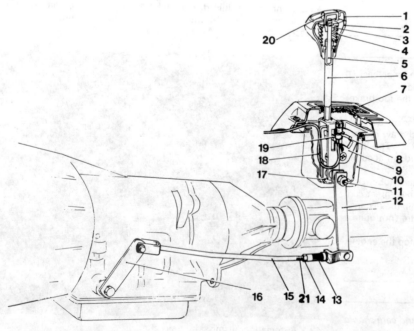

Fig. 6.51 Selector linkage assembly
(Sec 44)

 1   Selector lever knob, upper section
 2   Selector lever knob, lower section
 3   Washer
 4   Spring
 5   Pushrod
 6   Selector lever
 7   Shift positions cover
 8   Shift positions light
 9   Inhibitor plate
10   Housing
11   Shaft
12   Lever
13   Gearshift rod adjuster
14   Locknut
15   Control rod
16   Lever
17   Bracket
18   Cable, shift positions light
19   Detent
20   Button
21   Visible thread on linkage rod (35 mm max)

Note: *Increasing the link rod length reduces the clearance at 'D', and increases clearance at '2'.*
4   After adjustment, engage '1' then 'P', then repeat the check in paragraph 2.

45 Kickdown cable – renewal and adjustment

Caution: *Cable renewal involves removal of the transmission sump. Scrupulous cleanliness must be observed. If suitable working conditions are not available, have the job done by a Volvo dealer or other specialist.*

BW 35 – renewal

1   Drain the transmission fluid then remove the sump.
2   At the engine end of the cable, loosen the cable adjuster locknuts and release the cable from the bracket.
3   At the transmission end, rotate the cam of the kickdown valve until the cable end can be removed from the cam.
4   Unscrew the cable sheath bracket from the transmission casing and remove the cable.
5   The new cable is supplied with the stop on the cable at the engine end loose, which is crimped onto the cable once the adjustments are carried out. Do not lubricate the cable as it is already lubricated with silicone.
6   Screw the cable sheath bracket into the transmission casing, and attach the cable end to the cam on the kickdown valve.
7   Attach the engine end of the cable to the throttle pulley and cable adjuster bracket, but do not tighten the locknuts at this stage.
8   Check that the accelerator cable is fully released, then adjust the kickdown cable using the adjuster, so that the kickdown valve cam-to-plunger relationship is as shown in Fig. 6.52 – (A).
9   In this position, the stop at the engine end should be gently crimped onto the cable at the specified distance from the end of the sheath as shown in Fig. 6.55. Do not crimp it too tightly, as it may have to be moved.
10 Have an assistant fully depress the accelerator pedal, and check that the cam-to-plunger relationship is now as shown in Fig. 6.52 – (B).
11 The cable stop should now be as shown in Fig. 6.56.
12 Adjust as necessary on the adjuster, then tighten the locknuts and finally crimp the stop tight on to the cable.
13 Refit the sump, using a new gasket, and refill the transmission with the specified fluid.

BW35 – adjustment

14 In normal service, it should only be necessary to check and adjust the position of the crimped stop using the cable adjuster as described earlier. Further adjustment may be performed by a Volvo dealer or transmission specialist, using a transmission fluid pressure gauge.

BW55, AW70 and 71 – renewal

15 Drain the transmission fluid and remove the sump.
16 Cut through the cable at the engine end, between the crimped stop and the cable adjuster. Remove and discard the cable end from the throttle pulley.
17 Release the cable adjuster from the bracket.
18 Pull the inner cable through the sheath from the transmission end, and use the cable to pull the cam of the kickdown valve round so that the cable end is visible. Wedge the cam in this position using a screwdriver.
19 Remove the cable end from the cam.
20 Lever the outer sheath from the housing on the side of the transmission case.
21 Fit a new O-ring seal to the cable and push the sheath into the transmission housing.
22 Fit the cable end to the kickdown cam and remove the screwdriver.
23 Fit the cable adjuster loosely to the bracket at the engine end, and fit the cable end to the throttle pulley.
24 Pull the cable inner at the engine end until slight resistance is felt. Crimp the stop to the cable in this position so that it is the specified distance from the sheath (Fig. 6.55). Note that when the cable inner is released, the stop will be hard against the sheath.
25 Have an assistant depress the accelerator pedal fully. Adjust the sheath as necessary so that the distance between the sheath and the stop is as shown in Fig. 6.56. It should be possible to pull the

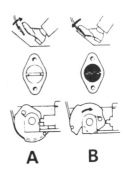

Fig. 6.52 Kickdown cam-to-plunger relationship (Sec 45)

A   *Accelerator pedal released*

B   *Accelerator pedal fully depressed*

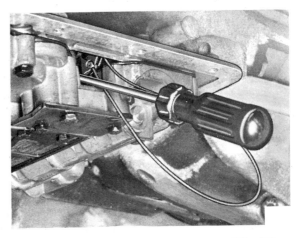

Fig. 6.53 Retaining kickdown cable cam (Sec 45)

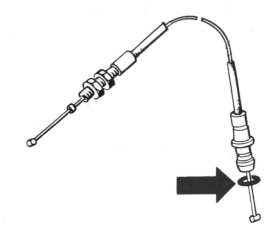

Fig. 6.54 Kickdown cable O-ring seal (arrowed) (Sec 45)

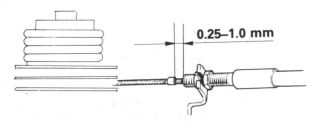

Fig. 6.55 Kickdown cable stop adjustment (accelerator released) (Sec 45)

kickdown cable inner out by a further 0.08 in (2 mm).
26 Tighten the adjuster locknuts when adjustment is correct.
27 Refit the sump, using a new gasket, and refill the transmission with the specified fluid.

BW55, AW70 and 71 – adjustment
28 Adjustment is as described above (paragraphs 24 to 26).
29 After adjustment, there should be no play in the cable with the throttle closed, and in the fully open position, it should be possible to pull out the cable by a further 0.08 in (2.0 mm).

46 Starter inhibitor switch – adjustment

BW35 type
1 The switch is located on the left-hand side of the transmission unit, and is operated by internal mechanism.
2 To remove the switch, first select 'P'. Raise and support the vehicle.
3 Disconnect the electrical leads.
4 Remove the switch by unscrewing it from the transmission casing. A cranked spanner will be needed to clear the lip of the casing.
5 Check that the operating pin projects by 0.55 in (14.0 mm). This check should also be carried out on new switches.
6 If the protrusion is less than that specified, press the switch pin in and out and measure the protrusion again. Each time the switch is pressed in and released, the pin will protrude a little more. Be careful not to let the pin come out too far.
7 If the pin protrusion is greater than that specified, fit a new switch.
8 Refitting is a reversal of removal, but use a new sealing washer under the switch.
9 On completion, check that the engine can only be started in 'P' or 'N', and that the reversing light comes on when 'R' is selected.

BW55, and AW70/71 types
10 Remove the selector lever cover, and check that the inhibitor switch lever aligns correctly with the 'N' and 'P' marks. If not, loosen the bolts, reposition the switch then tighten the bolts.

11 Move the selector lever through all positions, and check that the contact pin does not slide out of the switch lever. Check that the engine can only be started with the selector lever in positions 'P' and 'N', and that the reversing lights come on in position 'R'. If the reversing light flashes when the car is reversed, move the switch forward 0.04 in (1.0 mm), but check that the engine can only be started in positions 'P' and 'N'.

47 Brake band (BW35) – adjustment

1 The brake band adjuster is located on the right-hand side of the transmission casing, towards the rear end.
2 Access is difficult from underneath, and it may be better to remove the carpet from the front footwell and remove the transmission tunnel panel.
3 Loosen the locknut on the adjuster, then loosen the adjuster screw.
4 Tighten the adjuster screw to 10 lbf ft (14 Nm), then back off the screw one turn.
5 Tighten the locknut, being careful not to disturb the adjuster screw.
6 Refit the transmission tunnel panel and the carpet.

48 Overdrive solenoid valve (AW70/71) – removal and refitting

1 The overdrive solenoid is located on the left-hand side of the transmission unit.
2 Raise and support the vehicle. Disconnect the electrical connector on the right-hand side of the unit, and remove the cable clip securing the cable to the casing.
3 Clean off the area around the solenoid valve.
4 Remove the two bolts securing the valve to the transmission casing, and lift out the solenoid, retrieving the two O-ring seals.
5 The resistance of the solenoid can be checked using an ohmmeter

Fig. 6.56 Kickdown cable stop adjustment (accelerator pedal depressed) Sec 45)

On BW35: A = 1.694 to 1.852 in (43 to 47 mm)
On BW55, AW 70/71: A = 1.986 to 2.072 in (50.4 to 52.6 mm)

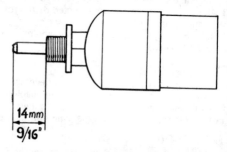

Fig. 6.58 Inhibitor switch pin protrusion (BW35) (Sec 46)

A Lever

Fig. 6.59 Inhibitor switch adjustment bolts (arrowed) (Sec 46)

Fig. 6.57 Unscrewing the starter inhibitor switch – BW35 (Sec 46)

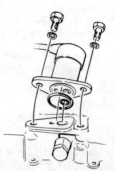

Fig. 6.60 Overdrive solenoid valve and fittings (Sec 48)

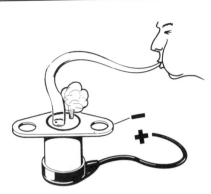

Fig. 6.61 The solenoid valve should pass air as shown with voltage applied (Sec 48)

connected between the valve body and the end of the electrical lead. Resistance should be 13 ohms.

6   The operation of the valve can be checked by applying 12 volts DC to the valve (positive to the lead, negative to the body). With voltage applied, air should pass through the valve. No air should pass with the voltage removed.

7   Refit in the reverse order, using new O-ring seals, lightly greased with petroleum jelly.

49 Transmission unit – removal and refitting

Note: *The procedure given here covers all types of unit, but it is pointed out that modifications to the various units mean that linkages and valves may be fitted in different positions, if fitted at all. It should also be remembered that the vehicle should be raised on ramps or axle stands, or driven over a pit, in order to give sufficient clearance for the transmission unit to be lowered and removed from under the vehicle.*

1   Disconnect the battery earth lead.
2   Drain the transmission fluid from the unit as described in Section 42.
3   Move the selector to '2'.
4   Disconnect the kickdown cable from the throttle pulley.
5   Remove the transmission crossmember and the rubber pad and bracket.
6   Disconnect the propeller shaft from the transmission output flange.
7   Disconnect the speedometer cable (when applicable).
8   Disconnect the selector lever linkage at the lever end.
9   Disconnect the fluid cooler pipelines at the transmission end, and

blank off the open ends. Flush the fluid cooler (Section 43) before refitting the transmission.

10 Disconnect the overdrive solenoid on AW70/71 units, and the starter inhibitor switch on BW35 units.
11 Remove the starter motor.
12 Disconnect and remove the fluid level dipstick tube.
13 Disconnect the exhaust bracket on the right-hand side of the converter housing. If necessary, also remove the exhaust downpipe.
14 Support the transmission unit securely on a trolley jack, then remove all but the top bolts from the transmission housing to engine.
15 Remove the torque converter cover plate and (if fitted) the cooling grilles. Turning the engine with a screwdriver levered against the starter ring gear, remove the bolts which secure the torque converter to the driveplate (photos).
16 Remove the remaining bolts from the converter housing.
17 Pull the unit backwards to release the transmission unit and lower it from the engine. It is heavy: the services of an assistant will be required.

Warning: *Do not tilt the unit forwards or the torque converter may fall out.*

18 Refitting is a reversal of removal, noting the following points:

   (a) Before offering the transmission unit up to the engine, ensure the torque converter is pushed fully to the rear so that the oil pump dogs are fully engaged.
   (b) Ensure the two dowel location pins are in position on the engine block.
   (c) Lightly grease the torque converter guide and female end.
   (d) There are two different lengths of torque converter retaining bolts, 0.55 in (14 mm) and 0.63 in (16 mm). The long bolts should be replaced by the shorter ones to avoid the risk of the bolts shearing in the torque converter. Tighten the bolts to the specified torque.
   (e) Make all connections and then adjust the throttle cable, kickdown cable and speed select linkage.
   (f) Fill the transmission unit with the specified fluid.

50 Fault diagnosis – automatic transmission

Without special test equipment, the DIY mechanic should not attempt any more than the adjustments and checks described in the preceding Sections.

Any fault not attributable to low fluid level or incorrectly set cables or linkages, should be dealt with by your Volvo dealer or local specialist.

Before removing a transmission unit for repair, make sure the repairer does not require in-car diagnostic checks carried out, as is often the case.

49.15A Removing a torque converter cooling grille

49.15B Removing a torque converter-to-driveplate bolt

Chapter 7 Propeller shaft

Contents

Specifications

Type .... Tubular, two-section with sliding centre joint and support bearing. Hardy-Spicer universal joints at centre bearing and at front and rear flanges, with rubber front joint on some later models

1 General description

1 The propeller shaft is of tubular construction in two halves, joined at the centre by a sliding splined joint, which allows for fore-and-aft movement between the engine and rear axle.

2 The front section is joined to the gearbox by a flanged universal joint, and supported at its rear end by the centre bearing.

3 The rear section is splined into the rear end of the front section, and joined to the rear axle by a flanged universal joint.

4 A third universal joint is situated just aft of the splined centre joint.

5 In 1985, a larger diameter propeller shaft was fitted, and in 1987, the front universal joint on manual gearbox models was changed in favour of a rubber type joint.

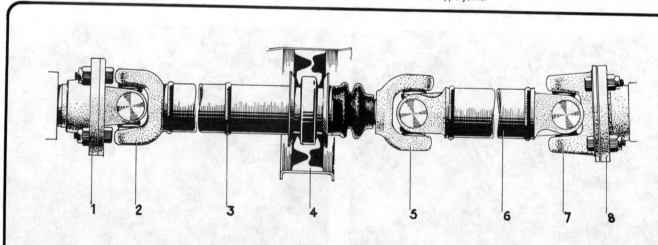

Fig. 7.1 View of the propeller shaft assembly (Sec 1)

1 Propeller shaft-to-gearbox
   flange
2 Front universal joint
3 Front section of shaft
4 Centre support bearing and
   splined sliding joint
5 Splined section universal
   joint
6 Rear section of shaft
7 Rear universal joint
8 Propeller shaft-to-rear axle
   flange

2 Routine maintenance

1 Apart from the lubrication of joints mentioned in the following Sections during overhaul, no routine lubrication operations are called for, the bearings being lubricated for life.
2 At the intervals laid down in the *Routine maintenance* Section at the beginning of this Manual, inspect the shaft and joints as follows.
3 Raise and securely support the vehicle, or drive it over a pit.
4 Check the flange bolts and the centre bearing bracket bolts for tightness.
5 Visually check the condition of the rubber coupling, if fitted. Renew it if it is damaged (Section 7).
6 Check for play in the universal joints, splined joint and centre bearing by attempting to lift, shake and twist the sections of the shaft relative to each other and to the flanges. Repair or renew as necessary (Section 4, 5 or 6).
7 Check that the centre bearing rubber boot is intact. To renew it, the two halves of the shaft must be separated.
8 Occasional oiling of the universal joint circlips is recommended to stop them rusting solid.
9 None of the above checks will detect a seized universal joint, which can cause heavy vibration – the shaft must be removed, or the flanges separated, so that the freedom of movement of the joint may be tested.
10 An out-of-balance or out-of-true shaft can also cause vibration, but these conditions are unlikely to arise spontaneously. Consult a Volvo dealer or a propeller shaft specialist.

3 Propeller shaft – removal and refitting

1 Before removing either the front or rear section of the propeller shaft, mark the relationship of each joint to one another by making a file cut or paint marks across the edge of the flanges. Also mark the two sections of the shaft relative to each other. The propeller shaft is balanced as a unit, and incorrect reassembly can cause vibration.
2 Raise and support the vehicle. Remove the four bolts from the rear flange (photo), lower the end of the propeller shaft, then pull the shaft rearwards to disengage the rear section from the splined centre joint (photo).
3 Remove the bolts from the front flange or rubber coupling (photo), and then from the support bearing frame and lower the front section of the shaft. Support the shaft while releasing the bearing frame.
4 Refitting is a reversal of removal, ensuring the relationship marks made in paragraph 1 line up. Apply molybdenum-based grease to the splines.
5 When correctly fitted, the yokes of both sections of the propeller shaft should be in the same plane. Do not fully tighten the support bearing bolts until the flange nuts and bolts have been tightened. The support bearing frame fixings are slotted to allow the bearing to take up an unstrained position.

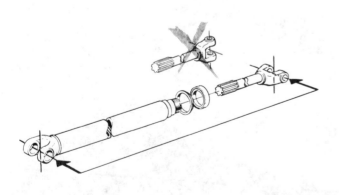
Fig. 7.2 Showing correct assembly of the propeller shaft with yokes in the same plane (Sec 3)

3.2A Removing the universal joint flange bolts

3.2B Pulling the rear shaft from the splined joint

3.3 Front rubber coupling on later models

4 Support bearing – removal, inspection and refitting

1   With the propeller shaft removed as described in Section 3, inspect the support bearing for wear and the rubber housing for deterioration and oil contamination causing sponginess.
2   The bearing should rotate freely without grating or harshness.
3   If either the bearing or rubber housing are not in good condition, renew them as follows.
4   Pull the rubber mounting from the propeller shaft.
5   Place the propeller shaft in a padded vice, and gently tap off the bearing, being careful not to damage the dust cover. Note which way the dust cover is fitted.
6   Clean the dust cover and the bearing seat on the propeller shaft.
7   Fit the dust cover, chamfered edge facing the bearing.
8   Tap the new bearing into place, using a suitable tubular drift on the inner race.
9   Fit the rubber mounting over the bearing, the spring and washer should be in the lower segment.
10 Check the condition of the rubber gaiter which fits over the splined centre joint, and renew it if perished or split.
11 Refit the propeller shaft as described in Section 3.

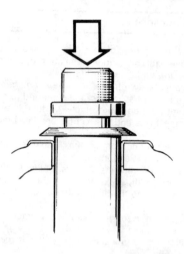

Fig. 7.3 Correct fitting of the dust cover (Sec 4)

5 Universal joints – renewal

Note: *Without a large workshop vice this operation is best left to your Volvo dealer.*
1   Remove the propeller shaft as described in Section 3.
2   Remove the circlips from the bearing cups. Use a punch to free them if they are stuck.
3   Place the propeller shaft onto the vice so that the yokes of the propeller shaft (not the flange) are resting on the open vice jaws. (Remember that the propeller shaft is hollow and easily damaged by too much vice pressure).
4   Using a socket which will just fit over the bearing cups and a hammer, gently tap the flange yoke downwards so that the uppermost bearing cup protrudes about 0.12 to 0.16 in (3.0 to 4.0 mm). Remove the cup (photos).
5   Turn the propeller shaft through 180° and repeat the operation on the opposite bearing.
6   The flange can now be removed from the propeller shaft (photo) and the same procedure used to remove the spider from the shaft.
7   Clean the bearing seats in the flange and propeller shaft yokes.
8   Remove the bearings from the new spider (photo) and ensure that the needle bearings are well greased. (This will ensure the needle bearings stay in place during the following fitting procedure).
9   Place the spider in the flange yoke (photo) and install one bearing cup onto the yoke (photo).
10 Using the vice and a socket of suitable diameter, press the bearing cup into the yoke by about 0.12 to 0.16 in (3.0 to 4.0 mm) (photo). Fit the circlip (photo).
11 Repeat on the opposite side, then fit the flange yoke and spider to the propeller shaft yoke (remember the alignment marks) and fit the remaining bearing cups (photos).
12 Fit the remaining bearing retaining circlips.
13 Check the joint for full and free movement, and if it feels excessively tight, rest it on the vice and just gently tap it with a plastic mallet, which will centralise the bearings and free the joint.
14 Refit the propeller shaft as described in Section 3.

6 Splined centre joint – inspection and renewal

1   Play in the splined centre joint can be tested by grasping the front and rear sections of the propeller shaft and turning them against each other. Any excessive movement should be investigated.
2   Remove the rear section of the shaft as described in Section 3.
3   Inspect the splines of the sliding joint for wear or cracking.
4   If the male splines only are worn or damaged, remove the splined section universal joint by following the procedure given in Section 5.
5   Fit a new splined section, grease the splines and fit a new rubber cover (photos), then refit the rear section of the propeller shaft.
6   If the female splines are also damaged, the complete propeller shaft may have to be renewed, and you should consult your Volvo dealer.

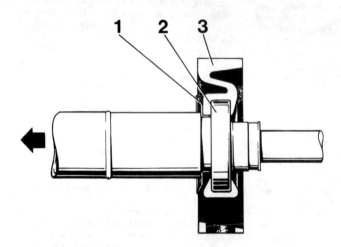

Fig. 7.4 Centre bearing and rubber mounting assembly.
Arrow points to front (Sec 4)

1 Dust cover	2 Centre bearing	
	3 Rubber mounting	

5.4A Tap the flange yoke downwards ...

5.4B ... and remove the bearing cup

5.6 Removing the flange

5.8 Spider, bearings and circlips

5.9A Placing the spider in the yoke ...

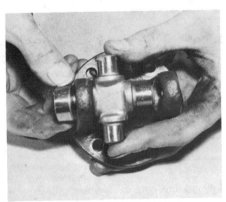
5.9B ... and fitting a bearing cup

5.10A Pressing the bearing cup into the yoke

5.10B Fitting the circlip

5.11A Tap the first cup into the shaft yoke ...

5.11B ... fit the other cup ...

5.11C ... and press it home in the vice

6.5A Internal splines of the front section

6.5B Fit the rubber cover

7.4 Rubber coupling locating plate

7 Rubber coupling – removal and refitting

1 Raise and securely support the vehicle.
2 Make alignment marks between the shaft and the gearbox output flange.
3 Remove the six nuts and bolts which hold the flanges to the coupling. (It may not be possible actually to remove the forward-facing bolts, which will stay on the flange.)
4 Pull the shaft rearwards and lower the front section. Remove the rubber coupling, the centre sleeve and the locating plate (photo).
5 Refit by reversing the removal operations, observing the alignment marks. Apply a little anti-seize compound to the locating plate pin.

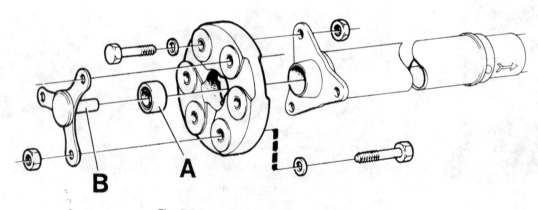

Fig. 7.5 Propeller shaft rubber coupling (Sec 7)

A Centre sleeve   B Locating plate

8 Fault diagnosis – propeller shaft

Symptom	Reason(s)
Vibration	Wear in sliding joint splines
	Worn universal joints (including front rubber joint where fitted)
	Propeller shaft unbalanced, bent or distorted
Knock or clunk when taking up drive	Worn universal joints
	Worn rear axle drive pinion splines
	Excessive backlash in rear axle gears
	Worn sliding joint splines
	Flange bolts loose

Chapter 8 Rear axle and suspension

Contents

Specifications

Rear axle

Type ....
Differential and final drive ....

Semi-floating
Bevel gear (hypoid) contained in integral housing in rear axle.
Limited slip available as option

Reduction ratios:
  Type 1030 ....
  Type 1031 ....
Lubricant capacity:
  Type 1030 ....
  Type 1031 ....
Lubricant type/specification:
  Without limited slip differential ....

  With limited slip differential ....

Drive shafts ....

Pinion bearing preload (models with compression sleeve):
  New bearings ....
  Used bearings ....

3.54:1, 3.73:1, 3.91:1, 4.10:1 or 4.30:1
3.15:1, 3.31:1, 3.54:1, 3.73:1 or 3.91:1

2.3 pints (1.3 litres)
2.8 pints (1.6 litres)

Hypoid gear oil, viscosity SAE 90, to API-GL-5 (Duckhams Hypoid
90S)
Hypoid gear oil, viscosity SAE 90, to API-GL-5, with Volvo additive
part number 1 161 129 0 (Duckhams Hypoid 90 DL)
Solid, splined to differential side gears, taper-roller bearings at outer
ends

1.8 to 2.6 lbf ft (2.5 to 3.5 Nm)
1.1 to 1.8 lbf ft (1.5 to 2.5 Nm)

Suspension

Type ....

Coil spring, trailing arms with reaction rods and track (Panhard) rod.
Telescopic, hydraulic or gas-filled shock absorbers, self-levelling
gas-filled as option

Rear wheel track:
  5 inch wheels ....
  5½ inch wheels (up to 1977) ....
  5½ inch wheels (1977-on) ....

53.15 in (1350 mm)
53.15 in (1350 mm)
53.58 in (1360 mm)

Torque wrench settings*

	lbf ft	Nm
Anti-roll bar front nuts	33	45
Anti-roll bar rear nuts	63	85
Shock absorber nuts/bolts	63	85
Spring upper mounting to body	33	45
Spring lower mounting	14	19
Brake caliper bolts	43	58
Differential cover bolts	20	27
Oil drain plug	36	50
Oil filler plug	18	25
Wheel nuts	83	115
Pinion nut (see Section 13):		
Without compression sleeve	148 to 184	200 to 250
With compression sleeve	133 to 207	180 to 280
Track rod to axle	44	60
Track rod to body	63	85
Reaction rod mounting	63	85
Trailing arm mounting	83	115

*Rear suspension torque wrench settings here are valid for models up to 1981. Later models are believed to be similar, but no definite figures have
been published.

1 General description

The rear axle and suspension are shown in Figs. 8.1 and 8.2. The rear axle is attached to the body by two trailing arms. Longitudinal stability is by two reaction rods, and lateral stability by the track rod. The trailing arms, track rod and reaction rods are attached to the body by rubber type mountings. On some models, an anti-roll bar is fitted between the trailing arms.

Suspension is by coil springs, and damping by two telescopic hydraulic or gas-filled shock absorbers, mounted independently of the springs. On some models, self-levelling gas-filled shock absorbers are fitted.

Most models are fitted with a type 1030 rear axle, although some high performance models may have a type 1031, one difference being in the differential reduction ratios. A limited slip differential is available as an option.

The drive shafts are carried in two taper-roller bearings at their outer ends. The brake disc assemblies (and the wheels) are attached to the driveshaft flange.

On later models with an electronic speedometer, the speedometer sensor is mounted in the differential rear cover.

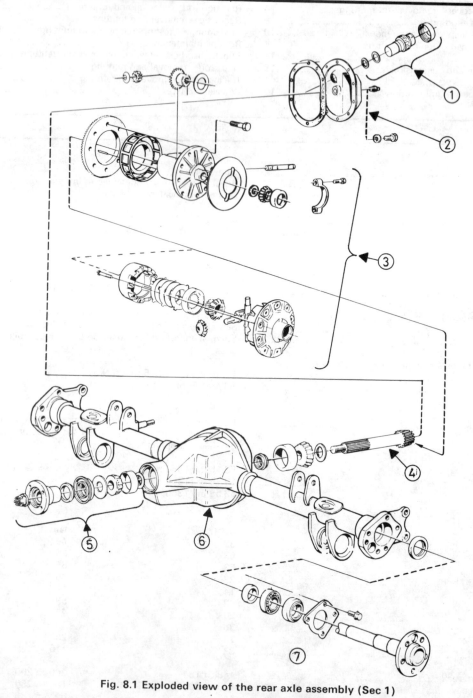

Fig. 8.1 Exploded view of the rear axle assembly (Sec 1)

1 Electronic speedometer sensor
2 Differential housing cover and gasket
3 Differential assembly (standard above, limited slip below)
4 Pinion shaft
5 Pinion flange and front bearing assembly
6 Differential housing and rear axle
7 Driveshaft and bearing assembly

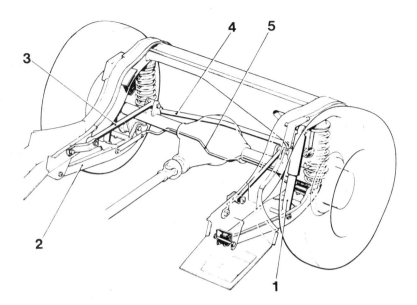

Fig. 8.2 Rear suspension components (Sec 1)

1   Shock absorber
2   Support arm
3   Reaction rod
4   Track rod
5   Anti-roll bar

2   Routine maintenance

1   At the intervals specified in the *Routine maintenance* Section at the beginning of this Manual, carry out the following operations.
2   With the vehicle in a level attitude, remove the filler/level plug from the rear axle cover (photo) and check the level of oil, which should be just up to the level of the filler plug hole. Top up as necessary with the recommended oil (photo). Check for leaks if frequent topping-up is required.
Note: *The oil in the rear axle is normally only renewed after the first 6 months, which would be done at a warranty service, and requires no periodic renewal thereafter. A drain plug is provided, however, and the prudent owner may wish to renew the oil every 36 000 miles or so as a precautionary measure.*
3   Check the rear suspension bushes (trailing arms, track rod, anti-roll bar) for wear and perishing. Raise the rear of the vehicle onto axle stands and use a stout lever to check for any movement in the bushes. Renew as necessary.
4   Check the condition of the suspension springs and their mountings.
5   Check the shock absorbers for leaks and correct operations (Section 3).
6   For rear tyres, refer to Chapter 10.

3   Shock absorbers – testing, removal and refitting

1   The shock absorber can be functionally checked using the 'bounce' method. Push down hard on the corner of the vehicle nearest to the shock absorber to be tested and release it immediately. Generally speaking, the vehicle should bounce once and return to rest. If it keeps bouncing, the shock absorbers should be renewed. As with the springs, shock absorbers should ideally be renewed as a pair and not singly, although the makers no longer specify this.
2   To remove a shock absorber, raise the rear of the vehicle onto axle stands, then just take the weight of the rear axle on a trolley jack positioned under the differential. Remove the rear wheel on the side concerned.
3   Remove the shock absorber top and bottom mounting nuts/bolts, and remove the shock absorber (photos).
4   No repairs are possible, and replacement units should be obtained and fitted.
5   Refitting is a reversal of removal, but note that the spacer is fitted on the inboard side of the shock absorber. Tighten the mounting nuts and bolts to the specified torque.
Note: *The procedure for renewing self-levelling gas-filled shock absorbers is similar to that described here. The self-levelling action is automatic by internal valves, and there are no external components.*

2.2A Removing the oil filler/level plug

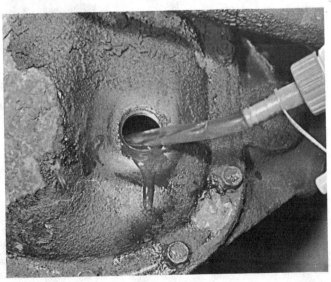

2.2B Filling the rear axle with oil

4   Rear springs – testing, removal and refitting

1   Testing of springs is best done with the springs removed and placed in a spring rate tester which your Volvo dealer may have. As a general guide, if the rear of the vehicle sags permanently, especially with a load, then the springs have become weak and should be renewed. Springs should be renewed in pairs, not singly, which could affect the handling of the vehicle.
2   To remove the springs, raise the vehicle onto axle stands and remove the rear wheels. Take the weight of the rear axle on a trolley jack placed under the differential.
3   Remove the nut from the spring lower mounting (photo), and disconnect the shock absorber lower mounting. Also disconnect the anti-roll bar, if fitted.
4   Lower the rear axle on the trolley jack until the spring tension is released, then lift the spring off the lower mounting and guide it out from under the vehicle.

5   Refitting is a reversal of removal, but guide the spring into location in the upper housing (photo) while raising the trolley jack. Tighten all nuts and bolts to the specified torque.

5   Track rod – removal and refitting

1   Raise the rear of the vehicle onto axle stands.
2   Remove the nuts from the track rod mountings (photos), then tap out the bolts using a soft drift.
3   Press out the rubber bushes using a mandrel of diameter just smaller than the bushes.
4   Press in new bushes using a little liquid soap as a lubricant. Note that there are different profile bushes in use, but this has no effect on procedures or performance.
5   Refit the track rod, but do not tighten any bolts to the specified torque (see Specifications) until the weight of the vehicle is back on the ground.

6   Reaction rod – removal and refitting

1   Raise the rear of the vehicle onto axle stands.
2   Remove the nuts from the reaction rod attachment points, then use a soft drift to tap out the bolts, and remove the rod.
3   The rubber bushes can be removed from the rod using a mandrel of diameter just smaller than the bush, and refitted in the same manner.
4   Use a little liquid soap as a lubricant, and ensure the flat sides of the rubber bush are parallel to the rod before pressing the bush home.
5   Refit the reaction rod, but do not tighten the nuts/bolts to the specified torque until the weight of the vehicle is back on the ground.
Note: *There are three different lengths of reaction rod. If the reaction rod is being renewed, replace it with a rod of the same length, unless suspension performance changes are required, in which case you should consult your Volvo dealer.*

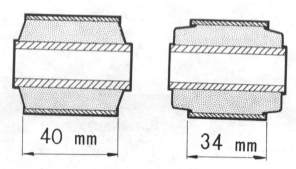

Fig. 8.3 Showing the different profile of track rod bushes (Sec 5)

3.3A Shock absorber lower mounting
1   *Trailing arm*   3   *Bolt*
2   *Shock absorber*   4   *Spacer*

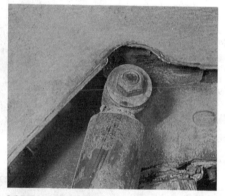

3.3B Shock absorber upper mounting

4.3 Spring lower mounting nut

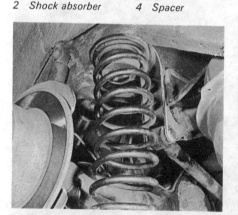

4.5 Spring upper housing

5.2A Track rod right-hand mounting

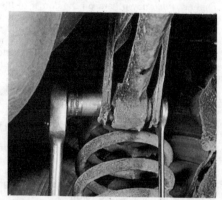

5.2B Removing the bolt from the left-hand mounting

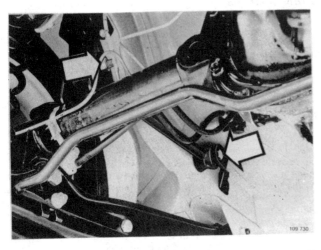

Fig. 8.4 Reaction rod attachment points (arrowed) (Sec 6)

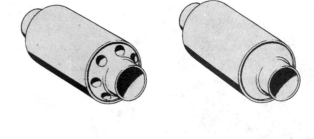

Fig. 8.5 Different types of trailing arm bush (Sec 8)

7 Anti-roll bar – removal and refitting

1   An anti-roll bar is fitted to certain models only, bolted between the two trailing arms.
2   To remove the anti-roll bar, raise the rear of the vehicle onto axle stands. Support the rear axle with a trolley jack to unload the shock absorber mountings.
3   Remove the shock absorber lower mounting bolts and the other nuts and bolts securing the anti-roll bar to the trailing arm on both sides of the vehicle (photo).
4   Remove the anti-roll bar.
5   Refitting is a reversal of removal, tightening all disturbed nuts and bolts to the specified torque (see Specifications) after lowering the vehicle back onto its wheels and bouncing the rear end a few times.

8 Trailing arm – removal and refitting

1   Raise the rear of the vehicle onto axle stands, and position a trolley jack under the rear axle and just take the weight. Remove the rear wheel.
2   Remove the shock absorber lower attachment bolt.
3   Remove the bolts from the anti-roll bar (when fitted).
4   Remove the nut from the spring lower housing.
5   Lower the rear axle on the trolley jack and remove the spring.
6   Remove the bolt from the trailing arm-to-rear axle bracket (photo) and lower the trailing arm rear end.
7   Remove the bolt from the trailing arm front mounting (photo) and lift the arm away.
8   If the front bushes are cracked or perished, renew them by drifting them out of the housing using a mandrel of suitable diameter (just smaller than the bush).
9   Note that an improved bush is fitted to later models, and if an early type bush has to be renewed (see Fig. 8.5), the bushes on both sides must be renewed with the later bush. (The early type are no longer available).
10 Use a little liquid soap as a lubricant when fitting the new bushes.
11 The rear bushes will still be in the housings on the rear axle, and may be difficult to remove and refit without special tools, and it is suggested that if the rear bushes need renewing, your Volvo dealer should do the job.
12 Refitting the trailing arm is a reversal of removal, but do not fully tighten any bolts to the specified torque (see Specifications) until the weight of the vehicle is back on the ground.

9 Driveshaft – removal and refitting

1   Remove the rear wheel on the side to be worked on.
2   Refer to Chapter 9 and remove the handbrake shoe assembly.

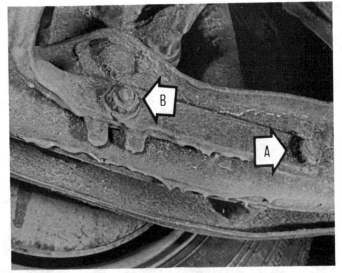

7.3 Anti-roll bar mounting details – (A) shock absorber lower bolt and (B) anti-roll bar nut

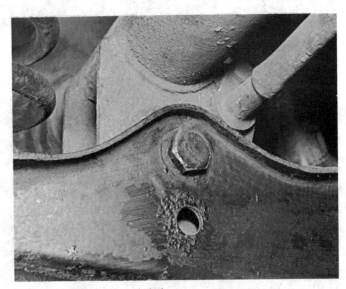

8.6 Trailing arm-to-rear axle bolt

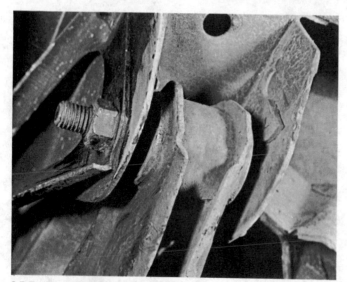

8.7 Trailing arm front mounting and bush

3   Remove the four bolts securing the retaining plate to the rear axle casing (photo), noting the brake shoe steady spring fitted under the bolt heads (photo).
4   Pull the driveshaft outwards from the rear axle casing (photo) using the brake disc temporarily fitted back to front as a puller if it is stiff. Be prepared for oil spillage. **Note:** *There is nothing to disconnect at the inboard end. If the driveshaft is broken, and half remains in the casing, it can be removed by taking off the differential cover and pushing the broken piece out with stiff wire through the differential.*
5   Refitting is a reversal of removal, remembering to fit the brake shoe steady spring under the retaining bolt heads.
6   Check the rear axle oil level and top up if necessary.

10 Driveshaft and bearing – inspection and renewal

Note: *Bearing renewal requires the use of press tools. The locking ring and bearing (see later text) can be removed by part-drilling through the locking ring, and then splitting it with a cold chisel, or grinding it off, but care should be exercised not to damage the driveshaft during the operation. Having removed the locking ring, the next problem is to remove the bearing, which would need a puller with arms the length of the driveshaft, or the bearing could be supported on its outer edge, with the driveshaft free, and the driveshaft driven through the bearing using a mallet and a block of wood as protection for the shaft. These methods are very 'Heath Robinson' affairs, and it should be remembered that the bearing and locking ring must be pressed back on in some way, which could be done using a length of metal tubing of suitable diameter, or pulled on with a puller if the arms will fit over the driveshaft flange and on to the bearing/locking ring. As the locking ring is basically what holds the driveshaft in the rear axle, these methods should only be used in an emergency, the best course of action being to take the driveshaft to your Volvo dealer.*
1   Remove the driveshaft as described in Section 9.
2   Clean the driveshaft and bearing thoroughly in solvent.
3   Inspect the driveshaft splines for cracks or wear, and the driveshaft for twisting or bending. If any of these signs are evident, the driveshaft should be renewed.
4   Inspect the bearing for signs of wear or blueing, and if it needs renewing or the outer seal is damaged, refer to the note at the beginning of this Section for removal procedures.
5   Remove the locking ring (2), bearing (3), oil seal (4) and retaining plate (5) from driveshaft (1) (photo).
6   Clean the bearing seat, pack the bearing and seal with grease, and ensure that the retaining plate is in position on the driveshaft before fitting the seal (lips towards the bearing), bearing and locking collar, again referring to the note at the beginning of this Section.
7   Press on the locking ring and bearing as far as they will go, so that they are hard up against the shoulder on the driveshaft.
8   Remove the bearing outer race and inner oil seal from the axle casing.

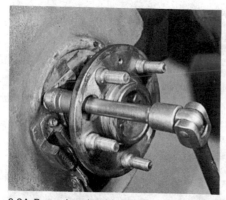

9.3A Removing the driveshaft retaining plate bolts

9.3B Brake shoe steady spring under the bolts (arrowed)

9.4 Pulling out the driveshaft

10.5 Driveshaft bearing assembly
Refer to text for item numbers

10.9A Tapping the oil seal home

10.9B Oil seal in position (arrowed)

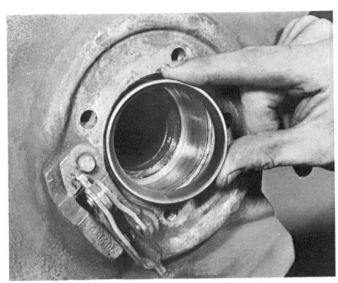
10.9C Fitting the bearing outer race

9   Clean out the bearing housing, then grease the new seal before fitting it (lips inwards) and the bearing outer race (photos).
10 Refit the driveshaft as described in Section 9, and then check the oil level in the rear axle.

11 Pinion oil seal – renewal

1   Raise the rear of the vehicle onto axle stands.

2   Drain the oil from the rear axle, or prepare for oil spillage.
3   Remove the rear section of the propeller shaft (see Chapter 7).
4   Remove the pinion flange nut by inserting two long bolts through the bolt holes in the flange and placing a crowbar between them while undoing the pinion nut – it will be tight.
5   Use a puller to remove the flange (photo).
6   Prise out the oil seal using a screwdriver, being careful not to damage the inner face of the pinion housing. Any scoring or scratches in this area will result in continued oil leakage.
7   Clean off the inner surface of the pinion housing, and check that there are no score marks or scratches. Blending any light marks out with fine emery cloth may effect a cure. Similarly check the seal rubbing surface of the pinion flange.
8   Grease the lips and the spring recess of the new seal.
9   Fit the seal with the 'outside' mark facing outwards (photos).
10 Tap the seal flush with the front of the housing using a block of wood and a hammer (photo).
11 Refit the flange and pinion nut (photos), with reference to Section 13 on pinion preload.
12 Refit the propeller shaft and fill the rear axle with oil.

12 Pinion front bearing – renewal and refitting

Note *This procedure is only intended for inspection of the front bearing. If bearing renewal is necessary, this should be performed by a Volvo dealer or other specialist, who will have the necessary equipment to determine bearing shim thickness.*
1   Remove the pinion oil seal as described in Section 11.
2   Remove the large washer (photo).
3   Remove the bearing, pulling it out with a puller with thin arms if it is tight (photo).
4   Remove the shim (photo).
5   Refit in the reverse order, fitting the oil seal as described in Section 11.

11.5 Using a puller to remove the flange

11.9A 'Outside' mark on oil seal

11.9B Fit the seal ...

11.10 ... and tap it home

11.11A Fit the flange ...

11.11B ... and tighten the pinion nut

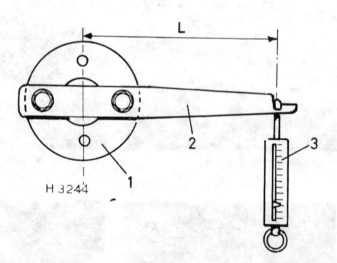

12.2 Remove the large washer ...

12.3 ... and bearing

12.4 Removing the shim

12.6A Dust cover on the flange

12.6B Using a socket to tap the dust cover on

6 Before refitting the pinion, check that the dust cover is in good condition and renew it if necessary (photos).
7 Refit the flange and pinion nut as described in Section 11.

13 Pinion preload – setting

1 Whenever the pinion drive flange is removed, on refitting the pinion preload must be checked as described in the following paragraphs.
2 On differentials without a compression sleeve (those axles without an 'S' in their serial number), it is simply a case of tightening the pinion nut to the specified torque (see Specifications), and no further action is required.
3 On differentials with a compression sleeve (those axles whose serial number begins with a letter 'S'), the procedure requires the use of a special torque wrench which measures the force required to turn the rear axle through the pinion shaft. This could be done by making up a tool similar to that shown in Fig. 8.6. Turning speed during the check should be approximately 1 rev/sec.
4 It should also be noted that this procedure is only intended for pinion nut tightening after an oil seal or bearing renewal, and is not fully descriptive where the pinion shaft or front bearing has been removed or renewed.
5 Tighten the pinion nut to the lower of the two figures given in the Specifications.
6 Check the force required to turn the rear axle (ensure the brakes are not binding), which should be between the values given in the Specifications.
7 If it is lower, tighten the pinion nut a little more, and re-check the turning force. Continue until the specified value is reached, but without exceeding the maximum value for pinion nut tightening torque.
8 If the pinion preload (the force required to turn the rear axle) is exceeded, a new compression sleeve will have to be fitted, which is best done by your Volvo dealer.

Fig. 8.6 Home-made tool for measuring pinion preload (Sec 13)

1 Pinion flange
2 Tool
3 Spring balance

Turning torque = length L x spring balance reading

14 Differential housing rear cover – removal and refitting

1 Raise the rear of the vehicle onto axle stands.
2 Drain the oil from the rear axle. Clean the rear cover and housing.
3 On vehicles equipped with an electronic speedometer, disconnect the leads on the sensor unit on the rear cover.

Note: *If only the rear cover is to be removed for gasket renewal, do not disturb the speedometer sensor in the cover, or the adjustment procedure in Section 17 will have to be complied with.*

4 Remove the bolts securing the cover to the rear axle, and lift the cover away.
5 Clean off both mating surfaces of the cover and the housing, removing all traces of old gasket. Check that the cover is not warped.
6 Apply grease to the face of a new gasket and fit it in position on the housing – the grease will make it stick.
7 Fit the cover and bolts and tighten them to the specified torque (see Specifications).
8 Reconnect the leads to the speedometer sensor.
9 Fill the rear axle with oil.

15 Differential – overhaul

1 Because of the precise nature of the reassembly procedures, and the need for special tools and measurement equipment, and the often disappointing results through lack of these tools, it is recommended that any repair or overhaul work on the differential, apart from those procedures already dealt with in earlier Sections, is left to your Volvo dealer.

16 Rear axle – removal and refitting

1 Raise the rear of the vehicle onto axle stands positioned just in front of the rear jacking points.
2 Drain the oil from the rear axle.
3 Remove the rear wheels.
4 Position a trolley jack under the differential housing of the rear axle.
5 Remove the driveshafts with reference to Section 9. (This is not essential, but it will reduce the weight of the axle considerably. If it is decided not to remove the driveshafts, just remove the handbrake shoes and disconnect the handbrake cable.)
6 If the exhaust pipe runs underneath the rear axle (certain models only), remove the rear section of the exhaust pipe.
7 Disconnect the propeller shaft from the rear axle (see Chapter 7).
8 Refer to the relevant Sections in this Chapter, and remove/disconnect the anti-roll bar, reaction rods, track rod, shock absorber lower mountings and spring mountings.
9 Remove the handbrake cable bracket from the top of the rear axle.
10 Disconnect the other brake pipe brackets which may be fixed to the axle (this differs between models).
11 Disconnect the rear axle breather pipe bracket.
12 On models equipped with an electronic speedometer, disconnect the electrical leads from the differential rear cover.
13 The rear axle can now be lowered slightly (check during this operation that all disconnections have been made and nothing is snagging), and the trailing arms released from the front mountings, or the rear axle released from the trailing arms.
14 Manoeuvre the rear axle from under the vehicle.
15 Refitting is a reversal of removal, referring to the relevant Sections of this Chapter, and Chapter 9 for the brakes, or Chapter 7 for the propeller shaft.
16 Do not fully tighten any bolts on the suspension side until the vehicle has been lowered to the ground (see Specifications for final torque load figures).
17 Fill the rear axle with the recommended oil.

17 Electronic speedometer sensor – removal , refitting and adjustment

1 Raise the rear of the vehicle onto axle stands (this will cause the oil level in the rear axle to fall below the level of the filler plug, and so the rear axle should not need draining).
2 Disconnect the leads to the sensor. There may be a tamperproof seal on the wiring plug: cut the seal off it so.
3 Unscrew the retaining collar on the sensor, and lift the sensor from the housing, retaining the shim and O-ring seal (photos).
4 Clean all parts and inspect their conditions. Always use a new seal on reassembly.

5 Apply a smear of grease to the new seal and slide it onto the sensor, followed by the shim.
6 Refit the sensor and tighten down the retaining collar.
7 Remove the filler plug, and using long feeler blades, check the clearance between the tip of the sensor and the sensor pick-up ring on the differential, which should be as specified in Fig. 8.8.
8 Adjustment is by shims placed under the sensor body, or (when refitting the cover) by moving the rear axle cover up or down as necessary.
9 On completion, refit the filler plug, connect the electrical leads and fit a new tamperproof seal if necessary, and remove the vehicle from the axle stands.
10 Finally, re-check the oil level.

18 Wheels and tyres

For information on general care of wheels and tyres refer to Chapter 10.

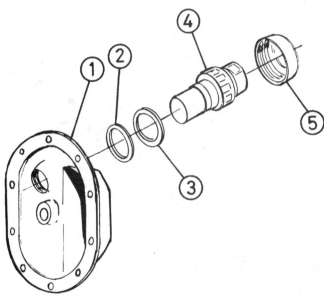

Fig. 8.7 Electronic speedometer sensor assembly (Sec 17)

1	*Rear axle cover*	*4*	*Sensor*
2	*Shim*	*5*	*Retaining collar*
3	*O-ring*		

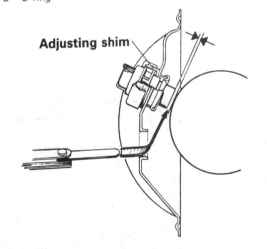

Fig. 8.8 Measuring the clearance between the sensor tip and pick-up (Sec 17)

Clearance = 0.334 ± 0.014 in (0.85 to 0.35 mm)

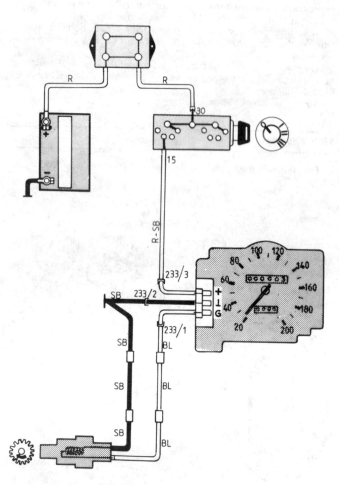

Fig. 8.9 Wiring diagram for electronic speedometer (Sec 17)

For colour code see wiring diagrams

17.3A Electronic speedometer removed showing the spacer (arrowed)

17.3B Electronic speedometer showing the O-ring seal (A) and wiring plug tamperproof seal (B)

19 Fault diagnosis – rear axle and suspension

Symptom	Reason(s)
Rear axle	

Note: *A defective propeller shaft or worn suspension bushes can cause noises which appear to emanate from the rear axle. Noise from the rear axle area can sometimes be hard to pinpoint. Try as many different combinations as possible, ie does it increase/decrease with speed, load, cornering, in or out of gear etc.*

Symptom	Reason(s)
Noise on drive or overrun	Oil level low or incorrect grade
	Bearings worn or damaged
	Gear teeth worn or damaged
Noise when turning (either way)	Differential worn or damaged
Noise when turning left only	Right-hand driveshaft bearing worn (and *vice versa*)

19 Fault diagnosis – rear axle and suspension

Symptom	Reason(s)
Knock when taking up drive	Propeller shaft flange bolts loose Wheel nuts loose Pinion flange loose Driveshaft splines worn Final drive worn or damaged
Oil leakage	Worn pinion oil seal Warped differential cover Worn driveshaft seals Differential breather hose blocked
Rear suspension Vehicle sags to one side	Spring weak or broken Shock absorber seized
Rear wheel skip on bumps	Shock absorber defective
Rear suspension noisy on bumps	Shock absorber defective Suspension bushes worn Loose suspension mounting bolts
Rear tyre wear excessive	Misalignment (due to worn or damaged suspension components) Shock absorbers defective Tyre pressures incorrect Unfavourable driving style or conditions of use

Chapter 9 Braking system

Contents

Specifications

General

System type	Disc brake on all four wheels; handbrake – drums on rear wheels only
Actuation	Dual hydraulic, split circuit with servo assistance. Handbrake mechanical.
Adjustment	Automatic (handbrake manual on early models)

Servo

Type	Double diaphragm, vacuum operated
Diameter	8 in (203.0 mm)

Front disc brakes

Disc diameter	10.35 in (263.0 mm)
Disc thickness:	
Solid, new	0.56 in (14.3 mm)
Solid, wear limit	0.50 in (12.7 mm)
Ventilated, new:	
ATE	0.94 in (24.0 mm)
Girling	0.87 in (22.0 mm)
Ventilated, wear limit:	
ATE	0.90 in (22.8 mm)
Girling	0.80 in (20.4 mm)
Disc run-out (all types)	0.0039 in (0.10 mm) maximum
Disc thickness variation	0.0008 in (0.02 mm) maximum
Brake pad friction material:	
Thickness (new)	0.39 in (10.0 mm)
Minimum (change at)	0.12 in (3.0 mm)

Rear disc brakes

Disc diameter	11.06 in (281.0 mm)
Disc thickness (new)	0.38 in (.96 mm)
Disc thickness (reconditioned)	0.33 in (8.4 mm)
Disc run-out	0.0039 in (0.10 mm) maximum
Disc thickness variation	0.0008 in (0.02 mm) maximum
Brake pad friction material:	

	Girling	ATE
Thickness (new)	0.32 in (8.0 mm)	0.39 in (10.0 mm)
Minimum (change at)	0.12 in (3.0 mm)	0.12 in (3.0 mm)

Handbrake
Drum diameter .... 6.32 in (160.45 mm) maximum
Run-out .... 0.006 in (0.15 mm) maximum
Out-of-round .... 0.008 in (0.2 mm) maximum

Master cylinder
Type .... Tandem, stepped bore
Primary bore diameter .... 0.88 in (22.3 mm)
Secondary bore diameter .... 0.62 in (15.75 mm)

Brake fluid type/specification .... Hydraulic fluid to DOT 4 (Duckhams Universal Brake and Clutch Fluid)

Torque wrench settings

	lbf ft	Nm
Front brake caliper mounting bolts	74	100
Rear brake caliper mounting bolts	43	58
Rear brake backplate	28	40
Wheel nuts	74 to 96	100 to 130
Master cylinder retaining nuts	22	30
Pipe unions	10	14
Rear brake valve hose	11	15

1 General description

The braking system is a four wheel hydraulic operated disc type. The hydraulic system is of dual circuit layout with each circuit operating two of the front four caliper pistons and a rear brake caliper. This arrangement ensures that half the braking system will be effective in the event of a failure of pressure in one circuit. The master cylinder is step-bored which ensures a braking power that is not noticeably diminished should one brake circuit fail. The driver is, however, warned by an indicator light which is activated by a pressure differential valve in the brake system.

The servo cylinder is directly actuated by the brake pedal. Vacuum assistance, obtained from the inlet manifold on carburettor versions, and from a vacuum pump on fuel injection versions, results in reduced pedal pressure being required for braking.

Pressure regulating valves are incorporated in each of the rear wheel brake lines to prevent the rear wheels locking in advance of the front wheels during heavy brake application.

The handbrake consists of cable operated brake shoes enclosed in small brake drums integral with the rear disc.

Since 1980, ventilated discs are used on the front brakes.

Work on the braking system should be careful and methodical. Scrupulous cleanliness must be observed when working on the hydraulic system. Replacement parts should preferably be the maker's own, or at least of known manufacture and quality.

Warning: Braking system hazards. *Some brake friction materials still contain asbestos. Assume that all brake dust is potentially hazardous for this reason; avoid inhaling it and do not dispense it into the air. Note also that brake fluid is toxic and attacks paintwork. Do not syphon it by mouth, wash thoroughly after skin contact and wash spillage off paintwork immediately.*

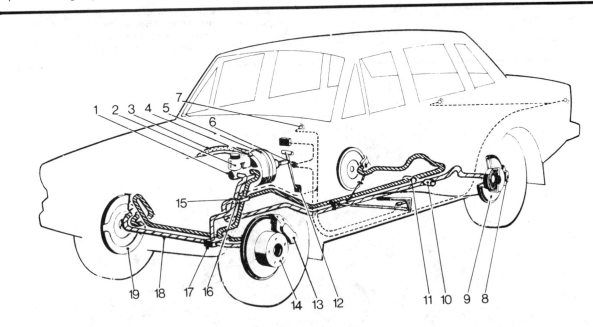

Fig. 9.1 Footbrake system layout – LHD shown, RHD similar (Sec 1)

1 Tandem master cylinder	7 Warning lamp	11 Brake valve, primary circuit	16 Warning valve
2 Brake fluid container	8 Rear brake caliper	12 Brake pedal	17 6-branch union (double
3 Vacuum line	9 Brake disc with drum	13 Front brake caliper	3-branch union)
4 Check valve	10 Brake valve, secondary	14 Brake disc	18 Brake pipe
5 Servo unit	circuit	15 Warning switch	19 Cover plate
6 Brake light switch			

2 Routine maintenance

1   At the intervals specified in the *Routine maintenance* Section at the beginning of this Manual, carry out the following operations.
2   Weekly, or before a long journey, check the fluid level in the master cylinder reservoir as follows.
3   The level of fluid in the brake master cylinder reservoir should be between the 'MAX' and 'MIN' marks on the outside of the reservoir. The reservoir is translucent, so the level can be checked without removing the cap.
4   If topping-up is necessary, wipe clean around the reservoir cap. Remove the cap and top up with fresh hydraulic fluid of the specified type. Only top up to the 'MAX' mark; do not overfill (photo).
5   Refit the reservoir cap. Wash any spilt fluid off paintwork immediately.
6   Regular need for topping-up shows that there is a leak somewhere in the system which should be found and rectified without delay. A slow fall in fluid level, as the pads wear, is normal; provided the level stays above the 'MIN' mark, there is then no need to top up for this reason. The level will rise again when new pads are fitted.
7   Other maintenance tasks, falling due at major service intervals, are as follows.
8   Check the brake servo booster for correct operation (Section 21).
9   Check the operation of the handbrake and adjust as necessary (Section 12).
10 Check the brake pads and shoes for wear (Sections 5 and 11).
11 Check all brake system pipelines and hoses (Section 24).
12 Renew the brake fluid (Section 25).

3 Front brake caliper – general description

1   The front brake caliper may be of ATE or Girling type, depending on year of manufacture (see note at beginning of Section 5). Both types are similar in operation, but differ slightly in construction.
2   The caliper is a two-piece casting, bolted together and attached to the suspension stub axle.
3   The upper and lower cylinders and pistons are completely separate from each other, but both pairs of cylinders are joined together by internal borings in the caliper.
4   The brake disc, which is bolted to the hub, rotates between the two halves of the caliper. When the footbrake is applied, the pistons, under

2.4 Topping-up the brake fluid level

the action of the hydraulic fluid, force the brake pads against the brake disc in a 'pincer' movement.
5   The piston has a rubber seal around its circumference to seal the hydraulic fluid in the cylinder, and this seal also acts as a return spring when the brakes are released. The seal also provides for automatic adjustment for brake pad wear.
6   A further seal, fitted to the piston where it contacts the brake pad backplate, prevents dust entering the cylinder.

4 Rear brake caliper – general description

1   The rear brake caliper may be of ATE or Girling type, depending on model (see note at beginning of Section 5).
2   Both types of caliper are similar to their front counterpart, except that they have single cylinders and pistons.

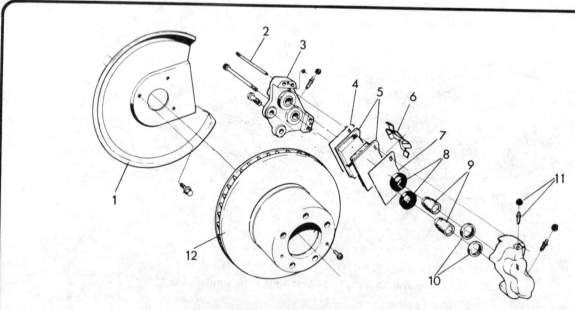

Fig. 9.2 Components of ATE type front caliper (Sec 3)

1 Disc shield	4 Anti-squeal shim	7 Anti-squeal shim	10 Seals
2 Pad retaining pin	5 Pads	8 Dust-excluding boots	11 Bleed nipple and dust cap
3 Caliper body	6 Anti-rattle spring	9 Pistons	12 Ventilated disc

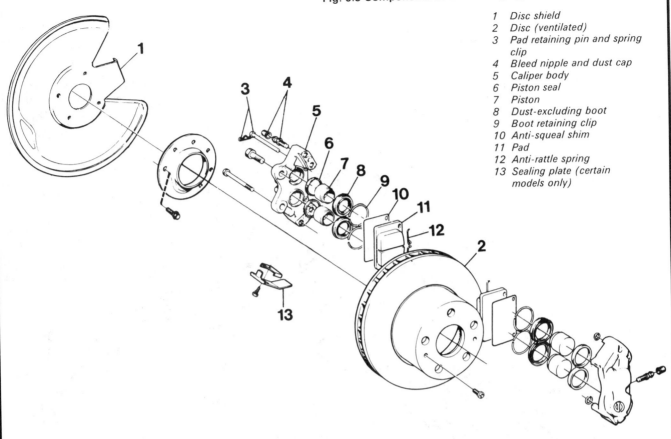

Fig. 9.3 Components of the Girling type front caliper (Sec 3)

1 Disc shield
2 Disc (ventilated)
3 Pad retaining pin and spring clip
4 Bleed nipple and dust cap
5 Caliper body
6 Piston seal
7 Piston
8 Dust-excluding boot
9 Boot retaining clip
10 Anti-squeal shim
11 Pad
12 Anti-rattle spring
13 Sealing plate (certain models only)

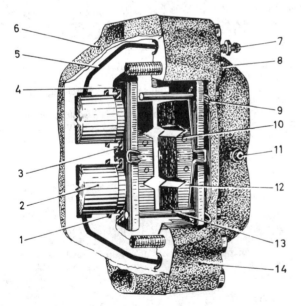
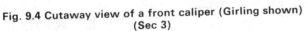

Fig. 9.4 Cutaway view of a front caliper (Girling shown) (Sec 3)

1 Seal
2 Piston
3 Rubber dust cover
4 Retaining ring
5 Channel
6 Outer half
7 Upper bleed nipple
8 Bolt
9 Retaining clip
10 Brake pad
11 Lower bleed nipple
12 Damping spring
13 Retaining pin
14 Inner half

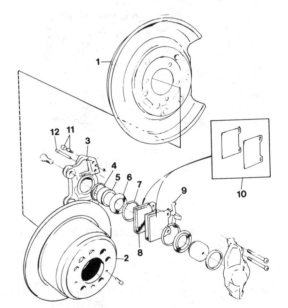

Fig. 9.5 Components of the ATE type rear caliper (Sec 4)

1 Disc shield
2 Disc/drum
3 Caliper body
4 Piston seal
5 Piston
6 Dust-excluding boot
7 Boot retaining clip
8 Pad
9 Anti-rattle spring
10 Anti-squeal shims (if fitted)
11 Bleed nipple and dust cap
12 Pad retaining pin

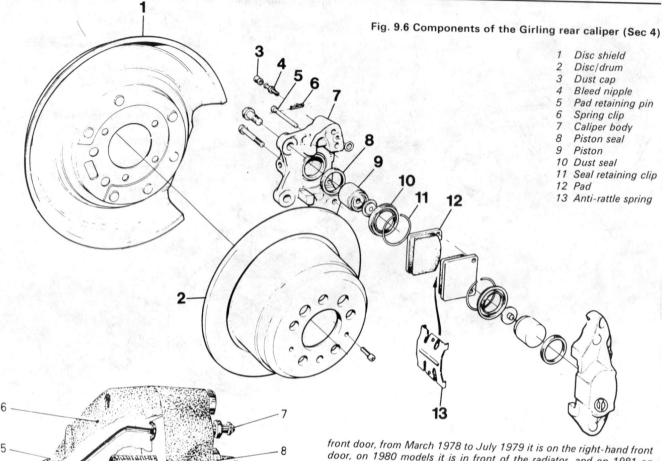

Fig. 9.6 Components of the Girling rear caliper (Sec 4)

1   Disc shield
2   Disc/drum
3   Dust cap
4   Bleed nipple
5   Pad retaining pin
6   Spring clip
7   Caliper body
8   Piston seal
9   Piston
10 Dust seal
11 Seal retaining clip
12 Pad
13 Anti-rattle spring

Fig. 9.7 Cutaway view of rear caliper (Girling shown)
(Sec 4)

1	Seal	8	Bolt
2	Piston	9	Retaining clip
3	Rubber dust seal	10	Brake pad
4	Retaining ring	11	Inner half
5	Channel	12	Anti-rattle spring
6	Outer half	13	Retaining pin
7	Bleedscrew	14	Washer

5   Front and rear disc brake pads – renewal

Note: *Both Girling and ATE type brake calipers are fitted, and the type fitted can be determined by the code numbers 1 and 2 which respectively refer to Girling and ATE. The code numbers are located on a plate. On early models the plate is on the pillar behind the right-hand*

front door, from March 1978 to July 1979 it is on the right-hand front door, on 1980 models it is in front of the radiator, and on 1981 on models it is in the engine compartment (Saloons) or luggage compartment (Estates). Note that for 1976 and 1977 models the code applies only to the rear calipers, as all front calipers are manufactured by Girling. On 1983 and later models, code number 2 indicates that the front brakes are Girling, and the rear brakes ATE.

1   The brake pads should be renewed when they have reached the limit given in the Specifications. The pads on both front or both rear brakes should be renewed at the same time. Renewing one side only can create braking imbalance.

2   Note also that high-friction rear pads should not be used in conjunction with early type front brake pads (Volvo part number DB818 or DB828), as this can cause braking imbalance between front and rear.

3   Raise the front or rear of the vehicle, as applicable, onto axle stands and remove the road wheels.

4   Measure the thickness of the friction lining of the brake pads and if they need renewing, proceed as follows.

ATE type (front)

5   Using a thin punch, knock out the pad retaining pins.

6   Lift out the anti-rattle spring.

7   Remove the pads, taking note of any anti-squeal shims which may be fitted to ensure they are refitted in the same position. Also identify the pad positions if they are to be re-used.

Girling type (front)

8   Remove the spring clips from the pad retaining pins (photo).

9   Remove the upper pad retaining pin (photo).

10 Prise out the pad anti-rattle spring (photo), then remove the lower pin.

11 Remove the brake pads, taking note of any anti-squeal shims which may be fitted between the pad the the piston, so that they can be refitted in the same position (photo). Also identify the pad positions if they are to be re-used.

ATE (type (rear)

12 The procedure is similar to that described for the front pads (photos).

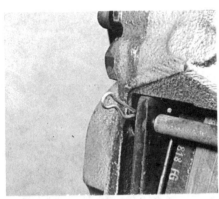

5.8 Pad retaining pin clip (Girling)

5.9 Removing the upper pad retaining pin (Girling)

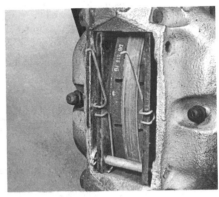

5.10 Anti-rattle springs and lower pin (Girling)

5.11 Removing the pads (Girling)

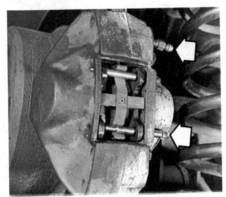

5.12A ATE type rear caliper pad retaining pins (arrowed)

5.12B ATE type rear caliper pads being withdrawn

Girling type (rear)

13 The procedure is similar to that described for the front pads, except that the spring-loaded cover plate should be removed first.

Inspection (both types)

14 Clean off all brake dust from the caliper (take precautions against inhalation), and take the opportunity to inspect the piston seals for leakage and the dust covers for deterioration. Refer to Sections 6 and 7 for overhaul of the calipers.
15 Use a block of wood as a lever to compress the pistons in the caliper (the new brake pads will otherwise be too thick). During this operation brake fluid may overflow from the reservoir, so be prepared for spillage. If the pistons cannot be compressed by this method, loosen the appropriate bleed nipple while compressing the piston, but the brakes may need bleeding on completion.
16 On ATE rear brakes, check the position of the stepped portion of the piston (refer to Section 7 for details).

Refitting (both types)

17 Smear the contact faces of the pistons, brake pad backplate and any shims with brake grease, or anti-squeal compound, but ensure that no grease gets on to the pads or disc.
18 Refitting of the pads is a reversal of the removal procedure for both types. Renew items such as anti-rattle springs and spring clips as necessary – they may be supplied with the new pad set.
19 On completion, operate the brakes several times to bring the pads up to the disc.
20 If any bleed nipples were slackened (paragraph 15), bleed the hydraulic system if necessary (Section 25).
21 Refit the wheels and remove the vehicle from axle stands.
22 Check the brake fluid level and top up if necessary.
23 Avoid harsh braking as far as possible for the next few hundred miles to allow the new pads to bed in.

6 Front brake caliper – removal, overhaul and refiting

Note: *The procedure given here covers both types of caliper, ATE and Girling. Before starting work, obtain a set of new seals and new caliper mounting bolts.*
1 Raise the front of the vehicle onto axle stands, and remove the front wheel.
2 Brush away any dirt and brake dust from the caliper.
3 Remove the cap from the brake fluid reservoir, place a square of cling film or polythene over the filler neck and refit the cap. This will reduce brake fluid loss when the brake pipes are disconnected.
4 Disconnect the brake pipe unions on the caliper. Cap the ends of the pipes, or clamp the flexible hoses, to reduce fluid loss.
5 Refer to Section 5 and remove the brake pads.
6 Remove the caliper-to-stub axle bolts (photo) and lift the caliper away. Discard the bolts.
7 Drain the fluid from the caliper. Carefully clean all traces of dirt and dust from the caliper before placing it on a clean bench.
Warning: *After removing the caliper, do not attempt to split the two halves of the caliper. Special tools are required, and the caliper halves cannot be reassembled outside of factory conditions.*
8 Remove the rubber dust caps from the pistons.
9 Place a piece of wood between the pistons, to act as a buffer, then blow the pistons from the cylinders by applying low air pressure to the pipe unions. **Caution:** *The pistons may be ejected with some force. Keep your fingers clear.*
10 Carefully remove the seals from the cylinder bore, being careful not to scratch the bore.
11 Clean the pistons in methylated spirit or clean hydraulic fluid, and wash out the bores in the same manner, before inspecting them for scratches or scoring. Light imperfections can be removed using steel wool or very fine emery cloth, but anything more serious will require renewal of the pistons (if available), or of the complete caliper.
12 Blow through the cylinder bores with air, and also check that the fluid transfer borings in the caliper body are clear.
13 Smear the cylinder bores, pistons and new seals with clean hydraulic fluid.

14 Fit the seals into the grooves in the cylinder bores, making sure they fit right down in the groove all the way round.
15 Fit the pistons into the cylinders (large diameter inwards – that is, facing away from the centre), ensuring they are kept square on to the bore.
16 Fit the dust cover over the piston and the caliper housing. If fitted, refit the dust cover retaining clips.
17 Refit the caliper to the stub axle, using new bolts, and tighten them to the specified torque.
18 Use feeler blades to check that the gap between the brake disc and the caliper is equal on both sides, to within 0.010 in (0.25 mm). If not, insert shims between the caliper and the stub axle to even up the gap.
19 Reconnect the brake pipes, fit the brake pads (Section 5), and bleed the hydraulic system (Section 25).
20 Fit the roadwheels, remove the vehicle from the axle stands, and carry out a road test.

7 Rear brake caliper – removal, overhaul and refitting

1 The procedure is similar to that described for the front calipers in Section 6 (photos). Again, use new bolts when refitting.
Note: *ATE pistons require a special tool to set the angle of the stepped shoulder to the caliper. The angle is 20 ± 2°. In the absence of this tool, a template of stiff card or alloy sheet could easily be made up to fulfil this requirement.*

8 Front brake disc – removal, inspection and refitting

1 Remove the caliper (Section 6). If care is taken, the hydraulic pipes need not be disconnected, but tie the caliper up with string or wire so that the hydraulic hoses are not strained.
2 Remove the brake disc retaining bolts (photo) and lift off the disc. Tap it off with a soft-faced hammer if it is tight. Note the spigot bolt for wheel location on later models.
3 If the discs are heavily scored, especially with radial marks, or badly corroded, they should be renewed. Light scoring is normal. The discs can be re-surfaced, provided the disc thickness is not reduced beyond the minimum thickness given in the Specifications.
4 Disc run-out should be checked using a dial test indicator, or feeler blades inserted between the disc and the caliper. Check thickness variation with a micrometer.
5 Obviously, any machining should be done by a specialist engineering firm.
6 Refitting is a reversal of removal. Bleed the brakes on completion, as described in Section 25, if the caliper hydraulic pipes were disconnected.
7 It is good practice to renew or refinish both front (or both rear) discs together, to maintain equal braking characteristics on both sides.

9 Front disc backplate – removal and refitting

1 The brake disc backplate is fitted to give protection against dirt and moisture ingress.

6.6 Front caliper retaining bolts (arrowed). Brake pipes should be disconnected

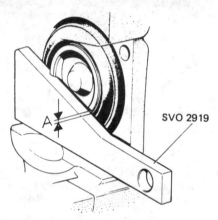
Fig. 9.8 Using the Volvo special tool to align ATE type caliper piston (Sec 7)
A (clearance between tool and stepped portion) = 0.04 in (1.0 mm)

2 To remove the backplate, first remove the caliper as described in Section 6.
3 Refer to Chapter 10, Section 4 and remove the front wheel bearings, hub, and disc.
4 Remove the bolts securing the backplate to the stub axle (photo).
Note: *On models built up to 1979, separate sealing plates were bolted to the backplate (see Fig. 9.9). These plates are still available as spares, although it would be better if the modified backplate which does not*

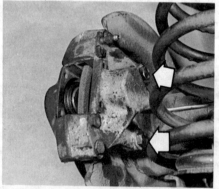
7.1A ATE rear caliper retaining bolts (arrowed)

7.1B Caliper bore showing piston seal (arrowed)

7.1C Pressing in a new piston

7.1D Fitting the dust seal

8.2 Front brake disc retaining bolts, showing the spigot for wheel alignment

9.4 Brake backplate securing bolts

have these plates, being more efficient, were fitted. Some models also have a separate dished collar bolted to the backplate (see Fig. 9.10). If no dished collar is fitted, it is desirable to fit one when the opportunity arises.

5 Refitting is a reversal of removal, bleeding the brakes on completion, and referring to Chapter 10 for bearing refitting and adjustment.

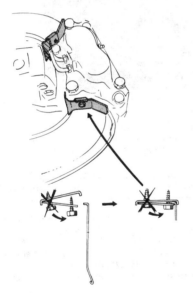

Fig. 9.9 Additional sealing plates on pre-1979 models (Sec 9)

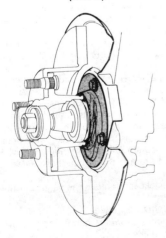

Fig. 9.10 Dished collar fitted to some models (Sec 9)

10 Rear brake disc/drum – removal, overhaul and refitting

1 Raise the rear of the vehicle onto axle stands.
2 Release the handbrake.
3 Remove the rear brake caliper as described in Section 7. If care is taken, there is no need to disconnect the hydraulic pipe, but release the pipe clip from the rear axle, and suspend the caliper with string or wire so that the pipe is not strained.
4 Remove the disc/drum retaining bolt and lift off the disc/drum (photos). If it is tight, refer to Section 12 and back off the brake shoe adjusters (if fitted) to loosen the drum.
5 The same comments as applied to front discs in Section 8 apply also to re-surfacing of the rear disc. The rear drum should be inspected for scoring and corrosion, and for ovality. Again, the drum can be re-surfaced, providing the limits are not exceeeded.
6 Refitting is a reversal of removal.
7 On completion, adjust the handbrake as described in Section 12.

11 Rear handbrake shoes – renewal

1 The handbrakes shoes must be renewed when they have worn down to the rivet heads, or in the case of bonded linings, when only 0.06 in (1.6 mm) of lining remains. (In practice the shoe linings are unlikely to suffer significant wear, unless there is a habit of applying the handbrake with the vehicle in motion). The shoes must also be renewed if they become contaminated with oil as a result of driveshaft oil seal failure.
2 Refer to Section 12, and loosen off the handbrake adjuster at the rear of the handbrake lever.
3 Remove the rear disc/drum as described in Section 10.
4 Take a note of which holes the return springs are hooked into (photo), then unhook the springs and remove the brake shoes and adjuster (if fitted) or spreader bar (photo).
5 Clean off all dust from the backplate area, being careful not to inhale it.
6 Inspect the adjuster mechanism (when fitted), cable end and lever for wear.
7 Apply brake anti-seize compound to adjuster or spreader bar and cable pivot points, and to the area of the backplate where the shoes are in contact with it. Keep anti-seize compound off the linings and drum friction surface.
8 Fit the lower return spring between the shoes, fit the shoes back over the hub, and then fit the upper return spring, locating the adjuster mechanism or spreader bar as you do so.
9 Ensure that the handbrake lever is slotted into the hole in the upper brake shoe (photo), and that the steady springs are located over the brake shoes.
10 Back off the adjuster and fit the brake disc/drum.
11 Refit the caliper and the brake pipe bracket on the rear axle if it was loosened.
12 Check that the disc/drum turns freely – it may bind until the shoes are centralised. (Apply the handbrake a few times to centralise the shoes.)

10.4A Removing a rear disc retaining bolt

10.4B Removing a rear brake disc

11.4A Brake shoe return spring (arrowed)

11.4B Brake shoes and spreader bar being removed

11.9 Handbrake lever in position

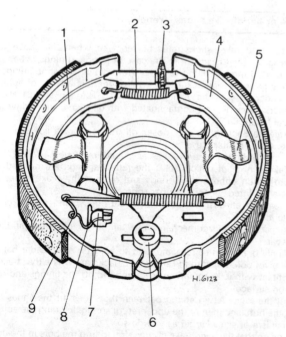

Fig. 9.11 Handbrake shoe arrangement (Sec 11)

1 Shoe	6 Anchor bolt
2 Return spring	7 Lever
3 Adjuster (some models)	8 Washer
4 Shoe	9 Spring
5 Shoe steady clip	

13 Adjust the handbrake as described in Section 12.
14 Refit the roadwheels and remove the vehicle from axle stands.

12 Handbrake lever, cables and shoes – adjustment

Note: *Handbrake adjustment should normally only be necessary to compensate for cable stretch, or after fitting new components. When a shoe adjuster mechanism is fitted, its main use is for initial setting-up after fitting new shoes. On models without shoe adjusters, adjustment is carried out only at the handbrake control.*
1 Raise the rear of the vehicle onto axle stands.

Models with shoe adjusters
2 Release the handbrake and remove the rear wheels.
3 Remove the ashtray from the handbrake console (see Chapter 11), and use a 17 mm socket and extension to undo the adjuster bolt and release all tension in the cables (photo).
4 Back off the adjuster mechanism in the rear drum by inserting a thin probe through the hole in the drum, and pushing the notched wheel round.
5 Now expand the adjuster until the shoes just begin to bind on the drum, then back it off 4 to 5 notches.
6 On the inside of the vehicle, adjust tension between the cables if necessary by using the cable end nuts, until the yoke at the rear of the handbrake is square on to the handbrake lever (photo).
7 Now tighten the bolt on the handbrake lever until it takes 2 to 8 clicks of the lever to obtain full braking efficiency. Make sure that the wheels are still free to turn with the handbrake released.
8 Refit the ashtray.
9 Refit the roadwheels and remove the vehicle from the axle stands.

Models without shoe adjusters
10 Removing the ashtray from the handbrake console.
11 Release the handbrake.
12 Proceed as from paragraph 6 above.

Fig. 9.12 Turning a handbrake shoe adjuster through the hole in the drum. Not all models have adjusters here (Sec 12)

12.3 Handbrake cable adjuster bolt (arrowed) – console removed for clarity

12.6 Handbrake cable end nuts (arrowed) – one side only shown

13 Handbrake cables – renewal

Note: *The procedure given here describes the renewal of a cable on one side only.*

1   Refer to Chapter 11 and remove the handbrake lever console.
2   Loosen the adjuster bolt at the rear end of the handbrake lever.
3   Loosen the nut at the end of the cable to be renewed.

Note: *The cables cross over underneath the vehicle, so the cable on the left of the handbrake lever operates the right-hand brake, and vice versa.*

4   Lift up the front end of the rear seat squab and fold back the carpet. This will reveal some cable clips which must be released.
5   Free the grommet where the cable runs through the floorpan.
6   Detach the rear brake disc/drum as described in Section 10.
7   Remove the brake shoes as described in Section 11.
8   Press out the pin securing the cable to the operating lever.
9   Remove the bolt from the cable bracket and guide tube on the trailing arm (photo), and withdraw the cable, plastic collar and rubber seal.
10 Pull the other end of the cable from the centre support and interior of the vehicle.
11 Fit the rubber seal and plastic collar to the guide tube on the trailing arm.
12 Route the cable through the centre support and grommet, and through the hole in the floorpan. Refit the grommet after both ends of the cable are connected.

Note: *The cable from the left-hand wheel should pass through the hole to the right of the propeller shaft, and vice-versa. The cable from the left-hand wheel should pass under the right-hand cable where they pass through the centre support (photo).*

13 Push the cable through the plastic guide tube on the trailing arm and reconnect it to the operating lever on the brake backplate.
14 Re-position the operating lever behind the backplate, and then refit the brake shoes, disc/drum and caliper.
15 Pull the other end of the cable into the interior of the vehicle, through the plastic tube, and reconnect it to the handbrake lever (photo).
16 Refit the cable clamps on the floorpan, and refit the carpet and seat squab.
17 Adjust the handbrake cable as described in Section 12, then refit the console.
18 Refit the rear wheels and lower the vehicle to the ground.

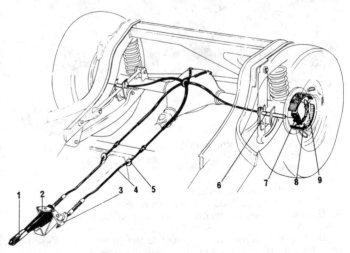

Fig. 9.13 Handbrake cable layout (Sec 13)

1 Lever	6 Plastic tube
2 Yoke	7 Levers
3 Lever	8 Brake shoes
4 Cable	9 Adjustment device (some
5 Rubber grommet	models)

14 Handbrake 'on' warning light switch – removal, refitting and adjustment

1   The handbrake 'on' warning light switch is mounted on a bracket under the handbrake.
2   To remove the switch, first remove the handbrake console as described in Chapter 11.
3   Disconnect the lead (photo).
4   Remove the securing screw and lift the switch from the bracket.
5   Refit in the reverse order.
6   To adjust the switch, check that with the handbrake fully released, the warning light goes out, and comes on when the handbrake lever is pulled up.
7   Bend the switch mounting bracket as necessary to achieve this condition.

15 Brake pedal – removal and refitting

1   Remove the panel under the dashboard.

Fig. 9.14 Pressing out the handbrake cable-to-operating lever pin (Sec 13)

13.9 Handbrake cable guide tube on the trailing arm
1   Retaining bolt   2   Guide tube

13.12 Route the cables correctly

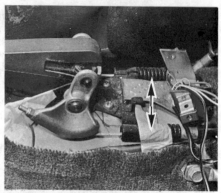

13.15 Plastic tubes (arrowed) through which the cables pass

14.3 Handbrake 'on' warning light switch
1   Electrical connection
2   Switch body   3   Securing screw

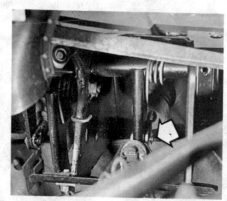

15.3 Pushrod link retaining pin (arrowed)

15.4 Brake pedal pivot bolt (arrowed)

2   Remove the brake light switch and bracket.
3   Disconnect the pushrod link from the brake pedal arm (photo).
4   Unscrew and remove the pedal pivot bolt and nut, and lift the pedal away (photo).
5   Bushes and sleeves can be fitted to the pedal and linkage by pressing out the old ones and fitting new ones. Apply grease to the bearing surfaces on reassembly.
6   When fitting the brake light switch, adjust it as described in Section 16.
7   Brake pedal travel can only be checked with all brake fluid drained from the system and all bleed nipples open.
Note: *Do not depress the brake pedal with the master cylinder removed, or damage to the servo booster may occur.*

8   With paragraph 7 complied with, the brake pedal travel and clearance from the bulkhead should be as shown in Fig. 9.15.

16 Brake light switch – adjustment

1   Remove the panel under the dashboard. Make sure that the footbrake pedal is fully released, and then measure the distance between the switch and the pedal arm (photo).
2   The distance should be as shown in Fig. 9.16. Adjust by slackening the retaining screws and moving the switch bracket. Retighten the retaining screws.

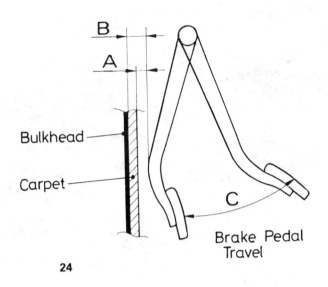

24

Fig. 9.15 Brake pedal travel (Sec 15)

A = 0.197 in (5.0 mm)   C = 6.3 ± 0.4 in (160 ± 10 mm)
B = 0.591 in (15.0 mm)

3   When adjustment is correct, the stop-lights should come on when pedal movement is between 0.32 and 0.55 in (8 and 14 mm).
4   Refit the panel under the dashboard.

17 Rear brake valves – removal and refitting

1   Any fault in either of the two brake valves which are incorporated in the rear brake lines can only be rectified in the rear brake lines can only be rectified by renewing the valve complete. Raise and support the rear of the vehicle for access.
2   To remove a valve, disconnect the rigid brake pipe from the valve and cap or plug the pipe to prevent loss of fluid (photo).
3   Using a close-fitting spanner, just release the flexible brake hose from the valve. Do not unscrew it more than a quarter of a turn.
4   Unbolt the brake valve, and then unscrew the valve body from the flexible hose. Do not twist the hose during this operation.
5   Refitting of the new valve is a reversal of the removal procedure.
6   On completion bleed the hydraulic circuit as described in Section 25.
Note: *Different models have different operating pressures. Make sure the correct brake valve for your model is fitted.*

18 Pressure drop warning valve – overhaul

1   The pressure drop warning valve is located in the engine bay, bolted to the left-hand chassis member (photo). On early models, it may be bolted to the right-hand side.
2   A repair kit is available for overhaul, and the valve does not have to be removed to do this. However, scrupulous cleanliness must be observed.
3   Blank off the breather hole on the brake fluid reservoir filler cap to prevent excess fluid loss.
4   Clean all dirt from around the valve and surrounding area.
5   Disconnect the electrical plug from the valve.
6   Remove the end-plugs and push out the piston, spring and seals.
7   Clean all parts in clean hydraulic fluid, and swab out the piston bore in the valve using a lint-free rag soaked in the same fluid. Discard the old seals.
8   Dip the new seals in hydraulic fluid before reassembling them to the piston.
9   Fit the rearmost end-plug, using a new copper washer under the plug.

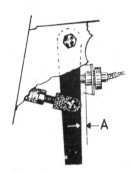

Fig. 9.16 Brake light switch adjustment (Sec 16)

A = 0.16 in (4.0 mm)

16.1 Brake light switch (arrowed)

17.2 Rear brake valve showing rigid pipeline (1), flexible pipeline (2) and securing bolt (3)

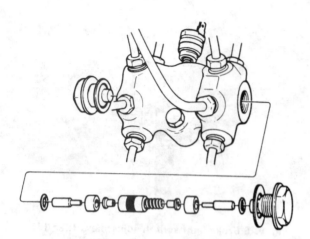

Fig. 9.17 Showing the internal components of the pressure drop warning valve (Sec 18)

10 Push in the piston and spring assembly from the other end and fit the remaining plug, again using a new copper washer.

11 If the electrical connector is to be renewed, unscrew it from the valve body and use a new sealing washer when fitting the new connector.

12 Reconnect the electrical plug.

13 Remove the blanking from the breather hole in the reservoir cap, and bleed the system as described in Section 25.

14 On completion, depress the brake pedal hard for 60 seconds and check the valve for leaks. If the valve leaks fluid from the electrical connector union, the complete assembly must be renewed.

19 Brake master cylinder – removal, overhaul and refitting

1 The master cylinder and reservoir are bolted to the brake servo booster unit in the engine compartment (photo). It is possible after a long service life that the seals in the cylinder can start to leak internally. An indication of this is when the brake pedal will continue to sink under pressure, when there are no exterior signs of leakage from other parts of the system. Repair kits are available, which contain all necessary seals and the piston assembly.

Warning: *Once the master cylinder is removed, do not depress the brake pedal or damage to the brake servo booster unit may occur.*

2 Place some rags beneath the cylinder to catch any spillage. Syphon as much hydraulic fluid as possible from the master cylinder reservoir.

3 Disconnect the fluid level warning electrical lead (where fitted).

4 Remove the nuts securing the cylinder to the servo unit.

5 On certain models, disconnect the fluid supply line to the clutch hydraulic system.

6 Disconnect all pipelines and remove the cylinder to a clean bench, being careful to keep hydraulic fluid off the car paintwork.

7 Separate the reservoir from the cylinder – it pulls out of the seals (photo).

8 Remove the locking ring from the end of the cylinder and withdraw the piston and spring (photo).

9 Clean all parts in hydraulic fluid and blow through the equalising and overflow holes in the cylinder with compressed air from a foot pump.

10 Examine the cylinder bores and if there are any heavy score marks or scratches, renew the cylinder as internal leakage will almost certainly continue, even with new seals.

11 The pistons, connector sleeve and seals come as one unit in the repair kit, and should be lubricated with clean hydraulic fluid before fitting.

12 Pour clean hydraulic fluid into the cylinder to lubricate the bore, then insert the piston and seal assembly, making sure the spring and spring seat are in position (photos). One way of doing this is to assemble the spring and seat to the piston assembly while holding the piston vertically, and to lower the cylinder over them.

13 Fit the lock ring back in the end of the cylinder.

18.1 Pressure drop warning valve
1 *Electrical connection*   2 *End-plugs*   3 *Retaining bolt*

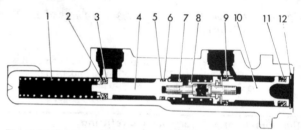

Fig. 9.18 Sectional view of the master cylinder (Sec 19)

1 *Spring*	7 *Spring*
2 *Spring seat*	8 *Connector sleeve*
3 *Seal*	9 *Seal*
4 *Secondary piston*	10 *Primary piston*
5 *Seal*	11 *Seal*
6 *Seal*	12 *Locking ring*

14 Refit the reservoir using new seals.

15 Refit the master cylinder to the brake servo – this is a reversal of removal.

16 Reconnect all pipelines, and finally bleed the system as described in Section 25.

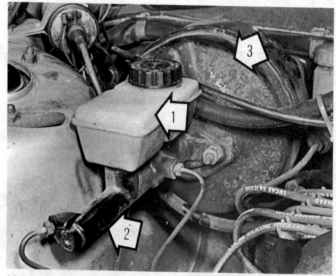

19.1 Brake master cylinder reservoir (1), also showing the master cylinder (2) and brake servo unit (3)

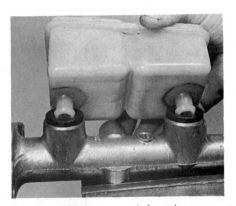

19.7 Removing the reservoir from the master cylinder

19.8 Remove the locking ring to release the pistons

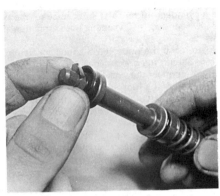

19.12A Fitting the spring seat ...

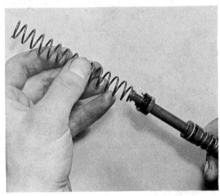

19.12B ... and the spring

19.12C Fitting the pistons into the master cylinder

20 Brake servo unit – general description

1   The brake servo unit is bolted to the engine bulkhead, with the brake master cylinder bolted to it.
2   The master cylinder is connected by a pushrod to the servo unit, which in turn is connected to the brake pedal, again by a pushrod.
3   With the engine running, a constant vacuum is maintained in the servo unit, derived from the inlet manifold on carburettor models, and from a vacuum pump on some fuel injection models.
4   This vacuum is used to pull a large diaphragm, which is connected to the pushrods, when the brake pedal is depressed, providing assistance to the driver. (On some versions a twin diaphragm unit is used.)
5   If the unit should fail in service the brakes will still operate, but will be much harder to apply.

21 Brake servo unit – checking, removal and refitting

Checking
1   Operate the brake pedal several times to release residual pressure in the system.
2   Keeping the pedal depressed, start the engine.
3   The pedal should move down slightly if the servo is correctly functioning. Keep the pedal depressed for a further 15 seconds, when it should not move any further.
4   If the servo fails this test, check the servo and all vacuum hoses for leaks and renew the non-return valve(s) in the system. When applicable, overhaul the vacuum pump. If this fails to improve the situation, consider renewal of the servo. Repair of the servo is not a DIY job.

Removal and refitting
5   Remove the brake master cylinder as described in Section 19. (If

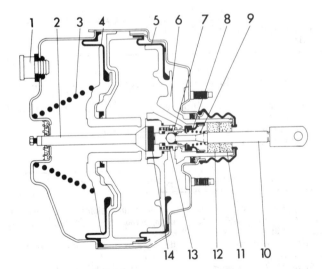

Fig. 9.19 Sectional view of the brake servo unit (Sec 20)

1 Non-return valve	8 Seal assembly
2 Front pushrod	9 Spring
3 Return spring	10 Rear pushrod
4 Diaphragm, front	11 Filter
5 Diaphragm, rear	12 Filter
6 Guide housing	13 Spring
7 Valve piston seat	14 Reaction disc

care is taken there is no need to disconnect the hydraulic unions from the cylinder, but be careful not to strain the pipes.)

6 Disconnect the vacuum hose from the non-return valve on the servo.

7 Remove the under-dash sound insulation, and the floor covering from behind the brake pedal.

8 Disconnect the brake pedal from the pushrod.

9 Remove the four nuts securing the servo to the bulkhead.

10 Lift the servo unit from the engine bay.

11 Refit in the reverse order, but where there is no sealing ring fitted to the servo unit-to-bulkhead contact area, apply a bead of sealant.

12 On completion, bleed the brake system (if the master cylinder was disconnected) as described in Section 25, and check the operation of the brakes.

22 Servo unit vacuum pump – removal, overhaul and refitting

Note: *Applies to some fuel injection models only.*

1 Disconnect both hoses from the vacuum pump.

2 Unscrew and remove the mounting bolts and withdraw the pump.

3 Clean away all external dirt and secure the pump in a vice. Remove the valve housing cover.

4 Scribe a line across the edges of the upper and lower body flanges to facilitate reassembly

5 Unscrew the flange screws and separate the upper and lower bodies.

6 Unscrew the centre bolt and remove the diaphragm, washers and spring from the lower housing.

7 Invert the pump and remove the lower cover.

8 Extract the lever shaft, lever and pump rod.

9 Renew worn components by obtaining the appropriate repair kits.

10 Reassembly is a reversal of dismantling, but make sure that the diaphragm centre bolt is fitted with its washer and O-ring. Clean the centre bolt threads and coat them with thread-locking compound.

11 Make sure that the raised side of the diaphragm is upwards and the dished sides of the washers are against the diaphragm.

12 Tighten the centre bolt, making sure that the hole in the diaphragm is opposite the one in the housing.

13 Refit the pump to the engine and reconnect the hoses to their respective connections.

23 Brake servo unit non-return valve – removal and refitting

1 Disconnect the vacuum hose (photo).

2 Use two flat-bladed levers to prise out the non-return valve from the unit.

3 Remove and discard the non-return valve seal. Obtain a new seal for reassembly.

4 Refit in the reverse order, but grease the seal before refitting, and ensure it is not dislodged on pushing in the valve.

24 Brake pipes and hoses – inspection and renewal

1 At the specified intervals or whenever leakage is suspected, examine the hydraulic hoses and pipelines, hose connections and pipeline unions.

2 Inspect the flexible hoses for chafing, kinking, cracking or swelling, and renew them as necessary.

3 Always unscrew rigid pipelines from the flexible part first, using two spanners to avoid twisting, then release the flexible hose end from its bracket and clip (photo).

4 On refitting, ensure the hose will not chafe against adjacent components, and that it is not twisted or in tension.

5 Rigid pipelines should be cleaned off and inspected for corrosion, chafing and other damage.

6 Check the security of all pipe clips or clamps. **Note:** *On post-1977 models, the routing of the brake pipe on the rear axle has been modified. A clamp and sleeve are now used to secure the pipeline, and the clamp should be positioned approximately 2.4 in (60.0 mm) from*

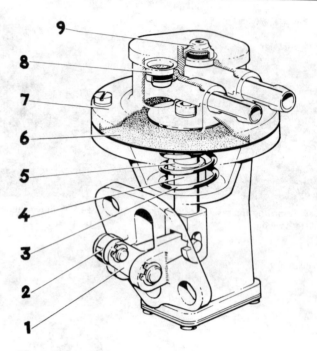

Fig. 9.20 Cutaway view of the vacuum pump (Sec 22)

1	This lever transfers the camshaft movements to the pump rod	5 Nylon bushing
2	Roller with needle bearing	6 Pump diaphragm
3	Pump spring	7 Valve housing
4	Pump rod	8 Suction valve
		9 Discharge valve (into the air)

23.1 Showing the vacuum hose connection (1) and non-return valve (2)

the reaction rod bracket (Fig. 9.21). If a new pipe is fitted to an earlier model, the new pipe must be clamped to the axle.

7 Any pipe which shows signs of corrosion should be renewed. Pipelines are available made up to length from motor factors.

8 Use the old pipe as a pattern to bend the new pipe to shape, being careful not to bend a pipe any more than is necessary, or it may collapse. This is best done professionally.

9 Special brake pipe spanners are available, which should be used in preference to normal spanners to avoid rounding off pipe union nuts (photo).

10 Bleed the hydraulic system on completion as described in Section 25.

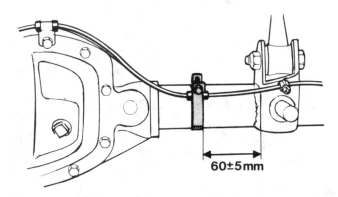

Fig. 9.21 Position of rear brake pipe clamp (Sec 24)

60±5mm

24.3 Typical rigid-to-flexible pipeline connection
1 Flexible pipeline 3 Spring clip
2 Rigid pipeline

24.9 Special brake pipe spanner in use

25 Hydraulic system – bleeding

1 Whenever the hydraulic system has been overhauled, a part renewed, or the level in the reservoir has become too low, air will have entered the system. This will cause some or all of the pedal travel to be used up in compressing air rather than pushing fluid against brake pistons. If only a little air is present, the pedal will have a 'spongy' feel, but if an appreciable amount has entered, the pedal will not offer any appreciable resistance to the foot and the brakes will hardly work at all.
2 To overcome this, brake fluid must be pumped through the hydraulic system until all the air has been passed out in the form of bubbles in the fluid.
3 If only one hydraulic circuit has been disconnected, only that circuit need be bled. If both circuits have been disconnected, or at time of fluid renewal, the whole system must be bled. The circuits are allocated as follows.

Primary*: Upper cylinders in both front calipers, and left-hand rear.
Secondary*: Lower cylinders in both front calipers, and right-hand rear.
*On pre-1977 models, primary and secondary circuits are reversed.

4 Bleed the system in the order shown in Fig. 9.22.
5 There are three bleed screws on each front caliper, and one on each rear caliper. When bleeding the front caliper lower cylinders, both the lower bleed screws should be opened and closed together.

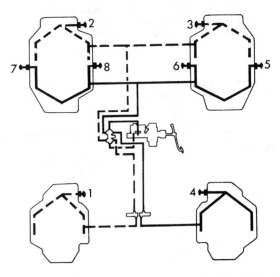

Fig. 9.22 Brake bleeding sequence (Sec 25)

1 Left rear wheel
2 Left front wheel, upper, inner
3 Right front wheel, upper, inner
4 Right rear wheel
5* Right front wheel, outer
6* Right front wheel, lower inner
7* Left front wheel, outer
8* Left front wheel, lower inner
*Bleed these in pairs (both right, then both left)

Bleeding with an assistant
6 Gather together two clear plastic tubes to fit over the bleed screws, a glass jar and a supply of fresh brake fluid.
7 Top up the master cylinder reservoir. Keep it topped up throughout the operation.
8 Attach the tube(s) to the bleed screw(s) of the first caliper to be bled (paragraph 4). Pour a little brake fluid into the jar and place the open ends of the tube(s) in the jar, dipping into the fluid.
9 Slacken the bleed screw(s). Have the assistant depress and release the brake pedal five times, stopping on the fifth downstroke. Tighten the bleed screw(s) and have the assistant release the pedal.
10 Top up the master cylinder reservoir.
11 Repeat paragraphs 9 and 10 until clean fluid, free from air bubbles, emerges from the bleed screw(s).

12 Repeat the process on the remaining calipers in the order given.
13 On completion, check that the brake pedal feels hard. Top up the master cylinder reservoir and refit the cap.
14 Discard the fluid bled from the system as it is not fit for re-use. Dispose of it in a sealed container.

Bleeding using a one-way valve kit

15 There are a number of one-man brake bleeding kits currently available from motor accessory shops. These devices simplify the bleeding process and reduce the risk of expelled air or fluid being drawn back again into the system.
16 To use this type of kit, connect the outlet tube to the bleed screw and then open the screw half a turn. If possible, position the tube so that it can be viewed from inside the car. Depress the brake pedal as far as possible and slowly release it. The one-way valve in the bleed kit will prevent expelled air or fluid from returning to the system at the end of each pedal return stroke (photo). Repeat this operation until clean hydraulic fluid, free from air bubbles, can be seen coming through the bleed tube. Tighten the bleed screw and remove the tube.
17 Repeat the operations on the remaining bleed screws in the correct sequence. Make sure that throughout the process the fluid reservoir level never falls so low that air can be drawn into the master cylinder, otherwise the work up to this point will have been wasted.

Bleeding using a pressure bleeding kit

18 These, too, are available from motor accessory shops and are usually operated by air pressure from the spare tyre.
19 By connecting a pressurised container to the master cylinder fluid reservoir, bleeding is then carried out by simply opening each bleed screw in turn and allowing the fluid to run out, rather like turning on a tap, until air bubbles are no longer visible in the fluid being expelled.

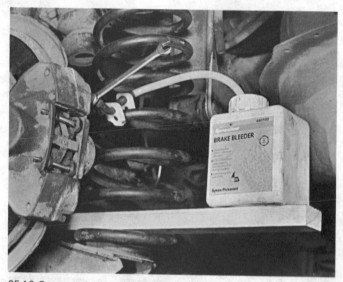

25.16 One-man brake bleeding kit in use

20 Using this system, the large reserve of hydraulic fluid provides a safeguard against air being drawn into the master cylinder during the bleeding process.

26 Fault diagnosis – braking system

Symptom	Reason(s)
Brake grab	Excessive run-out of discs Rust on disc Oil stained pads
Brake drag	Faulty master cylinder Foot pedal return impeded Reservoir breather blocked Seized caliper Incorrect adjustment of handbrake Crushed, blocked or swollen pipe lines
Excessive pedal effort required	Pads not yet bedded-in, or incorrect grade Pads or discs contaminated with oil or grease Scored discs Faulty vacuum servo unit
Brake pedal feels hard	Glazed surfaces of friction material Rust on disc surfaces Seized caliper piston
Excessive pedal travel	Low reservoir fluid level Disc run-out excessive Worn front wheel bearings Air in system Worn pads
Pedal creep during sustained application	Fluid leak Internal fault in master cylinder Faulty servo unit non-return valve
Pedal 'spongy'	Air in system Perished flexible hose Loose master cylinder mounting nuts
Fall in reservoir fluid level	Normal due to pad wear (slow fall) Leak in hydraulic system

Symptom	Reason(s)
Brake squeal	Pads worn Non-original pads fitted
Rear wheel lock under normal tracking	Faulty rear brake valve
Brakes pull to one side	Tyre pressures incorrect Pads contaminated on one side Caliper piston seized Pads renewed on one side only Suspension or steering fault
Brake judder	Pads contaminated, worn, or incorrect grade Disc(s) worn, rusty or damaged Disc run-out excessive Disc thickness variation excessive Wheel bearing worn or maladjusted Suspension or steering fault

Chapter 10 Front suspension and steering; wheels and tyres

Contents

Specifications

General

Front suspension type	Independent, Macpherson strut with anti-roll bar
Steering	Rack and pinion, manual or power-assisted

Front wheel alignment (unladen)

Castor:	
1979-on models with power steering	3 to 4° positive
All other models	2 to 3° positive
Camber	0°15' to 0°45' positive
Maximum side-to-side variation	0°30'
Kingpin inclination	12°
Toe-in (measured at wheel rim):	
Manual steering	0.10 ± 0.04 in (2.5 ± 1.0 mm)
Power steering	0.06 ± 0.04 in (1.5 ± 1.0 mm)

Steering gear – manual

Cam Gear and ZF

Ratio	21.4 to 1
Number of turns lock to lock	4.34
Steering gear lubricant*	Volvo part number 1 161 001-1
Quantity (applied to dry rack)	2.6 oz (75.0 g)

*Note: Some early models may be lubricated with engine oil

Steering gear – power-assisted

Cam Gear (except TRW, 1987 on) and ZF

Steering gear lubricant	Volvo part number 1 161 001-1
Quantity (applied to dry rack)	Approximately 3.5 oz (100.0 g)
Ratio	17.2 to 1
Number of turns lock to lock	3.5
Hydraulic fluid type	ATF type A, F or G (Duckhams Q-Matic)
System capacity:	
With separate reservoir	2.1 Imp pts (1.2 litres)
With combined reservoir	1.2 Imp pts (0.7 litre)
ZF control arm balljoint maximum clearance:	
Axial	0.118 in (3.0 mm)
Radial	0.02 in (0.5 mm)

Cam gear TRW (1987 on) – where different to above

Ratio	3.35
Number of turns lock to lock	17.3 to 1
System capacity	1.4 Imp pts (0.8 litre)

Roadwheels

Size .... 5, 5¹/₂ or 6J, depending on model

Lateral run-out:

Steel .... 0.039 in (1.0 mm)

Aluminium .... 0.032 in (0.8 mm)

Radial run-out:

Steel .... 0.032 in (0.8 mm)

Aluminium .... 0.024 in (0.6 mm)

Tyre sizes and pressures

Space restrictions prevent adequate coverage of details for all models. For individual model details, refer to the owner's handbook, or to the sticker inside the fuel filler flap

Wheel bearings

Lubricant type/specification .... Lithium based grease (Duckhams LB 10)

Torque wrench settings

	lbf ft	Nm
Steering wheel nut	44	60
Steering column lower bracket bolts	15	20
Steering shaft coupling flange bolts	17	23
Coupling pinch-bolts	15	20
Pinion cover bolts	14	19
Pre-tension housing cover bolts	14	19
Pinion nut (ZF type)	17	23
Steering tie-rod locknuts	52	70
Track rod-to-steering arm balljoint nut	44	60
Steering gear U-bolt nuts	15	20
Suspension strut upper housing nuts	15	20
Control arm-to-balljoint nuts	74 to 96	100 to 130
Control arm balljoint nut	37 to 52	50 to 70
Balljoint housing-to-strut	13 to 21	18 to 28
Control arm rear bracket bolts	30	40
Control arm rear bush	41	55
Control arm front bush	55	75
Wheel nuts	74 to 96	100 to 130
Hub bearing nut:		
Stage 1	41	55
Slacken, then Stage 2	See text (Section 3)	See text (Section 3)

1 General description

1 The front suspension is of the MacPherson type with a shock absorber inside the coil spring. It consists of a strut and coil spring assembly, attached at the top to the wheel housing and at the bottom to a control arm. A stabiliser bar, supported in rubber bushings, connects the control arms.

2 The strut assembly contains the shock absorber. The coil spring bottom support and the hub are welded to the strut casing. The shock absorber spindle functions as the strut upper guide and is pivoted in the strut upper attachment.

3 The steering gear is of the rack and pinion type. There are two versions: manual and power-assisted. There are two makes of manual steering gear.

4 The power pump is a vane-type pump driven by a belt from the crankshaft pulley.

5 The top section of the steering column is provided with a splined sliding joint which, in case of accident, prevents the shaft from being driven into the car. As a further safety measure the steering wheel is connected to the steering column by a steel sleeve which collapses under excessive pressure.

2 Routine maintenance

1 Check the tyre pressures at frequent intervals (Section 27).

2 At the intervals specified in the *Routine maintenance* Section at the beginning of this Manual, carry out the following checks and inspections.

3 Thoroughly inspect the tyres and wheels as described in Section 27.

4 Check and top up as necessary the power steering fluid level (Section 14).

5 Check the front wheel bearing adjustment (Section 3).

6 Check the steering and front suspension components for wear and damage. In particular, check all rubber bellows and balljoint covers for splits or deterioration, renewing them as necessary. Check balljoints for wear by levering them up and down, and by pushing them in and out. Wear tolerances can be found in the Specifications.

7 Check the steering for play by grasping a roadwheel and turning it in and out. Any play felt should be investigated. Also check for play at the steering wheel.

8 Check the front shock absorbers for leaks.

9 Check the power steering system for leaks.

10 Check the power steering pump drivebelt for correct tension (see Chapter 2), and for fraying or deterioration.

3 Front wheel bearings – checking and adjusting

Checking

1 Raise the front of the vehicle onto axle stands.

2 Grasp the top and bottom of the wheel, and try to rock it on the stub axle. Play should be barely perceptible.

3 Spin the wheel on the hub, and check that it runs freely without undue noise – any grating or squeal should be investigated.

Note: *During this operation, ensure the brake pads are not the cause of any noise or binding, removing them for the check if necessary.*

Adjustment

4 Remove the roadwheel.

5 Tap off the grease cap.

6 Remove the split pin from the hub nut and remove the nut, clean the nut and stub axle threads, then grease them thoroughly.

7 On vehicles with the old type hub nuts (see Fig. 10.3), fit and tighten the nut to the specified Stage 1 torque, while slowly spinning the wheel.

8 Slacken the nut by a half turn, then check that the bearing outer race is free to move.

9 Tighten the nut so that the washer underneath it can just be moved.

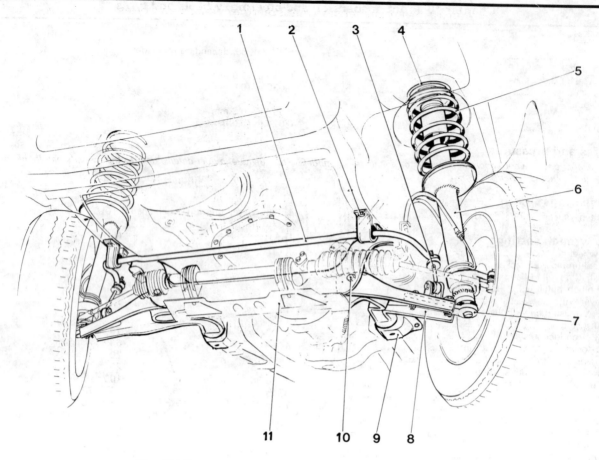

Fig. 10.1 Front suspension components – LHD shown (Sec 1)

1	Anti-roll bar	4	Suspension strut upper housing	6	Suspension strut assembly
2	Anti-roll bar bracket			7	Balljoint
3	Link rod	5	Coil spring	8	Control arm

9	Control arm rear bracket
10	Control arm front bushing
11	Front axle crossmember

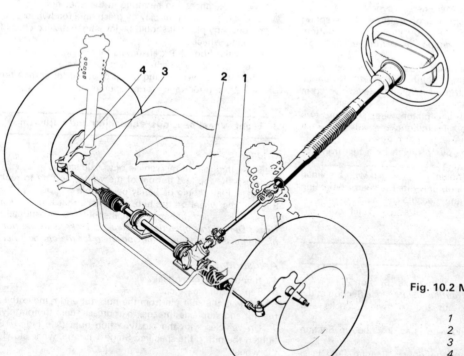

Fig. 10.2 Manual steering gear – LHD shown (Sec 1)

1 Steering column shaft
2 Steering gear
3 Steering track rod
4 Steering arm

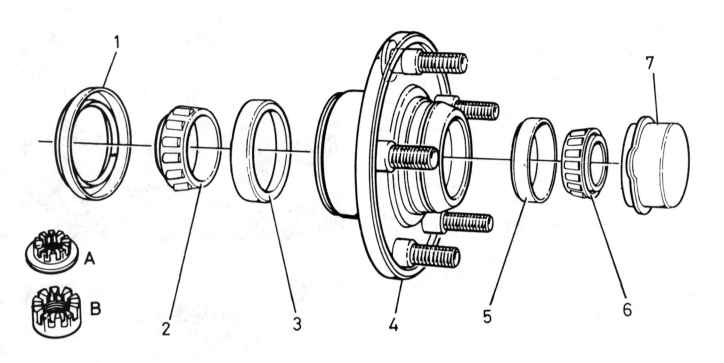

Fig. 10.3 Showing new (A) and old (B) type hub nuts and components of the front bearing (Secs 3 and 4)

1	Oil seal	3	Inner bearing outer race
2	Inner bearing	4	Hub

5	Outer bearing outer race	7	Hub cap
6	Outer bearing		

10 Slacken the nut to the next available split pin hole, then fit and lock a new split pin.
11 Check that the hub rotates freely, with no appreciable play.
12 Half-fill the cap with grease, and tap the cap back into position.
13 Refit the roadwheel and remove the vehicle from stands.
14 On 1980-on vehicles which have the new hub nut with fixed washer, the procedure is similar, with the following change. After slackening the nut by half a turn, tighten the nut by hand as far as is possible, then tighten to the next available split pin hole.

4 Front wheel bearings – overhaul

Note: *Wheel bearings of differing manufacture may be supplied. Bearing races of different manufacture should not be mixed, ie an SKF inner race should not have an outer race made by Koyo, and vice-versa.*
1 Remove the brake caliper as described in Chapter 9, Section 6.
2 Prise or tap off the hub cap (photo).
3 Extract the split pin and remove the hub nut.
4 Pull off the brake disc/hub, using a puller if it is tight, and retrieve the outer bearing (and washer, if separate from the hub nut).
5 Remove the inner bearing from the stub axle, again using a puller if necessary.
6 Use a soft drift to knock out the inner bearing outer race from the disc/hub.
7 Repeat the operation for the outer race of the outer bearing.
8 Clean the stub axle and disc/hub in solvent to remove all old grease. Discard the oil seals.
9 Smear some grease onto the inner bearing outer race, fit it to the hub and tap home with a block of wood (photos).

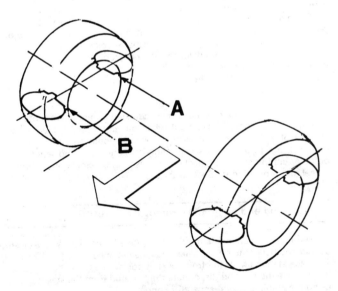

Fig. 10.4 Toe measurements. Arrow points forwards; for A and B see text (Sec 5)

10 Similarly, fit the outer bearing outer race.
11 Pack the new bearings with suitable grease, also applying grease to the hub and stub axle.
12 Place the inner bearing in the hub (photo).
13 Fit the inner bearing oil seal and tap it home (photos).
14 Grease and fit the inner sealing ring, chamfered edge facing inwards, to the stub axle (photo).
15 Fit the disc/hub to the stub axle (photo), then fit the outer bearing and (if applicable) the washer (photos).
16 Fit the hub nut, then adjust the wheel bearing as described in Section 3.
17 On completion of adjustment, fit a new split pin (photo), half-fill the hub cap with grease, and tap it into position.
18 Refit the brake caliper and roadwheel, remove the axle stands and lower the vehicle.

5 Front wheel alignment – general

1 Front wheel alignment is defined by camber, castor, steering axis (kingpin) inclination and toe setting. Incorrect toe will cause rapid tyre wear. Castor and steering axis inclination are determined in production, and can only be incorrect as a result of wear or damage. Camber can be adjusted by rotating the suspension strut top mountings, but this should only be done by a Volvo dealer or other specialist possessing the necessary measuring equipment.
2 Toe is defined as the amount by which the distance between the front wheels, measured at hub height, differs from the front edges to the rear edges. If the distance between the front edges is less than that at the rear, the wheels are said to toe-in; the opposite case is known as toe-out.
3 To measure toe, it will be necessary to obtain or make a tracking gauge. These are available in motor accessory shops, or one can be made from a length of rigid pipe or bar with some kind of threaded adjustment facility at one end. Many tyre specialists will also check toe free, or for a nominal sum.
4 Before measuring toe, check that all steering and suspension components are undamaged and that tyre pressures are correct. The vehicle must be at approximately kerb weight, with the spare wheel and jack in their normal position and any abnormal loads removed.
5 Park the vehicle on level ground and bounce it a few times to settle the suspension.
6 Use the tracking gauge to measure the distance between the inside faces of the front wheel rims, at hub height, at the rear of the front wheels. Record this distance; call it measurement 'A'.
7 Push the vehicle forwards or backwards so that the wheels rotate exactly 180° (half a turn). Measure the distance between the front wheel rims again, this time at the front of the wheels. Record this distance; call is measurement 'B'.
8 Subtract measurement 'B' from measurement 'A'. If the answer is positive it is the amount of toe-in; if negative it is the amount of toe-out. Permissible values are given in the Specifications.
9 If adjustment is necessary loosen the track rod end locknuts and the outer bellow clips, then rotate each track rod by equal amounts until the setting is correct. Hold the track rod ends in their horizontal position with a spanner while making the adjustment.
10 Tighten the locknuts and outer bellow clips.
11 Provided the track rods have been adjusted by equal amounts the steering wheel should be central when moving straight-ahead. The amount of visible thread on each track rod should also be equal to within 2 mm (0.08 in). If wheel alignment and track rod length are both correct but steering wheel position is wrong, remove the steering wheel and reposition it (Section 24).

6 Track rod end balljoints – removal and refitting

1 The track rod balljoints require no routine lubrication. When wear occurs, the balljoints on the track rods are renewed.
2 Place stands under the front jacking points.
3 Remove the nut and disconnect the ball stud from the steering arm using a suitable balljoint separator (photo).
4 Remove the splash guard from under the car.
5 Slacken the clips at the outboard end of the bellows.
6 Using an open-ended spanner on the flats provided to prevent the

4.2 Prising off the hub cap

4.9A Fit the inner bearing outer race ...

4.9B ... and tap it home

4.12 Place the inner bearing in the hub

4.13A Fit the inner bearing oil seal ...

4.13B ... and tap it home

4.14 Fitting the inner oil seal

4.15A Fitting the disc/hub to the stub axle ...

4.15B followed by the bearing ...

4.15C ... and washer (early type nuts)

4.17 Split pin correctly fitted

6.3 Using a balljoint separator

track rod rotating, release the locknut at the track rod end balljoint.

7   Unscrew the balljoint assembly from the track rod, counting the number of turns.

8   Screw the new balljoint onto the track rod by the same number of turns, and connect it to the steering arm. Tighten the balljoint nut to the specified torque. Check the wheel alignment as described in Section 5.

9   Tighten the bellows clips on completion.

7 Steering rack bellows – renewal

1   If, during routine inspection, the steering rack bellows are found to be split or otherwise damaged, they should be renewed at the earliest opportunity, as follows.

2   Remove the track rod end balljoint, as described in Section 6.

3   Undo the clips securing the bellows to the rack and track rod (photos). On early models be prepared for oil spillage. On later models the clips are of the plastic tie type, and must be cut off.

4   Clean off all oil or grease from the rack, and inspect the rack and inner balljoint for damage or wear due to grit getting inside.

5   On those steering racks which use grease as a lubricant, smear the rack and inner balljoint with the recommended grease (see Specifications).

Note: *The quantity of grease given in the Specifications is for a new, 'dry' rack, therefore modify the amount of grease to prevent overfilling, which could lead to the bellows being split by grease under pressure when the steering is on full lock.*

6   On early steering racks lubricated with oil (see Specifications), coat the rack and inner balljoint with oil, and squirt a further quantity into the bellows after fitting and before tightening the outer clip, bearing in mind the comments in paragraph 5.

7.3A Undoing the clips which secure the bellows to the rack ...

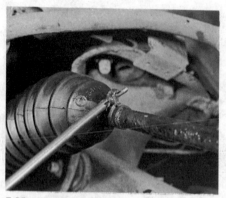

7.3B ... and the track rod

7.7 Sliding a bellows over the track rod

8.5A One U-bolt (arrowed) ...

8.5B ... and the other (arrowed)

8.5C U-bolt securing nuts (A) and the locating spigot (B)

7 Lubricate the necks of the bellows before sliding them over the track rod and onto the rack (photo).

8 Fit and tighten the inner clip to the rack housing, then with the steering central, allow the bellows to take up its natural relaxed position.

9 Refer to paragraphs 5 and 6, then fit and tighten the outer clip.

10 Refit the balljoint as described in Section 6.

11 Check the toe as described in Section 5.

8 Steering gear (manual) – removal and refitting

1 Remove the clamp bolt from the universal shaft joint flange. Open the flange slightly with a screwdriver. (On later models, the joint is protected by a plastic sleeve which will have to be pushed upwards for access to the flange.)

2 Raise the front end of the car and put stands under the jacking points: Remove the wheels.

3 Remove the track rod end balljoints as described in Section 6.

4 Remove the splash guard from under the car.

5 Remove the two 'U' bolts securing the steering gear to the front axle member (photos).

6 Disconnect the steering gear from the steering shaft flange and remove the steering gear, complete with track rods.

7 Refitting is the reversal of the removal procedure. Tighten all fastenings to the specified torque.

8 Check the toe (Section 5).

Note: Some steering gear rack mounting pads have locating spigots – (B) in photo 8.5C. If pads which have a spigot are being fitted to a vehicle without locating holes, the spigot should be cut off.

9 Steering gear (manual, Cam Gear type) – dismantling and inspection

1 Clean off all external dirt. Before dismantling check the inner balljoints for wear.

2 Undo the left side bellows clip, ease off the bellows and (on early models) drain the oil.

3 Bend up the peening lock on the inner balljoint (photo), and remove the left side track rod. Remove the right side track rod.

4 Remove the cover for the preloading device and lift out the spring, O-ring and piston.

5 Remove the pinion cover and lift out the pinion, top bearing and spacer sleeve. Collect the shims.

6 Pull out the rack towards the pinion side of the steering gear.

7 Clean all the parts in white spirit. Check the rack bush for wear and renew if necessary. Check the pinion lower bearing, if it requires renewing a puller and slide hammer will be required to remove it, see Fig. 10.5. Examine the rack and pinion for wear and damage. Renew all seals and gaskets.

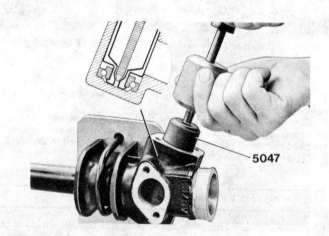

Fig. 10.5 Removing the pinion lower bearing (Sec 9)

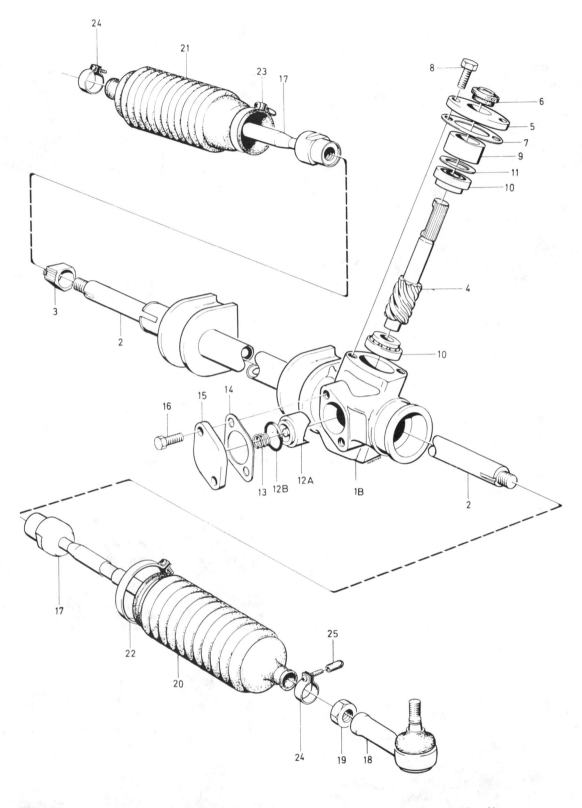

Fig. 10.6 Exploded view of the Cam Gear type manual steering gear (Sec 9)

1	Housing	8	Bolt	14	Shim
2	Rack	9	Spacer	15	Cover
3	Bearing bushing	10	Ball bearing	16	Bolt
4	Pinion	11	Shim	17	Steering rod
5	Cover	12a	Préload piston	18	Balljoint
6	Seal	12b	O-ring	19	Nut
7	Gasket	13	Spring		

20	Bellows
21	Bellows
22	Clamp
23	Clamp
24	Clamp
25	Cap

9.3 Steering gear inner balljoint

10 Steering gear (manual, Cam Gear type) – reassembly

1 Lubricate all parts with the specified oil or grease before reassembly.
2 If new rack bushing is being fitted, position it so that the locks on the bush align with the slots in the housing and drive it in with a drift.
3 Fit the pinion with upper bearing in the housing (no shims) and fit the spacer sleeve. Fit the pinion cover, with a gasket but without the seal.
4 Using a dial gauge, check the endplay of the pinion. Remove the pinion cover, and determine a shim thickness equal to the measured endplay plus 0.0039 in (0.1 mm) for preloading. Shims are available in thicknesses of 0.005 – 0.0075 – 0.01 in (0.127 – 0.191 – 0.254 mm).
5 Fit a new seal on the pinion cover. Apply a non-hardening gasket compound on the seal, and fit the seal on the pinion cover, using a suitably sized tube to drive it on.
6 Apply most of the specified quantity of grease to the rack, pinion and bearings, reserving a small quantity for the bellows. (For oil-lubricated models, wait until reassembly is complete before adding oil.) Fit the rack from the pinion side, taking care not to damage the bushing.
7 Fit the pinion, with upper bearing, shims and spacer sleeve. Note the relative positions of the pinion shaft and the rack (Fig. 10.8). Fit the pinion cover gasket and the cover.
8 Fit the preloading piston in the housing without the O-ring and

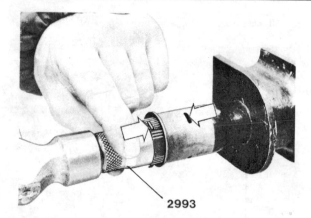

Fig. 10.7 Fitting the rack bushing. Lock and slot arrowed
(Sec 10)

spring. Use a steel ruler and feeler gauge to measure the end clearance, see Fig. 10.9. Determine the thickness of shims required. Shims and gasket together should equal the measured end clearance plus 0.0008 to 0.0059 in (0.20 to 0.15 mm) for the piston endplay. Shims are available in thicknesses of 0.005 – 0.01 – 0.015 – 0.02 in (0.127 – 0.254 – 0.381 – 0.508 mm).
9 Place the spring and O-ring in the piston, and fit the gasket and cover.
10 Connect a torque gauge to the pinion shaft and crank the rack back and forward to each end of its travel. The torque should be 5 to 15 lbf in (0.06 to 0.17 kgf m) if the preloading is correct (see Section 12).
11 Fit the left side track rod. If fitting the same rod, place a thin shim between the balljoint and rack shoulder so that an unused part of the balljoint can be used for locking by peening the edge of the balljoint into the rack groove. Fit the bellows and tighten the inner clamp. Fit the right side rod in the same way. Both rods should be the same length within 0.06 in (1.6 mm).
12 Fill the early type steering gear with specified oil by inserting an oil gun under the lip of the bellows.
13 Refit the steering gear as described in Section 8.

Fig. 10.9 Measuring the preload piston end clearance
(Sec 10)

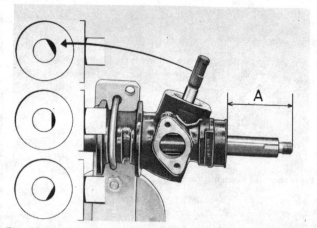

Fig. 10.8 With rack protrusion as shown, pinion shaft must be in one of three positions on left (Secs 10 and 12)

A (Cam Gear) = 2.835 in (72 mm)
A (ZF) = 2.874 in (73 mm)

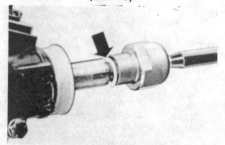

Fig. 10.10 Fitting a shim to provide a new locking position
(Sec 10)

11 Steering gear (manual, ZF type) – dismantling and inspection

1 Carry out the operations described in Section 9, paragraphs 1 to 3.
2 Remove the dust seal for the preloading device and remove the split pin (Fig. 10.11).
3 Remove the cover and spring for the preloading device, and remove the piston – tapping the rack with the palm of your hand will help to remove it.
4 Remove the pinion dust seal and the lockwasher. Remove the pinion nut.
5 To remove the pinion from the housing, clamp the pinion shaft in a vice with soft grips and tap lightly on the housing with a soft-nosed hammer.
6 Pull out the rack towards the pinion side of the housing.
7 Press in the locking tabs for the rack bushing and lever out the bushing.
8 Remove the thrustwasher and circlip from the pinion shaft and press off the bearing.
9 Clean all the parts and examine them for wear or damage. Renew O-rings and rack bushing.

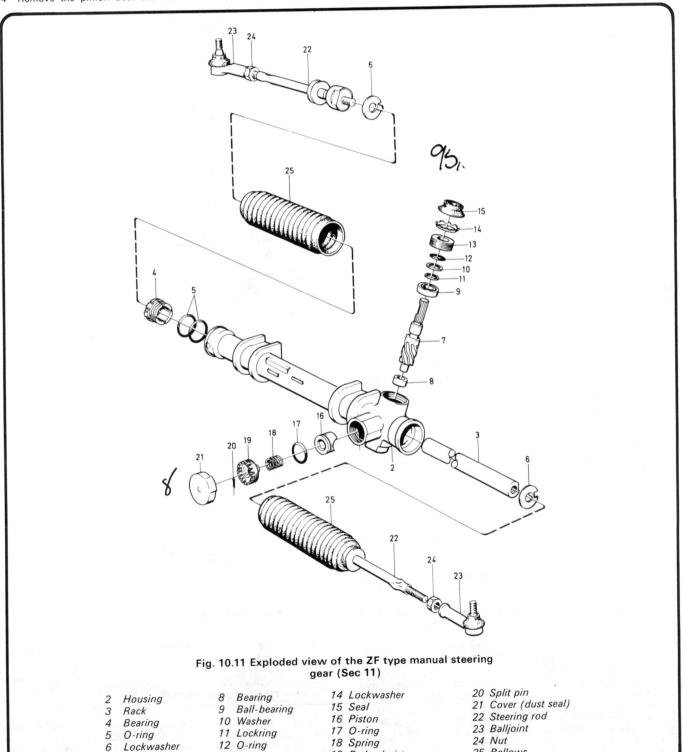

Fig. 10.11 Exploded view of the ZF type manual steering gear (Sec 11)

2 Housing	8 Bearing	14 Lockwasher	20 Split pin
3 Rack	9 Ball-bearing	15 Seal	21 Cover (dust seal)
4 Bearing	10 Washer	16 Piston	22 Steering rod
5 O-ring	11 Lockring	17 O-ring	23 Balljoint
6 Lockwasher	12 O-ring	18 Spring	24 Nut
7 Pinion	13 Pinion nut	19 Preload piston cover	25 Bellows

12 Steering gear (manual, ZF type) – reassembly

1   Press the ball-bearing on to the pinion shaft and fit the circlip and thrustwasher.
2   Fit new O-rings on the rack bushing and press it into the housing. Check that the locking tabs for the bearing fit correctly into the recesses in the housing.
3   Grease the rack with the specified grease and insert it in the pinion side of the housing. Be careful not to damage the bushing with the rack teeth.
4   Grease and insert the pinion, referring to Fig. 10.8. Pack the bearing with grease. Fit a new O-ring on the pinion nut, fit the nut and the locking circlip. Fill the cavity on top of the nut with grease and fit the pinion dust seal.
5   Fit a new O-ring on the preloading piston, grease the piston and fit the piston and spring. Fit the cover but do not finally tighten the cover yet.
6   Connect a torque gauge to the pinion and check the torque. Crank back and forward to each end of travel. The torque should be 5 to 15 lbf in (0.06 to 0.17 kgf m). To increase the torque, screw in the preload piston cover. When the correct torque is obtained, fit the split pin to lock the cover and fit the dust cover.
Note: *If the special torque gauge (see Fig. 10.13) is available, a reasonably accurate figure may be obtained using a spring balance and a length of cord wrapped round the pinion shaft. Multiply the spring balance reading (in lb or kg) by the radius of the shaft (in inches or metres) to find the torque. Do not mix metric and imperial units.*
7   Crank the rack fully out and fill the tooth spaces with grease. Crank in the rack, then out again and apply more grease. Most of the specified quantity of grease should now have been used; reserve a little for the bellows.
8   Fit the track rods, as described in Section 10, paragraph 11.

13 Power steering gear – general

1   Several types of power steering gear have been fitted to various models.
2   Up to 1979, a Cam Gear unit was used, with a cast iron housing. After 1979, a modified unit with aluminium housing was used, this being replaced with a further modified version in 1984.
3   Also in use are two versions of the ZF power steering gear, one with a fixed valve unit, and one with a removable valve unit.
4   In 1986, a further-modified Cam Gear unit was introduced.
5   Because of the complexity of power steering gear, the need for absolute cleanliness of working conditions, and the need for several special tools, we do not recommend the overhaul of such units by the home mechanic.
6   DIY maintenance should be restricted to those operations described in the following Sections.

14 Power steering system – filling and bleeding

1   On early models without a dipstick, keep the level in the reservoir filled almost to the bottom of the filler neck, checked when the fluid is cold.
2   Later models have a dipstick incorporated in the reservoir cap (photo).
3   Early dipsticks are marked 'HOT', 'COLD' and 'ADD' and the level can be checked with the fluid hot or cold, later types are only marked 'MAX' and (sometimes) 'MIN', and should be checked with the fluid cold (photo).
4   Use a clean funnel to pour the specified fluid slowly into the reservoir until the correct level is obtained. Mop up any spillage. Check for leaks if frequent topping-up is required.
5   To bleed the system free of air, which should only be necessary if the hoses have been disconnected or if major repair work has been carried out, proceed as follows.
6   Top up the fluid reservoir. Start the engine and allow it to idle, while turning the steering slowly from left to right (and back again) several times.
7   Keep turning the steering until no more bubbles are apparent in the reservoir.

Fig. 10.12 Fitting a new O-ring in the pinion nut (Sec 12)

Fig. 10.13 Checking the pinion torque (Sec 12)

Fig. 10.14 Markings on an early power steering fluid dipstick (Sec 14)

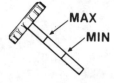

Fig. 10.15 Later dipstick markings (Sec 14)

8   Stop the engine, top up the reservoir to the correct level and replace the reservoir cap.

15 Power steering gear – removal and refitting

1   Removal and refitting of the power steering gear is basically the same as for the manual gear described in Section 8 (photo).
2   Additionally, the hydraulic hoses must be disconnected, and the unions blanked off to prevent entry of dirt. Scrupulous cleanliness should be observed at all times.

14.2 Power steering cap (arrowed) and reservoir

14.3 Power steering fluid level dipstick

15.1 Power steering gear U-bolt (arrowed)

3   After refitting, connect the hoses and bleed the system as described in Section 14.

Note: *If a new steering gear assembly has been fitted, or the existing one dismantled and reassembled for any reason, then the pressure balance between the left- and right-hand sides should be checked and adjusted by your Volvo dealer.*

16 Power steering pump – removal and refitting

ZF type (fitted to some early models)

1   This pump has a separate fluid reservoir.
2   Either clamp the hoses from the reservoir to prevent fluid loss before disconnecting the hoses, or place a container beneath the pump, disconnect the hoses and allow the fluid to drain.
3   Remove the nuts from the two long bolts through the mounting bracket.
4   Remove the tensioner locking screws on both sides of the pump, push the pump inwards and lift off the drivebelt.
5   Swing the pump upwards and remove the three bolts securing the mounting bracket to the engine block, then remove the pump and bracket.
6   If a new pump is being fitted, transfer the mounting bracket to the new pump.
7   Refit in the reverse order, then tension the drivebelt as described in Section 17, and fill and bleed the system as described in Section 14.

Saginaw type (pre-1985)

8   This type of pump is recognisable by the reservoir, which is integral with the pump.
9   Removal and refitting procedures are similar to those described for the ZF type.

Saginaw type (1985 on)

10 This is a lightweight pump, with separate reservoir mounted on the left inner wing, in front of the suspension strut tower.
11 Removal and refitting procedures are again similar to that for earlier types, but the belt tensioner is of the turn-buckle type.
12 If a replacement pump is to be fitted, then the pulley wheel and the mounting bracket have to be transferred to the new pump as follows.
13 Remove the centre bolt from the pulley wheel.
14 Screw a 3/8" x 2 3/4" UNC bolt into the vacant bolt hole, and use a puller against the bolt head, with the puller arms hooked under the pulley wheel centre boss, to pull the pulley from the pump shaft.
15 Transfer the mounting bracket to the new pump.
16 Apply a few drops of oil to the pump shaft and fit the pulley to the shaft.
17 This now has to be pressed onto the shaft, which can be done by using the same bolt as in removal, with a suitable socket or piece of tubing arranged as shown in Fig. 10.17.
18 Press the pulley on until its outer face is flush with the shaft end.
19 Make sure the bolt does not contact the inner face of the shaft during this operation by adding more washers as necessary.
20 Remove the press arrangement and fit the pulley centre bolt.

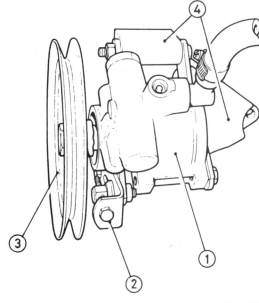

Fig. 10.16 Saginaw power steering pump (Sec 16)

1   Pump
2   Belt adjuster
3   Pulley
4   Mounting bracket

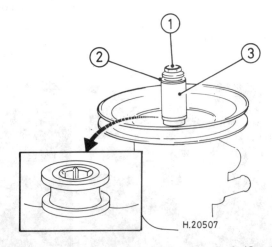

Fig. 10.17 Pressing a new pulley onto the shaft (Sec 16)

1   Bolt
2   Washers
3   Socket or tube

21 Refit the pump in the reverse order of removal, tension the drivebelt as described in Section 17, and fill and bleed the system as described in Section 14.

17 Power steering pump drivebelt – adjusting

Refer to Chapter 2, Section 14.

18 Power steering pump – overhaul

1 In general, power steering pumps are very reliable and require no maintenance, apart from the periodic checking of fluid level and belt tension.
2 If the pump should fail in service, or develop leaks, it is best to obtain a replacement unit.

19 Anti-roll bar – removal and refitting

1 Raise and support the front of the vehicle. Remove the front wheels and the undertray.
2 Remove the nuts from the anti-roll bar-to-link rod attachment points (photo).
3 Remove the bolts from the support brackets (photo).
4 Renew any rubber bushes which have perished.
5 Refit in the reverse order.

20 Anti-roll bar link rods – removal and refitting

1 Disconnect the upper link rod attachment to the anti-roll bar (see Section 19).
2 Remove the nut and bolt from the lower attachment (photo).
3 Renew any rubber bushes which are perished.
4 Refit in the reverse order.

21 Control arms and bushings – removal and refitting

1 Jack up the front of the car and place stands at the front jacking points. Remove the wheels.
2 Disconnect the anti-roll bar from the link rod.
3 Remove the three retaining nuts and disconnect the balljoint from the control arm (photo).
4 Remove the control arm front retaining nut and bolt (photo).
5 Remove the bolts securing the rear attachment bracket (photo) and lower the control arm. Remove the bracket from the control arm (photo).
6 Press out the bushings from the control arm and bracket.
7 When refitting the new bushing in the control arm, the flanged end of the bush is towards the front.

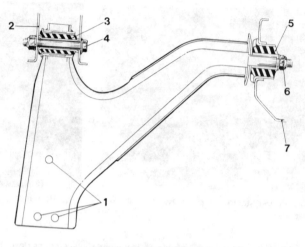

Fig. 10.18 Front control arm bushing (Sec 21)

1 Hole for balljoint	5 Rear rubber bushing
2 Front axle member	6 Nut
3 Front rubber bushing	7 Rear bracket
4 Bolt	

8 Fit the new bushing in the control arm bracket.
9 After replacing the bushings, fit the bracket to the control arm but do not tighten the nut.
10 Fit the rear end of the control arm in position, fit the three securing bolts but do not tighten them.
11 Fit the front retaining nut and bolt but do not tighten the nut.
12 Attach the balljoint to the control arm and tighten the nuts to the specified torque.
13 Position a jack under the outer end of the control arm, jack up and compress the spring.
14 Connect the anti-roll bar and link rod. Remove the jack.
15 Tighten the rear bracket bolts to the specified torque.
16 Refit the wheels, lower the vehicle and push it a few yards back and forth, at the same time bouncing the front end.
17 Tighten the rear bush nut to the specified torque. The weight of the vehicle must be on its wheels, or a jack raised under the control arm (paragraph 13) to simulate this. On B21-engined models, it will be necessary to disconnect the exhaust downpipe for access on the right-hand side.
18 Tighten the front bush nut and bolt to the specified torque.
19 Reconnect the exhaust pipe, if applicable, and lower the vehicle.
20 It is possible to remove the rear bracket for bush renewal without removing the control arm itself, but note the following points:

*(a) The anti-roll bar links on **both** sides must be disconnected to allow the control arms to move freely*
(b) Final tightening of the rear bush nut must only take place in the loaded condition (paragraph 17)

19.2 Anti-roll bar-to-link rod attachment nut (arrowed)

19.3 Support bracket bolts (arrowed)

20.2 Link rod lower attachment bolt

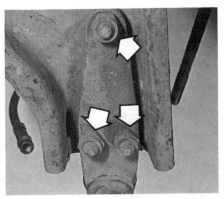

21.3 Balljoint-to-control arm retaining nuts (arrowed)

21.4 Control arm front retaining nut (arrowed)

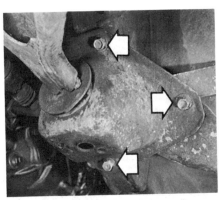

21.5A Rear attachment bracket bolts (arrowed)

21.5B Bracket-to-control arm nut (arrowed)

22.3 Preventing the strut from turning while undoing the nut

22.10 Balljoint-to-strut attachment bolts (arrowed)

22 Control arm balljoint – renewal

Early type

1 On early production models, the control arm balljoint is bolted to the control arm (see Section 21) and to the bottom of the suspension strut.
2 The nut which secures the balljoint to the strut is only accessible from inside the strut after the shock absorber has been removed, as described in Section 23.
3 With this condition met, use a socket and long extension inserted down inside the strut to loosen the balljoint nut by a few turns (socket size is 19 mm). It will be necessary to prevent the strut from turning while undoing the nut, using a strap wrench or pipe grips around the strut, fitted close to the weld mark at the top (photo).
4 With the nut loosened, use a long soft drift to tap the end of the ball joint spindle to free the socket from the ball.
5 Smear some grease on the inside of the socket and remove the nut. (The grease will stick the nut to the socket for easy removal when it comes off the threads.)
6 Remove the balljoint-to-control arm nuts and remove the balljoint.
7 Refitting is a reversal of removal, noting the following points:

   (a) *Before fitting the balljoint, clean all grease from the balljoint seat, or incorrect tightening may occur*
   (b) *Tighten all nuts and bolts to their specified torque*

Later type

8 On later type production models, the balljoint is connected to the suspension strut by a housing bolted to the bottom of the strut, and accessible from the outside. It is not necessary to remove the shock absorber.
9 Raise and support the front of the vehicle. Remove the front wheel. Loosen the shock absorber retaining nut a couple of turns (only applicable to pre-1978 models).

10 Remove the four balljoint-to-strut attachment bolts (photo). On some models these may be locked by a tab washer, which must be bent down.
11 Remove the balljoint-to-control arm nuts.
12 Ease the balljoint housing from the bottom of the strut.
13 Place the housing in a vice and undo the balljoint nut, then use a drift to drive the balljoint from the housing.
14 Clean all grease from the housing and new balljoint, then fit the balljoint to the housing and tighten the nut to the specified torque.
15 The remaining procedure is a reversal of removal, using new balljoint housing bolts (and tab washers, where fitted) and tightening all nuts and bolts to their specified torque.
Note: *From 1979 on, models with power steering, the balljoints for left and right sides are different and not interchangeable.*

23 Front suspension strut – removal, overhaul and refitting

Warning: *Spring compressors of sound design and construction must be used during this procedure. Uncontrolled release of the spring may result in damage and injury.*
1 Raise the front of the vehicle onto axle stands and remove the front wheels.
2 Loosen the shock absorber nut with a C-spanner.
3 Position a jack under the control arm, and just take the weight of the strut.
4 Disconnect the steering track rod balljoint.
5 Disconnect the anti-roll bar upper link attachment.
6 Remove the bolt from the brake pipe bracket on the inner wing.
7 Prise out the grommet from the top housing of the suspension strut (photo).
8 Loosen the centre nut while holding the piston rod stationary (photo).
9 Make an alignment mark on the plate opposite the 'pimple' mark on the suspension tower (photo), then remove the top housing nuts.

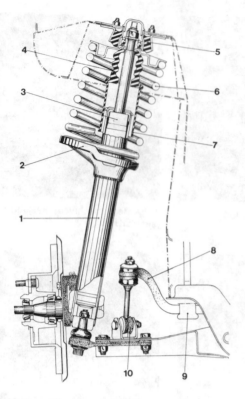

**Fig. 10.19 Components of the front suspension strut
assembly (Sec 23)**

1 Strut	6 Coil spring
2 Lower spring seat	7 Shock absorber cover
3 Shock absorber	8 Anti-roll bar link
4 Rubber buffer	9 Anti-roll bar bracket
5 Upper housing	10 Link rod

10 Lower the jack under the control arm, and guide the strut assembly
out from under the wing. Make sure the brake hoses are not strained
during this operation, and note that it may be necessary to remove the
jack completely and actually pull down on the strut to get it out.

11 Tie the strut to the wing to support it, then fit coil spring
compressors to the spring and compress it sufficiently to relieve
tension on the upper bearing housing.

12 Undo the centre nut, again preventing the piston rod from turning
(photo).

23.7 Prise out the grommet ...

23.8 ... and loosen the centre nut

23.9 Make an alignment mark (arrowed) before undoing the nut

23.12 Undoing the centre nut

23.13A Remove the nut ...

23.13B ... washer ...

23.13C ... upper housing ...

23.13D ... spring seat ...

23.13E ... and rubber buffer

23.15 Removing the shock absorber nut

23.16 Retrieve the rubber grommet

23.18A Stick the rubber grommet with grease ...

23.18B ... before inserting the shock absorber

13 Remove the nut and washer, then the upper housing, spring seat and rubber buffer (photos).
14 Lift off the spring, still compressed. Do not drop or jar it.
15 Remove the shock absorber nut using a C-spanner (photo).
16 Lift out the shock absorber and retrieve the rubber grommet from inside the strut (photo).
17 To remove the strut assembly from the lower balljoint, refer to Section 22, but it is not necessary to remove the balljoint from the control arm.
18 Fit a new shock absorber, sticking the rubber grommet in place with a little grease before inserting the shock absorber in the tube (photos).
19 The remaining refitting procedure is a reversal of removal, noting the following points:

(a) Tighten all nuts and bolts to their specified torque

(b) Do not loosen the coil spring compressor until the centre nut has been tightened, and ensure the spring locates correctly in the spring seats
(c) When fitting the top plate, line up the previously-made marks before tightening the nuts (photo)

Note: Later models may be fitted with gas-filled shock absorbers. The procedure for renewing them is similar to that described here.

24 Steering wheel – removal and refitting

1 Disconnect the battery negative terminal.
2 Prise out the centre impact pad (early models) or centre plate (later models).

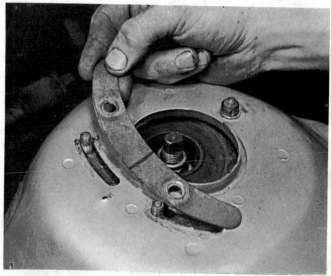

23.19 Line up the previously-made marks before tightening the nuts

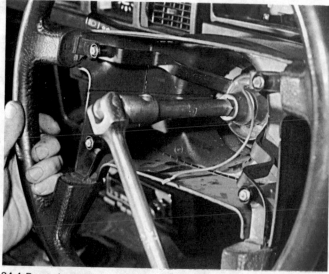

24.4 Removing the steering wheel nut

3   Disconnect the electrical leads to the horn push.
4   Remove the steering wheel nut (photo). On post-1979 models, a deep 27 mm socket is required.
5   On pre-1979 models, use a puller to ease the steering wheel from its taper seat. Do not try to use a hammer to knock the wheel off, or damage to the upper crumple shaft may result. On post-1979 models, knock the steering wheel off using both hands under the wheel, taking precautions against the wheel flying off into your face.
6   On some models there may be a spring and spring seat under the steering wheel nut – do not lose them.
7   Refitting is a reversal of removal, tightening the steering wheel nut to the specified torque.

25 Steering column and lock – removal and refitting

1   Disconnect the battery negative lead.
2   Remove the steering wheel as described in Section 24.
3   Remove the steering column shroud panels and column switches as described in Chapter 12, Section 34 and 35. Disconnect the ignition/starter switch.
4   Remove the under-dash soundproofing panels as described in Chapter 11, Section 34.
5   Working through the access holes in the support frame, drill out or extract the steering lock shear-head bolts (photo).
6   Disconnct the heater duct for access, and remove the steering column lower bracket (photo).
7   Remove the pinch-bolt from the upper coupling joint, after removing the locking pin (photos).
8   Remove the bolts from the flange, prise the flange apart and then remove the upper coupling assembly (photo). If no flange is fitted, separate the lower coupling.
9   Push the steering column down, and then out from underneath the support frame.
10 Remove the steering lock by undoing the two securing screws.
11 Check the steering column crumple unit has not been compressed. There should be no axial movement in the upper end, and the column overall length should be as shown in Fig. 10.22. If it is not, renew the column.
12 Fit the lock assembly, ensuring that the dimension in Fig. 10.23 is achieved.
13 Ensure the plastic guides are in position in the column support frame.
14 Refit the column, pushing its lower end through the engine bulkhead, and its upper end back over the support. Fit the shear-head bolts finger-tight only.
15 Fit the lower bracket, again only doing the bolts up finger-tight.
16 Adjust the position of the column up or down, so that the steering lock protrudes from the facia by the specified amount (photo).

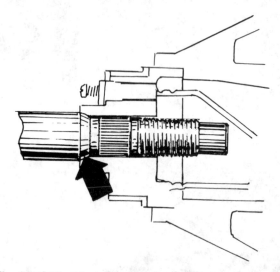

Fig. 10.20 Modified taper on post-1979 steering shafts
(Sec 24)

Fig. 10.21 Steering lock-to-column tube locating screws
(Sec 25)

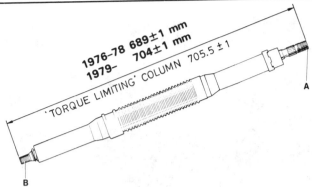

Fig. 10.22 Collapsible type steering column checking dimension (Sec 25)

A   Upper shaft   B   Lower shaft

Fig. 10.24 Ignition switch positions (Sec 25)

O   Locked (key withdrawn)   II   Ignition and all electrical
I   Radio, cigar lighter,   components on
     headlamp and blower on   III Starter energised

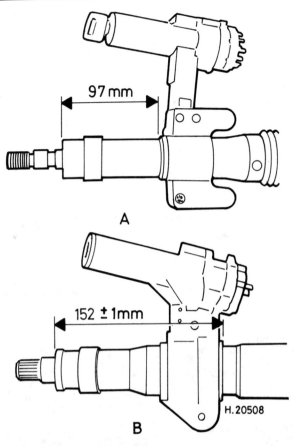

Fig. 10.23 Steering column lock position diagram (Sec 25)

A   Ordinary lock   B   Torque limited type

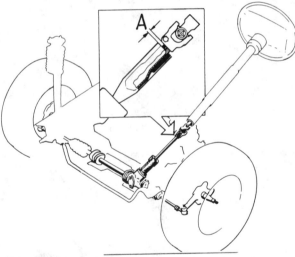

Fig. 10.25 Steering shaft coupling position (later models)
(Sec 25)

A = 0.39 to 0.75 in (10.0 to 19.0 mm)

17 Check that the steering column is not in contact with the plastic guides. If it is, loosen the support frame screws and move the frame, tightening them on completion.
18 Just 'nip' up the shear-head bolts in the upper attachment without shearing them.
19 Tighten the lower bracket bolts to the specified torque.
20 Refit the heater duct.
21 Fit the rubber grommet in the engine bulkhead if it has been dislodged, then loosely fit the upper coupling joint.
22 Where fitted, tighten the coupling flange bolts to the specified torque.
23 Now check the distance between the upper steering shaft coupling and the stop on the lower shaft, which should be as shown in Fig. 10.25. (This adjustment applies only to post-1979 models, and post-1978 models with ZF type power steering.)
24 Adjust by loosening the pinch-bolt in the lower coupling and

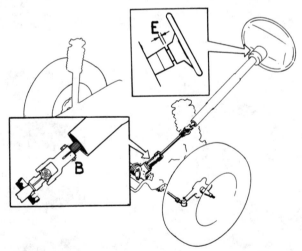

Fig. 10.26 Steering wheel-to-casing clearance (Sec 25)

B Coupling pinch-bolt   E = 0.039 to 0.079 in (1.0 to 2.0 mm)

moving the lower shaft up or down (photo).
25 Tighten the pinch-bolts to the specified torque on completion.
26 Temporarily refit the steering wheel, and check the distance between the steering wheel and the casing. Adjust to that specified in Fig. 10.26 by loosening the lower coupling pinch-bolt and moving the steering shaft up or down. Tighten the pinch-bolt on completion.
27 The remaining procedure is a reversal of removal. Check the operation of the steering lock before finally tightening the shear-head bolts until they shear, and check that the coupling joint pinch-bolt locking pins are inserted.

Note: *From 1986 model year, the steering column has been modified to accept a torque-limited steering lock. This comprises a strong outer sleeve pressed onto spring sleeves attached to the column. The tongue of the steering lock engages in the grooves of the outer sleeve, and if unreasonable force is applied to the steering wheel in an attempt to shear the lock tongue, the sleeve assembly slips in order to reduce the shear force.*

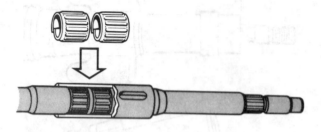

Fig. 10.27 Sleeves on torque limited steering lock (Sec 25)

25.5 Access holes in support frame for shear-head bolts (arrowed)

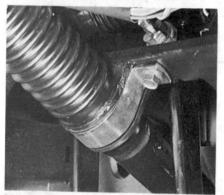

25.6 Steering column lower bracket

25.7A Upper coupling joint pinch-bolt (arrowed) ...

25.7B ... and lock pin (arrowed)

25.8 Steering shaft flange

25.16 Measuring the steering lock protrusion with a depth gauge. Measurement should be made from 'III' mark on lock   A = 0.6 in (15 mm)

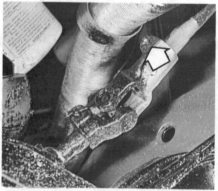

25.24 Lower coupling joint pinch-bolt (arrowed)

26 Wheel studs – renewal

Front

1 Remove the front hub end brake disc (Section 4).
2 Support the hub area of the disc, and press or drive out the studs.
3 Turn the disc over and press the new studs into the hub.
4 Refit the brake disc and adjust the wheel bearings (Section 3).

Rear

5 Remove the handbrake shoes (Chapter 9, Section 11).
6 If a tool similar to that shown in Fig. 10.28 is available, the studs can be renewed with the driveshafts *in situ*. If not, the driveshaft must be removed (see Chapter 8, Section 9), and a similar process as described for the front studs used.
Note: *It may be possible to adapt a carpenter's G-cramp and a socket in place of the special tool.*

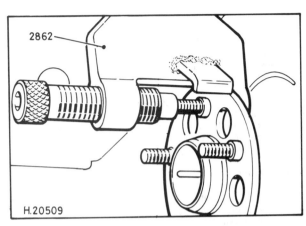

Fig. 10.28 Special tool for removing and refitting wheel studs (Sec 26)

27 Wheels and tyres – general care and maintenance

Wheels and tyres should give no real problems in use provided that a close eye is kept on them with regard to excessive wear or damage. To this end, the following points should be noted.

Ensure that tyre pressures are checked regularly and maintained correctly. Checking should be carried out with the tyres cold and not immediately after the vehicle has been in use. If the pressures are checked with the tyres hot, an apparently high reading will be obtained owing to heat expansion. Under no circumstances should an attempt be made to reduce the pressures to the quoted cold reading in this instance, or effective underinflation will result.

Underinflation will cause overheating of the tyre owing to excessive flexing of the casing, and the tread will not sit correctly on the road surface. This will cause a consequent loss of adhesion and excessive wear, not to mention the danger of sudden tyre failure due to heat build-up.

Overinflation will cause rapid wear of the centre part of the tyre tread coupled with reduced adhesion, harsher ride, and the danger of shock damage occurring in the tyre casing.

Regularly check the tyres for damage in the form of cuts or bulges, especially in the sidewalls. Remove any nails or stones embedded in the tread before they penetrate the tyre to cause deflation. If removal of a nail *does* reveal that the tyre has been punctured, refit the nail so that its point of penetration is marked. Then immediately change the wheel and have the tyre repaired by a tyre dealer. Do *not* drive on a tyre in such a condition. In many cases a puncture can be simply repaired by the use of an inner tube of the correct size and type. If in any doubt as to the possible consequences of any damage found, consult your local tyre dealer for advice.

Periodically remove the wheels and clean any dirt or mud from the inside and outside surfaces. Examine the wheel rims for signs of rusting, corrosion or other damage. Light alloy wheels are easily damaged by 'kerbing' whilst parking, and similarly steel wheels may become dented or buckled. Renewal of the wheel is very often the only course of remedial action possible.

The balance of each wheel and tyre assembly should be maintained to avoid excessive wear, not only to the tyres but also to the steering and suspension components. Wheel imbalance is normally signified by vibration through the vehicle's bodyshell, although in many cases it is particularly noticeable through the steering wheel. Conversely, it should be noted that wear or damage in suspension or steering components may cause excessive tyre wear. Out-of-round or out-of-true tyres, damaged wheels and wheel bearing wear/maladjustment also fall into this category. Balancing will not usually cure vibration caused by such wear.

Wheel balancing may be carried out with the wheel either on or off the vehicle. If balanced on the vehicle, ensure that the wheel-to-hub relationship is marked in some way prior to subsequent wheel removal so that it may be refitted in its original position.

General tyre wear is influenced to a large degree by driving style – harsh braking and acceleration or fast cornering will all produce more rapid tyre wear. Interchanging of tyres may result in more even wear, but this should only be carried out where there is no mix of tyre types on the vehicle. However, it is worth bearing in mind that if this is completely effective, the added expense of replacing a complete set of tyres simultaneously is incurred, which may prove financially restrictive for many owners.

Front tyres may wear unevenly as a result of wheel misalignment. The front wheels should always be correctly aligned according to the settings specified by the vehicle manufacturer.

Legal restrictions apply to the mixing of tyre types on a vehicle. Basically this means that a vehicle must not have tyres of differing construction on the same axle. Although it is not recommended to mix tyre types between front axle and rear axle, the only legally permissible combination is crossply at the front and radial at the rear. When mixing radial ply tyres, textile braced radials must always go on the front axle, with steel braced radials at the rear. An obvious disadvantage of such mixing is the necessity to carry two spare tyres to avoid contravening the law in the event of a puncture.

In the UK, the Motor Vehicles Construction and Use Regulations apply to many aspects of tyre fitting and usage. It is suggested that a copy of these regulations is obtained from your local police if in doubt as to the current legal requirements with regard to tyre condition, minimum tread depth, etc.

28 Fault diagnosis – front suspension and steering; wheels and tyres

Symptom	Reason(s)
Excessive play at steering wheel	Worn track rod end balljoints Worn control arm balljoints Worn steering gear
Vehicle wanders or pulls to one side	Uneven tyre pressures Incorrect wheel alignment Worn track rod end balljoints Worn control arm balljoints Faulty shock absorbers Accident damage
Steering heavy or stiff	Low tyre pressures Seized balljoint Seized suspension strut upper bearing Incorrect wheel alignment Steering gear damaged or lacking lubricant Power steering fault

Symptom	Reason(s)
Power assistance ineffective	Low fluid level
	Pump drivebelt loose or broken
	Faulty pump or steering gear
Wheel wobble or vibration	Wheel nuts loose
	Wheels out of balance or tyres damaged
	Wheel bearings worn
	Worn track rod end balljoints
	Worn control arm balljoints
	Faulty shock absorber
Excessive tyre wear	Incorrect tyre pressures
	Wheels out of balance
	Incorrect wheel alignment
	Faulty shock absorbers
	Harsh driving or braking

Chapter 11 Bodywork and fittings

Contents

1 General description

The name of Volvo has become synonymous with safety over the years, and the 240 series is the basis on which this reputation has been built.

The body is of welded steel construction with a built-in 'safety cage' surrounding the passenger compartment. Crumple zones at front and rear further enhance this safety angle. The front bumpers, which are made of aluminium, are fitted with impact-absorbing mountings to further reduce injury to occupants.

All steel panels used in construction of the bodywork undergo extensive anti-corrosion treatment, and this is further enhanced by ventilation of box sections, sills and double skins, especially on later models. The front wings are bolted in place for easy renewal.

Interior fittings, which are of a high standard, are carefully designed to reduce injury in the event of a collision.

The whole forms a rigid, durable and safe vehicle body which will give years of service with the minimum of maintenance.

2 Maintenance – bodywork and underframe

1 The general condition of a vehicle's bodywork is the one thing that significantly affects its value. Maintenance is easy but needs to be regular. Neglect, particularly after minor damage, can lead quickly to further deterioration and costly repair bills. It is important also to keep watch on those parts of the vehicle not immediately visible, for instance the underside, inside all the wheel arches and the lower part of the engine compartment.
2 The basic maintenance routine for the bodywork is washing – preferably with a lot of water, from a hose. This will remove all the loose solids which may have stuck to the vehicle. It is important to flush these off in such a way as to prevent grit from scratching the finish. The wheel arches and underframe need washing in the same way to remove any accumulated mud which will retain moisture and tend to encourage rust. Paradoxically enough, the best time to clean the underframe and wheel arches is in wet weather when the mud is thoroughly wet and soft. In very wet weather the underframe is usually cleaned of large accumulations automatically and this is a good time for inspection.
3 Periodically, except on vehicles with a wax-based underbody protective coating, it is a good idea to have the whole of the underframe of the vehicle steam cleaned, engine compartment included, so that a thorough inspection can be carried out to see what minor repairs and renovations are necessary. Steam cleaning is available at many garages and is necessary for removal of the accumulation of oily grime which sometimes is allowed to become thick in certain areas. If steam cleaning facilities are not available, there are one or two excellent grease solvents available such as Holts Engine Cleaner or Holts Foambrite which can be brush applied. The dirt can then be simply hosed off. Note that these methods should not be used on vehicles with wax-based underbody protective coating or the coating will be removed. Such vehicles should be inspected annually, preferably just prior to winter, when the underbody should be washed down and any damage to the wax coating repaired using Holts Undershield. Ideally, a completely fresh coat should be applied. It would also be worth considering the use of such wax-based protection for injection into door panels, sills, box sections, etc, as an additional safeguard against rust damage where such protection is not provided by the vehicle manufacturer.
4 After washing paintwork, wipe off with a chamois leather to give an unspotted clear finish. A coat of clear protective wax polish, like the many excellent Turtle Wax polishes, will give added protection against chemical pollutants in the air. If the paintwork sheen has dulled or oxidised, use a cleaner/polisher combination such as Turtle Extra to restore the brilliance of the shine. This requires a little effort, but such dulling is usually caused because regular washing has been neglected. Care needs to be taken with metallic paintwork, as special non-abrasive cleaner/polisher is required to avoid damage to the finish. Always check that the door and ventilator opening drain holes and pipes are completely clear so that water can be drained out (photos). Bright work should be treated in the same way as paint work. Windscreens and windows can be kept clear of the smeary film which often appears, by the use of a proprietary glass cleaner like Holts Mixra. Never use any form of wax or other body or chromium polish on glass.

3 Maintenance – upholstery and carpets

Mats and carpets should be brushed or vacuum cleaned regularly to keep them free of grit. If they are badly stained remove them from the vehicle for scrubbing or sponging and make quite sure they are dry before refitting. Seats and interior trim panels can be kept clean by wiping with a damp cloth and Turtle Wax Carisma. If they do become stained (which can be more apparent on light coloured upholstery) use a little liquid detergent and a soft nail brush to scour the grime out of the grain of the material. Do not forget to keep the headlining clean in the same way as the upholstery. When using liquid cleaners inside

2.4A Clearing a door drain hole

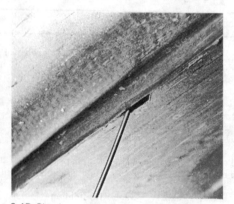

2.4B Clearing a sill member drain hole

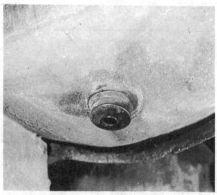

2.4C Rubber bung in rear wheel housing

the vehicle do not over-wet the surfaces being cleaned. Excessive damp could get into the seams and padded interior causing stains, offensive odours or even rot. If the inside of the vehicle gets wet accidentally it is worthwhile taking some trouble to dry it out properly, particularly where carpets are involved. *Do not leave oil or electric heaters inside the vehicle for this purpose.*

4 Minor body damage – repair

The photographic sequences on pages 238 and 239 illustrate the operations detailed in the following sub-sections.
Note: *For more detailed information about bodywork repair, the Haynes Publishing Group publish a book by Lindsay Porter called The Car Bodywork Repair Manual. This incorporates information on such aspects as rust treatment, painting and glass fibre repairs, as well as details on more ambitious repairs involving welding and panel beating.*

Repair of minor scratches in bodywork

If the scratch is very superficial, and does not penetrate to the metal of the bodywork, repair is very simple. Lightly rub the area of the scratch with a paintwork renovator like Turtle Wax New Color Back, or a very fine cutting paste like Holts Body + Plus Rubbing Compound, to remove loose paint from the scratch and to clear the surrounding bodywork of wax polish. Rinse the area with clean water.

Apply touch-up paint, such as Holts Dupli-Color Color Touch or a paint film like Holts Autofilm, to the scratch using a fine paint brush; continue to apply fine layers of paint until the surface of the paint in the scratch is level with the surrounding paintwork. Allow the new paint at least two weeks to harden: then blend it into the surrounding paintwork by rubbing the scratch area with a paintwork renovator or a very fine cutting paste, such as Holts Body + Plus Rubbing Compound or Turtle Wax New Color Back. Finally, apply wax polish from one of the Turtle Wax range of wax polishes.

Where the scratch has penetrated right through to the metal of the bodywork, causing the metal to rust, a different repair technique is required. Remove any loose rust from the bottom of the scratch with a penknife, then apply rust inhibiting paint, such as Turtle Wax Rust Master, to prevent the formation of rust in the future. Using a rubber or nylon applicator fill the scratch with bodystopper paste like Holts Body + Plus Knifing Putty. If required, this paste can be mixed with cellulose thinners, such as Holts Body + Plus Cellulose Thinners, to provide a very thin paste which is ideal for filling narrow scratches. Before the stopper-paste in the scratch hardens, wrap a piece of smooth cotton rag around the top of a finger. Dip the finger in cellulose thinners, such as Holts Body + Plus Cellulose Thinners, and then quickly sweep it across the surface of the stopper-paste in the scratch; this will ensure that the surface of the stopper-paste is slightly hollowed. The scratch can now be painted over as described earlier in this Section.

Repair of dents in bodywork

When deep denting of the vehicle's bodywork has taken place, the first task is to pull the dent out, until the affected bodywork almost attains its original shape. There is little point in trying to restore the original shape completely, as the metal in the damaged area will have stretched on impact and cannot be reshaped fully to its original

contour. It is better to bring the level of the dent up to a point which is about ⅛ in (3 mm) below the level of the surrounding bodywork. In cases where the dent is very shallow anyway, it is not worth trying to pull it out at all. If the underside of the dent is accessible, it can be hammered out gently from behind, using a mallet with a wooden or plastic head. Whilst doing this, hold a suitable block of wood firmly against the outside of the panel to absorb the impact from the hammer blows and thus prevent a large area of the bodywork from being 'belled-out'.

Should the dent be in a section of the bodywork which has a double skin or some other factor making it inaccessible from behind, a different technique is called for. Drill several small holes through the metal inside the area – particularly in the deeper section. Then screw long self-tapping screws into the holes just sufficiently for them to gain a good purchase in the metal. Now the dent can be pulled out by pulling on the protruding heads of the screws with a pair of pliers.

The next stage of the repair is the removal of the paint from the damaged area, and from an inch or so of the surrounding 'sound' bodywork. This is accomplished most easily by using a wire brush or abrasive pad on a power drill, although it can be done just as effectively by hand using sheets of abrasive paper. To complete the preparation for filling, score the surface of the bare metal with a screwdriver or the tang of a file, or alternatively, drill small holes in the affected area. This will provide a really good 'key' for the filler paste.

To complete the repair see the Section on filling and re-spraying.

Repair of rust holes or gashes in bodywork

Remove all paint from the affected area and from an inch or so of the surrounding 'sound' bodywork, using an abrasive pad or a wire brush on a power drill. If these are not available a few sheets of abrasive paper will do the job just as effectively. With the paint removed you will be able to gauge the severity of the corrosion and therefore decide whether to renew the whole panel (if this is possible) or to repair the affected area. New body panels are not as expensive as most people think and it is often quicker and more satisfactory to fit a new panel than to attempt to repair large areas of corrosion.

Remove all fittings from the affected area except those which will act as a guide to the original shape of the damaged bodywork (eg headlamp shells etc). Then, using tin snips or a hacksaw blade, remove all loose metal and any other metal badly affected by corrosion. Hammer the edges of the hole inwards in order to create a slight depression for the filler paste.

Wire brush the affected area to remove the powdery rust from the surface of the remaining metal. Paint the affected area with rust inhibiting paint like Turtle Wax Rust Master; if the back of the rusted area is accessible treat this also.

Before filling can take place it will be necessary to block the hole in some way. This can be achieved by the use of aluminium or plastic mesh, or aluminium tape.

Aluminium or plastic mesh or glass fibre matting, such as the Holts Body + Plus Glass Fibre Matting, is probably the best material to use for a large hole. Cut a piece to the approximate size and shape of the hole to be filled, then position it in the hole so that its edges are below the level of the surrounding bodywork. It can be retained in position by several blobs of filler paste around its periphery.

Aluminium tape should be used for small or very narrow holes. Pull a piece off the roll and trim it to the approximate size and shape required, then pull off the backing paper (if used) and stick the tape over the hole; it can be overlapped if the thickness of one piece is insufficient. Burnish down the edges of the tape with the handle of a screwdriver or similar, to ensure that the tape is securely attached to the metal underneath.

Bodywork repairs – filling and re-spraying

Before using this Section, see the Sections on dent, deep scratch, rust holes and gash repairs.

Many types of bodyfiller are available, but generally speaking those proprietary kits which contain a tin of filler paste and a tube of resin hardener are best for this type of repair, like Holts Body + Plus or Holts No Mix which can be used directly from the tube. A wide, flexible plastic or nylon applicator will be found invaluable for imparting a smooth and well contoured finish to the surface of the filler.

Mix up a little filler on a clean piece of card or board – measure the hardener carefully (follow the maker's instructions on the pack) otherwise the filler will set too rapidly or too slowly. Alternatively, Holts No Mix can be used straight from the tube without mixing, but daylight is required to cure it. Using the applicator apply the filler paste to the prepared area; draw the applicator across the surface of the filler to achieve the correct contour and to level the filler surface. As soon as a contour that approximates to the correct one is achieved, stop working the paste – if you carry on too long the paste will become sticky and begin to 'pick up' on the applicator. Continue to add thin layers of filler paste at twenty-minute intervals until the level of the filler is just proud of the surrounding bodywork.

Once the filler has hardened, excess can be removed using a metal plane or file. From then on, progressively finer grades of abrasive paper should be used, starting with a 40 grade productikn paper and finishing with 400 grade wet-and-dry paper. Always wrap the abrasive paper around a flat rubber, cork, or wooden block – otherwise the surface of the filler will not be completely flat. During the smoothing of the filler surface the wet-and-dry paper should be periodically rinsed in water. This will ensure that a very smooth finish is imparted to the filler at the final stage.

At this stage the 'dent' should be surrounded by a ring of bare metal, which in turn should be encircled by the finely 'feathered' edge of the good paintwork. Rinse the repair area with clean water, until all of the dust produced by the rubbing-down operation has gone.

Spray the whole repair area with a light coat of primer, either Holts Body + Plus Grey or Red Oxide Primer – this will show up any imperfections in the surface of the filler. Repair these imperfections with fresh filler paste or bodystopper, and once more smooth the surface with abrasive paper. If bodystopper is used, it can be mixed with cellulose thinners to form a really thin paste which is ideal for filling small holes. Repeat this spray and repair procedure until you are satisfied that the surface of the filler, and the feathered edge of the paintwork are perfect. Clean the repair area with clean water and allow to dry fully.

The repair area is now ready for final spraying. Paint spraying must be carried out in a warm, dry, windless and dust free atmosphere. This condition can be created artificially if you have access to a large indoor working area, but if you are forced to work in the open, you will have to pick your day very carefully. If you are working indoors, dousing the floor in the work area with water will help to settle the dust which would otherwise be in the atmosphere. If the repair area is confined to one body panel, mask off the surrounding panels; this will help to minimise the effects of a slight mis-match in paint colours. Bodywork fittings (eg chrome strips, door handles etc) will also need to be masked off. Use genuine masking tape and several thicknesses of newspaper for the masking operations.

Before commencing to spray, agitate the aerosol can thoroughly, then spray a test area (an old tin, or similar) until the technique is mastered. Cover the repair area with a thick coat of primer; the thickness should be built up using several thin layers of paint rather than one thick one. Using 400 grade wet-and-dry paper, rub down the surface of the primer until it is really smooth. While doing this, the work area should be thoroughly doused with water, and the wet-and-dry paper periodically rinsed in water. Allow to dry before spraying on more paint.

Spray on the top coat using Holts Dupli-Color Autospray, again building up the thickness by using several thin layers of paint. Start spraying in the centre of the repair area and then work outwards, with a side-to-side motion, until the whole repair area and about 2 inches of the surrounding original paintwork is covered. Remove all masking material 10 to 15 minutes after spraying on the final coat of paint.

Allow the new paint at least two weeks to harden, then, using a paintwork renovator or a very fine cutting paste such as Turtle Wax New Color Back or Holts Body + Plus Rubbing Compound, blend the edges of the paint into the existing paintwork. Finally, apply wax polish.

Plastic components

With the use of more and more plastic body components by the vehicle manufacturers (eg bumpers, spoilers, and in some cases major body panels), rectification of more serious damage to such items has become a matter of either entrusting repair work to a specialist in this field, or renewing complete components. Repair of such damage by the DIY owner is not really feasible owing to the cost of the equipment and materials required for effecting such repairs. The basic technique involves making a groove along the line of the crack in the plastic using a rotary burr in a power drill. The damaged part is then welded back together by using a hot air gun to heat up and fuse a plastic filler rod into the groove. Any excess plastic is then removed and the area rubbed down to a smooth finish. It is important that a filler rod of the correct plastic is used, as body components can be made of a variety of different types (eg polycarbonate, ABS, polypropylene).

Damage of a less serious nature (abrasions, minor cracks etc) can be repaired by the DIY owner using a two-part epoxy filler repair material, like Holts Body + Plus or Holts No Mix which can be used directly from the tube. Once mixed in equal proportions (or applied direct from the tube in the case of Holts No Mix), this is used in similar fashion to the bodywork filler used on metal panels. The filler is usually cured in twenty to thirty minutes, ready for sanding and painting.

If the owner is renewing a complete component himself, or if he has repaired it with epoxy filler, he will be left with the problem of finding a suitable paint for finishing which is compatible with the type of plastic used. At one time the use of a universal paint was not possible owing to the complex range of plastics encountered in body component applications. Standard paints, generally speaking, will not bond to plastic or rubber satisfactorily, but Holts Professional Spraymatch paints to match any plastic or rubber finish can be obtained from dealers. However, it is now possible to obtain a plastic body parts finishing kit which consists of a pre-primer treatment, a primer and coloured top coat. Full instructions are normally supplied with a kit, but basically the method of use is to first apply the pre-primer to the component concerned and allow it to dry for up to 30 minutes. Then the primer is applied and left to dry for about an hour before finally applying the special coloured top coat. The result is a correctly coloured component where the paint will flex with the plastic or rubber, a property that standard paint does not normally possess.

5 Major body damage – repair

Where major damage has been caused by impact, or large sections of panelling need renewal due to neglect, the work is best done by your local Volvo dealer or bodywork repair specialist.

After impact (even quite minor ones) the body alignment should be checked, which requires the use of special jigs. Misalignment is not always evident to the eye and can have serious effects on handling and cause excessive wear of tyres and suspension components.

Major panel renewal will probably require welding equipment and certainly the use of spray painting gear. These jobs are best done by experts who have the necessary equipment.

6 Bonnet – removal and refitting

1 Open the bonnet and support it in the open position.
2 Disconnect the washer tubing at the T-junction.
3 Where fitted, remove the bonnet light (refer to Chapter 12), and disconnect the wires. Tie a length of string to the wire (photo) and pull through the double skin of the bonnet. Undo the string on completion and leave it in position in order to pull the wire through again when the bonnet is refitted.
4 Mark the relationship of the bonnet to the bonnet hinges.
5 With the aid of an assistant, undo the hinge-to-bonnet bolts (photo) and lift off the bonnet, leaving the hinges in position on the inner wings.
6 The hinges can be removed from the inner wing by removing the

This photographic sequence shows the steps taken to repair the dent and paintwork damage shown above. In general, the procedure for repairing a hole will be similar; where there are substantial differences, the procedure is clearly described and shown in a separate photograph.

First remove any trim around the dent, then hammer out the dent where access is possible. This will minimise filling. Here, after the large dent has been hammered out, the damaged area is being made slightly concave.

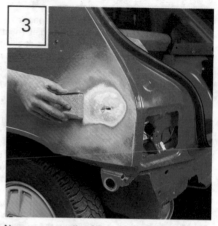

Next, remove all paint from the damaged area by rubbing with coarse abrasive paper or using a power drill fitted with a wire brush or abrasive pad. 'Feather' the edge of the boundary with good paintwork using a finer grade of abrasive paper.

Where there are holes or other damage, the sheet metal should be cut away before proceeding further. The damaged area and any signs of rust should be treated with Turtle Wax Hi-Tech Rust Eater, which will also inhibit further rust formation.

For a large dent or hole mix Holts Body Plus Resin and Hardener according to the manufacturer's instructions and apply it around the edge of the repair. Press Glass Fibre Matting over the repair area and leave for 20-30 minutes to harden. Then ...

... brush more Holts Body Plus Resin and Hardener onto the matting and leave to harden. Repeat the sequence with two or three layers of matting, checking that the final layer is lower than the surrounding area. Apply Holts Body Plus Filler Paste as shown in Step 5B.

For a medium dent, mix Holts Body Plus Filler Paste and Hardener according to the manufacturer's instructions and apply it with a flexible applicator. Apply thin layers of filler at 20-minute intervals, until the filler surface is slightly proud of the surrounding bodywork.

For small dents and scratches use Holts No Mix Filler Paste straight from the tube. Apply it according to the instructions in thin layers, using the spatula provided. It will harden in minutes if applied outdoors and may then be used as its own knifing putty.

Use a plane or file for initial shaping. Then, using progressively finer grades of wet-and-dry paper, wrapped round a sanding block, and copious amounts of clean water, rub down the filler until glass smooth. 'Feather' the edges of adjoining paintwork.

7 Protect adjoining areas before spraying the whole repair area and at least one inch of the surrounding sound paintwork with Holts Dupli-Color primer.

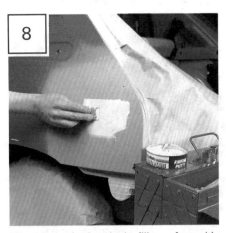

8 Fill any imperfections in the filler surface with a small amount of Holts Body Plus Knifing Putty. Using plenty of clean water, rub down the surface with a fine grade wet-and-dry paper – 400 grade is recommended – until it is really smooth.

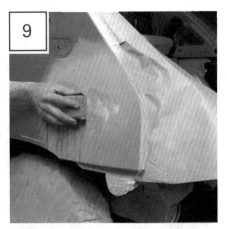

9 Carefully fill any remaining imperfections with knifing putty before applying the last coat of primer. Then rub down the surface with Holts Body Plus Rubbing Compound to ensure a really smooth surface.

10 Protect surrounding areas from overspray before applying the topcoat in several thin layers. Agitate Holts Dupli-Color aerosol thoroughly. Start at the repair centre, spraying outwards with a side-to-side motion.

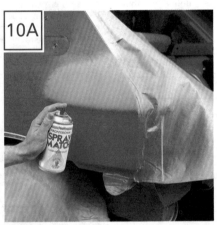

10A If the exact colour is not available off the shelf, local Holts Professional Spraymatch Centres will custom fill an aerosol to match perfectly.

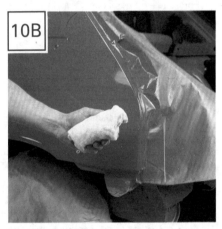

10B To identify whether a lacquer finish is required, rub a painted unrepaired part of the body with wax and a clean cloth.

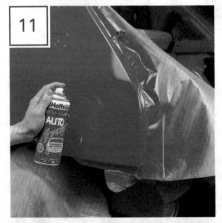

11 If *no* traces of paint appear on the cloth, spray Holts Dupli-Color clear lacquer over the repaired area to achieve the correct gloss level.

12 The paint will take about two weeks to harden fully. After this time it can be 'cut' with a mild cutting compound such as Turtle Wax Minute Cut prior to polishing with a final coating of Turtle Wax Extra.

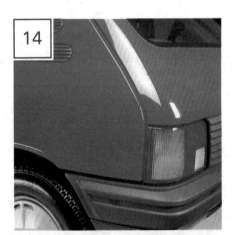

14 When carrying out bodywork repairs, remember that the quality of the finished job is proportional to the time and effort expended.

6.3 Tie a length of string to the wire

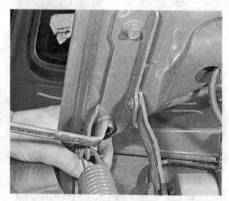
6.5 Removing the hinge-to-bonnet bolts

6.6 Hinge assembly is bolted to the inner wing

attachment bolts (photo), again marking the hinge-to-inner wing relationship before removal. Be extremely careful in dealing with the hinge springs if they are under tension.
7   Refitting is a reversal of this procedure, adjusting the bonnet as follows if necessary.
8   Fore-and-aft adjustment is by the elongated holes in the hinge-to-inner wing attachment.
9   Side-to-side adjustment is by the elongated holes in the hinge-to-bonnet attachment.
10 The height of the front of the bonnet is adjustable by screwing the rubber stops in or out.

7 Bonnet latch – removal and refitting

1   Remove the bolts securing the latch to the bonnet and lift off the latch (photo).
2   Adjustment of the lock pin is by undoing the locknut and using a screwdriver to screw the pin in or out to obtain satisfactory closing and opening of the bonnet.

8 Bonnet release cable and lock assembly – removal and refitting

1   To remove the cable, unhook the end from the bonnet lock; removing the front grille panel for access (Section 9).
2   Remove the cable clips securing the cable to the inner wing.
3   From inside the vehicle, grasp the release handle sleeve and pull the complete assembly into the interior of the vehicle.
4   Fit a new cable in the reverse order, sealing the hole in the engine bulkhead where the cable passes through with sealant.
5   Should the release cable snap in service, it is possible to release the bonnet by removing the splash guard from under the engine, and releasing the lock by levering against the operating lever with a screwdriver (photo).
6   The lock assembly can be removed by unhooking the cable and removing the bolts (photo).

9 Front grille panel – removal and refitting

1   Open the bonnet.
2   Depress the quick-release fasteners and turn them through 90° to release them (photo).
3   Pull the top edge of the grille forward, then lift the grille to release the locating spigots in the lower edge, and lift the grille away.
4   Refit in the reverse order, making sure the lower spigots are located properly.

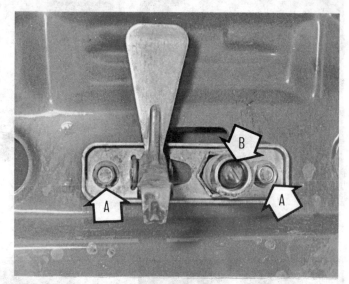
7.1 Bonnet latch showing (A) attachment bolts and (B) lock pin

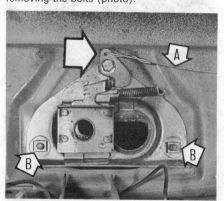
8.5 Bonnet lock assembly seen from below showing (A) release cable, (B) attachment bolts, and the release lever (arrowed)

8.6 Bonnet lock securing screws (arrowed)

9.2 Quick-release fasteners

10 Front wing – removal and refitting

1 Raise the front of the vehicle and remove the roadwheel.
2 Remove the plastic shield from under the wing (photos).
3 Remove the radiator grille, headlamp, front parking/direction indicator lamp cluster and headlamp wash/wipe if fitted.
4 Disconnect the bumper end fixing from the wing.

5 Remove the wing front fixing screws and those at the rear after opening the door fully for access.
6 Chisel through the spot welds at the bottom fixing plate.
7 Unscrew the top row of wing fixing bolts and remove the wing. The flange seal will have to be cut with a sharp knife to release the wing.
8 Refitting is a reversal of removal, spot welding is not essential. Apply undersealing compound and finish the exterior surface to match the body colour.

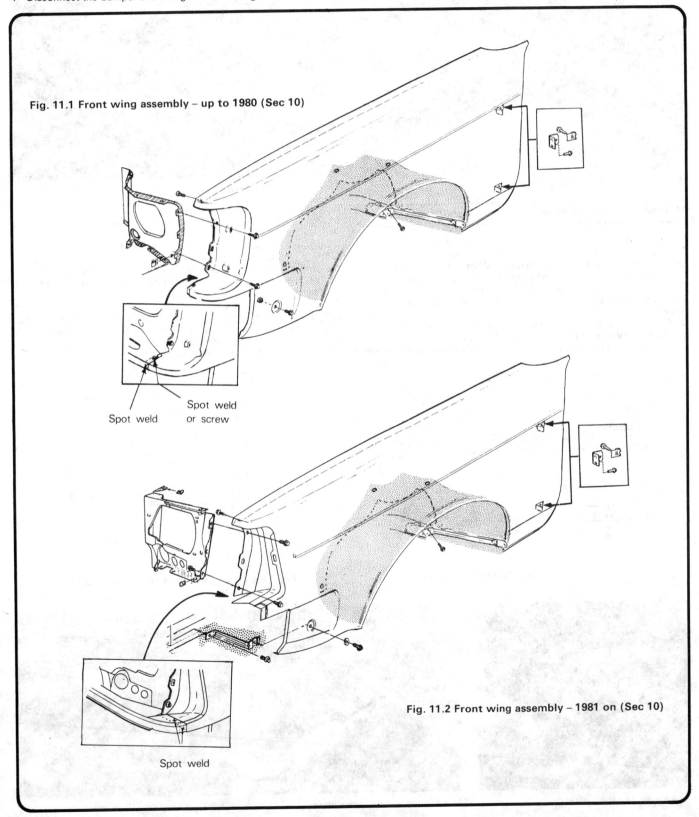

Fig. 11.1 Front wing assembly – up to 1980 (Sec 10)

Spot weld

Spot weld or screw

Fig. 11.2 Front wing assembly – 1981 on (Sec 10)

Spot weld

10.2A Plastic shield retaining bolt ...

10.2B ... and plastic button

11 Door interior trim panel – removal and refitting

Note: *The procedure for front and rear doors is similar.*

1   Prise out the plastic plugs from the armrest, and remove the screws securing the armrest to the door (photos). Where electric windows are fitted, slide the switch block out as the armrest is withdrawn.

2   The upper armrest attachment is in the form of a keyhole, and the armrest has to be swung downwards, around the upper attachment to release it (photo).

3   Prise off the cover from the window handle and remove the securing screw, then pull off the handle (photos).

4   Release the plastic fasteners from the door pockets by turning them through 90° and lift off the pocket.

5   Prise the trim panel from the door inner release handle and lift off the trim.

6   Unscrew the button from the door interior lock.

7   Prise off the interior trim panel, levering as close as is possible to the clips and working around the door until all the clips are free.

8   Disconnect any electrical wiring to door mounted components and then lift off the panel.

9   If access to the interior of the door is required, carefully remove the plastic sheet, which is stuck to the door by sealant. It is important that this sheet is refitted intact, as it is a moisture barrier. Where necessary, renew the sealant when refitting.

10   Refitting the trim panel is a reversal of removal.

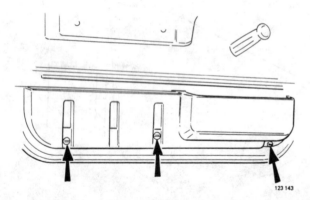

Fig. 11.3 Door pocket fasteners (Sec 11)

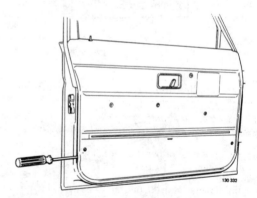

Fig. 11.4 Prising off the trim panel (Sec 11)

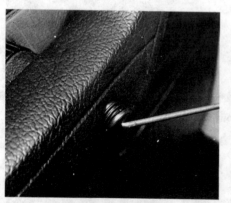

11.1A Prise out the plastic plug ...

11.1B ... and remove the screws

11.2 Releasing the upper armrest attachment

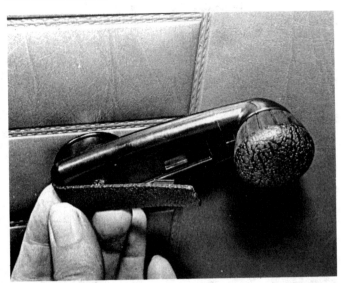

11.3A Removing the winder handle cover ...

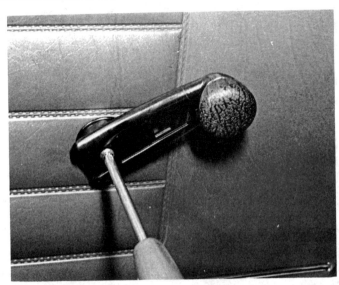

11.3B ... and securing screw

12 Doors – removal and refitting

1   Remove the door interior trim panel if necessary as described in Section 11.
2   Disconnect any wiring to electrical components in the door (refer to the relevant Section in this Chapter, or Chapter 12).
3   On early versions remove the pin from the door check strap.
4   On later versions the door check is part of the hinge assembly.
5   Support the door on a padded jack or axle stand, and have an assistant ready to steady the door.
6   Undo the hinge bolts from the door and lift the door away.
7   Refit in the reverse order, adjusting the door striker as described in Section 13.
8   Door positioning can be adjusted by adding or removing shims under the hinges.

13 Door locks, handles and latches – removal and refitting

Note: *The procedure for front and rear doors is similar. A general procedure is given here, and where differences occur, they are pointed out in the text.*
1   Remove the door interior panel as described in Section 11.

Exterior handle
2   Unhook the handle return spring and disconnect the handle-to-latch operating rod.
3   Remove the two screws securing the handle to the door and lift off the handle.
4   Refit in reverse order, adjusting the clearance between the operating rod eye end and the latch to the clearance shown in Fig. 11.9.
5   Adjustment is made by removing the clip securing the rod to the lever and screwing the rod in or out of the adjuster barrel (photo).

Lock and latch mechanism
6   Remove the two screws securing the lock cylinder retaining clip to the door edge and the Allen bolts securing the latch mechanism (photos).
Note: *On certain models produced around 1978-9, the lock cylinder clip was not screwed to the door edge. If a new lock cylinder is to be fitted, a retaining clip which can be screwed to the door edge should be fitted.*
7   Disconnect the operating rod from the exterior handle at the latch lever, and where fitted, the central locking motor control rod (see also Chapter 12) (photo).
8   On rear doors, disconnect the remote lock button operating rod.

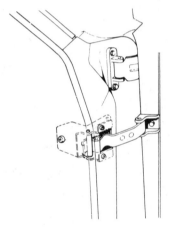

Fig. 11.5 Door check strap – early version (Sec 12)

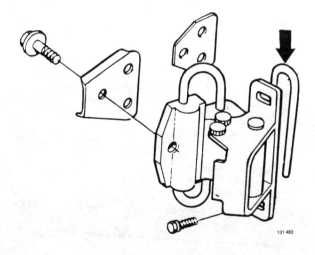

Fig. 11.6 Later type door check arrangement (Sec 12)

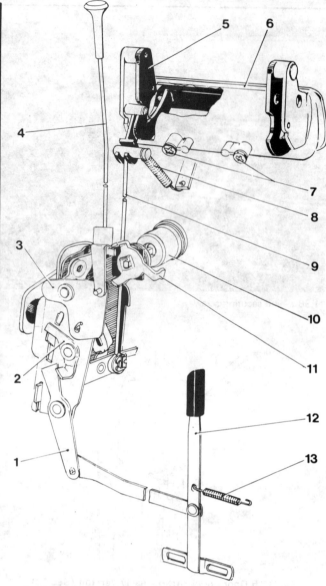

5
6
4
3
2
1
7
8
9
10
11
12
13

Fig. 11.7 Front door lock components (Sec 13)

1 Lever
2 Lever
3 Lever
4 Pullrod for lock button
5 Outer handle
6 Cover for outer handle
7 Screws for outer handle
8 Return spring for outer handle
9 Pullrod for outer handle
10 Lock cylinder
11 Lock device
12 Inner door opener
13 Return spring for inner door opener

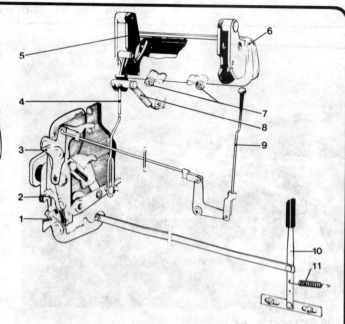

5
6
4
7
8
9
3
2
1
10
11

Fig. 11.8 Rear door lock components (Sec 13)

1 Lever for remote control
2 Lever for child safety door lock
3 Lever
4 Pullrod for outer handle
5 Outer handle
6 Cover for outer handle cover
7 Screws for outer handle cover
8 Return spring for outer handle
9 Pullrod for lock button
10 Inner door opener
11 Return spring for inner door opener

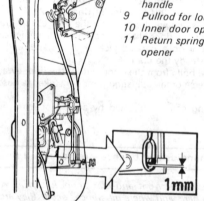

Fig. 11.9 Clearance between operating rod eye end and latch lever (Sec 13)

1mm

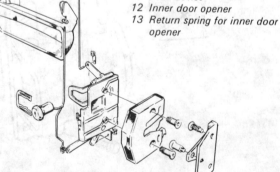

Fig. 11.10 Later type door lock component (Sec 13)

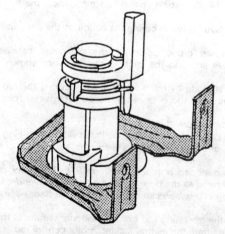

Fig. 11.11 Later type of lock cylinder securing clip (Sec 13)

13.5 Door exterior handle operating rod adjustment barrel (arrowed)

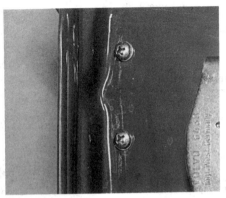

13.6A Lock cylinder securing screws

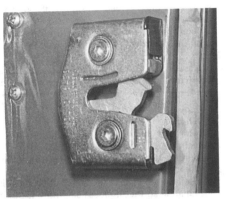

13.6B Latch mechanism securing bolts

13.7 Showing the spring clip (arrowed) which secures the operating rod(s)

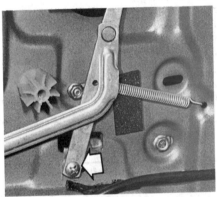

13.15 Interior release handle adjustment point (arrowed). Clearance should be 0.197 to 0.236 in (5.0 to 6.0 mm)

9   Lift out the latch assembly.
10 Prise out the lock cylinder retaining clip and lift out the lock. Disconnect the central locking system switch (when applicable).
11 The lock can be dismantled by removing the circlip, but if it is worn it is best renewed.
12 Refitting is a reversal of removal, but note the following. The door latch mechanism was modified in 1978, and if a new type latch mechanism is to be fitted to an old type door, then location holes must be drilled in the door edge as shown in Fig. 11.12.

Interior release handle
13 Unhook the return spring and the operating lever from the latch assembly.
14 Remove the screw and lift out the handle and lever.
15 On refitting, adjust the operating lever-to-handle clearance by means of the retaining screw elongated hole (photo).

Latch striker plate
16 Remove the striker plate securing screws and lift off the plate. Refit in the reverse order then adjust the plate as follows.
17 Loosen the securing screws so that the striker can just be moved by hand.
18 Close the door, holding the exterior handle in so that it cannot operate.
19 The striker plate will take up the correct position as the door is closed.
20 Open the door again. Tighten the striker plate screws, outboard screws first, then the inner.
21 Check that the door closes smoothly without undue force and does not lift as the latch engages with the striker.
22 If the latch striker plate is too far in, loosen the screws slightly and lever it outwards, keeping it at the same horizontal plane.
23 Fore-and-aft adjustment is by shims under the plate.

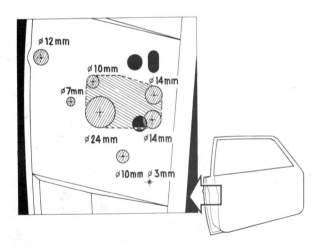

Fig. 11.12 Location of holes to be drilled when fitting a new lock assembly to an old door (Sec 13)

Shaded areas to be cut out

14 Front and rear door window lift mechanism – removal and refitting

Note: *For electric window components see Chapter 12.*
1   Free the window from the lift mechanism as described in Section
15. Raise the window and wedge or tape it securely in position.
2   Remove the bolts securing the lift mechanism to the door inner

skin, then lift the mechanism out through the lower aperture in the door.

3   Refit in reverse order, but do not fully tighten the securing bolts until the window is refitted and wound fully up.

15 Front and rear door windows – removal and refitting

1   Lower the window.
2   Remove the door inner trim panel as described in Section 11.
3   Remove the locking washers from the window lift arms, then detach the lift arms from the lift channel.
4   Lift the window and lift channel up and out of the door, swinging it to the inside of the door.
5   Refit in the reverse order, adjusting the window fore and aft in the lift channel so that it closes smoothly without binding.

16 Boot lid – removal and refitting

1   The boot lid is mounted on two hinges, which are attached to the boot lid by two bolts, and to the rear pillars by three bolts.
2   The lid is counter-balanced by spring dampers.
3   To remove the boot lid, mark across the lid and hinge before undoing the lid-to-hinge bolts and lifting off the lid.
4   If the hinges and balance spring assembly are to be removed, make up a tool as shown in Fig. 11.17 to keep the damper compressed before removing the mounting bolts.
5   Refitting is a reversal of removal, elongated holes in the hinge attachment providing for lid adjustment.

17 Boot lid lock and latch – removal and refitting

Note: For central locking types see Chapter 12.
1   On early types, the lock and latch are in the rear valance and the striker plate is in the boot lid. On later models this is reversed.

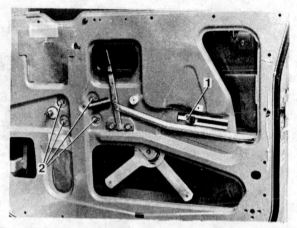

Fig. 11.13 Removing the window lift mechanism (Sec 14)

1   Locking washer   2   Securing bolts

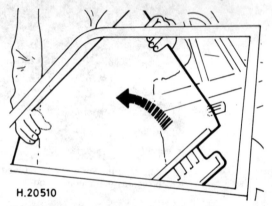

H.20510

Fig. 11.14 Lifting out a front door window (Sec 15)

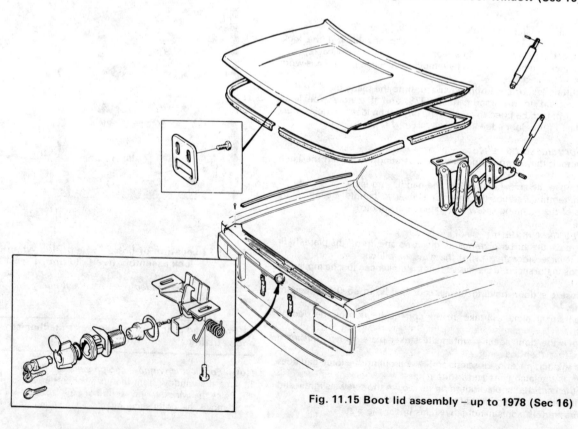

Fig. 11.15 Boot lid assembly – up to 1978 (Sec 16)

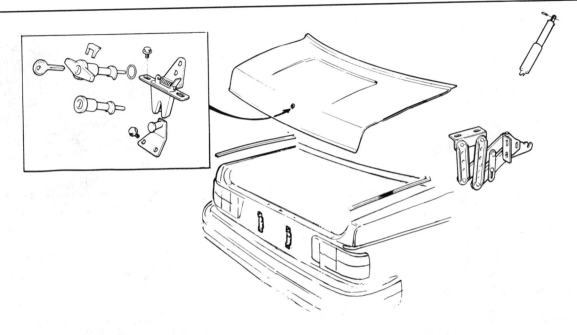

Fig. 11.16 Later type boot lid assembly – 1979 on (Sec 16)

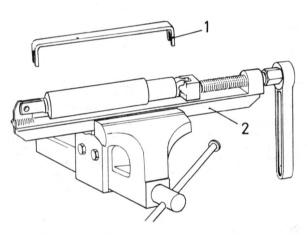

Fig. 11.17 Tool for keeping the damper compressed (1) and
for compressing new dampers (2) (Sec 16)

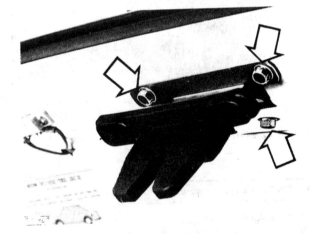

Fig. 11.18 Boot lid lock protective plate and securing bolts
(Sec 17)

2   To remove the latch or striker plate, undo the bolts securing them to
the valance or boot lid. **Note:** *On some models the lock cylinder may
be secured to the latch by a further screw or bolt which should also be
undone.*
3   Refit in the reverse order, adjusting the latch or striker in the
elongated holes to obtain correct closure of the boot lid.

Lock cylinder
4   The lock cylinder may be of the type only turned with a key, or may
have a handle, or have 'wings' with which to turn it.
5   To remove the lock cylinder, prise out the clip securing it to the
valance or boot lid. This can be awkward where the lock is in the
double skin.
6   Where fitted, remove the screw or bolt securing the cylinder to the
latch.
7   Lift out the lock cylinder.
8   The cylinder can be further dismantled by removing the circlip and
return spring, but if it is worn or broken it is better to renew the
cylinder.
9   If the cylinder is dismantled, on reassembly, tension the return
spring by engaging its end in the recess in the lock, connecting the
other end to the lock cylinder and turning the lock clockwise so that
the spring can be tensioned by one notch.
10   Refitting is a reversal of removal.

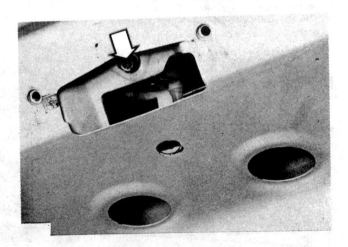

Fig. 11.19 Boot lock cylinder securing bolt (Sec 17)

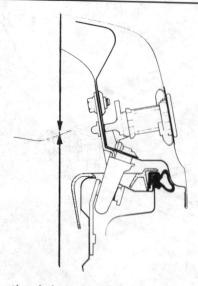

Fig. 11.20 Sectional view of later type boot lock (Sec 17)

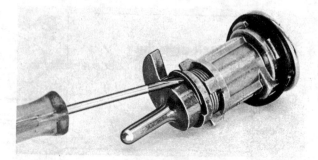

Fig. 11.21 Removing the lock cylinder securing clip (Sec 17)

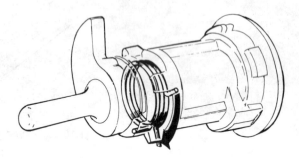

Fig. 11.23 Tensioning the boot lock cylinder return spring (Sec 17)

Fig. 11.22 Boot lock cylinder return spring (Sec 17)

18 Tailgate trim panel – removal and refitting

1   Open the tailgate.
2   Pull off the internal release handle plastic cover, then remove the screws from the plastic surround and remove the surround (photo).
3   Prise out the trim panel clips around the edge of the panel, levering as close as possible to the clips, working around the door edge and supporting the panel in the middle as you do so. Remove the panel when all the clips are released.
4   Refit in the reverse order.

19 Tailgate – removal and refitting

1   Disconnect the battery negative terminal.
2   Open the tailgate and remove the interior trim panel as described in Section 18.
3   Disconnect all electrical equipment in the tailgate, marking the terminals for refitting. Disconnect the washer tube. All the wires must be pulled out of the tailgate at the point where they enter near to the hinges.
4   Remove the spring retainer from the tailgate strut balljoint (photo).
5   Remove the spring clip from the other end of the strut (photo).
6   On early models, prise out the rubber covers which conceal the hinge bolts. On later models the hinge bolt is visible (photo). Loosen the hinge bolts, but do not remove them at this stage.
7   You will need at least two men to hold the tailgate open while the struts are removed (the balljoints pull off) (photo) and the hinge bolts are removed. Lift the tailgate away.
8   Refitting is a reversal of removal, only finally tightening the hinge bolts when the tailgate is adjusted for fit, which is provided for by

18.2 Pulling off the tailgate internal release plastic cover. The surround retaining screws are also visible

19.4 Balljoint retaining spring partly removed

19.5 Removing the spring clip from the door end of the strut

19.6 Tailgate hinge bolt on later models

19.7 Pull off the balljoint

elongated bolt holes.

9   If the hinge which is left in position on the roof structure has to be removed, the securing bolts are accessible after pulling down the roof lining material which is stretched over the lip of the roof edge.

20 Tailgate lock, latch and handle – removal and refitting

1   Remove the interior trim panel as described in Section 18.

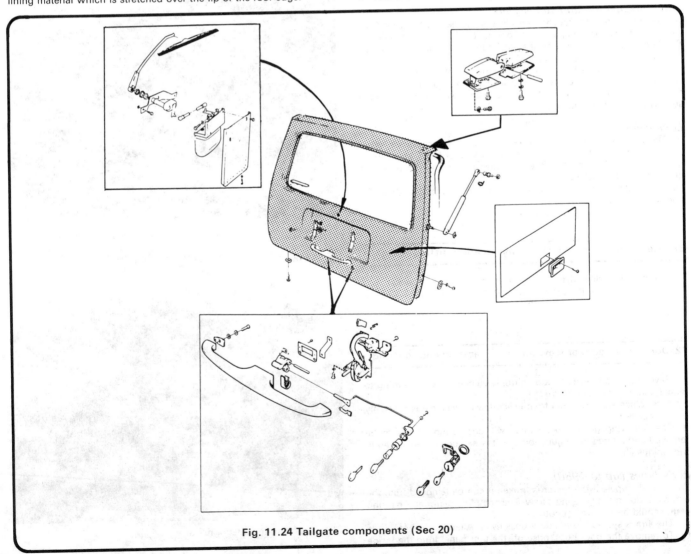

Fig. 11.24 Tailgate components (Sec 20)

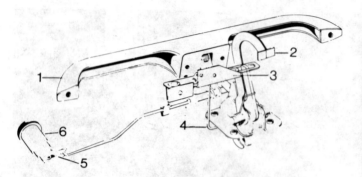

Fig. 11.25 Tailgate lock components (Sec 20)

1 Outer handle
2 Inside opener
3 Latching device for inner
   opener
4 Control for latching device
5 Eccentric
6 Lock cylinder

Exterior handle

2 Disconnect the lock-to-handle operating rod. Where fitted, also disconnect the central locking rod from the motor (refer to Chapter 12).
3 Remove the screws securing the handle to the tailgate skin and lift off the handle.
4 Refitting is a reversal of removal.

Latch mechanism and striker plate

5 To remove the latch mechanism, disconnect the operating rod from the lock, and where fitted, the rod from the central locking motor.
6 Remove the bolts securing the mechanism to the tailgate (photo) and lift off the latch assembly.
7 The striker plate is bolted to the luggage area floor (photo).
8 When refitting, which is a reversal of removal, adjust the striker plate in the elongated holes so that the tailgate closes firmly against the seal without undue slamming.

Lock cylinder

9 The lock cylinder is secured by a screw accessible from inside, or by a locking spring plate in similar fashion to the door locks, and can be removed after disconnecting the operating rods to the latch, and if fitted, the central locking motor.
10 Further dismantling of the lock cylinder is as described for door and boot lock cylinders.
11 Refitting is a reversal of removal.

---

21 Interior rear view mirror – removal and refitting

1 The mirror is clipped to the baseplate by a ball-and-socket type joint. Turn the mirror through 90° and pull it off the baseplate (photo).
2 The baseplate is screwed to the roof.
3 Refit in reverse order.

---

22 Door-mounted rear view mirrors – removal and refitting

1 Several different types of door mirror have been fitted according to model and year of manufacture.
2 Later types are adjustable from inside the vehicle, either manually or electrically.
3 The following general procedures will enable most types to be removed and refitted in conjunction with the exploded views given in the various illustrations.

Early types (up to 1980)

4 On early types, if the mirror is broken it can be removed from the arm by undoing the securing screw. The complete mirror and backing plate should be renewed (photo).
5 The arm is secured to the door boss by an Allen bolt (photo).
6 To remove the door boss, prise off the trim panel from the inside

20.6 Latch mechanism securing bolts

20.7 Striker plate retaining bolts

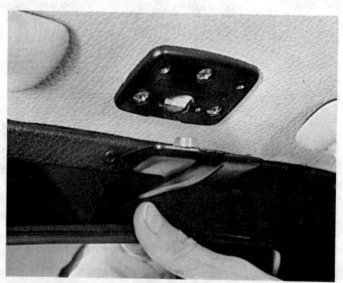

21.1 Removing the interior mirror

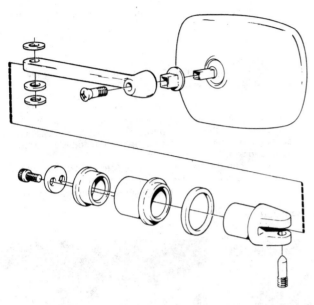

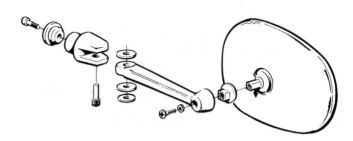

Fig. 11.27 Rear view mirror assembly – 1978 to 1979 (Sec 22)

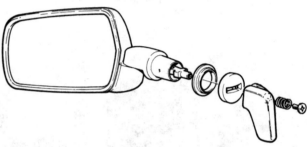

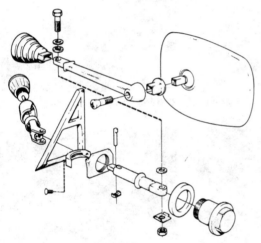

Fig. 11.26 Rear view mirror assembly – up to 1977 (Sec 22)

Fig. 11.29 Manually-adjustable mirror – 1980 on (Sec 22)

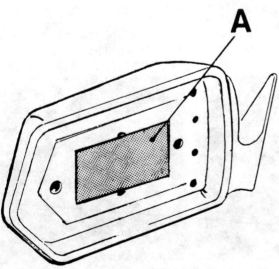

Fig. 11.28 Manually-adjustable mirror – 1975 to 1980 (Sec 22)

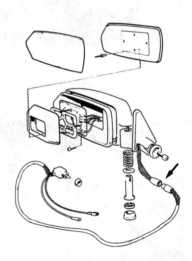

Fig. 11.30 Electrically-operated mirror (Sec 20)

Electrical connector on early types arrowed

front corner of the window and undo the Allen bolt securing the bolt to the window (photo). Refit in the reverse order.

Later types (1980 to 1985)
7 An exploded view of these types appears in Fig. 11-29.
8 The mirror is attached to the backplate by an adhesive pad.
9 To remove the mirror if it is broken, prise off the mirror glass with a wide-bladed tool (there is no need to remove the complete assembly from the door, and removal will be made easier if the mirror glass is gently warmed with a heat gun to soften the adhesive). Take precautions against being cut by wearing heavy gloves and eye protection.
10 Clean off the old adhesive using a solvent.
11 A new adhesive pad should be supplied with the new mirror glass. Peel off the backing paper and stick the pad to the backplate. If any air bubbles are trapped beneath the pad, puncture them with a pin.

Fig. 11.31 Mirror assembly secured by adhesive pad – A (Sec 22)

12 Press the new glass into positon, pressing only on the centre of the glass to avoid breaking it.

Later types (1985 on)

Note: *There is no need to remove the complete assembly from the door to change the glass. We did for photographic purposes.*

13 The mirror glass is secured to the mirror assembly by a plastic locking ring.

14 To remove the mirror, press the lower edge of the glass inwards to line up the locking ring with the hole in the lower edge of the mirror assembly, then insert a thin screwdriver into the hole and lever the locking ring to the right to unlock it and release the mirror glass (photos).

15 Fitting the new glass is a reversal of this procedure.

16 To remove the complete assembly from the door, first remove the door interior trim panel.

17 Pull or prise off the trim panel from the mirror control (photo).

18 Remove the spring clip and securing bolts (photo).

19 Pull the mirror away from the door, guiding the control lever through the hole in the door (photo).

20 Refit in reverse order, ensuring the rubber grommet is correctly located (photo).

Electrically-operated types

21 The motor is located in the mirror assembly, behind the glass.

22 On pre-1979 types, the connector for the electrical leads is located in the door, on later types it is located behind the fusebox.

23 Removal and refitting procedures are similar to that described for the manually-adjusted mirrors, with the addition of disconnecting the wiring and feeding the wires through as the mirror assembly is removed. Note that the mirrors may be fixed with adhesive, or on later types, with a locking ring.

24 The motor can be removed without removing the complete assembly from the door, by removing the glass and undoing the screws securing the motor to the backing plate, after removing the rubber cover over the motor.

25 Refit in reverse order.

22.4 Early type mirror-to-arm securing screw

22.5 Arm is secured to the door boss by an Allen bolt

22.6 Removing the door boss from the window

22.14A Releasing the locking ring to remove the mirror

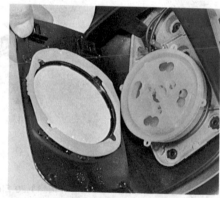
22.14B Mirror removed showing the locking ring

22.17 Pulling off the trim panel from the control lever

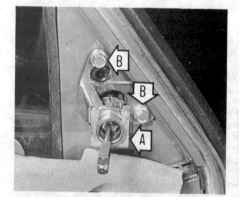
22.18 Spring clip (A) and securing bolts (B)

22.19 Removing the mirror assembly from the door

22.20 Ensure the rubber grommet (arrowed) is correctly located

24.2 Mudflap securing bolts

25.1 Underbody protective panel retaining bolt

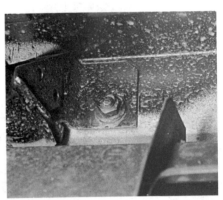

26.5 Typical impact absorber mounting bolt

23 Windscreen and fixed windows – removal and refitting

1   The removal and refitting of the windscreen and fixed windows is best left to specialist windscreen firms.
2   Apart from the need for special tools and adhesives, the risk of breaking a screen or window during removal or refitting is high, and replacement costs expensive, so let the specialist take the risk.

24 Mudflaps – removal and refitting

1   This procedure refers to original standard equipment only.
2   Remove the two bolts securing the mudflap to the wheel arch (photo).
3   Refit in the reverse order, using a sealant or anti-corrosion liquid on the bolt threads.

25 Underbody protective panels – removal and refitting

1   The underbody protective panels are secured by bolts (photo).
2   When removing them, support the centre of the panel until all the bolts are removed, then lift the panel away.

3   Refitting is a reversal of removal.

26 Bumpers – removal and refitting

1   The bumpers may be attached to the body by rubber type impact absorbers (early models) or by gas-filled absorbers (later models). Gas-filled absorbers are fitted to the front bumper only, the rear bumper being attached to an iron bracket.
2   To remove the bumper, first pull off the rubbing strip, being careful not to damage the rubber studs by which it is attached. Some types of rubbing strip use clips and a retaining strip, and may also have studs, secured by a nut accessible from inside the boot/luggage area after the flooring is removed.
3   Remove the nuts/bolts from the side wrap-around mounting.
4   Remove the nuts securing the bumper to the impact absorber or mounting bracket, and remove the bumper.
5   The impact absorber or mounting can then be removed by removing the bolts attaching them to the bodywork (photo).
6   The rubber cover over the bumper can be removed after prising off the clips on the inside of the bumper.
7   Refitting is a reversal of removal.
Note: *Do not weld or use excess heat near to gas-filled absorbers as there is a risk of explosion. Dispose of defective units safely.*

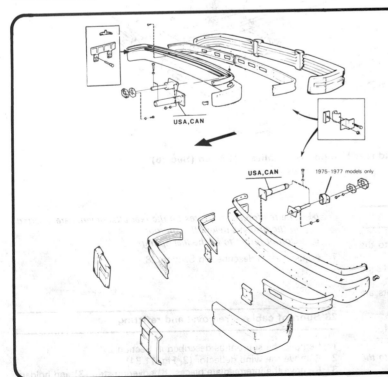

Fig. 11.32 Front and rear bumper assemblies – up to 1980 (Sec 26)

Large arrow indicates front of car

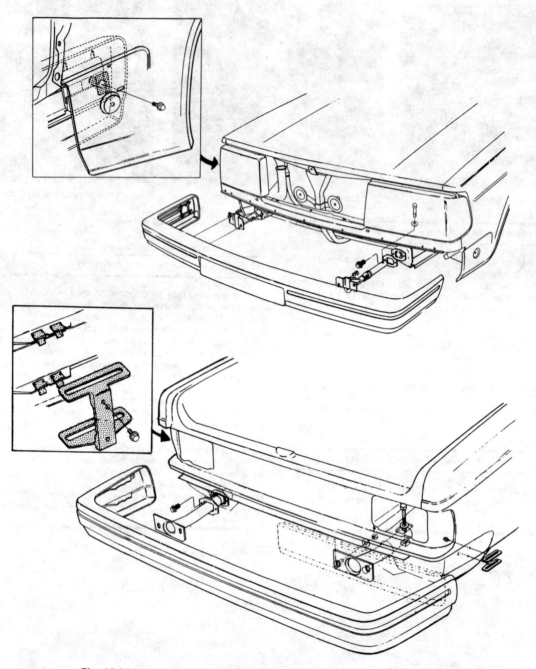

Fig. 11.33 Later type front and rear bumper assemblies – 1981 on (Sec 26)

27 Sunroof – removing and refitting

1   Remove the wind deflector if fitted, and wind the sunroof to the half-open position.
2   Release the headlining from the front edge of the sunroof and slide the headlining rearwards.
3   Now wind the sunroof forwards until the rearmost brackets are exposed.
4   Mark the relationship of the brackets to the sunroof.
5   Remove the screws from the brackets and lift off the sunroof.
6   Refitting is a reversal of removal, but note the following points:

   a)   Fit the sunroof with the roof attachments wound back to the rearmost position

   b)   The reinforcement plates on the rear attachments are inserted in the grooves below the sunroof
   c)   Do not forget to fit the leaf springs
7   Adjustment is described in Section 28.

28 Sunroof cables – removal and refitting

1   Remove the sunroof as described in Section 27.
2   Remove the wind deflector (2, Fig. 11.34).
3   Remove the intermediate pieces (8) covering strip (3) and holders

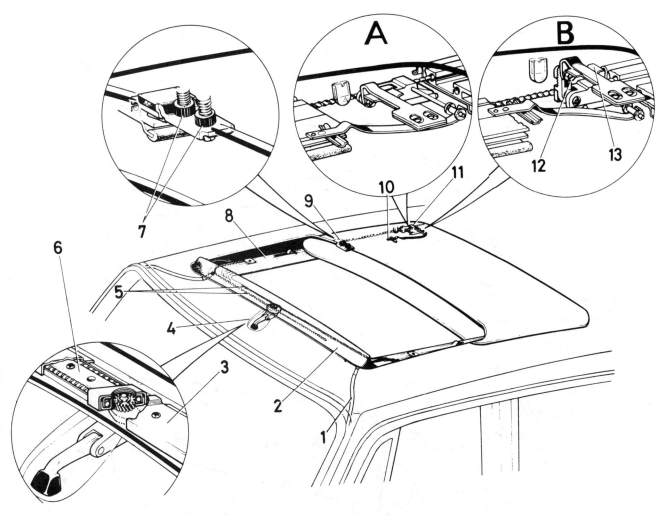

Fig. 11.34 Sunroof assembly (Secs 27 and 28)

1 Drain hose	5 Cables
2 Wind deflector	6 Front guide rail
3 Cover strip	7 Front adjustment
4 Crank housing with crank	8 Intermediate piece

9 Front attachment	13 Reinforcing plate
10 Leaf spring	A Rear attachment – roof open
11 Rear attachment	B Rear attachment – roof
12 Rear adjustment	closed

above the drive. Release the front guide rails (6) and pull out the cables (5).

4 Fit replacement cables so that the attachments for the sunroof come opposite each other at the rear end of the roof opening. Screw the front guide rails on securely.

5 Refit the intermediate pieces, holders, covering plate and the wind deflector.

6 Screw on the roof securely and put back the leaf springs.

7 Crank the sunroof forwards until it is completely closed and check that it is level with the main roof. If necessary, adjust at the front and rear attachments (7 and 12, Fig. 11.34). Check that the lifts on the rear attachments are pushed up when the roof is closed (B, Fig. 11.34).

8 When the roof is closed the crank should point straight forwards in the vehicle. If it does not, unscrew the crank and gear housing, turn the crank to the stop position and replace.

29 Heater fan control switch – removal and refitting

1 Disconnect the battery negative terminal.

2 Remove the side panels from the centre console and the sound proofing panel on the driver's side only.

3 Pull off the control switch knob.

4 Undo the nut securing the switch to the console panel.

5 Reach up behind the centre console, and locate and pull out the switch.

6 Take note of the cable connections before disconnecting the switch.

7 Refit in the reverse order.

30 Heater controls and cables – removal and refitting

1 Disconnect the battery negative terminal.

2 Remove the centre console side panels and the soundproofing panels from the footwell areas.

3 Remove the radio.

4 Remove the centre console plastic outer panel.

5 Remove the screws securing the metal support panel and the heater control panel (photos), and pull the support panel forward as far as is possible, giving sufficient room for the control panel to be manipulated.

6 Pull the knob off the control panel quadrant on which the cable is to be renewed.

Note: *Before carrying out the next operation, move the heater controls to minimum, and note which position the heater shutter or water valve lever has taken up. When refitting the cable, set the shutter or water control valve to that position before fitting the cable spring clips.*

7 Remove the cable clips at each end of the cable, then unhook the cable from the shutter/water valve end first, then from the control quadrant (photos).

8 Refitting is a reversal of removal. Make sure the shutter/water valve

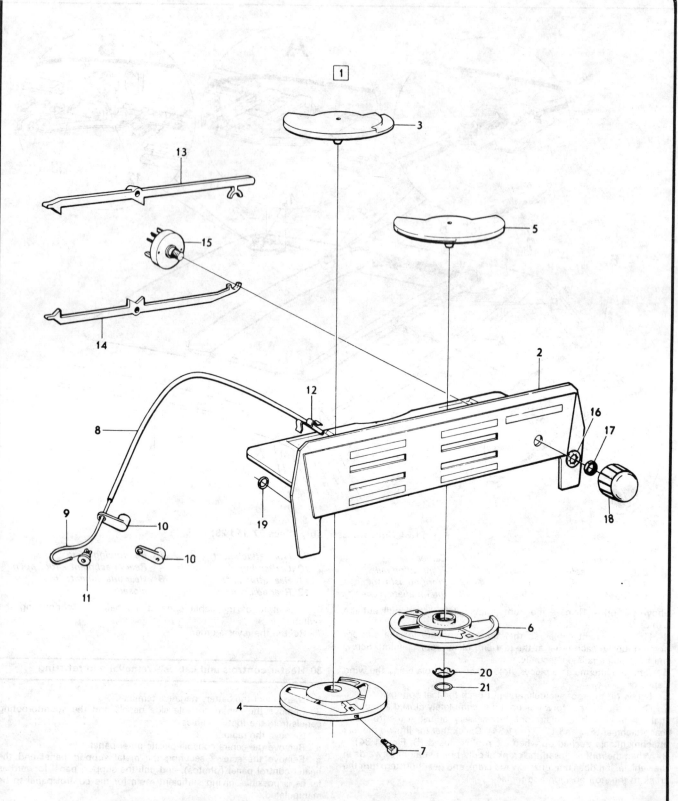

Fig. 11.35 Exploded view of heater controls (Secs 29 and 30)

1 Heater control	7 Knob	12 Clip	17 Nut
2 Control panel	8 Outer cable	13 Light distributor	18 Knob
3 TEMP control disc	9 Inner cable	14 Light distributor	19 Washer
4 AIRMIX control disc	10 Crank	15 Fan switch	20 Spring washer
5 DEF control disc	11 Cable holder	16 Washer	21 Washer
6 FLOOR control disc			

30.5A Metal support panel securing screw at lower edge

30.5B Upper securing screw (A) and heater control panel screw (B)

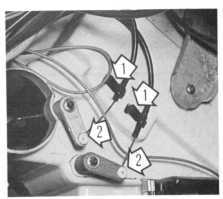

30.7A Control cable securing clips (1) and control levers (2)

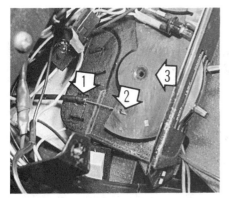

30.7B Control quadrant viewed from above showing (1) cable clip, (2) cable hooked into quadrant and (3) quadrant

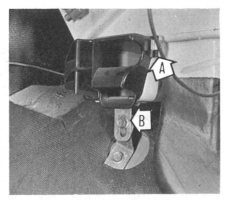

31.3 Floor air vent showing (A) clips and (B) lower mounting bolt

31.4 Rear compartment duct securing bolt

31.5 Hose clamps fitted to the heater hoses

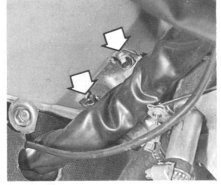

31.12 Upper bracket bolts (arrowed)

is positioned as previously noted, then fit the spring clips and check that they operate over their full range, adjusting the cables in the clips as necessary.

31 Heater unit – renewal and refitting

See note on water valve modification in Section 32 before starting work.

1   Disconnect the battery negative lead.
2   Remove the centre console side panels and the sound proofing panels from both footwell areas. Pull back the carpeting.
3   Remove the floor air vents, secured by clips, and remove the bolts from the lower mountings (photo).
4   Remove the rear compartment ducts secured by one bolt each (photo).
5   Either drain the cooling system as described in Chapter 2, or fit

hose clamps to the heater hoses where they pass through the bulkhead (photo).
6   Disconnect both hoses where they join the heater unit, being prepared for spillage as you undo the hose clips.
7   On early models, disconnect the water valve hose (after clamping it if the system has not been drained). Remove the screws from the valve mounting bracket and disconnect the valve control cable.
8   Lay the valve to one side, being careful not to bend the capillary tube too sharply. This point will also have to be watched when finally removing the heater.
9   On later models, the water valve remains in position, just carefully pull the capillary tube from the housing through the hole in the side casing.
10 Disconnect the heater control cables and fan switch connections. Also disconnect the earth wire for the switch.
Note: *The earth wire may be connected by a screw which secures the heater unit to an upper bracket. There is another screw higher up and*

both should be removed.

11 Remove the glovebox and facia side vents (Sections 35 and 37) and disconnect and remove the ducting behind them.

12 Remove the bolts from the heater upper brackets (photo).

13 Disconnect the heater drain hose on the right-hand side.

14 Lift the heater out sideways and to the left.

15 Refitting is a reversal of removal, adjusting the control cables as described in Section 30. Ensure that all ducting is refitted correctly and top up or refill the cooling system as described in Chapter 2 on completion.

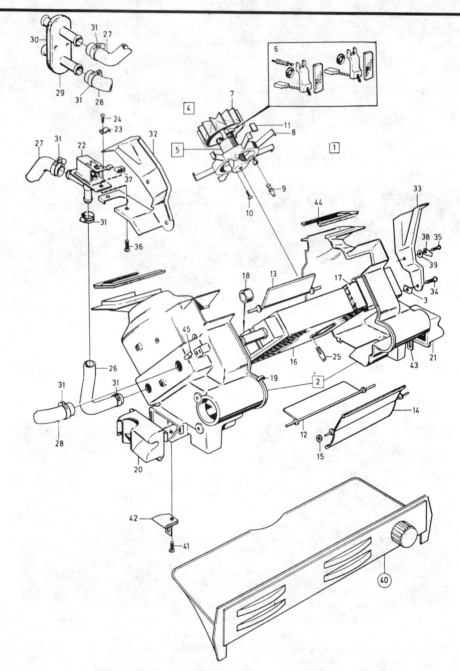

Fig. 11.36 Exploded view of the heater assembly (Sec 31)

1	Heater	13	Shutter, defroster
2	Casing	15	Catch washer
3	Clip	16	Matrix
4	Fan	17	Gasket
5	Motor	18	Seal ring
6	Carbon brush kit	19	Clip
7	Fan wheel	20	Air distributor, left
8	Flap	21	Air distributor, right
9	Pad	22	Control valve
10	Screw	23	Clamp
11	Gasket	24	Screw
12	Shutter, floor		

25	Capillary holder
26	Hose
27	Hose
28	Hose
29	Grommet
30	Spacer
31	Hose clamp
32	Bracket, left
33	Bracket, right
34	Screw
35	Screw

36	Screw
37	Spring nut
38	Flat pin
39	Washer
40	Heater control
41	Screw
42	Clamp, left
43	Clamp, right
44	Gasket
45	Clip

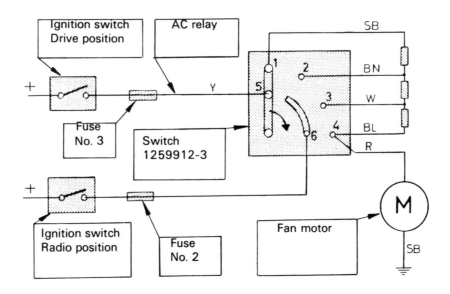

Fig. 11.37 Wiring diagram for later type blower motor (Sec 31)

For colour code refer to wiring diagrams in Chapter 12

32 Heater water valve – removal and refitting

Note: *On early models, the capillary tube was routed between the two halves of the heater casing and into the internal airflow. On later models, the heater as a hole and rubber plug in the casing for this purpose. When removing an earlier type valve, snip off the capillary tube close to where it enters the casing, retrieving the end from inside the ducting, and modify the casing as described later in the text.*

1 Carry out the operations described in paragraphs 1 to 3 in Section 31, but on the left-hand side only.

2 Clamp the water valve inlet and outlet hoses, or drain the cooling system as described in Chapter 2. Disconnect the hoses.

3 On earlier types, snip off the capillary tube where it enters the casing, as described above.

4 On later types, pull the capillary tube from the casing.

5 Remove the valve securing screws, lower the valve and disconnect the control cable.

6 Remove the valve.

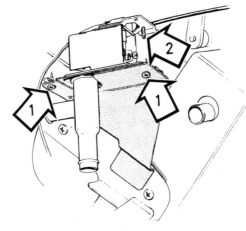

Fig. 11.38 Water valve securing screws (1) and control cable attachment (2) (Sec 32)

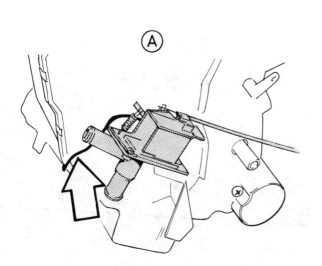

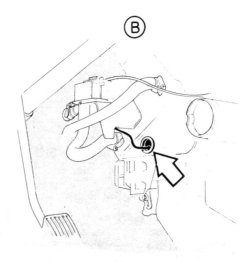

Fig. 11.39 Early type capillary tube (A) and later type (B) (Sec 32)

7   To modify an older type heater to accept the new capillary tube, cut a hole in the side casing using a hole saw, to the dimensions shown in Fig. 11.40. The hole must be positioned so that when fitted, the capillary tube will not foul the air shutter on the inside.

8   Fit the rubber plug to the new capillary tube (for the older types, these plugs are available from your Volvo dealer) then wind the tube loosely around a 1/2 in (14.0 mm) piece of tubing into a spring shape. Remove the tubing.

9   Connect the control cable and fit the valve back to the housing.

10 Push the capillary tube through the hole in the side casing, and ensure that it does not foul the shutter. Fit the rubber plug.

11 Reconnect the hoses and remove the clamps.

12 The remaining procedure is a reversal of removal. On completion, top up or refill the cooling system as described in Chapter 2.

33 Heater matrix and fan assembly – renewal

1   Remove the heater as described in Section 31.

2   Separate the two halves of the heater casing by removing the securing clips.

3   The heater matrix can now be lifted out. If a new matrix is being fitted, transfer the seal from the old to the new matrix before fitting the matrix back into the casing.

4   If the fan motor is to be renewed, lift it from the casing, and remove the two screws securing it to the fan frame. Transfer the fan to the new motor.

5   Refit the fan and motor assembly to the frame and re-install in the casing.

6   Before fitting the two casing halves together, apply sealant to the mating surface of one half, then fit the other half to it and fit the securing clips.

7   Refit the heater as described in Section 31.

34 Under-dash soundproofing panels – removal and refitting

1   The soundproofing panels under the dash and to each side of the centre console/heater assembly are secured either by large plastic screws, self-tapping screws, or clips. In some cases all three methods may be utilised.

2   Remove whichever fixing method is encountered and lift out the panels.

3   Refit in the reverse order.

35 Glovebox – removal and refitting

1   Open the glovebox lid.

2   Remove the securing screws (photo).

3   Pull the glovebox forward sufficiently to enable the wires to the light and microswitch (when fitted) to be disconnected.

4   Remove the glovebox.

5   Refit in the reverse order.

36 Centre console – removal and refitting

Note: *The centre console design was changed in 1980/81 model year. The procedure given here is a general guide only, as the specific procedure will vary according to model year and equipment levels.*

1   Disconnect the battery negative terminal.

2   Remove the ashtray.

3   Remove the radio if fitted.

4   Remove the screws securing the plastic outer panel to the inner metal support frame.

5   Pull the plastic outer panel off the support frame and disconnect all switches noting their connections (one way to do this is to remove each switch in turn and reconnect it to the leads after removal. See Chapter 12 for switch removal).

6   Remove the plastic outer panel.

7   If further dismantling of the support frame is required, the heater control panel should be removed as described in Sections 29 and 30.

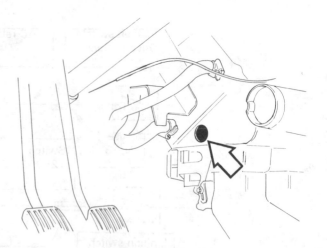

Fig. 11.40 Location of hole to be cut for modified capillary tube

(Sec 32)

Hole diameter is 0.827 in (21.0 mm)

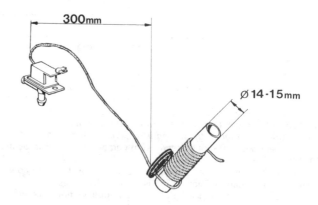

Fig. 11.41 Forming the capillary tube into a spring shape

(Sec 32)

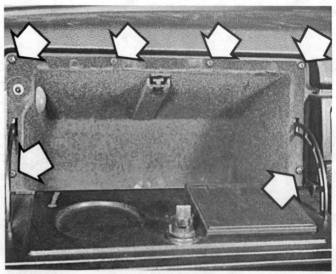

35.2 Glovebox securing screws (arrowed)

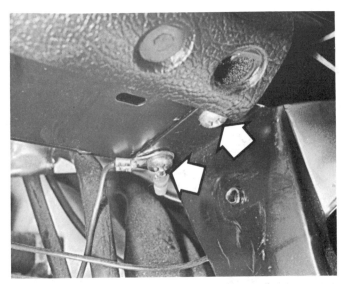

36.8A Support frame upper mounting screws (arrowed) ...

36.8B ... and the lower ones. Note the earth wires (arrowed)

8   Remove the support frame mounting screws, noting that some of them may have earth wires under them (photos) and pull out the frame.
9   Refitting is a reversal of removal, carrying out a functional check of all disturbed systems after the battery has been reconnected.

37 Facia panel – removal and refitting

Note: *The following procedure is a suggested method only, the specific procedure depending on the degree to which the facia panel and instruments etc. need to be removed, and the equipment level of the model being worked on. Reference should also be made to Figs. 11.43 and 11.44, which give an exploded view of the two types of facia, and to the relevant Sections of this Chapter and Chapter 12 for removal of heater controls, switches etc.*

1   Disconnect the battery negative terminal.
2   Remove the steering column shroud panels, and if required for greater access, the steering wheel (Chapter 10).
3   Remove the centre console (Section 36).
4   Remove the instrument panel (Chapter 12).
5   Remove the auxiliary instrument panel, if fitted.
6   Remove the glovebox (Section 35).
7   Pull off the padding strip from along the front edge of the facia panel.
8   This will reveal the screws which secure the air vent outlets to the facia. Remove these screws and pull out the vents (photos).

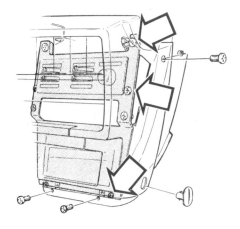

Fig. 11.42 Centre console securing screws (Sec 36)

37.8A Removing the screws from the left ...

37.8B ... and right-hand vent ...

37.8C ... and removing the vents (right-hand vent shown)

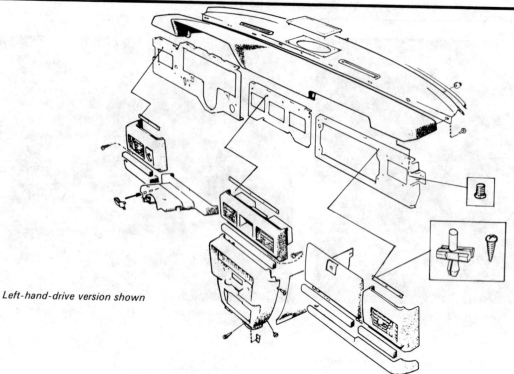

Left-hand-drive version shown

Fig. 11.43 Exploded view of the facia panel – up to 1980 (Sec 37)

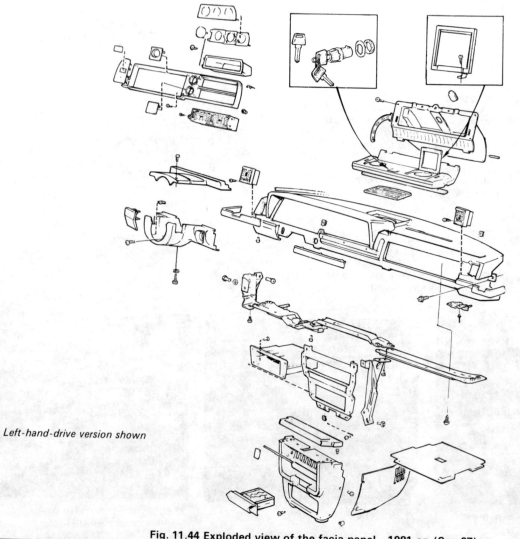

Left-hand-drive version shown

Fig. 11.44 Exploded view of the facia panel – 1981 on (Sec 37)

9 The remaining procedure consists of working around the facia panel, removing the screws and clips which secure the crash padding to the under-frame. The under-frame can then be removed if desired by removing its securing screws/bolts.

10 Take careful note of all the screws and bolts you remove, as they can be of different sizes for different locations, and some will have earth wires or relay clips secured under them.

11 Refitting is a reversal of removal, carrying out a functional check of all disturbed instruments and systems after the battery has been reconnected.

38 Handbrake level console – removal and refitting

1 Remove the rear ashtray and prise out the insert (photos).

2 Push out the seat belt warning light and rear courtesy light and disconnect the wiring (photo).

3 Similarly, prise out and disconnect the seat heating pad switches if they are fitted.

4 Slide both front seats forward as far as they will go and remove the screws from the rear sides of the console.

5 Lift the console rear edge, slide it forward off the locating tongue at the front (photo) and lift the console from over the handbrake.

Note: *On some models, the seat belt anchorages are fitted inside the console, and the console must be lifted off the anchorages.*

39 Rear air extractor vent (Estate) – removal and refitting

1 The outer grille is secured by screws (photo).

2 The inner duct can be reached after removing the luggage compartment trim panel. It is secured by screws (photo).

3 Refitting is a reverse of removal.

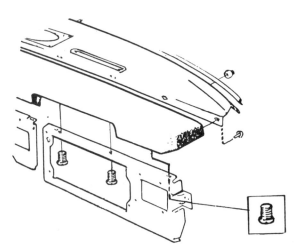

Fig. 11.45 Showing the crash padding attachment details
(Sec 37)

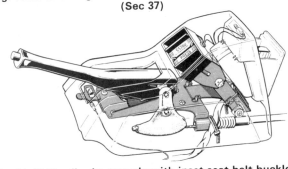

Fig. 11.46 Handbrake console with inset seat belt buckles
(Sec 38)

38.1A Remove the ashtray ...

38.1B ... and prise out the insert

38.2 Disconnect the warning and courtesy lights

38.5 Locating tongue at the front edge of console

39.1 Outer grille securing screws

39.2 Inner duct is secured by screws (arrowed)

40 Seats – removal and refitting

Front
1   If fitted, disconnect the seat heating pad connector.
2   Disconnect the 'fasten seat belt' warning light connector under the front passenger seat (photo).
3   Remove the bolts securing the seat runners to the floorpan (photo), there are four of them, and lift out the seat.

Rear seats – Saloon
4   Disengage the clips at the lower front edge of the seat cushion, pull the cushion forwards and remove it sideways from the vehicle.
5   The seat back should be pushed up to disengage the locating clips at its rear, after which it can be removed.

Rear seats – Estate
6   Tilt the seat cushion up, which will reveal the hinge mechanism, which should be pushed rearwards to unhook the hinge (photo). The seat cushion can then be removed.
7   To remove the seat back, operate the release handle of the fold mechanism and lower the seat back forwards.
8   Prise the seat swivel points from the brackets on the wheel arches, and remove the seat back.

Refitting
9   Refitting of all seats is a reversal of removal.

41 Front seat head restraints – removal and refitting

1   On early models (1975), it is necessary to remove the seat covering to release the bushes which secure the head restraints.
2   On later models (1976 on), the head restraints can be removed by pushing against the spring retainers (see Fig. 11.48) to release them, and lifting the head restraint off.
3   Refit in reverse order.

42 Front seat fittings – overhaul (general)

1   The runners are bolted to the seat (photos).
2   The reclining mechanism is bolted to each side of the seat and connected by a rod. If the mechanism is faulty it should be renewed as a complete unit.
3   The lumbar support is cable-operated. The cables are renewable if they should break.

43 Rear seat release mechanism (Estate) – general

1   The release mechanism is extremely durable and unlikely to give trouble during its service.
2   The latch mechanism is operated by a lever set in the seat back, which when operated releases the latches at each end of the seat back (photo). The latches are secured to the seat back by screws.
3   The fixed catch is bolted to the side-member (photo).

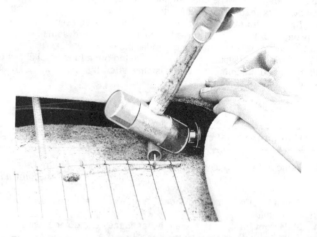

Fig. 11.47 Removing the head restraint retaining clips (Sec 41)

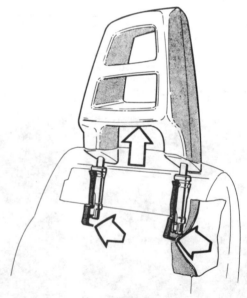

Fig. 11.48 Later type head restraint retaining clips (Sec 41)

40.2 'Fasten seat belt' warning light connector

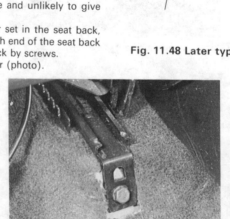

40.3 Seat runner securing bolt

40.6 Rear seat hinge mechanism on an Estate

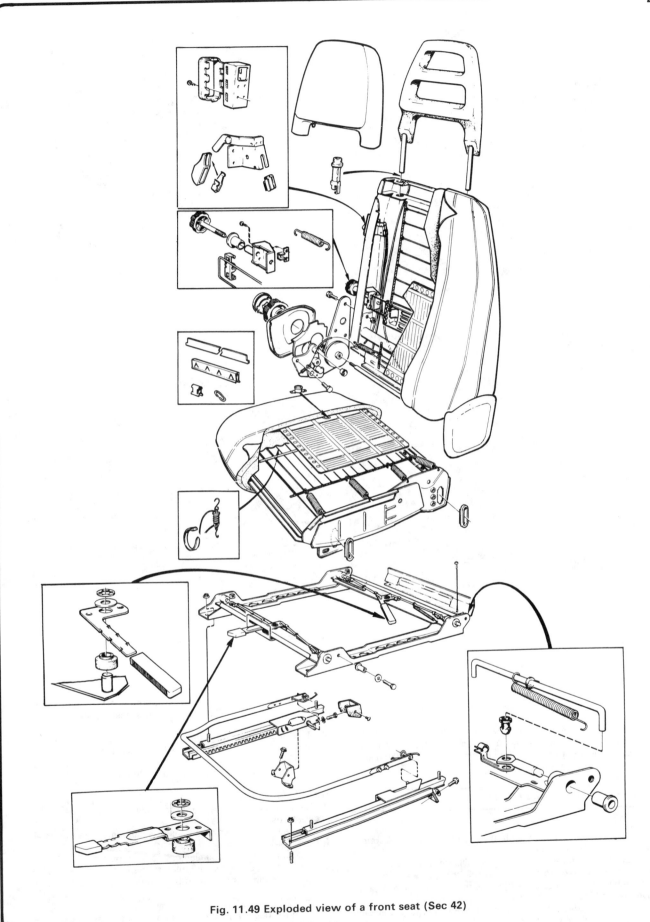

Fig. 11.49 Exploded view of a front seat (Sec 42)

42.1A Seat runner front ...

42.1B ... and rear mounting bolt (arrowed)

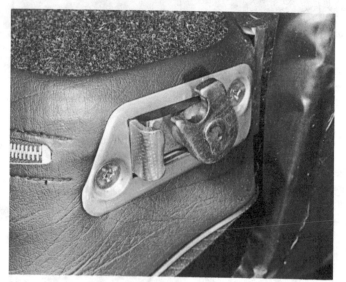

43.2 Seat back latch mechanism (Estate)

43.3 Seat back fixed catch (Estate)

44 Seat belts – general

1   Seat belts should be inspected at regular intervals for fraying, cuts or splits in the webbing, and for correct operation of the inertia lock mechanism. If any of these faults are found, the belts should be renewed. Belts should also be renewed after they have been used in a collision.
2   The belts should be kept clean by wiping with a mild detergent solution and keep the belt extended until it is dry. Oil and grease should not be allowed to contact the webbing, as it has a detrimental effect on the nylon if left to soak in.

45 Seat belts – removal and refitting

Front belts

1   The lower mountings are bolted to the inner floorpan at the bottom of the B-pillar. Remove the bolt to release the belt.
2   The upper mounting is bolted to the B-pillar at head height. Prise off the plastic cover and remove the bolt (photo).
3   The inertia reel is concealed behind the trim panel on the B-pillar. Remove the trim and undo the reel securing bolt (photo).
4   The inboard buckles are bolted to the transmission tunnel at each side of the handbrake console.

Note: *On some models, the buckles may be set inside the handbrake console, which must be removed for access to the steering bolts (see Section 38).*

Rear belts (Saloon)

5   The lower mountings are bolted to the floorpan in much the same way as the front belts. The bolts are accessible after removal of the seat cushion.
6   The upper mountings for the two outer belts are bolted to the C-pillars, again using a similar method as for the front belts.
7   The inertia reels are located under plastic covers at each end of the parcel shelf, and are similar to the units fitted to the rear of the Estate.

Rear belts (Estate)

8   Remove the trim panels from the side of the luggage area to gain access to the inertia reels.
9   The reel is mounted on a bracket, which is secured by three bolts (photo).
10   The upper mounting is clamped to a support bar (photo).
11   The lower mountings are bolted to the floorpan and wheel arches, and are accessible after folding back the seat cushion (photos).

All belts

12   Refit the reversing the removal operations, observing the originally fitted sequence of any washers, spacers etc. Tighten all bolts securely.

45.2 Front seat belt upper mounting with plastic cover removed

45.3 Removing the securing bolt from the inertia reel

45.9 Inertia reel mounting bracket (Estate – rear)

45.10 Upper mounting (Estate – rear)

45.11A Seat belt mounting on wheel arch

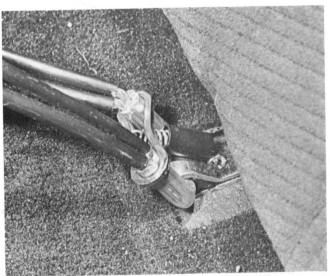

45.11B Seat belt buckle mounting (the bolt is hidden by the seat back)

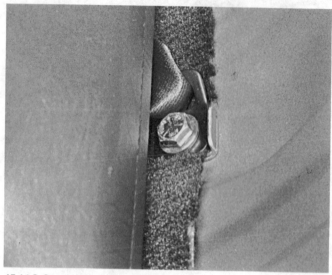

45.11C Centre lap strap securing bolt

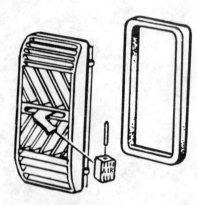

Fig. 11.50 Air vent control knob with securing pin (Sec 48)

46 Sun visors – removal and refitting

1   The sun visors are bolted to the roof panel in a hinged bracket at their outer end and clipped in a plastic holder at the inner.
2   Removal and refitting are self-evident.

47 Interior grab handles – removal and refitting

1   The grab handles are bolted to the inside of the roof above the doors.
2   To remove them, pull back the plastic covers at each end of the handle and remove the bolts thus uncovered.
3   Refit in the reverse order.

48 Interior trim panels – general

1   Interior trim panels are secured by a variety of means, mainly plastic screws or plugs, and self-tapping screws.
2   Removing the panels consists of gaining access to them by removing such interior fittings as is necessary (eg rear seats) to reach the trim panel securing screws.
3   Removal of some trim panels entails pulling off the door surround protection strip/seal. This pulls off quite easily, and it will be seen that it is in the form of a spring clip and is easily pushed back into place.
4   When removing the panels from the outer side of the footwell area, note that the air vent control knob, which has to be removed, may have a pin through it.

49 Roof lining – removal and refitting

Saloon
1   The roof lining is a moulded fibre panel.
2   Remove the interior fittings secured to the roof – grab handles, rear view mirror, sun visors and courtesy light.
3   On pre-1979 models, the rear window has to be removed. See Section 23.
4   On 1980-on models, remove the complete rear seat to gain access to the C-pillar trim panels.
5   Disconnect the heated rear window.
6   Remove the trim panel from above the windscreen, and the trim panels above the B-pillar.
7   Remove the screws from the roof lining, and lift the lining out

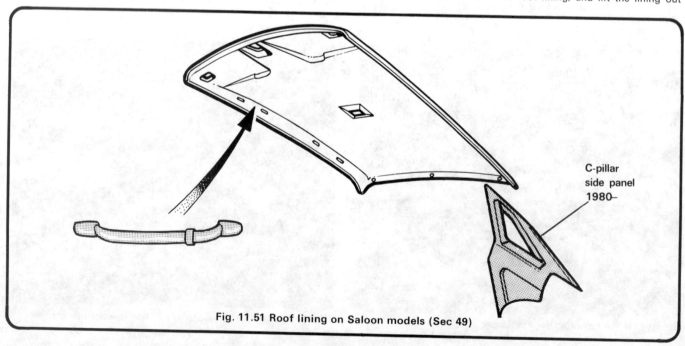

Fig. 11.51 Roof lining on Saloon models (Sec 49)

C-pillar
side panel
1980–

through the front driver's door. **Note:** *Select reverse gear or 'P', and handle the lining with care as it is easily damaged.*

Estate

8   The roof lining is made of cloth material, and is stretched over metal bows tensioned across the roof panel.
9   Carry out the preliminary operations as for the Saloon version, but there is no need to remove the rear seats.
10 Pull the edge of the roof lining from the lip of the roof panel, working round the roof until it is all free.
11 Starting from the rear, disengage the roof bows by bending them gently in the middle, working forwards to the front. Lift out the lining and bows.
12 If fitting a new lining or renewing the bows, ensure the bows have protective plastic end caps fitted to prevent damage to the lining.

Saloon and Estate

13 Refitting of both types of lining is a reversal of removal.

50 Air conditioning system – general

1   Three different types of system are shown in the accompanying illustrations.
2   In all three systems the refrigerant is circulated by a compressor driven from the engine crankshaft by belt.
3   Apart from the periodic checking of the drivebelt for wear and tension, there is little that can be done to the system without special tools, and all servicing should be undertaken by your local dealer.
Warning: *Never attempt to disconnect any part of the system, which may be under pressure, and the gasses given off are injurious to health.*
4   The air conditioning system should be operated for a few minutes each week, even in cold weather, to keep it in good condition.

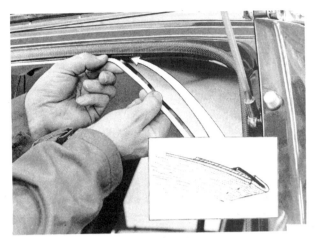

Fig. 11.52 Pulling the roof lining from the roof edge – Estate (Sec 49)

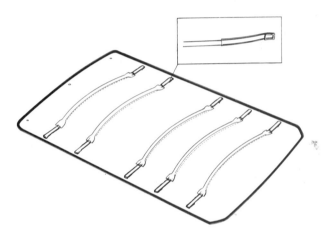

Fig. 11.53 Showing the metal bows in the roof lining – Estate (Sec 49)

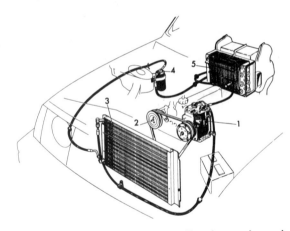

Fig. 11.54 Air conditioning system fitted to early models (Sec 50)

1 *Compressor*	4 *Drier*
2 *Idler pulley*	5 *Evaporator*
3 *Condenser*	

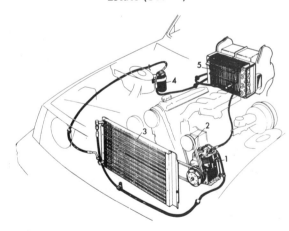

Fig. 11.55 Air conditioning system – B21 engine with power steering (Sec 50)

1 *Compressor*	4 *Drier*
2 *Steering pump*	5 *Evaporator*
3 *Condenser*	

◄ Fig. 11.56 Air conditioning system – 1978 on (Sec 50)

1 *Condenser*	3 *Receiver/drier*
2 *Compressor*	4 *Evaporator*

Chapter 12 Electrical system

Contents

Specifications

General

System type	12 volt, negative earth
Battery type	Lead-acid
Battery capacity	60 Ah

Alternator and regulator

SEV Marchal C14/55A

Maximum amperage	55A
Maximum wattage	770W
Minimum diameter slip rings	1.34 in (34.0 mm)
Radial throw:	
Slip rings	0.003 in (0.07 mm)
Rotor	0.002 in (0.05 mm)
Minimum brush length	0.20 in (5.0 mm)
Resistance:	
Rotor coil	3.5 to 4.3 ohms
Stator	0.17 to 0.23 ohms

SEV Marchal D14/70A

Maximum amperage	70A
Maximum wattage	980W
Minimum diameter, slip rings	1.34 in (34.0 mm)
Minimum brush length	0.20 in (5.0 mm)
Test values:	
Rotor winding resistance	3 to 5 ohms
Stator resistance	0.08 to 0.18 ohm/phase
Output at 14V	62A at 3000 rpm

Bosch N1 14V 70A 20

Maximum amperage	70A
Maximum wattage	980W
Minimum diameter, slip rings:	
With remote regulator	1.24 in (31.5 mm)
With integral regulator	1.06 in (27.0 mm)
Minimum brush length	0.20 in (5.0 mm)
Test values:	
Rotor winding resistance	4 to 4.4 ohms
Stator resistance	0.1 ohm/phase
Output at 14V	58A at 3000 rpm

Bosch K1/35A

Maximum amperage	35A
Maximum wattage	490W
Minimum diameter of slip ring	1.24 in (31.5 mm)
Maximum radial throw:	
Slip rings	0.001 in (0.03 mm)
Rotor	0.002 in (0.05 mm)
Minimum brush length	0.20 in (5.0 mm)
Resistance:	
Rotor coil	4 to 4.4 ohms
Stator	0.26 to 0.29 ohms

Bosch K1/55A

Maximum amperage	55A
Maximum wattage	770W
Specifications as for the Bosch K1/35A, except for following:	
Resistance:	
Stator	0.14 to 0.15 ohms
Note: *Where a built-in regulator is employed on this type of alternator, the following specifications apply:*	
Minimum diameter of slip rings	1.06 in (26.8 mm)
Resistance of rotor	3.4 to 3.75 ohms

Voltage regulator

SEV Marchal 727 105 02:	
Control voltage, after driving 10 minutes	13.5 to 14.1 V
Bosch AD – 14V:	
Control voltage, after driving 10 minutes	13.5 to 14.1 V
Load current, two lower contacts	44 to 46 A
Control range (between two upper and lower contacts)	0 to 0.4 V
Load current, two upper contacts	3 to 8 A

Transistorized remote regulator

Regulator temperature with fully charged battery	77°F (25°C)
Test voltage between B + and D − terminals (engine at 3000 rpm, alternator load 5 to 10A):	
Except Part No 1308030:	
Cold	13.7 to 14.5 V
Warm (30 minutes running)	13.5 to 14.1 V
Part No 1308030:	
Cold	14.3 to 15.0 V
Warm (15 minutes running)	14.05 to 14.35 V

Integral regulator

Regulator temperature with fully charged battery	77°F (25°C)
Test voltage between B + and D − terminals (engine at 3000 rpm, alternator load 5A):	
Cold	14.4 to 14.8 V
Warm (15 minutes running)	13.8 to 14.3 V

Wiper blades .... Champion C-4101 (all models)

Starter motor (Bosch)

Type	Bosch GF 12V 1.1 PS
Voltage	12 V
Earth connection	Negative terminal
Direction of rotation	Clockwise
Output	810 W (1.1 hp)

Number of teeth on pinion	9
Number of brushes	4
Test values:	
Mechanical:	
Armature endfloat	0.004 to 0.0118 in (0.10 to 0.30 mm)
Brush spring tension	3 to 3.5 lb (1.4 to 1.6 kg)
Distance from pinion to ring gear	0.047 to 0.173 in (1.2 to 4.4 mm)
Frictional torque of rotor brake	2.18 to 3.48 lb in (2.5 to 4 kg cm)
Pinion idling torque	1.22 to 1.91 lb in (1.4 to 2.2 kg cm)
Backlash	0.012 to 0.020 in (0.3 to 0.5 mm)
Minimum diameter of commutator	1.32 in (33.5 mm)
Minimum length of brushes	0.51 in (13 mm)
Electrical:	
Unloaded starter motor (11.5 volts and 30 – 50A)	5800 to 7800 rpm
Loaded starter motor (9 volts and 185 – 220A)	1050 to 1350 rpm
Locked starter motor (7 volts and 400 – 490A)	0 rpm
Control solenoid, cut-in voltage (minimum)	7.5 V

Starter motor (Hitachi)

Output	1.4 kW (1.9 hp)
Armature endfloat	0.001 to 0.004 in (0.03 to 0.1 mm)
Minimum diameter of commutator	1.535 in (39.0 mm)
Minimum length of brushes	0.433 in (11.0 mm)
Minimum solenoid cut-in voltage	8.0 V

Bulbs – typical

	Rating (W)
Headlights (1978)	55
Headlights (1979 on)	60/55
Parking/day running lights, front (certain markets)	21/5
Parking lights (other markets)	5
Direction indicators	21
Tail lights	5
Brake lights	21
Reversing lights	21
Rear foglights (certain markets)	21
Number plate light (1975 to 1978)	5
Number plate light (1979 on)	4
Courtesy light	10
Glove compartment light	2
Instrument panel light	2
Engine compartment light	15
Boot light	15
Lighting for:	
instrument panel	1.2
automatic transmission	1.2
ashtray, rear	1.2
seat belt lock	1.2
warning light	1.2
heated rear window	1.2
seat belts	2

Torque wrench setting

	lbf ft	Nm
Alternator pulley nut	29	40

1 General description

1 The electrical system is a 12 volt negative earth system.
2 Electricity is generated by an alternator, driven by belt from the crankshaft. A lead-acid battery provides power for starting, and for when the demand on the system cannot be met by the alternator. The battery is automatically charged when the engine is running.
3 Being a negative earth system, all components are fed positive current, the return negative being through the vehicle body. This means that loose or corroded component mountings can cause a break in the circuit.
4 Semi-conductors are used in many components, especially in later models, which are sensitive to excess voltage and wrong polarity. Observe the appropriate safety precautions at all times.
5 Modern electrical components are built to be non-user-serviceable, and if suspected of malfunction, often the only course of action is to renew the component. Those who wish to do more in repair than mere renewal, are advised to obtain the 'Automobile Electrical Manual'', also by the publishers of this Manual.
6 Before starting work on any part of the electrical system, read the *Safety first!* precautions at the beginning of this Manual.

2 Routine maintenance

1 At the intervals given in the *Routine maintenance* Section at the beginning of this Manual, carry out the following operations.
2 Check the operation of the windscreen, headlight and tailgate wash/wipe systems (Section 26).
3 Check the operation of all lights, horn and wipers, etc.
4 Check the level of the battery electrolyte and top up as necessary, clean the terminals and check the state of the battery charge (Section 3 and 4).
5 Check the tension and condition of the alternator drivebelt(s) (Chapter 2, Section 14).

3 Battery – maintenance

1 Periodically inspect the battery terminals for corrosion. If any is found, disconnect the negative terminal then the positive terminal, and clean the terminals on both the battery and the connections. Use a wire brush or scraper.

2 Sodium bicarbonate solution can be used to remove heavy corrosion, but make sure none of the liquid gets into the battery cells.
3 Smear the connections and terminals with petroleum jelly, then refit the terminals, negative connection last.
4 Also inspect the battery electrolyte level. The level in each cell should be about 0.25 in (6.0 mm) above the plates, or, on some batteries, there is a level mark on the outside. Some later-type batteries are translucent, and the level can be seen from outside, otherwise remove the cell covers and use a torch to see the level of the electrolyte. Remember not to smoke or use naked lights for this operation.
5 If topping-up is required, use distilled or de-ionised water, available from garages or accessory shops, to restore the level. Do not overfill, and mop up any spillage immediately.
6 Frequent need for topping-up would indicate a charging problem or a battery which is becoming defunct. Usually the two outer-most cells go first.
7 Some batteries may be of the 'maintenance-free' type, and as such, it is not always possible on these types to carry out any maintenance. Follow the maker's instructions.
8 Never try to replace the acid content of a battery without having first consulted your local specialist or auto-electrician.
9 Periodically remove the battery and wash down the battery tray. Neutralise and repaint any corrosion found.
10 Keep the top of the battery clean and dry at all times.

4 Battery – charging

1 The battery should not need charging from an external source during normal use. However, stop-start driving, especially in the dark, or in wintry conditions can rapidly drain even a battery in good condition, as the engine does not have time to recharge the battery. Batteries which are standing idle should be recharged every six weeks or so.
2 Battery charging can be done *in situ*, but it is better to remove the battery and charge it on a bench or remote corner of the garage because of the danger of spillage. (The battery can 'spit' during recharging).
3 Battery chargers are available from accessory shops, and should be used in accordance with the maker's instructions. The maximum output of the charger should be about 6 amps, and it should be set to deliver 12 volts before connecting to the battery.
4 Charging will probably take all night, and when complete, switch off at the mains before disconnecting from the battery. Charging releases hydrogen gas which is potentially explosive. Rapid or boost charging is not recommended.
5 During charging the temperature of the electrolyte should not exceed 38°C (100°F).

5 Battery – removal and refitting

1 Disconnect the battery negative terminal first. This will be marked with a minus sign.
2 Disconnect the battery positive terminal, marked with a plus sign.
3 Release the battery retaining clamp(s). These may take the form of a metal strap across the top of the battery, held by two long-threaded bolts, or a clamp bolted to the battery tray (photo). Later models have a quick-release plastic clip (photo).
4 Lift the battery out, keeping it upright, and be careful not to drop it.
5 Refit in the reverse order, connecting the positive connection first, and then the negative terminal.

6 Alternator – precautions

1 To avoid damage to the alternator semi-conductors, the following precautions should be observed:

   (a) *Do not disconnect the battery or alternator while the engine is running.*
   (b) *Do not allow the engine to turn the alternator while the alternator electrical connections are not made.*
   (c) *Never test the output of the alternator by grounding the alternator output lead.*
   (d) *Do not use a battery charger of more than 12 volts output.*
   (e) *Never use a battery charger as a starting aid.*
   (f) *Disconnect the battery and alternator before carrying out electric-arc welding on the vehicle.*
   (g) *Always ensure that the battery positive and negative terminals are correctly connected.*

7 Alternator – in-vehicle testing

1 If it appears that the alternator is not charging the battery, check first that the alternator drivebelt is in good condition, and that the tension is correct (see Chapter 2).
2 Check the security and condition of the alternator and regulator connections and the battery terminals.
3 Any further output testing is best left to your Volvo dealer or auto-electrician, who have the necessary test equipment. Different alternators are fitted to different models, and the test procedure and applied loading differs between models.
Note: *As from 1981, the charging regulator is integral with the alternator, and not separate as previously.*

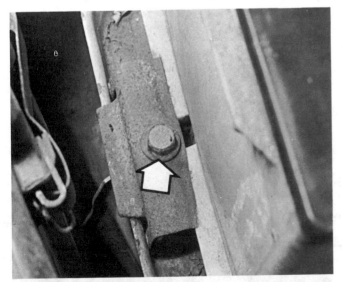

5.3A Battery clamp retaining bolt (arrowed)

5.3B Later-type battery quick-release clip (arrowed)

8 Alternator – removal and refitting

1 Disconnect the battery negative terminal.
2 Loosen the alternator drivebelts and slip them off the pulley wheel (see Chapter 2).
3 Make a note of the connections on the rear of the alternator, and then disconnect them (photo).
4 Remove the bolt from the alternator adjusting mechanism.
5 Remove the nut from the pivot bolt, then take careful note of any washers or spacers under the nut or the bolt head at the other end. It is important that these are refitted in the same order.
6 Remove the pivot bolt and withdraw the alternator.
7 Refitting is a reversal of this procedure, connecting the alternator terminals before connecting the battery. Adjust the tension of the drivebelt(s) (Chapter 2, Section 14).

9 Alternator – overhaul

1 In general, it is not a viable proposition to overhaul an alternator in terms of cost and time. It is better to obtain and fit a service exchange unit, which will certainly have the vehicle back on the road a lot sooner.
2 It is recommended that servicing be limited to the brush renewal procedure given later in this Section. However, for those determined to overhaul the alternator, general guidelines are also given, which in conjunction with the exploded views of the different alternators and the information given in the Specifications should enable overhaul to proceed.

Brush renewal

3 The brush holders are fitted to the outside of the alternator, and on some models may be renewed without removing the alternator. Disconnect the battery if this is the case.
4 Disconnect the battery negative terminal and remove the alternator, if necessary.
5 Remove the screws securing the brush holder to the rear of the alternator (photo).
6 Measure the length of each brush protrusion from the holder, and if they fall below the minimum length given in the Specifications, they should be renewed (photo).
7 Renewal of the brushes requires the use of a soldering iron, and it is pointed out that the inexpert use of this item can lead to damage where the voltage regulator is integral with the brush holder, as on later types.
8 Detach the wires from the brushes using the soldering iron, and fit the new brushes by the same method. Check that the brushes are free to move in and out of the holder on completion. Also check that the brushes are isolated from each other (see later text on overhaul).
9 Clean the slip rings with a cloth moistened in methylated spirit. Inspect the rings as described under overhaul.
10 Refit the brush holder to the alternator, and either connect the alternator leads or refit the alternator as described in Section 8.

Overhaul

11 If not already done, remove the alternator as described in Section 8.
12 Remove the brush holder as described earlier.
13 Use an old fan belt as a strap wrench to prevent the pulley wheel from turning, and undo and remove the pulley nut.
14 If it is tight, the pulley wheel may have to be removed using a puller. Take note of any washers or spacers, and refit them in the same positions on reassembly. Do not lose the key which locks the pulley wheel to the shaft.
15 Lift off the cooling fan.
16 Remove the two bolts holding together the alternator and take off the drive end shield holding the alternator in a vice by the driveshaft. Be careful when using screwdrivers to part the alternator – do not insert them further than $1/16$ in (2 mm) or you may damage the stator winding.
17 Remove the retaining plate which holds the rotor bearing in the drive end shield, and knock out the bearing by gently tapping on the rotor shaft with a hide mallet or a piece of wood.
18 In the SEV alternator, detach the isolation diode holder by removing the nuts and washers on terminal '61' and the corresponding ones on the other side of the isolation diode. This being done, it is a simple matter to detach the rectifier assembly from the slip ring end

8.3 Disconnecting the leads on the alternator

9.5 Removing the brush holder/voltage regulator screws ...

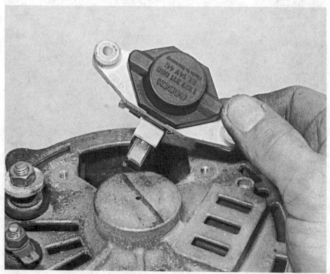

9.6 ... showing the brush protrusion

shield and withdraw the stator winding with the rectifier assembly still connected to it. The end shield may then be detached.

19 For the Bosch alternator, unsolder the stator winding leads from the terminals on the slip ring end shield, marking the leads and terminals so that you know which goes to which. The stator winding can then be withdrawn from the shield. Remove the positive diode assembly, the magnetizing rectifier assembly and the negative diode assembly from the slip ring end shield, which can then be separated from the stator.

Bearings

20 Generally speaking, the bearings for the rotor will stay on the rotor shaft when the alternator is dismantled, though sometimes they may remain in the end shields. Where these bearings are of the open type, they should be removed from the end shield or shaft, thoroughly cleaned in white spirit and examined carefully for signs of scoring, scuffing, wear or blueing. If such signs are present, or there is appreciable play in the bearing, it should be replaced. Otherwise, pack the bearing with a suitable grease for further use.

21 If the bearings are of the sealed type, check them for play and smoothness of operation, and replace them if you are in any doubt about their condition.

Brushes and slip rings

22 Using a 12V test lamp and battery, check that the brushes are isolated from each other (ie. the lamp must not light when connected between the brushes). Check that the connection between the brushes and their respective terminals on the holder are good – ie. the test lamp should light when connected between a brush and its terminal. (This test does not apply to models with integral regulator.)

23 The minimum length of the brush protruding from the holder should be as given in the Specifications.

24 The surface of the slip rings should be smooth. You may give them a polish with very fine sand paper (not emery paper), being careful to removal all traces of the sand paper when you have finished. If the slip rings are burnt or damaged in any other way, there is no reason why they should not be skimmed in a lathe, provided the minimum diameter is not exceeded (see Specifications).

Checking the rotor

25 Check the slip rings, as described previously.

26 Examine the winding for breakage or damaged insulation.

27 Check the insulation between the winding and the frame by connecting a test lamp and battery between the frame and one of the slip rings. The lamp should not light.

28 Measure the resistance between the slip rings with an ohmmeter or multi-meter. It should be as given in the Specifications.

Checking the stator

29 Examine the winding carefully for signs of burning. If this is found, it means that there is a short circuit in the winding and the stator should be replaced or rewound.

30 Connect a test lamp and battery between one of the winding terminals and the frame, the lamp should not light. If there is the smallest glow, the stator should be replaced.

31 Using an ohmmeter or multi-meter, measure the resistance between each pair of winding terminations (in the case of the Bosch alternator, these are the leads that are connected to the diodes – not the star point which has three wires going to it). The presence of the diodes on the SEV stator windings will not affect these measurements unless the diodes are defective. The three different measurements

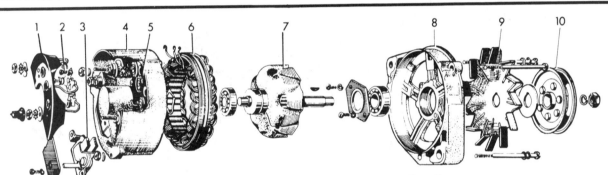

Fig. 12.1 Exploded view of Bosch alternator (Sec 9)

1	Rectifier (plus diode plate)	5	Rectifier (negative diodes)	8	Drive end shield
2	Magnetizing rectifier	6	Stator	9	Fan
3	Brush holder	7	Rotor	10	Pulley
4	Slip ring end shield				

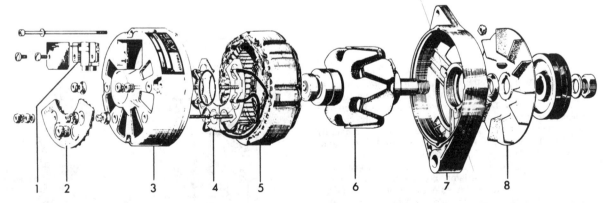

Fig. 12.2 Exploded view of SEV alternator (Sec 9)

1	Brush holder	3	Slip ring end shield	5	Stator
2	Isolation diodes with holder	4	Rectifier (silicon diodes)	6	Rotor

7	Drive end shield
8	Fan

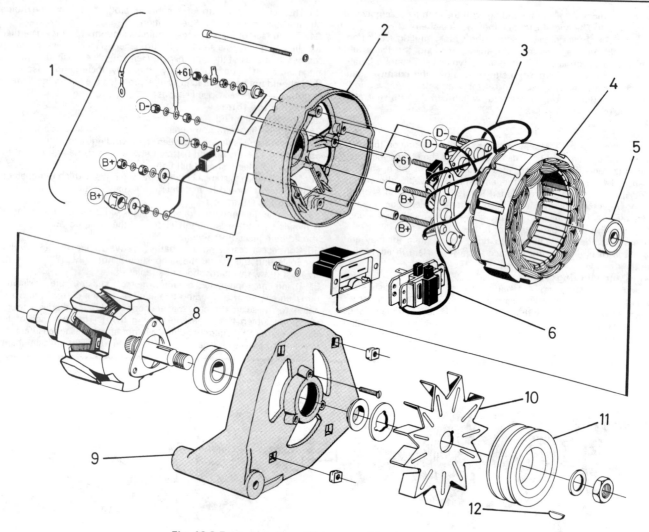

Fig. 12.3 Exploded view of later type SEV alternator (Sec 9)

1 Connections	4 Stator	7 Charge regulator	10 Fan
2 End cover	5 Bearing	8 Rotor	11 Pulley
3 Rectifier	6 Brush holder	9 Drive end shield	12 Key

should give the same value of resistance – certainly within 2% (see Specifications).

Checking the diodes

32 The diode is simply a device which will allow electric current to pass through it one way and not the other way. In diagrams such as Figs 12.4 and 12.5, the direction in which current is able to flow through the diode is indicated by the black arrowhead. Electric current flows from positive to negative, so if you connect a positive voltage (for example, the positive lead of your battery/test bulb combination) to the broad end of the arrow and the negative lead to the other end, current will flow and the lamp will light. If you reverse the connections, the lamp will not light. Normally, you do not have to worry about which way round you connect your lamp, because if the lamp lights when connected one way round and does not light when connected the other way round, the diode must be all right. A faulty diode either lights the lamp both ways or not at all. Note that the positive voltage on a rectifier diode appears at the pointed end of the arrow. The diodes are made up to produce positive voltage at the casing or at the centre lead as required; both types are used in the alternator.

33 Unless specialised apparatus is available, it is necessary to unsolder the leads from the SEV alternator to the diodes mounted on it in order to check them. To someone not experienced in working with electronic equipment, this soldering is a tricky business and best left to a

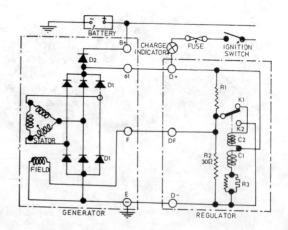

Fig. 12.4 Circuit diagram early type SEV alternator (Sec 9)

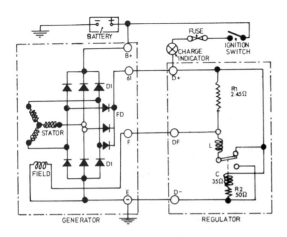

Fig. 12.5 Circuit diagram early type Bosch alternator (Sec 9)

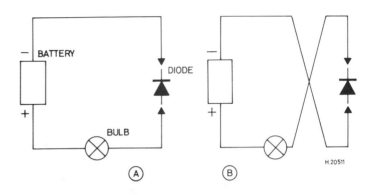

Fig. 12.6 Testing a diode with a test lamp and battery (Sec 9)

A   *Bulb lights*
B   *Connections reversed – bulb does not light*

specialist. There is no reason why the local radio shop should not do this for you. Check the diodes as just described with the test lamp and voltage source. In no circumstances should the test voltage exceed 14v. If any defective diodes are found, replace the relevant assembly or have a diode fitted to the existing plate by a specialist. In the Bosch alternator, the diode plate is disconnected from the stator winding when the alternator is dismantled and there is no need to unsolder the diodes themselves. The battery and lamp can be connected across each diode in turn.

Reassembly
34 Reassembly in the main is a reversal of the dismantling process, and present no special problems. In the Bosch alternator, fit the bearing and retaining plate to the drive end bearing shield before assembling this to the rotor. Coat the slip ring end shield bearing seat with a light layer of 'Molykote' paste or similar and assemble the alternator. Do not forget the spring ring, on the slip ring end shield bearing seat.
35 Be sure that the isolation diode holder on the SEV alternator is fitted with the full complement of plastic tube and isolation washers on its fixing screws.
36 Fit the spacer washer, key, fan, pulley, washer and finally the pulley nut in the order in which you took them off, tightening the pulley nut to the specified torque.

10 Regulator (charging system) – removal and refitting

1 The charging regulator which controls battery charge rate is separate from the alternator on early types, mounted down by the cooling system expansion tank (photo). On later types it is integral with the alternator brush holder.
2 Testing of the charging system regulator is best left to your dealer.
3 If it is suspected that the regulator is faulty, and should be renewed, it can be removed and refitted as follows:
4 Disconnect the battery negative lead. On early types disconnect the leads to the regulator, remove the securing screws and withdraw the unit. Refit in the reverse order.
5 On later types with integral regulator, refer to Section 9.

11 Starter motor – general description

1 The starter motor is of the pre-engaged type, in which the pinion is mechanically engaged with the flywheel ring gear before the motor is switched on, a roller clutch drive in the pinion assembly allowing the pinion to freewheel when the engine starts. The mechanical engagement is driven by a solenoid which operates the starter motor switch after it has pushed the pinion into position.
2 If properly lubricated before assembly, the self-lubricating bearings of the starter motor will last as long as the engine.

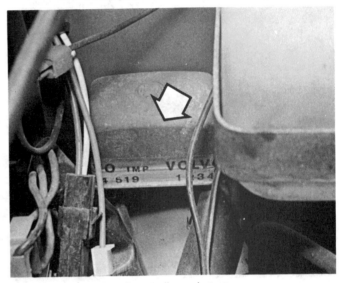

10.1 Charging regulator (arrowed) – early type

12 Starter motor – testing on vehicle

1 If the starter motor fails to operate, first check the condition of the battery by turning on the headlamps. If they shine brightly for several seconds and then gradually dim, the battery needs charging.
2 If the headlights remain bright and it is obvious that the battery is in good condition, check the connections between the battery and the starter – this includes the early lead from the battery terminal to the bodyframe and the lead from the starter switch to the solenoid.
3 If all the connections are sound, listen for a click from the solenoid when the starter switch is operated. If there is no click, a fault in the solenoid or starter switch is suggested. If there is a click but the starter motor does not turn, there is probably a fault in the motor itself. In either event the starter motor will have to be removed for inspection.

13 Starter motor – removal and refitting

1 Disconnect the battery negative terminal.
2 Disconnect the leads from the starter motor solenoid, making a note of them so that they can be refitted in the correct place (photo).
3 Remove the bolts securing the starter motor to the clutch bellhousing and engine flange (photo). On early B21 engines, there is also a bracket at the front of the motor. Remove the bolts securing the bracket to the cylinder block (photo).
4 Lift the starter motor from the engine.
5 Refitting is a reversal of removal.

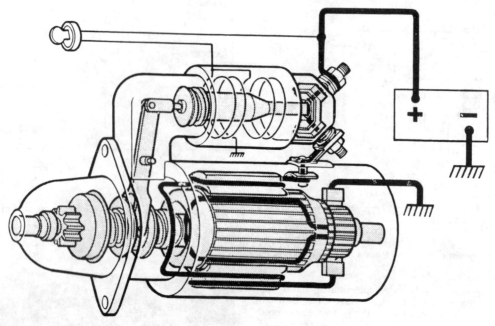

Fig. 12.7 Starter motor – general arrangement (Sec 12)

13.2 Starter motor leads

13.3A Starter motor securing bolts

13.3B Early engines have a bracket at the front

14 Starter motor – overhaul

Note: *Before attempting to overhaul the starter motor, consider the cost of a service exchange unit, which may be a better alternative in the long run.*

Bosch

1 Remove the small cover located at the front end of the shaft (photo).
2 Lift away the locking washer and the adjustment washer.
3 Suitably mark the drive bearing and commutator bearing brackets.
4 Undo and remove the two through-bolts.
5 Lift off the commutator bearing shield. The brushes and retainers will remain in position on the armature (photo).
6 Remove the brush retaining plate from the armature.
7 Note the position of the washers.
8 The brushes may now be pulled from their holders.
9 Remove the brush gear from the armature, taking care not to lose the shims.
10 When the brush gear is removed, the negative brushes will also be detached but the positive brushes will remain attached to the field winding (photos).
11 Unscrew the nut that holds the field terminal connection to the solenoid.
12 Undo and remove the screws which hold the solenoid to the driveshaft end. Lift away the solenoid.

13 Remove the drive end shield and armature from the starter body.
14 Remove the pivot pin from the engagement lever, lift away the rubber washer and also the metal washer.
15 Lift the armature, together with the pinion and lever, from the drive end shield.
16 Knock back the stop washer and remove the circlip from the armature.
17 Finally pull off the stop ring and drive pinion assembly.
18 Clean off the various components using a compressed air jet.
19 Carefully examine the rotor for signs of mechanical damage such as a worn or bent shaft, scored or burnt commutator or damaged windings. If the rotor shaft is bent or worn, it must be renewed.
20 If the commutator is scored or worn unevenly it may be skimmed on a lathe. Take small cuts each time so that the minimum amount of material is removed. The insulation between the laminations should now be undercut to a depth of 0.016 in (0.4 mm) using a hacksaw blade with the tooth sides ground off.
21 Examine the housing and the field winding for signs of damage caused by the rotor.
22 If possible, test the field winding to ensure that it is not earthed by connecting the contact points of a test light and battery to the housing and field winding. If the light comes on, the winding or lead through the body is damaged. Remove the through lead and re-test. If the light still remains on, the field coils are earthed and must be renewed.
23 Carefully examine the brush holders. If any parts are worn or damaged they must be renewed.

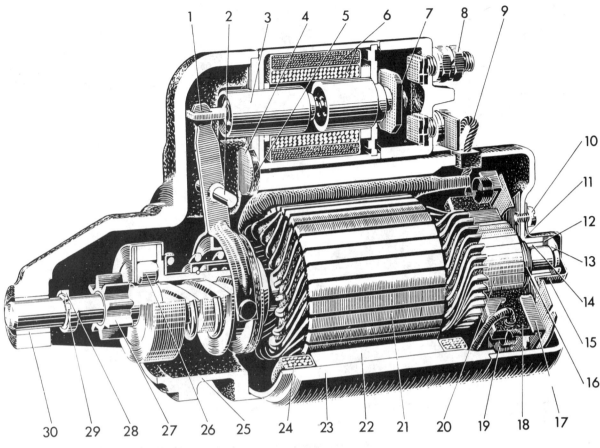

Fig. 12.8 Cut-away view of Bosch starter motor (Sec 14)

1 Shift lever	7 Contact plate	13 Snap ring	19 Brush spring	25 Drive end frame
2 Pivot pin (bearing screw)	8 Terminal for battery lead	14 Bush	20 Commutator	26 One-way clutch
3 Plunger	9 Connection lead to field	15 Commutator end frame	21 Armature	27 Pinion
4 Steel washer	10 Screw	16 Adjusting washers	22 Pole shoe	28 Stop ring
5 Rubber washer	11 Rubber gasket	17 Brush holder	23 Stator	29 Snap ring
6 Winding	12 Shims	18 Brush	24 Field winding	30 Bush

24 Generally inspect all other parts and renew any parts that are worn or damaged. During reassembly new circlips should always be used.

25 To remove the brushes they must be unsoldered from their attachments in the brush holder and field winding respectively. Solder the new brushes into position, taking care not to allow solder to run down onto the brush leads as this can prevent the necessary movement of the brushes in the brush holders and may also reduce brush spring. The brushes must be renewed when they have worn down to the specified minimum.

26 Reassembly of this starter motor is a direct reversal to the dismantling procedure. Lubricate the starter motor as shown in Fig. 12.9.

27 After reassembly, check the armature endfloat using a feeler gauge (photo). Adjust the clearance by fitting or removing shims from under the circlip.

Hitachi

28 Operations are similar to those described for the Bosch motor. Refer to Fig. 12.10 for an exploded view of the motor. During reassembly note the following points.

29 Measure the pinion endfloat. Connect up a 12 volt supply, positive to terminal 50 on the solenoid and negative to terminal 'M' on the solenoid. **Warning:** *The maximum connected time should not exceed 30 seconds, or the solenoid will overheat.*

30 With power applied, depress the pinion and measure the endfloat, which should be as shown in Fig. 12.11.

31 Adjustment of this clearance is by fitting shims under the solenoid,

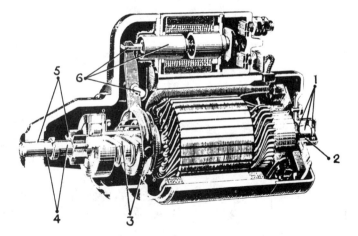

Fig. 12.9 Starter motor – lubrication points (Sec 14)

1 Lightly grease insulation washers, shaft end, adjusting washers and lock washer	4 Lightly grease rotor shaft
	5 Soak bush in oil for 30 minutes
2 Soak bush in oil for 30 minutes	6 Lightly grease engaging lever joints and iron core of solenoid
3 Well grease rotor thread and engaging lever groove	

14.1 Cover over the shaft (arrowed)

14.5 Showing the brushes which remain

14.10A Brush gear and negative brushes

14.10B Positive brushes attached to the field winding

14.27 Checking armature endfloat

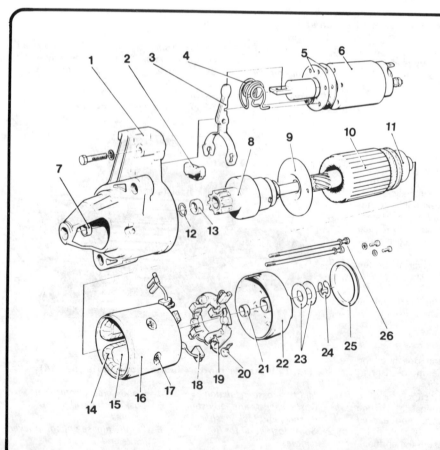

Fig. 12.10 Exploded view of Hitachi starter motor (Sec 14)

1   Drive end bearing housing
2   Rubber packing piece
3   Shift arm
4   Spring
5   Shims
6   Solenoid
7   Bush
8   Drive
9   Centre bearing
10 Armature
11 Commutator
12 Lock ring
13 Stop ring
14 Field coil
15 Pole shoe
16 Starter body
17 Screw
18 Brush
19 Brush holder
20 Spring
21 Bush
22 End cover
23 Shims
24 Lock ring
25 Seal
26 Tie-bolts

as shown in Fig. 12.12. Increasing the shim thickness will cause the clearance to be diminished by approximately twice the shim thickness. **Note:** *If two spacers are found under the solenoid on Hitachi type starter motors, they should be replaced upon reassembly. These spacers prevent the starter motor grinding. If this is a problem on a Hitachi type starter motor and the spacers are not fitted, then the fitting of these spacers will alleviate the problem. The pinion endfloat tolerance should still be observed.*

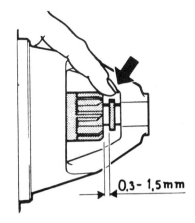

Fig. 12.11 Hitachi starter motor pinion endfloat (Sec 14)

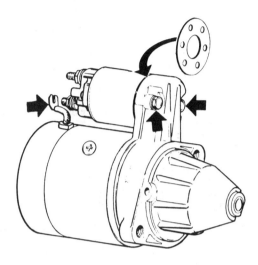

Fig. 12.12 Position of adjusting shim (Sec 14)

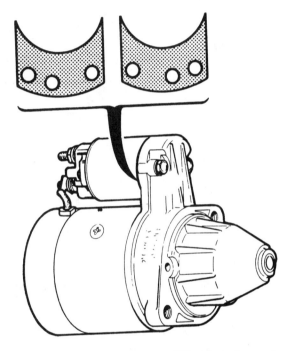

Fig. 12.13 Spacers fitted to some Hitachi starter motors (Sec 14)

15 Exterior light bulbs – renewal

Headlights
Note: *When renewing light bulbs, especially headlight bulbs, do not touch the bulb glass with the fingers. Grease thus released can give off a vapour when heated (when the lights are on) which will rapidly damage the reflector. If a bulb is accidentally touched, clean it with a soft rag and methylated spirit.*

Early models with round headlights
1   Open the bonnet.
2   Remove the two headlight surround quick-release fasteners and lift off the trim surround (photo).
3   Turn the chromed ring anti-clockwise to release it (photo) and lift it and the headlight out.
4   Pull the electrical connector off and remove the rubber cover (photo).
5   Release the spring clip securing the bulb and lift out the bulb (photos).
6   Fit a new bulb in the reverse order.

Early type square headlights
Note: *There are two types of early square headlight. A sealed type, on which no further dismantling can be done, and a type which has a removable lens, the dismantling of which is similar to the procedure described in Section 16 for later type square headlights.*
7   Carry out steps 1 and 2 above.
8   Grasp the upper part of the headlight and pull it forward to release the ball-and-socket fixture.
9   Insert a lever in behind one side of the headlight, and lever it forward from its housing. Repeat on the other side and lift the headlight out.
10 Disconnect the electrical connector.
11 There are two bulbholders in the back of the headlight, the upper being high beam and the lower, dipped beam. Bulb changing is similar to that described for round headlights.
12 Refit in the reverse order.

Later type square headlights
13 Both bulbs are accessible from within the engine bay.
14 On the left-hand side, the job is facilitated if the battery is removed.

Fig. 12.14 Releasing the ball-and-socket attachment on early type square headlights (Sec 15)

15 Disconnect the battery (if wished), or remove it as necessary.
16 Pull off the electrical connector (photo).
17 Remove the rubber cover (photo).
18 Release the spring clip (photo).
19 Remove the bulb (photo).
20 Fit a new bulb in the reverse order.

Front side and indicator lights
21 On early models, remove the two screws from the lens and remove the lens (photo).
22 On later models (1979-on) there are three screws (photo).
23 The bulbs are a bayonet fix in the holders (photo).

Side repeater light
24 Push the lens unit forward, at the same time prising up the rear edge.
25 Pull the bulbholder from the lens unit (photo).
26 The bulb is a push fit in the holder.

High level brake light
27 Pull off the outer cover (photo).
28 Prise the reflector unit from the plastic clips on the lens (photos).
29 The bulb is a bayonet fix in the holder.

Number plate light
30 Prise the light unit from the housing (Estates and early Saloons), or slide it rearwards to free it (later Saloons).
31 If fitted, remove the inner cover (photo).
32 The bulb is either of the bayonet type (push and twist), or of the festoon type, and clips between the two spring contacts (photo).
33 To remove the light unit, disconnect the wires, noting which terminal they serve.

Rear light cluster
Early models (Saloon)
34 Remove the four screws securing the lens to the baseplate (photo).
35 The bulbs are a bayonet fix in the holders (photo).
Early models (Estate)
36 The procedure is similar to that for the Saloon, the light cluster being a different shape.
Later models (Saloon)
37 Access to the bulbs is from inside the boot.
38 Unscrew the knurled knob and hinge the panel upwards and off.
39 Turn the bulbholders anti-clockwise to remove them.
40 The bulbs are a bayonet fix in the holders.
Later models (Estate)
41 For access to the left-hand light cluster, unclip the side cover in the luggage compartment and remove the spare wheel.
42 For the right-hand light cluster, lift up the floor panel, unclip and remove the side panel.
43 Turn the bulbholders anti-clockwise to release them (photo).
44 The bulbs are a bayonet fix in the holders.

Fig. 12.15 Levering out the lower attachment on early type square headlights (Sec 15)

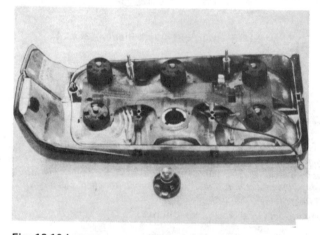

Fig. 12.16 Later type rear light cluster – Saloon (Sec 15)

Fig. 12.17 Rear light identification – Saloon (Sec 15)

1	Brake light	4	Tail light
2	Reversing light	5	Reflector
3	Indicator light	6	Foglight

Fig. 12.18 Rear light identification – Estate (Sec 15)

7	Indicator light	9	Brake light
8	Reversing light	10	Tail light

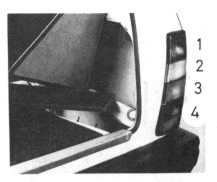

Fig. 12.19 Rear light identification –
Estate, later type (Sec 15)

1 Foglight   3 Indicator light
2 Reversing light 4 Brake and tail light

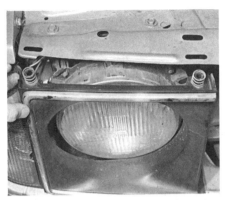

15.2 Removing the headlight surround on
early models

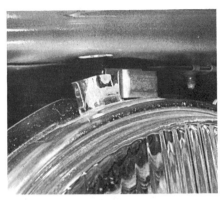

15.3 Removing the chromed ring

15.4 Pulling off the connector

15.5A Release the spring clip ...

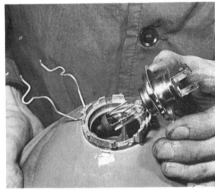

15.5B ... before removing the bulb

15.16 Pull off the connector

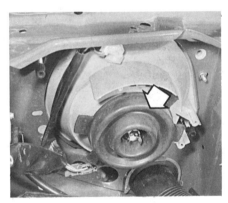

15.17 Remove the rubber cover

15.18 Release the spring clip

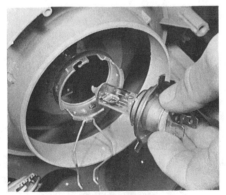

15.19 Remove the bulb

15.21 Two screws secure early type lenses

15.22 Later models have three screws
(arrowed)

15.23 Removing a bulb

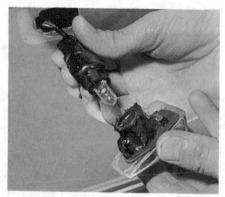

15.25 Pulling the bulbholder from the repeater light

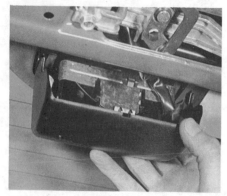

15.27 Pull off the outer cover

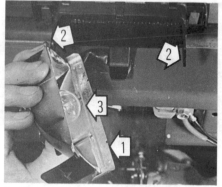

15.28A Reflector unit (1), plastic clips (2) and bulb (3)

15.28B Lens unit location for the clips

15.31 Remove the inner cover

15.32 Showing the festoon-type bulb

15.34 Securing screws on an early Saloon model (arrowed)

15.35 Lens removed showing the bulbs
1 Indicator   3 Rear light
2 Reversing light   4 Brake light

15.43 Removing a bulbholder on a later Estate model

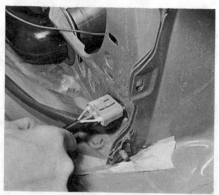

16.4 Disconnecting the sidelight lead

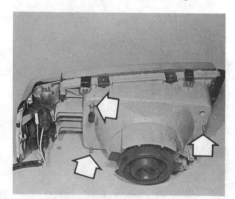

16.6A Headlight attachment points (headlight removed for clarity)

16 Exterior light units – removal and refitting

Headlights
Round headlights and early square headlights
1   The procedure for removing the headlight lens unit is covered in Section 15. The headlight support frame is bolted to the front frame.
2   Due to cosmetic changes in 1978, the headlight has a spacer and mounting frame behind it to bring it level with the new radiator grille.
Later type square headlights
3   Remove the battery. If only the right-hand unit is to be removed, it is only necessary to disconnect the battery if wished.
4   Disconnect the leads to the headlight and sidelight unit. The sidelight connection is remote from the sidelight unit, the cable being fed through the front frame after disconnection (photo). There is also a separate earth lead.
5   Where fitted, flip up or remove the wiper arms.
6   From inside the engine compartment, remove the nuts securing the headlight unit to the framework (photo), and pull the complete headlight and sidelight from the housing. The sidelight has locating dowels which fit into the wing (photo), so ease the unit out inboard side first.
7   The sidelight is clipped to the headlight unit (photo). Prise off the locking clip first (photo).
8   The trim strip is secured by screws on the inboard edge (photo).
9   The headlight lens and wiper buffer are secured by clips (photo).
10   Refitting is a reversal of removal. Check the beam alignment if necessary (Section 17).

Sidelights (front)
11   On early models, remove the headlight surround.
12   Remove the bolt securing the sidelight unit to the framework. This bolt is in between the headlight and the sidelight (photo).
13   Ease the sidelight forwards, inboard edge first, to release it (photo).
14   On later models, the procedure is included in headlight removal as described earlier.

Side repeater light
15   See Section 15.

Number plate light
16   See Section 15.

High level brake light
17   Should the lens become cracked and need renewal, consult your Volvo dealer. The lens is bonded to the rear screen. It may be possible to release it by applying gentle heat with a heat gun to soften the adhesive, and your Volvo dealer will also advise on the adhesive for refitting.

Rear light unit (all types)
18   The rear light unit can be removed after disconnecting the leads to the unit and removing the nuts which secure the unit to the rear wing (photo).
19   These are accessible from inside the vehicle as described for later model bulb renewal.

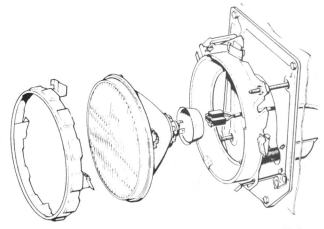

Fig. 12.20 Exploded view of early type round headlight assembly (Sec 16)

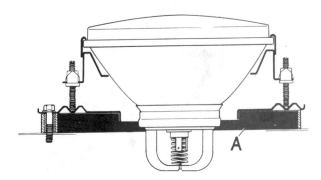

Fig. 12.21 Headlight assembly with spacer (A) (Sec 16)

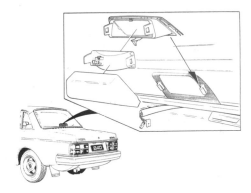

Fig. 12.22 High level brake light fitted to later models (Sec 16)

16.6B Sidelight locating dowels

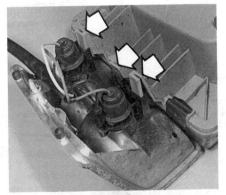

16.7A Sidelight retaining clips (arrowed)

16.7B Locking clip (arrowed)

16.8 Removing the trim strip securing screw

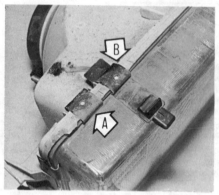

16.9 Headlight lens (A) and wiper buffer (B) securing clips

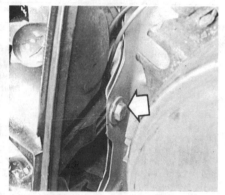

16.12 Sidelight retaining bolt (early models)

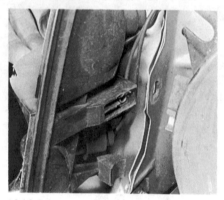

16.13 Easing out the sidelight

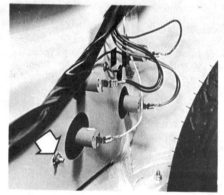

16.18 Rear light unit securing nut – arrowed (Saloon version shown)

17 Headlight beam alignment

1   For your own safety, and to prevent annoyance to other motorists, the headlamp beam alignment should only be carried out by a garage with beam alignment equipment.
2   In an emergency, the beam can be adjusted by turning the adjuster screws on the front of the headlamp on early models, and by turning the knurled adjusters on the back of later types (photo).
3   Holts Amber Lamp is useful for temporarily changing the headlight colour to conform with the usage on Continental Europe.

18 Interior light bulbs – renewal

Bonnet light
1   Remove the securing screw (photo).
2   Pull out the holder and disconnect the lead (photo).
3   The bulb is of the festoon type, held between two spring contacts.
4   The light is operated by a mercury switch which switches the light on when the bonnet is opened, and off when it is closed (photo).
5   Refit in the reverse order to removal.

Courtesy light
6   Prise off the plastic lens.
7   The bulb is of the festoon type, held between the spring contacts (photo).
8   To remove the complete unit, remove the two screws and lift the unit from the roof panel, disconnecting the leads.
9   Refit in the reverse order to removal.

Boot light (Saloon)
10 The procedure is similar to that described for the bonnet light.

Luggage area light (Estate)
11 The procedure is similar to that described for the courtesy light.

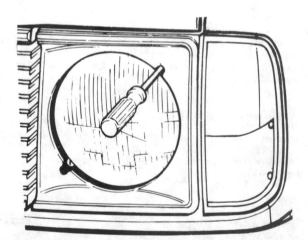

Fig. 12.23 Adjusting headlight beam on early models (Sec 17)

19 Courtesy light microswitches – removal and refitting

1   In general all the microswitches are secured to the bodywork by a screw (photo).
2   Remove the screw, disconnect the switch and remove it, being careful that the lead does not disappear back inside the double skin.
3   Refit in the reverse order.

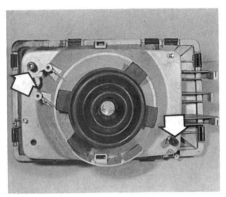
17.2 Headlight beam alignment adjusters

18.1 Removing the bonnet light securing screw

18.2 Pulling out the holder

18.4 Close-up of the mercury switch showing (1) bulbholder and (2) mercury switch

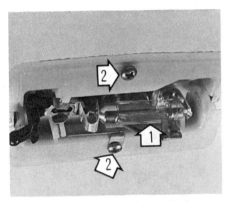
18.7 Courtesy light with lens removed showing (1) festoon bulb and (2) securing screws

19.1 Courtesy light microswitch showing (1) switch, (2) securing screw location and (3) electrical connection

20 Bulb failure warning system – general description

1   The bulb failure warning sensor is mounted on a clip under the dash above the left-hand footwell (photo).
2   The sensor is a type of relay, incorporating a number of reed switches surrounded by wire coils. The coils operate in pairs, one pair carrying the current for one pair of bulbs.
3   Under normal operation with both bulbs in a pair working, magnetic fields set up in each coil cancel each other out. When a bulb fails, the magnetic field becomes unbalanced and operates the warning light.
4   Because of the sensitivity of the system, it is advisable, before fitting any lighting system accessories, to seek the advice of your Volvo dealer. Incorrect wiring can cause malfunction of the warning system. This applies particularly to the installation of wiring for a trailer hitch.

21 Horns and horn push – general

1   Twin horns are bolted to the panelling behind the radiator grille (photo).
2   The horns normally require little attention, but if they fail to operate, first check the circuit fuse and wiring.
3   If the fuse and wiring are in order, lever out the centre crash pad from the steering wheel, disconnect the wire, and check the contacts (photos).
4   If all is in order here, renew the horn(s).

22 Windscreen wiper blades and arms – removal and refitting

1   To remove the blade assembly from the arm, unhook or unclip it from the arm (photo).

2   It is possible to obtain blade inserts, but it is more likely the blade will be supplied with the support arm. As the pivot points in the support arm are subject to wear, it is better to renew the whole assembly. Refit in the reverse order.
3   To remove the wiper arm, on early models depress the small clip and lever the arm from the splined spindle. On later models the arm is secured to the spindle by a nut. Lift up the cover to gain access (photos).
4   Refitting is a reverse of removal, but fit the arms to the spindle splines so that they are parallel to the lower edge of the windscreen.

20.1 Bulb failure warning sensor

21.1 Showing the twin horns location

21.3A Horn push electrical connection (arrowed)

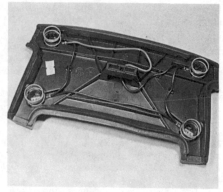

21.3B Showing the four contacts

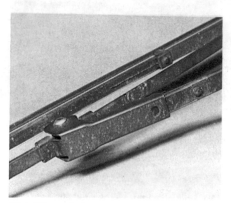

22.1 Wiper blade securing clip

22.3A Wiper arm removed from its spindle (early type)

22.3B Removing the wiper arm securing nut (later types)

23 Windscreen wiper motor and linkage – removal and refitting

1   The windscreen wiper motor is mounted in the engine bay, generally on the left-hand scuttle, although on some models it may be on the right-hand side.
2   Remove the wiper arms (Section 22). On later models, the drive spindles are also secured by a nut under the spindle seals, which can be removed once the arm is off.
3   Remove sufficient panelling from under the dash to gain access to the wiper linkage.
4   The motor spindle is held to the linkage by a clip which pulls off.
5   Disconnect the leads to the motor, remove the motor securing bolts, then withdraw the motor (photo).
6   Overhaul of the motor is not practical, and if it is unserviceable it should be renewed.
7   The linkage is held to the scuttle by screws. Do not forget to undo the nut under the spindle seals on later models.
8   Refitting is a reversal of removal, applying a little grease to the pivot points.

24 Headlight wiper blades and arms – removal and refitting

1   The wiper blade assembly clips into the wiper arm (photo). Pull it off to remove it.
2   The arm is secured to the motor spindle by a nut (photo). Lift up the cover to expose it.
3   Pull off the washer tube and remove the arm (photo).
4   Refit in reverse order, the longer half of the blade facing inboard.
5   Adjust the blade on the motor spindle as follows.
6   Slacken the arm-to-spindle nut, and set the arm so that it is immediately below the lower buffer.

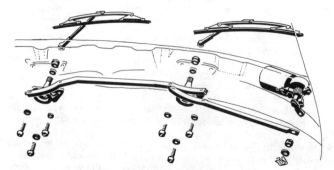

Fig. 12.24 Windscreen wiper motor and linkage (Sec 23)

7   Tighten the nut with the arm in this position, then lift the arm up and over the buffer.

25 Headlight wiper motors – removal and refitting

1   Early models had the motors mounted on the side of the headlight unit. From 1981 they are mounted on the underside.
2   The procedure for removing both types is similar.
3   Remove the wiper arm (Section 24).
4   Remove the radiator grille, and on early models the headlight surround. On later models, remove the headlight unit (Section 16).
5   Disconnect the motor leads.
6   Release the spindle locknut and lift the motor from the bracket, pulling the spindle through the framework (photo). This procedure is more simple on side-mounted motors.
7   Refitting is a reversal of removal.

26 Windscreen, tailgate and headlight washer system – general

1 On early models (pre-1981) the tailgate had its own reservoir and pump in the right-hand bootwell under the floor (photo), but since that date all systems utilise the one reservoir in the engine compartment, although the tailgate system retains its own pump, identified by a blue dot.
2 Fluid is supplied by the electric pumps to the washer jets through plastic tubing, which is clipped to the bodywork and also has junctions and valves in it (photos).
3 The pumps may be mounted either in the reservoir caps or on the side of the reservoir, depending on model.
4 Periodically flush the system through with clean water, as sediment can cause blockage.
5 If the pumps fail in service, they should be renewed, which presents no difficulties.

27 Tailgate wiper arm and motor – removal and refitting

1 The procedure for removing the wiper arms and blade is similar to that described for the windscreen wiper arm and blade in Section 22.
2 To remove the motor, remove the wiper arm, then open the tailgate.
3 Refer to Chapter 11 and remove the interior trim panel from the tailgate.
4 Reaching inside the double skin, prise off the wiper arm crank balljoint.
5 Disconnect the electrical leads to the wiper motor, not forgetting the earth lead, under which bolt the earth lead for the number plate light is also located.
6 Remove the remaining bolts from the motor support plate (photo).
7 Withdraw the motor and support plate.
8 Refit in the reverse order, not forgetting the number plate light earth lead.

23.5 View of the windscreen wiper motor

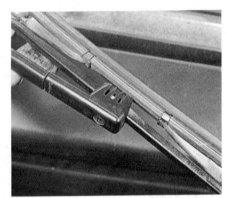
24.1 Headlight wiper blade clip

24.2 Wiper arm securing nut

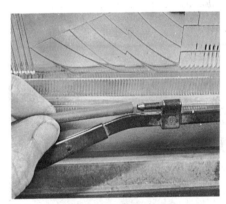
24.3 Pulling off the washer tube

25.6 Removing a headlight wiper motor (locknut arrowed)

26.1 Tailgate washer reservoir in the bootwell (pre-1981)

26.2A Typical washer tube junction

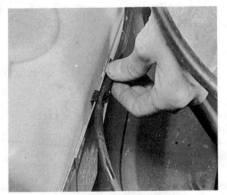
26.2B Unclipping a washer tube

27.6 Wiper motor securing bolts (A) and earth leads (B)

9   The wiper arm should be so positioned on the splines of the drive spindle that in the park position, the arm comes to rest approximately 1 in (25 mm) above the lower edge of the screen.

28 Fuses – general

1   The fusebox is located inside the vehicle under a plastic panel just inside the front left-hand door (photo).
2   If a fuse blows, the circuit protected by that fuse will cease to operate.
3   A list of fuses and the circuits they protect is shown on the inside of the plastic fusebox cover.
4   Blown fuses can be identified by examining the fuse to see if the wire link across it is intact.
5   Persistent blowing of a fuse indicates a fault in the circuit, and such fuses should not be bridged by metal foil paper. Fire could be the result. For the heated rear window fuse, see Section 31.

29 Relays – general

1   Relays are electrically-operated switches, installed in a circuit for two reasons:

   (a)   *to switch a heavy current source remote from the operating switch, allowing lighter switches and wiring to the switch.*
   (b)   *more advanced relays are now being used, which can receive more than one input and also perform computer-type logic functions.*

2   Relays can also be used as time switches, as in the case of intermittent wipe.
3   A faulty system can often be traced to the relay, and substituting a known serviceable relay is the best test. Remember that although relays may look identical externally, internally they may be different.
4   In the 240 series, relays are scattered in location and may be in the engine compartment, or more generally, behind the facia panelling. There are several under the left-hand dash in particular (photos), and behind the panel at the left of the front passenger footwell.

5   Identification of a particular relay is best done by identifying the coloured wiring to the relay and comparing it with the appropriate wiring diagram.

30 Direction indicator system – fault tracing

1   The direction indicator system consists of the external lights, control switch, flasher unit and the associated wiring and warning lights. The hazard warning system is included in the system.
2   Should the indicators flash either too quickly or too slowly, check the bulbs and wiring. Dirty contacts, incorrect bulb wattage and poor earth terminals are all causes of incorrect flasher rate.
3   If the direction indicators do not work at all, check the fuse before the flasher unit. If the hazard warning system works but not the indicators, it is not the flasher unit at fault.
4   The flasher unit is generally situated behind the centre control. Remove the side panels for access to it.

31 Heated rear window – general

1   Heating of the rear window is achieved by passing current through an electrical grid bonded to the inside of the window. The grid is resistant to the current and heats up, rather like the elements in an electric fire.
2   When cleaning the inside of the rear window, take care not to damage the grid element.
3   Small breaks can be repaired using a special conductive paint available from accessory shops.
4   As the rear heater uses a lot of power, it should be used sparingly, and not left on longer than necessary.
Note: *Fuse number 11 in the fusebox carries current for the heated rear window, overdrive and the heated seats. Under certain circumstances, where all three circuits are in use at the same time, the fuse may blow. If this becomes a problem, a 16 amp in-line fuse should be fitted and connected to fuse number 13 (before the fuse), the other end being connected to the heated rear window wire, which should be disconnected from fuse number 11. Your Volvo dealer will advise.*

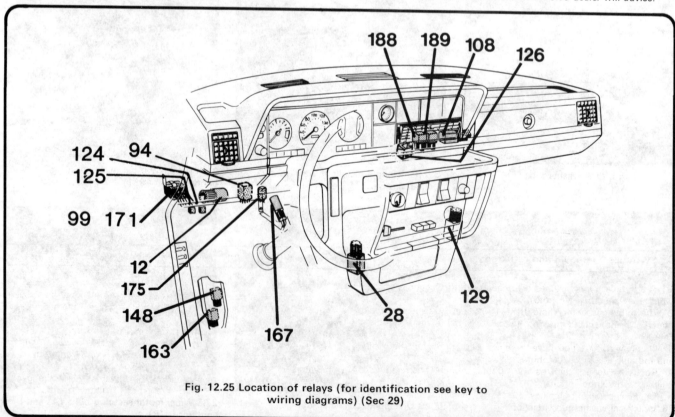

Fig. 12.25 Location of relays (for identification see key to wiring diagrams) (Sec 29)

28.1 View of the fusebox

29.4A Typical relays ...

29.4B ... located under the dash

32.1 Prising out a tumbler switch

32.2 Showing the spring clips and wiring connectors

32.3A An illuminated switch connection ...

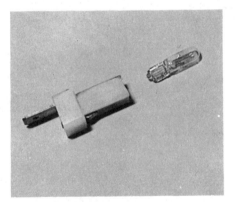

32.3B ... and bulb

32.4 Pulling off the knob on a rotary switch

32 Switches – removal and refitting

1   The tumbler type switches are prised from the facia or console in which they are housed (photo).
2   The spring clips which hold them in place can be seen clearly in the photo. Disconnect the wiring to remove the switch completely (photo).
3   Illuminated switches have a removable connection/bulbholder, and the bulb is a press fit (photos).
4   Rotary switches, such as the lighting switch, are removed by pulling off the knob (photo).
5   The facia panelling then has to be removed as described in Chapter 11, which will reveal the switch body.
6   Refit in the reverse order.

33 Instrument panel – removal and refitting

1   Disconnect the battery negative terminal.
2   Although the instrument panel and surrounding facia have been updated over the years, the removal procedure follows the same basic pattern.
3   Remove the steering column shroud panels (Section 34).
Note: *We also removed the steering wheel for clarity of photographic work, but this is not necessary in practice, unless more room is required.*
4   Remove the two screws securing the lower edge of the panel (photo). On some models these screws may be on the sides of the panel.
5   Ease the lower edge forwards, at the same time releasing the clips

at the top (photo).

6   The speedometer cable (when applicable) now has to be released, and there is little room to do this. Ease the panel forwards without putting undue strain on the speedometer cable, and disconnect all electrical cables and earth wires, taking careful note of their positions (photo).

7   Now release the speedometer cable, which is a bayonet type fix in the speedometer. There may be a plastic locking collar or a lead seal on the coupling to prevent speedometer tampering, and this will have to be broken.

8   Withdraw the instrument panel.

9   The various instruments are usually held by nuts in their housing in the rear of the panel. The voltage stabiliser is a push fit on its connectors (photo).

10 The warning lamp holders are clipped in position. Depress the plastic clips to remove them, the bulbs being a push fit in the holders (photos).

11 Refitting is a reversal of removal.

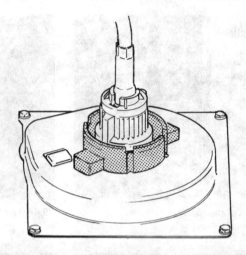

Fig. 12.26 Plastic collar tamperproof device (Sec 33)

34 Steering column shroud panels – removal and refitting

1   Remove the screws from the upper and lower panels (photos), separate the two halves and remove them.

2   Refit in the reverse order, ensuring that the two sections clip together correctly before tightening the screws.

Note: *For photographic purposes the steering wheel was removed. This is not necessary in practice.*

35 Steering column switches – removal and refitting

1   Remove the shroud panel as described in Section 34.

2   Disconnect the battery negative terminal.

3   Pull off the multi-plug connector photo).

4   Remove the screws securing the switches to the steering column.

5   Refit in the reverse order.

Note: *For photographic purposes the steering wheel was removed. This is not necessary in practice.*

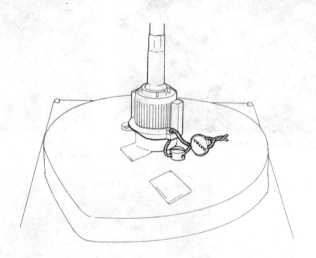

Fig. 12.27 Lead seal type tamperproof device (Sec 33)

36 Clock – removal and refitting

1   The clock is housed in different positions in the facia or console according to model year.

2   To remove the clock, refer to Chapter 11 for details of the facia or console section removal in which the clock is fitted.

3   Pull the section forward sufficiently to disconnect the wiring to the clock, then remove the clock and panel section (photo).

4   The clock is generally held in place by nuts (photo), and can be removed after these are undone.

5   Refitting is a reversal of removal, ensuring any air ducts are correctly refitted.

33.4 Instrument panel securing screws (arrowed)

33.5 Securing clip on upper edge

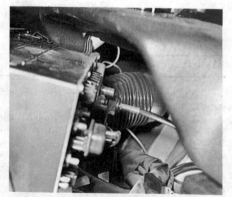

33.6 Rear view of the instrument panel being withdrawn

33.9 Rear view of the instrument panel showing the voltage stabiliser (A), tachometer (B) and speedometer (C)

33.10A Instrument panel warning lamp unclipped

33.10B Showing the bulb and holder

34.1A Removing the screws from the upper ...

34.1B ... and the lower shroud panel

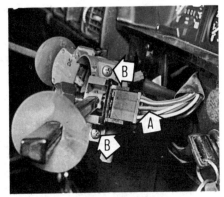

35.3 Column switch connector (A) and securing screws (B)

36.3 Electrical connections to the clock

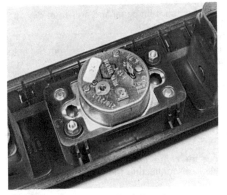

36.4 Rear view of the clock housing

37 Gearchange indicator – general description

1 Some later models are equipped with a gearchange indicator system as an aid to fuel economy.
2 A lamp indicates to the driver that a change to a higher gear is required.
3 The main components of the system are a control unit and a clutch pedal switch.
4 The control unit receives engine speed signals from terminal 1 on the ignition coil, and roadspeed information from a speed transmitter on the rear axle and, on vehicles so equipped, from the overdrive relay.
5 At engine start, the warning lamp comes on but goes out as soon as the vehicle is driven away.

6 By taking into account engine and roadspeeds, the control unit calculates the most desirable gear ratio, and if changing to another gear is required, the indicator lamp illuminates. Operation of the clutch pedal switch signals the control unit that a change of gear has occurred.

Memory reprogramming
7 If the battery is disconnected or the power supply to the control unit is interrupted, then the memory will be erased.
8 To reprogramme, drive the vehicle in 2nd gear and each higher gear for an eight second period (each gear). The indicator lamp will flicker once as each gear programming is completed. Make sure that the foot is lifted completely from the clutch pedal after each gearchange.
9 Refer to wiring diagram for further details.

38 Central locking components – removal and refitting

General description

1   On early models, only the four passenger doors operated on the system, but later models also include the tailgate/boot lock.
2   The system is operated by turning the key in the driver's door lock or pushing down the interior lock button.
3   All doors are unlocked by unlocking the driver's door. The driver's door is actually locked mechanically, but this operation causes switching gear in the door to operate the door lock motors in the other doors.
4   All the motors do is actuate the normal mechanical door lock mechanism, details of which will be found in Chapter 11.
5   The control relays are situated behind the clock panel above the centre console.

Door lock motors – front and rear doors

6   Remove the door trim panel as described in Chapter 11.
7   Where fitted, remove the plastic cover from the door lock link rod. This is an anti-theft device fitted to later models.
8   Disconnect the spring clip from the eye end (photo), and disconnect the link rod.
9   Disconnect the wiring from the motor.
10 Remove the two securing nuts and lift out the motor (photos).
11 Refit in reverse order.

Door lock motor – tailgate

12 The procedure is similar to that described above, but on refitting the motor should be adjusted as follows.
13 Attach the motor to the door loosely.
14 Move the lock cylinder lever to the locked position (towards the motor).
15 Move the motor towards the lock cylinder, compressing the rubber bellows.
16 Tighten the motor securing nuts.

Driver's door switches

17 One door switch is clipped to the door lock cylinder, the other is in the lock link rod.
18 To remove them, remove the door trim panel and anti-theft device.
19 Disconnect the wiring at the connector.
20 Unclip the switch from the lock cylinder.
21 To remove the link rod switch, remove the spring clips from the link rods and lift out the rods and switch.
22 When refitting, which is a reversal of removal, ensure the lock cylinder is positioned correctly (see Fig. 12.28) before fitting the switch and linkrod.

Control relays

23 The control relays are located behind the clock panel above the centre console.
24 To remove them, remove the centre console and clock panel and pull the relays from their clips, disconnecting the wiring.
25 Refit in reverse order.

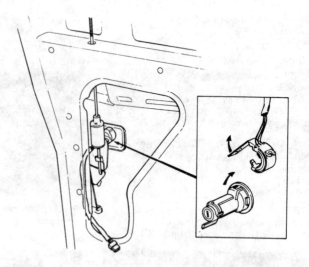

Fig. 12.28 Door lock switch removal (Sec 38)

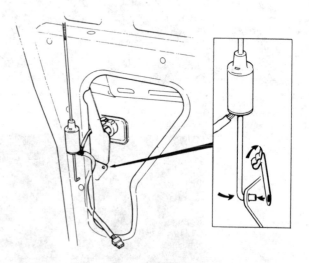

Fig. 12.29 Lock link rod and switch (Sec 38)

38.8 Disconnect the spring clip (arrowed)

38.10A Remove the two securing nuts ...

38.10B ... and lift out the motor

39 Electrically-operated window components – removal and refitting

General description

1   The electrically-operated windows are controlled by switches mounted in the door armrests. The driver's side contains a master control from which all four windows can be controlled.
2   The lift motors are fitted in the doors, and operate the lift mechanism in much the same way as the mechanical window winder.

Switches

3   To remove the switches, refer to Chapter 11, Section 11 and remove the door armrest. The switch block can then be slid from the armrest.
4   The tumbler-type switches are clipped into the plastic block (photo) – disconnect the wiring before prising out the switch.

Lift mechanism and motors

5   With the door interior panel removed as described in Chapter 11, peel away the waterproof sheet.
6   Fully lower the window to its stop.
7   Release the regulator arms from the glass rail. Do this by pushing the safety brackets to loosen them, extracting the washers and levering the arms towards you.
8   Raise the glass fully by hand and prop or wedge it.
9   Disconnect the battery negative lead.
10 Remove the panel from under the end of the facia, also the side panel from just forward of the front pillar.
11 Disconnect the electrical leads from the regulator motor. On some models, this will mean dismounting the fusebox to disconnect the leads. In this case, it is recommended that the leads are cut, and a suitable connecting plug fitted to facilitate the operation on any future occasion.
12 Release the lifting arm from the side of the rail in the door, extract the regulator mounting screws and withdraw the mechanism through the access hole in the door (photo).
13 To dismantle the mechanism, secure it in a vice and remove the electric motor.
14 Release the vice only very slowly, and keep the fingers away from the mechanism, as it is under spring tension.
15 When reassembling, grip the toothed ratchet quadrant in the vice and tension the regulator spring again, before fitting the electric motor.
16 Refitting to the door is a reversal of removal. Adjust in the following way.
17 Raise the wndow to its stop, and then release the stop lug.
18 Try to raise the window further by operating the lift button. Adjust the stop lug against the toothed quadrant, then tighten the lug locknut.
19 Lower the window fully to its stop, and then check that the lifting arm does not bottom in the slide fork. Adjust the stop lug if necessary to provide a clearance in the fork of approximately $1/32$ in (1.0 mm).

Fig. 12.30 Electric window stop lug adjustment (arrowed) – window raised (Sec 39)

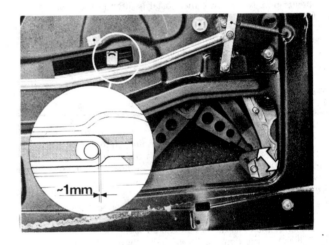

Fig. 12.31 Electric window stop lug adjustment (arrowed) – window lowered (Sec 39)

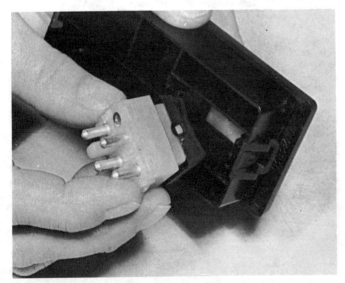

39.4 Removing a switch from the plastic block

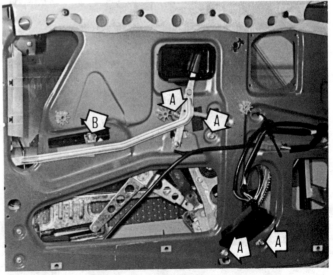

39.12 Regulator securing screws (A) and side rail clip (B)

40 Heated seat elements – removal and refitting

1 On some models the driver's seat and front passenger seat are heated. The elements are controlled by switches in the handbrake console.

2 Disconnect the leads to the seat heating pads at the junction box (Fig. 12.32).

3 Unbolt and remove the seat, complete with runners, from the car floor.

4 Disconnect the leads between the seat back panel and the seat cushion pad.

5 Remove the screws which secure the seat cushion and remove the cushion.

6 Place the seat upside down on the bench, and cut and remove the upholstery front retaining clamps.

7 Release the plastic hooks and pull out the heater pad from the seat back (Fig. 12.33).

8 When installing the new heater pad to the seat back, make sure that the barbed side of the elements faces the seat padding and the electrical leads run on the inner side of the seat back (nearer the transmission tunnel).

9 To renew the pad in the seat cushion, place the cushion upside-down and remove the cover plate.

10 Cut and remove the clamp at the rear end of the cushion. Withdraw the heater pad. Note that a thermostat is fitted in the cushion heater pad.

11 When installing the new pad, make sure that the barbed side of the heater element is towards the padding, and the electrical leads run on the inner side of the cushion (nearer the transmission tunnel).

12 Connect the upholstery using new clamps.

41 Radio – removal and refitting

1 The radio may be housed in either the centre console or in the facia panel above the centre air vents, depending on model year.

2 The type of radio fitted depends on the model year and personal choice. The procedure given here is for original equipment only.

Early types

3 Remove the centre console trim panel securing screws.

4 Pull off the radio control knobs.

5 Unscrew the locknuts which will be found under the knobs.

6 Pull the centre console forward slightly. Pull the radio mounting frame forward and lift out the radio, disconnecting the leads as you do so.

7 Refit in the reverse order.

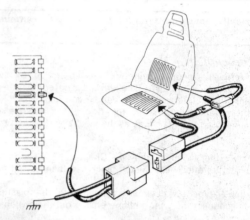

Fig. 12.32 Connector for heated seat elements (Sec 40)

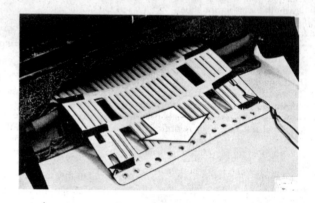

Fig. 12.33 Removing a heating element (Sec 40)

Later types

8 Pull off the radio control knobs (photo).

9 Bend a stiff piece of wire into a hook and use it to pull back the side clips as shown in the photographs, working through the space left by the knobs. Release each side clip and withdraw the radio (photo).

10 Disconnect the radio leads and remove the radio.

11 When refitting, reconnect the leads, then push the radio back into its housing until the clips snap into place.

12 Refit the control knobs.

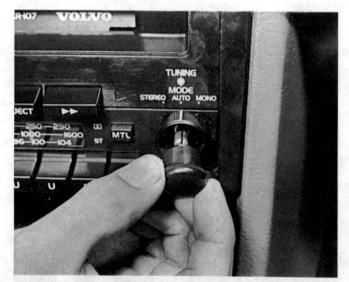

41.8 Pull off the radio control knobs

41.9A Insert a wire hook ...

41.9B ... and pull back the side clips (unit removed for clarity)

41.9C Withdraw the radio

42 Mobile radio equipment – interference-free installation

Aerials – selection and fitting

The choice of aerials is now very wide. It should be realised that the quality has a profound effect on radio performance, and a poor, inefficient aerial can make suppression difficult.

A wing-mounted aerial is regarded as probably the most efficient for signal collection, but a roof aerial is usually better for suppression purposes because it is away from most interference fields. Stick-on wire aerials are available for attachment to the inside of the windscreen, but are not always free from the interference field of the engine and some accessories.

Motorised automatic aerials rise when the equipment is switched on and retract at switch-off. They require more fitting space and supply leads, and can be a source of trouble.

There is no merit in choosing a very long aerial as, for example, the type about three metres in length which hooks or clips on to the rear of the car, since part of this aerial will inevitably be located in an interference field. For VHF/FM radios the best length of aerial is about one metre. Active aerials have a transistor amplifier mounted at the base and this serves to boost the received signal. The aerial rod is sometimes rather shorter than normal passive types.

A large loss of signal can occur in the aerial feeder cable, especially over the Very High Frequency (VHF) bands. The design of feeder cable is invariably in the co-axial form, ie a centre conductor surrounded by a flexible copper braid forming the outer (earth) conductor. Between the inner and outer conductors is an insulator material which can be in solid or stranded form. Apart from insulation, its purpose is to maintain the correct spacing and concentricity. Loss of signal occurs in this insulator, the loss usually being greater in a poor quality cable. The quality of cable used is reflected in the price of the aerial with the attached feeder cable.

The capacitance of the feeder should be within the range 65 to 75 picofarads (pF) approximately (95 to 100 pF for Japanese and American equipment), otherwise the adjustment of the car radio aerial trimmer may not be possible. An extension cable is necessary for a long run between aerial and receiver. If this adds capacitance in excess of the above limits, a connector containing a series capacitor will be required, or an extension which is labelled as 'capacity-compensated'.

Fitting the aerial will normally involve making a $7/8$ in (22 mm) diameter hole in the bodywork, but read the instructions that come with the aerial kit. Once the hole position has been selected, use a centre punch to guide the drill. Use sticky masking tape around the area for this helps with marking out and drill location, and gives protection to the paintwork should the drill slip. Three methods of making the hole are in use:

(a) Use a hole saw in the electric drill. This is, in effect, a circular

hacksaw blade wrapped round a former with a centre pilot drill.

(b) Use a tank cutter which also has cutting teeth, but is made to shear the metal by tightening with an Allen key.

(c) The hard way of drilling out the circle is using a small drill, say $1/8$ in (3 mm), so that the holes overlap. The centre metal drops out and the hole is finished with round and half-round files.

Whichever method is used, the burr is removed from the body metal and paint removed from the underside. The aerial is fitted tightly ensuring that the earth fixing, usually a serrated washer, ring or clamp, is making a solid connection. *This earth connection is important in reducing interference.* Cover any bare metal with primer paint and topcoat, and follow by underseal if desired.

Aerial feeder cable routing should avoid the engine compartment and areas where stress might occur, eg under the carpet where feet will be located. Roof aerials require that the headlining be pulled back and that a path is available down the door pillar. It is wise to check with the vehicle dealer whether roof aerial fitting is recommended.

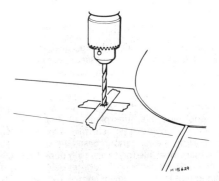

Fig. 12.34 Method of drilling the body (Sec 42)

Loudspeakers

Speakers should be matched to the output stage of the equipment, particularly as regards the recommended impedance. Power transistors used for driving speakers are sensitive to the loading placed on them.

Before choosing a mounting position for speakers, check whether the vehicle manufacturer has provided a location for them. Generally door-mounted speakers give good stereophonic reproduction, but not all doors are able to accept them. The next best position is the rear

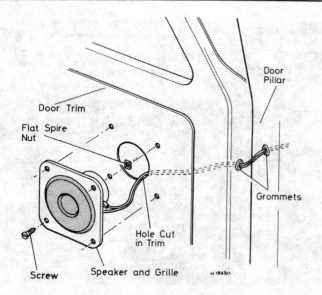

Fig. 12.35 Door mounted speaker installation (Sec 42)

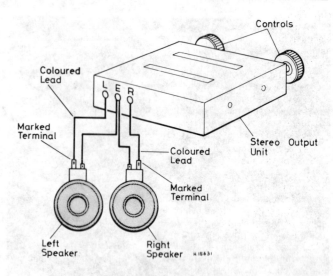

Fig. 12.36 Typical speaker connections (Sec 42)

parcel shelf, and in this case speaker apertures can be cut into the shelf, or pod units may be mounted.

For door mounting, first remove the trim, which is often held on by 'poppers' or press studs, and then select a suitable gap in the inside door assembly. Check that the speaker would not obstruct glass or winder mechanism by winding the window up and down. A template is often provided for marking out the trim panel hole, and then the four fixing holes must be drilled through. Mark out with chalk and cut cleanly with a sharp knife or keyhole saw. Speaker leads are then threaded through the door and door pillar, if necessary drilling 10 mm diameter holes. Fit grommets in the holes and connect to the radio or tape unit correctly. Do not omit a waterproofing cover, usually supplied with door speakers. If the speaker has to be fixed into the metal of the door itself, use self-tapping screws, and if the fixing is to the door trim use self-tapping screws and flat spire nuts.

Rear shelf mounting is somewhat simpler but it is necessary to find gaps in the metalwork underneath the parcel shelf. However, remember that the speakers should be as far apart as possible to give a good stereo effect. Pod-mounted speakers can be screwed into position through the parcel shelf material, but it is worth testing for the best position. Sometimes good results are found by reflecting sound off the rear window.

Unit installation

Provision is made for installing the radio in the facia or centre console. Later Volvo standard radio/cassette players are larger than many other units, so spacers or packing pieces may need to be used with a smaller unit.

Installation of the radio/audio unit is basically the same in all cases, and consists of offering it into the aperture after removal of the knobs *(not* push buttons) and the trim plate. In some cases a special mounting plate is required to which the unit is attached. It is worthwhile supporting the rear end in cases where sag or strain may occur, and it is usually possible to use a length of perforated metal strip attached between the unit and a good support point nearby. In general it is recommended that tape equipment should be installed at or nearly horizontal.

Connections to the aerial socket are simply by the standard plug terminating the aerial download or its extension cable. Speakers for a stereo system must be matched and correctly connected, as outlined previously.

Note: *While all work is carried out on the power side, it is wise to disconnect the battery earth lead.* Before connection is made to the vehicle electrical system, check that the polarity of the unit is correct. The Volvo uses a negative earth system, but radio/audio units often have a reversible plug to convert the set to either + or – earth. *Incorrect connection may cause serious damage.*

The power lead is often permanently connected inside the unit and

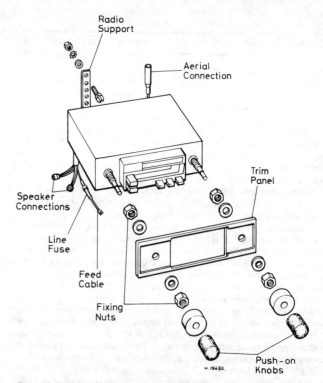

Fig. 12.37 Typical radio/cassette mounting components (Sec 42)

terminates with one half of an in-line fuse carrier. The other half is fitted with a suitable fuse (3 or 5 amperes) and a wire which should go to a power point in the electrical system. This may be the accessory terminal on the ignition switch, giving the advantage of power feed with ignition or with the ignition key at the 'accessory' position. Power to the unit stops when the ignition key is removed. Alternatively, the lead may be taken to a live point at the fusebox with the consequence of having to remember to switch off at the unit before leaving the vehicle.

Before switching on for initial test, be sure that the speaker connections have been made, for running without load can damage the output transistors. Switch on next and tune through the bands to ensure that all sections are working, and check the tape unit if applicable. The aerial trimmer should be adjusted to give the strongest reception on a weak signal in the medium wave band, at say 200 metres.

Interference

In general, when electric current changes abruptly, unwanted electrical noise is produced. The motor vehicle is filled with electrical devices which change electric current rapidly, the most obvious being the contact breaker.

When the spark plugs operate, the sudden pulse of spark current causes the associated wiring to radiate. Since early radio transmitters used sparks as a basis of operation, it is not surprising that the car radio will pick up ignition spark noise unless steps are taken to reduce it to acceptable levels.

Interference reaches the car radio in two ways:

(a) by conduction through the wiring.
(b) by radiation to the receiving aerial.

Initial checks presuppose that the bonnet is down and fastened, the radio unit has a good earth connection (not through the aerial downlead outer), no fluorescent tubes are working near the car, the aerial trimmer has been adjusted, and the vehicle is in a position to receive radio signals, ie not in a metal-clad building.

Switch on the radio and tune it to the middle of the medium wave (MW) band off-station with the volume (gain) control set fairly high. Switch on the ignition (but do not start the engine) and wait to see if irregular clicks or 'white' noise occurs. Tapping the facia panel may also produce the effects. If so, this will be due to the voltage stabiliser, which is an on-off thermal switch to control instrument voltage. It is located on the back of the instrument panel (see Section 33). Correction is by attachment of a capacitor and, if still troublesome, chokes in the supply wires.

Switch on the engine and listen for interference on the MW band. Depending on the type of interference, the indications are as follows.

A harsh crackle that drops out abruptly at low engine speed or when the headlights are switched on is probably due to the alternator voltage regulator.

A whine varying with engine speed is due to the alternator. Try temporarily taking off the fan belt – if the noise goes this is confirmation.

Regular ticking or crackle that varies in rate with the engine speed is due to the ignition system. With this trouble in particular and others in general, check to see if the noise is entering the receiver from the wiring or by radiation. To do this, pull out the aerial plug, (preferably shorting out the input socket or connecting a 62 pF capacitor across it). If the noise disappears it is coming in through the aerial and is radiation noise. If the noise persists it is reaching the receiver through the wiring and is said to be line-borne.

Interference from wipers, washers, heater blowers, turn-indicators, stop lamps, etc is usually taken to the receiver by wiring, and simple treatment using capacitors and possibly chokes will solve the problem. Switch on each one in turn (wet the screen first for running wipers!) and listen for possible interference with the aerial plug in place and again when removed.

Electric petrol pumps are fitted to some models and give rise to an irregular clicking, often giving a burst of clicks when the ignition is on but the engine has not yet been started. It is also possible to receive whining or crackling from the pump.

Note that if most of the vehicle accessories are found to be creating interference all together, the probability is that poor aerial earthing is to blame.

Component terminal markings

Throughout the following sub-sections reference will be found to various terminal markings. These will vary depending on the manufacturer of the relevant component. If terminal markings differ from those mentioned, reference should be made to the following table, where the most commonly encountered variations are listed.

Alternator	Alternator terminal (thick lead)	Exciting winding terminal
DIN/Bosch	B+	DF
Delco Remy	+	EXC
Ducellier	+	EXC
Ford (US)	+	DF
Lucas	+	F
Marelli	+B	F

Ignition coil	Ignition switch terminal	Contact breaker terminal
DIN/Bosch	15	1
Delco Remy	+	–
Ducellier	BAT	RUP
Ford (US)	B/+	CB/–
Lucas	SW/+	–
Marelli	BAT/+B	D

Voltage regulator	Voltage input terminal	Exciting winding terminal
DIN/Bosch	B+/D+	DF
Delco Remy	BAT/+	EXC
Ducellier	BOB/BAT	EXC
Ford (US)	BAT	DF
Lucas	+/A	F
Marelli		F

Suppression methods – ignition

Suppressed HT cables are supplied as original equipment by manufacturers and will meet regulations as far as interference to neighbouring equipment is concerned. It is illegal to remove such suppression unless an alternative is provided, and this may take the form of resistive spark plug caps in conjunction with plain copper HT cable. For VHF purposes, these and 'in-line' resistors may not be effective, and resistive HT cable is preferred. Check that suppressed cables are actually fitted by observing cable identity lettering, or measuring with an ohmmeter – the value of each plug lead should be 5000 to 10 000 ohms.

A 1 microfarad capacitor connected from the LT supply side of the ignition coil to a good nearby earth point will complete basic ignition interference treatment. NEVER fit a capacitor to the coil terminal to the contact breaker – the result would be burnt out points in a short time.

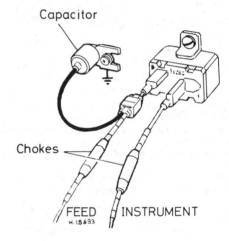

Fig. 12.38 Voltage stabiliser interference suppression (Sec 42)

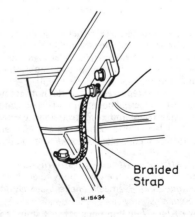

Fig. 12.39 Bonnet earth strap (Sec 42)

If ignition noise persists despite the treatment above, the following sequence should be followed:

(a) Check the earthing of the ignition coil; remove paint from fixing clamp.

(b) If this does not work, lift the bonnet. Should there be no change in interference level, this may indicate that the bonnet is not electrically connected to the car body. Use a proprietary braided strap across a bonnet hinge ensuring a first class electrical connection. If, however, lifting the bonnet increases the interference, then fit resistive HT cables of a higher ohms-per-metre value.

(c) If all these measures fail, it is probable that re-radiation from metallic components is taking place. Using a braided strap between metallic points, go round the vehicle systematically – try the following: engine to body, exhaust system to body, front suspension to engine and to body, steering column to body, gear lever to engine and to body, Bowden cable to body, metal parcel shelf to body. When an offending component is located it should be bonded with the strap permanently.

(d) As a next step, the fitting of distributor suppressors to each lead at the distributor end may help.

(e) Beyond this point is involved the possible screening of the distributor and fitting resistive spark plugs, but such advanced treatment is not usually required for vehicles with entertainment equipment.

Electronic ignition systems have built-in suppression components, but this does not relieve the need for using suppressed HT leads. In some cases it is permitted to connect a capacitor on the low tension supply side of the ignition coil, but not in every case. Makers' instructions should be followed carefully, otherwise damage to the ignition semiconductors may result.

Suppression methods – generators

Alternators should be fitted with a 3 microfarad capacitor from the B+ main output terminal (thick cable) to earth. Additional suppression may be obtained by the use of a filter in the supply line to the radio receiver.

It is most important that:

(a) Capacitors are never connected to the field terminals of the alternator.

(b) Alternators are not run without connection to the battery.

Suppression methods – voltage regulators

Alternator regulators come in three types:

(a) Vibrating contact regulators separate from the alternator.

(b) Electronic regulators separate from the alternator.

(c) Electronic regulators built-in to the alternator.

In case (a) interference may be generated on the AM and FM (VHF) bands. For some cars a replacement suppressed regulator is available. Filter boxes may be used with non-suppressed regulators. But if not available, then for AM equipment a 2 microfarad or 3 microfarad capacitor may be mounted at the voltage terminal marked D+ or B+ of the regulator. FM bands may be treated by a feed-through capacitor of 2 or 3 microfarad.

Electronic voltage regulators are not always troublesome, but where necessary, a 1 microfarad capacitor from the regulator + terminal will help.

Integral electronic voltage regulators do not normally generate much interference, but when encountered this is in combination with alternator noise. A 1 microfarad or 2 microfarad capacitor from the warning lamp (IND) terminal to earth for Lucas ACR alternators and Femsa, Delco and Bosch equivalents should cure the problem.

Suppression methods – other equipment

Wiper motors – Connect the wiper body to earth with a bonding strap. For all motors use a 7 ampere choke assembly inserted in the leads to the motor.

Heater motors – Fit 7 ampere line chokes in both leads, assisted if necessary by a 1 microfarad capacitor to earth from both leads.

Electronic tachometer – The tachometer is a possible source of ignition noise – check by disconnecting at the ignition coil CB terminal. It usually feeds from ignition coil LT pulses at the contact

breaker terminal. A 3 ampere line choke should be fitted in the tachometer lead at the coil CB terminal.

Horn – A capacitor and choke combination is effective if the horn is directly connected to the 12 volt supply. The use of a relay is an alternative remedy, as this will reduce the length of the interference-carrying leads.

Electrostatic noise – Characteristics are erratic crackling at the receiver, with disappearance of symptoms in wet weather. Often

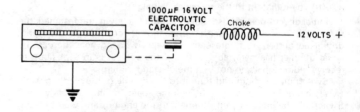

Fig. 12.40 Suppressor in radio supply line (Sec 42)

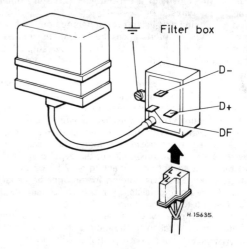

Fig. 12.41 Typical filter box for vibrating contact voltage regulator (alternator) (Sec 42)

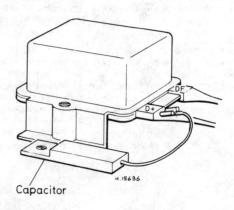

Fig. 12.42 Suppression of AM interference by vibrating contact voltage regulator (Sec 42)

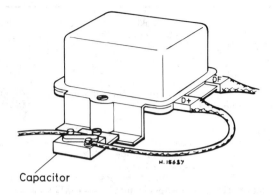

Fig. 12.43 Suppression of FM interference by vibrating contact voltage regulator (Sec 42)

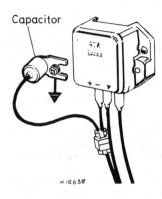

Fig. 12.44 Suppression of electronic voltage regulator (Sec 42)

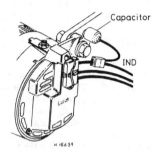

Fig. 12.45 Suppression of alternator integral type electronic voltage regulator (Sec 42)

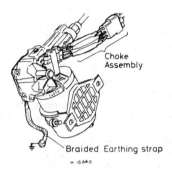

Fig. 12.46 Suppression of wiper motor (Sec 42)

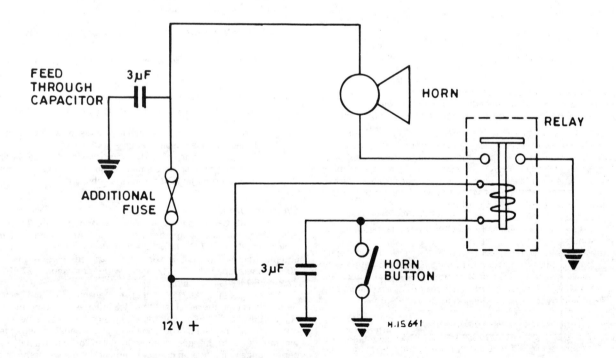

Fig. 12.47 Relay used to reduce horn interference (Sec 42)

shocks may be given when touching bodywork. Part of the problem is the build-up of static electricity in non-driven wheels and the acquisition of charge on the body shell. It is possible to fit spring-loaded contacts at the wheels to give good conduction between the rotary wheel parts and the vehicle frame. Changing a tyre sometimes helps – because of tyres' varying resistances. In difficult cases a trailing flex which touches the ground will cure the problem. If this is not acceptable it is worth trying conductive paint on the tyre walls.

Fuel pump – Suppression requires a 1 microfarad capacitor between the supply wire to the pump and a nearby earth point. If this is insufficient a 7 ampere line choke connected in the supply wire near the pump is required.

Fluorescent tubes – Vehicles used for camping/caravanning frequently have fluorescent tube lighting. These tubes require a relatively high voltage for operation and this is provided by an inverter (a form of oscillator) which steps up the vehicle supply voltage. This can give rise to serious interference to radio reception, and the tubes themselves can contribute to this interference by the pulsating nature of the lamp discharge. In such situations it is important to mount the aerial as far away from a fluorescent tube as possible. The interference problem may be alleviated by screening the tube with fine wire turns spaced an inch (25 mm) apart and earthed to the chassis. Suitable chokes should be fitted in both supply wires close to the inverter.

Radio/cassette case breakthrough

Magnetic radiation from dashboard wiring may be sufficiently intense to break through the metal case of the radio/cassette player. Often this is due to a particular cable routed too close and shows up as ignition interference on AM and cassette play and/or alternator whine on cassette play.

The first point to check is that the clips and/or screws are fixing all parts of the radio/cassette case together properly. Assuming good earthing of the case, see if it is possible to re-route the offending cable – the chances of this are not good, however, in most cars.

Next release the radio/cassette player and locate it in different positions with temporary leads. If a point of low interference is found, then if possible fix the equipment in that area. This also confirms that local radiation is causing the trouble. If re-location is not feasible, fit the radio/cassette player back in the original position.

Alternator interference on cassette play is now caused by radiation from the main charging cable which goes from the battery to the output terminal of the alternator, usually via the + terminal of the starter motor relay. In some vehicles this cable is routed under the dashboard, so the solution is to provide a direct cable route. Detach the original cable from the alternator output terminal and make up a new cable of at least 6 mm² cross-sectional area to go from alternator to battery with the shortest possible route. *Remember – do not run the engine with the alternator disconnected from the battery.*

Ignition breakthrough on AM and/or cassette play can be a difficult problem. It is worth wrapping earthed foil round the offending cable

run near the equipment, or making up a deflector plate well screwed down to a good earth. Another possibility is the use of a suitable relay to switch on the ignition coil. The relay should be mounted close to the ignition coil; with this arrangement the ignition coil primary current is not taken into the dashboard area and does not flow through the ignition switch. A suitable diode should be used since it is possible that at ignition switch-off the output from the warning lamp alternator terminal could hold the relay on.

Connectors for suppression components

Capacitors are usually supplied with tags on the end of the lead, while the capacitor body has a flange with a slot or hole to fit under a nut or screw with washer.

Connections to feed wires are best achieved by self-stripping connectors. These connectors employ a blade which, when squeezed down by pliers, cuts through cable insulation and makes connection to the copper conductors beneath.

Chokes sometimes come with bullet snap-in connectors fitted to the wires, and also with just bare copper wire. With connectors, suitable female cable connectors may be purchased from an auto-accessory shop together with any extra connectors required for the cable ends after being cut for the choke insertion. For chokes with bare wires, similar connectors may be employed together with insulation sleeving as required.

VHF/FM broadcasts

Reception of VHF/FM in an automobile is more prone to problems than the medium and long wavebands. Medium/long wave transmitters are capable of covering considerable distances, but VHF transmitters are restricted to line of sight, meaning ranges of 10 to 50 miles, depending upon the terrain, the effects of buildings and the transmitter power.

Because of the limited range it is necessary to retune on a long journey, and it may be better for those habitually travelling long distances or living in areas of poor provision of transmitters to use an AM radio working on medium/long wavebands.

When conditions are poor, interference can arise, and some of the suppression devices described previously fall off in performance at very high frequencies unless specifically designed for the VHF band. Available suppression devices include reactive HT cable, resistive distributor caps, screened plug caps, screened leads and resistive spark plugs.

For VHF/FM receiver installation the following points should be particularly noted:

(a) Earthing of the receiver chassis and the aerial mounting is important. Use a separate earthing wire at the radio, and scrape paint away at the aerial mounting.

(b) If possible, use a good quality roof aerial to obtain maximum height and distance from interference generating devices on the vehicle.

(c) Use of a high quality aerial downlead is important, since losses in cheap cable can be significant.

(d) The polarisation of FM transmissions may be horizontal, vertical, circular or slanted. Because of this the optimum mounting angle is at 45° to the vehicle roof.

Citizens' Band radio (CB)

In the UK, CB transmitter/receivers work within the 27 MHz and 934 MHz bands, using the FM mode. At present interest is concentrated on 27 MHz where the design and manufacture of equipment is less difficult. Maximum transmitted power is 4 watts, and 40 channels spaced 10 kHz apart within the range 27.60125 to 27.99125 MHz are available.

Aerials are the key to effective transmission and reception. Regulations limit the aerial length to 1.65 metres including the loading coil and any associated circuitry, so tuning the aerial is necessary to obtain optimum results. The choice of a CB aerial is dependent on whether it is to be permanently installed or removable, and the performance will hinge on correct tuning and the location point on the vehicle. Common practice is to clip the aerial to the roof gutter or to employ wing mounting where the aerial can be rapidly unscrewed. An alternative is to use the boot rim to render the aerial theftproof, but a popular solution is to use the 'magmount' – a type of mounting having a strong magnetic base clamping to the vehicle at any point, usually the roof.

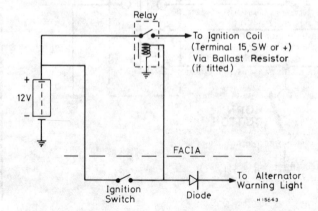

Fig. 12.48 Ignition coil relay used to suppress case breakthrough (Sec 42)

Aerial location determines the signal distribution for both transmission and reception, but it is wise to choose a point away from the engine compartment to minimise interference from vehicle electrical equipment.

The aerial is subject to considerable wind and acceleration forces. Cheaper units will whip backwards and forwards and in so doing will alter the relationship with the metal surface of the vehicle with which it forms a ground plane aerial system. The radiation pattern will change correspondingly, giving rise to break-up of both incoming and outgoing signals.

Interference problems on the vehicle carrying CB equipment fall into two categories:

(a) Interference to nearby TV and radio receivers when transmitting.
(b) Interference to CB set reception due to electrical equipment on the vehicle.

Problems of break-through to TV and radio are not frequent, but can be difficult to solve. Mostly trouble is not detected or reported because the vehicle is moving and the symptoms rapidly disappear at the TV/radio receiver, but when the CB set is used as a base station any trouble with nearby receivers will soon result in a complaint.

It must not be assumed by the CB operator that his equipment is faultless, for much depends upon the design. Harmonics (that is, multiples) of 27 MHz may be transmitted unknowingly and these can fall into other user's bands. Where trouble of this nature occurs, low pass filters in the aerial or supply leads can help, and should be fitted in base station aerials as a matter of course. In stubborn cases it may be necessary to call for assistance from the licensing authority, or, if possible, to have the equipment checked by the manufacturers.

Interference received on the CB set from the vehicle equipment is, fortunately, not usually a severe problem. The precautions outlined previously for radio/cassette units apply, but there are some extra points worth noting.

It is common practice to use a slide-mount on CB equipment enabling the set to be easily removed for use as a base station, for example. Care must be taken that the slide mount fittings are properly earthed and that first class connection occurs between the set and slide-mount.

Vehicle manufacturers in the UK are required to provide suppression of electrical equipment to cover 40 to 250 MHz to protect TV and VHF radio bands. Such suppression appears to be adequately effective at 27 MHz, but suppression of individual items such as alternators/ dynamos, clocks, stabilisers, flashers, wiper motors, etc, may still be necessary. The suppression capacitors and chokes available from auto-electrical suppliers for entertainment receivers will usually give the required results with CB equipment.

Other vehicle radio transmitters

Besides CB radio already mentioned, a considerable increase in the use of transceivers (ie combined transmitter and receiver units) has taken place in the last decade. Previously this type of equipment was fitted mainly to military, fire, ambulance and police vehicles, but a large business radio and radio telephone usage has developed.

Generally the suppression techniques described previously will suffice, with only a few difficult cases arising. Suppression is carried out to satisfy the 'receive mode', but care must be taken to use heavy duty chokes in the equipment supply cables since the loading on 'transmit' is relatively high.

43 Dim-dip system – general

1   A reduced intensity dipped headlight system, known as dim-dip, was introduced in 1987.
2   The system provides a reduced headlight dipped beam (10% of normal power), when the parking lights are on, and the ignition is switched on. Thus it is no longer possible to drive using parking lights only.
3   The parking lights revert to normal operation when the ignition is switched off.
4   The reduced beam regulator is located on the pillar to the left of the front passenger footwell area.
5   Refer to the wiring diagram for further details.

44 Headlights 'on' warning buzzer – general

1   The headlights 'on' warning buzzer, introduced in 1979, is located under the facia panel, above the foot pedals.
2   The buzzer sounds if the headlights are left on, or if the ignition key is left in the lock, when the driver's door is opened.
3   The 1986-on models where the headlights are wired through the ignition switch, the warning buzzer is no longer fitted.
4   See wiring diagrams for details.

45 Fault diagnosis – electrical system

Symptom	Reason(s)
Starter motor does not turn – no voltage at motor	Battery terminals loose or corroded Battery discharged or defective Starter motor connections loose or corroded Starter switch or solenoid faulty Automatic transmission not in P or N Automatic transmission inhibitor switch faulty
Starter motor does not turn – voltage at motor	Internal defect in starter motor
Starter motor turns very slowly	Battery discharged or defective Battery terminals loose or corroded Starter motor internal defect
Starter motor noisy or rough	Mounting bolts loose Pinion or flywheel ring gear teeth damaged or worn
Alternator not charging battery	Drivebelt slipping or broken Alternator brushes worn Alternator connections loose or corroded Alternator internal defect Fault in charging system
Alternator overcharging battery	Alternator regulator faulty

45 Fault diagnosis – electrical system

Symptom	Reason(s)
Battery will not hold charge	Short-circuit (continual drain on battery) Battery defective Battery case/terminals dirty or damp
Gauge or speedometer (electronic) gives no reading	Sender unit defective Earthed or broken wire Gauge faulty
Fuel or temperature gauge reads too high or low	As above Instrument voltage stabiliser faulty (will affect both gauges)
Horn operates continuously	Horn push stuck down Horn cable earthed
Horn does not operate	Fuse blown Loose cable connections or broken cable Horn push switch defective
Lights do not come on	Battery discharged Fuse or fuses blown Light switch faulty Bulbs blown Relays (where fitted) defective
Lights very dim	Dirty lenses Corroded internal reflectors Bulbs blackened Incorrect bulb wattage Battery discharged
Wiper motor fails to work	Fuse blown Connections loose or broken Relay defective Switch defective Motor defective
Wiper motor works slowly	Worn brushes Seized linkage Motor defective
Wiper motor works but blades do not move	Linkage seized Drive spindle broken Worn motor gearbox
General defects in other components	Blown fuse(s) Faulty relay Broken or corroded wiring/connections Faulty switch Incorrect earthing of component Faulty component

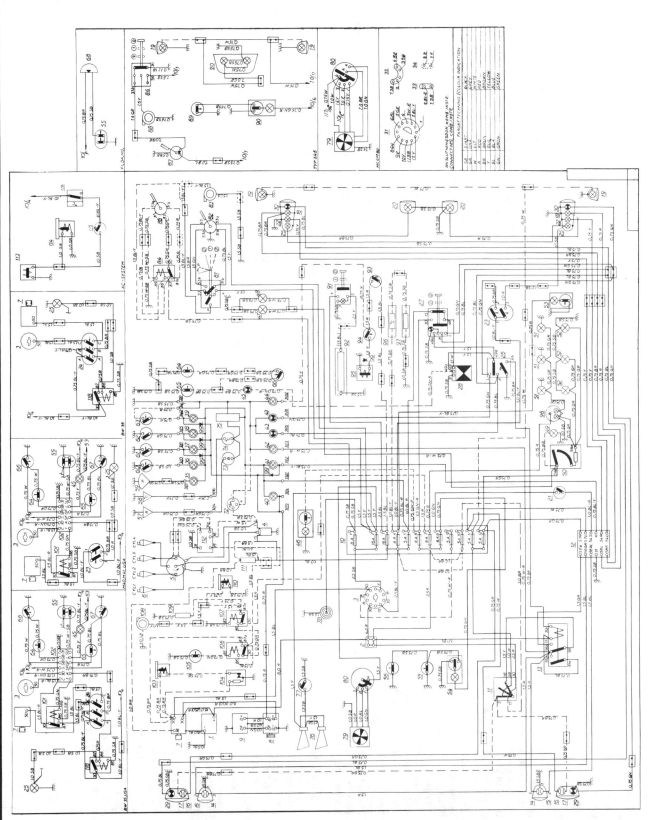

Fig. 12.49 Wiring diagram for models up to 1975

Key to Fig. 12.49

1 Battery
2 Connection plate
3 Ignition switch
4 Ignition switch
5 Distributor, firing sequence 1-3-4-2
6 Spark plug
7 Starter motor
8 Alternator
9 Charging regulator
10 Fusebox
11 Lighting switch
12 Bulb failure warning unit
13 Step relay for full beam, dipped beam and headlight flasher
14 Full beam
15 Dipped beam
16 Parking light
17 Day notice light
18 Tail light
19 Side marking light
20 Sign light
21 Stop light contact
22 Stop light
23 Contact on M 40, M 41 gearbox
24 Contact on BW 35 automatic transmission
25 Back-up stoplight
26 Direction indicator lever
27 Hazard warning lights switch
28 Flasher unit
29 Front flasher light
30 Rear flasher light
31 Conn. to instrument
32 Conn. to instrument
33 Conn. to instrument
34 Conn. to instrument
35 Oil pressure warning light
36 Choke light
37 Parking brake warning light
38 Brake warning light
39 EGR – indicator light
40 Battery charging warning light
41 Bulb failure warning light
42 Full beam indicator light
43 Flasher indicator light
44 Overdrive indicator light
45 Fasten seat belt light
46 Engine compartment
47 Buckle lighting
48 Rear ashtray lighting
49 Gear position lighting
50 Rheostat for instrument panel light
51 Instrument panel light
52 Control panel light
53 Glove locker light
54 Courtesy light
55 Door contact, driver's side
56 Door contact, passenger's side
57 Fuel level sender
58 Temperature sender
59 Oil pressure sensor
60 Choke control contact
61 Parking brake contact
62 Brake warning contact
63 EGR – warning contact
64 Contact, seat belt, pass. seat
65 Contact, seat belt, driver's seat
66 Contact, passenger seat
67 Contact, driver's seat
68 Light buzzer
72 Rev counter
73 Fuel gauge
74 Thermometer
75 Voltage stabilizer
76 Horns
77 Horn ring
78 Cigar lighter
79 Fan
80 Fan switch
81 Windscreen wiper/washer switch
82 Windscreen wipers
83 Windscreen washers
84 Relay for headlight wipers
85 Headlight wipers
86 Switch for tailgate window wiper/washer
87 Tailgate window wiper
88 Tailgate window washer
89 Rear door contact
90 Rear cargo space light
91 Electrically heated rear window switch
92 Electrically heated rear window
93 Switch for overdrive M 41
94 Contact for overdrive on M 41 gearbox
95 Control magnet for overdrive on M 41 gearbox
96 Heater element with thermostat, driver's seat
97 Heater element, driver's seat
98 Clock
99 Diode
100 Joint
101 Relay, start inhibitor
102 Start inhibitor unit
103 Start valve
104 Thermal timer contact
105 Air pressure gage
106 Main relay, fuel injection
107 Fuel pump relay
108 Fuel pump
109 Pressure regulating valve
110 Auxiliary air valve
111 Resistor
112 Ignition control unit
113 Solenoid on compressor
114 Solenoid valve
115 Switch, AC compressor
116 Thermostat
118 Relay for back-up light

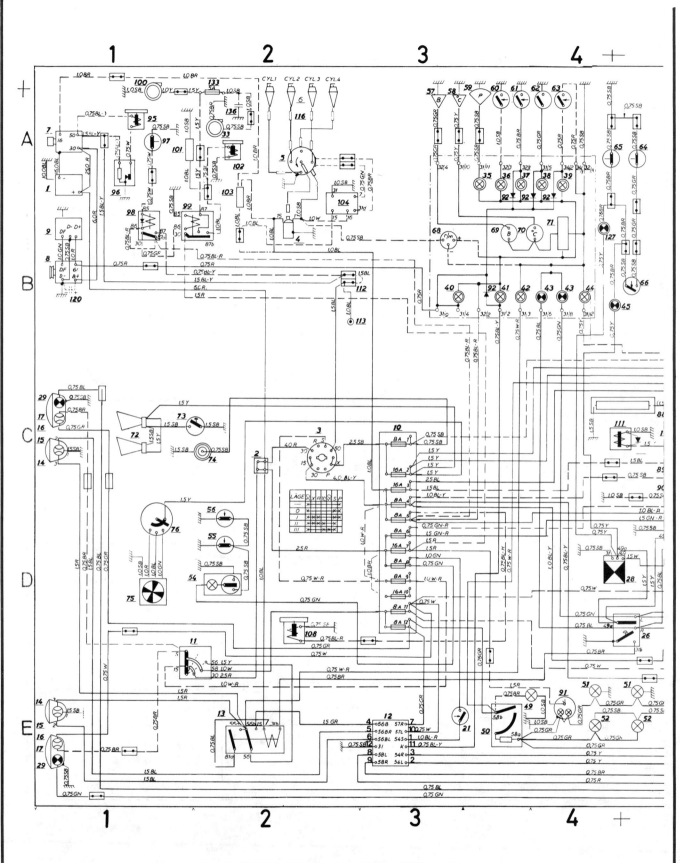

Fig. 12.50 Wiring diagram for **1976 to 1977 models**

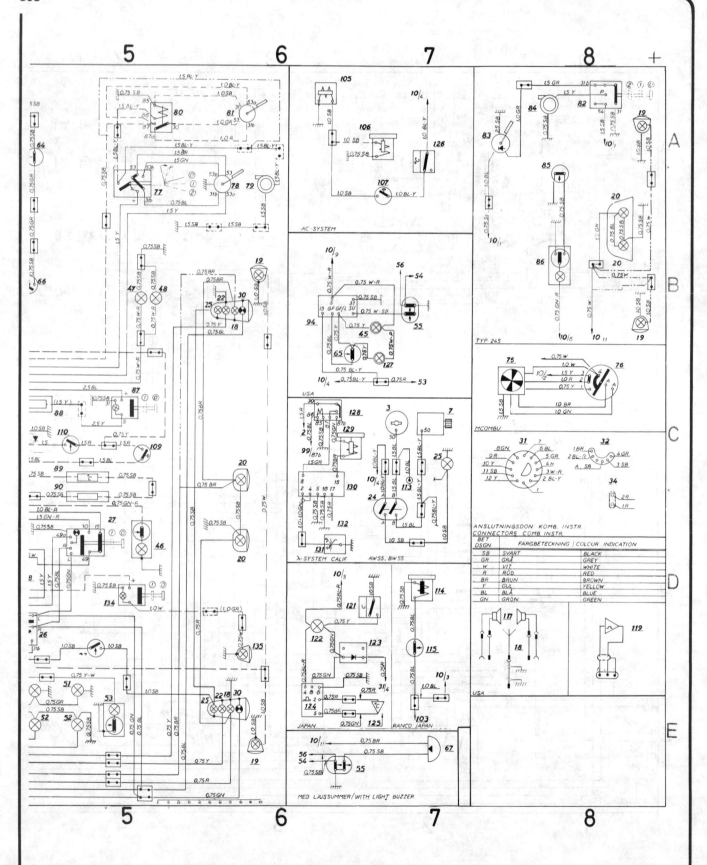

Fig. 12.50 Wiring diagram for 1976 to 1977 models (continued)

Key to Fig. 12.50

1	Battery	A1
2	Connection plate	C2
3	Ignition switch	C2,C7
4	Ignition coil 1.2 A	B2
5	Distributor	A2
6	Spark plugs	A2
7	Starter motor, 800 W	A1,C7
8	Alternator, 760 W	B1
9	Charging regulator	B1
10	Fusebox	C3
11	Lighting switch	D2
12	Bulb failure warning sensor	E3
13	Step relay for full beams and dipped beams and headlight flasher	E2
14	Mainbeam 60 W max	C1,E1
15	Dipped beams, 55 W max	C1,E1
16	Parking lights, 5 W	C1,E1
17	Day running lights, 21 W	C1,E1
18	Tail lights, 5 W	B6,E6
19	Side marker lights, 3 W	A8,B6
20	Number plate light, 5 W	C6,B8
21	Stop-light switch	E3
22	Stop-light, 21 W	B6, E6
23	Switch on gearbox	D5
24	Switch on automatic transmission	C7
25	Reversing lights, 21 W	B6,C7
26	Direction indicator stalk	D4
27	Switch for hazard warning lights	D5
28	Flasher device	D4
29	Front direction indicator light, 21 W	C1,E1
30	Rear direction indicator light, 21 W	B6,E6
31	Connection at instrument	C8
32	Connection at instrument	C8
33	Tank pump, 1.6 A	A2
34	Connection at instrument	C8
35	Oil pressure warning light, 1.2 W	A3
36	Choke light, 1.2 W	A4
37	Parking brake indicator light, 1.2 W	A4
38	Brake warning light, 1.2 W	A4
39	EGR indicator light, 1.2 W	A4
40	Battery charging warning light, 1.2 W	B3
41	Bulb failure warning light, 1.2 W	B4
42	Mainbeam indicator light, 1.2 W	B4
43	Direction indicator panel light, 1.2 W	B4
44	Overdrive indicator light, 1.2 W	B4
45	Fasten seat belt warning light, 1.2 W	B4,B7
46	Engine compartment light, 15 W	D5
47	Fasten seat belt light, 1.2 W	B5
48	Ashtray light, 1.2 W	B5
49	Selector lever light, 1.2 W	E4
50	Rheostat for instrument panel light	E3
51	Instrument panel light, 2 W	E4,E5
52	Control panel light, 1.2 W	E4,E5
53	Glove locker light, 2 W	E5
54	Courtesy light bulb, 10 W	D2
55	Door switch, driver's side	B7,D2,E6
56	Door switch, passenger's side	D2
57	Fuel gauge sender	A3
58	Temperature gauge sender	A3
59	Oil pressure sensor	A3
60	Choke contact	A3
61	Parking brake switch	A4
62	Brake warning switch	A4
63	EGR/EXH warning switch	A4
64	Switch, seat belt, passenger's seat	A4
65	Switch, seat belt, driver's seat	A4
66	Switch, passenger's seat	B4
67	Headlights on reminder buzzer	E7
68	Rev counter	B3
69	Fuel gauge	B3
70	Thermometer	B4
71	Voltage stabilizer	B4
72	Horn 7.5 A	C1
73	Horn pad	C2

Key to Fig. 12.50 (continued)

No.	Description	Ref
74	Cigar lighter, 7 A	C2
75	Fan, 115 or 170 W	C8,D1
76	Fan switch	C8,D1
77	Switch for windscreen wipers/washers	A5
78	Windscreen wipers, 3.5 A	A6
79	Windscreen washer, 2.6 A	A6
80	Relay for headlight wipers	A5
81	Headlight wipers	A6
82	Switch for tailgate wiper/washer	A8
83	Tailgate wiper, 1 A	A7
84	Tailgate washer, 2.6 A	A8
85	Rear door switch	A8
86	Rear cargo space light, 10 W	B8
87	Switch for electrically heated rear window	C5
88	Electrically heated rear window, 150 W	C5
89	Heater element with thermostat, driver's seat cushion, 30 W	C5
90	Heater element, driver's seat backrest	C5
91	Clock	E4
92	Diode	
93	Joint	
94	Fasten seat belt reminder	A1
95	Cold start valve	A1
96	Thermal timer switch	A1
97	Fan, combined system	A1
98	Fan switch, fan combined system	A1
99	Relay for fuel pump	A1
100	Fuel pump, 6.5 A	A1
101	Control pressure regulator	A2
102	Auxiliary air valve	A1
103	Resistance, 0.4 to 0.6 ohm	A2
104	Control unit, ignition system	A6
105	Control magnet, compressor	A7
106	Solenoid valve	A7
107	Switch for air conditioning	D2
108	Solenoid valve, carburettor	C5
109	Switch for overdrive	C5
110	Switch for overdrive on gearbox M 46	C4
111	Control magnet for overdrive 2.2 A on gearbox M 46	B3
112	Coupling	B3,C7
113	Power output	D7
114	Thermostat	D7
116	Suppressor	A2
117	Loudspeaker, front doors, 4 ohms	D7
118	Antenna, windscreen	D8
119	Top dead centre sender	D8
120	Capacitor, 2.2µ F	B1
121	Thermostat, floor, 149°C	D6
122	Exhaust temp. indicator light	D6
123	Diode box	D7
124	Temperature sensor, 850°C	E6
125	Thermoelement, catalyst	E7
126	Thermostat AC	A7
127	Fasten seat belt warning light	B4
128	Switch for rear foglights	C6
129	Relay for Lambda system	E1
130	Control unit, Lambda system	C6
131	Lambda-sond	D6
132	Test point, Lambda-sond	D6
133	Cable fusing, tank pump	A2
134	Motor for window winder, RH side front	D5
135	Rear foglights	D6
136	Condenser, tank pump	A2

Colour code

BL	Blue	R	Red
BR	Brown	SB	Black
GN	Green	W	White
GR	Grey	Y	Yellow

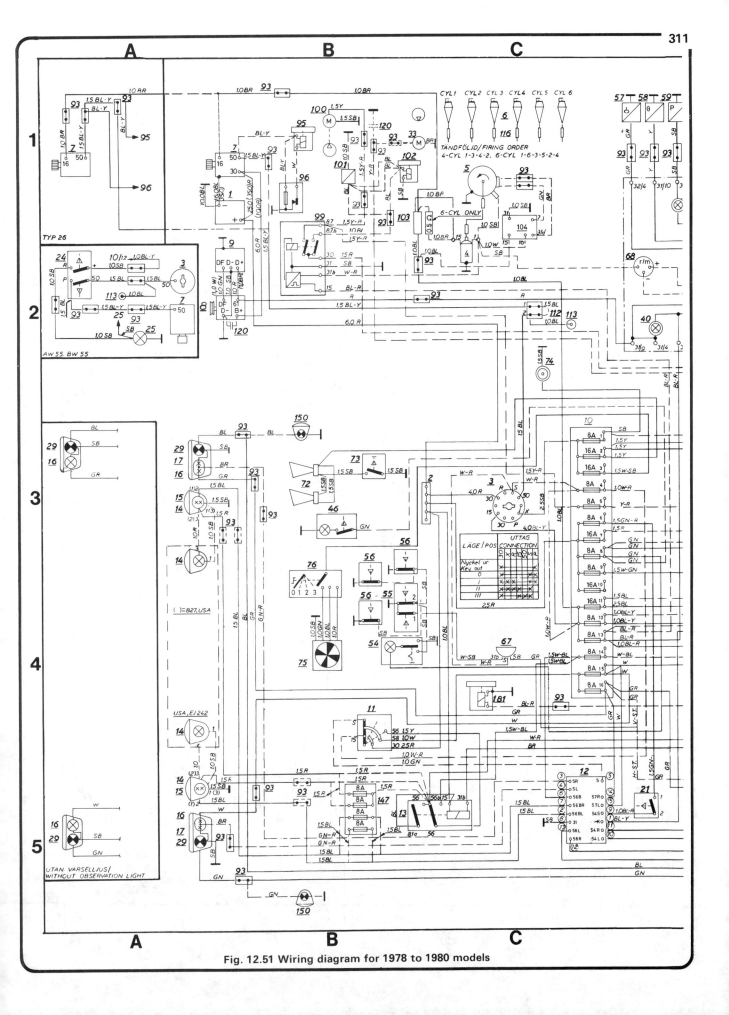

Fig. 12.51 Wiring diagram for 1978 to 1980 models

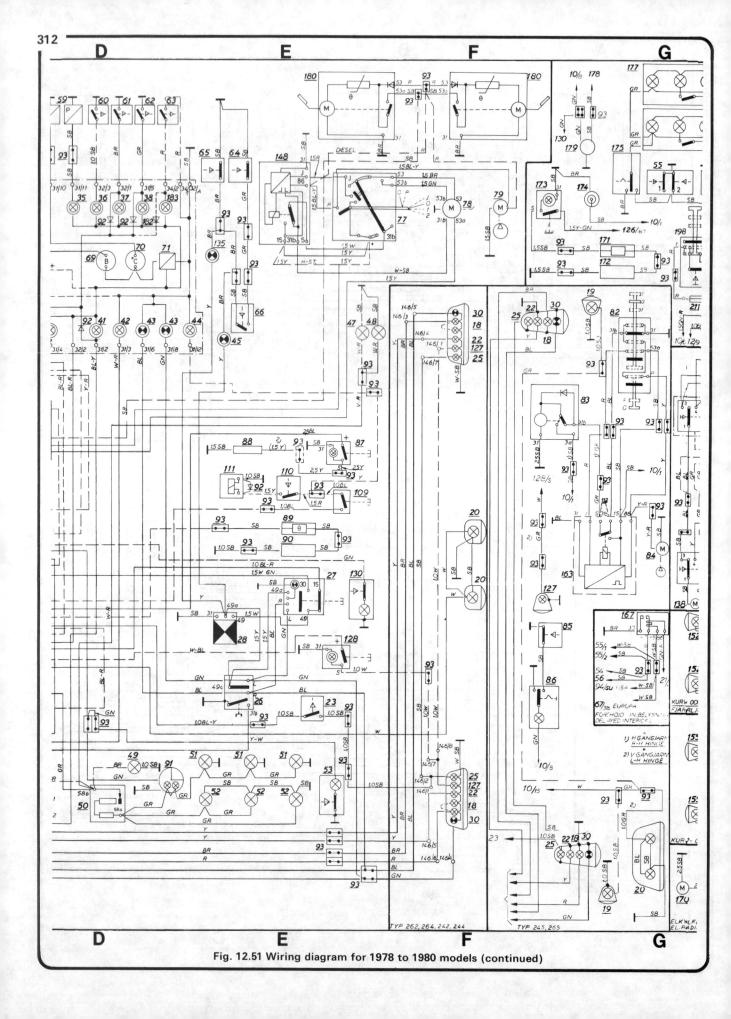

Fig. 12.51 Wiring diagram for 1978 to 1980 models (continued)

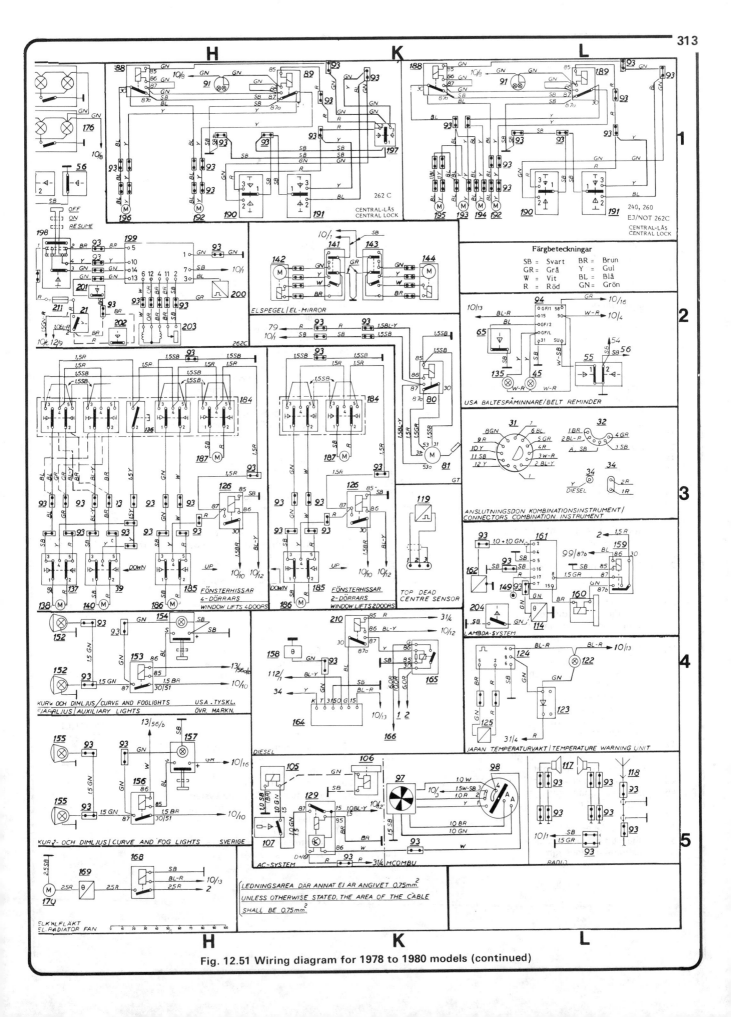

Fig. 12.51 Wiring diagram for 1978 to 1980 models (continued)

Key to Fig. 12.51

1	Battery	B1
2	Connection plate	C3
3	Ignition switch	A2,C3
4	Ignition coil	C2
5	Distributor	C1
6	Spark plugs	C1
7	Starter motor	A1,A2,B1
8	Alternator	A2
9	Charging regulator	B2
10	Fusebox	C3
11	Light switch	B4
12	Bulb failure warning sensor	C5
13	Step relay for full beams and dipped beams and headlight flasher	B5
14	Full beams	A3,A4,A5
15	Dipped beams	A3,A5
16	Parking lights	A3,A5
17	Day running lights	A3,A5
18	Tail lights	F2,F5,G5
19	Side marker lights	G5
20	Number plate lights	F3,G5
21	Stop-light switch	D5,G2
22	Stop-light	F2,F5,G5
23	Reversing lights contact, manual gearbox	E4
24	Reversing lights contact, automatic transmission	A2
25	Reversing lights	A2,F2,F5
26	Direction indicator stalk	E4
27	Switch for hazard warning flashers	E3
28	Flasher device	E4
29	Front direction indicator light	A3,A5
30	Rear direction indicator light	F2,F5,G5
31	Connection at instrument	L3
32	Connection at instrument	L3
33	Tank pump	B1
34	Connection at instrument	L3
35	Oil pressure warning light	D1
36	Choke light	D1
37	Parking brake indicator light	D1
38	Brake warning light	D1
40	Battery charging warning light	D2
41	Bulb failure warning light	D2
42	Full beams indicator light	D2
43	Direction indicator panel light	D2
44	Overdrive indicator light	E2
45	Fasten seat belt warning light, front	E2,L2
46	Engine compartment light	B3
47	Belt lock light	E2
48	Ashtray light	E2
49	Selector lever light	D5
50	Rheostat for instrument panel light	D5
51	Instrument panel light	E5
52	Control and panel light	E5
53	Glove locker light	E5
54	Courtesy light bulb	B4
55	Door switch, driver's side	B4,C1,L2
56	Door switch, passenger's side	B3,B4,G1
57	Fuel gauge sender	D1
58	Temperature gauge sender	D1
59	Oil pressure sensor	D1
60	Choke contact	D1
61	Parking brake switch	D1
62	Brake warning switch	D1
63	Lambda-sond switch	D1
64	Switch, seatbelt, passenger's seat	E1
65	Switch, seatbelt, driver's seat	E1,K2
66	Switch, passenger's seat	E2
67	Headlights ON ignition key IN reminder buzzer	C4
68	Rev counter	D2
69	Fuel gauge	D2
70	Temperature gauge	D2
71	Voltage stabilizer	D2
72	Horn	B3
73	Horn pad (button)	B3
74	Cigar lighter	C2
75	Car heater (standard)	B4
76	Switch for car heater blower	B3
77	Switch for windscreen wipers/washers	F1
78	Windscreen wipers	F1
79	Windscreen washers	F1
80	Relay for headlight wipers	K2
81	Headlight wipers	K3
82	Switch for tailgate wiper/washer	G2
83	Tailgate wiper	G2
84	Tailgate washer	G3
85	Rear door switch	G4
86	Rear cargo space light	F4
87	Switch for electrically heated rear window	E3
88	Electrically heated rear window	E3
89	Heater element and thermostat, driver's seat cushion	E3
90	Heater element, driver's seat, backrest	E3
91	Clock	D5,H1,L1
92	Diode	D1,D2,E3
93	Connector	
94	Fasten seat belt reminder	L2
95	Cold start injector	B1
96	Thermal timer switch	B1
97	Fan heater, combined system	K5
98	Switch for fan combined system	L5
99	Relay for fuel pump	B1
100	Fuel pump	B1
101	Control pressure regulator	B1
102	Auxiliary air valve	B1

Key to Fig. 12.51 (continued)

103	Resistance	B1	161	Control unit, Lambda system	L3
104	Control unit, ignition system	C1	162	Lambda-sond	K3
105	Control magnet, compressor	H5	163	Interval wipe relay, rear window	G3
106	Solenoid valve	K5	164	Control unit, preheating, diesel	H4
107	Switch for air-conditioning (with thermostat)	H5	165	Relay, preheating (glow) current	K4
109	Switch for overdrive M46	E3	166	For glow plugs	K4
110	Switch for overdrive on gearbox M46	E3	167	Relay, delayed courtesy lighting	G4
111	Control magnet for overdrive on gearbox M46	E3	168	Relay for elec. cooling fan	H5
112	Coupling	C2	169	Thermostat for elec, cooling fan	G5
113	Power socket, starter motor	A2,C2	170	Motor for elec. cooling fan	G5
114	Thermostat	L4	171	Heater element with thermostat, passenger's seat cushion	G2
116	Damper resistance	C1	172	Heater element, passenger's seat backrest	G2
117	Loudspeaker, front doors	L5	173	Switch, heater element, passenger's seat	F1
118	Antenna, windscreen	L5	174	Cigar lighter, rear	G1
119	Top dead centre sender	K3	175	Switch, rear cargo space light	G1
120	Capacitor	B2	176	Courtesy light, left	G1
122	Exhaust temperature indicator light	L4	177	Courtesy light, right	G1
123	Diode box	L4	178	To switch for motor-driven antenna	G1
124	Temperature sensor	L4	179	Motor-driven antenna	G1
125	Thermo element, catalyst	K4	180	Headlamp wipers	E1,F1
126	Relay for window winders	H3	181	Solenoid valve, carburettor, or fuel valve diesel	C4
127	Rear foglights	F2,F4,F5	182	Diode, Lambda-sond indicator light	D1
128	Switch for rear foglights	E4	183	Lambda-sond indicator light or indicator light for glow current, diesel	D1
129	Delay relay for air-conditioning	K5	184	Switch for window winder, driver's side	H2,K2
130	Rear cargo space light	E3	185	Switch for window winder, passenger's side, front	H4,K4
135	Fasten seatbelt warning light, rear	E2,L2	186	Motor for window winder, passenger's side, front	H4
136	Main switch for window winders, rear	H2	187	Motor for window winder, driver's side	H3,K3
137	Switch for window winder, LH side rear	G4	188	Relay for central lock, opening all doors	H1,K1
138	Motor for window winder, LH side rear	G4	189	Relay for central lock, locking all doors	K1,L1
139	Switch for window winder, RH side rear	H4	190	Switch for central lock, link rod	H1,L1
140	Motor for window winder, RH side rear	G5	191	Switch for central lock, key	K1,L1
141	Switch for electrically operated rear view mirror, LH side	K2	192	Motor for central lock, passenger's side	H1,L1
142	Electrically operated rear view mirror, LH side	H2	193	Motor for central lock, LH side, rear	K1
143	Switch for electrically operated rear view mirror, RH side	K2	194	Motor for central lock, RH side, rear	K1
144	Electrically operated rear view mirror, RH side	K2	195	Motor for central lock, tailgate (245, 265)	K1
147	Fusebox, headlights, Italy	B5	196	Motor for central lock, driver's door 262 C	H1
148	Relay for windscreen interval wipe	E1	197	Switch for central lock, armrest 262 C	K1
149	Test point, Lambda-sond	L4	198	Switch for cruise holder	G1
150	Side direction indicators	B3,B5	199	Control unit for cruise holder	H2
152	Spotlights	G4	200	Pick-up coil for cruise holder	H2
153	Relay for spotlights	H4	201	Retardation switch for cruise holder	G2
154	Switch, spotlights	H4	202	Switch, clutch pedal, for cruise holder	H2
155	Road bend and foglights	G4,G5	203	Servo for cruise holder	H2
156	Relay for road bend and foglights	H5	204	Microswitch, Lambda-sond	K4
157	Switch for road bend and foglights	H4	210	Relay for control unit, diesel	K4
158	Temperature gauge sensor	H4	211	Cable fusing 4 A	G2
159	Relay for Lambda-sond	L3			
160	Frequency valve	L4			

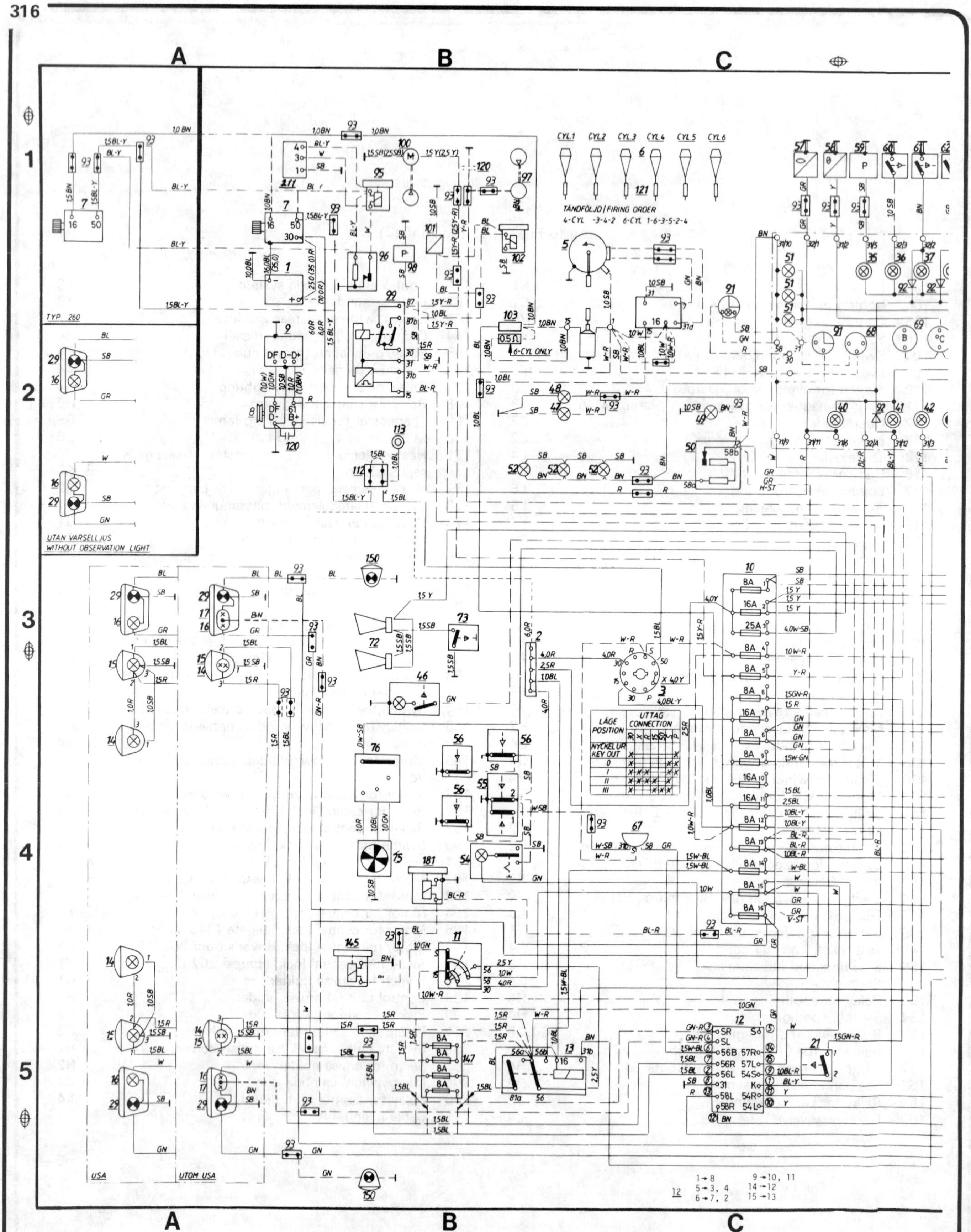

Fig. 12.52 Wiring diagram for 1981 to 1984 models

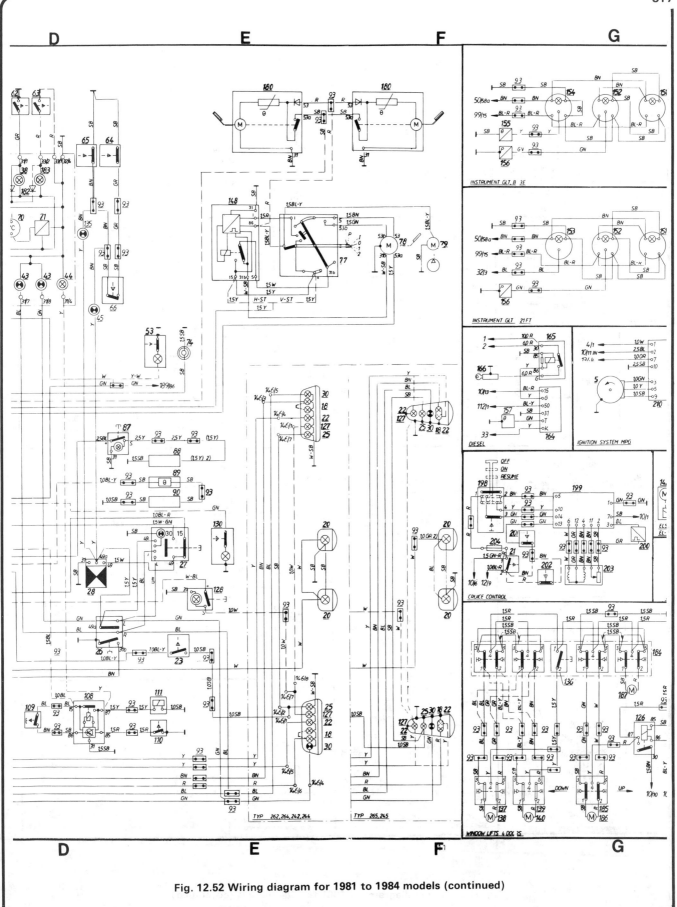

Fig. 12.52 Wiring diagram for 1981 to 1984 models (continued)

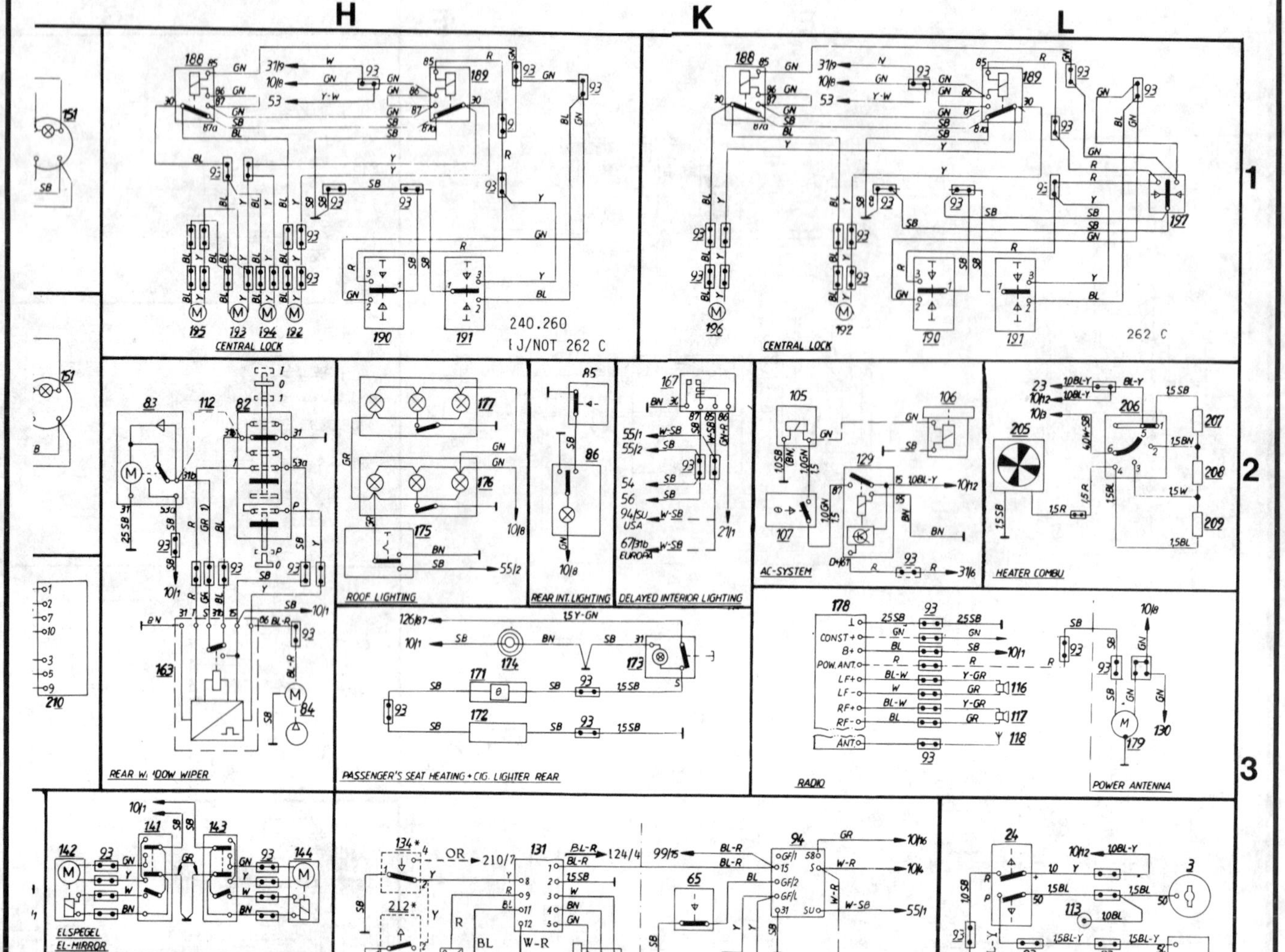

Fig. 12.52 Wiring diagram for 1981 to 1984 models (continued)

Key to Fig. 12.52

1	Battery	A1
2	Junction box	B3
3	Ignition switch	C3,L3
4	Ignition coil	B2
5	Distributor	B1,G3
6	Spark plugs	C1
7	Starter motor	A1,L4
8	Alternator	A2
9	Charging regulator	A2
10	Fusebox	C3
11	Light switch	B4
12	Bulb failure warning sensor	C5
13	Step relay for full/dipped beams and headlight flasher	B5
14	Full beams	A3,A4,A5
15	Dipped beams	A3,A5
16	Parking light	A2,A3,A5
17	Day running lights	A3,A5
18	Tail light	E3,E5,F3,F5
20	Number plate light	E4,F4
21	Brake light switch	C5,F4
22	Brake light	E3,E5,F3,F5
23	Reversing light contact, man. gearbox	E4
24	Reversing light contact, auto transmission	L3
25	Reversing light	E3,E5,F3,F5
26	Direction indicator stalk	D4
27	Switch, hazard warning flasher	E4
28	Flasher device	D4
29	Front direction indicator	A2,A3,A5
30	Rear direction indicator	E3,E5,F3,F5
31	Connection at instrument	L4
32	Connection at instrument	L4
33	Connection at instrument	L4
35	Oil pressure warning light	D1
36	Choke light	D1
37	Parking brake indicator light	D1
38	Brake warning light	D1
40	Battery charging warning light	C2
41	Bulb failure warning light	D2
42	Full beams indicator light	D2
43	Direction indicator panel light	D2
44	Overdrive indicator light	D2
45	Fasten seat belt warning light	D2,K4
46	Engine compartment light	B3
47	Seat belt lock light	B2
48	Ashtray light	B2
49	Gear selector light	C2
50	Rheostat for instrument panel light	C2
51	Instrument panel light	C1,C2
52	Control and panel light	B2,C2
53	Glove compartment light	E2
54	Courtesy light	B4
55	Door switch, driver's side	B4
56	Door switch, passenger's side	B3,B4
57	Fuel level sender	C1
58	Temperature sender	C1
59	Oil pressure sensor	C1
60	Contact: choke control	D1
61	handbrake	D1
62	brake warning	D1
63	Lambda-sond	D1
64	seat belt, passenger's seat	D1
65	seat belt, driver's seat	D1,K3
66	passenger's seat	D2
67	Headlights ON ignition key IN reminder buzzer	C4
68	Rev counter	D2
69	Fuel gauge	D2
70	Temperature gauge	D2
71	Voltage stabilizer	D2
72	Horn, 7.5A	B3
73	Horn pad (button)	B3
74	Cigar lighter 7A	E2
75	Heater fan (standard) 115W	B4
76	Switch for heater fan	B3
77	Switch for windscreen wash/pipe	E2
78	Windscreen wiper 3.5A	F2
79	Windscreen washer 3.4A	F2
80	Boot lock motor 0.6A	K4
81	Boot lock contact	K4
82	Switch for tailgate wash/wipe	H2
83	Tailgate wiper 1A	G2
84	Tailgate washer 2.6A	H3
85	Rear door switch	K2
86	Rear courtesy light	K2
87	Switch, heated rear window	D3
88	Heated rear window 150W	E3
89	Heater element and thermostat, driver's seat cushion 30W	E3
90	Heater element, driver's seat backrest 30W	E3
91	Clock	C1,C2
92	Diode	D1,D2
93	Connector	
94	Fasten seat belt reminder	K3
95	Cold start device	B1
96	Thermal timer switch cold start device	B1
97	Tank pressure 1.6A	B1
98	Air pressure sensor for turbo	B1
99	Relay for fuel pump	B1
100	Fuel pump 6.5A	B1
101	Control pressure regulator	B1
102	Auxiliary air valve	B1
103	Resistance 0.9 Ω/4cyl. 0.5 Ω/6 cyl	B2
104	Control unit, ignition system	C2
105	Control solenoid, for compressor, air cond. 3.9A	K2
106	Solenoid valve	L2
107	Switch for air conditioning (with thermostat)	K2

Key to Fig. 12.52 (continued)

108	Relay for overdrive	D5
109	Switch for overdrive, M46	D5
110	Contact for overdrive on M46	E5
111	Control magnet for overdrive on M46 2.2A	E5
112	Coupling	B2,H2
113	Power socket for running starter motor	B2,L3
114	Thermostat, Lambda system	H5
115	Pressure contact, Lambda system	H5
116	Loudspeaker, LH front door 4	L3
117	Loudspeaker, RH front door 4	L3
118	Antenna, windscreen	L3
119	TDC sender for monotester	K5
120	Capacitor 2.2mF	A2,B1
121	Damper resistance, spark plugs	C1
122	Exhaust temperature indicator light (Japan)	K4
123	Diode box (Japan)	H4
124	Temperature sensor (Japan) 850°C	H4
125	Thermal element, catalyst (Japan)	H5
126	Relay for window winders	G5,H5
127	Rear foglight	E3,E5,F3,F5
128	Switch, rear foglight	E4
129	Delay relay for air-conditioning	K2
130	Boot light	E4
131	Control unit CIS (constant idle speed system)	K3
132	Idle valve CIS	K4
133	Temp. sender CIS	H4
134	Microswitch CIS	H3
135	Fasten seatbelt warning, rear	D2,K4
136	Main switch for window winders, rear	G4
137	Switch for window winder, LH side rear	F5
138	Motor for window winder, RH side, rear 5A	F5
139	Switch for window winder, RH side, rear	G5
140	Motor for window winder, RH side, rear 5A	G5
141	Switch for elec. rear view mirror, LH side	G3
142	Elec. rear view mirror, LH side	G3
143	Switch for elec. rear view mirror, RH side	H3
144	Elec. rear view mirror, RH side	H3
145	Hot start valve	B4
146	Junction 8 poles	E3,E5
147	Fusebox, headlamps Italy	B5
148	Relay for intermittent windscreen wipe	E2
149	Test point, Lambda-sond	H5
150	Side direction indicators	B3,B5
151	Voltmeter	G1,G2
152	Oil pressure gauge	G1,G2
153	Charge pressure gauge for Turbo	G2
154	Ambient temp. gauge	G1
155	Ambient gauge sender	F1
156	Oil pressure sender	F1,F2
157	Temperature sender, diesel	F3
158	Microswitch Lambda-sond	H5
159	Relay for Lambda-sond	K5
160	Frequency valve	K5
161	Control unit, Lambda system	H5

162	Lambda-sond	H5
163	Intermittent wipe relay, tailgate	H3
164	Control unit, preheating, diesel	G3
165	Relay, preheating (glow) current – diesel	G2
166	Glow plug – diesel	F3
167	Relay, delayed courtesy light	K2
168	Relay for elec. cooling fan	H4
169	Thermostat for elec. cooling fan 100°C	H4
170	Motor for elec. cooling fan 13A	G4
171	Heater element with thermostat, passenger's seat cushion 30W	H3
172	Heater element, passenger's seat backrest	H3
173	Switch, heater element, passenger's seat	K3
174	Cigar lighter, rear 7A	H3
175	Switch, courtesy light	H2
176	Courtesy light, left	H2
177	Courtesy light, right	H2
178	Radio	K2
179	Elec. antenna 3A	L3
180	Headlamp wiper 1A	E1,F1
181	Solenoid valve, carburettor, or fuel valve diesel	B4
182	Diode, Lambda-sond indicator light	D1
183	Lambda-sond indicator light or indicator light for flow current – diesel	D1
184	Switch for window winder, driver's side	G4,H4
185	Switch for window winder, passenger's side, front	G5,H5
186	Motor for window winder, passenger's side, front 5A	G5,H5
187	Motor for window winder, driver's side 5A	G5,H5
188	Relay for central lock, opening	H1,K1
189	Relay for central lock, locking	H1,L1
190	Switch for central lock, link rod	H2,L1
191	Switch for central lock key	H2,L1
192	Motor for central lock, passenger's side	H1,K1
193	Motor for central lock, LH side, rear	H1
194	Motor for central lock, RH side, rear	H1
195	Motor for central lock, rear door (245/265)	H1
196	Motor for central lock. driver's side 262C	K1
197	Switch for central lock, arm rest 262C	L1
198	Switch for cruise control	F3
199	Control unit for cruise control	G3
200	Pick-up coil for cruise control	G4
201	Retardation switch for cruise control	F4
202	Switch, clutch pedal, for cruise control	G4
203	Servo for cruise control	G4
204	Fuse, cruise control 4A	F4
205	Heater fan CU	L2
206	Switch, Heater fan CU	L2
207	Resistance 1.9 ohms	L2
208	Resistance 0.7 ohms	L2
209	Resistance 0.2 ohms	L2
210	Control unit, ignition system MPG	G3
211	Impulse relay, cold start device	A1
212	Microswitch	L5

Colour code

BL	Blue	R	Red
BN	Brown	SB	Black
GN	Green	VO	Violet
GR	Grey	W	White
OR	Orange	Y	Yellow

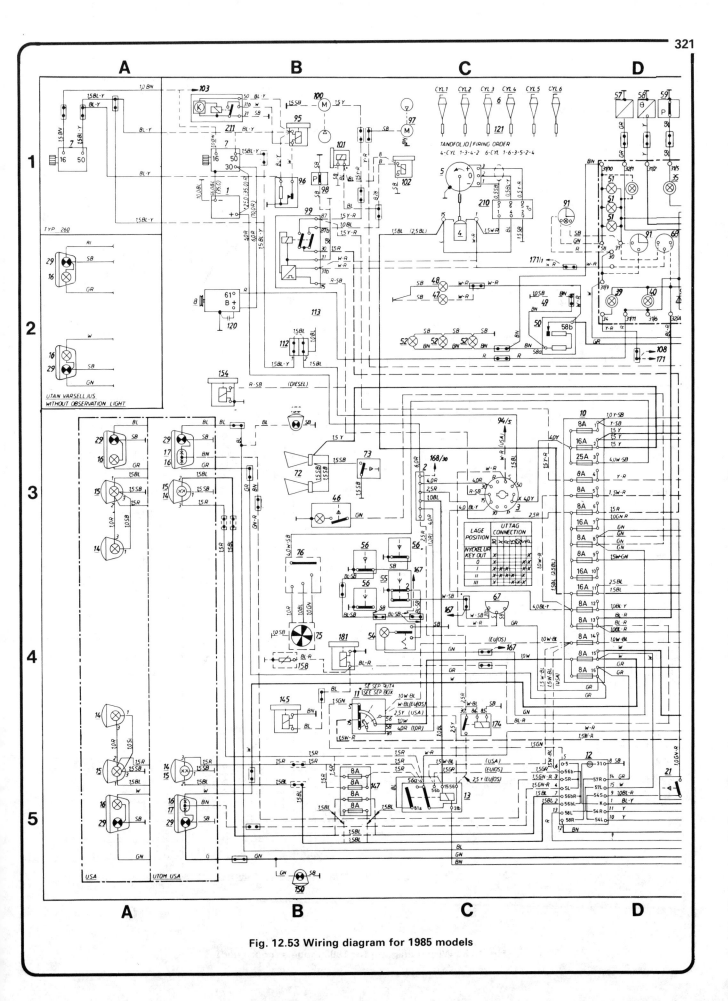

Fig. 12.53 Wiring diagram for 1985 models

Fig. 12.53 Wiring diagram for 1985 models (continued)

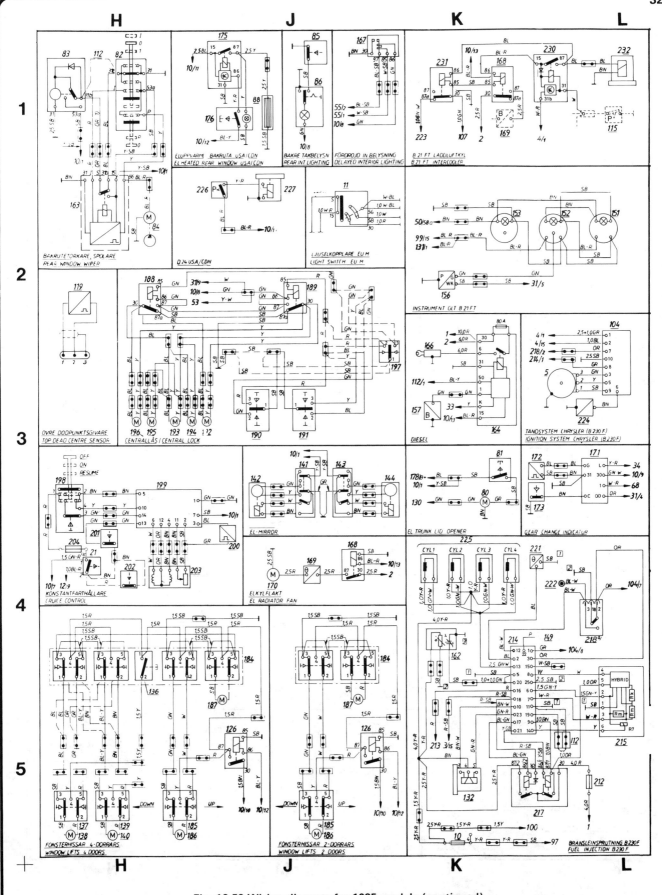

Fig. 12.53 Wiring diagram for 1985 models (continued)

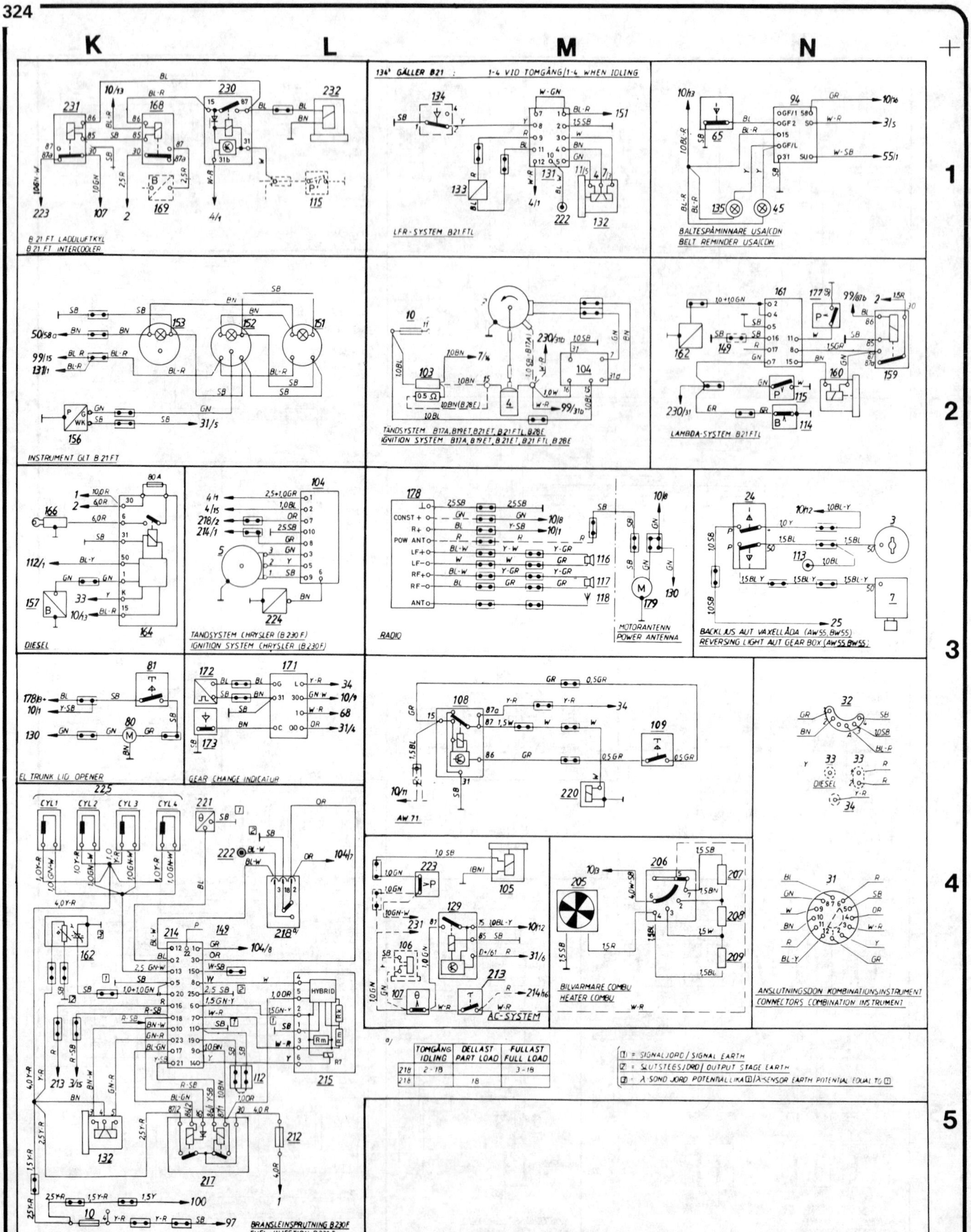

Fig. 12.53 Wiring diagram for 1985 models (continued)

Key to Fig. 12.53

No	Description	Ref
1	Battery	B1
2	Fusebox	C3
3	Ignition switch	C3,N2
4	Ignition coil 12 A	C1
5	Distributor	C1,L3,M2
6	Spark plug	C1
7	Starter motor	A1,B1
8	Alternator	A2
10	Fusebox	D3,K5,L2
11	Light switch	B4,J1
12	Bulb failure warning sensor	D5
13	Step relay for main and dipped beams and flash	C5
14	Main beam bulb 75 W max	A3,A4,A5
15	Dipped beam bulb 55 W max	A3,A5
16	Parking light 4cp/5 W	A2,A3,A5
17	Day running light 32 cp/21 W	A3,A5
18	Tail light 4 cp/5 W	G3,G5
20	Number plate light 4 cp/5 W	G3,G4
21	Brake light switch	D5,H4
22	Brake light	G3,G5
23	Reversing light switch, manual gearbox	F4
24	Reversing light switch, automatic gearbox	N2
25	Reversing light 32 cp/21 W	G3,G5
26	Direction indicator switch	E4
27	Hazard warning light switch	F4
28	Flasher device	E4
29	Direction indicator, front	A2,A3,A5
30	Direction indicator, rear	G3,G5
31	Instrument connection	N4
32	Instrument connection	N4
33	Instrument connection	N3
34	Instrument connection, AW71	N4
35	Oil pressure indicator lamp	D1
36	Choke indicator lamp	D1
37	Parking brake indicator lamp	D1
38	Brake failure warning lamp	E1
39	Overdrive (AW71) indicator lamp	D2
40	Battery charging indicator lamp	D2
41	Bulb failure warning sensor lamp	D2
42	Main beam indicator lamp	D2
43	Direction indicator indicator lamp	E2
44	Overdrive indicator lamp	E2
45	Seat belt reminder light	E2, N1
46	Engine compartment light 15 W	B3
47	Seat belt buckle light	C2
48	Ashtray light 1.2 W	C2
49	Gear selector panel light	C2
50	Adjustment knob, panel light intensity	C2
51	Instrument lighting 2 W	D1
52	Instrument and panel lighting	C2
53	Glove compartment light 2 W	E2
54	Courtesy light 10 W	B4
55	Door switch, driver side	C4
56	Door switch, passenger side	B3,B4,C3
57	Fuel level sensor	D1
58	Temperature sender	D1
59	Oil pressure sender	D1
60	Choke switch	D1
61	Parking brake switch	D1
62	Brake failure warning switch	E1
63	Lambda-sond switch	E1
64	Seat belt switch, passenger	E1
65	Seat belt switch driver	E1,N1
66	Seat belt switch passenger	E2
67	Reminder buzzer for key and lights	C4
68	Tachometer	D1
69	Fuel gauge	D1
70	Temperature gauge	E1
71	Voltage stabilizer 10 ± 0.2 V	E1
72	Horn, 7.5 A	B3
73	Horn switch	B3
74	Cigar lighter 7 A	F2
75	Standard heater fan 115 W	B4
76	Heater fan switch	B3
77	Windscreen wash/wipe switch	G2
78	Windscreen wipe 3.5 A	G2
79	Windscreen washer 2.6 A	G2
80	Boot release motor 0.6 A	F3,K3
81	Boot release switch	K4
82	Tailgate wash/wipe switch	H1
83	Tailgate wiper 1A	H1
84	Tailgate washer 3.4 A	H2
85	Rear door switch	J1
86	Rear courtesy lighting 10 W	J1
87	Heated rear window switch	E3
88	Heated rear window 150 W	F3,J1
89	Heater pads + thermostat, driver seat 30 W	F3
90	Heater pad driver backrest 30 W	F3
91	Clock	D1
92	Diode	D1,D2,E1
94	Fasten belt reminder light	C3,N1
95	Start injector	B1
96	Thermal timer switch, start injector	B1
97	Tank pump 1.6 A	C1
98	Charge air overpressure switch (turbo)	B1
99	Fuel pump relay	B1
100	Fuel pump 6.5 A	B1
101	Control pressure regulator	B1
102	Auxiliary air valve	C1
103	Resistance 0.9Ω/4 cyl,0.5Ω/6 cyl	L2
104	Ignition system control unit	L2
105	AC compressor solenoid 3.9 A	M4
106	Solenoid	L4
107	AC switch (thermostat type)	L4
108	Overdrive relay	E5,M3
109	Overdrive switch M46	E5,M3
110	Overdrive casing switch M46	E5
111	Overdrive solenoid (M46) 2.2 A	E5
112	Bridge connector	B2,H1
113	Service socket for cranking starter motor	B2,N3
114	Lambda-sond cut-out device	N2
115	Pressure switch, Lambda system	L1,N2
116	Loudspeaker 4 ohms, front left door	M3
117	Loudspeaker 4 ohms, front right door	M3
118	Aerial, (windscreen pillar)	M3
119	TDC transmitter for monotester	H2
120	Capacitor 2.2µF	B2,H2
121	Spark plug suppressor	C1
126	Power window relay	J5
127	Rear foglight 32 cp/21 W	G3,G5
128	Rear foglight switch	F4
129	AC delay relay	E4,M4
130	Boot light	F3
131	CIS control unit	M1
132	CIS air control valve	K5,M1

Key to Fig. 12.53 (continued)

133	CIS temperature sender	M1	181	Carburettor solenoid valve (fuel valve diesel)	B4
134	CIS microswitch	L1	182	Lambda-sond diode lamp 1.2 W	E1
135	Rear seat belt light 2 W	E1,N1	183	Lambda-sond lamp (glow lamp diesel) 1.2 W	E1
136	Power window switch (main), rear	H4	184	Power window switch, driver side	J4,K4
137	Power window winder switch, rear left	H5	185	Power window switch, passenger side	H5,J5
138	Power window motor, rear left 5 A	H5	186	Power window motor 5 A, passenger side	H5,J5
139	Power window switch, rear light	H5	187	Power window motor 5 A, driver side	J5
140	Power window motor, rear right 5 A	H5	188	Central lock motor, unlocking	H2
141	Power door mirror switch, left	J3	189	Central lock motor, locking	E2,J2
142	Power door mirror, left	J3	190	Central lock link rod switch	J3
143	Power door mirror switch, right	J3	191	Central door lock switch	J3
144	Power door mirror, right	K3	192	Central lock motor, passenger side	H3
145	Warm start injector	B4	193	Central lock motor, rear left	H3
146	Connector 8-pole	F3,F5	194	Central lock motor, rear right	H3
147	Fusebox, headlights, Italy	B5	195	Central lock motor, tailgate	H3
148	Windshield wiper relay	F1	196	Central lock motor, driver door	H3
149	Lambda-sond test socket	N2,L4	197	Central lock motor armrest 242	K3
150	Side marker light 2-4 W	B3,B5	198	Cruise control, switch	H3
151	Voltmeter	L2	199	Cruise control, control unit	H3
152	Oil pressure gauge	L2	200	Cruise control, pick-up	J4
153	Boost pressure gauge, (turbo)	K2	201	Cruise control, deceleration switch	H4
154	Fuel valve (diesel)	B2	202	Cruise control, clutch switch	H4
155	Heated seat switch	E3	203	Cruise control, servo unit	H4
156	Oil pressure sender	K2	204	Fuse	H4
157	Coolant temperature sender	K3	205	Heater fan CU	M4
158	Solex carburettor PTC resistor	B4	206	Heater fan switch CU	M4
159	Lambda-sond relay	N2	207	Resistor 1.9 ohms	N4
160	Frequency valve	N2	208	Resistor 0.7 ohm	N4
161	Lambda-sond control unit	N1	209	Resistor 0.2 ohm	N4
162	Lambda-sond (heated = B230F)	K4,M2	210	TZ-28H ignition system control unit	C1
163	Tailgate wipe relay	H2	211	Impulse relay	B1
164	Control unit (diesel)	K3	212	Fuse 25 A	L5
166	Glow plug	K4	213	AC Microswitch	M4
167	Delayed courtesy light relay	C3,J1	214	Control unit B 230 FLH Jetronic 2.2	K4
168	Electric cooling fan relay	C3,C4,J4,K1	215	Air mass meter	L5
169	Electric cooling fan thermostat 100°C	J4,K1	216	Gearbox switch	L4
170	Electric cooling fan motor 13 A	J4	217	Main relay B 230 F	K5
171	Shift indicator control unit	C2,D2,E2,L3	218	Microswitch (idling and full load)	L4
172	Rear axle impulse sender	K3	220	Overdrive (AW 71) solenoid	M4
173	Clutch switch	K3	221	Temperature sender B 230 F	K4
174	Headlamp relay	C4	222	Idle speed adjustment	L4,M1
175	Heated rear window delay relay	J1	223	AC receiver/driver	L4
176	Switch, delay relay	J1	224	Knock sensor	L3
177	Pressure differential switch	N1	225	Injector	K4
178	Radio	D2,L2	226	Altitude compensation pressure switch	J1
179	Power aerial 3 A	M3	227	Altitude compensation solenoid valve	J1
180	Headlamp wiper 1 A	F1,G1	230	Engine rpm relay	L1
			232	On-off valve	L1

327

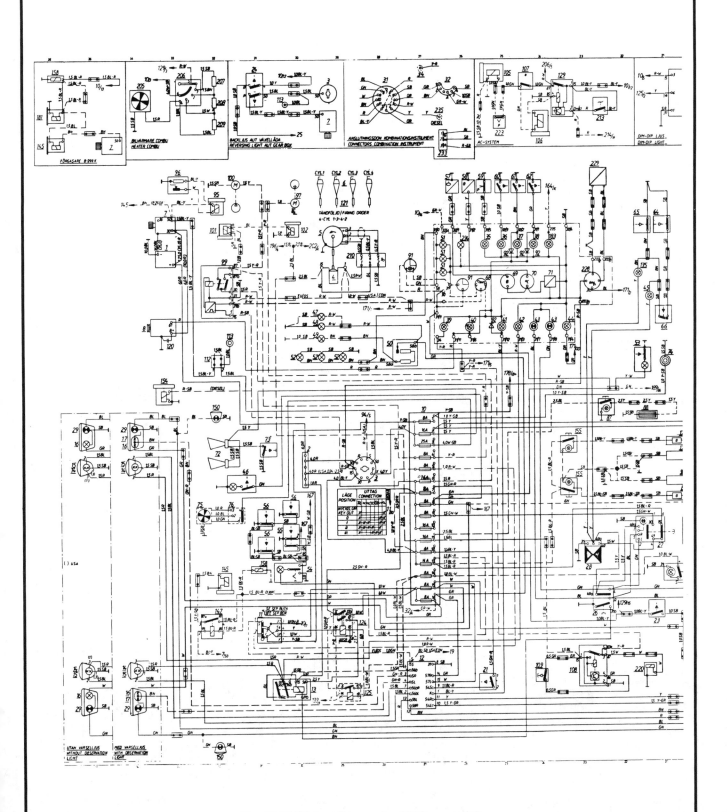

Fig. 12.54 Wiring diagram for 1986-on models

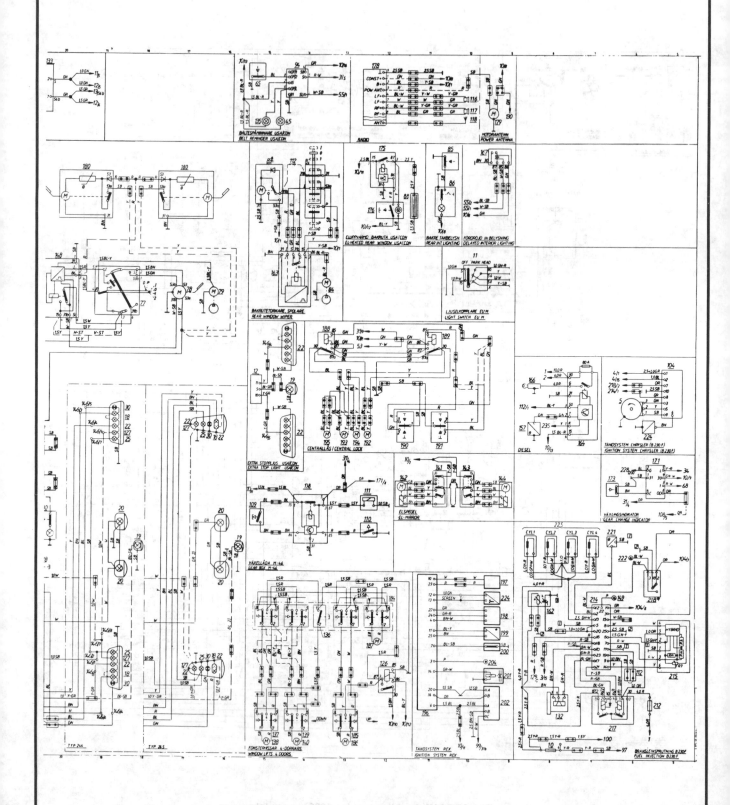

Fig. 12.54 Wiring diagram for 1986-on models (continued)

Key to Fig. 12.54

1	Battery	63	Lambda sond switch
2	Fusebox	64	Seat belt switch, passenger
3	Ignition switch	65	Seat belt switch, driver
4	Ignition coil 12 A	66	Seat belt switch, passenger
5	Distributor	68	Tachometer
6	Spark plug	69	Fuel gauge
7	Starter motor	70	Temperature gauge
8	Alternator	71	Voltage regulator 10 ± 0.2 V
10	Fusebox	72	Horn 7.5A
11	Light switch	73	Horn switch
12	Bulb failure warning sensor	74	Cigar lighter 7 A
13	Step relay for main and dipped beams and flash	75	Standard heater unit 15 W
14	Main beam bulb 75 W max	76	Heater fan switch
15	Dipped beam bulb 55 W max	77	Windscreen wash/wipe switch
16	Parking light 32cp/21 W	78	Windscreen wiper 3.5 A
17	Day running light 32 cp/21 W	79	Windscreen washer 2.6 A
18	Tail light 4cp/5 W	82	Tailgate wash/wipe switch
20	Number plate light 4cp/5 W	83	Tailgate wiper 1 A
21	Brake light switch	84	Tailgate washer 3.4 A
22	Brake light	85	Rear door switch
23	Reversing light switch, manual gearbox	86	Rear courtesy lighting 10 W
24	Reversing light switch, automatic gearbox	87	Heated rear window switch
25	Reversing light 32 cp/21 W	88	Heated rear window 150 W
26	Direction indicator switch	89	Heater pads + thermostat, driver seat 30 W
27	Hazard warning light switch	90	Heater pad, driver backrest 30 W
28	Flasher device	91	Clock
29	Direction indicator, front	92	Diode
30	Direction indicator, rear	94	Fasten seat belt reminder light
31	Instrument connection	95	Start injector
32	Instrument connection	96	Thermal time switch, start injector
34	Instrument connection, AW71	97	Tank pump 1.6 A
35	Oil pressure indicator lamp	99	Fuel pump relay
36	Choke indicator lamp	100	Fuel pump 6.5 A
38	Brake failure warning lamp	101	Control pressure regulator
39	Overdrive (AW71) indicator lamp	102	Auxiliary air valve
40	Battery charging indicator lamp	104	Ignition system control unit
41	Bulb failure warning sensor lamp	105	AC compressor solenoid 3.9 A
42	Main beam indicator lamp	106	Solenoid
43	Direction indicator indicator lamp	107	AC switch (thermostat type)
44	Overdrive indicator lamp	108	Overdrive relay
45	Seat belt reminder light	109	Overdrive switch M 46
46	Engine compartment light 15 W	110	Overdrive casing switch M 46
47	Seat belt buckle light	111	Overdrive solenoid (M 46) 2.2 A
48	Ashtray light 1.2 W	111	Bridge connector
49	Gear selector panel light	113	Service socket for cranking motor
50	Adjustment knob, panel light intensity	116	Loudspeaker 4 ohms, front left door
51	Instrument lighting 2 W	117	Loudspeaker 4 ohms, front right door
52	Instrument and panel lighting	118	Aerial, (windscreen pillar)
53	Glove compartment light 2 W	120	Capacitor 2.2 F
54	Courtesy light 10 W	121	Spark plug suppressor
55	Door switch, driver side	122	Heater pad, passenger seat backrest
56	Door switch, passenger side	123	Heater pad, passenger seat
57	Fuel level sensor	124	Main headlight relay
58	Temperature sender	125	Rear foglight relay
59	Oil pressure sender	126	Power window relay
60	Choke switch	127	Rear foglight 32 cp/21 W
61	Parking brake switch	128	Rear fog light switch
62	Brake failure warning switch	129	AC delay relay

Key to Fig. 12.54 (continued)

130	Boot light		184	Power window switch, driver side
132	CIS air control valve		185	Power window switch, passenger side
135	Rear seat belt light 2W		186	Power window motor 5 A, passenger side
136	Power window switch (main), rear		187	Power window motor 5 A, driver side
137	Power window switch, rear left		188	Central lock motor, unlocking
138	Power window motor, rear left 5 A		189	Central lock motor, locking
139	Power window switch, rear light		190	Central lock link rod switch
140	Power window motor, rear right 5 A		191	Central lock door lock switch
141	Power door mirror switch, left		192	Central lock motor, passenger side
142	Power door mirror, left		193	Central lock motor, rear left
143	Power door mirror switch, right		194	Central lock motor, rear right
144	Power door mirror, right		195	Central lock motor, tailgate
145	Hot start valve		205	Heater fan CU
146	Connector 8-pole		206	Heater fan switch CU
148	Windscreen wiper relay		207	Resistor 1.9 ohms
149	Lambda wiper relay		208	Resistor 0.7 ohm
149	Lambda sond test socket		209	Resistor 0.2 ohm
150	Side marker light 2-4 W		210	TZ-28H ignition system control unit
154	Fuel valve (diesel)		212	Fuse 25 A
155	Heated seat switch		213	AC Microswitch
157	Coolant temperature sender		214	Control unit B 230 F LH Jetronic 2.2
158	Solex carburettor PTC resistor		215	Air mass meter
162	Lambda sond (heated = B 230 F)		216	Gearbox switch
163	Tailgate wipe relay		217	Main relay B 230 F
164	Control unit (diesel)		218	Microswitch (idling and full load)
166	Glow plug		220	Overdrive (AW 71) solenoid
167	Delayed courtesy light relay		221	Temperature sender B 230 F
171	Shift indicator control unit		222	Idle speed adjustment
173	Clutch switch		223	AC receiver/driver
175	Heated rear window delay relay		224	Knock sensor
176	Switch, delay relay		225	Injector
178	Radio		228	Speedometer
179	Power aerial 3 A		229	Impulse wheel, rear axle
180	Headlamp wiper 1 A		233	Instrument connection
181	Carburettor solenoid valve (fuel valve diesel)		235	Instrument connection
183	Lambda sond lamp (glow lamp diesel) 1.2 W		236	Indicator lamp, glow plugs

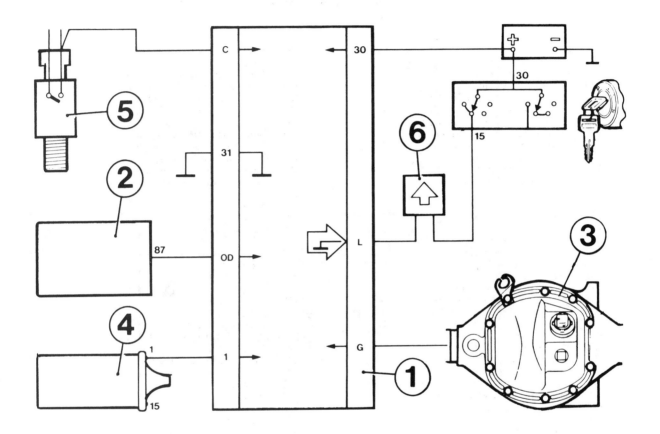

Fig. 12.55 Wiring diagram for gear change indicator system (fuel economy system)

1 Control unit, gear change indicator
2 Overdrive relay
3 Speedometer transmitter

4 Ignition coil
5 Clutch pedal switch
6 Indicator lamp

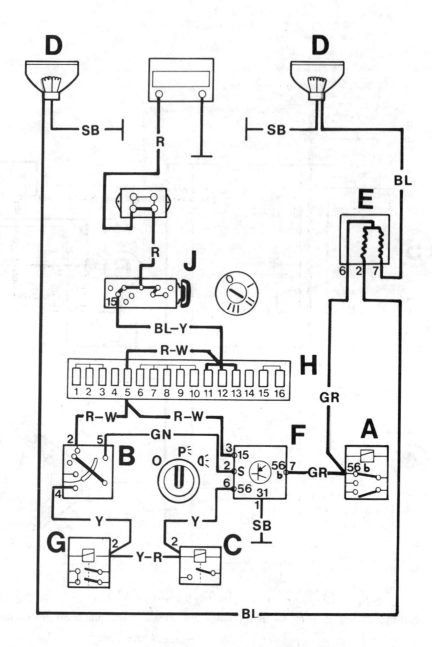

Fig. 12.57 Wiring diagram for headlights wired through ignition switch

A   Step relay   D   Headlamps   G   Headlamp relay
B   Main light switch   E   Bulb failure sensor   H   Fusebox
C   Turn signal switch   F   Main beam indicator lamp   J   Ignition switch

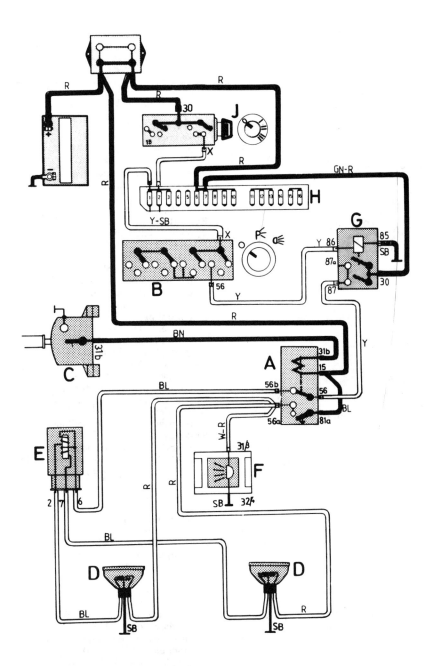

Fig. 12.56 Wiring diagram for dim-dip system

A	Stepping relay	D	Dipped beam	G	Main beam regulator
B	Light switch	E	Bulb failure warning sensor	H	Fusebox
C	Rear foglight relay	F	Dim-dip regulator	J	Ignition switch

Index